D1799779

Franz Rosenzweig and Jehuda Halevi
Translating, Translations, and Translators

Franz Rosenzweig (1886–1929), one of the most daunting modern Jewish thinkers, exercises a profound influence on contemporary philosophy and modern Jewish thought. In this seminal study, Barbara Galli provides the first English translation of Franz Rosenzweig's *Jehuda Halevi: Zweiundneunzig Hymnen und Gedichte*, a German translation of the poems of the great medieval Jewish poet Jehuda Halevi, followed by a lively, interpretive response.

Galli's primary aim is to explore Rosenzweig's statement that his Notes to Halevi's poems exemplify a practical application of the philosophic system he set out in *The Star of Redemption*. Through an extended, multifaceted investigation of Rosenzweig's thought, Galli uncovers his philosophy of translation, out of which she determines and unravels his philosophic conclusion and his belief that there is only one language. In the final chapters, she concentrates on the Notes to the poems, and in doing so attempts to philosophize according to Rosenzweig's own mandate: full speech is word *and* response.

"This is a huge, daring, and important contribution. Galli's achievements are remarkable, and the book is studded with important and original discussions."

Michael Fishbane, Nathan Cummings Professor of Jewish Studies, University of Chicago.

BARBARA ELLEN GALLI is adjunct assistant professor in the Department of Religion, Concordia University, and the Faculty of Religious Studies, McGill University.

Franz Rosenzweig, 1928
Photo courtesy of the Leo Baeck Institute, New York

Franz Rosenzweig and Jehuda Halevi

Translating, Translations, and Translators

Barbara Ellen Galli

FOREWORD BY
PAUL MENDES-FLOHR

McGill-Queen's University Press
Montreal & Kingston • London • Buffalo

© McGill-Queen's University Press 1995
ISBN 0-7735-1288-8

Legal deposit second quarter 1995
Bibliothèque nationale du Québec

Printed in Canada on acid-free paper

This book has been published with the help of a
grant from the Canadian Federation for the Humanities, using funds provided by the Social Sciences and Humanities Research Council of
Canada.

McGill-Queen's University Press is grateful to
the Canada Council for support of its publishing
program.

Canadian Cataloguing in Publication Data

Galli, Barbara E. (Barbara Ellen), 1949–
Franz Rosenzweig and Jehuda Halevi:
translating, translations, and translators
Includes a translation of Jehuda Halevi:
Zweiundneunzig Hymnen und Gedichte, a
German translation, with interpretations, of the
poems of Jehuda Halevi, by Franz Rosenzweig.
Includes bibliographical references and index.
ISBN 0-7735-1288-8
1. Rosenzweig, Franz, 1886–1929.
2. Translating and interpreting –
Philosophy. 3. Philosophy, Jewish. 4. Judah,
ha-Levi, 12th cent. – Criticism and
interpretation. I. Rosenzweig, Franz, 1886–
1929. II. Title.
B3327.R64G34 1995
121'.68   C95-900138-7

This book was typeset by
Typo Litho Composition Inc.
in 10/12 Baskerville.

Dedicated, with Filial Devotion, to Joseph Nicholas Galli and, with Love Stronger than Death, to Bessie Cooley Birch

Contents

Preface   ix

Foreword by Paul Mendes-Flohr   xv

PART ONE
JEHUDA HALEVI   FRANZ ROSENZWEIG

Poems   1

Afterword   169

Notes   185

PART TWO
RESPONDING TO ROSENZWEIG'S HALEVI BOOK

Chapter One
Placing the Halevi Book, Rosenzweig, and the *Star*   289

Chapter Two
Rosenzweig's Philosophy of Translation   322

Chapter Three
"There is only one language"   360

Chapter Four
The Notes as Application of the New Thinking   399

Chapter Five
The Sub-themes of Revelation in the Notes   434

Appendix A
The Problem of the English Aids to Understanding   469

Appendix B
Translation of Rosenzweig's "Reversed Fronts" 479

Notes 489

Bibliography 509

Index 515

Preface

This book comprises two parts. Each constitutes a stage in a response to Franz Rosenzweig's philosophy of speech-thinking, and each also attempts to remain within the speech-thinking method itself. The cue for the first stage, translating, began with Rosenzweig's own direct prompting. In "Das neue Denken," the supplementary essay to *The Star of Redemption*, Rosenzweig states that his Notes to the poetry of Jehuda Halevi provide an example of the practical application of his philosophic method, speech-thinking. The investigation of this directive proved irresistible for one whose interest in the *Star* deepens with the passing years, and who repeatedly returns to its endless riches.

Part one of this book offers the first English translation of the 1927 edition of Rosenzweig's Halevi book. Through translating, that is to say through the use of Rosenzweig's own words through translation, I seek to present to English readers what Rosenzweig was doing philosophically and religiously. Thus part one is not by me, but by Franz Rosenzweig. I have tried to give to the reader Rosenzweig's own words by literally and laboriously following his own speech word by word, and to speak it through a new language.

For the Afterword and the Notes I accept responsibility as translator. The poems, which I find myself incapable of translating in the first place, are untranslatable also on philosophical grounds. Only translations of originals are permitted and possible. Also Rosenzweig, as he makes clear in the Afterword, and in his remarks on the translations at the conclusion of each note, while far from construing himself as a free renderer, does occasionally introduce a word or phrase for reasons of rhyme or metre. As well, he actually from time to time even alters the content, in order to retain the contours and the spirit of the verse, and all the while, rightly I would argue, defends himself as a true translator. The problem of the untranslatability of a translation is, of course, not solved in this case by translating from the Hebrew, or offering, when available, translations from the original.

The project here is to translate *Rosenzweig's* book, and to retain Rosenzweig's own remarks on his own translations, which make sense only with the presence of his translations. Within the narrower confines of scholarship, Alan Udoff, with his usual blend of sharpness and eloquence, helped to solve, or at least to shift the weight of this circularly insoluable, burdensome problem I must carry right into the printing of this book. On 16 October 1991, in personal correspondence concerning my work, Udoff wrote that "the inclusion of an English translation of the Hebrew from a scholarly point of view is unnecessary and, on another level, a virtual impossibility for [a translator] going from Halevi's Hebrew to Rosenzweig's German and coordinating on some distant English horizon! It is simply a delusion, based on a profound misunderstanding of the nature of translation, to believe that the Hebrew could be translated into English such that it could stand as the index for Rosenzweig's interpretation of the Hebrew."

To alleviate this problem, then, I am doing two things. First, I am placing Rosenzweig's translations on the righthand pages, that is to say on the dominant side as it were, and, on the lefthand pages my English aids, in as interlinear a fashion as possible, will appear for those who have no or very little German. Second, in Appendix A I supply a practical example of the intricacies of transmission through two of Jehuda Halevi's poems translated into English by Olga Marx and by Nina Salaman. The aim of this appendix is to look more closely at this problem in terms of translation theory. Also provided here are samples of lines from poems with insights offered by Rosenzweig's son, Rafael.

To Rosenzweig, translating is an integral aspect of genuine speech, already the beginnings of a response. And no speech, furthermore, is complete without a response.

Part two, a response to and analysis of certain aspects of Rosenzweig's Halevi book, tries to understand and to convey some of the ways in which the Notes to the poems exemplify speech-thinking.

Rosenzweig worked on these poetry translations and corresponding Notes during the latter part of his life, and he considered them to be of great importance, the centre of his life. The Notes contain a plenitude of responses. These are not to Jehuda Halevi alone, nor are they responses only to the Spanish medieval philosophical and theological contexts, but they speak as well to the early twentieth-century European thinkers. Indeed, the Notes are indescribable in their breadth and depth of scope, in their widely varying thrusts, from sublime devotional moments, humorous anecdotes and irony, to the briefest, or densest, of theological treatises. The Notes do not follow "logically" from one to the next, but instead follow the "logic" of events of life which can be planned but not predicted, but yet which make sense when one is open to the present commandments of revelation.

Bringing these Notes in translation to English readers, accompanied by some commentary based on some of Rosenzweig's other writings, may serve to facilitate further worthwhile exploration of Rosenzweig's vast world of thought and action.

To date very little attention has been paid to Rosenzweig's later work, and none has been given to the Notes as a whole. Rosenzweig viewed the *Star* as a foundational and a theoretical starting point, from which theory he never deviated. The Notes, as a practical application of his speech-thinking philosophy, can therefore be regarded as one of the *Star*'s more instructive fruits, and ultimately more important than the *Star*. This book, representing the first definitive, but by no means exhaustive statement with regard to the Notes, seeks to open the already lively discussions and enjoyment of Rosenzweig's philosophy to new conversants, especially in respect of his views on language.

Of Jehuda Halevi and Franz Rosenzweig I would like to say nothing here except that to both of them I owe my greatest thanks. Their own writings, consistently healthy-minded, more than anything or anybody else, freshened me again and again whenever I began to wilt from recklessly overworking.

I am grateful for two major financial contributions. This book has been published with the help of a grant from the Canadian Federation for the Humanities, using funds provided by the Social Sciences and Humanities Research Council of Canada (SSHRCC).

A donation by Mitchell Fenton saved the book from shipwreck. When it became clear that this double-sized book could not be published without funds of an amount nearly equivalent to the already generous SSHRCC contribution, Mitchell, a remarkable human being, with no ado offered, from his own pocket and heart, the required amount. May good-humoured gods who really do not mind his brand of non-belief shower upon this atheist who believed in this book all the blessings, and more, that *he* requires, or desires, for life.

Several other people have been interested in and supportive of this project and those who were not already have become friends during its development. In the order of getting to know them, I wish to mention a few names.

Anna M. Rosenberg, Carleton University, (retired), was my first teacher of German, twenty years ago. When I showed her my first translating efforts for this book, she was appalled, and in her admirably fastidious manner, she insisted on reviewing the whole. Our subsequent sessions together, sometimes spanning several successive intense days, and our frequent arguments not only drew us closer to each other, but showed me how much more German and English there is to learn. The blame for faults in the translation lies on my shoulders; for many of the more elegantly translated passages all praise lies with her.

To Joseph C. McLelland, of McGill University, I offer warm thanks for his excellent and inspiring teaching that leads me to an ever deeper appreciation of and sensitivity toward philosophical thinking and living.

Helen Shepherdson has been an inordinate source of both practical and spiritual strength, which are often the same thing.

Michael D. Oppenheim, of Concordia University, often steadied me by maintaining a calming, unswerving confidence and interest in all my reactions to Rosenzweig. I treasure his loyally engaged support and keen involvement that began even before the inception of this work. Only through conversations with him did strands of cloudy ideas start to take on distinct shapes in clear skies.

Harold M. Stahmer, of the University of Florida, was the first to publish a comprehensive book on speech-thinkers. I knew his work long before I met him personally. He and his wife, Paula, extend warm hospitality to scholars, and it was they who organized a meeting between me and Paul Mendes-Flohr. As well, Professor Stahmer introduced me, through correspondence, to Rosenzweig's son, Rafael.

Paul Mendes-Flohr, with his refined sense of Rosenzweig scholarship, with his gift of an expansive intellect, and his highly tuned ability to listen has a way of unobtrusively demanding the best in others. He insists that people speak their own speech, and at all times carefully, and that their writing be crafted with an accuracy that blends with a moral responsibility toward those written of and to. I am deeply honoured that he has agreed to write the Foreword to this book.

I am in awe of Alan Udoff. I hope that his profoundly sensuous yet playfully poetic philosophical creations, many of which are tucked away in learned journals, reach and benefit all those who would appreciate them.

Samieun Khan offered gracious help in preparing the manuscript, and many a soothing word and gesture.

Don Akenson, Professor of History at Queen's University, editor of McGill-Queen's Press, truly a gentleman and a scholar, has eased every ruffle in the procedure of publishing with a rare prowess and finesse.

The warmth of Philip Cercone, executive director of the Press, created just the right mood for that troubled, interminable last inch of travel toward the final manuscript. That I could laugh while traversing that inch is a tribute to Philip.

In the final stages of this book, Frances Rooney has worked closely with the manuscript and with me. Her highly talented and adept light editorial touch has clarified and illuminated the text's own speech.

Tewfik Saïd, with his penetrating inner gentleness, opens my mind and my soul toward a new prospect of peacefulness.

Foreword

On the face of it, this is a strange volume: a translation of a translation, which seeks to present in English Franz Rosenzweig's German translation of the Hebrew poems of the twelfth-century Spanish Jewish philosopher and poet Jehuda Halevi. One could have of course simply translated Rosenzweig's accompanying "Notes," so marvelously rich in theological and philosophical insight. But that would have raised even more disturbing incongruities, since the "Notes" are Rosenzweig's pointed response – perhaps more correctly dialogue – with each of Halevi's poems he translated. This problem could have been solved by reprinting existing English translations of the poems, but that would also have been absurd, since it would have obscured the very principle that Rosenzweig sought to exemplify through his project, namely that translation should be a "speech thinking," cognition that is grounded in dialogue or genuine conversation – and "true conversation takes place only after true translating (*qua* conversion) of another's speech into one's own." Only when the voice of the other reverberates through one's own lips, and thus through one's soul, does true conversation take place. Across generations and linguistic barriers, such conversation can only take place through a translation marked by genuine conversation.

Although Rosenzweig knew Hebrew well – and had consistently argued that even the best translations could never be but more than veiled imitations – he nonetheless once confided that only after having translated Halevi's poems did he truly understand them. He undoubtedly meant that through his efforts he gained more than intellectual clarification; the understanding he achieved was preeminently existential and dialogical. What he sought was to resonate the spoken – felt – word that gave birth to Halevi's poem; through translation he hoped to hear the living word embodied anew in the poems. "Translating,"

Rosenzweig wrote even when he was making his first, fledgling steps along the road to religious faith, "is after all the actual goal of the mind (*Geist*); only when something is translated has it become really *audible*, no longer to be disposed of." He tellingly adds, "in a corresponding way, [this is true] also of translating from person to person."

One might have adopted this method and gone to the Hebrew original of Halevi's poems, translating them much as Rosenzweig would have. But that would not only have been pretentious; it would also have vitiated the value of Rosenzweig's "Notes," which are in effect elaborations of the "conversation" he initiated with Jehuda Halevi through the translations of the poems. The translations and the "Notes" together serve to capture the unique inflections of Rosenzweig's own voice.

Thus Barbara Galli decided wisely to render Rosenzweig's translations into English and re-sound his voice for those who do not have easy access to the original German. To be sure, Galli is duly aware of the inherent limitations of this project, and humbly offers her efforts as but an approximation of Rosenzweig's text. Nonetheless with manifest intelligence, linguistic sensitivity, and grace, she provides us with an uncanny sense of the tonality, cadence, passion, and verbal dexterity of Rosenzweig's voice as it resonates through Halevi's original voice. The publisher is also to be commended for accepting Galli's suggestion that the format of Rosenzweig's original text be used for her translation and that the poems be included in German as well, allowing the reader ready reference to Rosenzweig's and Halevi's words.

Martin Buber once observed that "Rosenzweig's translation of Jehuda Halevi's poems is among the greatest works of linguistic conscience that I know in all literature – of the linguistic conscience of the translator, who in relation to the mystery of two languages [Hebrew and German] is responsible for his attempt to bring them together in unison. In 1923 Rosenzweig would often ask my advice in this project, and I could see with what élan and tenacity he was, despite his worsening bodily paralysis, wrestling with the spirit of both languages to win their blessings." I wish to thank Barbara Galli for allowing us to share in these blessings.

Paul Mendes-Flohr
Jerusalem
16 January 1995
Tu Bi-Shvat 5475

PART ONE

Jehuda Halevi
Franz Rosenzweig

LEO BAECK AND FRANZ ROSENZWEIG
IN CORRESPONDENCE ON THE HALEVI BOOK
LEO BAECK TO FRANZ ROSENZWEIG ON 27 JUNE 1924

I first wanted to read and read again your Jehuda Halevi before I wrote to you; for already after the first poem it happened to me that the first one did not let me go, and that I only continued after the again and once again. He who wants already to have read your book for the first time should rather leave it lying unopened. So now your book has been an ever-renewed gift for me for a month in the hour that remain to me.

Can anyone read Jehuda Halevi himself any other way? I don't know if anyone has anywhere already "reviewed" your book, and whether a dissatisfaction has maybe been expressed about the "long-short way," to use the words of the Midrash. I would ask him whether he has already read Jehuda himself and whether he has read him other than each song three or four times before the identity of language and content, of rhythm and train of thought became clear. A "readable" Jehuda Halevi! חס ושלום!

Thank you very much!

And an especially big thank you for the Notes. If the translation only had brought only them to us – דינו. I almost might wish them as a separate book for those who cannot read the poems.

During the next weeks I want still to give away the homiletic exercises at the educational establishment for mutual absorption in your book, in a few pages, as far as the weeks grant it. Everyone who is using the exercises will have a book.

FRANZ ROSENZWEIG TO LEO BAECK ON 9 OCTOBER 1924

A year ago you did wonderful work regarding the scenic remarks of the second [galley] sheet of the "Freitagabend," with luck, I'm glad to say, it's the turn of the fourth, and it asks for your help, as the translator still knows no Hebrew...

I have not thanked you at all for your letter about my Jehuda Halevi, it made me very happy. I hope that through the use of the Notes as a means for rabbinical education, none of our future shepherds of the soul has become a mushrik [Arabic: heretic]; I would be disconsolate.

Rosenzweig wrote the following signpost in "Das neue Denken," the supplementary essay to his *Star of Redemption*, published in 1925:
The Notes to my Jehuda Halevi *contain instructive examples of the practical application of the new thinking.*

FRANZ ROSENZWEIG

JEHUDA HALEVI

NINETY-TWO
HYMNS AND POEMS

GERMAN

WITH AN AFTERWORD
AND WITH NOTES

THE SIXTY HYMNS AND
POEMS SECOND EDITION

BERLIN

VERLAG LAMBERT SCHNEIDER

FRANZ ROSENZWEIG

JEHUDA HALEVI

ZWEIUNDNEUNZIG

HYMNEN UND GEDICHTE

DEUTSCH

MIT EINEM NACHWORT
UND MIT ANMERKUNGEN

DER SECHZIG HYMNEN UND
GEDICHTE ZWEITE AUSGABE

BERLIN
VERLAG LAMBERT SCHNEIDER

Contents

GOD	GOTT	POEM	NOTE
Praised be He	Gelobt	10	185
Almighty One	Gewaltiger	20	186
Yearning	Sehnsucht	20	187
During the Night	Nachts	20	187
Event	Ereignis	22	188
All My Limbs	All Meine Glieder	22	190
The Incomparable One	Der Unvergleichliche	24	191
None Other!	Keiner Sonst!	26	192
The Lovers	Die Liebenden	28	193
The Day of Judgment	Gerichtstag	28	193
Homecoming	Heimkehr	32	194
Hear	Hör	38	197
The True One	Der Wahre	40	198
Your God	Dein Gott	42	199
His Peace	Sein Friede	44	201
The Universe	Das All	46	201
The Far-and-Near One	Der Fern-und-Nahe	52	204
The Name	Der Name	54	206
Consecrated	Geweiht	56	208
Your Dwelling Places	Deine Wohnungen	62	208
The God of the Spirits	Der Gott der Geister	62	209
Holy	Heilig	64	209
The Helper	Der Helfer	64	211

6

SOUL	SEELE	POEM	NOTE
Here I am	Hier bin ich	68	212
Soul	Seele	70	213
Soul in Exile	Seele im Exil	72	214
With You	Bei Dir	72	215
Prayer	Gebet	74	216
Human Frailty	Menschenschwäche	76	218
Return	Umkehr	78	219
Reward	Der Lohn	80	220
This Soul Here	Diese Seele hier	82	223
Illusion and Truth	Wahn und Wahrheit	84	224
Lady World	Frau Welt	84	225
Wise Teachings	Weise Lehren	86	226
Servants	Knechte	88	227
World	Welt	88	227
The Sick Doctor	Der kranke Arzt	88	228
To the Sabbath	An den Sabbat	90	229
Free	Frei	92	229
Sabbath Morning	Sabbatmorgen	92	230
Life	Leben	94	231
The Day	Der Tag	94	233
Return, Return!	Kehr um, kehr um!	96	233
The Ascent	Der Aufstieg	96	234
Breath of All Life	Hauch allen Lebens	98	234

PEOPLE	VOLK	POEM	NOTE
In Eternity	In Ewigkeit	102	235
God Speaks	Gott spricht	102	235
Festival of Lights	Lichterfest	104	236
Morning Service	Morgendlicher Dienst	104	237
Light	Light	106	237
Conquered Darkness	Besiegte Finsternis	106	237
On Reed Sea Day	Am Schilfmeertag	108	238
My King	Mein König	110	239
Out of Distress	Aus dem Elend	110	241
To the Redeemer	An den Löser	112	241
Looking Upwards	Aufblick	114	245
Bride of Israel's Sabbath	Jungfrau Israels Sabbat	116	246
Home	Heim	118	248
The Miracles of Elijah	Die Eliawunder	120	249
The Jew	Der Jude	122	250

The Promise	Die Verheißung	122	250
Love of the Enemy	Feindesliebe	124	252
Miracle of Love	Liebeswunder	126	253
Angry Love	Zürnende Liebe	126	254
Dream Vision	Traumgesicht	126	255
Faithfulness	Treue	128	255
Love's Solace	Liebestrost	130	256
Finding Again	Wiederfinden	132	257

ZION	ZION	POEM	NOTE
Awake	Auf	138	258
The Happy Message	Die frohe Botschaft	138	259
The Calculation of Salvation	Heilsrechnun	140	260
In the Sanctuary	Im Heiligtum	140	261
Solomon's Tapestries	Teppiche Salomos	142	262
Tears at Night	Nächtliche Träne	142	263
The City on High	Die hohe Stadt	146	263
Between East and West	Zwischen Ost und West	146	264
Reply	Antwort	148	264
The Pilgrim	Der Pilger	152	266
All Weighs Lightly	Leicht wiegt das alles	154	266
The Compulsion	Der Zwang	154	267
Praying	Bitten	156	268
The Flood	Die Flut	156	268
Spoken to the Heart	Zum Herzen gesagt	156	279
Calm after the Storm	Stille nach dem Sturm	158	280
To the Westwind	And den West	158	280
In the Harbour	Im Hafen	160	281
Egyptian Soil	Ägyptischer Boden	160	281
The River	Der Strom	160	282
Thither ...	Hin ...	162	282
Foreboding	Vorgefühl	162	283
Ode to Zion	An Zion	164	284

| AFTERWORD | | 169 | |
| NOTES | | 185 | |

God   Gott

PRAISED BE HE!

Yes, Lord, You
You I praise;
Your justice, through
    me may it shine widely.

Hark, a tone —
I obey already,
Question melts away
    and strife.

And was it not as
if the clay
accused the potter:
    "What are you doing?"

Whom I desired,
Whom I received
as a tower and defense
    and security:

Shining all around,
    sending forth light,
without a veil
    freed of a cover —

That He be praised,
    Oh that He be garlanded,
    Oh that He be extolled,
    and consecrated.

GELOBT!

Ja Herr Dich
   dich rühme ich;
dein Recht, durch mich
   leucht' es weit.

Horch, ein Ton —
   gehorch ich schon,
Frage schmilzt
   und Widerstreit.

Und glich' es dem
   nicht, wie wenn Lehm
den Töpfer: „Was
   Tust du!" zeiht?

Des ich verlang,
   den ich empfang
zu Turm und Wehr
   und Sicherheit:

All-um glühnd,
   Geleucht aussprühnd,
schleierlos,
   verhangbefreit —

Daß gelobt,
   o daß umkränzt,
      o daß gerühmt
         er, und geweiht.

Lord, of your splendour,
the work of your might —
the heavens are
its telling.

Their rising and
their bowing and
when deeply they bow
their faces.

And angels,
wandering about
between walls of
flood and light,

Acknowledge You
and name You,
You who created
the sound that speaks.

For You do balance
without effort, and carry,
and not in arms,
not upon hands;

The deepest ground,
heaven-high sphere,
the throne and
those who attend Him —

That He be praised,
Oh that He be garlanded,
Oh that He be extolled,
and consecrated.

Herr: Deiner Pracht,
   Werks Deiner Macht —
die Himmel sind
   sein Bericht.

Ihr Steigen und
   ihr Neigen und
wenn tief sich beugt
   ihr Gesicht.

Und Engel, hin-
wandelnd in
Gemäuer aus
   Flut und Licht,

Bekennen dich
   und nennen dich,
der du schufst
   den Laut, der spricht.

Denn du wägst
   ohn' Müh, und trägst,
und nicht im Arm,
   auf Händen nicht:

Tiefsten Grund,
   hochhimmlisch Rund,
den Thronsitz und
   die sein Geleit —

Daß gelobt,
   o daß umkränzt,
      o daß gerühmt
         er, und geweiht.

And whose mouth, whose
would be worthy of Him
who forms clouds
    with His word,

Eternally lives
— a secret weaves
on heights of heights
    around His place —

And yet from the throne
into the tent to the son
descended
    to live there.

Appearance of reflection
to His seers
He grants out of
    the treasure of His Being.

Yet without form
and without norm
His Spirit moves
    and without harbour.

Prophecy
only saw Him as
in the grandeur
    of royal garb —

That He be praised,
    Oh that He be garlanded,
    Oh that He be extolled,
        and consecrated.

Und wes Mund, wes,
   wär würdig Des,
der Wolken ballt
   mit seinem Wort,

Ewig lebt
— Geheimnis webt
auf Höhn der Höhn
um seinen Ort —

Und doch vom Thron
ins Zelt zum Sohn
herab sich ließ,
zu wohnen dort.

Wohl Abglanz-Schein
den Sehern sein
vergönnt er aus
des Wesens Hort.

Doch ohne Form
und ohne Norm
zieht hin sein Geist,
und ohne Port.

Profetie
nur sah ihn wie
in Königkleids
Erhabenheit —

Daß gelobt,
o daß umkränzt,
o daß gerühmt
er, und geweiht.

The great works,
countless forms —
who can encircle
    the stature of praise?

Blessed be the man
who started early
to see in Him
    omnipotence,

And boldly founds himself
Him Who holds
the universe firmly
    in eternal hold,

with a lively spirit
praises Him highly
and never accused as unjust
    His judgement

And freely admits
that, whatever God does,
the deed serves consistently
    His purpose

And that He brings
near the day
when the judgement of the world
    stands in readiness —

That He be praised,
    Oh that He be garlanded,
    Oh that He be extolled,
        and consecrated.

Die Werke groß,
Gebild zahllos —
wer umzirkt
    des Lobs Gestalt?

Heil dem Mann,
der früh begann,
in ihm zu sehn
    die Allgewalt,

Und kühn sich stellt
auf den, der hält
fest das All
    in ewgem Halt,

Mit regem Geist
hoch ihn preist
und sein Gericht
    nie Unrecht schalt

Und gibt frei zu,
daß, was Gott tu',
seinem Ziel
    das Tun stets galt

Und daß er nah
den Tag bringt,
da der Welt ihr Spruch
    hängt bereit —

Daß gelobt,
    o daß umkränzt,
        o daß gerühmt
            er, und geweiht.

Melt,
and build yourself anew,
clearly see yourself
    in the depths of your bosom!

Grasp, oh spirit,
what you are,
that out of nothing
    came all your blossoming.

Who gave you strength?
Who knowledge?
Who called you once?
    Are you aware?

So look upon
the power, and in it
enflame your heart
    to holy joy!

Recognize his work!
But, Him, take heed,
You must leave
    untouched.

Search and search!
The seed and goal rest
in miracle
    and concealment —

That He be praised,
    Oh that He be garlanded,
    Oh that He be extolled,
    and consecrated.

Auftaue dich,
neu baue dich,
klar schaue dich
in tiefster Brust!

Erfaß, o Geist,
was du seist
und daß aus Nichts
kam all dein Blust.

Wer gab dir Kraft?
wer Wissenschaft?
wer ruft dich einst?
ist dirs bewußt?

So schaue an
die Macht, und dran
entflamm dein Herz
zu heilger Lust!

Erkenn sein Werk!
Ihn doch, merk,
unberührt
lassen mußt.

Forsch wie viel!
Keim ruht und Ziel
in Wunder und
Verborgenheit —

Daß gelobt,
o daß umkränzt,
o daß gerühmt
er, und geweiht.

ALMIGHTY ONE

Almighty One! Who   is without Him!   who would contend His rank!
    He, Source of the universe   around Him,   whose creation
    sprang from Him!
His form —   no eye   has seen it, only the
    Heart soulfully,   gazing out and   recognizing, has penetrated
    to Him.
His mighty splendour   rings 'round   the universe; thus He is   called
    The universal "Place",   because no   place has surrounded Him.
Seeing soul, who can never   be seen!   To the one seeing, never   to
    be seen,
    Draw near and bring   thanksgiving   and the sound of blessing to
    Him!

YEARNING

To Him, source of true life, I strive thither.
    The life around, the vapid and empty, I disdain.
To see my King's countenance — what more do I desire!
    I know no other might and no other magnificence.
Oh that I might be allowed to see Him, were it only in a dream!
    I would gladly sleep eternal sleep and never awaken.
And if I saw His countenance in the shaft of my heart,
    I would not give my eye leave to be on the lookout any longer.

DURING THE NIGHT

Recently thoughts belonging to you awakened me
    and let me look upon the round-dance of your grace.
They taught me illuminatingly how your creation, the soul,
    intertwined with me — a miracle, never to be silent!
And did not my believing heart see You, as if it had
    been permitted to be a witness at Sinai?
My visions sought You. Into me entered
    Your brilliance, to descend into my clouds.
Then my reflections roused me from the bed,
    to bow down, Lord, before your magnificence.

GEWALTIGER

Gewaltger! Wer   ohn' Ihn!   wer stritte den Rang Ihm!
 Er Bronn des All   ringsum,   des Schöpfung entsprang Ihm!

Seine Gestalt —   kein Aug   hat sie gesehn, nur das
 Herz seelenvoll,   schaun und   erkennend, zudrang Ihm.

Sein mächtger Glanz   umringt   des Weltalls Rund; so heißt
 „Raum" Er dem All,   weil kein   Raum rings sich umrang Ihm.

Schaunde, die nie   zu schaun!   Schaundem, der nie zu schaun,
 nah' du und bring   Preisdanks–   und Segensworts Klang Ihm!

SEHNSUCHT

Zu ihm, des wahren Lebens Quell, hintracht ich.
 Das Leben drum, das schal und leer mißacht ich.
Schaun meines Koenigs Antlitz — was begehrt' ich noch!
 Nicht kenne andre Macht und andre Pracht ich.
O dürfte ich ihn sehen doch, wärs nur im Traum!
 Gern schlief' ich ewgen Schlaf und nie aufwacht' ich.
Und säh sein Antlitz ich in meines Herzens Schacht,
 Nicht gäb dem Aug, hinauszuspähn, noch Macht ich.

NACHTS

Jüngst weckten mich Gedanken Dir zu eigen
 und ließen schaun mich Deiner Gnaden Reigen.
Hell lehrten sie, wie Dein Gebild, die Seele,
 mit mir verflochten — Wunder, nie zu schweigen!
Und sah mein gläubig Herz dich nicht, als hätt es
 gedurft sich mit am Sinai erzeigen?
Dich suchten meine Schauungen. In mich trat
 dein Glanz, in mein Gewölk herabzusteigen.
Aufscheuchte da mein Sinnen mich vom Lager,
 vor Deiner Herrlichkeit mich, Herr, zu neigen.

EVENT

Heaven's spheres   saw your brilliance, then they reeled.
The billows of the abyss, when   you drew away, they fell still.

And how should the souls stand,   there where your secret dwells,
Where the fire beats through the cliffs,   that, flaming, they
    flicker and fade,
Yet their heart becomes strong through You,   if You want to
    strengthen them.
So that following the spirits who   see Your Being they give thanks.
That is why the praise of all souls rises up   to You, oh Lord God,
For words of praise find You,   around Whom they twine
    magnificently.

ALL MY LIMBS

All my limbs   call out: Lord, who is like You!

Body and life   I have from You.
My heart, when sorely agitated, I comfort it with You.
My poetic striving,   I surrendered it to you,
The measure of my songs   — draws near Your dwelling,   adjusts to You.

The breath which I inhale,   originates from You,
The ray in my eye   flames out of You,
The counsel which is good for me beats down in You,
My spirit, against whatever it reflects,   looks upon You,   yields to You.

And may my languishing   reach for You,
Envelop You   in the depths of my breast —
Which were thinking about You,vainly struggled,
My feathers, however dream-high they wave,   do not reach You.

But You billow out the banner of those who surround You,
You raise the standard high   to those who follow You,
So that You never slip out   of the memory of those
                                imploring You —
My impulse again   is at work so that I forsake   You, alas, easily.

Ah see, You saw   all my thoughts,
When once you built   my beginning,
Then You entrusted   to me this innermost:
My heart — down   to the narrowest rampart   nothing escapes You.

EREIGNIS

Die Sphären des Himmels sahn   dein Glänzen, da wanken sie.
  Die Wogen des Abgrunds, als   du auszogst, still sanken sie.

Und wie solln die Seelen stehn,   dort wo Dein Geheimnis haust,
  wo Feuer durch Felsen schlägt,   daß flammend zerschwanken sie.

Doch stark wird ihr Herz durch Dich,   wofern Du sie stärken willst,
  daß folgend den Geistern, die   dein Sein schauen, danken sie.

Drum Lob aller Seelen steig'   zu Dir auf, O Herregott,
  denn Lobworte finden Dich,   den prächtig umranken sie.

ALL MEINE GLIEDER

Meine Glieder   rufen all-alle: Herr, wer gleicht dir!

  Ja Leib und Leben,   von Dir hab ichs,
  Mein Herz, wills beben,   in Dir lab ichs,
  Mein dichtend Streben,   Dir ergab ichs,
Meiner Lieder   Maß — Deiner Halle   nahts, geeicht dir.

  Hauch, den ich sauge,   von Dir stammt er,
  Strahl, mir im Auge,   aus Dir flammt er,
  Rat, den ich tauge,   in Dir rammt er,
Mein Geist, wider   was er auch pralle,   schaut Dich, – weicht dir.

  Und mag mein Schmachten   nach dir langen,
  In Busens Schachten   Dich umfangen –
  Die Dich umdachten,   fruchtlos rangen,
Mein Gefieder,   wie's traumhoch walle,   nicht zureicht dir.

  Doch Fahne schwellst du   Dich Umstehnden,
  Panier hoch stellst du   Dir Nachgehnden,
  Daß nie entfällst du   Dich Anflehnden –

Mein Trieb wieder   wirkt, daß abfalle   ich, weh, leicht dir.

  Ach sieh, du schautest   all mein Sinnen,
  Als einst du bautest   mein Beginnen,
  Da du vertrautest   mir dies Innen:
Mein Herz — nieder   zu engstem Walle   nichts entschleicht dir.

THE INCOMPARABLE ONE

Who is like You, to whom the depth is light,
Whispered praise surrounds You, source of miracles!

He created nothingness suddenly into being-so;
He approaches hearts, his image fled
From eyes; hence do not ask, how and where!
Filled with Him is every place in the universe.

If you keep evil desire far from you
You will find God in your breast;
You must only wander with a quiet heart —
He lowers, raises life's waves.

And see the riddle: paths of the soul!
In this wisdom bathe blissfully, —
You will find therein the grace of freedom:
Indeed you are a prisoner, the world is the cell.

Thinking — send it to join yourself to Him!
Dissolve your will and do His!
Whither would his eye not shine?
His doing knows no borders nor thresholds.

He, first of all, lives before the speck of the world's dust.
And He created. And bears. Like the flower,
Which whithers, so goes the fame of man:
As a leaf withers, withers he fast.

DER UNVERGLEICHLICHE

Wer gleicht Dir, dem Tiefen helle,
Lobumraunt du, Wunderquelle!

Jäh umschuf er Nichts ins Sosein;
Herzen naht er, Augen floh sein
Bild; drum frag nicht, wie und wo! Sein
Voll im All ist jede Stelle.

Hältst dir ferne böse Lust du,
Findest Gott in deiner Brust du;
Herzensstill nur wandeln mußt du —
Er senkt, hebt des Lebens Welle.

Und Rätsel sieh: der Seele Pfade!
In dieser Weisheit selig bade, —
Findest drin der Freiheit Gnade:
Bist ja Häftling, Welt die Zelle.

Denken — sends, dich Ihm zu einen!
Lösch deinen Willen und tu Seinen!
Wohin würd nicht Sein Auge scheinen?
Sein Tun kennt Grenze nicht noch Schwelle.

All-erst lebt vor Weltstaubs Krume
Er. Und erschuf. Und trägt. Wie Blume,
Die welkt, so gehts des Menschen Ruhme:
Wie ein Blatt welkt, welkt er schnelle.

NONE OTHER!

Each who sees me lamenting fans my heart's flame.
"What sweeter trumpery," revilers ask, "does Your Friend offer above
all friends?"

Hymn and wisdom might draw around His image,
Wholly beauty — praise rings itself endlessly around Him.
I donned the dress of a cry of lament for his fleeing.
Would that He have compassion, may He feel it for me anew!
Would that He speak comfort to me! how do I bear it: Loving — and
He disappeared!

The original fire is locked in me — thus His Name burns me,
Sealed up into my heart and marrow.
And stirred up the ones who spit at my Law,
Rebuke and plague me who turned to His service,
They dare blasphemies, when I guard the pledge of His honours.

When they threaten to eradicate Your entire action,
Shame and pain do I choose before such a flight,
Save, and share with the heart the fruit of Your Law!
Should I reject You, so forget me, right hand!
Should a foreign word please me, cleave, tongue, to my palate!

Onto this ear resounded the news of Your fame,
Reed Sea and Sinai are full of Your greatness.
How could my mouth, how indeed, bring tribute to a second?
Heart, eyes lack courage to loosen the band of my foot,
If I see Him towering above, the Only One. Beside Whom no second stood.

KEINER SONST!

Jeder, der klagen   mich sieht, schürt meines Herzens Brand.
„Was beut", schmähn Fragen,   „Dein Freund vor Freunden süßern
                       Tand?"

Hymnus und Weisheit   möchten sein Bild umziehn,
Ganz Schöne — Preis reiht   sich endelos um ihn.
Klagegeschreis Kleid   anlegt ich um sein Fliehn.
Wollt Mitleid tragen!   macht, daß er neu für mich empfand!
Wollt Trost mir sagen!   wie trag ichs: Lieben — und er schwand!

Urfeu'r geriegelt   in mich — so brennt mich Sein
Name, versiegelt   ins Herz mir und Gebein.
Und aufgewiegelt,   die mein Gesetz bespein,
Schelten und plagen   mich, der zu Seinem Dienst sich wandt',
Lästrungen wagen   sie, wahr' ich Seiner Ehren Pfand.

Drohn auszumerzen   sie Deine heilge Zucht,
Schande und Schmerzen   wähl ich vor solcher Flucht.
Heil, Teil dem Herzen   Deines Gesetzes Frucht!
Wollt' ich ausschlagen   Dich, so vergiß mich, rechte Hand!
Würd mir behagen   fremd Wort, kleb, Zung', an Gaumens
                       Wand!

An dies mein Ohr die   Maer Deines Ruhmers scholl,
Schilfmeer und Sinai   sind Deiner Größe voll.
Wie brächt mein Mund, wie   wohl einem Zweiten Zoll?
Herz, Augen zagen,   zu lockern meines Fußes Band,
Seh Ihn ich ragen,   Einzgen. Bei dem kein Zweiter stand.

THE LOVERS

Him His lovers entreat,   they ask about his love,
    yet they dare to await   the late rain of his grace.
Does not His mercy dwell nearby,   even though throned on high and
    towering above?
    thus are his acts great,   widely reigning, they tower up.
And those gladly would see His light,   with eyes, therefore they test
    their heart; they see then the light,   His exalted light, thus they
    lack courage.
But the word of His Law,   His Kingdom — they shoulder it,
    borne by His fame,   and His fame — they carry it.
All splendour, all magnificence   they call up and announce,
    and as their throat orders it,   they say what is greatest.

THE DAY OF JUDGMENT

Countless, they come
                the children of the earth,
And are all taken
                under the staff like the herd,
The desecrators as the pious ones,
                so that there be judgement for all,
Before the Lord, for He is coming,
                indeed is coming, to judge the earth.

Today the fate is assigned
                and World must stand before the Judge.
The powers which once created it,
                God allowed to see today for the first time.
He erected today the steps of the throne
                high, whether to become, to pass away,
Deep, yet viewing furthest distances
                in heaven and on earth.

DIE LIEBENDEN

Ihm flehn seine Liebenden,   sein Lieben umfragen sie,
   des Spätregens seiner Huld   zu harren doch wagen sie.
Haust nicht seine Gnade nah,   er thron hoch und ragend gleich?
   so sind seine Taten groß,   und weitherrschend ragen sie.

Und jene sähn gern sein Licht,   mit Augen, drum prüfen sie
   ihr Herz; sehn dann das Licht, sein hehres, so zagen sie.

Doch seines Gesetzes Wort,   sein Reich — auf sich nehmen sies,
   getragen von seinem Ruhm,   und sein Ruhm — den tragen sie.
All Glanz, alle Herrlichkeit   errufen und künden sie,
   und wie's ihre Kehle beut,   das Größeste sagen sie.

GERICHTSTAG

Ja Unzählige kommen
            sie, die Kinder der Erde,
Und werden sämtlich genommen
            untern Stab wie die Herde,
So die Frevler, die Frommen,
            daß allen Spruchsprechung werde,
Vor dem Herrn, denn er kommt,
            ja kommt, zu richten die Erde.

Heut wird Schicksal berufen
            und Welt muß dem Richter stehen.
Die Kräfte, die einst sie schufen,
            ließ heut Gott erstmalig sehen.
Erstellte heut des Throns Stufen,
            hoch ob Werden, Vergehen,
Tief doch schaund fernste Hufen
            im Himmel und auf der Erde.

Today all rounds of the universe are surrounded.
      The foundations of the world's structure, they stood.
Today the barrenness of the three women
      has vanished, they gave birth to holy ones.
Those who experienced the burden of service
      heard today the news of freedom.
Thus these hours bring one day
      the journey home from the foreign earth.

You, flock, invited today! Say
      "King!" — your King chases away from you
The kings. So that he notices you,
      Alarm bugles, ring forth, blow, you!
To save you from the danger of the grave,
      and so that His countenance illuminates you
Nay, he fashions you anew, young like the eagle,
      may he water the earth like rain.

From the Land far away may there sound,
      Dove, your poor stammering.
You who calls out of the swell of waves
      your song, may it reflect heavenward!
So that the judgement soon may resound
      to the rose in the rocky mounds:
Your people, may they all be just,
      the eternal heirs of the earth!

Umründet sind heut Alls Runden.
       Des Weltbaus Pfeiler, sie stunden.
Unfruchtbarkeit ist heut schwunden
       drei Frauen, Heilger entbunden.
Die der Fron Druck empfunden,
       hörten heut Freiheitskunden.
So bringen einst diese Stunden
       den Heimzug aus fremder Erde.

Du heut geladene Schar! Sprich
       „König!" — dein König scheucht dir
Die Kön'ge. Daß er gewahr' dich,
       Lärmhörner, schmettert, keucht, ihr!
Zu retten aus Grabs Gefahr dich,
       und daß sein Angesicht leucht' dir,
Schaff' neu er jung wie den Aar dich,
       tränk' wie Regen die Erde.

Aus der Ferne Land halle,
       Taube, dein arm Gelalle.
Rufrin aus Wogenschwalle,
       Dein Sang himmelan pralle!
Daß der Spruch dann bald schalle
       der Rose im Felsenwalle:
Dein Volk Gerechte sie alle,
       die ewigen Erben der Erde!

HOMECOMING

'Every straying, You bear it for me. Stretch out
    Your arm to the one returning homeward!
Yet if I follow Your guidance,
    I must renounce my own counsel.
Spread Your light around my eye!
    Heal the perversion of my heart!
Prepare the homecoming for us, Lord,
                To you, so that we return home.'

"A precious possession to me indeed
    is your heart! My bosom burns for you.
Before there dawns for me my day of retribution.
    I warned you in your wretchedness.
A call to me in my sanctuary
    rang out, to make you finally better.
Return home to me,
                then I shall return home to you."

'You have taught us Your Law
    which we did not exchange nor distort,
we who desired only Your service
    knew only Your Name.
How are the men whom You love,
    like berries, burnt in fire!
The enemy, thresh him like corn! Your sword,
    draw it up upon them who are unmanned by terror,
They are unburdened by fear of You,
    we the ones captivated therein!
The stylus wrote, adamantine,
                Judah's revolt.'

HEIMKEHR

‚Jed Irrn, du trägst mirs. Breite
    den Arm dem Heimwärtskehren!
Doch folg ich deiner Leite,
    muß eignen Rats entbehren.
Dein Licht ums Aug mir spreite!
    Heil' Herzens Sichverkehren!
Heimkehr uns, Herr, bereite
    zu dir, daß heim wir kehren.'

„Ja köstlich Eigentum mir
    eu'r Herz! Mein Busen brennt um euch.
Eh tagt Vergeltertum mir,
    warnt ich im Elende euch.
Ruf im Heiligtum mir
    erscholl, zu bessern endlich euch.
Kehrt heim zu mir,
    so kehr ich heim zu euch."

‚Hast uns dein Gesetz gelehrt,
    das wir nicht tauschten, wandten,
Die wir nur deinen Dienst begehrt,
    nur deinen Namen kannten.
Wie sind die Männer, die dir wert,
    gleich Beeren, glutverbrannten!
Den Feind, drisch ihn wie Korn! Dein Schwert,
    zücks auf den Schreckentmannten.
Deiner Furcht sie unbeschwert,
    wir die drein Gebannten!
Stift schrieb, diamanten,
    Judas Aufbegehrn.'

"Make yourselves holy, be pure, flee from
    the decay of every corpse!
And approach, enter here
    as living souls.
Flesh melts away, bones, which
    the throats of graves swallow up
Like shards they will be consecrated
    to the mute concealment of caves,
The souls, to be anew, which float up,
    jewels of light.
Hurry! upward! let not your eye go moist
        for shards."

'And can blood-red become white?
    as wool behaves like purple?
Heart become granite, gneiss —
    ah, make it into tender flesh.
Do you watch for the false glitter in the Son
    of the inherited sin, which was preserved?
They who were clay before you,
    could their spirit move boldly onward?
You can build, tear down,
    When we matched word to word.
Can chaff and straw withstand
        the hot flame?'

"And God's sons end up
    dug into the grave of desires?!
When spirits send you bread,
    the rock's breasts will give you drink!
Atonement — you have that which would have to
    turn about the souls' sickness:
The strict gifts of God:
    The armour of the Commandments, of the Law.
Leave the niche of the prison-wall!
    to the most distant coasts of hope!
Gird your loins,
        Put on your shoes."

„Heiligt euch, seid rein, flieh'
    jeder Leichnams Schwelen!
Und nahet euch, geht ein hie
    als lebendge Seelen.
Wegschmilzt Fleisch, Gebein, die
    verschlingen Gräberkehlen.
Wie Scherben wird man weihn sie
    der Höhlen stummen Hehlen,
Die Seelen neu zum Sein, die
    aufschweben, Lichtjuwelen.
Eilt! hinan! nicht feucht' um
        Scherben sich das Auge euch."

  ,Und kann Blutrot sich weißen?
    wie Wolle Purpur arten?
Herz graniten, gneißen —
    o machs zum fleischern zarten.
Spähst du am Sohn das Gleißen
    der Erbschuld, der bewahrten?
Die Ton vor dir geheißen,
    ihr Geist zög kühn auf Fahrten?
Erbaun kannst du, einreißen,
    wenn Wort zu Wort wir paarten.
Kann Spreu und Stroh der heißen
        Flamme sich erwehren?'

  „Und Gottes Söhne enden
    gewühlt ins Grab der Lüste?!
Da Brot euch Geister senden,
    getränkt euch Felsens Brüste!
Sühnwerk — ihr habts, das wenden
    der Seelen Siechtum müßte:
Gottes strenge Spenden:
    Gebots, Gesetzes Rüste.
Laßt Kerkers Mauerblenden!
    zu fernster Hoffnung Küste!
Gurte um die Lenden,
        Schuhe an den Füßen euch."

'Your spirit, your power pours
    out the spirit, the powers.
Yours is all the authority! did you
    lend it to anyone that he might ape it?
On the shaft of your scales you see
    the transactions of man.
Only the sap of your hope shoots
    in the shafts of the terrestrial tribes.
The clasp of your key-bolt locks
    the clasps of all keybolts.
If you flee from me in anger
               to whose favour should I aspire?'

"Call delivery to the souls
    from the service of corpses.
Accept the giving of your inheritance,
    instead of passing through the universe.
On the day of the world's new order
    when the graves open
And in the disunion of spirit and flesh
    I put together the hoard of bones:
Then, then consecration radiates around you,
    to reach crowns, —
When the signs of abomination
             were washed off."

'Ah, him, the nearest to you, you pushed away, —
    who shows him the stars of consolation?
Who helps him — you have abandoned him,
    he fell — , that he might learn to stand!
If you do not pour salvation around
    and have pity on him
if you do not enclose him in a cherub-flight
    and the centre of a citadel's cliffs,
awaiting the day which you promised,
    him You lift out of cisterns of mud —
Ah do not be far from us,
             for devastation approaches.'

,Dein Geist, dein Kraft geißt
    aus den Geist, die Kräfte.
Dein die Allherrschaft! liehst
    du wem, daß er sie äffte?
An deiner Wage Schaft siehst
    du, was des Manns Geschäfte.
Nur deiner Hoffnung Saft schießt
    in irdscher Stämme Schäfte.
Deines Riegels Haft schließt
    aller Riegel Häfte.
Wenn du mir zornentrafft fliehst,
        wes Huld soll ich gehren?'

„Den Seelen ruft Befreiung
    von dem Dienst der Leichen.
Annehmt Erbbeleihung,
    statt durchs All zu streichen.
Am Tag der Weltneureihung
    wenn Grabeshüllen weichen
Und in Geist-Fleisch-Entzweiung
    ich füg der Knochen Speichen:
Dann, dann umstrahlt euch Weihung,
    Kronen zu erreichen, —
Wenn der Greuel Zeichen
        abgewaschen ward von euch."

,Ach ihn, dir nächst, fern stießest du, —
    wer zeigt ihm Trostes Sterne?
Wer hilft dem — ihn verließest du,
    er fiel — , daß stehn er lerne!
Wenn nicht Heil rings gießest du
    und sein erbarmst dich gerne,
In Cherubflug ihn schließest du
    und Burgenfelsgekerne,
Des Tags harrnd, den verhießest du,
    ihn hebst aus Schlammzisterne —
Ach sei uns nicht ferne,
        denn es naht Verheeren!'

HEAR

Hear, the shyly daring ones
Who lie down before You, beseeching.
Father, from the child's stirring
Did you want to hide your ear?

Indeed they cried out of the depths,
Out of much distress they flee.
Oh, do not let them move away empty
Today from your paths.

The heart's hot swelling
Wanted to still the surging of guilt.
You are not doing it for their sake,
Do it, Refuge, for Your own.

And their going astray today forgive it.
Take their simple supplication as a sacrifice.
Direct their heart towards You.
And incline your ear.

Their tearstained faces, take notice.
Seek the lamb, the one gone astray,
Make it that your shepherd arises,
Gently take care of the flock.

They are going on the wrong path,
Let them today see forgiveness,
If late in the day they now beseech.
Let Your blessing find them.

HÖR

Hör, die scheu-verwegen
Flehnd vor dich sich legen.
Vater, Kindesregen
Wolltst dein Ohr verhegen?

Ja aus Tiefen schrien sie,
Aus viel Nöten fliehn sie.
O laß leer nicht ziehn sie
Heut von deinen Stegen.

Herzens Heißaufquillen,
Schwall der Schuld woll stillen.
Tusts nicht ihretwillen,
Tus, Hort, deinetwegen.

Und ihr Irrn heut schwicht es.
Opfer nimm ihr schlichtes
Flehn. Ihr Herz dir richt es.
Und neig dein Ohr entgegen.

Die verweint, bewirte,
Das Lamm such, das verirrte,
Mach, daß ersteh ihr Hirte,
Woll mild der Herde pflegen.

Auf Richtsteigen gehn sie,
Lass heut Vergebung sehn sie,
Wenn spättags nun flehn sie,
Finde sie dein Segen.

THE TRUE ONE

With all my strength, You, Truth, with all my soul
   do I love you, in the light, in the secret of my bosom.

Your Name is mine! — where could there be anyone, if someone stole
      it from me?
   My Beloved, He! — who could there be who would be missing
      there?
My Light, He! — could my wick be devoid of oil?
   Could there be stumbling? where I rely on such a staff?

Their mockery derides — fools! yet derisive mockery
   of your crown becomes for me the crown jewel!

My fountain of life! may my life be a praise for You
   and my song, as long as there is breath in me.

DER WAHRE

Mit ganzer Kraft, Du Wahrheit, ganzer Seele
    hab ich Dich lieb, im Licht, in Busens Hehle.

Dein Name mein! — wo gäbs, der den mir stehle?
    Mein Liebster Er! — wen gäbs, der da mir fehle?

Mein Licht Er! — meinem Docht gebrächs an Öle?
    Gäbs Wank? wo solchem Stab ich mich empfehle!

Ihr Hohn schmaelt — Toren! wird doch Hohngeschmaele
    ob Deiner Krone mir zum Kronjuwele!

Mein Lebensborn! sei Dir Ein Preis mein Leben
    und Sang, solang noch Hauch in meiner Kehle.

YOUR GOD

Still slumbering? Hasn't your rest been sufficient?
Renounce the fool's derisions!
Look upon heaven's steps of the spheres,
    far from human footfalls.
Move towards the arch-eternal rock's service!
    Thus moves the fleet of stars.
But enough, not more rest?
    Up! call to your God!

Arise to look upon his heavenly vault,
    His fingers created it.
And the edifice of His tent high in the blue,
    He hung it in his arms.
And stars, his seal, marvel at,
    he engraved His ring.
Tremble before His dreadfulness,
    await the salvation, of which He is the carrier —
so that the world may not decay around you,
    and thus also your heart become rotten.

And rise up at midnight,
    to tread upon the footprints of the great ones,
who, the splendour of the Psalms on their tongues,
    with reflection, reflective constantly,
spent their day fasting,
their night with praying,
    God a shaft in their heart,
they are planets around the throne —
Climb up your way, up, with might,
    to Him, to your God.

Let your eye stream tears on and on,
    that your repentance might atone for sins.
And implore to the place of your steward
    that it might wean you of the hate of men
And bend your pride up to there
    and choose the good: it is beautiful.
Honour God out of your riches, —
    until the Redeemers travel to the heights
and from your flock resounds the word:
    Turn to your God!

DEIN GOTT

Im Schlummer noch? Genug der Ruh?
Sag ab dem Narrenspotte!
Himmels Sphärentritt schau du,
fern der Menschen Trotte.
Urewgen Felsens Dienst fahr zu!
so fährt der Sterne Flotte.
Doch genug, nicht fürder ruh?
Auf! ruf deinem Gotte!

Heb dich, sein Gewölb zu schaun,
es machtens seine Finger.
Und seinen Zeltbau hoch im Blaun,
in seinen Armen hing er.
Und Sterne, Siegel ihm, bestaun,
eingrub seinen Ring er.
Bebe du vor seinem Graun,
des Heils harr, des er Bringer, —
Dass Welt dich nicht umrotte,
und so dein Herz verrotte.

Und stehe auf um Mitternacht,
der Großen Spur zu treten,
Die, auf der Zunge Psalmenpracht,
mit Sinnen, sinnig-steten,
Fastend ihren Tag verbracht,
ihre Nacht mit Beten,
Gotte in ihr Herz ein Schacht,
sie um den Thron Planeten —
Steig ihr Weg, hinauf, mit Macht,
Ihm zum deinem Gotte.

Dein Aug ström' Tränen fort und fort,
daß Sünden deine Reu versöhn'.
Und fleh zu deines Walters Ort,
daß Menschenhaß er dir entwöhn'.
Und beuge deinen Stolz bis dort,
und wähl das Gute: es ist schön.
Ehre Gott aus deinem Hort, —
bis einst Heilande walln zu Höhn
Und deiner Schar entbraust das Wort:
Zuricht dich deinem Gotte!

The poor ones! Earthly brood!
    where is wisdom to be there?
Man's particular good distinguished from
    the beast: such a small nothing.
Only: his gazing radiated around the shelter
    — the heart's vision! not the eye's illusion —
And the flood of the dark wells,
    more precious than wine.
But thus, flesh and blood,
    you approach your God.

"I am Who I am," thus He speaks,
    Whose Will tests deeds,
Who sends death, life, close to each other,
    lowers grave-deep, raises high up.
You, endure His final judgement
    and live! Leave the blustering
which is intent on "When?" and "Where?",
    "What is below?" and "What is above?" —
No, rather you be wholly and simply
    with Him, with your God.

HIS PEACE

The hand of the living — its shadow becomes your roof,
    if you simply and sincerely place only upon Him your
    concerns.
When you are walking, He takes care that your foot does not stumble.
    When you are taking action — he brings it about that your
    arm is not weak.
Seek peace, chase after Him! Do you not confess that
    He is: "Lord of Peace," and: "He Who makes peace"?

Die Armen! Erdenbrut!
      wo soll da Weisheit sein?
Des Menschen Sondergut
      vorm Tier: ein Nichts so klein.
Nur: Schaun umstrahlte Hut
      — Herzschau! nicht Augenschein — ,
Und dunkler Bronnen Flut,
      köstlicher denn Wein.
So aber, Fleisch und Blut,
      nahst du deinem Gotte.

‚Ich bin, der ich bin‘, so spricht,
      des Willen Taten proben,
Der Tod schickt, Leben, dicht bei dicht,
      grabtief senkt, hebt nach oben.
Du stehe seinem Weltgericht
      und lebe! Laß das Toben,
Das auf ‚Wann?‘ und ‚Wo?‘ erpicht,
      ‚Was drunten?‘ und ‚Was droben?‘ —
Nein, sondern sei du ganz und schlicht
      mit Ihm, mit deinem Gotte.

SEIN FRIEDE

Des Lebendgen Hand — ihr Schatten wird dein Dach,
  stellst du schlicht und redlich nur auf Ihn dein Sach.

Wenn du wandelst, sorgt er, daß dein Fußnicht schwank;
  wenn du handelst, — Er wirkt, daß dein Arm nicht schwach.

Suche Frieden, jag ihm nach! Bekennst du nicht,
  Er sei: ‚Herr des Friedens‘, und: ‚Der Frieden mach‘?

THE UNIVERSE

Let the mouth exult,
what you allow this sphere
of eye to look upon
in the wonderful display!

As well as it can,
let it start —
not because you
are fearful.

The wheel of the spheres
rises around your path,
and never does its
edifice contain you.

And whatever lives there,
however boldly it lifts itself
high over it
You are enthroned in the blue.

Round about in the
army of creatures —
it bears exact witness to
you who creates.

What does their call witness?
The One Who created them.
The How dwells far away
in the region of the riddle.

In the pre-creation mass,
in the final ruin
intones the echo
awe-filled.

God only He
in the divine halls!
He the Lord
of Lords all!

Today and Now
always is replaced, —
always irreplaceably
shines His brilliance.

Erects twelve spheres,
He hews the ascent
for the seven
who are there as guests.

The sun moves
at His word,
rises,
goes to rest.

Traversing its realm
like the king
from palace
to palace;

The moon, whose light,
though it does not circle
in a higher sphere,
yet grows pale in purity.

Then far around
star upon star,
the numbers are
adjusted Him.

He Who clearly sees
the Pleiades:
seven around
the candlestick's branches.

The largest circle,
which during the day
inclines westward
its load,

DAS ALL

Jauchz' der Mund,
was Du dies Rund
des Augs läß schaun
    an Wunderschau!

So gut er kann,
so heb' er an, —
nicht weil er vor
    Dir sichs trau'.

Der Sphären Rad
umhöht dein Pfad,
und nimmer faßt
    Dich ihr Bau.

Und was da lebt,
wie kühn sichs hebt,
hoch ob ihm
    thronst Du im Blau.

Es rings in der
Geschöpfe Heer —
dich Wirkenden
    bezeugts genau.

Was zeugt ihr Ruf?
Wer sie schuf.
Das Wie haust fern
    in Rätsels Gau.

Im Urgeball,
im Endzerfall
tönt ehrfurchtbang
    Widerhall:

Der sieht klar
Plejadenschar:
sieben um
    Leuchters Ast;

Gott nur Er
im Göttersaal!
Er der Herr
    der Herren all!

Heut und Jetzt
stets ersetzt, —
ersatzlos stets
    glänzt Sein Glast.

Zwölfkreis baut,
den Sieben haut
Er den Steig,
    die dort zu Gast.

Die Sonn' rückt fort
auf Sein Wort,
macht sich auf,
    geht zur Rast,

Durchziehnd ihr Reich,
dem König gleich,
von Palast
    zu Palast;

Der Mond, des Licht,
kreist auch nicht
in höhrm Kreis,
    rein doch blaßt;

Dann rings fern
Stern an Stern,
die Zahlen Ihm
    angepaßt,

Was sich haßt
und was sich faßt,
allem rolln
    sie im Blut.

Bowed down
it mutely gives testimony:
One holds
the universe embraced.

Lofty surely,
but apparent
to the eye how it
is reflected on His work:

God only He
in the divine halls!
He the Lord
of Lords all!

And around He places
a tent,
to which He gave the earth
for protection.

That the earth might not stand
on the ground,
no, floating in the
void, it rests;

Its impetus
attempts flight downward,
towards the abyss
is its intention;

Homewards the fire flames,
from whence it comes,
upwards towards
heaven's glow;

And to the two
right in between
the wind's blowings
and water's floods;

That which hates each other and
that which is bound to each other,
they roll all
in the blood.

Out of them shot
sprouting of plants
as Adam's son
and animal's brood.

And moisture gives a drink,
is reduced
according to kindness, and according to
Anger's fury;

For his arrow
becomes portion of the slanderer,
and to whom He is well-disposed,
overbrimming with divine mercy.

God only He
in the divine halls!
He the Lord
of Lords all!

Constant passing away
and constant arising —
Constant only He
without year and count.

Before all Being
He alone,
thus again at the
end some time.

Not power of the arms,
Only spirit creates
creation, which
He commanded:

Der größte Kreis,
der tagesweis
westwärts neigt
 seine Last, —

Hingebeugt
stumm er zeugt:
Einer hält
 das All umfaßt.

Erhaben zwar,
doch offenbar
Dem Aug, wie's auf
 Sein Werk prall':

Gott nur Er
im Göttersaal!
Er der Herr
 der Herren all!

Und ringsum stellt
Er ein Zelt,
dem gab die Erd
 Er zur Hut,

Daß sie stund
nicht auf Grund,
nein schwebend im
 Leeren ruht;

Ihre Wucht
sucht abwärts Flucht,
nach tiefstem Ort
 steht ihr Mut;

Heim Feuer flammt,
von wos stammt,
aufwärts gen
 Himmels Glut;

Aus ihnen schoß
Pflanzensproß
wie Adamssohn
 und Tieresbrut.

Und Feuchte tränkt,
wird eingeschränkt,
nach Güte, nach
 Zornes Wut;

Denn sein Pfeil
wird Lästrers Teil;
wem er hold,
 Huldüberschwall.

Gott nur Er
im Göttersaal!
Er der Herr
 der Herren all!

Dau'rnd Vergehn
und dau'rnd Entstehen —
Sein Dauern nur
 ohn Jahr und Zahl.

Vor allem Sein
Er allein,
so wieder am
 End einmal.

Nicht Arms Kraft,
Geist nur schafft
Schöpfung, die
 Er befahl:

Seelen viel,
Wissens Spiel
und klugen Sinns
 Leuchtfanal;

Many souls,
Game of knowledge
the beacon light
of balanced judgement;

Splendour of the vault
He arches, makes
the water's ray
to rise above it;

Source of the day
and light of the stars
that shine into the
valley of the earth.

And threatening
and blazing
call, which
commended His praise.

And precious stones
cascading consecrations
to Him with a hymn
with a chorus;

Praising ones,
Circling ones,
Flaming ones,
around Him a wall:

God only He
in the divine halls!
He the Lord
of Lords all!

Ah, He Who thinks
and, ah, He Who guides
and, ah, He Who makes
known the future.

Whose glance finds
medicine, poison
and knows beforehand
the result!

Oh, retrieve them
the flocks of Yours
from right out of
the lion's throat!

Tender lambs,
crowded together
among strangers they
are round about.

You tormented them,
hurt them,
and plunged them
into hell's ground.

And when You heaped up sorrow —
their arm holds You
and they trust
in Your Covenant.

Your Name rings
through Your world
up and down the streets
out of their mouths.

Aloud they praise, —
like the flock which
was, so that
Your Throne should stand and

of the "Thrice-
Holy"may the ray
fall upon His Head
Who is their Creator:

God only He
in the divine halls!
He the Lord
of Lords all!

Und zu den zwein
mittzwischenein
Windeswehn
und Wasserflut;

Tages Quell
und Sterne hell,
die scheinen ins
Erdental;

Und Drohender
und Lohender
Ruf, der Sein
Lob empfahl;

Und Edelstein-
sprühnde weihn
mit Hymnus Ihn,
mit Choral;

Preisende,
Kreisende,
Flammende
um Ihn ein Wall:

Gott nur Er
im Göttersaal!
Er der Herr
der Herren all!

Ach, der denkt
und, ach, der lenkt
und, ach, der macht
Künftges kund,

Des Blick trifft
Heiltrank, Gift
und weiß voraus
den Befund!

Gewölbes Pracht
wölbt er, macht
ob ihm sich staun
Wassers Strahl;

O hol sie ein
die Herde Dein
mitten aus
Löwenschlund!

Lämmer zart,
zwanggeschart
bei Fremden sie
rings im Rund.

Quältest sie,
strähltest sie,
und tauchst sie in
Höllengrund.

Und häufst du Harm —
Dich hält ihr Arm,
und sie traun
Deinem Bund.

Dein Name gellt
durch Deine Welt
straßuf, straßab
aus ihrem Mund.

Laut preisen sie, —
der Schar gleich, die
ward, auf daß
dein Thron steh' und

des „Dreimal-
Heilig" Strahl
aufs Haupt Ihm, der
ihr Schöpfer, fall':

Gott nur Er
im Göttersaal!
Er der Herr
der Herren all!

THE FAR-AND-NEAR ONE

God, where are You found,
   Whose space the breadths of aether veil.
And where would You not be found,
   Whose border fills the breadths of the earth.

Dweller in my heart's core,
   He, and establishes the ends of the earth.
To those near He is the arch-refuge
   for those far the gleam of hope.
You, — enthroned among cherubim!
   You, — crowned amid clouds!
Entwined with songs of Your host, You —
   they praise You, the blessed ones.
You burst open the rounds of the spheres —
   as once the Temple's sides!

And You have raised Yourself
   high into the secrets of darkness
To them You remain mingled
   more than body, than soul.
Hear how they promise:
   He only should command us.
When would You have freed from fear
   him who has accepted Your yoke?
Let You Yourself grant a respite for his supplications —
   You must prepare his bread for him.

For the sake of Your nearness
   my heart went out, glimmered up to You.
Thus it came towards You —
   see! You come towards me.
With the rain of miracles,
   flowing forth as at once, oh, You profit me.
To whom do You remain unfelt!
   Heaven, pavillions of stars
Must declare You, You,
   in silent stepping.

DER FERN-UND-NAHE

Ja Gott wo wirst funden Du,
      des Raum hülln Ätherweiten.
Und wo nicht wärest funden Du,
      des Saum füllt Erdenbreiten.

Herzensgrund-Bewohner
      Er, und stell Erd-Gränzen.
Nahen Erzbastion er,
      Fernen Hoffnungsglänzen.
Du, — Cherubenthroner!
      Du, — in Wolkenkränzer!
Heerscharliedumwunden Du —
      es lobt Dich Benedeiten.
Sprengest Sphärenrunden Du —
      wie erst Tempels Seiten!

Und hast Dich erhoben
      hoch in Dunkels Hehle,
Ihnen bleibst verwoben
      mehr als Leib, als Seele.
Hoer, wie sie geloben:
      Er nur uns befehle.
Wann hättst furchtentbunden Du
      den Deinem Joch Gefreiten?
Wolltst sein Flehn selbst stunden Du —
      sein Brot mußt ihm bereiten!

Deiner Nähe wegen
      ging aus mein Herz, aufglomms zu Dir.
So kams Dir entgegen —
      sieh! entgegen kommst du mir.
Mit der Wunder Regen,
      quellnd wie einst, o, frommst du mir.
Wem bleibst unempfunden Du!
      Himmel, Sterngezeiten
Müssen Dich bekunden, Du,
      in schweigendem Schreiten.

Ah! does God want to share
                    His dwelling place with Adam's sons?
Can their spirit overtake Him?
                    disaccustom itself to the primaeval dust?
But yes! Where You want to linger,
                    their song of praise may crown You.
Forms of beasts stood, to
                    bear the consecrated one.
Your Throne, bound. You
                    bear them, in eternities.

THE NAME

Year out, year in, in Your house a camping place
     holds the happy people, where Your Name found its place.
High, world high dwells the Name and has Being yet in
     the stricken heart and where anyone writhed in wretchedness.
And the heights of heaven do not contain Him,
     whether He descends to Sinai, lives in the flaming bush.
For near is His way, very near, at the same time very far,
     for, what He created, He bound to Himself and the Other.
I thank God alone, when my heart spun thoughts
     and Him only, if my mouth spoke and answered.

Ach! will Wohnsitz teilen
      denn Gott mit Adams Söhnen?
Kann Ihn ihr Geist ereilen?
      des Urstaubs sich entwöhnen?
Doch ja! wo Du willst weilen,
      darf Dich ihr Loblied krönen.
Tiergestalten stunden, zu
      tragen den geweihten.
Deinen Thron, verbunden. Du
      trägst sie, in Ewigkeiten.

DER NAME

Jahraus, jahrein   in Deinem Haus   faßt Lagerstand
   das Glücksvolk, wo   Dein Name drin   sein Lager fand.
Hoch, welthoch wohnt   der Name und   hat Sein doch in
   zerschlagnem Herz   und wo sich wer   in Jammer wand.
Und Himmelshöhn   fassen ihn nicht,   ob er herab
   zum Sinai   stieg, wohnt in Buschs   Dornflammenbrand.
Denn nahe ist   sein Weg gar sehr   und gleich sehr weit,
   da, was er schuf,   ans Selbst er und   ans Andre band.
Allein Gott dank   ichs, wenn mein Herz   Gedanken spann,
   und ihm nur, wenn   Rede mein Mund   und Antwort stand.

CONSECRATED

Call three
Times: "Consecrated,"   to consecrate Him
                                         like the seraphim!

May jubilation ring
to the creator, who   gently received
                                         the beseeching of the creature.

The ring of the camp
He places around the throne   opposite
                                         the ring of the camp.

Let swing around the servant
crowd of the fire,   in which once the thorn
                                         was not consumed.

Seeking his
Countenance, therein Grace   and Truth stand
                                         in unison,

The appearance of fire
admixing wetness,   and neither of the two
                                         grows weak.

"Present!"
reports your   army of wind at the goal
                                         for the roll-call.

They are the sources
of the teaching, as   circles of Your space
                                         swell.

They brightly announce
Your sacred praise   which they spread
                                         quickly into the world.

They wrap themselves up
in shyness, crowning   Your head with
                                         precious jewels.

GEWEIHT

Ruft zu drein
   Malen: „Geweiht",   seraphenhaft
                       Ihn zu weihn!

Jubel kling'
   zum Schöpfer, der   mild des Geschöpfs
                       Flehn empfing.

Lagers Ring
   stellt um den Thron   genüber er
                       Lagers Ring.

Ihn umschwing'
   Dienstschar aus Feu'r,   drin einst der Dorn
                       nicht verging.

Suchen sein
   Antlitz, drin Gnad'   und Wahrheit stehn
                       im Verein,

Feuers Schein
   beimengend Nass,   und schwach wird keins
                       von den zwein.

„Hier zur Stell!"
   meldet sich Dein   Wind-Heer am Ziel
                       zum Appell.

Sind so Quell
   der Lehre, wie   rings Deines Raums
                       Ründe schwell'.

Künden hell
   Dein Weihelob,   das welthin sie
                       breiten schnell.

Hülln sich ein
   in Scheu, dein Haupt   umkrönend mit
                       Edelstein.

And that they are
Your work,   their breath says Yes,
                                        never No.

And now I,
out of the tomb of misery,   a ship, which the blowing
                                        of the storm surrounded, —

See me here,
calling "Consecrated,"   so that my ring
                                        matches the highest ring.

Never did my word
escape the circle   which suffering enclosed
                                        in a brotherly manner;

They became small
before the sons   of the maid too, who
                                        once were free men,

But they alone await
Your salvation,   they never want
                                        to accuse You of an injustice.

Though oppression
oppressed them,   which removed them far
                                        from the Land's splendour,

They called
what always at the end   a mouth cried out
                                        of the depths of suffering,

Did they not find
in You the original sources   of salvation, which
                                        still have never disappeared.

Of His Name —
original knowledge of it   is whispered from mouth to
                                        mouth a universal inheritance.

Und nun ich,
    aus Elends Gruft,   ein Schiff, das Sturms
                             Wehn umstrich, —

Hier sieh mich,
    rufend „Geweiht",   daß höchstem Ring
                             mein Ring glich.

Nie entwich
    mein Wort dem Kreis,   den Leiden schloß
                             brüderlich;

Wurden klein
    sie vor der Magd   Söhnen auch, die
                             einst die Frein,

Harrn allein
    sie Deines Heils   doch, wolln dich nie
                             Unrechts zeihn.

Drückte sie
    Druck auch, der Lands Herrlichkeit fern
                             rückte sie,

Riefen sie,
    was je ums End   ein Mund aus Leids
                             Tiefen schrie,

Fanden sie
    in Dir doch Heils   Brunnquelln, die noch
                             schwanden nie.

Namens Sein —
    Urwissen drum   raunt Mund zu Mund
                             erbgemein.

Busens Schrein
    entrauschts: Auch ich   kenn Ihn — doch, o,
                             schweiget fein.

From the crying of the bosom
there comes a murmur: I, too,	know Him — yet, oh,
					be silent.

Universally known reigns
Your brilliance: for their		word tells how Your
					grace gives rewards.

Clearly stresses
Your witness, how			it is Your work which
					Your arm sustains.

He who serves you,
commands the people,			who dwell near
					to Your counsel:

You should sing
your songs afresh,			know all this, and
					be valiant.

Shout three
times: "Holy."				to consecrate Him
					like the seraphim!

Allkund thront
  Dein Glanz: denn ihr   Wort sagts, wie Dein
                                     Holdsinn lohnt.

Und daβ Dein
Werk sie, dazu   spricht Ja Ihr Hauch,
                                   nimmer Nein.

Klar betont
Dein Zeuge, wie's   Dein Werk, was Dein
                                   Arm umschont.

Der dir frohnt,
  entbeut das Volk,   das Deinem Rat
                                  nahe wohnt:

Lieder reihn
  sollt neu ihr, all   dies wissen, und
                                   wacker sein.

Ruft zu drein
  Malen: „Geweiht",   seraphenhaft
                                   Ihn zu weihn!

YOUR DWELLING PLACES

Beautiful are Your dwelling places
        and your four surrounding boundaries.
You have the splendour of a lion and the power of a steer
        holding up Your throne.
And Jacob's camp divisions thus
        on earth Your forbearances.
You arrange them to banners, You teach
        them the voicings of Your names.
To look upon You the Holy One, and Your work
        to announce — oh, rewards!

THE GOD OF THE SPIRITS

Every mouth, it praises God highly, the God of the spirits.

        Throne adorned with grace, Raising
        those who have raised it,
        A place which silences
        Every raging;
He who is called wise, he Who is the speaker — from there He shines.

        And in the heart of
        Your servants stand tablets, genuine
        Witnesses; Your right hand
Dug into it the original behest of the duty, which no one ever wears to
shreads.

        Solid are the wheels of the throne chariot
        Near the paths of the souls;
        For Your spirit in grace,
He motions them towards waters of bliss, circled by bliss!

        Ah — ringing of the souls: Yours,
        Downfall of bodies: Yours,
        Everyone's hope: all Yours,
Service pulls them, maidlike before You, the Master.

DEINE WOHNUNGEN

Ja lieblich deine Wohnungen
    und deine vier Umzonungen.
Hast Löwenpracht und Stierskraft
    als deine Unterthronungen.
Und Jakobs Lagerzonen so
    auf Erden deine Schonungen.
Du ordnest sie zu Fähnlein, lehrst
    sie deiner Namen Tonungen.
Anschaun dich Heilgen, und dein Werk
    zu künden — o Belohnungen!

DER GOTT DER GEISTER

Jeder Mund, hoch preist er   Gott, den Gott der Geister.

Hochsitz huldumwoben,
Hebend, die ihn hoben,
Ort, der jedes Toben
Schweigt; wer weise heißt, wer   Redner — dorther gleißt er.

Und in deiner Knechte
Herz stehn Tafeln, echte
Zeugen; deine Rechte
Grub drein Urgeheiß der   Pflicht, das nie zerschleißt wer.

Dicht Thronwagens Rade
Nahe der Seelen Pfade;
Denn dein Geist in Gnade
Wonnewassern weist er   zu sie, Wonnumkreister!

Ach — der Seelen Schall: Dein,
Leiber Niederfall: Dein,
Aller Hoffen: all Dein,
Hin magdgleich sie reißt der   Dienst vor dir, dem Meister.

HOLY

Jubilating hosts of saints entone "Holy" for Him,
and choruses of seraphim standing above around Him.

Sublime splendour purified, invisible to the eye,
But His blue sky attests to it, thus the troop of heaven
And its shadow unites the spirit pair of flame and flood.
Souls' rays live on the gleam that gleams out from Him,
His call let loose fire out of cloud-blossoms.

And the stream of the holy spirit ran around the ones related to Him.
Into the one who burns for Him He fans an ardent spirit.
Those who recognized His word live in it. Note this:
Human necks desire to kneel under His yoke,
Weary sighs long for His roof, to flee thither.

Cherubic footfalls are heard in the seam of the world,
His radial hubs draw the trace easily like fluff,
His good gifts, they yet approach our space,
Rare works, whose brilliance and strength are borrowed from Him,
Manifest miracles — they originate prophecies out of the loftier source.

Up! With holy calls make yourself equal to those above,
Make yourselves holy territories of inheritance in their realm.
Hearts, storm the steps up to the Lord of Lords! who richly
Honours the one who guards His honour as his paladin.
But rebellious ones he never allows into the kingdom.

THE HELPER

Solace to the stricken heart which, sick, already saw itself decayed,
    in Him, Him the God of Hosts, Who says "I Who live!" draw near.
If He has the power of death over us in rancour, so that we pass away,
    So he helps us to life in grace — and indeed we live.
And so calls forth the mouth to the new light — there it stands in that
        moment —
    the mouth which once spoke "let there be light" and it was there.

HEILIG

Jubelnd Heilgenheeren
  Und Seraphenchören

  Hohe Pracht gereinigt,
  Doch sein Blau bescheinigt
  Und sein Schatten einigt
Seelenstrahlen zehren
Feur aus Wolkenflören,

  Und die Ihm-Verwandten
  In den Ihm-Entbrannten
  Die sein Wort erkannten,
Menschennacken gehren,
Müde Seufzer koeren

  Des cheruben Traben
  Seine Rädernaben
  Seine guten Gaben,
Rare Werke, deren
Klare Wunder — hoeh'ren

  Auf! Mit Heilig-Rufen
  Selgen Erbes Hufen
  Herzen, stuermt die Stufen
Ehrt, wer seine Ehren
Doch, die sich empören,

'Heilig' ent-töts für ihn,
oben rings stehnd um ihn.

zwar dem Aug unsichtbar,
sie, so des Himmels Schar,
Flamm- und Flut-Geistespaar.
vom Schein, der ihm entschien,
hat sein Ruf losgeschrien.

heilgen Geists Strom umrann.
bruenstgen Geist facht er an.
leben drin. Merks daran:
unter sein Joch zu knien,
gern sein Dach, hinzufliehn.

hoert man am Weltensaum,
ziehn die Spur leicht wie Flaum,
sie doch nahn unserm Raum,
Glanz und Kraft ihm entliehn,
Quells quelln sie Prophetien.

machet euch Obern gleich,
schafft euch in ihrem Reich.
zu der Herrn Herrn! der reich
schirmt als sein Paladin.
läßt nie ins Reich er ziehn.

DER HELFER

Ja Trost dem verstörten Herz,   das, krank, sich verwest schon sah,
  in Ihm, ihm der Heere Gott,   der spricht „Ich, der wese!" nah'.
Hat Macht uns zum Tode Er   im Groll, dass wir gar vergehn,
  so hilft uns zum Leben Er   in Huld — und wir leben ja.
Und so ruft dem neuen Licht   — da steht es im Augenblick —
  der Mund, der „es werde Licht"   einst sprach, und da war es da.

Soul   Seele

HERE I AM

How do I attain service   with Him, whom I thank for my beginning!
Gladly would I give up   anyone, if I have his love.

Indeed Lord and Shepherd,   body, soul, which are Yours, You sur-
   round;
This self unravels   itself for You, my innermost You saw,
From whose way I strayed.   In going, in resting: You approach, testing.
You, oh, remember,   You helped when my foot dragged wearily.
Whether it was like the spider's,   you lifted me out of the middle of the
   web.

Heart, entrails,   fervently desire to take lodgings near You, Lord,
But when I suffer,   my suffering drives them far from You
So that both go   again, to forget to pursue You —
Let Your word wrap me closely.   Lead me high to Your pinnacle.
Look gently upon me,   and say that I am free of sin.

Ill luck! — when my desire was   still wanton, then I was too tired for
   You.
What still remains   of my portion, if old age snatches me away?
Oh, God, oh, heal me!   with You, God, is what creates healing.
When strength once waned,   toothless and hanging loose the chin
   gave way,
Then do not strike me out,   and do not break the reed that I am.

Parched, broken,   I sit in an eternal narrowness,
Barefoot, dragging   the mere body, where mockery can scorch me,
Defiled by great   sins, by a multitude of outrages —
Dividing You, me,   there crept in between my sinful mind,
Woe, sensual worldly glitter   — Your radiance whitened the inner
   mind.

Ah, incline my heart   to service, Lord, to serve Your Kingdom.
What are sport and levity to me!   far away, if I look upon Your God-
   head, it yields!
In my deep pain,   oh quickly, oh reach me, Your healing herb!
If I could turn Your mind!   do not be silent to the need in which I am!
Help, that I might escape!   Say to Your servant: "Here I am."

HIER BIN ICH

Wie Dienst gewinn ich
Gern geb dahin ich

bei Ihm, dem danke Beginn ich!
jedweden, hab Seine Minn' ich.

Ja Herr und Hirte,
Dies Selbst entwirrt
Wes Wegs ich irrte.

Du, o besinn dich,

Obs dem der Spinn' glich,

Leib, Seele, die Dein, umfahst du;
sich Dir, mein Inneres sahst du;
Gehn, Ruhen; ihm prüfend nahst
du —
halfst, wenn mein Fuss müde hin-
schlich.
hobst aus dem Netz mittenin mich.

Herz, Eingeweide
Doch wenn ich leide,
Daß wieder beide
Dein Wort umspinn' mich.
Schau mild doch in mich,

glühen nach Einkehr, Herr, nah Dir;
führt sie mein Leiden fernab Dir,
gehn, nachzugehn verlernen Dir —
Hoch leite zu Deiner Zinn' mich.
und daß ich sühnefrei bin, sprich.

Unstern! — als geil noch

Was bleibt mein Teil noch,
O Gott, o heil' doch!
Wenn Kraft einst hinwich,

Nicht tilg dann hin mich,

mein Blust, da war ich Dir er-
schlafft.
wenn einst das Alter mich errafft?
bei Dir ist, Gott, was Heilung schafft.
zahnlos und schlotternd das Kinn
wich,
und nicht das Rohr, das ich bin, brich.

Dorrend, zerstoßen
Barfuß, den bloßen

Entweiht von großen
Dir, mir mittinn schlich
Weh, Weltgranz sinnlich —

sitz ich in ewiger Enge,
Leib schleppend, wo Spott mich
senge,
Suenden, von Freveln die Menge —
trennend mein sündiger Sinn sich,
Dein Strahl dem inneren Sinn blich.

Ach, neig mein Herz mir,
Was Spiel und Scherz mir!

Im tiefen Schmerz mir
Wändt' Deinen Sinn ich!
Hilf, daß entrinn ich!

Dienst, Herr, zu dienen Deines Reichs.
fern, schau ich Deine Gottheit,
weichs!
Dein Heilkraut, o geschwind, o reichs.
nicht schweig der Not du, darin ich!
Sag deinem Knecht es: „Hier bin ich".

SOUL

Soul —
    most beautiful maiden of all, joyful in her most youthful ones, of
        his sweetness.
Every day
    she exults: My companion's song from his vineyard — oh,
    Song of Songs, that of Solomon.

Soul —
    the maiden goes out, to draw the water of salvation full of longing,
Strikes up
    brightly in going, in coming, the playmates with her:
    If You draw us to You, we make haste.

Soul —
    and God's spirit rouses her: Do not flinch!
You still adorn yourself with kettledrums
    and go in the round-dance of the joyful ones and are mine, —
        proudly tower above!
    With me from Lebanon, oh Bride, with me from Lebanon oh hunt.

Soul —
    who is clasped by envy, surrounded by the enemy, speaks
Calmly her utterance:
    He who is my Friend, — white and red out of thousands he
        streams light.
    Mighty waters may not extinguish the love.

Soul —
    She accuses herself today: woe that His anger has not yet van-
        ished!
Then she sings happily:
    Look at me, I am a wall, a wall of precious jewels!
    Then I was in his eyes like one who had found peace.

SEELE

Seele —
   Jungfrau allerschönste, ihres Jugendlichsten, seiner Süße
      froh,
Tagtäglich
   jauchzt sie: Meines Gesellen Lied von seinem Weinberg — o
Lied der Lieder, das von Salomo.

Seele —
   hinaus geht das Mädchen, zu schöpfen Heils Wasser voll Begier,
Stimmt
   hell an beim Gehn, beim Kommen, die Gespielinnen mit Ihr:
Zeuch uns dir nach, so eilen wir.

Seele —
   und Gottes Geist erwecket sie: Nicht zage du!
Noch schmückst du dich mit Pauken
   und gehst im Reigen der Fröhlichen und bist mein, — stolz rage
      du!
Mit mir vom Libanon, o Braut, mit mir vom Libanon o jage du.

Seele —
   die neidumschlungene, feindumrungene, spricht
Still ihren Spruch:
   Der mein Freund, — weiß und rot aus Tausenden strahlt er
      licht.
Mächtge Wasser mögen löschen die Liebe nicht.

Seele —
   anklagt sie sich heute: weh daß sein Zorn noch nicht
      schwand!
Dann singt sie froh:
   Anseht mich, ich bin eine Mauer, von Edelstein eine Wand!
Da war ich in seinen Augen wie eine, die Frieden fand.

SOUL IN EXILE

Ah, she who laments full of longing around the Father's house
    and, in order to see it, ventured upward in the dream,
Ventured upward, to find solace, but the dream
    does not protect, once its foam vanished, the awakening tormented,
The day tormented her sick, where His smile does not
    radiate to you, without whose light she withers and wavered.
Wavered! to a new deed! and toiling heavily? to the victory!
    because she did not renounce the brilliance for the sake of chaos.
If she renounced the brilliance, then she opened the fountain,
    whose depth only she henceforth asked after,
Asked after the nucleus — and the band of the oath bound her,
    Wisdom, to you, as long as the day dawned for her.

WITH YOU

I was with You, before the troubles of the earthly body —
    may You now be willing to protect, to increase, Your Spirit in me.
If I had strength to stand, would You wish to disturb me?
    and power to walk, would You wish to hinder me?
And what I think — it remains yet Your thought;
    what I start — how could I do without You.
I seek You at time of grace — may You be willing to hear me;
    with the shield of Your mercy protect me.
Set me up in service before Your gate
    and awaken me to the honouring of Your Name.

SEELE IM EXIL

Ach, die ums Vaterhaus voll Sehnsucht klagete
und, es zu schaun, im Traum hinauf sich wagete,
Wagte hinauf sich, Trost zu finden, doch der Traum
schützt nicht, daß, schwand sein Schaum, Erwachen plagete,
Plagte sie krank der Tag, wo nicht Sein Lächeln dir
strahlt, ohne dessen Licht sie welkt und zagete.
Zagte! zu neuer Tat! und müht sich schwer? zum Sieg!
weil nicht ums Chaos sie dem Glanz absagete.
Sagte dem Glanz sie ab, so schloß den Born sie auf,
des Tiefen einzig sie hinfort nachfragete,
Fragte dem Kernpunkt nach — und Schwures Band sie band,
Weisheit, an dich, solang der Tag ihr tagete.

BEI DIR

Ich war bei Dir, vor Erdenleibs Beschweren —
in mir nun Deinen Geist woll schirmen, mehren.
Hätt Kraft zu stehn ich, wolltest Du mich stören?
und Macht zu gehen, wolltest Dus mir wehren?
Und was ich sinn — es bleibt doch Dein Gedanke;
was ich beginn — wie wollt' ich Dich entbehren.
Dich such zur Gnadenzeit ich — woll mich hören;
mit Deiner Gnade Schild woll mich bewehren.
Anstelle mich zum Dienst vor Deiner Schranke,
und weck mich auf zu Deines Namens Ehren.

PRAYER

Oh God You, when I extend my prayer to you,
    hear my voice, my cry, oh You God.
Oh God You, let Your Hand be seen, unveil
    the omnipotence and bless me, oh You God.
Oh God You, my heart beats stormily in my breast,
    I envelop myself in my distress, oh You God.
Oh God You, may my remembrance come near You with kindliness,
    think of me and look after me, oh You God.
Oh God You, I always await Your help,
    may Your love be a solace to me, oh You God.
Oh God You, my Creator, You, my Rock,
    who is my helper, except for You, oh You God.
Oh God You, may your compassion flow over me,
    heed not the number of my sins, oh You God.
Oh God You, only You does all my thinking desire,
    and my soul speaks: my part, oh You God.
Oh God You, my fear covers my heart,
    to You do I pour out my soul, oh You God.
Oh God You, hear me for Your sake
    and accept today my prayer, oh You God.

Oh God You, see my meditations in Your hand,
    the secret of my heart, it is known to You, oh You God.
Oh God You, bring balsam to my anguish
    open Your eyes and see, oh You God.
Oh God You, place my foot on the ground
    before all people I acknowledge You, oh You God.
Oh God You, look on me awaiting Your help,
    till You look here and turn, oh You God.
Oh God You, incline Your ears to my cry,
    be merciful to me and listen, oh You God.

GEBET

O Gott Du, wenn ich Dir mein Flehen breite,
    hör meine Stimme, meinen Schrei, o Du Gott.
O Gott Du, Deine Hand laß sehn, enthülle
    die Allmacht und begnade mich, o Du Gott.
O Gott Du, stürmisch geht mein Herz in Busen,
    ich hüll mich ein in meine Not, o Du Gott.
O Gott Du, nah' dir freundlich mein Gedächtnis,
    gedenke mein und walte mein, o Du Gott.
O Gott Du, Deiner Hilfe immer harr ich,
    werd' Deine Liebe mir zum Trost, o Du Gott.
O Gott Du, mein Erschaffer Du, mein Felsen,
    wer ist mein Helfer außer Dir, o Du Gott.
O Gott Du, über mich wall' Dein Erbarmen,
    nicht acht' auf meiner Sünden Zahl, o Du Gott.
O Gott Du, einzig Dich will all mein Denken,
    und meine Seele spricht: mein Teil, o Du Gott.
O Gott Du, meine Angst umhüllt mein Herze,
    dir schütt ich meine Seele aus, o Du Gott.
O Gott Du, höre mich um Deinetwillen
    und annimm heute mein Gebet, o Du Gott.

O Gott Du, sieh in Deiner Hand mein Sinnen,
    mein Herzgeheimnis, Dir ists kund, o Du Gott.
O Gott Du, bringe Balsam meinen Schmerzen,
    tu Deine Augen auf und sieh, o Du Gott.
O Gott Du, stelle meinen Fuß auf Boden,
    vor allen Volk bekenn ich Dich, o Du Gott.
O Gott Du, sieh mich Deiner Hilfe harren,
    bis her Du blickst und wendest Dich, o Du Gott.
O Gott Du, neige meinem Schrei die Ohren,
    sei gnädig mir und merke her, o Du Gott.

Oh God You and my God, for You I yearn,
    my heart, it longs for Your salvation, oh You God.
Oh God You, be surety for Your servant's good,
    do not look at the number of his sins, oh You God.
Oh God You, will the one bound to You still sit long
    ensnared in the prison of his sins, oh You God?
Oh God You, its reasoning advises my heart
    to devote itself to You in its plight, oh You God.
Oh God You, yes then! I — I exult in You,
    rescue the poor one from his torment, oh You God.
Oh God You, Lord of the world, for You I yearn,
    as You love the yearning for You, oh You God.

Oh God You, show your patience to Your servant,
    who has appealed to Your grace, oh You God.
Oh God You, see, I lay my prayer down here, —
    before I call, You answer, oh You God.
Oh God You, make me strong through Your love,
    and offer balsam to the sick heart, oh You God.
Oh God You, my sorrow has made me sick,
    the soul fevers day and night, oh You God.
Oh God You, You, tear me out of the abyss
    and change Your servant's prison, oh You God.

HUMAN FRAILTY

Why do you trust to time in which there is no lasting truth?
    Ah, how long my labour lasts! how swiftly my day disappeared!
Yet each man warns his brother not to sin:
    "Take care that what is working in you does not overpower you!"
If sin draws near, he says: "The human hand — what can it do?
    The creature and what works in it are in the Creator's Hand."

O Gott Du und mein Gott, zu Dir hin hang ich,
    mein Herz, nach Deinen Heil verlangts, o Du Gott.
O Gott Du, bürg für Deinen Knecht zum Guten,
    nicht blick auf seiner Sünden Zahl, o Du Gott.
O Gott Du, sitzt noch lang, der Dir verhaftet,
    in seiner Sünde Haft verstrickt, o Du Gott?
O Gott Du, meinem Herzen rät sein Denken,
    sich Dir zu weihn in seiner Not, o Du Gott.
O Gott Du, ja denn! ich — in Dir frohlock ich,
    erlös den Armen seiner Pein, o Du Gott.
O Gott Du, Herr der Welt, zu Dir hin hang ich,
    dieweil Du liebst den Hang zu Dir, o Du Gott.

O Gott Du, Deinem Knecht zeig Deine Langmut,
    der sich an Deine Huld gewandt, o Du Gott.
O Gott Du, sieh, ich leg Gebet hier nieder, —
    bevor ich rufe, antwortest o Du Gott.
O Gott Du, mach mich stark durch Deine Liebe,
    und Balsam reich dem kranken Herz, o Du Gott.
O Gott Du, krank gemacht hat mich mein Kummer,
    die Seele fiebert Tag und Nacht, o Du Gott.
O Gott Du, reiße Du mich aus dem Abgrund
    und Deines Knechts Gefängnis wend, o Du Gott.

MENSCHENSCHWÄCHE

Was trauest du der Zeit, in der nichts Treue ist?
    Ach wie währt lang mein Werk! wie rasch mein Tag schwand!
Mahnt jeder doch den Bruder, nicht zu sündigen:
    sorg, daß, was in dir schafft, dich nicht überwand!
Naht Sünde dann, heißt: „Menschenhand — was kann sie tun!
    Geschöpf und, was drin schafft, ist in Schöpfers Hand".

RETURN

Oh, God, for You alone is my desire,
    even if it has never passed my lips.
If I lived for a moment in Your grace,
    how gladly would I then embrace death.
Commend the residue of my spirit to Your hands,
    and I would sleep gently, a smile on my face.
Far away from You — oh, death in the cup of life!
    Nestled close to you — oh, life in the pincers of death!
Yet I do not know how I should approach You
    and which service, which deeds do reach You.
Oh, God, do deign to teach me Your ways,
    to pluck me from the bonds of folly which constrained me.
And show me, as long as strength for repentance is still
    in me, and do not disdain my repentant dread,
Ere I am a burden to myself, ere the bones below
    yield to the pressure above,
And I lay myself down against my will, and moths
    devour the bones, which for a long time moved until weary,
And I move towards the place where the Patriarchs moved,
    and find rest, where they found a place of rest.
Belonging, yet a stranger on the back of the earth,
    in its belly I shall be the resplendent heir.
Youth was busy only for itself —
    when shall I plant the poles of my tent?
He put the world into my heart — whose delights
    sang me into a sleep, which forgot the end,
How can I serve my sculptor, where I,
    ensnared in creation, still a slave to desire.
They who are tomorrow brothers to earthworms, — would one think
    that today they strove after honour and offices?
How may my heart be glad on days of joy!
    perhaps they already die away for me tomorrow.
Together the days and nights restlessly struck against
    my flesh, to put an end to it.
Into air dispersed, into dust I am returned — those are the two
    who in the end attain their hate.

UMKEHR

O Gott nach Dir allein steht mein Verlangen,
    auch wenns mir von den Lippen nie gegangen.
Lebt einen Augenblick in Deiner Huld ich,
    wie gern würd ich dann den Tod umfangen,
Beföhle meines Geists Rest Deinen Händen
    und schliefe sanft, ein Lächeln um die Wangen.
Von Dir entfernt — o Tod in Lebens Bechern!
    an Dich geschmiegt — o Leben in Tods Zangen!
Jedoch nicht weiß ich, womit ich dir nahn soll
    und welcher Dienst, welch Tun zu Dir hindrangen.
Woll Deine Wege doch, o Gott, mich lehren,
    mich ziehn aus Torheits Banden, die mich zwangen.
Und weise mich, solang noch Kraft zur Buße
    in mir, und nicht mißacht mein büßend Bangen,
Eh ich mir selbst zur Last bin, eh sich beugen
    dem obern Druck der untern Knochen Spangen
Und ich mich lege wider Willn, und Motte
    die Knochen frißt, die lang sich müde schwangen,
Und hin ich zieh, wohin die Väter zogen,
    und finde Ruh, wo sie sich Ruhstatt dangen.
Ein Beisaßfremdling auf der Erde Rücken,
    in ihrem Bauch werd ich als Erbherr prangen.
Die jungen Jahre schafften für sich selbst nur —
    wann werd ich stecken meines Zeltes Stangen?
Die Welt gab er ins Herz mir — deren Lüste
    in Schlummer, der des Ends vergaß, mich sangen.
Wie kann ich meinem Bildner dienen, wo ich
    gebildumstrickt, ein Knecht noch dem Verlangen.
Die morgen Brüder Erdgewürmen, — dächt man,
    daß heut sie noch um Ehr' und Würden rangen?
Wie mag mein Herz an Freudentagen froh sein!
    vielleicht daß sie schon morgen mir verklangen.
Vereint die Tag' und Nächte rastlos an dies
    mein Fleisch, den Garaus ihm zu machen, sprangen.
In Luft verstreut, in Staub verkehrt ich — die zwei
    sinds, die am Ende ihrem Haß gelangen.

What do I say, whom the desire drove on like an enemy
    from youth on, until they swallow me up!
What do I have in time if not Your grace?
    If I do not receive You, what shall I receive?
Naked am I and bare of all good works —
    Your justice alone wrapped around me as a cloak.
Why do I talk so much, for what am I pressing —
    Oh, God, You alone are my desire.

REWARD

She is a jewel who lingers in the body,
    a light wedged in the dark —
She is enticed to prepare for flight
    to the workplace where her jewels are filed
To where, when she prepares for flight, whatever
    fruit she craves, is distributed;
Original honey from Eden, sap of bliss,
    and wisdom rich and finished.
Then she looks upon the path of the Creator,
    healed of the memory of suffering,
The line of each and every soul
    ringed around, who sing God's praises.

Was sag ich, den die Triebe hetzten, feindgleich
    von Jugend an, bis daß sie mich verschlangen!
Was hab ich in der Zeit, wenn Deine Huld nicht?
    Empfang ich Dich nicht, was werd ich empfangen?
Nackt bin und bloß ich aller guten Werke —
    Dein Recht allein als Mantel mir unhangen.
Was reg ich noch die Zunge viel, was dräng ich —
    o Gott, nach Dir allein steht mein Verlangen.

DER LOHN

Juwel sie, das im Leibe weilt,
    ein Licht in Dunkel eingekeilt —
Es lockt sie, Flucht zu rüsten hin
    zur Werkstatt, wo ihr Schmuck gefeilt,
Hin, wo, wenn Flucht sie rüstet, was
    von Frucht sie lüstet, wird verteilt:
Urseim von Eden, Wonnesaft,
    und Weisheit reich und ausgefeilt.
Des Schöpfers Wandel schaut sie dann,
    von Leids Erinnerung geheilt,
All-aller Seelen Zeile rings,
    die Gott lobsingen, eingezeilt.

THIS SOUL HERE

We strive to arrange the song   to show His radiance,
The very One Who has given   to us this soul here.

The loftier the thoughts   the further his flight
While I must creep along the earth,   He can move world high.
And yet: in the limits of the spirit —   the heart finds Him,
Because pearls of light sank   from the throne canopy,
Those who are now in the realm of the ray   desire for Him seizes them,
The very One Who has given   to us this soul here.

Here my being is afraid in   the night, my light sank.
What I valued little in youth, —   it gives me to the judgement.
Ah, desire, the archenemy,   fascinates like a snake.
In the day I tremble full of pain   where the soul does not
Follow me, into   this ground here, —
No, to Him, Who has given   to us this soul here.

Would the deposit of dust want   to consider itself equal to Him?
Which is only able to languish,   only to want?
Oh silence, heart! your striving,   oh silence it! be afraid for every-
    thing!
Close to You I would like to spend the night!   And when Your day of
    grace comes,
Chase, oh, do not chase away,   one Who tarries here as a maid,
The very One Who has given   to us this soul here.

The soul of Your servant   seeks You in the blue sky.
And if she may not look upon You,   she looks left and right.
Yet she may look upon You here: a miracle, break the dark!
The maid therefore —   put her among the women of the lineage of
    the covenant.
Who take shelter with You   and look upon, Lord, Your embellishment,
The very One Who has given   to us this soul here.

If the light goes out,   kindle it wondrously anew!
That the night might disappear,   where Your anger pitched a tent,
The wall of sin between us,   roll it apart,
Into the dark grounds of wrath   the starlight of grace flowed!
Deign to look from heaven upon the vine here, —
The very One Who has given   to us this soul here.

DIESE SEELE HIER

Lied zu reihn streben,
Der selber gegeben

Je höh'r die Gedanken,
Muß erdlang ich ranken,
Und doch: in Geists Schranken —
Weil Lichtperlen sanken
Die nun in Strahls Revier
Der selber gegeben

Hier zagt mein Sein in
Was jung mir galt klein, — hin
Ach Lust, die Erzfeindin,
Zum Tag beb' voll Pein hin
Folgt mir, hinein in
Nein Ihm, der gegeben

Und Ihm gleich sich achten
Der nur zu schmachten,
O still, Herz! dein Trachten,

Dir nah möcht ich nachten!

Jag, o nicht verjag,
Der selber gegeben

Dich sucht im Blaun die
Und darf Dich nicht schaun sie,
Darf doch dich schaun hie:
Die Magd drum — den Fraun sie

Die bergen sich bei Dir
Der selber gegeben

Auslosch Licht, zünde
Daß die Nacht schwünde,
Die Dustwand von Sünde
In Zorns finstre Gründe
Vom Himmel schaun du woll
Der selber gegeben

zu schaun sein Leuchten wir,
uns diese Seele hier.

ferner nur sein Fliehn
welthoch kann er ziehn.
das Herz findet Ihn,
vom Thronbaldachin,
ergreift nach Ihm Begier,
uns diese Seele hier.

Nacht, es sank mein Licht.
gibts mich dem Gericht.
schlangengleich besticht.
ich, wo Seele nicht
diesen Boden hier, —
uns diese Seele hier.

wollt' des Staubes Schlag?
nur zu wolln vermag?
o stills! um Alles zag'!

Und kommt dein Gnadentag,

die als Magd weilt hier,
uns diese Seele hier.

Seele Deines Knechts.
schaut sie links und rechts.
das Dunkel, Wunder, brechts!
reih' des Bundgeschlechts,

und schaun, Herr, Deine Zier,
uns diese Seele hier.

neu es wundervoll!
drin schlug Zelt dein Groll,
zwischen uns zerroll',
Sternlicht der Gnade quoll!
auf die Rebe hier, —
uns diese Seele hier.

ILLUSION AND TRUTH

Yes, beloved of the Truth, you must disturb the delusion;
    live here, as those who live in the grave beneath flowers.
Rise up and beautify service to God, because you live,
    let the beauty of the world belong to the others.
May your service help rather to adjure the dawn
    than that the dawn must adjure your sleep.
And far away from today is your tomorrow, and willingly leave
    the world to those who delude themselves with it.
Better that you serve at God's countenance
    than that spectres choose you for a servant.
At the countenance of God, Whose Being and Whose Name
    every soul should praise in exultation and choruses.

LADY WORLD

The globe of this earth became forbidden to me as a husband,
    whilst this Self became more precious to me than the universe.
Now she distributes her brilliance on others;
    she saw, one portion only, my God, pleased me.
Should she choose me, and I am her mortal enemy?
    Should I choose her, who became for me the fall of man?
I, husband to duty, scorn her; she strips off my shoe,
    spits into my face a torrent of spittle.

WAHN UND WAHRHEIT

Ja Traute der Wahrheit, den Wahn mußt du stören;
    wohn hier, wie, die wohnen im Grab unter Flören.
Erheb und verschön Gottes Dienst, weil du lebest,
    der Welt Schönheit laß du den andern gehören.
Helf' lieber dein Dienst, zu beschwören die Frühe,
    als daß deinen Schlaf muß die Frühe beschwören.
Und fern aus dem Heute dein Morgen, und gern laß
    die Welt denen, welche an ihr sich betören.
Denn besser, du dienest am Antlitze Gottes,
    als daß dich zum Diener sich Larven erkören.
Am Antlitze Gottes, des Sein und des Namen
    lob' jegliche Seele in Jubel und Chören.

FRAU WELT

Verwehrt Gemahl ward dieser Erde Ball mir,
    dieweil dies Selbst ward teurer als das All mir.
Nun teilt sie ihre Herrlichkeit an andre;
    sie sah, Ein Anteil nur, mein Gott, gefall' mir
Soll sie mich wählen, und ich bin ihr Todfeind?
    ich wählen sie, die ward zum Sündenfall mir?
Ich Pflichtgemahl verschmäh sie; ab den Schuh streift
    sie mir, sprüht ins Gesicht des Speichels Schwall mir.

Heart, on guard! Would anybody keep his courage,
    Whose heart rests on His scales?
That which is hidden do not strive to see,
    so that the glow does not burn you.
Hand, desist from His deed! not to you
    does He reveal the statute of His might.
You are not an angel, your presumptuousness should not press
    to the place of the great ones.
Direct your paths to Him,
    in the flood of restlessly fleeting times.
And be blissful, not a ne'er-do-well,
    not oppressed by fear before the whip of unhappiness.
The enticing call of men, do not heed it,
    heed only whither your Lord has invited you.
Why do you serve the sovereigns of the earth?
    does not one kiss the whip of the other!
In its favour — what frivolous happiness,
    in their wrath — what wild fury!
Salvation to you therefore when you serve the Lord,
    whose might alone rules absolutely.
He gave to you richly in the keeper's lap,
    and He never withholds his wealth from you.
Await His counsel and do not trust
    the doctorate of the nine-times wise.
Then you yourself will see fruit and once
    in the most distant distance yet your blood.
Build an altar of atonement and bind
    upon it the brood of your sinful desire.
For He is favourably inclined to the rooster, but even
    he who is far, let him hasten home, with a light tread.
Thus do not inquire into His action,
    await quietly in the protection of his gate.
He who, whether he slays, whether he revives,
    does what is good in His eyes.
He spoke: Let there be light — and it was;
    commanded — the earth pays tribute.
And God looked at what He had made,
    and behold: it was very good.

WEISE LEHREN

Herz, auf der Hut! Blieb Einem Mut,
   der Herz auf Seiner Wage ruht?
Verborgnes trachte nicht zu schaun,
   auf daß dich nicht verglüh' die Glut.
Hand laß von Seinem Tun! nicht Dir
   enthüllt er Seiner Macht Statut.
Kein Engel bist du, nicht zum Platz
   der Großen dräng' dein Übermut.
Befiehl du deine Wege Ihm,
   in unstet flüchtger Zeiten Flut.
Und sei, beglückt, kein Tunichtgut,
   nicht angstgedrückt vor Unglücks Rut'.
Der Menschen Lockruf horch ihm nicht,
   horch nur, wohin dein Herr dich lud.
Was dienst der Erde Herrschern du?
   küßt einer doch des andern Knut'!
In ihrer Gunst — welch windig Glück,
   in Zornesbrunst — welch wilde Wut!
Heil drum dir, wenn du dem Herrn dienst,
   des Macht allein herrscht absolut.
Er gab dir reich in Wärters Schoß,
   und nimmer sperrt er dir sein Gut.
Harr Seines Rats und traue nicht
   der Neunmalweisen Doktorhut.
Dann wirst du selbst Frucht schaun und einst
   in fernster Ferne noch dein Blut.
Bau einen Bußalter und bind
   drauf deines sündgen Triebes Brut.
Denn hold ist Er dem Hahn; doch auch
   wer fern, heim eil' er, leichtbeschuht.
So spüre Seinem Tun nicht nach,
   harr still in seines Torraums Hut.
Der, ob er tötet, ob belebt,
   was gut in Seinen Augen tut.
Er sprach: Es werde Licht — da wards;
   befahl — die Erde zollt Tribut.
Und Gott sah an, was er gemacht,
   und siehe da: er war sehr gut.

SERVANTS

Servants of time   are servants of   servants;
   only God's servant   as the only one   is free.
That is why when for his   portion everyone   prays,
   my heart, it says: God Himself, my portion   may he be!

WORLD

Oh, heart, why are you chasing after possessions and riches,
   after the world, which is crooked and never — thus its curse —
   simple!
See: whoever makes the train of his coat long,
   how easily he falls onto his knee over his own cloth.
The betrayal of the world is obvious, and just the same
   are you still seeking a high rank in it? oh, seek not!

THE SICK DOCTOR

Heal me, You, my God, then I will be healed.
   Do not let the fire of Your anger burn me.
Extracts and medicine are Yours — whether good,
   or ill, whether strong, or weak, they act.
It is You Who chooses, You, not I, and Your
   Omniscience quides or does not guide the arrow to the mark.
I do not place trust in my healing potion,
   only of Your healing potion let me partake.

KNECHTE

Knechte der Zeit   sind Knechte von   Knechten;
   nur Gottes Knecht,   als einzger ist   frei er.
Drum, wenn um sein   Teil jeder Mensch   bittet,
   mein Herz, es spricht: Gott selbst, mein Teil   sei er!

WELT

O Herz, was jagst du nach Besitz und Reichtum,
   nach Welt, die krumm und nie — so wills ihr Fluch —
schlicht!
Sieh: wer erst seines Mantels Schleppe lang macht,
   Wie leicht ins Knie er übers eigne Tuch bricht.
Der Welt Betrug ist offenkund, und gleichwohl
   suchst hohen Rang in ihr du noch? o such nicht!

DER KRANKE ARZT

Heile mich Du, mein Gott, so bin ich heil.
   Nicht brenn mich Deines Zornes Feuerkeil.
Extrakt und Medizin sind Dein, — ob gut
   ob bös, ob stark ob schwach sie tun. Dieweil
Du es, der auswählt, Du, nicht ich, und Dein
   Allwissen lenkt, lenkt nicht, zum Ziel den Pfeil.
Nicht setz auf meinen Heiltrank ich Vertraun,
   nur Deines Heiltranks werde mir zuteil.

TO THE SABBATH

Yes, I drink the drink of love to you:
Awake happily, oh Day, awake happily, my seventh one!

Six days are work days, bound to your service,
I have found already enough labour in them,
Yet they seemed to me like single hours,
So do I love you, my day of rest —
Awake happily, oh Day, awake happily, my seventh one!

I go on the first day the worker's ways,
For whom other than you, Sabbath, do I prepare myself!
He who guides all Heaven gives you the blessing.
Be you my portion, whatever else do I act and do —
Awake happily, oh Day, awake happily, my seventh one!

Holy ray of light out of holy source,
Sun, stars, wish to bask in light from you.
On the second, third, what have I attained!
Let the host of lights of the fourth veil the chest of darkness —
Awake happily, oh Day, awake happily, my seventh one!

I hear the fifth preparing tidings of happiness.
Will blessings flower for you, Soul, tomorrow night?
Still early in the servant's constraint night brings free escort,
When my Shepherd invites me to His kingly meal —
Awake happily, oh Day, awake happily, my seventh one!

Joyfully your morning dawns, oh sixth, for my soul.
Does she sense already the approaching care-free time?
Unsteadily and fleetingly watching for where she is sheltered,
Taking a breath at night: flight vanished, displaced in a flash —
Awake happily, oh Day, awake happily, my seventh one!

Exquisitely then your evening shadow approaches me,
In which anew, eye to eye, I look upon the holy bride,
Arise then, with apples draw near, with brimming plates!
Oh blessed Day, my Friend, you my Beloved —
Awake happily, oh Day, awake happily, my seventh one!

AN DEN SABBAT

Ja Trank der Liebe   ihn trink Dir ich zu:
Glück auf, o Tag, Glück auf,   mein Siebter Du!

Sechs Tage Werktag, Dir   zu Dienst verbunden,
Hab ich an ihnen schon   Müh satt gefunden,
Deuchten mir all doch gleich   einzelnen Stunden,
So hab ich Dich lieb, Tag   Du meiner Ruh —
Glück auf, o Tag, Glück auf,   mein Siebter Du!

Geh ich am Ersten Tag   auf Werkers Wegen,
Wem sonst als, Sabbat, Dir   rüst ich entgegen!
Der all Himmel lenkt,   schenkt Dir den Segen.
Sei Du mein Teil, was sonst   ich treib und tu —
Glück auf, o Tag, Glück auf,   mein Siebter Du!

Heiliger Lichtstrahl aus   heiligem Bronnen,
Sonn', Sterne wolln in Licht   von Dir sich sonnen.
Am Zweiten, Dritten was   hab ich gewonnen!
Des Vierten Lichterheer   hüll' Dunkels Truh —
Glück auf, o Tag, Glück auf,   mein Siebter Du!

Glückskunde hör ich ihn,   Fünften, bereiten.
Blühn, Seele, morgen Nacht   dir Seligkeiten?
Früh noch im Knechtsbann, bringt   Nacht frei Geleiten,
Lädt Seinem Königsmahl   mein Hirt mich zu —
Glück auf, o Tag, Glück auf,   mein Siebter Du!

Froh meiner Seele graut,   Sechster, dein Morgen.
Spürt sie wohl nahe schon   Zeit frei von Sorgen?
Unstet und flüchtig späh'nd,   wo sie geborgen,
Aufatmend nachts: schwand Flucht,   Unstatt im Nu —
Glück auf, o Tag, Glück auf,   mein Siebter Du!

Ja köstlich kommt dann mir   Dein Abendschatten,
Drin neu ich Aug in Aug   schau heilgem Gatten.
Auf doch, mit Äpfeln naht,   schwellenden Platten!
O selger Tag, mein Freund,   Geliebter Du —
Glück auf, o Tag, Glück auf,   mein Siebter Du!

So I sing to you, Sabbath, a song to your praise
that I might pay homage to your loveliness.
A day full of bliss for me, three meals,
Blissful table splendour, blissful rest —
Awake happily, oh Day, awake happily, my seventh one!

FREE

A servant who, to   seek You, joyful,   awakens
    at dawn and   asks You for freedom —
Today is the day of rest!   the sun of Your might bestow upon
    the son of Your maid,   when free time comes blissfully to him.
The day when a song   would like to prepare your   soul
    and freely dedicates   herself to Your fame   and call.

SABBATH MORNING

Beautiful are you,   unique one, as long as you are mine,   sweeter to
    me
Is today, when you stand   before the Lord Whose Name is my
    Redeemer here.
And reward for the toil   will be the rest,   for which you ask   full of
    desire.
Therefore be silent and bow down   under the yoke which   you have
    to bear.
But you sense the mysterious   power of time — open the heart's   ear
    to it!
Learn to do good,   not evil! such action — it would be   sheer
    madness.
Dedicate to the Protector   — let every breath sing praises to Him—
    precious ornament
In the song of jubilation,   and before Him, Whose Name is
    Lord,   exult!

So sing ich, Sabbat Dir,   Sang Deinem Preise,
Daß Deiner Holdheit ich   Huldgung erweise.
Tag voller Wonne mir,   dreifacher Speise,
Wonnvolle Tafelpracht,   wonnvolle Ruh —
Glück auf, o Tag, Glück auf,   mein Siebter Du!

FREI

Ein Knecht, der, Dich   zu suchen, froh,   aufweckt
    die Frühe und   Dich bittet um   Freiheit —
Ruhtag ist heut!   Sonn' Deiner Macht   spend dem
    Sohn Deiner Magd,   kommt selig ihm   Freizeit.
Tag, wo dir Sang   möcht rüsten die   Seele
    und Deinem Ruhm   und Ruf ihr Selbst   frei weiht.

SABBATMORGEN

Ja schön bist Du,   Einzge, so lange du mein,   wonn'ger mir

Heut, da du stehst   vor dem Herrn, des Name mein   Heiland hier.

Und Lohn der Müh   wird die Ruh,   nach der du fragst   voll Begier.

Drum schweig und bück   unter das Joch Dich, das zu   tragen Dir.

Ahnst doch der Zeit   Rätselmacht — des Herzens Ohr,   öffn' es ihr!

Lern Gutes tun,   Böses nicht! solch Tun — es wär'   Tollheit schier.

Weihe dem Hort   — jeder Hauch lobsinge ihm —   edle Zier

Im Jubelsang,   und vor ihm, des Name Herr,   jubilier!

LIFE

"Rejoice, one soul, in the God of faith, in the One,
   heap up songs, luxuriate in exquisite melodies,
Let fathoming His Law be yours. And full powers
   beg for always, to pour out beseeching weeping.
Consider worthless the acquisition of earthly goods, and may the
   acquisition of wise action and intention be dear to you.
Leave what is evil in the line of generations for what is simple:
   foolish people! they have virtually no sense:
Your existence, if it has already been long — it is like a smaller track,
   like a moment in the lapse of time, to a small one."
She answers: "I understood it early,
   my friend, that all this is right and correct.
Begin, you beggar, for God's countenance,
   to unite the voices of thanks and exultation.
Even when you think that I am disturbed, know:
   my heart is awake, though it might appear to be asleep.
I left the heights behind, I am now a prey to death,
   spellbound in shadows and to skeletons.
Before God, powerfully swift, calls me to rest and of life's
   bond I am bound in dark shrines.
Because my Redeemer lives, He will still bless
   His memory and so incorporate me
'Into life!' to the living rejoicing, souls,
   still living in life's ground, — Yours."

THE DAY

For my life's source should my desire entreat
   before my days spin to my grave.
But if only the soul knew who chases after wind,
   that wholly alone she herself is my fief in the world.
And if yet my heart would awaken, it would think of my end,
   the day which will be my sleep and my rising up,
The day which allows my handiwork to look into my eye,
   the day when soul and spirit enter His granary.

LEBEN

„Jauchz, Eine, Glaubens Gotte du, dem Einen,
    häuf Lieder, schwelg in Melodieen, feinen.
Erforschen sein Gesetz sei deins. Und Vollmacht
    heisch allzeit, auszuschütten flehend Weinen.
Halt unwert irdschen Guts Erwerb, und teuer
    sei dir Erwerb von weisem Tun und Meinen.
Um Schlichtes laß du Schlechtes, des Geschlechtes
    Schar: Torenvolk! hat Geist so gut wie keinen.
Dein Dasein, wärs schon lang, — geringer Spur gleichts,
    dem Augenblick im Zeitablauf, dem kleinen."
Antwortet sie: „Ich hab es bald verstand,
    mein Freund, daß all dies richtig und im reinen.
Heb an, ein Bettelmann zu Gottes Antlitz,
    um Dank und Jubels Stimmen zu vereinen.
Auch wenn du meinst, dass ich verstört sei, wisse:
    mein Herz ist wach, mag ich zu schlafen scheinen.
Ließ rückwärts Höhen, bin nun todverfallen,
    gebannt in Schatten und zu Totenbeinen.
Eh Gott, gewalt-rasch, ruhn mich heißt und Lebens
    Bund eingebunden ich in dunklen Schreinen.
Weil mein Erlöser lebt, wird sein Gedenken
    noch segnen er und so mich eingemeinen,
‚Ins Leben!' dem Lebendgen jubelnd, Seelen,
    noch lebenden in Lebens Grund, — der Seinen."

DER TAG

Nach meines Lebens Quell   soll mein Verlangen flehn
    eh' meine Tage sich   zu meiner Erde drehn.
Wüsst es die Seele doch,   die hinter Wind her jagt,
    daß ganz allein sie selbst   rings in der Welt mein Lehn.
Und würd mein Herz doch wach,   dächts an mein Ende, den
    Tag, der mein Schlafengehn   wird und mein Auferstehn,
Tag, der mein Händewerk   läßt mir ins Auge sehn,
    Tag, da in Seine Scheu'r   Seele und Geist eingehn.

RETURN, RETURN!

Put, oh heart, your raging to rest!
He has already guaranteed it for you above.

Jewel out of the treasury of your Creator!
Up! Do you want to settle down to rest here?
Long is the way! Take something to refresh yourself —
It's time! Do what He can praise!

Here is one who belongs, like the ancestors,
My years, presentiments of a shadow —
When if not now, be reminded,
Do you create life for yourself removed from death?

And did you glow to seek Him
And have you removed yourself from what is ordinary —
Venture courageously to come to Him!
Examples of your deeds are your escort.

You, presumptuous one, see your tracks!
Do not stray in dream circles!
Short is the day and long the journey —
What do you say if the semblance has flown away!

Did your eye suffer for thirst of heaven?
Eternally before Him did your step come to a standstill?
Return, return, oh Sulamit,
Home again to the Father above!

THE ASCENT

Turn, you only one,   to your place,   oh turn!
   desire always   to sit upon   God's throne!
Thrones of the world —   refuse them!   but you know: you climbed
   to the height, you won   the magnificence of victory,   highly exalted.
So bow down   and give God   praise and fame,
   where God   stands, give the tribute   of your song.

KEHR UM, KEHR UM!

Kehr, o Herz, zur Ruh dein Toben!
Schon gewährt hat Ers dir oben.

Juwel aus deines Schöpfers Schätzen!
Auf! Willst hier zur Ruh dich setzen?
Lang der Weg! Nimm, dich zu letzen, —
Zeit ists! Wirk, was Er kann loben!

Hier ein Beisaß, gleich den Ahnen,
Meine Jahre Schattens Schwanen —
Wann wenn jetzt nicht, laß dich mahnen,
Schaffst dir Leben todenthoben?

Und bist, zu suchen ihn, entglommen
Und hast Gemeinem dich entnommen —
Mutig wags, zu Ihm zu kommen!
Geleit sind deiner Taten Proben.

Du Hochfahrge, sieh dein Gleise!
Verirr dich nicht in Traumeskreise!
Kurz dein Tag und lang die Reise —
Was sprichst du, wenn der Schein zerstoben!

An Himmelsdurst dein Auge litt?
Ewig vor Ihm stockt' gern dein Schritt?
Kehr um, kehr um, o Sulamith,
Wieder heim zum Vater droben!

DER AUFSTIEG

Kehr, Einzge Du,   an Deine Statt,   o kehre!
    an Gottes Thron   zu sitzen stets   begehre!
Throne der Welt —   ausschlage sie!   weißt doch: stiegst
    zur Höh, errangst   Siegs Herrlichkeit,   hochhehre.
So beuge Dich   und Gotte gib   Preis Du und Ruhm,
    wo Gottgeschlecht   steht, zolle Du   Sangs Ehre.

BREATH OF ALL LIFE

I offer to God the smoke of my song of thanks,
In Whose hand is the breath of all life.

    The origin of every cause and effect:
    God, in the heights where no measure has reached.
    To see Him, my eye ardently strove for;
    Yet known to the heart, still constrained to fleshly bonds.
I shall someday look upon Him too, free of the body,
In Whose hand is the breath of all life.

    He has sunk the soul into the offspring of the earth:
    To be wise and clever, he loaned
    To her the reflection of the light above — see:
    Even the reflection makes her sweetly pure,
Of my years let her have use and usage! —
In Whose hand is the breath of all life.

    And up to the original ground she pines away,
    Awaits the day when she is free of earthly fetters.
    While she still inhabits me, she desires
    That my praise reveres her Creator,
That my speech blooms for Him like buds on the bush —
In Whose hand is the breath of all life.

    That He is unique: the passing away and the gliding away
    Of the Creature bears witness time and again,
    In it He alone remains. He will prepare
    Judgement for the secrets of the wanton mind.
He looks to see if I am devout or a cheat,
In Whose hand is the breath of all life.

    Ah, incline to the maid's son, Your servant,
    When he places himself before Your people!
    When I enter into Your netting of inheritance:
    I teach the brothers: "Praise, let His praise speak!"
That I might immerse myself into the relationship of Your Covenant —
In Whose hand is the breath of all life.

HAUCH ALLEN LEBENS

Gotte opfre ich Dankgesangs Rauch,
In Dessen Hand allen Lebens Hauch.

Jeder Ursach und Wirkung Anfang:
Gott, in Höhn wo kein Maß hinandrang.
Ihn zu schaun, das Aug heiß anrang;
Dem Herz doch kund, das noch Fleisches Bann zwang.
Schaun einst werd ich, des Leibs los, Ihn auch —
In Dessen Hand allen Lebens Hauch.

Hat gesenkt dem Erdsprossen ein die
Seele: weise und klug zu sein, lieh
Er ihr obern Lichts Widerschein — sieh:
Noch der Abglanz macht lieblich rein sie,
Meiner Jahre hab' Nutz sie und Brauch! —
In Dessen Hand allen Lebens Hauch.

Und hinauf zum Urgrund verzehrt sie
Sich, harrt des Tages, wo erd-entschwert sie.
Dieweil sie noch mir einwohnt, begehrt sie,
Dass mein Lob ihren Schöpfer verehrt, die
Rede Ihm blühe gleich Knospen am Strauch —
In Dessen Hand allen Lebens Hauch.

Daß er einzig: zeugt, Zeit an Zeiten,
Des Geschöpfs Vergehn und Vergleiten,
Drin Er allein bleibt. Rechtspruch bereiten
Wird er freveln Sinns Heimlichkeiten.
Herschaut Er, ob ich ein Frommer, ein Gauch,
In Dessen Hand allen Lebens Hauch.

Ach zum Magdsohn neig, Deinem Knecht, Dich,
Wenn er stellt vor Dein Volksgeschlecht sich!
Tret hinein in Dein Erbgeflecht ich:
Lehr die Brüder „Lob, Sein Lob sprecht!" ich,
Daß in Deines Bunds Kindschaft ich tauch' —
In Dessen Hand allen Lebens Hauch.

People   Volk

IN ETERNITY

Sun, moon both move   eternally on guard;
   Day, night, their course   never deviates from the track.
They are established as a symbol   for Jacob's seed,
   A people, he, in eternity   and never annihilated.
When God's left hand distances them,   the right hand draws them near.
   Thus even in distress they have   never considered blasphemy.
No, they firmly trust that   they are eternal, and
   That their end will never come   before day and night cease.

GOD SPEAKS

May hope remain young!   let your heart be   strong for it!
   why do you calculate   the purpose of misery,   nearly despondent?

Rise up, speak,   and compose afresh   words of song!
   Your disgraced Name   still says: My   tent in you.

And despise the one who   scoffs, however   loud he roars!
   Gently is driven the flock,   — you come finally   to the quarters.

Your Beloved torments you,   but He, He also causes happiness   to
      swell in you.
   Your part, the sick one, is He.   He is the elixir   of the healing
      draught.

You love most beautifully   hoping for Him Who   redeems you.
   Do not push! You will still look   upon the radiance and
   ornament   of my deed.

When they boast   of their king,   you sing praise:
   He, Jacob's Holy One,   is my King,   my Redeemer.

IN EWIGKEIT

Sonn', Mond, die beiden ziehn   in Ewigkeit auf Wacht;
    Tag, Nacht, ihr Gleichlauf wird   nie aus dem Gleis gebracht.
Sinnbild verordnet sind   dem Samen Jakobs sie,
    Volk er in Ewigkeit   und nie zunichtgemacht.
Fernt Gottes Linke sie,   die Rechte bringt sie nah.
    So haben auch in Not   sie Lästrung nie gedacht.
Nein, fest vertraun sie, daß   in Ewigkeit sie, und
    Daß nie ihr Ende kommt,   eh enden Tag und Nacht.

GOTT SPRICHT

Jung bleib' die Hoffnung!   dein Herz es sei   stark zu ihr!
    was rechnest aus Du   des Elends Ziel,   mutlos schier?

Hochrichte Dich, sprich,   und Liedeswort   dichte frisch!
    Dein Schandenname   noch sagt es: Mein   Zelt in dir.

Und acht gering, wer   da höhnt, ob schon   laut er dröhnt!
    Sacht trieb die Herde,   — du kommst zuletzt   ins Quartier.

Dein Liebster quält Dich,   doch Er, er quillt   Glück dir auch.
    Dein Teil, der krank, Er.   Er Heiletranks   Elixier.

Am schönsten liebst Du,   des hoffend, der   Dich erlöst.
    Dräng nicht! noch schaun wirst   du meiner Tat   Glanz und Zier.

Wenn ihres Königs   sich rühmen die,   rühme du:
    Er, Jakobs Heilger,   mein König ist,   Löser mir.

FESTIVAL OF LIGHTS

At times through Your light, Lord of Lights, we look upon light.

Hope — for the people whose worldly path points
Through the night, how long does its lustre gleam
And does sin bite them in the heel?
Oh, that upon them, like a glow upon light, Light might reign!

Around the bare head bind priestly vestments,
Torn clothing — by priestly garments
Replaced it, let the seed of the original light
Blossom anew, as in the "Let there be light" and there was light.

Your sign may it raise up the staggering knees,
Let the angel walk before them.
And, oh, that soon the day may appear
Where salvation surrounds the pious, shame those who scorn light!

Ah, he, a servant, gasps for shade,
Pour out upon him the light of Your salvation,
And call to him: "Where darkness creeps,
How long will you sit? Come, be light. Light has risen."

"Grace, grace!" oh, call it! Let olive trees
Come to be in two rows, so that
In the Temple the liquid of the oil may stream,
To kindle lights to the One Who is Light, a light for Him!

MORNING SERVICE

The morning stars all sing up to You,
For the original sources of their ray originate from You.
And the offspring of God, holding fast on their guard
By night, by day swell in exuberance of praise.
And the companions of the kingdom learned it from them, when
They joyfully bring into Your House the light of the dawn.

LICHTERFEST

Jeweils durch Dein Licht, Herre licht, schaun wir Licht.

Hoffnung — dem Volk, des Weltpfad weist
Nachtdurch, wie lang ihr Schein nur gleißt
Und Sünd' es in die Ferse beißt?
O daß auf ihm, wie Glut auf Licht, throne Licht!

Ums bloße Haupt bind Weih-Ornat,
Zerrissen Kleid — durch Priesterstaat
Ersetz es, laß des Urlichts Saat
Neu blühn, wie beim „Es werde Licht" und es ward Licht.

Dein Zeichen höh' den wanken Knien,
Laß ihnen vor den Engel ziehn.
Und o daß bald der Tag erschien',
Wo Fromme Heil, Schmach die umflicht, die verschmähn Licht!

Ach der, ein Knecht, nach Schatten keucht,
Umgieß ihm Deines Heils Geleucht,
Und ruf ihm zu: „Wo Dunkel kreucht,
Wie lang noch hockst du? Komm, sei licht! Aufging Licht."

„Huld, Huld" — o rufs! Ölbäume laß
Erstehen zweigereiht, auf daß
Im Tempel ström' des Öles Naß.
Lichter zu zünden Dem, der licht, Ihm zum Licht!

MORGENDLICHER DIENST

Morgengestirne all   zu Dir aufsingen,
    Denn ihres Strahls Urquelln   aus Dir urspringen.
Und die Gottes-Sprossen,   festgebannt auf ihre Wacht,
    Nachts, Tags den Überschwang   des Lobs ausschwingen.
Und die Reichs-Genossen   lernten es von ihnen, wenn
    Froh sie der Frühe Licht   in Dein Haus bringen.

LIGHT

Youthfully let songs bloom around Him by day, by night,
   He allowed the glow of His eye to glow into mine.
Kindling the shining light on high, He chases away the night,
   thus he boldly tore a window for me into the vault.
And His own ray He bestowed upon me,
   His spirit became word for me through the labour of saints.
The stream of the original light paved a way for me,
   from Seïr it shone upon Sinai's mountain-ridge, —
I lap up the seed of His word and rejoiced:
   Oh come, oh see my eye sparkle forth light!

CONQUERED DARKNESS

They hunted you, little dove, until
Grief ripped away the lament itself —
Around Him who, sure of heart,
Raised the banners of your troops!
For you, too, a day still shone —
   He creates light, He creates darkness.

Loudly echoed His creative Yes,
In a moment all stood there.
That the world saw Him as mighty,
It did not get back Chaos,
He called up from the east
   His light, chased away darkness.

A host of clouds heard the words,
"Let there be light." A Rock
Exists, they recognized at once,
Rent in two; in its place
Sank the foundation stone, it was made known there:
   Light higher than darkness.

Into my darkness may His light penetrate!
May He send him who establishes me,
That my people break into the light,
That my jewel be surrounded by fame —
Rock, of Whom my praising speaks,
   He is mine in the darkness.

LICHT

Jung sollen tags, nachts   Ihn Lieder umblühn,
   Glut seines Augs ließ   in meines er glühn.
Hoch zündend Geleucht   verjagt er die Nacht,
   so riß ins Gewölb   mir Fenster er kühn.
Und eigenen Strahls   beschenkte er mich,
   sein Geist ward mir Wort   durch Heiliger Mühn.
Der Urlichtstroms Weg   zur Bahn mir gebahnt,
   von Seïr her schien   ob Sinais Flühn, —
Aufschlürft seines Worts   den Seim ich und jauchzt:
   O kommt doch, o seht   mein Auge Licht sprühn!

BESIEGTE FINSTERNIS

Jagten sie dich, Taüblein, bis
Harm den Klaglaut selbst zerriß —
Um Ihn her, der herzgewiß,
Deiner Streitmacht Fahnen hiß!
Auch für Dich ein Tag noch gliß —
   Er schafft Licht, Er Finsternis.

Laut erscholl sein schaffend Ja,
Augenblicks stand alles da.
Daß die Welt ihn mächtig sah,
Chaos nicht sie rückempfah',
Rief vom Ost herauf er nah
   Sein Licht, scheuchte Finsternis.

Wolkenschar vernahm das Wort
„Werde Licht". Ein Felsenhort
Ist — erkannte sie sofort,
Riß entzwei; an seinen Ort
Sank der Grundstein. Kund ward dort:
   Höher Licht als Finsternis.

In mein Dunkel fahr' sein Licht!
Send' er ihn, der mich erricht',
Daß mein Volk ins Helle bricht,
Daß mein Kleinod Ruhm umflicht —
Fels, vom dem mein Rühmen spricht,
   Er mir in der Finsternis.

ON REED SEA DAY

Let it rejoice brightly in the morning ray on the festival-day of Your
    might,
Devoted to You, flock, shaded by You, sheltered.

Here they stand destitute of Your world before You in languishing
    prayer
And bring before Your throne a heavy load of words.

They walk the little temple's path, of whom You have eternal tenancy,

Like a guide is Your justice, so my ear heeds Your word.

Help Your Messiah! out, Protector, on guard!

All the days of the world when he bore Your yoke, let them be
    remembered.
Let Your redeeming arm which once fought Your battle

Shine forth as then, tear the banner out of the night!

Full of breath the human breast, all united in Your might,

In the exultation of the morning star let it exult in Your splendour.

AM SCHILFMEERTAG

Jauchz' hell sie im Morgenstrahl   am Festtag   Deiner Macht,

Ergebne dir, Schar, von Dir   beschattet,   überdacht.

Hier stehn arm sie Deiner Welt   vor Dir in   Bittgeschmacht

Und bringen vor Deinen Stuhl   der Worte   schwere Tracht.

Des Kleintempels Pfad gehn, die   du hast zu   ewger Pacht,

Als Richtpunkt dein Recht, so hat   das Ohr Dein   Wort in acht.

Hilf Deinem Messias Du!   heraus, Hort,   auf die Wacht!

All Welttage, die er trug   dein Joch, sei'n   ihm gedacht.

Laß Deinen Erlöserarm,   der einst schlug   Deine Schlacht,

Erglänzen wie damals, reiß   die Fahne   aus der Nacht!

Voll Hauches die Menschenbrust,   geeint all   Deiner Macht,

Im Morgensternjubel soll   sie jubeln   Deine Pracht.

MY KING

Let my Prince radiate youthfully, everywhere,
That a banner may wave to the beat of the march-step,
That the word of scorn may fade away, and he who felled, may he fall,
Into his ear may it echo: Prepare the universe for God!

He hurls down the city into deep ruins.
Listen! The watchman's horn: gush forth, bloody fountain.
The wrath flashes, grasses wither,
Ripe stands the corn — sickles into the swell!

And fast as a wheel runs the sound of the happy message
To You city, saying: "Rise high! rise!
Sing a poetic song! Sight the Messiah!
Stand up, be light! See the Prince, the huge army."

For the son He chose a path of crystal,
Raised the riot of sins, opened the eye's gate,
Until, he who lost him, newly may swear to him,
And, King before Him, entered Gilgal.

His word went out; the sphere revolves.
He tears open a window: a valley, a mountain points
Out, brilliantly lit by stars, the pure spirit of light.
Moon, sun, circles on the wall of the spheres.

OUT OF DISTRESS

Let Your fountain of life gush forth blessings for me
    as Your wrath caused rains of fire!
Eternally should my sins
    separate me and You?
Have I not sought You for a long time, and
    You never come to meet me?
Dwelling under wings of cherubim,
    which protect Your shrine
Do You enslave me to strangers, instead
    of caring Yourself for Your young plant?
Arise, my Redeemer, to redeem me,
    stand! Look here from the paths of stars!

MEIN KÖNIG

Jung strahl' mein Fürst
    Daß Fahne wall'
    Spotts Wort verschall',
Ins Ohr ihm hall':

        allüberall,
        zu Marschtritts Prall,
        der fällte, fall',
        Bahnt für Gott das All!

Hoch stürzt die Stadt
    Horch! Wächters Horn:
    Es zückt der Zorn,
Reif steht das Korn —

        er tiefen Fall.
        quill, blutger Born!
        die Gräser dorrn,
        Sicheln in den Schwall!

Und radschnell läuft
    Dir Stadt zu, spricht:
    Sing Singgedicht!
Steh auf, sei licht!

        Frohbotschafts Hall
        „Richt hoch dich! richt!
        Messias sicht!
        Fürst sieh, Heergewall."

Dem Sohn kor Pfad
    Hob Sündenflor,
    Bis, der verlor
Und, König vor

        er von Kristall,
        erschloß Augs Tor,
        ihn, neu ihm schwor
        Ihm, betrat Gilgal.

Ausfuhr sein Wort:
    Ein Fenster reißt
    Sternübergleißt
Mond, Sonne kreist

        umrollt der Ball.
        er: Tal, Berg weist
        Lichts lautren Geist.
        auf der Sphären Wall.

AUS DEM ELEND

Ja so quell' Dein Born mir Segen,
    wie dein Zorn quoll Feuerregen!
Ewig sollte meine Sünde
    zwischen mich und Dich sich legen?
Hab ich Dich nicht lang gesucht, und
    nimmer kommst Du mir entgegen?
Unter Cherubsflügeln hausend,
    welche Deinen Schrein umhegen,
Du, versklavst Du Fremden mich, statt
    Deinen Setzling selbst zu pflegen?
Auf, mein Löser, mich zu lösen,
    steh! schau her von Sternen-Wegen!

TO THE REDEEMER

Dove — you have borne her   on wings of eagles,
She has nested in Your lap   for beloved safekeeping —
Why have you smitten her, now   she has to fly through the forest
Where all around there were   trappers in hordes,
Enticing her, barbarians,   to alien altars;
But she — cries the clear   tears for Him and her years of youth.
When the tongue of the enemy, the smooth one,   had already en-
snared her, —
Her eye, in dimness, asks: Where stays my first husband?
Why do You leave my   soul to the grave?
I know that besides You   I have no redeemer.

Lovely one, did He tear apart   forever your veil?
Will he be the victim and remains   of ravens and vultures?
The maid's son, now a suitor —   woe, the horrifying suitor!
He is all strength without consecration,   when he stretches the horns
of the bow.
My tent: place of celebration —   in there monotonous words sound
loudly!
My refuge from the world, where is He   I ask! Does He stand by me
still?
No more miracles, no signs.   Visions, dreams pale.
And when I ask: when will we reach   the day without compare —
Prophets, alas, elude: bury your inquiries.
I know that besides You   I have no redeemer.

And daughters, the slender ones,   dragged out of the city-gates,
Out of bed-linen, bright,   out of arboured surroundings,
Who totter towards peoples,   with sick understanding,
Towards mockery of barbarians   and scolding in foreign tongues,
But faithful to the thought,   to whom they owe care,
Before the painted boards of the horrible idol   they never sank to
their knees!
Now, when the mild one who was   my shield moved away
Into cloud regions,   now the barbarian pursues me!
Dig to the end of days,   demand, oh dig!
I know that besides You,   I have no redeemer.

AN DEN LÖSER

Jungtaube — trugst sie   auf Flügeln von Aaren,
   Sie nistete im Schoße dir   zu trautem Verwahren, —
Was schlugst du sie, nun   mußte walddurch sie fahren,
Wo ringsum in Scharen   Schlingenbreiter waren.
Sie lockend, Barbaren,   zu fremden Altaren;
Doch sie — weint die klaren   Tränen nach Ihm und den jungen
   Jahren.
   Wenn Feinds Zunge, die glatte,   sie umgarnt schon hatte,
   Ihr Aug fragt, das matte: wo bleibt mein Urgatte?
Was läßest du meine   Seele dem Grab?
Ich weiß, daß außer dir   ich keinen Löser hab.

Holde, riß entzwei er   auf ewig, dein Schleier?
   Raben und Geier   Raub und Gespei er?
Der Magd Sohn, nun Freier, —   weh der grause Freier!
Ganz Kraft ohne Weih er,   spannt Bogens Geweih er.

Mein Zelt: Ort der Feier,   drein gellt Wortgeleier!

Mein Welthort, wo sei er,   ich frags! Steht noch bei er?
   Nicht Wunder mehr, nicht Zeichen.   Gesichte, Träume blei-
   chen.
   Und frag ich: wann erreichen   den Tag wir ohne gleichen —
Propheten, ach, ausweichen: dein Fragen begrab!
Ich weiß, daß außer dir   ich keinen Löser hab.

Und Töchter, die schlanken,   verschleppt aus Stadtschranken,
   Aus Linnen, den blanken,   aus Laubenumranken,
Die Völkern zuwanken,   einsichtskranken,
Barbarengespött zu   und Fremdzungenzanken,
Doch treu dem Gedanken,   dem Betreuung sie danken,
Vor Greulbilds bunten Planken   aufs Knie nimmer sanken!

   Da, der mir zum Schilde,   in Wolkengefilde
   Jetzt wich, der Milde,   hetzt mich der Wilde! —
Zum Ende der Tage   grab, Frage, o grab!
Ich weiß, daß außer dir   ich keinen Löser hab.

The banner of accord,   alas it has flown from me.
And arrogance struck me   with a heavy blow on my neck.
I am open to punishment,   in the lap of cruelty,
Excommunication and fetters my fate,   listless, joyless.
No commander, no chief,   no king, no one great.
He attacks me vehemently!   the protector is away from me!
    Destroys the place in ecstasy of rage   which his soles had chosen
        for himself.
    Kindles in angry rage   the timbrework, the foundations,
Fire blasts out of his blowing,   which burns until the grave —
I know that besides You   I have no redeemer.

Alas, will he eternally   shun me in anger?
    Visions — can they   confirm no goal for me?
Awake, God! to tend   to me, to disperse those who envy me!
Be content anew   behind the curtain's silk.
As at Sinai appear to both   my eyes in Your radiant jewels.
And settle with the heathens   the debt of my suffering.
    Let the light of salvation flow down   on him, whom anxiety breaks.
    Send down the maid's son,   the wight, from the throne into
        judgement
Soon! so that I do not   go to the grave in sorrow.
I know that besides You   I have no redeemer.

LOOKING UPWARDS

Draw out Your arm, Your strong right hand,
    to help Your remnant of the flock in battle!
For doesn't Your arm have the strength to save?
    time and chance touch you like those made from dust.
And yet, lights of heaven, they circle 'round You
    and stand slaves of Your mouth, of Your word.
Your word, the flocks on high await it tranquilly,
    starlight bears witness to Your treasure's authenticity.
Its brightness is kindled by Your splendour,
    its ray by the garland of Your network of stars.

Der Einmut Panier,   ach von mir entfloh's,
  Und Hochmut trat mir   in Nacken schweren Stoß.
Ich der Züchtigung bloss,   in der Grausamkeit Schoß,
Bann und Bande mein Los,   verdrossen, freudelos.
Kein Feldhaupt, kein Schwerttos,   kein König, keiner groß.
Der hart, auf mich los!   der Hort von mir los!
  Zerstört den Ort in Grimms Extasen,   den seine Sohlen sich
    erlasen,
  Entzündet in Zorns Rasen   das Gebälk, die Basen,
Feuer schlägt aus seinem Blasen,   das brennt bis zum Grab —
Ich weiß, daß außer dir   ich keinen Löser hab.

Ach wird er ewig   mich grollend meiden?
  Gesichte — können   kein Ziel sie mir beeiden?
Auf, Gott! zu weiden   mich, zu zerstreun, die mich neiden!
Woll neu dich bescheiden   hinter Vorhangs Seiden.
Zeig sinaigleich dich den beiden   Augen in Strahlgeschmeiden.
Und zahle den Heiden   den Lohn meiner Leiden.
  Herab tau Heils Licht   auf ihn, den Angst zerbricht.
  Vom Thron ins Gericht   stürz den Magdsohn, den Wicht.

Bald! auf daß ich nicht   in Kummer fahr zu Grab.
Ich weiß, daß außer dir   ich keinen Löser hab.

AUFBLICK

Jach zück Deinen Arm, Deine starke Rechte,
  zu Hilf Deiner Restherde zum Gefechte!
Hat Kraft zu erlösen dein Arm denn nicht?
  rührt Zeit Dich und Zufall gleich Staubs Geschlechte.
Und doch — Himmelslichter, sie kreisen um Dich,
  und stehn Deines Munds, Deines Wortes Knechte.
Dein Wort, still erharrn es die Scharen der Höh;
  Gestirnlicht bezeugt Deines Schatzes Echte.
Anzündet ihr Glanz sich an Deinem Gepräng,
  ihr Strahl sich am Kranz Deiner Sterngeflechte.

BRIDE OF ISRAEL'S SABBATH

Jewel of a day around which peace
And life are set —
You consecrate it so that it should separate
Israel from the heathens.

They would like to have — with a twist of words! —
Theirs the same as my Holy Day:
Rome the first already from long ago,
The sixth most recently Arabia.
Their mockery — as if it may ever
Make me stray from the masters of Truth!
Can one not separate dirty clothes from silken adornment,
Death from life?

And my neighbours would like
Very much to go up to the king's throne
Which is the rest of God and man.
To which He allotted the reward of bliss
The original Here and Now of the festive call,
Already from the days of Creation —
Your word sows meadows of life:
On which we live among heathens.

To be a priestess to You — her proud lot!
Your Name in a rushing wave her raft!
She sobs her pain into Your lap,
She rejoices only at Your table,
Manna satisfies her, free from suffering,
A portion was left over, a little jugful,
So that islands afar envy her,
Her fame runs to the heathens.

Extend Your arm again, Lord,
Have mercy anew on Your old kingdom.
Though Your people live deeply in sorrow,
Dispersed in zones cold and warm:
How poor Arabia stands, and Greece.
You lead home Aaron's troop of priests!
In Levi's camp be
Consecrated, You praise of the heathens!

JUNGFRAU ISRAELS SABBAT

Juwel von Tag, das Friede
Und Leben rings umschmeiden, —
Du weihst ihn, daß er schiede
Israel und die Heiden.

Hätten gern — mit Wortesdreh! —
Die ihren meinem heilgen Tag
Gleich: Rom den ersten schon von eh,
Den sechsten jüngst Arabiens Schlag.
Ihr Gespött — als ob es je
Irrn der Wahrheit Herren mag!
Kann Schmutzkleid man, Schmuck seiden,
Tod, Leben wohl nicht scheiden?

Und meine Nachbarn möchten zu
Gern hinauf zum Königsthron
Der Gottes- und der Menschenruh,
Der Er beschied den Segenslohn,
Festrufs urerstes Hie und Nu,
Von der Schöpfung Tagen schon —
Dein Wort sät Lebensweiden:
Drauf leben wir bei Heiden.

Dir Priestrin sein — ihr stolzes Los!
Dein Nam' in Wogendrang ihr Floß!
Sie schluchzt ihr Leid in deinen Schloß,
Sie jauchzt an deinem Tische bloß,
Satt macht sie Manna, leidenlos,
Ein Maß blieb übrig, krügleingroß,
Daß Inseln fern sie neiden,
Ihr Ruhm läuft zu den Heiden.

Ausstreck wieder, Herr, den Arm,
Des alten Reichs dich neu erbarm.
Lebt dein Volk auch tief in Harm,
Zerstreut in Zonen kalt und warm:
Wie stehn Arabien, Hellas arm,
Führst heim du Ahrons Priesterschwarm!
In Levis Lager sei denn
Geweiht, du Lob der Heiden!

HOME

The flock wandering about behind enemy's walls — let it go
Home where Your promised One may bear its eternal support.

Let the demand for salvation some day exult in the exile,
When the messenger points out to those who are unhappy in their
sin that the gate is near.
He Whom the womb of time never enveloped, let Him play joyfully
and whoever still dares temptation, let him flee.
Let him be purified, for whom torment was meant.

Hark! "Let the axe eat up the stump!" the enemy's behest.
That my wreath may go around his head, his diligence intends,
Boasts: "Now no more branch will sprout from the root of Jesse"-
That the barren staff may bud, be implored,
Be gracious, and let the scales of fate turn.

Free from rent and slavery, lead us on.
Watch above Zion's crown of hills You Yourself henceforth
In the shade of the Highest One Your people will then dwell —
Deluge of desecration, of ruinous conditions, let them pass away.
Let the wild death-lamentations of the sea rest.

The cry of the oppressed, may it float up to You,
Among lions the lamb — free it from bloody voracity,
Shepherd! Your heart, in compassion may it tremble for Your crea-
ture —
Your flock, fainthearted with yearning, do not let it stay.
Light of salvation, it was almost extinguished, let it be newly promi-
nent, let it be seen.

The seed of light shoots up, now that the night is torn.
You give counsel to the afflictions of Your firstborn.
Well for him the knowledge of Your light to whom it approaches!
Then You reign. From that day forth extend afar
Your salvation. And all my suffering — like a fable let it blow away.

HEIM

Herd' umirrnd in Feinds Verschlage —
Heim, wo Dein Verheißner trage

Juble einst das Heilsverlangen
Weist der Bote Sündenbangen

Den nie Zeitschoß sanft umfangen,
Und wer noch Versuchung wage,
Läutrung ihm, dem galt die Plage,

Horch! „Den Stumpf die Axt abfresse!"
Dass mein Reif sein Haupt ummesse,
Prahlt: „Nun sproßt der Wurzel Jesse
Dass der dürre Stab ausschlage,
Hold sei, und des Schicksals Wage

Uns aus Zins befreit und Frohnen
Wach ob Zions Hügelkronen
In des Höchsten Schirm wird wohnen
Frevels Flut, getürmter Lage,
Ruhn die wilde Totenklage

Des Bedrängten Weinen, schweb' es
Unter Leun das Lamm — entheb es
Hirt! Dein Herz, in Mitleid beb' es

Deine Herde, sehnsuchtzage,
Heilslicht, fast schon loschs, neu rage

Aufschießt, nun die Nacht zerrissen,
Deines Erstlings Kümmernissen
Wohl dem Deines Lichts Gewissen,
Dann herrschst Du. An jenem Tage
Dein Heil. Und all mein Leid — wie Sage

laß sie gehn
ihr ewges Lehn.

im Exil,
nah das Ziel.

froh er spiel'
fliehn laß den.
laß geschehn.

Feinds Geheiß.
sinnt sein Fleiß,
mehr kein Reis" —
laß dich flehn.
laß sich drehn.

führ hinan,
du selbst fortan,
Dein Volk dann
laß zergehn.
laß der Seen.

auf zu Dir,
blutger Gier,
um Dein Tier —

laß nicht stehn.
laß es sehn.

Lichtes Saat.
schaffst Du Rat.
dem selbst es naht! —
weithin dehn
laß verwehn.

THE MIRACLES OF ELIJAH

Miracle, missed daily by us —
Alas, Elijah's God, where is He?

His seed hearkens to his words,
Cries out in distress, when enemies come.
Speaks: where is the Protector, the names?
For a thousand years already He has forgotten us.

Because of the wantonness of the Northern Kingdom
Elijah locked the gates of heaven;
That by his word should descend
Fire, water, he ventures.

He said prayers over the jar and the bowl,
Blesses them to luxuriant rays,
Plucks the child out of death's valley —
Who saw, heard it whom you know, who?

He caused warlords and mighty ones to burn,
Fasted for forty days and nights;
Ravens came, so that one might think:
Enticed — their bread, he eats it.

When he went up in a storm
In the trembling glow of a chariot of fire
Elisha remained, crying bitterly:
Father, Father! And answer was missing.

See the floods of Jordan dry up,
That they were not even ankle deep,
And they yielded also to Elisha —
If anybody saw it they were amazed without delay.

Those hoping for signs of the prophets,
When will they see the wondrous events?
When will He do the same for them
And raise the banner of God!

DIE ELIAWUNDER

Wunder täglich uns vermißter —
Ach, Elias Gott, wo ist er?

Seinen Worten horcht sein Samen,
Schreit vor Not, wenn Feinde kamen,
Spricht: wo bleibt der Hort, die Namen?
Tausend Jahr schon uns vergißt er!

Wegen Nordreichs Ungebühren
Schloß Elia Himmels Türen;
Daß auf sein Wort niederführen
Feuer, Wasser, sich vermißt er.

Er besprach so Krug als Schale,
Segnet sie zu üppgem Strahle,
Reißt das Kind aus Todes Tale —
Wer sah, hört' es, den ihr wißt, wer?

Er verbrannt Kriegsherrn und -mächte,
Fastet vierzig Tag und Nächte;
Raben kamen, daß man dächte:
Hergelockt, — ihr Brot, das ißt er.

Als er auffuhr in Gewitter,
Feuerwagens Glutgezitter,
Blieb Elisa, weinend bitter:
Vater, Vater! Antwort mißt' er.

Jordans Fluten sieh versiegen,
Daß sie nicht zum Knöchel stiegen,
Und Elisan auch sich schmiegen —
Sah wer's, starr ward sonder Frist er.

Hoffer auf Propheten zeichen,
Wann sehn sie die wunderreichen?
Wann tut er für sie dergleichen
Und die Gottesfahne hißt er!

THE JEW

I am reviled on your account by those who wander through the nights,
    The servants of deluded powers of brazen images,
I replied: To serve God is the right thing.
    What did those people effect that He did not accomplish?
When He frowns upon me, I am the servant of servants.
    When He is gracious to me, I am the might of mights.

THE PROMISE

"Young doves who are precipitously misplaced
        in a land waste and windy,
Up! as here no rest comforts you,
        The brilliance of the homeland, now fades away.
Home! thither where you take delight in
        Air soft and gentle —
    May God give it to you now,
            that you may find rest!"

'Lord, since we flew out of Jerusalem,
        To the daughters, who surrounded it,
And high up drew away from Zion,
        Whose meadows are buried in desert,
We — the path is bent nightwards!
        Land — it wants years of peace!
    Hoping yet not betrayed
            that the sound of prayer will never vanish from Him

And who gives me wings of doves!
        I would fly up, and soar homeward.
I would ride upon horses of the south, of the north,
        but I would ask only for the wind of Zion.
That the time of the end, time of the beginning is rid of,
        the footfall of shepherds, princes approach,
    when the cut of the sword, deaf to pain,
            the sword of revenge delivers the sword of revenge.'

DER JUDE

Es schmähn mich Deinethalb, die irrn durch Nächte,
die Diener erzgegossner Wahngemächte,
Erwidert' ich: Gott Dienen ist das Rechte.
Was wirkten jene, was nicht Er vollbrächte?
Wenn Er mir grollt, bin ich der Knecht der Knechte.
Ist Er mir hold, bin ich die Macht der Mächte.

DIE VERHEISSUNG

„Jungtauben, die jäh versetzt
    in Land wüst und umwindet,
Auf! da hier nicht Ruh euch letzt,
    Heimatglanz, nun erblindet.
Heim! dorthin wo euch ergetzt
    Luft gesänftet, gelindet —
So gebe es Gott euch jetzt,
    daß ihr Ruhe findet!"

‚Herr! seit wir Salem entflogen,
    Töchtern, die's rings umgaben,
Und hoch aus Zion weg zogen,
    des Aun in Wüste begraben,
Wir — Pfad nachtwärts gebogen!
    Land — Ruh-Jahre wills haben!
Hoffen doch unbetrogen,
    daß nie Gebetslaut Ihm schwindet.

Und wer gibt mir Taubenfittich!
    Aufflöge, heimzu glitt' ich.
Auf Süds, Nords Rossen ritt ich,
    doch Zionswind nur erbitt ich.
Daß Endzeit, Urzeit quitt sich,
    naht Hirten-, Fuersten-Schritt sich,
Da schmerztauben Schwertes Schnitt sich
    Rachschwert, Rachschwert entbindet.'

"You wandering on the hills of hope,
    the distant shimmer does not lie.
You broke away from the reins of harmony,
    but never from harmony with me.
Beautiful little daughter returns on wings
        of youth to my room.
    I'll try to find out from the cherub of salvation,
            floating through the air, where you will find rest.

Be watchful! Solace shall cover you,
    like dew in an arid year.
Cultivates the desolate patches of land.
    May the city wake up on its ruins.
He awakens, like war heros,
    Love out of the heart's prison,
He who makes the barren one
        into the mother happily surrounded by children."

LOVE OF THE ENEMY

From ere You were the firmament of love,
    my loving nested with You in the nest.
The invectives of my enemy, they gladden me, for Your sake;
    let him — his oppression crushes him whom Your oppression
        has long crushed.
The enemy learned Your fierceness: that is why I love him;
    for his fist meets the ailments of Your blow.
If You spurned me, I myself would spurn the day,
    how could I wish the best for him whom You spurned!
Until Your anger passes away and You send redemption,
    the remnant of the heritage once saved by You.

„Du wallnd auf der Hoffnung Hügeln,
   nicht lügt der ferne Schimmer.
Entbracht ihr der Eintracht Zügeln,
   der Eintracht mit mir doch nimmer.
Schön Töchterlein kehrt auf Flügeln
   der Jugend meinem Zimmer.
Vom Heilscherub-Luftdurchschwimmer
   späh ich, wo Ruh ihr findet.

Acht habt! Trost soll euch decken,
   gleich Tau in dürrem Jahre.
Anpflanzt verödete Flecken.
   Auf Trümmern die Stadt hochfahre.
Er weckt, wie kriegrischen Recken,
   Liebe aus Herzverwahre,
Der macht die Unfruchtbare
   zur Mutter froh umkindet."

FEINDESLIEBE

Von eh warst Du der Liebe Himmelsveste,
   mein Lieben nistete bei Dir im Neste.
Scheltworte meines Feinds, sie freun mich, Deinethalb;
   laß ihn — sein Druck preßt, den dein Druck längst
   preßte.
Es lernte Deinen Grimm der Feind: drum lieb ich ihn;
   denn seine Faust trifft Deines Schlags Gebreste.
Verwarfst du mich, den Tag verwarf ich selber mich,
   wie gönnt' ich dem, den Du verwarfst, das Beste!
Bis einst dein Groll vergeht und Du Erlösung schickst
   des einst von Dir erlösten Erbes Reste.

MIRACLE OF LOVE

Do You look gently upon the jewel and sifting out
  of my song and praise?
Beloved, who flew far from me
  because of the errant striving of my wickedness!
And if I hold His seam only,
  oh, miraculous power, which would still remain to me!
Your Name would be enough of a reward for me,
  when my toil would grind me down.
Alas, increase the suffering — more shall I love!
  The miracle of my life: Your love.

ANGRY LOVE

Beloved, have You ever forgotten the place of rest upon this bosom?
  and how could You ever sell me to my exterminators?
Did I ever once waver in following you in the desert?
  Your mountains, oh Sinai, bear witness of what you know.
And You rich in my love and I full of Your grace —
  Ah, woe, that I now must apportion the glory among others.
Whom I dragged to Edom, whom I cast out to Hagar's lineage,
  oppressed under the Persian yoke, carried off in Greek blossoming.
Ah, are You not the only God? and does another than I await you?
  Oh, give Your strength to me! To You I give anew love's delight.

DREAM VISION

In starlight my ground of twilight shines.
  Does my fruit-harvest return to me anew at this hour?
A delightful meadow, a vineyard mine,
  mine the kettledrum, mine the mouth of the flutes.
The bracelet returns home onto my arm,
  to my nose the golden roundness.
And His palace and my room
  stood facing threshold to threshold.
Then I returned home to His understanding,
  heart, senses, all in union.
By Him let the soul be intoxicated.
  Let the tongue make Him known in jubilation.

LIEBESWUNDER

Je blickst du hold auf meines Lieds
      und Lobs Geschmeid und Ausgesiebe?
Herztrauter, der mir ferne floh
      ob meiner Bosheit irrem Triebe!
Und halt ich Seinen Saum auch nur,
      o Wunderkraft, die noch mir bliebe!
Dein Name wär mir Lohns genug,
      wenn meine Arbeit mich zerriebe.
Ach mehr' du Leid — mehr liebe ich!
      Mein Lebenswunder: Deine Liebe.

ZÜRNENDE LIEBE

Je, Liebster, vergaßest Du   den Ruhplatz auf dieser Brust?
      und konntst mich verkaufen je   du meinen Vertilgern just?
Hab einst ich gezögert, Dir   zu folgen in wüstes Land?
      Ihr Berge, o Sinai, gebt   mir Zeugnis, wie euchs bewußt.
Und Du meiner Liebe reich   und ich Deiner Gnade voll —
      ach weh, daß ich nun den Glanz   an andre verteilen mußt'.
Die Edom ich zugeschleppt,   verstoßen zu Hagars Stamm,
      gedrückt unter Perserjoch,   entrückt in hellen'schen Blust.
Ach bist nicht der einzge Gott?   und harrt noch ein andrer Dein?
      O spend Deine Kraft mir! Dir   spend' neu ich der Liebe Lust.

TRAUMGESICHT

In Sternlicht strahlt mein Dämmergrund.
      Kehrt neu mein Fruchtherbst mir zurstund?
Ein wonnger Hag, ein Wingert mein,
      mein Pauke, mein der Flöte Mund.
Heim kehrt an meinen Arm der Reif,
      an meine Nase goldnes Rund.
Und sein Palast und mein Gelaß
      genüber Schwell gen Schwelle stund.
Dann ich zu seiner Einung heim
      gekehrt, Herz, Sinne all im Bund.
An ihm berausch' die Seele sich,
      ihn mach' die Zunge jauchzend kund.

FAITHFULNESS

"Year after year, Beloved One, pushed me wretchedly
To the snakebite, to the scorpion's sting
Into the dungeon —
Have mercy, mercy!

Yet my heart still hopes until weary! In the morning
Every day it sees the goal as far away as ever.
Ah, Beloved, what should I say, since
Edom slunk into my hall as proprietor,
Arabians, Northmen rule over me,
All dogs, as they
Ran around my flock,

And the sweet melody of my name
Spat at me as an insult out of foreign mouths,
They — against me! — boast with prophecy,
Every maniac among all the people,
Without heed of the spiritual judgement over him,
Oppressed me and pushed
So that I yielded to lies!

You! let us wander through the Garden's air,
Savour the spikenard's and rose's fragrance.
What is the chamois doing in the foxes' lair!
Wake up to my harp, speak to my bell,
Drink my wine, and oh, pluck my fruit!
My paradise
Open up, of which the splendour turned pale for me!"

" "Hold out! be it still countless years.
I have wedded myself to no other people.
You chose Me, so I have chosen you
Where would be a stock, in which part under the heavens,
Which was like My son, sacrifice, firstborn,
Whom I called friend, —
And where a God like me!" "

TREUE

„Jahr, Trauter, stieß um Jahr elendiglich
        Zu Schlangenbiß, zu Skorpionstich
        Mich ins Verließ —
      Erbarm, er- barme dich!

Hofft doch mein Herz sich müd! Zur Morgenzeit
Tagtäglich siehts das Ziel entfernt gleich weit.
Ach Liebster, was soll ich noch sagen, seit
Edom in meinen Saal als Eigner schlich,
        Araber, Norrman herrschen über mich,
        Samt Hundsvolk, wie's
        Um meine Herde strich,

Und meines Namens süße Melodie
Als Schimpf aus fremden Munde mich anspie,
Sie — wider mich! — großtun mit Prophetie,
Von allem Volk jedweder Wüterich,
        Ohn' Acht des Geisterurteils über sich,
        Mich drängt' und stieß,
        Daß ich zu Lügen wich'!

Du! laß uns wandeln durch der Gärten Luft,
Schmecken der Narden und der Rosen Duft.
Was soll die Gemse in der Füchse Kluft!
Wach meiner Harfe, meiner Glocke sprich,
        Trink meinen Wein, und meine Frucht, o, brich!
        Mein Paradies
        Tu auf, des Glanz mir blich!"

„ „Ausharre! seis noch Jahre ungezählt.
Ich hab mich keinem andern Volk vermählt.
Du wähltest Mich, so hab ich Dich erwählt.
Wo wär ein Stamm, in welchem Himmelsstrich,
        Der meinem Sohn, Schlachtopfer, Erstling glich,
        Den Freund ich hieß, —
        Und wo ein Gott wie Ich!" "

LOVE'S SOLACE

"What good, Sister, is the account
of the days, in which you lie imprisoned?

You pursue, you Dove, and you wander flitting
Lonely from mountain ridge to mountain ridge,
You ask: "When, you my day, will you come?"
Have courage, heart, which bursts from fear,
The witnessing of hope did not lie,
oh, only hope — already the sap rises."

" "Did I still hope for medicine
For my sickness, when I was sick
From Your anger? In darkness sank
My image because of the wavering of my deeds.
In flaming pain of widowhood
I sit, my happiness night has snatched up.

And enemies say: 'For her salvation
is lacking! it seems a long time coming.
Her Redeemer lives? Why doesn't He come?
Into our hand fell her judgement,
Surely, she deceived the Prophets,
and it is deception, what her seer saw.' " "

"You Love! May this satisfy you:
That I am raising anew My banner,
I purify the estate of your inheritance.
I spread My Name. For Me
I redeem My family inheritance
and save those who sleep the sleep of death.

If My heart surges up, I remember
The love, here from the beginning of times.
The word can no longer express it.
Love burns like coal-fires.
A storm of passion blows through Me:
strong as death is the power of love."

LIEBESTROST

„Was Schwester, soll die Rechenschaft
        der Tage, die du liegst in Haft?

Jagst, Taube Du, und flatternd irrst
Du einsam hin von First zu First,
Fragst: ‚Wann, mein Tag du, kommen wirst?‘
Hab Mut, Herz, das vor Angst zerbirst,
Nicht log der Hoffnung Zeugenschaft,
        o hoffe nur — schon steigt der Saft.“

„ „Hofft’ wohl ich noch auf Heiletrank
Fuer meine Krankheit, da ich krank
An Deinem Zorn? In Dunkel sank
Mein Bild ob meiner Taten Wank.
In Flammenpein der Witwenschaft
        sitz ich, mein Glück hat Nacht gerafft.

Und Feinde sprechen: ’Der gebricht
Das Heil! es läuft auf lange Sicht.
Ihr Heiland lebt? was kommt er nicht?
In unsre Hand fiel ihr Gericht.
Gewiss, sie trog Prophetenschaft,
        und Trug ists, was ihr Seher gafft.‘ “ “

„Du Liebe! Dies genüge Dir:
Ich richte neu auf mein Panier.
Ich rein’ge Deines Erbs Revier.
Ich breite meinen Namen. Mir
Ausloes ich meine Stammerbschaft
        und heil, die Todesschlafs erschlafft.

Aufwallt mein Herz, gedenk ich der
Liebe, die von Urzeiten her.
Aussprechen kanns das Wort nicht mehr.
Wie Kohlenfeuer brennt sie sehr.
Sturm weht durch mich der Leidenschaft:
        stark wie der Tod ist Liebeskraft.“

FINDING AGAIN

"How can I atone
                to my sweet one? — alas, He has vanished!
Oh, may He yet bloom anew
                for me out of the East!"

" "Maiden, gentle as a dove,
                you are brought to Me,
Gird around fabrics woven in many colours, —
                May my eye smile on you!
Then I gird on armour, wild,
                avenging passion.
Still in the dust? see already salvation
                greeting in bud-form!
Loyalty of the one whom my "Go!"
                dispatched carries to the sons." "

"Love of my heart, I have cried
                to You out of the water's swell,
Hear the echo of my melodies,
                up into heaven.
The degree of punishment of the prophesies —
                when will my fall fulfill it?
You recorded a sprouting of sins
                already in the tome,
sprinkle the rain of mercy upon it,
                delete it with a kindly hand.

For me, the wretched one, abandoned,
                grant the hour of grace!
The remnant of the flock
                let it pasture on Your meadow!
How long may the poison of mockery
                seize me, corroding?
Ishmael, Edom lock
                me in prison walls,
My head, fearing the knife,
                loses its pledge of dedication.

WIEDERFINDEN

„Wie kann ich meinem Süßen
      Büßen? — ach er schwand!
O blüht' er doch aufs neue
      mir aus Morgenland!"

„ „Jungfraue, taubenmilde,
      bringt man dich zu mir,
Guert um webbunt Gebilde, —
      lach' mein Auge dir!
Dann gürt ich Wehr um, wilde,
      rächender Begier.
Im Staub noch? sieh schon grüßen
      Heil im Knospenstand!
Den Söhnen trägt des Treue,
      den mein ‚Geh!' entsandt." "

„Herzlieb, ich hab geschrieen
      dir aus Wassers Schwall,
Hör meiner Melodieen
      himmelauf den Hall.
Strafmaß der Prophetieen —
      wann erfüllts mein Fall?
Schriebst ein der Sünd' Aufschießen
      gleich schon im Foliant,
Drauf Gnadenregen streue,
      tilgs mit gütger Hand.

Unselger mir, verlassen,
      Gnadenstunde stift!
Den Rest der Herdenmassen
      weid auf Deiner Trift!
Wie lang darf beizend fassen
      mich des Spottes Gift?
Ismael, Edom schließen
      mich in Kerkerwand,
Einbüßt das messerscheue
      Haupt sein Weihepfand."

" "Give thanks! It was done for the remnant,
  which I did not expel.
Your salvation — you are seeing it near now.
  Who was it Who promised it!
He who remains silent, he saw it.
  Come! those whom I never left.
Like the flowing of myrrh-spice
    your sacrificial offering smells.
Let your festival now gladden Me,
    where I once found horror.

Wake up, oh, you my own,
  they are still afflicted with grief.
To the ascent of your garden
  came, who plucks the fruit for himself.
Your light, already about to incline,
  it flames! arise, be light!
Your friend, on hart's feet
  escaped your lap,
Come! The blue of God's heaven
    is stretched around you." "

„ „**D**anks! Um den Rest geschah es,
    den ich nicht verstieß.
Dein Heil — nun schaust du nah es.
    Wer wars, ders verhieß!
Der stille bleibt, der sah es.
    Komm! die nie ich ließ.
Wie Myrrhngewürzes Fließen
    riecht dein Opferbrand,
Dein Fest mich nun erfreue,
    dran ich Graun einst fand.

Aufwach, o du mein Eigen,
    die noch Gram umflicht.
Zu deines Gartens Steigen
    kam, der Frucht sich bricht.
Dein Licht, schon wollt sichs neigen,
    flammt! steh auf, sei licht!
Dein Freund, auf Hirschesfüßen
    deinem Schoß entrannt,
Kommt! Gotteshimmels Bläue
    ist um Dich gespannt." "

Zion   Zion

AWAKE

Sleeper, your heart is still awake,
Full of flame and roaring storm, —
Awake! leave the slumberer's roof,
    Come into the ray of my glance!

Start the journey happily!
Already your star has risen for you.
The one you believed dead, he climbed
    Up to Sinai.

Let the one be quiet in the meantime, who
Exults: "Zion is heavily laden
With sins!"— Lo, I never turn away
    My heart, my eye, from her.

I open and I close.
Let anger burn, I sow the seed of salvation.
How could I forsake
    Them, my children, them!

THE HAPPY MESSAGE

Young dove far away, your most beautiful song — oh, sing it,
    To Him, Who calls you, what is sweet in You — bring it forth.
It is He, Your God Himself, Who calls you: oh, be quick.
    Incline down to the earth! Give a gift — bring it there.
Raise yourself to Your nest, the way to Your tent,
    To Zion, — set up signposts for Yourself, which is the way.
First friend, who pushed You away, because Your action seemed evil,
    He Himself saves You today. Praise — where did it start?
You prepare for the homecoming into the beautiful land;
    Kingdom of Arabia, of Edom — oh, fight it into dust!
The house of all who once forced You — may wrath force it,
    And the house of Your friend, — may the wreath of love encircle it.

AUF

Schläfer, das Herz doch wach,
Voll Glut und Wetterkrach, —
Auf! laß des Schlummers Dach,
    In Meines Blicks Strahl zieh!

Glückhaft beginn den Lauf!
Schon ging dein Stern dir auf.
Der totgeglaubt, hinauf
    Stieg er zum Sinai.

Still sei dereinst noch, wer
Jauchzt: „Sündenlast drückt schwer
Zion!"— sieh, dennoch kehr
    Herz, Aug ich von ihr nie.

Auftu ich, schließe mich,
Zorn brenn, Heil sprieße ich:
Wie wohl verließe ich
    Sie, meine Kinder, sie!

DIE FROHE BOTSCHAFT

Jungtaube fern,   Dein schönstes Lied —   o sing es,
    Ihm, der dich ruft,   was süß in Dir —   zudring' es.
Er ists, dein Gott   selbst, der dich ruft: o sei geschwind,
    Neig Dich herab   erdtief! Geschenk —   darbring es.
Heb Deinem Nest   Dich zu, den Weg   zu Deinem Zelt,
    Nach Zion, — setz   Dir Zeichen, wes   Wegs ging es.
Urfreund, der Dich   fortstieß, weil Dein   Tun bös sich wies,
    Er selbst erlöst   Dich heut. Lob — wo   anfing' es?
Du schick dich an   zur Heimkehr ins   vielschöne Land;
    Arabiens Reich,   Edoms, — o in   Staub ring es!
Aller, die Dich   einst zwangen, Haus —   Zorn zwing' es,
    Und Deines Freunds   Haus — Liebeskranz   umschling' es.

THE CALCULATION OF SALVATION

Young dove, far away, she flies away to the woods;
    she fell: strength now fails her, which raises her.
She flew there, she veered there, she moved there
    around her friend, a whirlwind, she swirls.
And she reckons a thousand years as its end,
    but each number brings her more deeply into debit.
The friend, who now torments her already "eight! eight times!"
    years longer is at fault for her living near the brink of the grave.
She cries out: "no longer do I think the Name": there
    he became a flame — kindled deep in her heart she trembles.
Do You live, to be her enemy? and she — parched
    strives for the wetness of late rain of your salvation.
How steadfast her heart! it does not falter, whether Your Name,
    proudly raises her, or whether deep in the dust she cleaves to Him.
Come soon, You strength of God, be not silent,
    and, storms, all around, flaming, encompass her!

IN THE SANCTUARY

My God, how lovely are Your dwelling places!
    to be near to You in a vision, not in allegorical paths!
A dream brought me into God's sanctuary,
    I was permitted to bathe my eye in its works:
The burnt-offering, and the meal, and the drink-offering,
    and round about the thick vapours of smoke.
And blissfully I heard the Levis' song,
    in their circle, assembled according to the rank of their service.
I woke up, and I was still with You, oh, God,
    and thanked You — to thank You, oh, for the grace!

HEILSRECHNUNG

Jungtaube fern,   waldeinwärts fort   schwebet sie;
   sie fiel: ihr fehlt   wohl Kraft nun, die   hebet sie.
Hinflog sie dort,   hinbog sie dort,   zog sie dort,
   um ihren Freund,   ein Wirbelwind,   webet sie.
Und rechnet aus   eintausend Jahr   als Termin,
   doch jede Zahl   bringt tiefer ins   Debet sie.
Der Freund, der sie   nun quält schon „acht!   acht mal!" Jahr
   länger, ist schuld,   daß Grabs Rand nah   lebet sie.
Ausrief sie: „nicht   mehr denk ich den   Namen": da
   ward Flamme er —   herztiefentfacht   bebet sie.
Lebst du, ihr Feind   zu sein? und sie —   lechzend hin
   zu deines Heils   Spaetregennaß   strebet sie.
Wie fest ihr Herz!   nicht wankts, ob sein   Name sie
   stolz hebt, ob um   ihn tief am Staub   klebet sie.
In Bälde komm,   du Gotteskraft,   schweige nicht,
   und, Wetter, rings,   flammende, um —   gebet sie!

IM HEILIGTUM

Mein Gott, wie lieblich Deiner Wohnung Gaden!
   in Schau Dir nah sein, nicht auf Gleichnispfaden!
Es brachte mich ein Traum in Gottes Weihstatt,
   ich durft den Blick in ihren Werken baden:
Das Brand- samt Speise- und samt Trankgußopfer
   und ringsumher des Rauches dichte Schwaden.
Und selig hört das Lied ich der Leviten,
   in ihrem Kreis, geschart nach Dienstes Graden,
Ich wachte auf, und noch war ich bei Dir, Gott,
   und dankte Dir — dir danken, o der Gnaden!

SOLOMON'S TAPESTRIES

"You tapestries of Solomon
                in the tent of a desert-dweller,
    how has your splendour been worn down
         and your weaving disfigured!"

" "The mighty flock entered here,
           which was at home amidst us,
   and left us desolate and unprotected —
       where could there be recompense for the loss?

And the consecrated instruments taken
          into foreign lands became profane,
    do you expect roses not disfigured
       which are amidst a thorny thicket?" "

"Everyone hunts them, near, far,
          they ascertained only by their own Lord,
   Who calls all by name
        — no one falls out of His world,

Out of spring splendour of blossoms
        May He weave their autumn crown,
   so that lights like the lights of Creation
       will illumine their darkened lamp."

TEARS AT NIGHT

Jerusalem, lament,
   Zion, let your tear flow,
Your sons' eye, thinking of You,
   cannot seal off its wetness.
Hand, forget me, if I should forget
   You, City, whence the Psalms spring!
Cleave, tongue, to my palate, if I ever let
   my mind freely enjoy!

TEPPICHE SALOMOS

„**I**hr Teppiche Salomos
         in Wüstenbewohners Zelt,
    wie ist eure Pracht zermürbt
       und euer Gewirk entstellt!"

„ „**H**inging die gewaltge Schar,
         die zwischen uns heimisch war,
    und ließen uns wüst und bar —
       wo gäbs dem Verlust Entgelt?

Und zog das geweihte Gerät
         ins Ausland und ward gemein,
    wollt Rosen ihr unentstellt,
       die Distelgestrüpp gesellt?" "

„**D**ie jagt jedermann, nah, fern,
         erfragt nur dem eignen Herrn,
    der alle beim Namen ruft
       — fällt keiner aus seiner Welt —,

Aus lenzlichem Blütenglanz
         flecht' Er ihren Erntekranz,
    dass Leuchten wie Schöpfungslicht
       ihr dunkles Geleucht erhellt."

NÄCHTLICHE TRÄNE

Jerusalem, weheklage,
         die Träne, Zion, laß fließen!
Deiner Sohne Aug, denkts dein,
         Kann sein Naß nicht verschließen.
Hand, vergiß mich, vergäß ich
         Stadt dich, der Psalmen sprießen!
Kleb, Zung', am Gaumen, ließ' den
         Sinn je froh ich genießen!

If my sins should drive me away
    from my mother's teaching
My father's punishment seeks me
    for the gravity of my sins,
And if my brother and the son of my
    maid should take from me the inheritance of the firstborn,
With all that, the soul could imploringly
    pour itself out before God!

And give blows to the cheek,
    do not hide your face from spittle,
So that after such castigation
    burdens of guilt may be light,
And live where jackals cry,
    with ostriches in the wilderness,
And wander with a heart like the night,
    shrouded in bleak vexation.

But be silent to him who does not
    eternally forget the poor one,
Who does not wholly destroy,
    no, he turns to mercy
Until Israel's day comes,
    in Zion they embrace salvation,
On cords of love He pulls
    you out of the prison of misery.

Alas, God, do not be too wrathful,
    may you not eternally remember the guilt.
Be ardent for Zion! may you not further
    give away your remnant.
Speak to your heir's heart,
    do not push it deeper into sorrow —
And in the morning there will be exultation, where
    at night tears still pour.

Hetzten mich meine Sünden
        aus meiner Mutter Lehre,
Verlangt nach mir Vaters Strafe
        ob meiner Sünden Schwere,
Und nahm mein Bruder und meiner
        Magd Sohn mir Erstlings Ehre, —
Könnt' mit all dem die Seele
        vor Gott sich flehend ergießen!

Und gib Schlägen die Wange,
        nicht birg dein Antlitz vor Speien,
Dass nach solchem Kasteien
        Lasten der Schuld leicht seien,
Und leb, wo Schakale schreien,
        mit Straußen in Wüsteneien,
Und nachtgleichen Herzens wandle
        gehüllt in schwärzlich Verdrießen.

Doch sei still zu ihm, der nicht
        ewig vergißt des Armen,
Der nicht gänzlich vernichtet,
        nein wendet sich zum Erbarmen,
Bis daß Israels Tag kommt,
        in Zion Heil sie umarmen,
An Seilen der Liebe Er dich
        zieht aus Elends Verließen.

Ach, Gott, zürne nicht zu sehr,
        der Schuld woll nicht ewig denken.
Eifre um Zion! woll nicht
        dein Restvolk fürder verschenken.
Zum Herzen sprich deinem Erbe,
        nicht tiefer in Gram wolls senken —
Und früh wird Jubel sein, wo des
        Nachts die Tränen noch schießen.

THE CITY ON HIGH

Steeply you rise, you are resplendent on the enraptured sphere,
        You City, throne of the Lord of the World.
My heart is sick for you here from out of
                the world's western bastion.
Hotly does my interior boil up,
                   when I think of long ago how it was,
      of the glory, now in misery,
                     of the dwelling place, now a mockery.
And if I flew on wings
           of the eagle, I would soon mix
      the eye's tears with your dust,
                until it is pliant like clay.
You I seek, even when Your Lord
          is far from you and, where
      your Gilead, a land of balsam,
              is now a viper, a scorpion.
Alas, to caress, to kiss
          your rock still is my desire,
      and the taste of your clod of earth would be
             for me a honeysweet reward.

BETWEEN EAST AND WEST

My heart is in the east, and I on the westernmost edge.
How could I enjoy drink and food? how? did I ever delight in it?
Woe, how shall I fulfill the pledge? how my dedication? while
Zion is still in Roman chains, I in Arabian bond.
All good things of Spanish soils are chaff to me, while
The dust where once the sanctuary stood is gold to my eyes!

DIE HOHE STADT

Jäh steigst, prangst entzücktem Ball
   Du Stadt, des Weltherrn Thron.
 Nach Dir krankt mein Herz hin aus
    der Erde Westbastion.
Heiß wallt mir mein Innres auf,
    denk ich des Einst, wie's war,
 der Glorie, im Elend nun,
     der Wohnstatt, nun ein Hohn.
Und flög ich auf Fittichen
    des Aars, so mischt' ich bald
 des Augs Naß mit Deinem Staub,
    bis bildsam er wie Ton.
Dich such ich, auch wenn Dein Herr
    Dir ferne ist und, wo
 dein Balsamland Gilead,
    nun Viper und Skorpion.
Ach noch Dein Gestein Begehr
    zu kosen, küßen ich,
 und Schmack Deiner Scholle wär'
    mir honigsüßer Lohn.

ZWISCHEN OST UND WEST

Mein Herz im Osten, und ich selber am westlichsten Rand.
Wie schmeckte Trank mir und Speis! wie? dran Gefalln je ich fand?
Weh, wie vollend ich Gelübd? wie meine Weihung? da noch
Zion in römischer Haft, ich in arabischem Band.
Spreu meinem Aug alles Gut spanischen Bodens, indes
Gold meinem Auge der Staub drauf einst das Heiligtum stand!

REPLY

Your word — it is permeated by the fragrance of myrrh,
    and wrested from the cliffs of mountains of myrrh;
For your worth and that of your father's house
    any praise can only wearily yearn.
You approached me with words, with pleasant ones,
    but in them was an ambush, armed;
And behind façades of gentle speech — bees,
    and under honeycombs, thorns.
Are we not supposed to seek Jerusalem's bliss
    because today the blind and lame are there?
Thus we would have to do it, for the sake of our God's Temple
    and because the neighbours, our brothers, press toward it.
Yes, if it were as you say, oh, see: sin
    would encircle, who on their knees bow down before it,
And sin [encircle] the ancestors who as strangers dwelled there,
    and received only domestic authority for their dead.
And a useless deed then was the embalming
    of the fathers, and the sending home — their corpses.
And see: the land for which their sighs sounded, —
    was yet held prisoner by a reprobate nation.
For nought the altars they built there!
    In vain, that fragrances of sacrifices wafted upwards!
Should the dead be remembered — and yet the Ark
    and the Tablets be swallowed by the night of forgetting?
Should we seek the place of death, of worms — not the spring
    out of which the waters of eternal life sprang?
Does any inheritance beckon us except for God's sanctuary?
    Could the memory ever be dispersed for us?
Does the orient a place of hope beckon us
    or the occident with guarantees of life?
The Land alone, full of gates, facing which
    the gates of heaven burst open:
Mount Sinai, Karmel, Bethel and that of the
    Prophets' houses surrounded by the sound of the fame of the mission,
The thrones of the priests of God's throne and that
    of the kings with the grace of the oil.
And he is taking care of it for us and our children,
    and even if the birds of the desert soared above it!
Had it not like this been given once to the fathers,
    a field, which only thorns and thistles fertilized?

ANTWORT

Dein Wort — es ist von Myrrhenduft durchdrungen,
    und Myrrhngebirges Felsen abgerungen;
Nach dein und deines Vaterhauses Werte
    kann müde nur jedwedes Lob sich langen.
Du nahtest mir mit Worten, mit gefäll'gen,
    doch drin ein Hinterhalt, gewehrumhangen;
Und hinter sanfter Rede Mienen — Bienen,
    und Dornen unter Honiganhäufungen.
Wir sollen Salems Seligkeit nicht suchen,
    weil drin heut Blind-und-Lahme sich ergingen?
So müßten wirs um unsres Gottes Tempel
    und weil die Nächsten hin, die Brüder drängen.
Ja wär es wir ihr sagt, o seht: würd Sünde,
    die dorthin knieend sich verneigt, umfangen,
Und Sünd' die Ahnen, die dort, Fremde, wohnten,
    Hausrecht für ihre Toten nur empfingen.
Und wüstes Tun war dann die Balsamierung
    der Väter, ihrer Leichen Heimsendungen.
Und sieh: das Land, dem ihre Seufzer klangen, —
    doch wars in schlechten Volkes Haft gefangen.
Um nichts, die dort sie bauten, die Altäre!
    Umsonst, daß Opferdüfte aufwärts drangen!
Der Toten soll gedacht sein — und die Lade,
    die Tafeln von Vergessens Nacht verschlungen?
Wir suchen Tods, Gewürms Ort auf — den Born nicht,
    daraus die Wasser ewgen Lebens sprangen?
Winkt Erbe noch uns außer Gottes Weihtum?
    Erinnrung dran könnt je sich uns versprengen?
Winkt uns im Morgen- oder Abendlande
    ein Hoffnungsort mit Lebenssicherungen?
Das Land allein, das voller Tore, welchen
    genüber Himmelstore aufgesprungen:
Berg Sinai, der Karmel, Bethel und der
    Propheten Haeuser sendungsruhmumklungen,
Der Gottesthrones-Priester Throne und die
    der Kön'ge mit des Öls Begnadigungen.
Und uns verwahrt er es und unsern Kindern,
    und wenn der Wüste Vögel sich drob schwüngen!
Wards so nicht auch den Vätern einst gegeben,
    ein Feld, das Dornen nur und Disteln düngen?

And they wandered through the length and breadth,
    as one who wanders through a garden's splendour,
And were foreign, without full citzenship, begging for
    lodging and a grave in the highest leaps of their wishes.
Thus they wandered there before God's countenance,
    upon paths which always get narrower towards the goal.
And it is said that there the dead rise up
    out of the graves which thickly encase them,
And that the bodies rejoice there, the souls
    enter there in the bliss of rest.
And yet see, see, my good one, and understand,
    avoid nets and traps which ensnare.
And do not be seduced by the wisdom of the Greeks,
    which never got fruit, only flowers.
And its fruit: the earth never rooted,
    the arches of the tents of heaven never stretched out;
There was no first beginning to the first laws of the universe,
    no goal, when again and again the months renewed themselves.
Hear the misguided words of their wisest men,
    where night and chaos are the presuppositions —
You will come back, your heart empty and confused,
    your mouth full of verbiage and remote things.
Would it be right if I, seeking side-paths,
    crooked ones, would have deviated from the original path??

Und sie durchwandeltens die Läng' und Breite,
    wie wer durchwandelt eines Gartens Prangen,
Und waren fremd, Beisassen nur, Herberge
    und Grab erflehnd in Wunsches höchsten Sprüngen.
So wandelten sie dort vor Gottes Antlitz,
    auf Pfaden, die sich zielwärts stets verjüngen.
Auch heißts, daß dort die Toten auferstehen,
    aus Grabeshüllen, die sie dicht umschlingen,
Und daß die Leiber jubeln dort, die Seelen
    dort eingehn in der Ruh Beseligungen.
O sieh doch, sieh mein Guter und begreife,
    weich aus vor Netz und Fallstrick, die rings hängen.
Und nicht verführe dich der Griechen Weisheit,
    die nimmer Frucht, nur Blüten hat empfangen.
Und ihre Frucht: die Erde nie gegründet,
    nie ausgespannt des Himmels Zeltwölbungen;
Uranfang keiner Weltalls Urgesetzen,
    Ziel keins, wenn neu und neu sich Monde schwangen.
Hoer ihrer Weisesten verirrte Worte,
    wo Nacht und Chaos die Voraussetzungen —
Du kehrst zurück, das Herz leer und verworren,
    den Mund voll Wortkram und entlegnen Dingen.
Wärs recht drum, wenn ich Seitenpfade suchend,
    gewundne, waer vom Urpfad abgegangen??

THE PILGRIM

Longing for Him, the only One immune from death,
    drove me to the throne site of my consecrated ones,
Until it no longer let me kiss the children
    in the house, and those who are a close second after them for me,
I do not weep for the garden which I planted
    and watered, whose shoots happily sprout,
And I think no longer of Judah and Asarel,
    they the most precious blooms of my flowerbed,
And of the fruit of my sun, growth of my moon,
    of Isaac, who stood at my side like a son,
And I could almost forget the house of prayer, the schoolhouse,
    which stood open to me for classes, free from anxiety,
Forget the bliss of my Sabbath days,
    the splendour of the Festivals, the proud Passover,
And give my honours to others
    and leave my fame to the unconsecrated.
I exchange the shadows of bushes for my rooms,
    thorn-hedges for the security of the key-bolts,
And my soul, tired of sweet scents,
    revels in the scent of logs of wildwood,
And I cease to go where there is road and path,
    and direct my path through width of the sea
Towards the footstool of the feet of my God,
    in order to spread out there my mind, my soul,
And want to stride to His holy mountain, through
    gates, facing the gates of the clouds
And let my spikenards bloom anew in Jordan,
    in the flood of Siloa let my flowers glide.
God is mine — what could frighten and terrify me,
    while His angels of mercy accompany me.
I bring praise to His Name, because I live,
    and thanks forever and ever.

DER PILGER

Nach Ihm Sehnsucht, dem einig Todgefeiten,
    trieb mich zur Thronstatt meiner Salbgeweihten,
Bis sie mich nicht mehr kuessen liess die Kinder
    im Haus und die nach ihnen mir die Zweiten,
Ich nicht bewein den Garten, den ich pflanzte
    und wässerte, des Sprossen froh sich spreiten,
Und nicht mehr denke Judas und Asarels,
    sie meines Beetes Blühndste Kostbarkeiten,
Und meiner Sonne Frucht, Wuchs meiner Monde,
    des Isak, der mir sohngleich stand zuseiten,
Und fast vergäß das Bethaus ich, des Lehrraum
    mir offenstand zu Stunden, drangbefreiten,
Vergäß die Wonnen meiner Sabbat-Tage,
    Der Feste Pracht, die stolzen Osterzeiten
Und gebe meine Ehren fort an andre
    und lasse meinen Ruhm den Ungeweihten.
Strauchschatten tausch ich ein für meine Stuben,
    Dornhecken für der Riegel Sicherheiten,
Und meine Seele, satt der Wohlgerüche,
    schwelgt im Geruch aus wilden Holzes Scheiten,
Und ich hör auf, zu gehn wo Weg und Steg ist,
    und richte meinen Pfad durch Meeresweiten
Zum Schemel hin der Füße meines Gottes,
    um dort den Sinn, die Seele hinzubreiten,
Und will zu seinem heilgen Berg, durch Tore,
    der Wolkentoren gegenüber, schreiten
Und laß im Jordan neu blühn meine Narden,
    in Flut Siloas meine Blumen gleiten.
Gott ist mir — was soll mich graun und ängsten,
    da seiner Gnade Engel mich geleiten.
Lob bring ich Seinem Namen, weil ich lebe,
    und Dank in Ewigkeit der Ewigkeiten.

ALL WEIGHS LIGHTLY

Yours is this heart, whether trusting, whether oppressed by fear,
    Yours is my kneeling, my gratitude unlimited.
I will be glad of You when wandering and on the run,
    call Your Name when flight and restlessness devour me.
When my ship stretches its wings over dark floods
    like stork's wings over cypress woods,
When the deep then rages under me and surges
    — does it learn this from my innermost or from whose? —
And lets the flood boil like a kettle
    — like a hot brew the sea becomes in the meantime —
When the ship of the western shore comes into the sea, then of the
    Philistines, Hittites, much intent on piracy,
And when the wild sea monsters mock the little ship
    and sea-dragons, hoping for a feed,
When misery oppresses, like the first-time mother,
    — the children ready, powerless the labour pains:
May Your Name be food for my mouth,
    for which I would gladly go without drink and food,
And I shall not care about gain, loss,
    and shall not be troubled about markets and fairs,
Amd even abandon them, offspring of my loins,
    the sister to my soul, the only one I ever had,
I will forget her son, an arrow in my heart,
    whose image fills me instead of intellectual tricks,
Fruit of my body, child of my bliss —
    Jehuda, can he ever forget Jehuda?
All weighs lightly compared to your love,
    When I shall approach Your hearth thankfully
And dwell there and bind my heart
    to the altar, more precious than animal-meat
And will have my grave in Your land
    so that it may be my testimony for me for all this.

THE COMPULSION

Already my heart swelled to the house of the high time,
    but I was still dreading homelessness.
There the One rich in counsel sent me reason to be homeless;
    thus I found myself ready for Him.
Therefore I fall upon my face at each repose,
    thank Him for the step, each one, that I step forward.

LEICHT WIEGT DAS ALLES

Dein ist dies Herz, mags traun, mag Angst es pressen,
 dein ist mein Knien, mein Danken ungemessen.
Dein werd ich froh sein, dann, unstet und flüchtig,
 dich nennen, wolln mich Flucht und Unrast fressen.
Spannt über dunkler Flut mein Schiff die Flügel,
 wie Storchenflügel über Waldzypressen,
Tobt unter mir die Tiefe dann und toset
 — lernt sies von meinem Innern oder wessen? —
Und läßt die Flut wie einen Kessel brodeln
 — wie heiß Gebräue wird das Meer indessen — ,
Kommt Weststrands Schiff ins Meer dann der Philister,
 Hethitervolks, auf Seeraub sehr versessen,
Und höhnt das wilde Flutgetier des Schiffleins
 und Meeresdrachen, hoffend auf ein Fressen,
Drängt Not dann wie bei erstgebärndem Weibe,
 — die Kinder reif, kraftlos der Wehen Pressen:
Dein Name sei in meinem Mund mir Speise,
 um die ich Trinken gern entbehr und Essen,
Und nicht werd sorgen um Gewinn, Verlust ich,
 und nicht um Märkte kümmern mich und Messen,
Verlassen sie sogar, Sproß meiner Lenden,
 mir Seelenschwester, einzge je besessen,
Vergessen ihren Sohn, Pfeil mir im Herzen,
 des Bild mich füllt statt geistiger Finessen,
Frucht meines Leibes, Kindlein meiner Wonnen —
 Jehuda, kann Jehudas er vergessen?
Leicht wiegt das alles gegen deine Liebe,
 werd dankend nahn ich deinen Feueressen
Und wohnen dort und binden dir mein Herz auf
 den Altar, köstlicher als Tiereshessen,
Und werd mein Grab in deinem Lande haben,
 und daß es dort mir Zeugnis sei all dessen.

DER ZWANG

Schon schwoll mein Herz zum Hause der hohen Zeit,
 doch graute michs noch vor der Heim- losigkeit.
Da schuf, der reich an Rat, mir Grund heimlos zu sein;
 so fand für Ihn den Sinn ich mir wohlbereit.
Drum falle ich an jeder Rast aufs Angesicht,
 dank' Ihm den Schritt, jeglichen, den vor ich schreit.

PRAYING

Oh, God, do not cradle the waves to rest
    and do not command the bottom of the sea to dry up
Until I thank You for Your mercy, thank
    the sea for its swelling and the west wind for its flying.
They draw me near to the place of Your yoke of love,
    no longer do I have to yield to the Arabian yoke.
And how could my wish not be fulfilled!
    In You I trust — Your pledge is genuine.

THE FLOOD

Has the flood come again, in which land and sea sank down?
    No longer to see the bounds of firm ground?
No human being, no beast, no bird — has all then
    come to an end? Has it gone where shadows stagger?
And if I saw mountain and rocks — oh, rest for me!
    my heart could yearn for thorny bushes.
I peer towards all sides — not a soul.
    Only water, heaven, and the ark,
And Leviathan, — the abyss grey like old age,
    when he strikes the deep with his flanks.
The heart of the sea would like to conceal the little ship,
    as if she were a stolen good in the sea's paws.
So the sea rages. My heart rejoices, for soon it will be permitted
    to give thanks in the holy place of its God.

SPOKEN TO THE HEART

I speak in the heart of the seas to the heart
    which fears and trembles when the rage of their din shrills:
If you trust in God Who made the sea,
    the Name in which the world rests eternally,
Then you will not tremble, even if the sea towers up,
    for He Who sets boundaries to the sea is with you.

BITTEN

O Gott, woll nicht zur Ruh die Woge wiegen
und nicht befiehl dem Meergrund zu versiegen,
Bis ich Dir danke Deine Gnade, danke
der Flut ihr Wallen und dem West sein Fliegen.
Sie nähern Deines Liebesjoches Ort mich,
nicht mehr muß ich arabschem Joch mich schmiegen.
Und wie ging' in Erfüllung nicht mein Wünsche!
dir trau ich — Deine Bürgschaft ist gediegen.

DIE FLUT

Kam neu die Flut, drin Land und Meer versanken?
Nicht mehr zu sehn der festen Erde Schranken,
Nicht Mensch, nicht Tier, nicht Vogel — ist denn alles
zu Ende? gings dorthin, wo Schatten schwanken?
Und säh ich Berg und Felsenfluh — o Ruhe!
nach Steppdornranken könnt das Herz mir kranken.
Ich späh nach allen Seiten — keine Seele.
Nur Wasser, Himmel, und der Arche Planken.
Und Leviathan, — greisengrau der Abgrund,
wenn er die Tiefe peitscht mit seinen Flanken.
Das Herz des Meers verhehlte gern das Schifflein,
als wär es Diebsgut in des Meeres Pranken.
So tobt das Meer. Mein Herze jauchzt, denn bald darfs
im Heiligtume seines Gottes danken.

ZUM HERZEN GESAGT

Ich sprech im Herz   der Fluten zum   Herzen,
das graust und bebt,   wenn ihres Lärms   Wut gellt;
Traust du auf den   Gott, der die Flut   machte,
den Namen, drin   in Ewigkeit   ruht Welt,
Dann bebst du nicht,   ob auch die Flut   sich türmt,
denn bei dir ist,   wer Grenzen der   Flut stellt.

CALM AFTER THE STORM
Fragment

The night then! the sun has departed — in hierarchies are the flocks
    of the heights, and He, field captain to His companions.
Like a Mooress draped in gold-fabrics,
    like royal purple surrounded by crystals.
And stars, wandering through the heart of the sea, like
    heavenly offspring banished from their seat.
According to their image and likeness they brighten the heart
    of the sea, as if workers in fireworks had a good time.
The face of the water and of heaven — wide as the sea
    and deep as the night they rest, clear, like moulded in brass.
The sea looks like the firmament: both
    are now two seas, the one having flowed in the other.
In between yet a third sea: my heart when
    the waves of its new songs surged high.

TO THE WESTWIND

It is Your wind, oh west! its wingbeats as gentle
    as the scent of spikenard and perfume of apple!
Your place of origin is in the shopkeeper's spice cupboard,
    not in the cupboard where the winds are kept.
Soar, little swallow, and announce me free like a swallow, like
        myrrh,
    removed from the bundle of fragrance, like a swallow's flight.
How longs for you whoever might be riding
    on the back of the sea and the back of the plank!
Oh, do not remove Your hand here from the ship,
    whether the day be bright or whether it goes blind in the night.
Put a rope over the gulf of the abyss, you, divide the heart of the seas,
    ˋ hurry! before you go to rest, swiftly to the holy mountain.
And now threaten the eastwind which agitates the sea until it is like a pot
    which the servants set upon the fire of the hearth. —
What should one do, bound to a creature which
    now squats like an old man, now plays freely like a child!
Yet the secret of my imploring stands in the heights with the one
    Who formed the heights of the mountain and created the winds.

STILLE NACH DEM STURM
Bruchstück

Die Nacht dann! Sonne schied, — gestuft die Scharen
    der Höh, und er, Feldhauptmann den Genossen.
Wie eine Mohrin goldgewirkumhangen
    wie Purpur von Kristallen rings umschlossen.
Und Sterne, durch das Herz des Meeres irrnd wie
    von ihrem Sitz verwiesne Himmelssprossen.
Nach ihrem Bild und Gleichnis hellen sie des
    Meers Herz, als trieben Feuerwerker Possen.
Des Wassers und des Himmels Antlitz — meerweit
    und nachttief ruhn sie, klar, wie erzgegossen.
Das Meer sieht gleich dem Firmament: die beiden
    sind nun zwei Meere, die ineinsgeflossen.
Dazwischen noch ein drittes Meer: mein Herz, wenn
    hoch seiner neuen Sänge Wogen schossen.

AN DEN WEST

Dein Wind ists, West!   Sein Flügelschlag   so linde
    wie Nardenruch   und Apfelduft!   im Spinde
Des Krämers mit   Gewürzen ist   dein Ursprungsort,
    nicht in dem Spind,   wo aufbewahrt   die Winde.
Schwing, Schwälblein, dich   künd schwalbenfrei mich,
    Myrrnsaft gleich,
    schwalbflüchtgen Dufts   entnommen dem   Gebinde.
Wie krankt nach dir,   wer immer um   dich rittlings auf
    Meers Rücken und   Bretts Rücken sich   befinde!
O lasse doch   nicht deine Hand   hier von dem Schiff,
    ob hell der Tag,   ob nächtlich er   erblinde.
Seil' Abgrunds Kluft   du, teil' das Herz   der Meere, eil',
    eh ruhn du gehst,   zu heilgem Berg   geschwinde.
Und dräu dem Ost,   der wühlt im Meer,   bis es dem Topf
    gleicht, den aufs Feu'r   des Herds stellt das   Gesinde.
Was soll man tun,   an ein Geschöpf   gebunden, das
    bald greishaft hockt,   bald frei spielt gleich   dem Kinde!
Doch meines Flehns   Geheimnis steht   in Hoehn bei dem,
    der bildete   Berghöhn und schuf   die Winde.

IN THE HARBOUR

Be still, surging of the sea! until the bow of the ship's keel
    draws the disciple near to the kiss, to the clever eyes of the master,
and his hands, Aaron's master, whose staff
    was always beautiful, fresh, and always budded anew.
He teaches — he never says to his mouth: it is enough!
    he gives — never does he say to his hand: it is sufficient!
Today I thank the east for the waving of its wings,
    because tomorrow I curse the westwind's flight.
How could one leave the balsam of Gilead,
    in whose flesh dug the plough of the snake's tooth?
Would anyone exchange the thick roof of leafage
    and glow and frost and the lies of the mirror of air?
The home of the highest for me instead of the beam of a roof.
    My roof is the city which bore His throne!

EGYPTIAN SOIL

See the cities, open your mind to the lands
    which Israel received as meadow-pastures
And pay tribute to Egypt, set your foot down softly
    and do not stride in self-confidence.
The streets here — the Divine Presence walked upon them,
    seeking doorposts dipped in the blood of His Covenant,
The pillars of fire and the pillars of cloud,
    and all eyes hoping and watching for them.
Here the bearers of God's Covenant are broken,
    the stones of the eternal people hewn here.

THE RIVER

God, Your miracles moved through the generations
    from father's mouth to sons, without lies.
The Nile attests to it here, which You changed into blood,
    — not a work of necromancers, sorcerers.
Your Name only, through Moses and through Aaron,
    the staff, earlier bent into the body of a snake.
Therefore help the believing servant who comes journeying
    to look upon the places of Your miracles.

IM HAFEN

Schweig, Meergebraus! bis nahbringt Schiffskiels Bug
    zum Kuß den Jünger Meisters Augen klug
Und Händen, Meister Ahrons, dessen Stab
    stets schön und frisch und immer neu ausschlug.
Er lehrt — nie sagt er seinem Mund: es reicht!
    er schenkt — nie sagt er seiner Hand: genug!
Heut danke ich dem Ost sein Flügelwehn,
    weil morgen ich verwünsche Westwinds Flug.
Wie ließe wer den Balsam Gileads,
    in dessen Fleisch grub Schlangenzahnes Pflug?
Vertauschte jemand dichten Laubes Dach
    und Glut und Frost und Luftgespiegels Lug?
Des Höchsten Heim mir statt Dachbalkenfug!
    mein Dach die Stadt, die Seinen Thronsitz trug!

ÄGYPTISCHER BODEN

Die Städte sieh, den Sinn tu auf den Gauen,
    die Israel empfing zu Weideauen,
Und Ehre zoll Ägypten, setz den Fuß auf
    fein sacht und schreite nicht in Selbstvertrauen.
Die Straßen hier — die Gottheit zog drauf, spähend
    nach Pfosten, die vom Blut des Bundes tauen,
Die Feuersäule und die Wolkensäulen,
    und aller Augen hoffen drauf und schauen.
Hier sind gebrochen Gottesbundes Träger,
    des ewgen Volkes Quadern hier behauen!

DER STROM

Gott, Deine Wunder durch Geschlechter wogen,
    aus Vaters Mund zu Söhnen, unzerlogen.
Der Nil hier zeugts, den Du in Blut gewandelt,
    — kein Werk von Nekromanten, Mystagogen,
Dein Name nur durch Mose und durch Ahron,
    der Stab, zuvor zum Schlangenleib gebogen.
So hilf dem gläubgen Knechte, der, zu schauen
    die Stätten Deiner Wunder, kommt gezogen.

THITHER ...

Oh, carry me to Zoan,
        to the Reed Sea, to Horeb, the waters,
Then I shall wander to Silo and
                where deep in the rubble the sanctuary rests,
And go the ways
        of the Ark of the Covenant, until I
Have tasted the dust of its grave,
                which is gentler than honey,
Looked upon the dwelling place of
        blissful ones, which forgot its nest,
Out of which doves have been driven away,
                and now a brood of ravens lives there.

FOREBODING

Your heart — if it wants that my will be done,
        leave me, so that I may see the countenance of my Lord.
For I shall not find rest for these two feet
        until, where He dwells, I procure my dwelling.
My step, do not hold it back from setting out,
        for I have a presentiment that my sorrow will meet me beforehand.
My prayer: a place under the gleaming of wings and
        that, where my fathers rest, I may go to rest!

HIN ...

O trag hin nach Zoan mich,
          zum Schilfmeer, zum Horeb, Flut,
Dann schweif ich nach Silo und
          wo schuttief das Weihtum ruht,
Und gehe den Zügen nach
          der Lade des Bunds, bis ich
Geschmeckt ihres Grabes Staub,
          der linder als Honig tut,
Die Wohnung der Wonnigen
          geschaut, die ihr Nest vergaß,
Draus Tauben vertrieben sind,
          nun haust drin der Raben Brut.

VORGEFÜHL

Euer Herz —   will es, daß   mein Wille   geschehe,
     laßt mich, daß   meinem Herrn   ins Antlitz   ich sehe.
Denn nicht find   Ruhe ich   für diese   zwei Füße,
     bis, wo Er   haust, ich mir   Behausung   erstehe.
Meinen Schritt,   haltet ihn   zurück nicht   vom Aufbruch,
     denn mir schwant,   daß zuvor   mich treffe   mein Wehe.
Mein Gebet: unterm Glanz   der Flügel   ein Platz und
     daß, wo mir   Väter ruhn,   zur Ruhe   ich gehe!

ODE TO ZION

Zion! are you not asking about your people bearing a yoke,
    Remnant of your flock who ask only for You?
West, East, North storm, South — oh, let them give the greeting to You
    of the One Who is far and near, all around you.
The greeting of the One Whom yearning ensnares, whose tears are
    like the dews of Hermon,
    Oh, that it also would sink down to your mountain groves!
When I cry for your suffering, I become a jackal; when I dream of You
    being freed from bondage,
    I am the harp playing to your songs.
To Machanaim, to Bethel and Pniel my heart sorely urges,
    And wherever else your people still abided in the presence of God.
Here the Highest One came down to you; and He Who created you
    Broke open your gates according to the situations of the gates of
    heaven.
And God's splendour bathed you in light, — how could then
    The sun and moon and stars still be lights for you?
How could I pour out my soul there where God's spirit
    Poured out upon your great ones — how could I tremble.
You are the king's palace, you God's throne, how may the grandchildren
    Of your servants dare sit upon the throne of your Lords.
Oh, may my foot carry me where God gave
    Answer to the questions of Your messengers and Your prophets.
Oh, that I had wings, how I would rush to You to hide
    My rent heart in your clefts.
I would fall upon my face, upon your soil, and your stones
    I would caress, and would fondle your dust with lament;
And I would stand before the graves of my fathers wholly shaken,
    In Hebron before your proudest tombs,
I would pass through your woodland, vineyards, and would stand in
    the south
    Before your mountain-borders, newly shaken, full of trembling.
Hor and Abarim, where they, your great double star,
    Your two lights and teachers once lay in death.
The life of souls is your air! Fragrance of myrrh
    Wafts through your dust, the breaking of the wave drips honey.
Barefoot and naked would I wander through the desolate ruins which
    Were your temple — where would there be equally delightful
    comfort.
There where your cherubim dwelled in the innermost places,
    There where rested, now hidden, the chambers of your sanctuary.

AN ZION

Zion! nicht fragst Du den Deinen nach, die Joch tragen,
    Rest Deiner Herden, die doch nach Dir allein fragen?
West, Ost und Nordsturm und Süd, — o laß von ihnen den Gruß
    Dessen, der fern ist und nah, von ringsher Dir sagen.
Gruß des, den Sehnsucht umstrickt, des Träne wie Hermons Tau;
    O sänk' auch sie doch hinab zu Deinen Berghagen.

Wein ich dein Leid, Schakal werd ich; träum ich Dich
        fronbefreit,
    Bin ich die Harfe, zu Deinen Liedern zu schlagen.
Nach Machanajim, nach Bethel, Pniel hindrängt mein Herz,
    Und wo die Deinen noch sonst der Gottesschau pflagen.
Hier kam der Höchste zu Dir herab; und der Dich erschuf,
    Brach Deine Tore gemäss den Himmelstor-Lagen.

Und Gottes Lichtglanz umstrahlte Dich, — wie konnten da noch
    Sonne und Mond und der Sterne Lichter Dir tagen?
Wie könnt die Seel' ich da auszugießen, wo Gottes Geist
    Auf Deine Großen sich goß — wie könnt ich wohl zagen.
Königspalast Du, du Gottesthron, wie dürfen des Knechts
    Enkel, zu sitzen auf Deiner Herren Thron, wagen.
O trüge dort mich der Fuß, wo Deinen Sendboten Gott,
    Deinen Propheten er Antwort gab auf ihr Fragen.
O hätt ich Flügel, wie wollt ich, mein zerrissenes Herz
    In Deinen Rissen zu bergen, hin zu Dir jagen.
Aufs Antlitz sänk ich, auf Deinen Boden, und Dein Gestein
    Herzt ich, und liebkoste Deinen Staub mit Wehklagen;
Und stünde dann vor der Ahnen Grüften durchschüttert ganz,
    In Hebron vor Deinen stolzesten Sarkophagen,
Durchstrich' dein Waldland, die Traubengärten, und stünd
        im Süd
    Vor Deinen Randbergen, neu erschüttert voll Zagen,
Hor und Abarim, wo sie, Dein großes Doppelgestirn,
    Deine zwei Leuchter und Lehrer einst im Tod lagen.
Leben der Seele o Deine Luft! Gewürzduft vor Myrrh'n
    Duftet dein Staub, Honig träuft der Welle Anschlagen.
Barfuß und bloß durch die Trümmerwüsten wandern, die einst
    Dein Tempel waren — wo gäbs gleich köstlich Behagen.

Dort wo gewohnt Deine Cherubim im innersten Raum,
    Dort wo geruht, der entschwand, des Heiligtums Schragen.

I shall cut off, throw away the adornment of my head; may my curse
    charge the time,
    Which pushed consecrated heads into an unclean land.
How can food and drink taste good to me, at a time when I see
    Dogs dragging and persecuting your lions.
Or how could my eyes still find the light of day sweet,
    When I must see ravens gnawing on the flesh of your eagles.
Cup of suffering, oh, cease! a little rest! for long already
    Is my heart heavy from your poison, my stomach full of bitterness.
From the foam to the dregs I empty you, when I look upon Aholibah's
    And Jerusalem's fate in the raiment of prophetic tradition.
Zion, you splendid circlet, surrounded of old by grace and love,
    See your faithful ones surround themselves with you like a wall.
They brightly rejoice in your wellbeing, and bear the grief
    of your devastation, and cry for the torment of your end;
They fall down where it be, turn to, where your gate rose,
    And flee from prisons to you on chariots of the dream of longing;
The flock of your herds, driven away, wandering from mountain to valley,
    But they never forgot the time in Your sheds;
They who hold fast to your garment's seam, who gladly would swing
        themselves up
    To your palmtrees, grasping the boughs.
Land of the Euphrates and the Nile — how small before you with all
        their splendour.
    Their knowledge turned to wind when your justice, your Light
        prophesied.
Where did your king, your seer, where your priest,
    And where your singer, where did he find around Him any kin,
Change and transformation threaten every heathen realm;
    Your treasure is eternal, your crowns tower eternally young.
Your God Himself desires you as a dwelling place — and blessed is he
    Who may rest near to Him on the stones of your courts.
Blessed is he who waits, and experiences it, and who sees how your
        shining light rises,
    Whose beams of the rays will break through the nocturnal shadows,
So that he may look upon your chosen ones in happiness, to rejoice
        with you,
    Whom you make newly resplendent in youthfulness as once in
        ancient days.

Ich schere, werfe des Haupts Schmuck hin; mein Fluch mag
    die Zeit,
    Die Hauptsgeweihte in unrein Land stieß, anklagen.
Wie schmeckte Speise und Trank mir wohl, zur Stund' da ich seh
    Hundegezücht Deine Löwen zerren und plagen.
Oder wie wär meinen Augen noch des Tags Leuchten süß,
    Muß sehn ich Raben an Deiner Aare Fleisch nagen.
Becher der Leiden, o laß! ein wenig Ruh! denn schon lang
    Ist Deines Gifts schwer mein Herz, voll Galle mein Magen.
Vom Schaum zur Hefe ausleer ich Dich, wenn Schomrons ich schau
    Und Salems Los im Gewand prophetischer Sagen.
Zion, du Prachtreif, von Huld und Liebe seit je umkragt,
    Sieh Deine Treuen mit Dir wie Wall sich umkragen.
Die hell mitjubeln dein Wohlergehn, und tragen den Gram
    Deiner Verwüstung, und weinen Deines Ends Plagen;
Hinfalln sie, wo's sei, dorthin gewandt, wo Dein Tor sich hob,
    Und fliehn aus Kerkern zu Dir auf Sehnsuchttraums Wagen;
Schar Deiner Herden, vertriebne, irrnd von Bergen zu Tal,
    Doch nie vergaß sie der Zeit in Deinen Verschlagen;
Die Deinen Schleppsaum erfassen, die sich schwängen wie gern

Auf Deine Palmbäume, in des Astgezweigs Tragen.
Euphrat- und Nilland — wie klein vor Dir mit all ihrer Pracht!

Wind ward ihr Wissen, wenn Dein Recht, Dein Licht
    weissagen.
Wo fand dein König, dein Seher, wo dein Priester und wo
    Dein Sänger, wo fand er rings noch Sippen, noch Magen?
Wechsel und Wandel umdroht jedwedes heidnische Reich;
    Dein Schatz besteht, Deine Kronen ewig-jung ragen.
Dich gehrt zur Wohnstatt er selbst, Dein Gott — und selig der Mensch,
    Der nah ihm ruhn darf auf Deiner Höfe Steinlagen.
Selig, wer harrt, und erlebts, und schaut, wie aufgeht dein Licht,

Des Strahlgeschosse die nächtgen Schatten durchschlagen,
Deine Erwählten zu schaun im Glück, zu jubeln mit Dir,

Die neu du jugendlich prangst wie einst in Urtagen.

Afterword

Oh dear Reader, learn Greek
and throw my translation
into the fire.
Friedrich Leopold von Stolberg
Translation of *The Iliad* Note to VI, 484

Jehuda Halevi was a great Jewish poet in the Hebrew language. This small selection tries to give an idea of this to the German reader. So it was not my aim to make the reader believe that Jehuda Halevi composed in German, nor that he composed Christian church songs, nor that he is a poet of today, even if only a *Familienblatt*[1] poet of today – all this as far as I can see the aims of my predecessors in translation, especially the most recent ones. Instead, these translations want to be nothing but translations. Not for a moment do they want to make the reader forget that he is reading poems not by me, but by Jehuda Halevi, and that Jehuda Halevi is neither a German poet nor a contemporary. In a word: this translation is not a free rendering, and yet if here and there it is so, then only for need of rhyme. Basically my intention was to translate literally, and in approximately five-sixths of these lines of verse I may have succeeded. For the sixth sixth where, even I, if only to the most careful extent, had to resort to "free renderings," here I formally beg the pardon of the reader.

The notion of free rendering has been so commonly accepted today as the measure for the value of translations that it demands further elucidation. When a great German poet declares that he wants to translate a foreign one freely, I cannot stave off mild amazement that he would not rather compose something himself. After all, a Goethian Reinecke Fuchs based on the middle-low German Reineke Vos obliges me to feel respect for it as a Goethian work, even if I cannot wholly suppress the suspicion that he couldn't himself think of anything much at that time; – which the Goethe-philologists will then confirm. But when Mr. Müller or Mr. Schulze or, to stick to the case at hand, Mr. Cohn begins to translate freely,[2] the events will interest me as little as Mr. Müller's, Schulze's etc. own poems. He who cannot write poetry should also leave "free translation" alone. It does not become more beautiful.

The patron saint of contemporary free-renderers of poetry is that famed professor from Berlin, who right away in his first public appearance revealed the chief attributes of a competent philologist: "tact" and a feeling for what is great, in tracing the greatest thinker, the (still) greatest artist and the greatest philologist of his epoch in order to attack them. This Wilamowitz[3] has disclosed to us the aim of his generally popular translations of Greek tragedians: into *Gartenlauben* German.[4] He would like to make Aeschylus more understandable to the modern reader than he was to his Greek contemporaries. A very meritorious admission. The work of these gentlemen Free Renderers amounts indeed to such "making more understandable." They would very much like to give some help to the unfortunate original. Now poetry is not quite as understandable as prose. Obviously this is because the poet did not quite know how to express himself properly, just as the characteristic distance from life of an Egyptian sculpture means only that the artist could not yet do it quite right.[5] Nothing is easier and nothing more gratifying than to engage in corrective action and to add a little. The notion that things that are foreign to us can occasionally be so for reasons of style does not make sense to the creative renderer, as he is altogether unsympathetic to the idea of style. His ambition is to dress the masterpieces of the past and of foreign lands in "modern garb". But would the Apollo of Belvedere really gain substantially from a cutaway and a stiff collar?

The task of translating is entirely misunderstood if it is seen as the Germanizing of what is foreign. I demand Germanization in this sense if I as a merchant receive an order from Turkey and send it to a translation office. Already in the case of a letter from a Turkish friend a translation office would no longer do for me. Why not? Maybe because it would not be accurate enough? It will turn out just as accurate as that of the business letter. That then is not the point. It will be German enough. But not – Turkish enough. I shall not hear the person, his tone, his meaning, his heartbeat. But is that possible? Will this not be asking something impossible of language with this task to reflect the foreign tone in its foreignness: not to Germanize what is foreign, but rather to make foreign what is German?

Not the impossible, but rather the requisite, and the requisite not merely in translating. The creative achievement of translating can lie nowhere else than where the creative achievement of speaking itself lies. The Germanization of what is foreign, then, as in the legitimate case of the office translation of the business letter, is done in the German that is already there. Its understandability is based upon that, and the "popularity" is based upon that – which only envy could dispute in the translations of Müller, Schulze, Cohn, Wilamowitz. They translate as a person speaks who – has nothing to say. Since he has nothing to say, he does not need to demand anything of the language; and the language of which its speaker demands nothing, rigidifies to a means of communication, which any Esperanto can competently bring about. He who has something to say will say it in a new way. He becomes the creator of language. After he has spoken, the language has a different face from before. The translator makes himself the mouthpiece of the foreign voice, which he makes audible over the gulf of space or time. If the foreign voice has something to say, then the language must afterwards appear different from before. This result is the criterion of the translator's conscientiously carried out achievement. It is not at all possible that a language into which Shakespeare or Isaiah or Dante has really spoken into would remain untouched thereby. It will experience a renewal, just as if a new speaker had stood up within the language itself. But still more. For indeed the foreign poet calls into the new language not merely what he himself has to say, but rather he brings along with it the heritage of the general language-spirit of his language to the new language, so that here not merely a renewal of the language occurs through the foreign person, but rather through the foreign language-spirit itself.

That such a renewal of a language through a foreign one is at all possible certainly presupposes that just as the language itself has given birth to each of its speakers, so too all human speaking [*Sprechen*], all foreign languages which ever were spoken and ever will be spoken, are contained in it in germ-cell at least. And that is the case. There is only one language. There is no language trait of one language that does not evidence itself, at least in germ, in every other language, be it in dialects, nurseries, peculiarities of trades. Upon this essential oneness of all language and upon the dependent commandment, namely that of universal human mutual understanding [*Verständigung*], is based the possibility as well as the task of translating, its Can, May and Shall. One can translate because in every language is contained the possibility of every other language; one may translate if one can realize this possibility through cultivation of such linguistic fallow land; and one should translate so that the day of that harmony [*Eintracht*] of languages, which can grow only in each individual language, not in the empty space "between" them, may come.

An example may illustrate this. Luther could translate the Bible because it is possible in German to render peculiarities of the Hebrew as well as the Hebraisms of the New Testament Greek, such as the co-ordinate, and not subordinate joining together of sentences. If he had wanted to translate here into the language of his own publications, which indeed betray entirely the humanistically schooled master of language, then a Kautzsch-Weizsäcker[6] or something even worse would have emerged, but not the Lutheran Bible. But he had the courage to import into the German the sentence construction of the Hebrew, even then cyclopean for the cultivated German consciousness of language, and in this way he created a work which outlives the language consciousness of his time – conquering for the realm of contemporary German the new province of Bible-German, which now could have its own history within the German history of language. And hence it was not washed away without further resistance by the development of the collective body of the language; instead it actively engaged in this development, and by this itself remained preserved in its originality.

And Luther was permitted to translate because he possessed for this linguistic conquest the necessary courage as well as the necessary circumspection. His well-known battle against the translating "donkeys" and their scholastic literalness may not be understood as if he had on the other hand advised a blind arbitrariness. For indeed not indiscriminate literalness leads to the goal which is meant here and which Luther has achieved. The dictionary may *not* be the chiefest authority for the translator. Language does not consist of vocabulary but of words. The schoolboy and the schoolmaster translate vocabulary. Vocabulary [*Wörter*] stands in the dictionary. Words [*Worte*] stand only in the sentence. "Stand" is actually already a false picture that does not do justice to the wavelike flow of words through the sentence-bed. The contours with which the word fits into the sentence and those in the dictionary, which is obliged in accordance with its function to forge ahead of the contours to the centre or centres of gravity of the word, can not be found. These contours and precisely these contours are what want to be and must be translated, as the above example of the co-ordinate and subordinate sentence constructions is such an example of contours, only for the sentence, not for the word. How far this search for contours can forge ahead into the elements of the grammatical structure, whether only as far as the sentences or as far as the words or even as far as the root that can be excavated under the word – that can be determined only in each individual case. But it is always a matter of contours; and when Luther in his famous example refuses to translate the word of the English salutation with "You full of grace", he has thus caught the contour of the word with his translation "*holdselig*" without on this account dispensing with the root contained in the Greek word, which precisely "*hold*" [well disposed] renders much better than the school dictionary translation "*Gnade*" [grace] would do. That he has, however, in the translation itself, preferred to relinquish his "*Du liebe Maria*," on which he had insisted in the exuberance of his

polemics, is not, as the donkeys of today would like to have it, coward-
ice before its own consequences, but a proof of the genuine caution of
his translating. With "*Du liebe Maria*" he would have changed the scene
into a German folksong and thus destroyed just the tension through
which it was capable of becoming ground for the folksong. Only the
respected distance makes the leap over the ditch possible; he who fills
it up at the beginning cripples the others' powers for leaping.

And Luther had to translate, because the German people now
needed this influx of the foreign language-spirit. Among all books, the
Bible is the one whose destiny it is to be translated, and hence it is also
the one translated the earliest and the most. That which is the meaning of all translation, the coming of "that Day", is for the Bible (with its
joining together, unique in all literature, of telling, demand, and
promise) the circlet which holds together these elements. Thus the entry of a nation into world history is marked by the moment when it
makes the Bible its own by translating it. This entry also always demands a sacrifice of national isolation, a sacrifice that is reflected in
the recasting of the national language which is necessarily joined with
a translation of the Bible. For while other translations always touch
only a part of life, as a translation of Shakespeare only the theatre, a Bible translation engages in all spheres of life. There is no "religious
sphere." The *Heliand* was consequence and symptom that the German
people were not yet ready for world history; none of their achievements in the medieval centuries has been effectively received [*rezipiert*]
by the world, whereas the German people have effectively received to
the greatest degree on all fronts. The Reformation is the first German
event that had an effect on the world and did not vanish again out of
it. Since then German destiny has been woven into the world's destiny.
Luther's act of translating demonstrates this point. The so-called "religious genius" as such is never a personality of world history alone –
Meister Eckhart was not one – , still another, a worldly side belongs to
it. Luther's other side was the translator. This "worldliness" of his completed him as a person of world history.

But now back to medieval Jewish poetry. The problem of translation is here first of all quite simply an external problem of form. In
the history of translation it is almost typical that the first ones to appear shy away from the poetic form of the original. Homer is translated first in blank verse, Alexandrines, *ottave rime*, before one dares
to construct modern hexametres. That a German hexametre is not a
Greek one remains true, even after Voß. But still less is a German Al-
exandrine a Greek hexametre, and thus the translator cannot in the
long run avoid erecting a structure as equivalent as possible to the
form of the original. He will thereby be compelled possibly to estab-

lish even stronger technical bonds than the original form imposed
upon the poet – if, that is, through such increased bonds of the language being translated into, the impression of the original form can
be achieved in a closer approximation. One example is the necessary
preferance for monosyllabic vocabulary in the German Shakespeare,
which is linguistically [*sprachwegen*] natural to the poet, whereas the
translator consciously imposes this preferance.

Until now not a single one of the translators of Jehuda Halevi has
recognized in principle this duty with regard to metre, and even with
regard to the rhyme Heller alone, who also otherwise towers heads
above all his predecessors and successors and who for this reason of
course is designated *communis opinio* as "unpalatable."[7] The aversion to
imitation of the rhyme-form is for the simple reason which, at a closer
look, surprisingly many human matters share, that is – laziness, quite
simply laziness, laziness without qualification [*sans phrase*]. For imitation of even the most complicated rhyme-forms are entirely possible in
German, as Rückert proves. In the worst case one may easily resort to
the rhymeword dictionary; indeed one makes use of it when one wants
to figure through and through as a free renderer in order to betray no
one; I, who am only a translator, would like to confess herewith that I
am grateful to Mr. Steputat's dictionary of rhyming words for many a
facilitation, even if for the most part the most beautiful rhymes have
not occurred to him. But just how important the rendering of the
rhyme-form is, that is based on the fact that in the poetry in question
the rhyme is not merely the mortar that glues stone to stone, as in the
modern forms, but almost without exception, is at least also the building material itself, whose uniform tone determines the collective impression of the façade. One may just imagine a master-builder who – at
a time where such commissions were given – had copied the Pitti Palace in every section in stone of different colours. In some such way,
compared to the original, we are struck by the copies which recklessly
tear apart either the strictly uniform rhyme, or, in the poems with stanzas, the unity of rhyme of the stanza conclusions. What is still left over
then of the beauty of the "*Gürtelgedichte*" [round-poetry], in which the
rhymes of the individual stanzas are locked together by the precious
clasp of the round rhyme system, if one splinters them into German
song stanzas? Yet that has happened almost invariably with the single
exception of Heller.

The question of the metre is more difficult. Here lies a really
marked foreignness. True, the rhyme cannot without further ado be
equated with the occidental rhyme, which always begins with a vowel
whereas the rhyme of the poems translated here always draws in a consonant into the rhyming element, thus for example not "ajich" but "ra-

jich" or not "im" but "bim" are rhymed. That of course cannot be imitated.[8] But the foreignness of the metre goes much deeper.

The metre of the Spanish Hebraism is customarily disposed of by calling it an imitation [*Nachahmung*] of the Arabic one. When put in short words like that it is misleading. The taking over of the Arabic metre did not occur in blind imitation; that was ruled out, although in itself it would have been entirely possible, through the prevailing theory of Hebrew syllables among the Hebrew philologists of the time. But the launchers of the new poetry in Hebrew seized with a bold grip the peculiarity of the prose-rhythm of their language which differentiates it from the Arabic, the silent syllables which sound roughly like the syllable "*ge*" in "*Gewand*" or the "*Be*" in "*Bezug*", and gave to this sound the value of that Arabic kind of syllable, which according to the theory is absent in Hebrew. Thus both elements of Hebrew metre came into being, a kind of iambus from a silent-syllable and a stressed syllable, and a stressed syllable which could be increased to two, three and virtually, through the tandem rowing of the metrical feet, even to a yet greater number. Of course now the metre thus arisen led far away from the prose accents, both from the Sephardic one of the endings and from the Ashkenaz one of the stem.[9] And here lies the root of the difficulty for the translator as well. For in German, the following principle has been arising since the seventeenth century and has been impenetrably immured through the classical poetry of 1800: that the prose stress of the words in the verse must be preserved, a principle that only in the the most recent decades begins to experience a certain modification through the George[10] school with its demand of the equal level stress. The domination of this principle is now so absolute that it is difficult for someone today correctly to comprehend even the possibility of other principles which applied for the past. That Greco-Roman antiquity had an entirely different principle is taken more as fact than it is aesthetically understood. Yet the thing is not at all so difficult to grasp. Modern man needs only to think of the musical declamation in which he also puts up with a stress foreign to the word accent. The charm lies here – and obviously also lay here in the Homeric hexametre – in the constantly alternating tension between prose and verse tones which reciprocally flee and return. Every Homeric hexametre thus has its own wholly individual metre, – an opulence of which the school metrics can not conceive and which, by the way, in modern music for voice the Wagnerian rule of stress wastes with its one-sided domination of the recitative style.

From this then the so-called "unnaturalness" of these Hebrew metrics can also be understood. He who wants to acquire a feeling for this metre does well to read the verses "George-like," thus with equal level stress of all vocal-syllables, which may not, however, permit the word-stress to disappear completely – in this case Sephardic of course. The task of the translator is to construct verses in German that force upon the reader this level stress, and to overcome the natural inclination of the German language towards iambic, trochaic and to a certain extent dactylic, and in all cases anapaestic rhythms, that by no means comply with these Hebrew verses with their accumulations of stressed syllables. Here is a case in hand, like the one I mentioned before, where the translator must strive through artificial means of increased bonds to achieve, in the language being translated into, as close an impression as possible of the original. The following ways present themselves: artificial evocation of a floating stress through destruction of the iambic or trochaic inclination of a line of verse in the next; a strong application of such two-syllable words that consist of equal weighted syllables like "Mißwachs," "Lichtstrahl" [English examples: bookcase, moonbeam] and the like, as well as an accumulation of equally stressed single-syllables for just this purpose; and finally the artificial introduction of caesurae, which within the line of verse over and over again permit the rhythm, which now begins to wander off into the step of the iamb or the troche, to adjust itself. All these means, however, are only for poems with a strict metre. In the numerous poems with a freer metre (precisely in the cultic poetry), which counts only the stressed syllables and scatters or does not scatter silent syllables without rules and singly between them, the task of an exact rendering of the metre remains unresolvable. For by no means will the German reader be forced in recited poetry – singing to familiar tunes is a different matter – to take as rhythmically essential only a selection of the syllables making up the line, for such a marked difference between full syllables and silent syllables, as there is in Hebrew, in German is certainly orally present, but is not metrically usable. Here the only help is the resolve to limit oneself in German to the count of syllables that is counted in Hebrew, thus an adjustment of the stream of syllables that flows along much more freely in Hebrew.[11] The single place where even in German the freedom [Befreitheit] of the metre can be imitated (and thus, according to my principle, must be) is the beginning of the verse. Yet the syllable placed ahead here may not lose the character of a grace-note [the blank space on a book's front page] and that is to say a grace-note before a line which is rather trochaic than iambic. Otherwise even the gender of the rhyme will have to be determined for the translation by the metre, in all the cases where the original rhymes with masculine endings, but the line closes with an even number of stressed syllables and consequently the translation must rhyme with feminine endings, which incidentally is no misfortune, as the consonantal initial rhyming

sound for our feeling also allows the masculine rhymes of the original
to appear almost like the feminine ones. In the reverse case – feminine
rhyme in a verse-ending of an odd number of syllables – the feminine
rhyme can be rescued if one places a stress-toned syllable in front of it.

The sum of all these means will then add to an impression which lies
at least in the direction of the goal aspired to, of an introduction of the
foreign rhythm into German. A third point to be noted does not fall as
do rhyme and metre into the problem of form, but concerns the nature of the content. It is what is denoted with the catchword "Mosaic
style" ["*Musivstil*"] and is considered just as non-reproducible as rhyme
and metre. What is the point in question?

All Jewish poetry in exile scorns to ignore this being-in-exile. It
would have ignored its exile if it ever, like other poetry, took in the
world directly. For the world which surrounds it is exile, and is supposed to remain so to it. And the moment that it would surrender this
attitude, when it would open itself to the inflow of this world, this
world would be as a home for it, and it would cease to be exile. This exiling of the surrounding world is achieved through the constant presence of the scriptural word. With the scriptural word another present
thrusts itself in front of the surrounding present and downgrades the
latter to an appearance, or more precisely, as parable. Thus it is not
that the scriptural word is drawn out as parables for illustrations of
present life, but exactly reversed, that events serve as illucidation of the
scriptural word and become the parable for this scriptural word. Thus
the relationship is exactly the opposite to what we imagine with the expression *Musivstil.* The *Musivstil* is an appearance of epochs that are lit-
erarily in the age of minority. When Einhard[12] depicts Charlemagne
with words taken from Suetonius' biography of Augustus, he wants to
show him in the costume of Augustus, to show him in the light of Augustus, not vice versa. When a Jewish poet describes Christianity and Islam through Edom and Ishmael, he is not commenting on the present
from Scripture, but rather on Scripture from the present. It is not literary immaturity that lies at the base of this but much rather literary
overripeness. It is not that he lacks a style of his own, but that his style
is so much his own that it is not at all possible for him to lapse into lack
of style. Such a relationship to the written word does of course presup-
pose that this word is classical not only according to form, but content
as well, and that indeed the classical traits of content and form are considered inextricably interwoven. The way Europeans quote offers a remote companion of this today. He who has heard Englishmen quote
Shakespeare knows how often they quote his "fine passages." Shakespeare quoted by an Englishman certainly gives a "*musiv*" effect.
Namely he quotes him without feeling a serious sense of identity with

him. The worldview [*Ansicht*] of the modern Englishman stems from Cromwell's century, not from Shakespeare's. On the other hand, when an educated German quotes Goethe or Schiller, along with these, he is quoting Kant, Fichte, Hegel – in other words: he believes in the spirit [*Geist*] that he is quoting; he quotes not merely for conversational entertainment. As far as one can speak of a superiority of the Germans over the western nations, it is grounded in this historical stroke of luck of the bond between the most recent highpoints of its culture with regard to form and with regard to content. Among the older nations, at best the Italian with his Dante, and among the younger perhaps the Russian with Dostoyevsky, has a comparable firm ground under his feet that allows him to use the most beautiful word for the most elevated thing that he has to express. Now this fortunate unity of speech and thought belongs in the highest measure to the medieval Jew, and indeed in a dearly bought exclusivity. Not only does he find an established form for his highest thoughts, but also every thought that generally wants to legitimate itself as thought seeks this form. Here the quotation is by no means an adorning pendant, rather it is the label for the envelope of his speech.

But this again results in a task for the translator. He may not suppress the innuendos of the language. This task has been not merely considered insoluble; to a certain degree it really is so. For of course it would not be a solution if one wanted to impart by additional commentary the knowledge of the Bible to the reader. For the Hebrew reader the bond with the scriptural word is no additional matter, but rather is a succession accompanying the reading of immediate connections of currents which precisely in their continuous sequence effect the fluorescing of what is being read. With this analogy of the problem the possibility of solution is now indicated at the same time. The succession of the individual connections of currents can not be as fast as in Hebrew, simply because the scope for quoting the German Bible is less than for the Hebrew. But still, here there is also a certain scope for quoting, – thanks to the Lutheran Bible, thanks to a few of the church-songs drawn from Biblical passages and thanks as well to the fact that some Biblical content is still known to people today. And because Biblical quotation is less common in German, it is by comparison all the more powerful that even in sparser frequency it manifests a certain fluorescing. Thus the translator has the task of working out every Bible quotation of the text, which he wants to bring to awareness really as such, and possibly to substitute a quotation which is foreign to a contemporary with one more familiar to him. That he commits the hitherto denounced errors of "making things more understandable" is something he need not fear; the person of today is barely familiar with the fact that the Arabs stem from Ishmael and that Ishmael's mother was named Hagar, as the readers or hearers of Jehuda Halevi's poems that Epher was a son of Ketura and that she is identified according to tradition with Hagar. Incidentally, it helps today's reader, that precisely the Books of the Bible still best known to the educated person today, like the Psalms, Isaiah, the Song of Songs, are the same ones that most often come to the lips of the Hebrew poet.

I did not mention a fourth point in the first edition because I thought it self-evident. But it is not, as I noticed in the meantime. I shall therefore now speak of the choice of words.

This is a somewhat tender point for the translator to touch upon. He is even more exposed than the real poet to the suspicion of passing off his technical deficiencies as poetic virtues. Especially the rhyme is always suspect of being transformed from an obedient servant into the lord of poetic thought. Every servant does it because it is the reparation of service lying in the fact itself. The poet can submit to it without worry, to whom the word is given to service only for the purpose of getting power over him. Otherwise the translator. He does not have the right to allow himself to be carried by his own word, the word personal to him. He must reproduce word for word as they are given to him. Thus every word places him before the question of reproduction, that is, before a scientific question in the widest sense. He, and only he, not a poet, chooses his words. He must know the place of the word on the language's field of vision, and of this special language of this poet, he must strive to know, of what nearer or farther derivation this word is whose trace he is following, whether it is at home in the core of the language, or in its peripheral regions.

In the Hebrew of the Spanish poets this ascertainment in itself is not all that difficult on account of the limited vocabulary, that is, in the essentially purely Biblical vocabulary. Mechanical working with dictionary and concordance is ruled out here also; a word for instance that occurs in the daily prayer is familiar even if the concordance has it as a *hapax legomenon*[13]. But in spite of this, as I had the occasion to establish between the first and second editions of this book, the awareness of theses differences is spread to a remarkably narrow degree. Jehuda Halevi particularly has the reputation of an effortless charm and special polish. People obviously think since they are pretty much without exception dependent on a dictionary, that Jehuda Halevi would have been as well. But he was more capable in Hebrew, not merely more than I, but even – let this be said in all modesty seemly to the author – than my critics. He was an intimate servant in the whole vast house of the Holy Language. And he had a feeling for whether a word belongs to the daily tableware of the language, or whether it was kept in a

locked cupboard only for special occasions. That for him the two keys
turn equally easily in his hand testifies to his faithful diligence as a
steward, which does not allow even the less often used lock to rust, says
nothing, however, about the difference of the chinaware, for which
both keys open the latch.

Here the translator has to follow the poet and reproduce, if not
word for word, at least sentence for sentence, the novel content of the
vocabulary in his language, as well as it can go. Even at the risk that
readers whose knowledge of development of the German language has
advanced only to the point of the Song of Songs, and for whom the discovery of the *Westöstliche Divan* and Hölderlin's hymns, to say nothing
of more recent writings, still lies ahead, might find his German incomprehensible.

Or does the poetry of Jehuda Halevi himself stand under conditions
that make the praised polish possible for him, and not for his translator? That at any rate is the instruction that these connoisseurs of Hebrew and non-connoisseurs of German impart to him with uncommon
unanimity. The problems with rhyme which coerced the translator into
his curious word constructions – which are to be found oddly enough
just as much in the middle of the verse and even in his, the translator's,
totally un-rhymed prose writings – did not, they say, exist for Jehuda
Halevi. He could without hesitation make rows of rhyme after rhyme in
a charming stream, they say, and there was no need to degenerate into
the sublime. The legend of the suffix rhyme is unanimously cited as a
foundation for this view.

Suffix rhymes are end-rhymes, as for example in German the rhyme
of *jubilieren* with all other verbs ending in *-ieren*. Actually they are more
readily possible in Hebrew than in German. Precisely for this reason
the respectable poets avoid them and use them only in the way that
even Goethe after all sometimes rhymes *Liebe* and *Triebe*, *Sonne* and
Wonne. But among the connoisseurs the legend has spread that the
Spanish-Hebrew poets made most extravagant use of this convenient
possibility and rhymed their long poems of single rhymes as happily as
for instance a German professor of philosophy facilely fills an entire
class hour with only rhymes of -isms. This legend – the legend with reference to the Spanish-Jewish poets, not the professors of philosophy –
has, however, like every legend that has something in it, a real foundation, and my enquiries into it have been crowned with success. In the
Viennese morning newspaper the connoisseur instructs me as follows:
"When for example Jehuda Halevi in his Zion poetry uses the rhyme
ajich (the ending that means 'your') more than sixty times, it is certainly a more difficult task for the German translator who has to find
sixty rhymewords to *Fragen*. In Hebrew a suffix which is common to in-

flected words often rhymes; in German the word itself rhymes." Now this is roughly as if a Frenchman would claim that the translation of the Zion poetry in this book rhymes with the endings *-en*. The connoisseur did not recognize that the rhyme is *rajich* and thus consists of a word-element and an ending exactly as the German rhyme to *agen*. He obviously does not know the differentiating feature of this whole technique of rhyme compared to our own, although it is placed before him needlessly on page 112 of the Afterword (page 158 of this edition [i.e. the 1927 edition]): – the always consonantal initial rhyme sound. This sounds unlikely. But he who is acquainted with the practically fabulous ignorance, which reigns among us in all matters more scientific than routine, and which makes the fame of a connoisseur on the one hand very difficult to attain (that is in everything that can be gained only through routine), but on the other hand disproportionately easy (that is in everything that can be gained with a little reason and scientific sense), – he will not wonder further about it. Years ago I asked a friend once about the metre of the Zion songs which he was accustomed to recite since childhood every year on the Ninth of Av.[14] He answered, he had often tried to find it, but none was there, they were free rhythms!

But one sees precisely in the Zion poetry how even in Hebrew it is by no means child's play to find thirty-five (let alone sixty) rhymes, from which by the way one can conclude the very early appearance of rhyme-dictionaries with certainty. To the demand of words ending in *r* there is added still the binding of the metre, which permits only certain groups of words that are in keeping with the demand of the rhyme. Actually – in the sixth and twenty-sixth couplets – the same rhymeword appears twice with the same meaning. Thus, the rhyming was at that time also, or rather was just as difficult, as the believers in the myth of the suffix-rhyme think, as it is today, – and thus also the composing. And among the thirty-five rhyme-words of the Zion songs are two that appear only once in the entire Bible, and a further two words which appear only two or three times. And on the other hand for instance in the hymn, "Dein Gott" ["Your God"] the rhyme possibilities of the words of this title, which drives forth out of the whole, with regard to content and form, are used up in the original no less than in the translation that follows the original, – because the poet has just not permitted himself the suffix-rhyme that is possible here, but honestly in spite of the difficulties allows the stem to take part in the rhyme. So it's all nonsense about the charming polish of this poet and his unerring choice of words – at least as far as he himself comes into consideration. The foregoing criteria may fit that which his translators have made out of him.

The foregoing selection was originally chosen quite accidentally. For every single one of the poems translated first I could give an account as to how I came to the translation, but the reasons would be only personal and in part really accidental. It is no accident that I do omit the worldly poetry that takes up a fair bit of space in the collected works of the poet (though not by a far cry that which the usual German collections are zealous to include). It was not quite the timidity that S.D. Luzzatto, the great and genuine philologist among those who worked at Jehuda Halevi, states for his selection from the *Diwan*: he did not want to mix the holy with the profane; rather here also it is a personal reason. There always comes in translating a moment when the dividing wall between poetry and translation falls down, if only for a moment. For the sake of this moment one translates, even if one does not know it oneself; but this moment is also the barrier which restricts one in the selection.

The accident of the selection got lost then in the course of the work. I began to take care that the translated poems should as far as possible supply, in terms of content and form, a collective picture of the poet. At a certain stage of the work that was more or less achieved. But this stage, scarcely achieved, was already again overstepped. And the position now reached, although aesthetically less delightful than the one already achieved, was nevertheless the more faithful, if this word is permitted. For even the repetitions which occurred belong to the picture.

It is not the case that just whole parts of a poem are repeated – for which nevertheless world literature offers examples – but what is repeated are rather thoughts and images. Not merely in the individual poem, but precisely whole poems appear in many ways as variations of set types. And since that really is the case, then this collection would lack something if it did not give the reader any picture of this.

But it would be entirely remiss if this were attempted through a grouping together one beside the other of the like types, of the *Meorot* [Light], *Ahabot* [Love], *Geulot* [Redemption], and whatever else they may be called. This museum method would give precisely the most perverted impression. Then whence comes the typical here? These poems originally of course are not intended for reading, but, as in all ages where poetry, or a part of the poetry, was a popular event, for performing and hearing. Goethe's impotent wish: "Only not to read, always to sing!" – impotent, for still in his time, through Schubert, music, which in the case of Goethe's house composers, had still served poetry unpretentiously, now precisely under the pretext of following it faithfully, began to get dominion over it – that wish, already powerless then, in such ages or circles, for which the same holds true as for those times denoted, is carried out as a matter of course. What is important is the presence of the circle, of the "people", much more than the "time". It is not at all an occasion for the usual, sanctimonious, in truth only indolent, expressed sadness about the "senseless" or the "God-distanced" present; where poetry was composed for a certain circle of men and is received by them, by their throats of course, not only in spirit, then the "time" is there. Thus for example in the evil present in every army and in every Protestant church congregation, and not for example in the beautiful Middle Ages for Walther von der Vogelweide.

The poems of Jehuda Halevi and his contemporaries are at least for the most part, such art with a purpose; and insofar as they are not, they (even in the case of decidedly worldly ones) are determined linguistically and formally by the laws of that artform. The purpose, however, is in this case a performance by the cantor and the singing along of the congregation at set points of the liturgical year. The flow of the words known to all and of old has to be, interrupted by them, dammed up into the lakes, that bring into view unaccustomed shorelines. In the recurrence they are the variable, but because in their variation they are bound nevertheless to recurrence, they are necessarily forced into a certain similarity. That is not conspicuous as long as they stand in their natural relationship to application; the different poems indeed were then divided by a full, really a full year full of events of the life of the synagogue. Repetitions were not experienced as such, or, as far as they are experienced, it is entirely in order. For this recurrence in the year is after all the essence of the festival. As in the final analysis repetition is altogether the great and only form which man has for expressing what is entirely true for him. In these poems one can encounter the always renewed words of humility and devotion, of despair and of trust in redemption, of world-aversion and longing for God, of repentance of sins and of faith in mercy – one can do it, but one does not thereby remove the fact from the world that the heart of the poet and the hearts of those for whom he has composed are full of these feelings and demand expression for them. The lie has many possibilities, the truth only a few, at base always only one. That it does not become tired of saying anew this always One again and again testifies to its enduring power. In the mouth of the lover the word of love never becomes old, the word which from the mouth that shams love already withers when it is spoken for the first time.

But the practical problem of how one should conduct oneself as a publisher and reader of a collection is not solved by this. One could say: as Jehuda Halevi himself, that is, not at all. For he did not collect his "divan." Only after his death did it come to be, but soon after many times. Practically, it would mean for our age that the authorized place, that is the synagogue, and in particular the "Reform"-Synagogue of

Middle and Western Europe and America would remember this poetry more extensively than ever before. What an opportunity for the songleaders and the conductors of local synagogue choirs who delight in composing! But, above all, what an opportunity for the rabbis! They could here, by basing their sermon on the simple interpretation of the poem of the day, find their way back to the only genuinely Jewish preaching style, to the instructive one, from which the exhorting and appealing would result unsought on occasion, in the best sense.

But what I have just spun out is only valid for the originals. Nothing is gained by this for the policy of the translator. How could I prevent the reader of this collection of translations from behaving as a reader, in other words, how could I bring him to consume the poems not like cherries but like peaches, that is not to begin the next one when he still has hardly finished the previous one, but instead each neatly one by one and with deliberation and with the idea: perhaps there will not be one like this again so soon.

The Notes are supposed to serve this purpose. Of course, not this alone. They should accomplish besides the usual purpose of notes, to impart to the reader, while keeping to civilized manners, that is, more in passing and as if he already knew it all, the things useful for the understanding of the poem, which he surely does not know. But the main purpose is the other: to induce the reader to take each poem as a thing for itself, just as the poet has composed it as a thing for itself and just as the singer and the hearer, in the place for which it is meant, sang and heard it, sings and hears it, will sing and hear it. Thus, to change the reader from a reader and consumer into a guest and friend of the poem.

About Jehuda Halevi himself I do not want to speak here. A better, because direct, opportunity for this will be given in the Notes to the individual poems. The Notes will also demonstrate the apology expressed at the beginning of this Afterword because of the "free rendered"-parts that are found occasionally in spite of the best of intentions for literalness, by supplementing the wording in these places.

If finally I may express a wish, then it is the double one that the level established here in this small selection will soon be flooded, but that not one of my successors in this territory may have again the daring of laziness to fall behind the measure of exactitude reached here. The excuse that it "is not possible" now is no longer at anyone's disposal.

Franz Rosenzweig

Notes[1]

PRAISED BE HE! / יה שמך

Luz., Div. Nr. 65.Harkavy II 104ff. Brody III 230ff. Hamburger Tempelgebetbuch 68ff. Gebetbuch der Neuen Synagoge Berlin II 420ff. Seligmannsches Gebetbuch 307.[2]

This hymn is an introduction to the Kaddish prayer; the poem's refrain is taken from the second paragraph, and the rhythm of the whole
is derived and developed from this eulogy's rhythm. Thus, the refrain
here, as is so often the case, is the germ-cell of the poem, the point toward which each stanza flows, and which, as its pivot, determines its
course. This emptying into the familiar sound of the prayer, which in
Jewish ritual plays a role with which "The Lord's Prayer" in Christian
rituals be compared – this emptying determines the effect of the
poem: now is splendrous breadth, now in a sublime cascade, now in a
ferocity brisk as a river, now in mysterious rustling. (No coincidence
then, that both the earliest and the most recent translators simply omit
the refrain, apparently because it is repeated five times and therefore
would be "fatiguing.")

The streams of the five stanzas which empty into the common ocean
of the "Daβ gelobt ..." ["That He be praised ..."] all come from a different direction. The first stanza starts from the position of the creature, of the creature to which the creature's demand for the Creator's
help is rhymed immediately by his receiving this help. Heaven opens
up to the one so certain of help, and, blinded, he falls down.

The second stanza dares to open its eyes again. Heaven has closed.
Nature lies spread out. But the poem swings from sphere to sphere up to
its First Mover, Himself at rest. When it arrives here it sees the wonders
of the divine throne of Ezekiel's vision and falls prostrate once again.

Shaken by the tension between height and depth which he presently experiences, the poet now fathoms the riddle of Redemption: the peg-tent closes around the Eternal One for whom the world does not offer enough room. The thinker knows that all our knowledge, even prophetic knowledge, sees only a reflection – and yet knows that this Only is not a mere Only but the form by which, the human being participates in "the treasure of being" ["*des Wesens Hort*"]. But the thought of the "Only" throws him anew to the ground.

And now he looks around into the world of human beings which surrounds him. He recognizes the lot of man in his dependence and his salvation in the free and joyous acceptance of this dependence, in the recognition of providence, and in the expectation of judgment. This time the words of the prayer are only the tranquil and self-evident consequence of what Wisdom has understood.

But this repose of knowledge is not everything. Man reaches more deeply into his breast. He is not wise, he is – Nothing. And yet out of this last and innermost experience of his Nothingness he looks up again to the greatness of his Lord. Trembling, only now does he express the last thought which his thinking [*Denken*] has reached: he perceives, is conscious only of the divine action; upon God Himself he – he says it with the same words with which God denies power to the Tempter over Job's life – may "not lay a hand." And shuddering from this feeling of the mystery over him, he stammers the words of the prayer which, now whispered in solitude, carry further, as when in the beginning they had been accompanied by the chorus of the Creation and of the created spirits.

On the translation:[3] Stanza 2, lines 23 and 24: "those who attend Him" ["das Geleit"] are of course the four animal forms of Ezekiel 1.

MIGHTY ONE / משגיב בכחו מי בלתו וכמהו

Brody-Albrecht 105.

What the previous poem spreads out over five stanzas, this one compresses into eight brimful lines, which despite the short form, are of a hymnal quality through the heavily thundrous rhythm. This enormous concentration, with respect to content, is achieved by the means which man generally has for transmitting his knowledge about God for himself and others across the ages: the dogmatic formula. Precisely because it is frozen, it awakens an infinity of co-vibrating tone, if only the formula is brought rightly to those hearing it. The Incomparable! The

Creator! the Invisible! the Manifest to the Heart! the All-Embracing –
"space" – as the Talmud calls Him! and the kindred essence [*Wesensver-
wandte*] of the human soul which was created after His own image, the
soul which, like Him, seeing, is yet invisible! – these are truly familiar
words of the Biblical-Talmudic circle, which unite here like blocks into
one colossal monument.

On the translation: Nothing to note.

YEARNING / לקראת מקור חיי אמת ארוצה

Luz., Div. Nr. 39. Harkavy II 88f. Brody II 296. Brody-Wiener 171.

A sensitive interlacing of world weariness and longing for heaven. The
nodal point in the desire for "eternal sleep." For this poet, the forerunner of the great Kabbalistic movements for whom the vision of God
served as Israel's topical heritage and always to be newly actualized on
the holy ground, sleep and dream are the legitimate ways to this goal.
But here the longing for vision overshoots deep sleep and true dream
to the "Sleep of Eternity."

On the translation: Nothing to note.

DURING THE NIGHT / יעירוני בשמך רעיוני

Luz., Div. Nr. 81. Harkavy II 120ff. Brody III 65. Brody-Wiener 153.

The longed for event has happened. A night-vision has brought the
poet the experience of the sight of God. In the state between dream
and waking, a state which derives its autonomy from dream and its validity from waking, as the poet reflects upon the connection of body
and soul, he sees God, as if his heart "had been allowed to stand by at
Sinai." The experience of today confirms and repeats the historical
revelation.

What confirms revelation and what repeats it? What is revealed?
That upon which he reflected has certainly been called a problem before. Does revelation bring a solution to that problem? Does it render
the never-silenced miracle a manageable, practical dogma, as Catholi-
cism has somehow presented it? Indeed no word about it stands firmly,
although every reason would have been given for it. What then?

God reveals in revelation always only just this – revelation. In other
words: he reveals always only Himself to the human, to the human

only. This accusative and dative in its union is the peculiar content of revelation. Whatever does not follow immediately from this bond established here between God and human, whatever cannot verify its unmediatedness to this bond, does not belong in it. The problem has not been solved for the seer of the vision, but rather – it moves into the past. The miracle does not astonish him, but rather the vision has given to him the courage to bow down before the source of the miracle. Out of the problem of thought has arisen a strength of heart.

On the translation: Nothing to note.

EVENT / גלילי זבול ראו הדרך ונבעתו

Luz., Div. Nr. 60. Harkavy II 98. Bordy III 3.

Revelation is experience and event. Genuine experience only, because and when it also has been event, genuine event only, because and when it can become experience again and again. The present shies away from this relationship. It would like to confine God, in the most different forms and in the most different ways, to experience which happens at night and to impede His road into the daylight of event. But God does not permit His roads to be impeded. Event is not farther from Him than experience, nature is not more inaccessible than the soul. Nor, as the fearful ones dread, will He be pulled down into coarse objectivity; he has already taken care of that. Today, for instance as regards the War [i.e., World War I], which was a comparable revealing experience for mankind, it is no different from the Revelation at Sinai; there also the *Midrash* knows how to report: that the nations heard each a different thing and answered each a different thing. The answer is what matters – here also.

Hence belonging as it does to the Festival of Freedom [Passover], as the first of the three festivals of the historical revelation – the little powerful poem plunges right away into the abyss of the question, how souls can endure in the fire-kernel of the self-revealing mystery, and knows that the strength to bear it must come out of Revelation itself, but that Revelation also comes out of the strength. The human finds himself again thankful and praising after the event, just as after the experience.

On the translation: Nothing to note.

EXCURSUS: DAY OF REVELATION / יורד עלי הרים ולא יכילו

Luz., Div. Nr. 23. Harkavy II 83f. Brody III 114f.

Mountain-ridge, mountain-top,   if You descended,   they would
    not contain You, before Whose   force, trembling,   they split off.
Would my heart have strength to stand before You in the day when You
    threaten stars: and they grow cold.
And the heavenly multitude – Your Name demands: they appear;
    and the earthly multitude awaits Your faithfulness, of old.
The law of fire, they receive it from Your mouth; remembrance, deed,
    thanks should rule therein.
Oh hear with gladness the singing of those who are close to You.
    Exult in the multitude which itself is exultant, when it adores Your
    rule.

Joch, Bergeshöh,   stiegst Du herab,   nicht halten sie Dich, vor
    des   Wucht zitternd sie   sich spalten.
Hätt' Kraft zu stehn   mein Herz vor Dir   am Tage, da Gestirne
    Du   bedräust: und sie   erkalten.
Und Himmelsvolk –   Dein Name beischt: sie stelln sich ein;
    und Erdenvolk   harrt Deiner Treu,   der alten.
Das Feurgesetz,   aus Deinem Mund   empfingen sie's; Erinn-
    rung, Tun,   Gedanke soll   drin schalten.
Anhör, oh, gern   Sang derer, die   Dir nah. Frohlock des Volkes,
    das selbst   frohlockt; verehrts   Dein Walten.

It was admitted already by the collector of the Divan that Luzzatto used
– a few decades after the poet's death – that he would not be able to
vouch for the claim that really only poems by Jehuda Halevi were in his
collection.[4] He even names the others which, on the basis of the same
acrostic, could be considered as mistakenly Halevian. The poem translated here belongs to those for which I would like to use this permission of the ancestor of Jehuda Halevi philology. The comparison with
"Event," very much related in substance, precisely demonstrates the
quality it lacks to be a "genuine" Jehuda Halevi. It is not a matter of the
linguistic aspects taken individually – the handling of language on the
basis of biblical language material is so common to the whole Spanish
school that in general it would be difficult or impossible here to argue
assignation or denial from these criteria. Rather, the poets differ from
one another in thought content and, more properly still, in the direction of the thought. Jehuda Halevi's charisma is a very characteristic

terseness, I would say: slenderness of the line of thought. He knows exactly how much space a thought needs for its arc. Just this the poet of
the above poem, whoever he might have been, does not know. Each
line begins as a new one, and none has a sequel. Those noblest words
and images are vainly conjured up and suffocate in this short-winded-
ness, which contrasts most sharply with the free outflowing which
both thoughts of the first two couplets of the "Day of Revelation" find
in "Event". But there is no reason to deny the poem to Jehuda Halevi
with any certainty on the basis of such impressions. Philology can
never reckon enough with Homer's nodding. Precisely among poets
who, like Jehuda Halevi (especially in the verse poems) have a
strongly personal, often even a confessional trait, one must at times
reckon with surprising failures. In the mature Goethe, poems of
lesser value are found, which never happen with Schiller, the master,
who on account of his "being in command of poetry" was alway looked
upon by Goethe to the end with a kind of timidly shocked awe.

On the translation: Nothing to note.

ALL MY LIMBS / כל עצמותי

Luz., Div. Nr. 71. Sachs 37f. Harkavy II 113ff. Brody III 7f. Brody-Albrecht 103f.

There is a hymn contained in the Sabbath and Festival morning services where the transition is made from their preluding parts as it were
to the main prayers. The one who says the prayers lets course broadly
into this hymn all that he has only touched like a survey in the hasty
"mumbling" of the wealth of the Psalms. The hymn is very old – the
French medieval Jews in all seriousness ascribe it to the Apostle Peter –
the language of the Psalms resounds in it, but here heightened to the
monumental. And the poets have allowed their ivy to twine around this
edifice so that it is completely covered with it. Just as in the Catholic liturgy there are certain points of the mass-text upon which are built up
the great phrases of the musical masses, so traditionally in Jewish liturgy there are firmly located points. In this prayer one such a place occurs over which the accompanying insertions have accumulated since
the revival of our poetry after the Talmud-inspired centuries. It is the
place where it leads, after a powerful messianically convoked crescendo, "every mouth," "every tongue," "every knee," "every heart,"
into the word of the Psalm, "as it is written" (Psalm 35:10), and in it
for a moment into the individual praying person: "All my limbs must
say: Lord, who is like unto You?"

Jehuda Halevi's hymn deepens into this moment where the We, the "Breath of all things living" – the opening words of the prayer – sinks into the I. "My limbs," "my songs," "my spirit," "my plumage," "my driving force," "my heart" – always again "my": it is man, the individual man before God. He is not looking inwards, he is extending himself outwards; he only says My in order to place that which is his again and again at God's feet. He says I, but only to forget himself. Again and again his words begin with My and end again and again with: to You.

On the translation: Stanza 1, lines 2ff.: My limbs acknowledge / that they live in You, // with the offering of my songs / they strive toward You, / and as my offering / they bring before You / my thankful thoughts. [Es bekennen meine Glieder, / daß in dir sie leben, // mit dem Opfer feiner Lieder / zu dir sie streben, // und als mein Hebopfer / mein dankend Sinnen / bringen sie vor dich.] – Stanza 2, line 4: And my thoughts / constant before my countenance / they set You as a sign. [Und mein Sinnen / stets vor mein Antlitz / stellt Dich als Zeichen.] – Stanza 4, line 4: Only my sins / before my eyes / they conceal You. [Nur meine Sünden / vor meinen Augen / Dich verbergen.] – Stanza 5, line 4: My secret / and what is deeply hidden – / do not escape You. [Mein Geheimnis / und tief Verborgnes – / nicht entgehts dir.]

THE INCOMPARABLE ONE / מי כמוך עמקות גלה

Brody-Albrecht 104f.

The incomparability of God which this poem sings in the same place in the prayer as the last one, can induce man to reflective comparison: What is he beside the Incomparable, he, the very comparable, the "leaf that withers"?; he whose knowledge of the Creator has its zenith in not asking questions; he, who finds divine support for his life in the commitment to human duty; he, for whom the bliss of freedom awakens only out of the mystery which he remains to himself; he, who can realize his own particular will only through subordinating to His? In this pensively described comparison, the poem paraphrases the omnipotence of the Incomparable One.

On the translation: Pre-stanza, line 1: "… who reveals depth;" ["… der Tiefen offenbart;"] – line 2: "… performer of miracles!" ["… Wundertäter!"] – Stanza 2, line 4: "to the threshold of heaven" ["zur Himmelsschwelle"] is an addition. – Stanza 4, line 4: "no thing is too miraculous for Him" ["kein Ding ist ihm zu wunderbar"].

NONE OTHER! / יודעי יגוני

Luz., Div. Nr. 84. Harkavy II 15f. Brody III 89f. Brody-Albrecht 109f. Badisches Gebetbuch 372f.

The great German scholar Lagarde, whose bitterness was possibly still greater than his scholarship – and that says something – , once said that for the Jews monotheism meant: of God there is only one model. What the truth of this is, that is, seen from the inside, if one does not already know it, is seen in this poem, which belongs to those that revolve around David's morning prayer (1 Chron 17:20;[1*] compare Is. 45:5 and 21;[2*] Hoshea 13:4;[3*] Psalm 18:32[4*]): And there is no God but You. This "keiner denn du" [no one but you], "keiner sonst" [no one else], "kein Zweiter" [no second], this true root word of faith in the One, is produced from the doubting question of the bride's handmaids in the Song of Songs (5:9): "what is your Friend among other friends, oh you most beautiful among women?" and surges up in the answer out of the wavy crests of the song of praise, of the destiny of being called (Jer. 20:9[5*]), of the suffering of martyrdom, and of the present time in history, over all of which at the conclusion it rises monumentally. For the uniqueness of God is the exclusiveness of love. Of God there is only One Model.

On the translation: Nothing to note.

1* 1 Chronicles 17:20: Oh Lord, there is none like thee, and there is no God besides thee, according to all that we have heard with our ears.

2* Isaiah 45:5 and 21: I am the Lord, and there is none else, there is no God beside me: I girded thee, though thou hast not known me. 21 Declare and bring them near; let them take counsel together; who declared this from ancient time? who told it from that time? did not I the Lord? and there is no God else beside me; a just God and a deliverer; there is none beside me.

3* Hoshea 13:4: Yet I am the Lord thy God from the land of Mizrayim [Egypt]; and thou knowest no God but me: for there is no saviour besides me.

4* Psalm 18:32: For who is God save the Lord? And who is a rock save our God?

5* Jeremiah 20:9: Then I said, I will not make mention of him, nor speak any more in his name. But his word was in my heart as a burning fire shut up in my bones, and I am weary with containing myself, and I cannot.

THE LOVERS / יחלו פני אל חי חסידיו

Luz., Div. Nr. 24. Harkavy II 84f. Brody III 3f.

But love is difficult. Even love for God. That is the most difficult love. Unhappy love, which is in all love, even in the happiest, through the tension between the infinitude of the desire for loving, the having to love, and the finitude of the capacity for loving, here ascends by degrees to the infinite. To love God is always at once happy and unhappy, the happiest and the unhappiest love. It comes close to the human being, the closest – and draws itself away from him again into the most distant distance. It is the most ardently desired and at the same time the least bearable thing. The refuge for the most ardently desired thing is under the eternal arms, but the eternal countenance no one sees and remains alive. Thus the beloved returning love to the lover must nevertheless beg and always ask about it – for "to beg" and "to enquire" in Hebrew are the same word. The solution of this predicament and conflict lies, however, as the solution of all predicaments and conflicts, with the lover, with his strength for the For-All-That, who endures the For-All-That, and who For-All-That permits Himself to be endured. Here then it is the human's prerogative and his strength to demand that God – loves him in return.

On the translation: Line 1: God the Living One they entreat ... [Zu Gott dem Lebendgen flehn ...]

THE DAY OF JUDGMENT / יעלו לאלף ולרבבה

Brody III 252f.

Judaism has kept alive the thought of the judgment of the world, which always awakens in man when the seasons renew themselves and fall asleep when the seasons decline and "yet all remains as before," in that it has drawn the thought, irrespective of the end of the seasons, into the year. The New Year's Day in the autumn has become the "Day of Judgment" which places the individual once each year before the full dreadfulness of world judgment. Of a world judgment of course only in the microcosmos of the soul, of all souls. For the soul, for the souls, today the fate is sealed. To this internal knowledge, of which the external realization must be lacking – for the end of the world, of course, can happen only once, and not every year – the reading creates now at least a substitute of this worldly reality in placing on the Today of this Day the great Day of the World, its beginning and its messianic completion. But man now sees the yearly turning point of his own life framed into the Days of Remembrance and of Hope of the World. And besides there is reflected for him in that day – which makes the hearing of the final trumpets [Shofar] a duty in the circle of Jewish duties and tells Israel to anticipate the universal acknowledgment of God's dominion – there is reflected also the destiny of the Patriarchs, exactly at the point where man feels his dependence most intimately and yet at the same time quite concretely, at the point where the unbeliever is as believing as the believer and the believer cannot be more believing than the other. The reading places onto this day the reprieve of the three barren mothers, Sarah, Rachel, Hannah; one of these three fates, that of Hannah (1 Sam. 1), has therefore become the passage for this day of the Last Judgment that is interwoven by the most ardent and most private prayers.

On the translation: Stanza 1, line 3: For "all" ["sämtlich"] line 4 of the original: "without exception and without omission" ["ohne Ausnahme und ohne Lücke"]; line 6: "in the valley (Josaphat) …" ["im Tal (Josaphat) …". – Stanza 2, lines 5f.: "… the elevated Throne / He Who is enthroned on high" ["… den erhabenen Thron / Er der hoch Thronende"]; line 7: "furthest distances" ["fernste Hufen"] is an addition. Stanza 3, line 6: "today help came to them out of their misery" ["heut kam ihnen Hilfe aus ihrem Elend"]. – Stanza 4, lines 2f: "… will be king over you / …" ["wird über dich König sein / … "]. – Stanza 5, lines 5f: "Perhaps He will then bring on the day, to fulfill His Word …"].

HOMECOMING / ימינך נשא עוני

Harkavy II 31ff. Brody III 298ff.

Does God or does the human being take the first step? That is a real question, not, as Protestant theologians today would like to believe, a preliminary question already solved. Nor indeed is it "the difference between Judaism and Christianity," as the Jewish theologians in their understandable demand for harmless "distinctions for teaching purposes" would like to believe. Rather, it is a real question of the real heart of the human. For, referring once more to the Neo-Protestant theologians, it is rather a different matter whether one proclaims the paradox of the "slavish will" in the role of an emperor of world history or whether one proclaims it in the role of an undisturbed professor and writer. In the former case the theory is supplemented in life with the stamp of truth. In the latter, the theory raises itself to a higher power through life solely to a magnified – and therefore false – theory. If Luther had died on 30 October 1517, then all the audacities of his commentary on the "Letter to the Romans" would have been only the extravaganza of a late scholastic.

The real question arises because the human always senses his own lack of power whenever he stands before God, and thus necessarily must await and request the first step from God. And yet at the same time he hears that which he cannot help but hear: that God demands the first step from him, from the human. No theory can get away from this, neither one that seeks to discredit the demanding voice of God that is heard, nor one that seeks to discredit the perceived lack of power as a deception of Satan. And of course absolutely not one that might steer between such a crude alternative through clever distribution or a meticulous apportionment of roles. Instead, the matter remains an unending conversation, where therefore, as in every conversation, the one who speaks last is "right" – and so God after all on that account must be right, because at the very End He has the last word!

When the *Midrash* presents the human being and God, the community of Israel and its God in conversation, it grasps the problem in this way. With reference to the conclusion of Lamentations (4:21)[6*] and the prophecy in Malachi (3:7),[7*] the demand for the first step is held out against a condition for the second step, and only then will either take it himself. Upon this *Midrash* Jehuda Halevi has built up the great conversation between a human being and God, which is intended, as a fifth half-double stanza hymn, for the noon-hours of the great Day of Atonement.

The first double stanza is shorter than the following ones, and, in motto fashion, it opposes the two guiding principles by a stark contrast between the human entreaty and the divine necessity to refuse. Then the actual dialogue begins: and it is carried out very differently from the many other dialogues between Israel and God composed by Jehuda Halevi. For, while in these others – our collection offers three examples from pages 190 to 196 [i.e., "Treue," "Liebestrost," "Wiederfinden," pages] – a real conversation takes place, face to face, here a fearful distance remains, precisely the distance that is marked out in the two introductory and lead-in stanzas. The human voice – through

---

6* Lamentations 4:21: Turn us to thee, O Lord, and we shall be turned; renew our days as of old.

7* Malachi 3:7: From the days of your fathers you have turned aside from my ordinances, and have not kept them. Return to me, and I will return to you, says the Lord of hosts. But you have said, With what shall we return?

lawful demand, profound despair, resolute humility, impassioned pleading remains – a cry out of the depths; and the divine voice – in demand, warning, promise – remains a call from the heights. Just on this day, wholly to do with reconciliation, the tension between God and the human being appears to be irreconcilable.

And just that by which this tension at other times is most easily off-set, here serves only to add to it. When at other times God's ways are distant from human ways, the way of Israel's God and the way of his people meet at the eternally flaming Sinai. Even today, on this day, when the Jew is wholly human, and his God is wholly Judge of the world, this bridge does not disappear from consciousness. It is even trod upon by both sides, but it does not lead to the other shore. When the human being – second double stanza – addresses God as the bearer of his Jewish Law and of his Jewish suffering, God answers with the most stringent demand on the human being and on the human being only. And when – third double stanza – he stammers out from his whole and simple humanness, God reminds him of his Jewish son-ship of God, of miracle and Law. The nearness itself on this fearful day thus becomes an element of the distance. The conversation between the two voices continues in that unending distance with which it be-gan.

But here the last word belongs to the human. The concluding stanza is no longer a double stanza, God's voice is silent here. What does this silence mean? When one considers the poem by itself it is not possible to determine the reason – just because the last cry of the human, his totally naked cry of despair, remains without an answer. But the poem is as little detached from the day and the hour for which it is meant, as the individual chorus is detached from its tragedy and the place where it stands in the tragedy. The poem belongs to the mid-hours of the "long day." And even if there were any doubt as to whether it were writ-ten for that day – as in the beginning, with its citation from the con-cluding prayer – you offer your hand to sinners and your right hand is extended to welcome the homecoming; then even there everything is still preliminary and there is no last word. A last word is only possible at the last moment. And if the human being is to be the one to speak that which is God's concern, then the last word – of the day, of life, of history – can be only the word that stands behind all God's speech, – in the way in which the human can take this divine "I" into his mouth, namely as a profession of the "He." In this profession of the last mo-ment of the day, the entire day as well as our poem finds its solution for the first time. The human himself, under God's eyes, gives himself the answer, which presents him with the gift of the fulfilment of his prayer of return, of homecoming for this one, anticipated last moment. At

this moment he is as near to God, as close to his throne as human beings can be. In the rapture of this nearness the "You" is silent to him,
not merely the You of his cry of despair, but also the You of his yearning and of his love. Like the angel under the throne he turns around
and professes, testifies to – Him. But he is permitted to anticipate this
highest, final moment because a few minutes later when the sound of
the ram's horn (Leviticus 25:9f)[8*] announces the close of the Holy
Day, he will again recite the evening prayer of his everyday life which
has broken through once again: Forgive us, our Father, for we have
sinned.

On the translation: Stanza 3, line 6: ... berries on the tip of the
branch! [Beeren auf der Spitze des Zweigs!] lines 7 and 8 are changed
compared to the original "... spill upon him Your terror" ["schütt auf
ihn dein Schreck"]. Stanza 4, line 10 ... to the highest heights [... zu
höchsten Höhen. Lines 7 and 8 are reversed. Line 7: What should they
feel and think ... [Was sollen sinnen und denken ...] – Stanza 7,
line 4: and besides You there is no rule [und nicht gibt es außer dir
Herrschaft]. lines 7f. And who is Lord besides You / for hoping and
awaiting? [Und wer ist Herr außer dir / zum Hoffen and zum Harren?] line 12: where should I get away? [wohin soll ich mich scheren?]
– Stanza 9, line 1: The people, ... [Das Volk, ...]. line 5: If he may not
live surrounding you [Wenn er nicht wohnen darf rings um dich ...]

HEAR / יה שמע אביונך

Brody III 301. Hamburger Tempelgebetbuch 424. Seligmannsches Gebetbuch 351.

This prayer of the prayer leader on the Day of Atonement meant for
the afternoon service, as the conclusion shows, is, unlike the foregoing
hymnic dialogue, all demand. In its centre it has the words which,
taken from Ezekiel (36:22)[9*], always recur in the liturgy of the day. But

8*Leviticus 25:9f: Then shalt thou cause the shofar to sound on the tenth day
of the seventh month, on the day of atonement shall you sound the shofar
throughout all your land. 10 And you shall hallow the fiftieth year, and proclaim liberty throughout all the land to all its inhabitants: it shall be a jubi-
lee for you; and you shall return every man to his possession, and you shall
return every man to his family.

9*Ezekiel 36:22: Therefore say to the house of Yisra'el, Thus says the Lord
God: I do not this for your sakes, O house of Yisra'el, but for my holy name's
sake, which ye have profaned among the nations, to which you came.

if they are founded in Ezekiel, as in the sections of Torah which prepare their formulation (Exodus 32:12ff),[10*] (Numbers 14:13ff),[11*]
(Deuteronomy 9:28),[12*] on the relationship of God to His people, so
they are founded today, commensurate with the meaning of the day,
only on the sin of man and the forgiving grace of God. People have
been terrified about this, have found blasphemous this demand of
man for forgiveness – quite literally – for God's sake. There has even
been a movement to erase it from the prayers. And certainly it is as ridiculous as the clever psychology children use with their parents: it
serves my father right if I freeze my hands – why doesn't he buy me any
gloves! But after all – isn't this parent-psychology right?

On the translation: Stanza 1, line 1: God, hear your beggar [Gott, hear
your beggar]. – Stanza 3, line 1: Their wantonness and their flaw
[Ihren Frevel und ihren Fehl]. – Stanza 5, line 1: Look at the tears of
their face [Blick auf die Träne ihres Angesichts]. – Stanza 6, line 4: Let
them find your ... [Laβ sie finden deinen ...]

THE TRUE ONE / בכל לבי אמת ובכל מאדי

Luz., Div. Nr. 12. Harkavy I 56. Brody II 221. Brody-Wiener 170.

10*Exodus 32:12ff: Wherefore should Mizrayim [the Egyptians] speak, and
say, In an evil hour did he bring them out, to slay them in the mountains,
and to consume them from the face of the earth? Turn from thy fierce anger, and relent of this evil against thy people. 13 Remember Avraham,
Yizhaq, and Yisra'el, thy servants, to whom thou didst swear by thy own self,
and didst say to them, I will multiply your seed as the stars of heaven, and
all this land that I have spoken of will I give to your seed, and they shall in-
herit it forever. 14 And the Lord relented of the evil which he thought to
do to his people.

11*Numbers 14:13ff: And Moshe said to the Lord, Then Mizrayim [the Egyp-
tians] shall hear it, (for thou didst bring up this people in thy might from
among them;) 14 and they will tell it to the inhabitants of this land: who
have heard that thou Lord art among this people, that thou Lord art seen
face to face, and that thy cloud stands over them, and that thou goest before
them, by day time in a pillar of a cloud, and in a pillar of fire by night. 15
Now if thou shalt kill all this people as one man, then the nations which
have heard the fame of thee will speak, saying.

12*Deuteronomy 9:28: lest the land from which thou didst bring us out say, Because the Lord was not able to bring them into the land which he promised
them, and because he hated them, he has brought them out to slay them in
the wilderness.

This poem is an address to Truth, or to the One who is True – both are the same thing in the Hebrew language and for Jewish feeling. That is, neither of them make the concept of truth separate; he who says "Truth" knows that God is it. So says Jeremiah (12:12);[13*] and so the daily rite has learned it from him, when it draws together the last word of the Hear-Oh-Israel prayer, "the Lord your God" with the first word of its repetition, "Truth" into one loud call. Thus this poem as a matter of course also finds its beginning in the first words of that prayer: in the command to love God (Deuteronomy 6:5),[14*] which here now becomes the love of truth and yet retains all the sensual and suprasensual ardour of love for God. And he who has understood this "and yet" will know what "Jewish rationalism" is about, and that this rationalism may be very rational, and yet can never be as rational as it – is Jewish. Whoever has known Hermann Cohen – he also will know this.

On the translation: Lines 3 – 5 are in the second half somewhat paraphrased. Literally: line 3: "… and how may I go alone" ["… und wie mag ich allein gehn"]; line 4: "… how may I sit lonely" ["… wie mag ich einsam sitzen"]; line 5: "… how can my light die out" ["… wie kann mein Licht erlöschen"].

YOUR GOD / יִשַׁן אל תרדם

Sachs 34, Brody III 203f. Brody-Wiener 166f.

For God is your God. If we were not permitted to know anything else about Him other than that He is God – and to the question what He is, this of course would be the most adequate answer – : then it would be in vain to call to Him; and glancing up to the stars would be only an escape from the world; and if there could be no way up to His height (Hoshea 14:2)[15*]; and the hope of being permitted to turn to Him completely once again on this earth and to prepare oneself (Obadiah 1:21)[16*] would be in vain; and it would be a delusion of the ones born

---

13*Jeremiah 12:12: The spoilers are come upon all high hills through the wilderness: for the sword of the lord devours from the one end of the land to the other end of the land: no flesh has peace.

14* Deuteronomy 6:5: And thou shalt love the Lord thy God with all thy heart, and with all thy soul, and with all thy might.

15* Hoshea 14:2: O Yisra'el, return to the Lord thy God; for thou hast stumbled in thy iniquity.

16* Obadiah 1:21: And liberators shall ascend upon mount Ziyyon to judge the mountain of "Esav; and the kingdom shall be the Lord's.

of dust to find Him in the love-intoxicated heartbeats of the vision
(Song of Songs 1:2)[17*]; and there would be no other intercourse with
Him, the pure Being [Sein] (Exodus 3:12),[18*] than those questions
forbidden in the Talmud about When and Where, the Below and
Above of Creation, and precisely not those questions of the whole and
simple life (Deut. 18:9-15).[19*] [5] which the Scriptures have opposed
(Deut. 18:13)[20*] to all such magic compulsion for knowledge. This
would be so if we really knew nothing more than that. But just as we
have to heed the limits of our knowledge, so too, and not less, the
limits of our not-knowing. Beyond all our knowledge God lives. But
before our not-knowing begins, your God presents Himself to you, to
your call, to your ascent, to your readiness, to your glance, to your
life.

On the translation: Stanza 2, lines 9f.: That time not elevate you / and
your heart become proud in your elevation [Daß nicht Zeit dich
erhöhe / und stolz werde dein Herz in deiner Höhe]. – Stanza 3,
line 8: and a place for them at His throne [und ihnen an seinem
Thron eine Stätte]. – Stanza 5, line 10: you find your God [findest du
deinen Gott] – Stanza 6, line 3: "close to each other" ["dicht bei
dicht"] is an addition; line 9: "wholly and simply" ["ganz und schlicht"]
in Hebrew is one word.

17* The Song of Songs 1:2: Let him kiss me with the kisses of his mouth: for thy
love is better than wine.
18* Exodus 3:12: And he said, Certainly I will be with thee; and this shall be a
token to thee, that I have sent thee. When thou hast brought the people out
of Mizrayim [Egypt], you shall serve God upon this mountain.
19* Deuteronomy 18:9-15: When thou art come to the land which the Lord thy
God gives thee, thou shalt not learn to do after the abominations of those
nations. 10 There must not be found among you any one that makes his son
or his daughter to pass through the fire, or that uses divination, a soothsay-
er, or an enchanter, or a witch, 11 or a charmer, or a medium, or a wizard,
or a necromancer. 12 For all that do these things are an abomination to the
Lord: and because of these abominations the Lord thy God drives them out
from before thee. 13 Thou shalt be perfect with the Lord thy God. 14 For
these nations, which thou shalt dispossess, hearken to soothsayers, and to
diviners: but as for thee, the Lord thy God has not permitted thee so to do.
15 The Lord thy God will raise up to thee a prophet from the midst of thee,
of thy brethren, like unto me; to him you shall hearken.
20* Deuteronomy 18:13: Thou shalt be perfect with the Lord thy God.

HIS PEACE / צל ירי אל חי יהי לך מחסה

Luz., Div. Nr. 35. Harkavy II 147f.

The main prayer, recited three times a day, ends with the plea for peace to the "Lord of Peace"; the concluding prayer and the Kiddush end with "The One who makes peace in His heights, let Him also make peace upon us and all His people." This conclusion of the prayers is also the final conclusion of human wisdom. But in order that it may become the conclusion of wisdom, it must be the beginning of action. Of an action which is, of course, doing.

On the translation: Nothing to note.

THE UNIVERSE / יחו לשון חזות אישון

Luz., Div. Nr. 67. Harkavy II 107ff. Brody III 75ff.

For the four concluding lines of each stanza, this hymn picks up word for word a verse from Deuteronomy (10:17).[21*] This verse as well as the hymn that he develops out of it are unfamiliar to people today in that it assumes the reality of the gods. And today it is generally regarded as an "achievement of religious development" that humankind has learned that gods do not exist. Even the atheist is accustomed, with confident good will, to pronounce "monotheism" as a necessary developmental step on the route from many gods to no god. The poet who composed this hymn, however, would have to refuse to tolerate this good will. For him the gods are real, and God is "only" more real. And that this is the truth is hidden from us today by the madness that "monotheism" is something self-evident. "Monotheism" perhaps. Not belief in the One. Experience of life very much resists this belief and is likely to compel us all to believe in all kinds of powers. The names change, but the diversity remains. Culture and civilization, people and state, nation and race, arts and science, ethics and religiosity – this comprises, although certainly it is not complete, an overview of the pantheon of today. Who will deny the reality of these powers? But never has a "pagan" served his gods more faithfully and been in more readiness to sacrifice to them than we humans of today. And if the One meets us, then even today the battle with the many is unavoidable, and

---

21*Deuteronomy 10:17: For the Lord your God is God of gods, and Lord of lords, a great God, a mighty, and a terrible, who favours no person, and takes no bribe.

its outcome, to be sure, only as far as it touches us, is uncertain. If God wanted – the Talmud knows this – to annihilate the gods once and for all, if He wanted to destroy the powers which the human is tempted to make into gods – He would have to annihilate no less than his world.[6] And yet it is His world, coming from Him, and returning to Him. It is His Universe.

And thus the hymn, which is woven around that verse, sings of the universe, God's world. But here the child of the present is alienated once more, and the more present so much the more alienated; for it is a comparatively young – not yet a hundred and fifty years old – a fundamental dogma of modern education and consequently also of modern religiosity, that one may not seek God in nature. At the source of this prejudice sits Kant with his refutation of the "physico-teleological proof of God," through which the previously obvious step from the Creation to the Creator all at once appeared forbidden even to the grounding of modern natural science. Truly only apparent; no one knew it better than Kant himself, Kant, who concludes the story of how he observed during one insect-scarce summer that the swallows were even pushing their young out of the nest with an outcry: For my understanding stood still, for there was nothing to do about it except to fall down and to worship. He had wanted to criticize the "proof," not the "worshipping."

But certainly mankind would not so lightly have cut short this worshipping if in the last century the world itself had not now plainly become ever more invisible to the eye. That is above all the fault of the dogmatic popularizing of the Copernican-Newtonian theory that took place in all the public schools of the last century. In the vaporous light of the large cities worshipping cannot be located, for the builder has become just as obtuse. In this point the whole nation consists of "educated people." Today one finds at most one among ten people who knows that the stars also rise and set. The other nine, if asked, answer: Only the planets. Then the first one also usually falters.

It was the enormous advantage of the Ptolemaic system before the Copernican – which maybe we can acknowledge today, when indeed neither one is true any longer – , that in the Ptolemaic the understanding of things went together at least in its initial steps in a harmonious fashion with the view of the childish mind. Thus he did not lose the courage really to look around himself now and to see also what he "knew." For one saw, one believed that he saw the circles of the spheres ordered in each other and simultaneously over each other, in which the seven planets, the sun and the moon as the lowest, closest to the earth, reckoned with them, around which, at the deepest point of this funnel of spheres, suspending earths were swinging up to the outermost husk of the globe of the heaven of fixed stars which once a day completed its orbit. What was beyond – was the Beyond. For one followed still with his eyes the movement of the individual planets through the twelve houses of the Zodiac. For one still had the good conscience that Below really was Below, and Above, Above. Similarly we also know today: Copernicus – the "fool" after Luther's sentences that were lacking in and yet full of ideas, – detracted from humanness. To his sister's question why the Antipodes did not fall off a small child answered: "Where one stands is always below." And because one knew it, so in that which was always under, and in that which was always above, and in that which was always between below and above, one could again not merely know the elements of all things, but rather see them. Wherever, then, knowledge by seeing ceased, there one always replaced the final cause with a system of between-powers, exactly as now at the limit of our calculated knowledge. The angel of medieval Aristotelianism and the basic understanding of modern physics approach this the most closely in that here, as there, the whole world believes in it; and concerning it, the uninitiated envisage for the most part nothing, the knowledgeable for the most part nonsense. For the spiritual righteousness which it brings upon itself has seldom been a case of expressing the really experienced thing purely, and not mythologically growing forth with those former knowledges that shoot up directly in the experience for the one experiencing. Real and great experiences of the work of God have been set down in the Talmudic study of the angels. But they have been all too lightly choked by the ramblings of fantastic reason lacking in experience, as the real and great knowledges of science have been choked through the ramblings of a fantasy that is a stranger to experience and a possessor of reason.

To be sure, there is a danger in praising God out of nature, and this danger smoulders even in this hymn. In the third stanza's last four lines there is an attempt, unbroken from nature to overlook – not the human, that would be permitted, but: – our very selves, and to drown out the seriousness of the individual destiny with an all too cheaply purchased Hallelujah, that is not with the particular body. Against this danger the Jobs and the Ivan Karamazovs remain, who believe in God, but do not accept his world, the eternally necessary antidote.

But Jehuda Halevi does not need this cure. He is a Jew and therefore not in danger of singing Hallelujah hastily. The powerful middle four lines of the concluding stanza, which at first glance interrupt the coherence and once more push aside the already reached Angel conclusion, certainly in order to let it in again in unprecedented concentration, have an extremely profound reason for being in this place. As hard, as daring, as proud of suffering and as certain of being right as

the poet speaks here is almost nowhere in such evidence in the poems
which were dedicated expressly to this theme. It is this undertoned
consciousness of suffering alone that gives him the right to accept
God's world. Yet. The suffering one alone has the permission to praise
God in his works. But all men suffer. That is why humanity has that
right. Only he who wants to deny or to forget his suffering, only to him
is it not permitted. For whoever wants to lie himself away, he lies also
whenever he speaks about Him. Only in the mouth of the upright ones
does He want to be praised.

On the translation: Stanza 1, lines 23f.: "But they never know the
How" ["Doch nimmer wissen sie das Wie"]; line 30: "of the gods!"
["der Götter!"] – Stanza 2, line 1: "the times" ["die Zeiten"]; line 8 is
an addition; lines 23f.: "He calculates the number of all" ["allen rechnet Er die Zahl"]. Stanza 4, line 16 is an addition; the angels' names
from lines 25, 26, 29f., 33, 34, 35 correspond to the Erillim, Chash-
mallim, Tarshishim, Cherubim, Ofannim, Seraphim of the text. –
Stanza 5, lines 15f.: "to Ishmaelite and Edomite" ["zu Ismaelit und
Edomit"]; lines 30 – 32: "to resemble the / Cherubim / and Chayot"
[zu gleichen den / Cherubim / und Chajjoth"].

THE FAR-AND-NEAR ONE / יה אנה אמצאך

Sachs 32f. Harkavy II 131f. Brody III 150f. Brody-Wiener 157.

This hymn is assigned to that section of the morning prayers consisting
mostly of hymns. It speaks of the heavenly wheel and animal forms of
the vision of Ezekiel, and it is animated by one particular thought. But
it is the last thought that human thinking can grasp, and the first that
Jewish thinking grasps: that the faraway God is none other than the
near God, the unknown God none other than the revealed one, the
Creator none other than the Redeemer. The poem sings this thought
which the brief opening stanza presents in epigrammatic brevity;[22*]
and the following four stanzas let it swing in wide hymnic sweeps from
heaven's throne to the human heart and back again. This thought has
been repeatedly discovered anew in the sphere of revelation; and inside as well as outside its sphere, from Paul and Marcion to Harnack
and Barth repeatedly forgotten anew.

22* Lord, where shall I find Thee?
   High and hidden is Thy place;
   And where shall I not find Thee?
   The world is full of Thy glory.
   (translated by Nina Salaman)

Always discovered anew, always forgotten anew. For what people discover, the theologians forget. And the more they do so, the better theologians they are. The most accurate theology is the most dangerous. After a long drought, today we have a theology, mostly Protestant, that leaves nothing to be desired as to accuracy. We have it now: that God is Wholly Other, that to talk about Him is to talk Him away, that we can only say what He does to us. The result of this monstrous accuracy is that we accurate people today all stand together like children in a circle. One person asserts one accurate point; his neighbour scorns him with the even more accurate statement that this assertion was false because it was accurate. And so it goes around the circle until we arrive back at the first. The whole thing is called theology.

We theologians cannot help but make prescriptions for God's conduct out of our knowledge. We know that God can be known only in His presence, and at once we make out of this a law for Him: that He does not permit Himself to be known in His absence. In truth, however, we could easily leave it to Him as to when and how and what of Himself He wants to be known. And we have to say only what we know in utter calm or in utter unrest – but whether in calm or in unrest is not up to us; that is as accurately as we can – and this accuracy *is* up to us.

When God comes near to us, of course we know only the inexpressible. But that is not our duty (and as it is called in our innermost hearts instead: our due – because we are such excellent modern theologians). Rather, we cannot do anything else; it is solely a matter of His nearness. That is why we have no reason at all for scorning each other because we express the inexpressible. As long as it is inexpressible and wants to be so, it itself will take care that we cannot express it. Thus when we do begin to express it, that probably happens because it itself makes it possible for us to speak, be it ever so imperfectly, in that it – no, in that He, God, begins to retreat from us, distances Himself from us. In distancing Himself from us He gives Himself to us to know Him as the Faraway One. And when He is totally distant, that is when He has totally distanced Himself, we can even – deliver me up to the worldly arm of the law, you inquisitors of the new theology! – prove him.

The possibility of the proof of God is the simple result of the fact that God, as you will never tire of repeating, is Wholly Other. No, not even a result. Rather this "wholly-other" is itself the modern proof of God, namely the residue of the other proofs thinned out to the outermost distance of abstraction. But the proofs reach, before this last point of distance, the point where they, each from its own distance, represent the accurate expression of what is visible here. Thus it is not at all a sign of being hopelessly lost with respect to knowing that God is the wholly perfect being or the first cause, or indeed even that He is the ideal of ethics. Rather, wherever it is expressed as honest knowledge, it is only a sign that at the moment of acquiring this knowledge, God really was very far away from the one who was acquiring it. But what does this mean: "honest knowledge"? Nothing other than what it always means. To say nothing about what does not concern us and what we ourselves do not concern. Without such a concern even research on fifteenth-century German agriculture is worthless, while with it, sentences like "God is holy" or even "God exists" are just as true as our modern approximations.

For nearness and distance in themselves signify nothing as to whether that mutual concern, which all knowledge first has to render true, does prevail, and thus here whether the human concerns [German wordplay: "*an-geht*": goes to] God and God the human. Even in the most dreadful nearness the human can look away and then does not know in the least what has happened to him. And in the farthest distance the glance of God and of the human can burn into one another, so that the coldest abstractions become warm in the mouth of Maimonides or Hermann Cohen – more than all our distressed prattle. Near, far, it doesn't matter! What does matter is that here as there, what is spoken is spoken before His countenance – with the You of the refrain of our poem, the You that never turns away for a moment.

On the translation: Stanza 2, line 2: "up to the highest throne" ["auf zum höchsten Thron"]; lines 7 – 10: "Who could there be who does not fear You? / The yoke of your kingdom is his yoke! / Who could there be who does not beseech You? / His bread You prepare for him!" [Wen gäbs, der nicht fürchtet Dich? / Joch Deines Reichs ist sein Joch! / Wen gäbs, der nicht anfleht Dich? / sein Brod bereitest Du ihm!"] – Stanza 3, line 2: "... cry up to You" ["aufschreies zu Dir"]; line 6:"I gazed upon You in the sanctuary" ["schaut' ich Dich im Heiligtum"]. Stanza 4, line 7 – 10: "Animals praise Your might, / standing atop world, – Your throne rests on their heads, / yet You bear them all" ["Tiere loben Deine Macht, / stehnd auf Weltenhöh', – auf / ihren Häuptern ruht Dein Thron / jedoch Du trägst sie Alle"].

THE NAME / יפה וטוב לאחוז בביתך מחנה

Luz., Div. Nr. 31. Harkavy II 86. Brody III 66.

The paradox that God is near and far at the same time is smashed to pieces by the fact that He has a name. Whatever has a name can be spoken of and spoken to, depending on whether it is absent or present. God is never absent and that is why there is no concept of God (of the false gods definitely, but of the true none). God is the only one whose name is at the same time His concept, whose concept is at the same time His name. One names God only God, and each name has only this meaning.

The Far-and-Near helps the poet also to solve the problem of the purpose of the world, about which the philosophy of religion of that time toiled. Everything created has a double function: first, it is simply wholly there, has being, self-being, is a purpose in itself. But then it is also there for the sake of something else, in the final resort for the sake of everything else. In its selfness it experiences the near God, in its bondedness to the other the far God. For the far God is the God of the world, which always is the whole, and a whole made up of totally different parts. The near God is the God of the heart, of the heart which is never so much self and only self as when it suffers.

It is striking that in the second couplet, which formulates the content of the poem very briefly and simply, the concrete word "dwell" is used for the Being of God that is high above and far away from the world. The word usually indicates the dwelling of God's glory on earth, among his people, in his house, whereas here it is used for the dwelling in the crushed heart and is the most abstract word imaginable, even in deviation from the biblical verse on which it is based (Is. 57:15).[23*] It is the word "is" ["Sein"], this typical word of philosophers, which Western scholastics rendered as "exists" – strictly speaking one would have had to have translated it "Being there" ["*Dasein*"]. This contradiction discloses the ultimate depth of Jewish knowledge [*Wissen*] and faith. The "Boreh Olam", the Creator of the world, does not mean here, as one would have thought, something distant as indicated by the content of the words. But rather: in popular speech words are filled with emotion, and with the God of the heart, the heart does not forget for a moment He is the one who "is." So here the spark does not merely jump back and forth between the two poles of far and near; but rather the poles themselves are each laden with two polar charges, only ordered differently. The Creator above the world sets up a "dwelling," and the abstract God of Philosophy has "being" in the crushed heart.

When Hermann Cohen was still in Marburg, he once explained his idea of God in his "Ethics" to an old Marburg Jew. The Jew listened full of reverence, but when Cohen was finished, he asked: "And where does the Boreh Olam fit?" Cohen did not answer and broke into tears.

23* Isaiah 57:15: For thus says the high and lofty One that inhabits eternity, whose name is Holy; I dwell on high and in a holy place, yet with him also that is of a contrite and humble spirit, to revive the spirit of the humble, and to revive the heart of the contrite ones.

On the translation: Line 1: "Year in, year out" ["Jahraus, jahrein"] is an addition.

CONSECRATED / שלשו קדוש

Luz., Div. Nr. 68. Harkavy II 6ff. Brody-Albrecht 105f.

This hymn, sparkling with rhyme, like the previous one is assigned to that place in the morning services that portrays the thrice holy of the heavenly host, as Isaiah heard it. For all the "Below" corresponds to an "Above": thus should Israel echo the threefold-consecration of the angels on earth, Israel whose city faces the heavenly city of God – or as it is also written in memory of the preliminary form of the city during the wandering in the desert: the earthly camp faces the heavenly. The hymn is entirely embued with the view of this divine double-dominion in heaven and on earth. This is miraculous, where the dominion unites the angelic powers of mercy and truth, which usually neutralize like fire and water, and where it confronts again at the destination the messengers it has sent out – for this divine double-dominion governs at the destination just as it does in the place of instruction. And it is no less miraculous where it steels the human powers of the people to unlimited patience for suffering and untiring witnessing, the people whom the poet summons to do as the angels do.

On the translation: Stanza 3, lines 11f.: "... and / not freed" ["... und / nicht befreit"]. – Stanza 4, lines 5f.: "in the days of their final end, which are wonderful" ["um die Tage ihres Endtermin, die wunderbar sind"].

YOUR DWELLING PLACES / ידידות משכנותיך וארבע מחנותיך

Luz., Div. Nr. 18. Harkavy II 82.

The lens of these few lines gathers the rays of the great hymn that precedes it: the doubleness of the heavenly and earthly sanctuary of the "tents," there the animal-angels from the vision of Ezekiel (1:10),[24*] who bear the chariot throne, here Jacob's sons, the bearers of the Name, the witnesses of the Works of God.

24* Ezekiel 1:10: As for the likeness of their faces, they had the face of a man, and they four had the face of a lion, on the right side: and they four had the face of an ox on the left side; they four also had the face of an eagle.

On the translation: Line 10: "oh, rewards!" ["o Belohnungen!"] is an addition.

THE GOD OF THE SPIRITS / יאתו לך תשבחות

Luz., Div. Nr. 82. Harkavy II 121ff. Brody III 67f.

The spirit, His Spirit, is the proudest possession of the human. The word of the God of the Spirits, which Moses speaks to God in one of his great entreaties (Ex. 4:16,22),[25*] shakes this pride. A completely gentle shaking, one that allows the spirit to stand where it stands, in "all flesh," and which yet entirely uproots his pride. There remains for him, undoubted, the wisdom, the sparkle of the word, but he owes to wisdom and word the place at the heavenly throne, whence they spring. And certainly: the Tables of the Commandments stand in the heart of man – but God's finger has written them. And the soul has a nearby path to heavenly delight, but God's spirit must show that path to the soul. Always only a small But, upon which after all the "self-glory" of the human spirit, his "autonomies" are dependent. And thus in the last stanza the ingenious edifice of the spiritual order collapses, where the soul has its legitimate place above the body in a great side-by-side and confusion of bodies and souls – of "all" together. And there remains, in the image of the prostrate maidens, in place of the proud spiritual order the chaos of humiliation.

On the translation: Stanza 1, lines 1f.: "… grounded in grace, / ele-vated, raised, … ["… huldgegründet, / erhaben, hebend, …]

HOLY / יהי בפי קדושים

Luz., Div. Nr. 83. Harkavy II 124ff. Brody III 124f.

The word Holy in Hebrew originally had the meaning of having been set apart. God's work is at one time the quiet, almost inaudible work of the first beginning; and there everything remains, for the time being, standing as it stands. The creation seems so very old that it could al-most be "eternal," and the voice of conscience so absolute that it might almost be called "autonomous." And strict believers in Kant could well

---

25* Exodus 4:16,22: And he [Aaron] shall be thy [Moshe] spokesman to the people: and he shall be to thee instead of a mouth, and thou shalt be to him instead of God. 22 And thou shalt say to Par'o, Thus says the Lord, Yisra'el is my son, my firstborn.

come to the idea that it actually would alter nothing if one were to surrender to the "religious position": God as the creator of starry heavens and conscience. But this "position" is not to be purchased so cheaply. God is not merely the one who was. He is not merely base, supporter, of the world and of the human. For surely, this is an empty faith, a mere "surrender," if it lacks the experience of the living present, indeed if it does not directly spring from it. Without the God who takes action, powerfully working in the day of our present life, the quiet and inaudible, which preserves the world and our hearts that he created, becomes a fairy tale, no, worse: a dogma. It is the Holy One who sets Himself apart and who everywhere makes a setting apart, an unheard of thing, an election, a holiness. Without the revealed miracles of this today, the concealed miracles of everyday would be invisible, at least invisible as miracles. Only the revelation of things set apart teaches us to revere the Creator even in "natural things." Only the tremors of holiness sanctify the everyday of the profane.

Thus it is essential for miracle that it be drawn into the living present of holiness, thus into sanctification: "Arise! with shouts of holiness ... ." The question, why "today" miracles no longer happen as they "once" used to happen, is sheer foolishness. Miracles never "happened" at all. The past is a murderous atmosphere for the miracle. The Bible itself explains the miracle of the Reed Sea after the fact as "natural." After the fact every miracle can be explained. Not because the miracle was not a miracle, but because the explanation is an explanation. The miracle always stands in the present and perhaps in the future. One can ask for and experience it; and as long as the present of the experience lasts, one can be thankful. But if this present is extinguished, then one can of course only explain it. Every miracle is possible, even the most ludicrous, even that an axe floats (2 Kings 6:1-7).[26*] If it has happened, one will not be discouraged from finding an explanation. The sole condition for its coming to pass is that one can pray

---

26* 2 Kings 6:1-7: And the sons of the prophets said to Elisha, Behold now, the place where we dwell with thee is too small for us. 2 Let us go, we pray thee, to the Yarden [Jordan], and take fom there every man a beam, and let us make us a place there, where we may dwell. And he answered, Go. 3 And one said, Be pleased to go with thy servants. And he answered, I will go. 4 So he went with them, And when they came to the Yarden, they cut down wood. 5 But as one was felling a beam, the axe head fell into the water: and he cried, and said, Alas, master! for it was borrowed. 6 And the man of God said, Where fell it? And he showed him the place. And he cut down a stick, and threw it in there; and made the iron float. 7 Then he said, Take it up to thee. And he put out his hand, and took it.

for it. With genuine prayer, naturally one that is extracted from the will, not with the wilful prayer of the magical technique of a medicine man or of the American absence of such technique. Only herein is there something like a difference of the times, in that the one time can pray for something, for which the other time cannot pray. But when a genuine prayer is possible, then the most impossible is possible; and where it is not possible, the most possible becomes impossible. Therefore it can be possible that the dead rise up, and impossible that the sick get well. There is nothing in itself impossible, but there is much that we deem so impossible that we are not capable of praying for it, and much else we deem possible but nevertheless we for some reason do not have the strength to pray for it.

Actually there is nothing miraculous about the miracle other than that it – does come. The east wind had perhaps already hundreds of times opened the path in the Red Sea, and it will do it again hundreds of times. That it does so at that moment, however, when the people advanced into it in their need, that is the miracle. What was still a future that was prayed for now becomes a present that is entered into. This enrichment of a present moment with a past, its own past, gives to it a strength to endure as a present and not as a past moment, and thus raises it out of the stream of moments, whose companion it nevertheless remains. Thus the miracle becomes the germ-cell of holiness which holds its power as long as it is bound with this origin, as long as it remains miraculous. The Creator, who created only one creation, laughs at the divisions that the human being tries to establish, and lets them again and again be flooded over by the onslaught of primordial chaos. But the divisions which God himself establishes stretch out over the whole creation and make manifest in their becoming the oneness and the all-ness of the silent secret of the one creation.

On the translation: Stanza 1, line 1: "purified" ["gereinigt"] is an addition. Stanza 3, line 5: ... – in them He reveals, yes, He reveals Himself [... – in ihnen offenbart, ja offenbart er sich].

THE HELPER / ינוחם לבב נפעם ונחלה ונהיה

Luz., Div. Nr. 15. Harkavy II 140f.

This little poem is very noteworthy not merely with respect to form, that is to say through the odd metre, which concludes a heavily dragging line with a nimble doubleiambic, but even more through the way in which this form is achieved. In each of the three half-endings and the three full-endings the peak of the poetic thought is driven into the

doubleiambic: the first time, knowledge concerning the God who reveals Himself to us the decaying ones as the living being; to us who are
destined for passivity and for being finished with the I of eternally
present activity; the second time, the restrained joy that we – are not
gone, but indeed live; the third time, the joyous certainty of the future
moment from the "And there was light" of the first moment. "I the living!" [Ich der wese], "Indeed we live" [wir leben ja], "for it was there"
[da war es da] – three times out of the nocturnal severity of distress a
breakthrough into the winged light of help, each time is amplified, because each time a more interior line of the fortress is assaulted in
which the treasure of help is guarded.

The third time this assault occurs under the battle cry of the word of
the "new light." Thus precisely in this sense have the men who originated the Order of Service [*Siddur*] for the synagogue rendered this
word, when they were teaching in the morning prayer, directly before
the praise of God as the Creator of the lights of heaven, who day after
day renews the work of the Creation, in order to pray for the new light
for Zion. For human beings there are two kinds of certainty of divine
help. The one is the certainty of the one to whom help has already been
given; we know from Jehuda Halevi that he asked why God appeals to
the deliverance from Egypt at Sinai, and not to the creation of the
world, and, since we have his *Kuzari*, we need not attribute to him the
foolish answer which Ibn Ezra, the transmitter of his question, gives to
this. There is however a depth of despair in which that certainty fails,
because even the memory of the former help itself chokes in it. When
in this way that which is nearest is for man removed into the distance
of unbelievability, then there remains only the help which comes to
him from the furthest distance; then, and only then, is it time for the
final appeal, for the appeal to the Creator, not in the cultic prayer,
where also other laws serve for this, but rather in the fervent prayer of
the heart. For in this depth of despair nothing more than the creature
remains of man, and thus it is indeed the Creator alone with whom he
can learn anew to believe in the Revealer and to hope for the Redeemer.

On the translation: Nothing to note.

HERE I AM / מִי יִתְּנֵנִי עֶבֶד אֱלוֹהַּ עוֹשִׂנִי

Luz., Div. Nr. 73. Sachs 36f. Harkavy II 118ff. Brody III 228f. Brody-
Wiener 154f.

In the Jewish community of a southern Black Forest village there was a
man named Mendele who, being a little feeble-minded, was cared for
by the community. One day he was in the square beside the synagogue,

busy woodchopping. The little synagogue stood, as is fitting, on the highest ground of the area, right up against the steep slope of the mountain on which the village lay. Now when a couple of lads coming along the path over the steep slope saw the fool down below, they had a bit of fun and called aloud: "Mendele!" Mendele looked up, but nothing could be seen. A while later they called again, this time from another spot: "Mendele! Mendele!" He looked up, confused. Again nothing. After awhile there is a third call: "Mendele, Mendele!" Then he throws down the axe, runs into the synagogue to the raised section in the middle where the Torah is read, stretches out his arms and as Abraham once did, calls out in Hebrew: "Here I am."

Man can call "Here I am," because the echo returns out of God's mouth. The poem longs, laments, atones and prays for this divine "Here I am" in twenty-three beats of its rhyme until the twenty-fourth, where the answer to the longing, lamenting, atoning and praying rhymes with it.

And the answer is not merely longed, lamented, atoned and prayed for: No, the divine answer must be so humanly spoken that in this poem a moment can arrive where the answer is demanded almost with a threat: "but when I suffer … ." The human heart has the inalienable right to deny again and again the great truth of Revelation, that suffering is a gift from God, whenever it becomes a theological schematization, as it does again and again, and to reinstate against this the primaeval position of nature. For this position suffering is suffering and nothing else. God answers only the word that rises out of the depth of all human powers, of the created as well as of the awakened.

On the translation: Stanza 1, lines 4f.: When You are my helper, / who could still get me to stumble? // When You bind me, / who, if not You, frees me? – Stanza 2, lines 4f.: God, enlighten me! / In Your Truth guide me! // And gently lead me / in judgment, and pronounce me free! – Stanza 3, line 1: "Ill luck!" is an addition. Lines 4f.: If some time old age / plucks me out, and my strength leaves me, // Then do not eradicate me, / my God! and do not abandon me. – Stanza 4, line 5: And surrounds me with darkness, so that … – Stanza 5, line 2: Purify my thinking, / that I might look upon Your Godhead.

SOUL / נשמת יפת עלמות

Brody III 43f.

This wholly tender, wholly floating, wholly soulful fantasy on the Song of Songs motif is meant to be read on the Sabbath of the week of Passover. It belongs to those metrically free pieces which assume more space, especially in scope, in the collected works of the poet than this selection shows. Even with regard to content this poem is conceived out of this freedom of the form. Because of its volatile movement it would be hardly thinkable in a bound metre. It is meant to be an introduction to the aforesaid Sabbath and Festival prayer "The Soul of all Living Things," the first word of which – just this "soul" – it sings five times as a prelude, and that is to say sings it in the grammatical form which in Hebrew is possible only immediately before a genitive.[7] But five times the genitive does not appear. Instead it holds itself evasively throughout the stanza, which builds itself up on the bittersweet non-resolution of that diminished seventh chord – until the sixth time where there is no longer any stanza, but finally the resolution: Soul of all Living Things – may she praise Your Name …

On the translation: Nothing to note.

SOUL IN EXILE / נפש לבית אב נכספה גם כלתה

Luz., Div. Nr. 57. Harkavy II 151f. Brody-Albrecht 98. Brody II 306.

The highly contrived form of this poem, which repeats the rhyming word of each couplet in the first word of the next couplet (only shortened to two syllables by omitting the silent "e" of the middle-syllable), has been transmuted by the poet from a technical feat into a spiritual vehicle of the small entity. The rhyme endings become only apparent endings from which, out of the similar sound beginnings, a new beginning, which was already concealed in them, directly unfolds. Thus there arises the characteristic impression of floating at the junctions of the couplets, through which the whole poem, apparently so formed, acquires something of a loosened breath structure. At the same time the centre of the whole poem, the transition from the third to the fourth couplet becomes a powerful focal point. At first there was a lamenting, pale, tormented backward glance, from couplet to couplet, to the bliss in God's mansion before birth, lost by the descent to earth: then after the nadir is reached, or rather immediately at this nadir, comes the reversal which, from the despairing consciousness of withering, achieves in a wonderful soaring (incomprehensible through logic, but absolutely authentic) the certainty of the new blossoming – a certainty not despite this withering but out of it. And from then on the tone changes, and the transitions of the couplets become proudly assured triumphal cries of a conqueror over life.

　　This lack of transition in this two-part poem – shocking to the "modern man's" need for gradualness – this change of mood, violently unfounded because at its profound depth powerfully founded, is the same as that which could be familiar to this modern man after all from countless Psalms, as long as his own experience knows nothing of it; if he did not prefer rather to cut these Psalms into two halves, and by attributing each to different authors, he then protects himself from the disconcerting experience of what can happen in a human soul.

On the translation: Line 4 "its foam vanished" is an addition; in the original the play on words with "dream" of the previous line is in "does not protect." Line 12, second half is an addition; in the original the doubling of "the band bound her" of line 11 through "she swore the oath" ["Schwur sie schwor"].

WITH YOU / ידעתני בטרמ תצרני

Luz., Div. Nr. 30. Harkavy II 85. Brody II 116f. Brody-Wiener 153.

For the Jewish poet there has been no previous need of Platonism in order to know what Isaiah knew (45:4)[27*] and the Psalmist (103:14 and 139:1),[28*] and what was said to Jeremiah (1:5)[29*] word for word when he was called, that God, even before a human steps into life, knew and loved him – Hebrew expresses both to know and to love in one word, which is untranslatable. This knowledge is a supporting base of human life, still more than even the hope for that which awaits us beyond the grave; for this hope is based only on that knowledge which has a certainty, that is confirmed in life itself. Every birthday confirms it. About this knowledge of the soul concerning its descent, my unforgettable teacher in Torah, Nehemiah Nobel, preached on his fiftieth and last birthday.

On the translation: The first four words attempt to bring out the double meaning of the "You knew me" which was just now pointed out in the Note.

27* Isaiah 45:4: For Ya'acov my servant's sake, and Yisra'el my elect, I have even called thee by thy name: I have surnamed thee, though thou hast not known me.

28* Psalm 103:14: For he knows our frame; he remembers that we are dust. 139:1 O Lord, thou hast searched me, and known me.

29* Jeremiah 1:5: Before I formed thee in the belly I knew thee; and before thou didst come out of the womb I sanctified thee, and I ordained thee a prophet unto the nations.

PRAYER / אדני יום לך אערך

Brody III 225f.

This litany – for that is what this piece is and wants to be – is intended
for the services of the New Year's Day as it judges souls. It is not composed for reading but for praying. He who reads it as one reads a poem
will find it monotonous and without development of thought, and
rightly so; one could also arrange most of the lines in another order
without it being noticeable. But it does not want to be read so but
rather each line for itself, as it is closed off by the double call. Each line
is a complete prayer, simple, and sufficient in itself. That these almost
similarly formed rings yet are arranged in a chain may not be grasped
by one who thinks that the soul must give lectures to God, and does
not know that the soul always has only one thing to say to Him, and
that one thing over and over again.

Yet the original text has an external, but not merely external, articu-
lation which the translation, however, could not render. Just as each
couplet begins and ends with the call to God, which since days of old –
already the Septuagint says "Lord" – is used as a veil for the unutter-
able divine name of revelation, so is this name itself hidden in its four
silent consonants [יהוה (yod, hay, vav, hay)] in the four stanzas: so that
the first word of each line that immediately follows the call always begins with the letter for the whole stanza, and the number of lines in
each stanza – 10, 5, 6, and again 5 – accords with the numerical value
of its letter.

What does the unutterability of God's name actually mean? A student friend of mine once came over after visiting a renowned re-
searcher on Humboldt[8] and related with every sign of horror: "And he
speaks of Frau Humboldt as Li!" Obviously here it is exactly as it is with
all other genuine theological problems: they are not theological problems. Names on the whole of course are utterable only under quite
specific conditions. It is dissonant with good tone and natural feeling,
in a conversation with three people, when one of them is essentially
taking part only by listening, to say the name of this one person; instead, the speaker will invite this one into the conversation, for a moment at least, and – address him. The name is thus in the presence of
the one who is named, not to be expressed but only to be addressed;
and this applies to every name. Every name stands originally in the vocative. Only when its bearer has left are the other cases possible. If the
name of someone present is expressed, without his being addressed,
then that person feels, at least in this moment, something like "placed
on the outside." God, however, never leaves; and the attempts to ex-

press His Name would make sense only as attempts to externalize Him.

But that is really the intention. At least with regard to the "old God of the Jews". Theological science pounced upon the quotation of the late Greek author which tells the "true pronunciation" of the Name of four consonants (among the Samaritans!) with a confidence and enthusiasm which it usually does not have to the same degree – which a scientific Protestant theologian would otherwise be permitted, to mention only the nearest at hand, to speak still of Jesus and Mary rather than of Yeshua and Miriam, of course with stressed final syllables. Not to mention that in the days when that science is in the habit of colloquializing most of the Bible's wording, the pseudonym had commonly occurred in place of the actual one, so that allowing for that time of origin, the favoured reading is roughly as scientific as if one were to publish Goethe's name each time in place of Hafiz' in the *Westöstlichen Diwan*, which, as is well known, is once even demanded of the rhyme.

That concealing thus has other reasons which only hide in the learned ass's skin. One would like to put out the old God of the Jews, one would like to make him into a departed, "dead God" in the same way that Zeus and Apollo, Baal and Astarte are dead for today's world. That is something very different from the old-Protestant naïveté that expressed the Name with the vowels from the transmitted Hebrew text vowels which were not intended as vowels of this Name at all, and which in Gellert and Klopstock sang "dir, dir, Jehova." That was genuine naïveté, which did not want to objectify the name but precisely to be as close as possible, eye-to-eye with it; only impossible in the way, as when a child has snapped up the given name of the mother and now tries to address the mother with this name that is impossible on his lips.

For of course it is only a matter of whether the name on my lips is an addressed name and not merely an expressed one. If the danger threatens it to become the latter, then I save myself in a new name which, spoken only between me and the addressed other, covers the original name. The first then becomes inexpressible to me, although it still shimmers through the second and is mutely spoken along with it; but the second becomes the actual name, as the address for the one who belongs to it. He who tries to retrieve the old name artificially, shuts himself out of the circle of those who belong.

One can explain this situation as name-magic and the like through subsequent rationalization. These are subsequent even when they come from the name-givers themselves. He who does not place such enormous value in differentiating himself from Blacks, as perhaps at any rate a German professor of philosophy must do, can discover in the names which are on his own lips and with which he addresses people nearest to and farthest from him, all primitivenesses, all the numinosities and fascinations [*Fascinositäten*] of the science of comparative religion.

But does God have a name? Are not all names here nothing but attempts to name the unnameable? Is one thus permitted to take any name, even if it is the name 'God' itself – for even this is a name, and today The Name – as seriously, that is, as being as real as the names that a human has? This is a very serious question.

But then does the human "have" his name? Is it not also only given to him? And does he have it elsewhere than on the lips of those who give it to him? Does his name have a reality other than – to be named? If Jehuda Halevi and the Judaism of the millennia address God with the familiar name of this poem [*Adonai*] through which the mysterious and ineffable shines, as is likewise quite clear in this poem, God is so called only when he is the living God and not a dead idol, really so as He is addressed. And when Shabbatai Zvi dares to force the arrival of the kingdom of heaven into this world by expressing the name according to its letters, his failure is shown plainly in this: that he can express only the vowels which do not at all have the meaning of giving the right pronunciation, and that thus the attempt to force ahead the end of Jewish world history fails for him exactly as for those today who try by saying the declared "scientific pronunciation" instead of "God", to get again out of the circle of this Jewish world history, which has already encircled them.

"But is God called the God of the world and of world history really just as Jehuda Halevi named him and you name Him?" – Is Frau v. Humboldt "called" Li?

On the translation: Third paragraph, line 12: "while He is gracious to all who yearn for Him."

HUMAN FRAILTY / מה תאמין בזמן אשר אין בו אמת

Luz., Div. Nr. 46. Harkavy II 149f. Brody II 300.

This small, thoroughly fleet and stirring reflection which moves from pure soliloquy into dramatization, indeed a two-act drama – and all this in three couplets – , leads to a wordplay that yet is more than play. For the derivative of the root "*schaffen*" [to create] which in its form lives a double life between an active and a passive possibility – Luther translates it with sense, thought, poetry, poetry and striving, something made – in its equivocal in-between position between creature and creator designates really most accurately of all the place of our own weakness. This lies precisely in the fact that we are strong, and that this strength breaks down only when it is called for. In this desperate experience that our own being [*Wesen*] ceases again and again to be our own, time, the faithless one, which we must nevertheless again and again trust, even through its faithlessness, teaches us that our work belongs to us as little as does our day.

So closely together do human strength and weakness dwell that the question of intentionality can actually be posed only in theory, only for the sake of abstract differentiation. Thus it is practical only in law where we seek to procure for concepts dominion over life. The criminal judge may try to define how much intention and how much diminished responsibility is involved in an act. But wherever the act is not subsequently analysed, but operates in its present totality, this apparently meaningful difference becomes meaningless. Thus first of all for the violated world order, which demands restitution through a healing counteraction – a counteraction which always must retain something symbolic because indeed there are only immediate acts and no "counteracts." Secondly, however, also before the divine grace which according to the great word of the Talmud, turns acts of intention into acts of madness.[9] And finally, most astonishing, even for the doer's own consciousness, which, when and because it is not permitted to face the deed, its own deed, with attempts at scientific analysis, but must face the deed, which for it is still present tense, a pressing, not disposed of, present tense, as an indivisible whole and which consequently cannot know where the consciousness has stopped and the confusion has begun. It must disdain for itself as an unworthy evasion the appeal to its own creatureliness, which its advocate puts forth for it loudly before God's throne – as does the poet of this poem.

On the translation: Nothing to note.

RETURN / אדני נגדך כל תאותי

Luz., Div. Nr. 52. Sachs 35f. Harkavy II 90ff. Brody III 226ff. Brody-Wiener 167f.

This poem does not look back to the origin, but out of the midst of life. It has been taken up in some places into the morning liturgy of Yom Kippur. Out of the midst of life which, here also, as in the famous Latin hymns, is encircled by death. Or, as the poet puts it: which can be death already in the midst of life. But also – and this is the expression particular to this poem – life still in the midst of death. This either-or of being distant from God and of being pressed close to him gathers all the energy into what lies between the two: the return to repentance. The end arises in ever new images before the eye: youth has gone by; the power of desires, of the world, which God Himself has put into the heart of the human, seems tremendous, invincible (Eccl. 3:11).[30]* The cloak of good works has fallen off. Man, naked and uncovered, can cover himself with no other righteousness than with that of God Himself. And thus the last word of his return can be none other than the one with which the return started, the word as that which came from his lips first and as the first. For this yearning is the fulfilment, as it was the void. This necessity for yearning becomes being allowed to yearn. Having found God is not the end, but rather itself a beginning. Seeking and finding are here differentiated not as present tense and perfect tense, but rather both are future tense, only the former a temporal future and the latter an eternal future. Both speak the word of yearning.

On the translation: Page 77 [62 in the original], lines 7f.: The "cups" as is "pincers"are additions. Lines 15f.: … ere / a part of me becomes heavy for the other part. Line 24: when finally shall I work for my house? – p. 63, lines 11f. in : Into wind they disperse one half of me, the other they will turn toward the dust.

REWARD / יקרה שכנה גויה

Luz., Div. Nr. 14. Harkavy II 139f. Brody-Wiener 154.

The third couplet of this little poem which makes the transition from the longing of the soul to the description of the reward that awaits her – in the original with the words with which the emissaries (Numbers 13:27)[31]* introduce the portrayal of the fruit of the land – encompasses a series of thoughts which are as self-evident to the poet as they are foreign to his readers of today.

Already the basic presupposition that the human may think at all of reward during his actions has been overcome by the people of today. The whole pride of the human takes refuge today in the citadel of the thought of the unrewarded action. From there, he looks down contemptuously on the "ethic of the Bible," unfortunately, of the New Tes-

30* Ecclesiastes 3:11: He has made everything beautiful in his time: also he has set the mystery of the world in their heart, so that no man can find out the work which God has made from the beginning to the end.

31* Numbers 13:27: And they told him, and said, We came to the land where thou didst send us, and indeed it flows with milk and honey; and this is the fruit of it.

tament no less than of the Old, the ethic which travels the same highway as the entirely unethical morality of the everyday, which demands honesty because it "lasts the longest," and cautions against "all too much," because it is "unhealthy." The relationship is undeniable. When the discrepancy with the philosophical ethic became all too unbearable for a pious thinker, one sought help with the concept of education, but from the standpoint of the strictly rewardless ethic, for which it may by a matter only of the attitude and not at all of the act, such education [*Erziehung*] would be only distortion [*Verziehung*]. But shouldn't there be a more profound reason for that meeting of the "ethic of the Bible" and of the immorality of the everyday? For what is the flat country called in which both meet each other far beneath the cloud citadel of ethics?

The plain into which the Bible moves, is the plain of experience. The warnings and counsels that healthy human understanding of the adage has to give, are nothing but experiences – from the golden foundation of crafts to the fall which follows pride. Just from this lowland of experience the philosophical ethic flees into its purer heights. Precisely into these lowlands does the Bible descend. And now of course experience, to which it points, includes not everything indiscriminately that the horizon of life encloses, as is the case with the moralistic world-experience of the adage, but only a small selected segment that to be sure has the tendency to keep expanding up – not to the horizon, but to the ends of the world. In other words: this experience is not simply the sum of accumulated experience, but given and promised experience. It is experience only for those who are aware of coming out of that gift and determined to come into that promise. To the others it is invisible. To these it is experience.

But it is a great thing that this experience has the same brutal reality as the experience of the everyday. So great a thing that surely it seldom occurs. For it can happen only when the human is wholly stretched out between that certainty and this determination. It is absolutely not suited for education. For it to happen, it demands people already educated – educated by life. Let everybody at some time ask himself whether it is really so easy to live in the certainty that every, but really every deed will have its consequences for the one who does it – not for "the world". Easier, really easier than in the certainty that only the deed that comes out of a good will – not: may be done; but: may be counted as good? What does this theory actually require other than to be accepted? Does it require a deed? Or does it not much rather warn caution about the deeds? From the Daimon of Socrates to the categorical imperative, to the rationality of the real, to the pathos of distance?

The second presupposition self-evident to the poet, but not self-evident to the reader, is the full equivalence of the "sensual" and the "spiritual" reward, of nectar and of wisdom. Here the poet seems to see as little a difference as does the Bible, for which what one calls today other-worldly and what one calls today worldly also hopelessly merges. Our concepts of That Side and This Side are Platonic; they are much too static; they make out of this and that world two essences existing side by side, whose chief difference to all practical purposes is that we believe in this world and not in that one. In the sense of that unfruitful differentiation the other world, promised by God and hoped for by man, is other-worldly as well as worldly: other-worldly, totally other-worldly compared to this world of today; worldly, totally worldly for us who await it. This world passes away when that one comes; we remain. What meaning does the question still have in the view of this certainty, whether it is "that-worldly" or "this-worldly" – a question which our Prophets and the Apostles of Christianity would not have understood at all. Give a hungry person a piece of bread – he will not ask whether it was baked with domestic or foreign flour.

But on this ground that final freedom has been able to grow up which, in the exuberance of God's love, already felt in the world of now, scorns the bliss of the future one, something *toto coelo* – really by a whole heaven – other than the arrogant Stoic scorn of the Kantians for reward, for here the loving one believes and knows that "an hour of bliss of the world to come is more than the whole of life in this world,"[10] and yet prefers the one hour of active nearness to God in this world to the whole life of the future world, from the utmost overflow of love, for which no future can any longer displace the entirely fulfilling present.

Such final blending of both worlds finds a boundary, however, and just at the point where people of today would gladly tear down the dividing-wall: in death. This is the third of those presuppositions which are contained in both lines. The day of "its separation" from the body, which – with still much greater wordplay in the original than in the translation – becomes the day when the soul feasts upon the "fruit of its belief"; this day does not cease to be a day, and is not displaced by any "being-eternal in every moment." What does prevent the poet from setting in the place of the day of separation this "being-eternal in the moment", which he nevertheless – many places in this poem indicate this – knows just as well as his modern readers and their guarantor?

Eternity can of course break into every moment, but what it then seizes is only just this moment. Life on the whole is contained in a few moments in such a way that it can grasp them in these moments.

At the moment of birth as a life ahead; in one or two moments during life as a decisive one; and in death as a perfected one. Thus, only in death as a real, "present" whole. This worldly reality has life only here, and to want here to withdraw it from the clasp of eternity would mean that life never would be allowed to be an experienced whole.

Of the things that happen in life we know something. Of death we know less and more, namely nothing and everything. Everything that it is for us the living, nothing of what it will be for us when dead. Knowledge of death from this side is our most precious possession and through every increment is augmented in genuine knowledge; he who does not respect the secret of that Nothing of our hither-side knowledge of death from the other side, but attacks it, with the fools who exist under changing names in every age, loses as a punishment even that genuine knowledge of the universe [*Allwissenheit*] that he has. Indeed there is a relation between that which from here can be much better known to us than anything, only because it is totally unknown from there. It is the same thing that we see from here entirely and from there not at all. What is true here, is also true there. But this certainty, which does not allow the foot to stumble when it nears the border that separates the all-known from the all-unknown, does not illuminate the darkness wherein the unknown lies.

On the translation: Nothing to note.

THIS SOUL HERE / לערוך שיר באנו ונעם צור לחזות

Luz., Div. Nr. 64. Harkavy II 100ff.

The soul is not a thing. On this truth all psychology runs aground, from Aristotle and Thomas to Häckel[11] and Wundt.[12] The appearance that it must nevertheless be a thing, "matter," "something," is raised up by the fact that, like things, it is "here." But things can, be "here" just as easily as they can also be "there." The soul can always only "be here." A soul "there," a soul in the third person – there is no such thing. The soul is always present – my soul, your soul, our soul, hence always: this soul here.

The poem, connected with the hymn of the morning prayer for the Sabbaths of the Festivals [i.e., Passover, Shavuot, Succot] "The Soul of All Living Things," turns to this matter of being here with an intensity that goes beyond the demands of art. In three of the six end-rhymes the poem rhymes the "this here" ["*diese hier*"] of the soul (Jeremiah

38:16)³²* with the "this here" [i.e. the "this here" of "Boden"; "Magd";
"Rebe"] of another biblical passage which can be seen in this connection as referring to soul. Thus the forms of the biblical women, a
Rachel, a Hagar rise up metaphorically in the place of the pearl that
has fallen from the divine throne, a pearl which now does menial service on earth, – "metaphorically" is already saying too much for this
mere singling out of the one expression "this here." Finally the expression finds its highpoint in the application to the soul of the psalmic
comparison of Israel with the vine (Psalm 80:15).³³*

On the translation: Stanza 1, lines 1f.: "The hands of the thought are
too short / to reach his wonder, // and for me too high are / the lofty
towers of his greatness."

ILLUSION AND TRUTH / ידועת אמונות דחי השקרים

Luz., Div. Nr. 29. Harkavy II 144f. Brody III 143.

But the soul does have one place, only it is not a place to which the finger can point, but rather an in-between. She moves, can be moved, between two poles, illusion and truth, world and service, masks and
countenance. Those are the three designations which indeed do not
"mean the same thing" at all – this favourite category of both scholarly
and popular metaphysics offends not merely the poet's healthy linguistic understanding, but also that of the one who speaks, of everyone
who speaks altogether – , but which lie in the same line of vision for
the soul which moves between them. By getting entangled in illusion,
it perseveres also in service and stands before the divine countenance.
The soul's "spiritually destined order", "bodily form", and "secret vision" are not one, but they coincide in this poetic life, whose oneness is
precisely a oneness [Einheit] of the before and after. Even in "olden
Jewish" life this oneness is only too often split apart.

On the translation: Line 2: "beneath flowers" is an addition. Line 8:
the world to the barbarians.

32*Jeremiah 38:16: So Zidqiyyahu [Zekediah] the king swore secretly to Yirm-
eyahu [Jeremiah], saying, As the Lord lives, that made us this soul, I will not
put thee to death, neither will I give thee into the hand of these men that
seek thy life.

33*Psalm 80:15: Return, we beseech thee, O God of hosts: look down from
heaven, and behold, and be mindful of this vine.

LADY WORLD / כנדה היתה תבל לפ

Luz., Div. Nr. 32. Harkavy I 58. Brody II 292.

This little poem, laden with enormous explosives, deals with the common medieval type of "Lady World". But neither his relation to woman
nor his relation to the world permits the Jewish poet, as does the medieval Christian master of word and image, to represent woman simply
and the world simply as temptress. He must specialize the image in
many ways so that it is in tune with Jewishness. The law [*Gesetz*] gives
him the means for such a specialization.

Not woman as temptress, but conjugal relations form the material
for the parables. The reciprocal disdain, which in the middle of the little poem uses the general, judiciously neutral word, "choice of mate"
separates in the corner-couplets into two images of quite specific relationships of the Jewish marriage law: in the introductory verse that falls
like a hammer blow, the physical impurity (Leviticus 15:19 ff),[34*]
which forbids to the husband any contact with the wife, and only to
him, but to him absolutely; in the concluding couplet that cuts like a
razor the ceremony (Deuteronomy 25:5 ff)[35*] with which the brother's
widow makes the brother-in-law, unwilling to marry her, despicable as a
"barefooter." Both are founded on a natural feeling, both are enormously intensified by the law. The one is intensified to a prescription
that rules half the time of married life far beyond the natural basis.
The other, from a natural reaction (shaped by the law) to a voluntary
act is intensified to a mere gesture that acknowleges receipt of the refusal now exactable and enforceable by tradition and law; and at the

---

34* Leviticus 15:19ff: And if a woman have an issue, and her issue in her flesh
be blood, she shall be seven days in her menstrual separation: and whoever
touches her shall be unclean until evening. 20 And everything that she lies
upon in her separation shall be unclean: everything also that she sits upon
shall be unclean. 21 And whoever touches her bed shall wash his clothes,
and bathe himself in water, and be unclean until evening.

35* Deuteronomy 25:5ff: If brothers dwell together, and one of them die, and
have no child, the wife of the dead shall not marry abroad to a stranger: her
husband's brother shall go in to her, and take her to him to wife, and perform the duty of a husband's brother to her. 6 And it shall be, that the firstborn which she bears shall succeed in the name of his brother who is dead,
that his name be not wiped out in Yisra'el. 7 And if the man like not to take
his brother's wife, then let his brother's wife go up to the gate to the elders,
and say, My husband's brother refuses to raise up to his brother a name in
Yisra'el, he will not perform the duty of a husband's brother.

same time, however, out of an individual situation, is intensified to a general norm. And both nevertheless in the framework of the sanctifying of marriage, grounded equally in law and tradition. Of an absolute sanctifying, not merely of one relative to "human weakness."

This is in all accuracy the Jewish relationship to the "world." It is full of asceticism and yet not at all ascetic. In principle it is even entirely unascetic. To the Jew the world is not the harlot enticing to sin, but the sanctified wife. But she has become "unclean", and the law extends the fence so widely around the abstention from idol worship until finally half the world is forbidden to the Jew. But what is allowed to him he should not "have, as if he did not have it", rather he should really have it. Innumerable foods are forbidden to him but those allowed he should enjoy, and for the Sabbath the Law commands heightened joy in the meal. And now the opening image must be abandoned as insufficient, for it does not adequately express the dramatic alternation of the disdain. The poem steers towards its concluding image: the world, despising its despisers; what was originally suffering out of a free personal act, martyrdom of the Prophet, now becomes accustomed, destined suffering from traditional and dutiful doing – Jewish destiny. Because, however, it is tradition, therefore it is no longer experienced as asceticism, but as the natural life that cannot be otherwise. The knowledge that the world "actually" belongs to him, for work and enjoyment, permits no ascetic mood to emerge in the face of all asceticism, but at most the defiant battle rhythm of this poem. Whereas the consciousness of the medieval Christian is full of asceticism and precisely for this reason in his life the ascetism occupies – and can occupy – only a very narrow, and moreover carefully, socially fenced off space.

On the translation: Nothing to note.

WISE TEACHINGS / לבי עמוד כי מי בסוד

Luz., Div. Nr. 10. Harkavy II 79ff. Brody II 218ff.

"Wisdom," to whom the poet has sworn allegiance, wisdom, however much it amounts to the "Be satisfied" on the whole which at all times was the self-imposed discipline precisely of passionate natures, has also its casuistry. Such a consequence of maxims lies before us here. One senses behind the content the rich possibilities, but also the dangers, which the Spanish soil with its countless small princely courts presented to the Jew at that time. The charm of this little didactic poem's form lies in its brisk rhythm, which strongly stresses the caesura right at the beginning through the inner-rhyme of the first line and thereby itself experiences, so to speak, an inner acceleration. The beauty of the content depends on the inclusion of moral rules of prudence in the trust in God (situated before all prudence) which finds an infinitely stirring, tranquil finale in the last couplet with its simple literalness of its Bible quotation that seems now to have lain dormant in the rhythm from the start.

On the translation: Lines 11 and 12: "Do not make yourself impertinent in the time of the dance and do not flinch in the time of lamenting." – Line 16: "Servants of servants you only serve." – Line 20: "to whom splendour and magnificence is due." – Line 24: "whatever friend and neighbour counsel."

SERVANTS / עבדי זמן עבדי עבדים הם

Luz., Div. Nr. 50. Brody II 300. Brody-Wiener 171.

"They are my slaves," says the Torah upon the establishment of the great freeing of the slaves in the fiftieth year and on the standardization of the rule which man exercises over his brother (Leviticus 25:42 and 55).[36*] Out of this source from which a good part, the best part, of all subsequent world history has flowed the poet has filled also the cup of this epigram, which begins quite epigrammatically as a tightly argued summary of all the disseminated moral wisdom which ever was to be known, and ends quite lyrically, with the Book of Lamentations' cry of longing (3:24)[37*] for the God of the heart.

On the translation: Nothing to note.

WORLD / לבבי מה תרדף הון ועשר

Luz., Div. Nr. 48. Harkavy II 150. Brody II 289.

With few words the little poem says the same as many another does with many. The word in which it captivates the object of its denial and which I have translated with "world," actually means: time. The reason why the poet does not say, as does for example his great inspiration, Ghazali, "world," is very noteworthy. In the language of the Bible the

36* Leviticus 25:42 and 55: For they are my servants, whom I brought out of the land of Mizrayim [Egypt]: they shall not be sold as bondmen. 55 For to me the children of Yisra'el are servants; they are my servants whom I brought forth out of the land of Mizrayim: I am the Lord your GOD.

37* Lamentations 3:24: The Lord is my portion, says my soul; therefore will I hope in him.

word which is later used for "world" means "eternity." In later language
of course "this" world and "that" world are differentiated, but "world"
pure and simple can assume no pessimistic meaning; the word is too
much filled with the meaning "eternity"; thus the word "time" must do,
which contains no value judgement in the language of the Bible, neither positive nor negative.

Scripture has gone into the world as a power of separation. Just on
that account it itself was not allowed to contain the final and most fundamental split which was meant to arise out of it. The cutting edge of a
knife may not itself be cut into two. Thus Scripture itself does not have
the schism of this and that world, which everywhere, even in Judaism,
opens up under its breath, (and which because both worlds are known
as equally real, is entirely different from the Greek "real" and "apparent" world). And just for this reason it is the guarantee that this opposite which it has called forth in the first place, is not final and that this
and that world are destined to come together once again in eternity,
out of which they have separated from one another.

Jehuda Halevi's poem is medieval, not biblical and not messianic. Of
course he who would be of the opinion that these Middle Ages [*Mittelalter*]
were today already superseded by a "New Age" would be sorely mistaken.
These Middle-Ages [*Mittel-Alter*] embrace the whole – world history.

On the translation: Besides the above still: Line 2: "... , which is twisted
and crooked?" – Line 4: "in the end may it happen that it becomes a
snare for him."

THE SICK DOCTOR / אלי ופאני וארפא

Luz., Div. Nr. 36. Harkavy II 87f. Brody II 294.

Jehuda Halevi was a doctor. That is why he is free from that faith in any
miraculous power of the medical arts, a faith to which even he submits
helplessly as soon as he himself becomes sick, who in healthy days cannot mock "the doctors" enough. Free from that superstition, he can
therefore sense all the more strongly the relationship between healing
[*Heil*] and redemption [*Heilung*], which in German the language already indicates and which Jeremiah's words mean (17:14).[38*]

On the translation: Line 6: it is according to Your discernment, what is
bad, what good.

38*Jeremiah 17:14: Heal me, O Lord, and I shall be healed; save me, and I
shall be saved: for thou art my praise.

TO THE SABBATH / עַל אַהֲבָתְךָ אֶשְׁתֶּה נְבִיעִי

Harkavy II 126f.

This Sabbath song, which Nobel sang at the family table to a marvellous melody that he had composed, belongs in the "Soul" section. With this its originality is marked among the Sabbath songs, even those of Jehuda Halevi himself, which otherwise would all belong in this collection's "People" section, or perhaps even in the "God" section. Hebrew Sabbath poetry is marvellously objective. The subjective, the Sabbath, goes without saying, which, as the ancients certainly also knew, "is given to man" (not merely man to the Sabbath). The Lurianic *Kabbala* was the first to develop the forms in which this subjective side comes into its objective right. But Jehuda Halevi's song paves its own way for itself and wholly by itself. It deals with man and with his Sabbath – no, it does not deal with, it speaks to the Sabbath and grasps the simplest, the primeval phenomenon, in the fact of the Seventh Day, which here is not somewhat polemically turning it against the celebration of the first and the sixth days, but is quite simply looking at them. Because the Sabbath is the seventh day, the week leads up to it; the days become "single hours," as for the Patriarch Jacob the seven years of service for Rachel became single days – "so had he loved her." In five stanzas this inner rhythm of the week is caught up in the mirror of the soul. Then the sixth stanza empties into the wonderful comparison with the prescription for the "seven days of the banquet," the seven-day wedding celebration during whose length the whole "seven blessings" of the marriage ceremony may always be newly repeated in the blessing at the table when new guests, "new faces" in the language of the Law, join at the table: thus the Sabbath is welcomed as a "new face," like a bride, but not as guest, rather himself as the always new groom, the beloved of the soul. And thus the poet drinks to the Sabbath the cup of love in this song, which nowhere departs from the immediacy of the address, of I and You.

On the translation: Stanza 6, line 2: "to look upon the face of the Sabbath as upon a new face" (compare what is said in the Note).

FREE / עֶבֶד אֲשֶׁר יָעִיר לְשַׁחְרֶךָ

Luz., Div. Nr. 49. Harkavy II 89f.

And still, as late as it was understood in mystical thinking, the Sabbath in its origins was already the day of the soul. Already the opening

words which celebrate it, in the community in the evening, at home in
the morning, as the sign of creation between God and Israel (Exodus
31:16f),[39] use a strange word for the portrayal of the divine rest of the
Creator, which even if it originally may mean the sigh of relief, nevertheless for the mature linguistic feeling makes the Sabbath the day
when the human comes to his self, to his soul.

This triad of freedom, blissful sigh of relief, perfecting of the soul's
coming to itself, now shapes the fundamental chord of the poem into
the three rhyme-endings of the three couplets. But it also shapes the
fundamental chord of the Sabbath itself from which no note can be
omitted without destroying the harmony. Should one like to play off
the "social" meaning of the command of the Sabbath, as the formulation of the fifth Book of Torah [Deuteronomy] emphasizes it, against
the "religious" meaning of the second Book [Exodus], our poem demonstrates the folly of such a risky undertaking with its joining of the
first and third couplets through that blissful word [*Ruhtag*] which,
taken from the Rest of the Most High, yet is applicable to the sigh of
relief of the servant (Exodus 23:12)[40]. Each separation of the "social"
from the "religious," or the reverse, makes the social an eternally open
question, the religious an ever ready answer. The separation deprives
that question of the healing power of recurrent possibilities of answers,
and deprives this answer of the verification of recurrent possibilities of
being questionable. The freedom of the servant is devoid of content if
it is not freedom of the master; the freedom of the master is unreal if it
does not transform into freedom of the servant. For each is master and
each is servant.

On the translation: Line 3: For "the son of Your might" the corresponding play on words of the original has only "Your truth."

SABBATH MORNING / יפית יחידה בעודך בי

Luz., Div. Nr. 25. Harkavy II 141f.

---

[39] Exodus 31:16f: Wherefore the children of Yisra'el shall keep the sabbath,
to observe the sabbath throughout their generations, for a perpetual covenant. 17 It is a sign between me and the children of Yisra'el for ever: for in
six days the Lord made heaven and earth, and on the seventh day he rested,
and was refreshed.

[40] Exodus 23:12: Six days shalt thou do thy work, and on the seventh day thou
shalt rest: that thy ox and thy ass may rest; and the son of thy handmaid,
and the stranger, may be refreshed.

A soliloquy of the one praying with his "unique one" – so the Psalmist (22:21 and 35:17)[41*] calls his own soul – about the "mystery of time": the alternation between work and rest, which the Sabbath brings to the soul in its rhythm of every seven days and which at the same time is intended – this is the mystery – to be more than rhythm of the soul: a prognostic sign of the way of the world.

On the translation: Nothing to note.

LIFE / יהידה יחדי נא אל אמונה

Luz., Div. Nr. 33. Harkavy II 143ff.

The one acknowledges the One – Hermann Cohen referred to this poem in his great defence when he proclaimed to his students his mature perception of the necessary "transgression" from "ethics" to "religion," the perception that before the Unique God even man becomes unique, one, alone. This poem is again a soliloquy of the human with his soul. Just as the prayer leader knows himself as authorized by the community to pray for the people and to lead their prayers – whence after all this whole genre of short introductory poems without stanzas has its name for the prayerleaders: authorizations – so, just so, should souls speak when entering for and before man, the unique ones to the Unique. And as the employer tells the deputy first the meaning and content of the office in lofty words, but then descends easily into those words of the service and its demands, so likewise here. But with a slight motion this deputy eludes the pedantic demand. The deputy does not need authorization, it has full powers. Full powers from elsewhere, from above, from the homeland, out of which the soul, an alien guest – what wonder that to an earthly eye it seems to dream, just when it is most awake! (Ezekiel 5:2)[42*] – , sank down into this world of flesh and of death.

Of death. It and the brevity of earthly existence, with which the warning speech of man wanted to drive it to its duty, thus do not frighten it: the soul awaits precisely for the call which will be for it a

41*Psalm 22:21; 35:17: Deliver my life from the sword; my only one from the power of the dog. 35:17: Lord, how long wilt thou look on? rescue my soul from their destructions, my only one from the lions.

42*Ezekiel 5:2: Thou shalt burn with a fire a third part in the midst of the city, when the days of the siege are fulfilled: and thou shalt take a third part, and smite about it with the sword: and a third part thou shalt scatter to the wind; and I will draw out a sword after them.

call to come home. The soul was death-bound in life; but on the stone, under which its body is hidden, sheltered, the word will be written: Let soul be tied into the skein of life.

Of life. At this point – the transition from the ninth to the tenth couplet – , in the Hebrew even given prominence through the opening jubilant cry of the acrostic of the name, this time not to be reproduced in its division into three which organizes the whole poem, – at this point then the speech of the soul, oddly strange from the start, begins to shed completely the answer form. These last six lines of the poem are entirely a floating away of immediate – I might say musical – power. Indeed, more accurately, with its unceasing repetitions of the same motif, following one after the other more and more closely, rising more and more exuberantly, and sounding more and more ethereal, more and more distant it is reminiscent of the vanishing finales of some of Beethoven's slow movements. The ever repeated motif is just the word "life." From its first appearance in the quotation of the burial speech until the end, the original has twenty-two words; six of these, that is almost every third word, are words of life. Of ever intensified, ever more rapturous, ever calmer certainty.

Such certainty, however, which in earthly life is itself only a weak, flickering little flame, which threatens at every moment to be extinguished – and yet never goes out, all the same derives its whole nourishment from this earthly life, from that which is in him, in life – is life. Because, in the double meaning of this word, earth and heaven touch each other, and because that epitaph full of supra-terrestrial hope, is said in its Biblical place of origin (1 Samuel 25:29),[43*] in a terrestrial way, because therefore not merely I live, today and here, but also "my Saviour lives" (Job 19:25),[44*] and because a soul knows itself to be thought of and considered (Psalm 115:12),[45*] today and always, here and there, for these reasons the soul is also certain of its further blessing, today and always, here and there, because – He lives. And thus the call "Life!", "To Life!", "Into Life!", with which we intend to greet earthly life (1 Sam.25:6)[46*] now becomes permission for the soul to

---

43* 1 Samuel 25:29: Though a man rises to pursue thee, and to seek thy soul: yet the soul of my lord shall be bound in the bond of life with the Lord thy GOD; and the souls of thy enemies, them shall he sling out, as out of the hollow of a sling.

44* Job 19:25: For I know that my avenger lives, and that he who outlives all things, will rise when I shall be dust.

45* Psalm 115:12: The Lord has been mindful of us: he will bless us; he will bless the house of Yisra'el; he will bless the house of Aharon.

46* 1 Samuel 25:6: and thus shall you say to him: "A hearty greeting! Peace be both to you, and peace to thy house, and peace be to all that thou hast.

enter into the "community of the souls of His pious ones." These "still"
live, in the secret lap of life – because the call acclaims Him who is
alive, today and always, here and there – now for the third and last and
final time this is expressed through one of the sad utterances of the
Preacher (Ecclesiastes 4:2):[47*] the praise of the dead and of the ones
not yet born, before those who are "still" alive, the turn from the Today
and Here into the There and Always! – they "still" live.

On the translation: Line 7: Drive away grief before joy, ... Line 20: ...
I, concealed in darkness. Lines 22ff.: and so "to Life!" to the living God
the sound of rejoicing / the community of souls of his pious ones will
prepare / in the secret of life, as those who are in life – still.

THE DAY / לקראת מקור חיי אתן מנמתי

Luz., Div. Nr. 56. Harkavy II 97. Brody III 118.

A glance out of the life of time into the life of eternity which breaks at
the wall that is erected between the two, on the day of death, and
which taking up his position here surveys both worlds from this water-
shed in a threefold great opening of the eye.

On the translation: Nothing to note.

RETURN, RETURN! / שׁוּבִי נפשׁי למנוחיכי

Sachs 33f. Brody III 35f. Brody-Wiener 156.

The poet developed not only the end-rhyme of the five stanzas and the
rhythm of the whole out of the seventh verse of Psalm 116, but the
content as well (Psalm 116:7).[48*] The rhymed couplet at the beginning of his poem is word for word as that verse stands written. The
word for turning around and homecoming [Um-und Einkehr: return
and introspection] to the peace of the certainty that God has already
made for him, for which his heart still rages, calls forth the image of
life's journey, which now becomes a journey home. Like the Patriarchs
(Genesis 23:4)[49*] the soul is only a stranger and a sojourner on earth,

---

47* Ecclesiastes 4:2: So I praised the dead that are already dead more than the
living that are yet alive.
48* Psalm 116:7: Return to thy rest, O my soul; for the Lord has dealt bounti-
fully with thee.
49* Genesis 23:4: I am a stranger and a sojourner with you: give me a possession
of a buryingplace with you, that I may bury my dead out of my sight.

but the homeland is promised to it. And the conclusion of the last stanza in its first word picks up again, in precisely that "return", the first word of the opening verse of the Psalm and announces fulfilment. It does this with its change of meaning of the rhythmical call of the wedding guest to the dancing bride of the Song of Songs (7:1)[50*] into the call to the soul to turn and come home – and "Sulamit," who has "found peace" (8:10),[51*] is the festive soul.

On the translation: Pre-stanza, line 1: "… to your rest." – Stanza 4, line 4: "Consider what you say to your Master!"

THE ASCENT / שׁוּבִי אֵל מְנוּחֵךְ שׁוּבִי   שׁוּבִי יְהִידָה אֵל מְנוּחֵךְ שׁוּבִי

Luz., Div. Nr. 5. Harkavy II 139. Brody II 217.

The meaningful word of return opens this little poem as well, but here it is set in the key that could conclude the previous great poem. Here soul is not first the restless wanderer, but right away the ascending one, indeed the ascended, the conqueress – God's daughter, who worships among God's sons.

On the translation: Line 4: …, you took booty.

BREATH OF ALL LIFE / שֵׁם אֱלֹהִים אוֹדֶה בְּשִׂיחִי

Luz., Div. Nr. 63. Harkavy II 98ff.

May this great hymn, also composed for the prayer "The Soul of Every Living Thing," serve as the conclusion of the songs about the soul. The poem's circular rhyme picks up its opening words almost literally. For the hymn contains almost everything that the individual poems of this section have sung: the longing for a vision of God while still in the flesh and their certainty of the day of separation from these limbs; the heavenly origin of the soul and her desire to go home to her source; the submission of her secrets to the law court of the Judge; and finally

---

50* The Song of Songs 7:1: Return return, O Shulammite; return, return, that we may look upon thee. What will you see in the Shulammite: as it were the dance at Mahanayim.

51* The Song of Songs 8:10: I was a wall, and my breasts were like towers: then was I in his eyes as one who finds content.

the deeply moved and moving words in which the poet humbly returns to this people his special position in relation to his people, precisely that of the poet, without denying it, and wraps himself, as into a prayershawl, into the new folds [*Kinderschaft*] of the covenant that envelops him and everyone. Now follow the songs of the People.

On the translation: Transposed compared with the original are Stanza 1, lines 1 and 2; Stanza 3, lines 4 and 5; Stanza 5, lines 4 and 5. – Stanza 1, line 2: "The hand of God, the master of all, high, lofty." – Stanza 3, line 5: "That my speech might drip" (that is "like the rain," Deut. 32:2). – Stanza 4, line 5: "And from heaven he looks upon my paths." – Stanza 5, line 4: "Proclaim Your Name to my brothers."

IN ETERNITY / שמש וירח לעולם שרחו

Luz., Div. Nr. 61. Harkavy I 72. Brody II 307.

Thus saith the Lord, who gives the sun to the day for light and the moon and the stars to the night for light according to their orbit, who stirs the sea so that its waves roar, Lord of Hosts (Zeboath) is his name: When such patterns depart before me, saith the Lord, then also will the seed of Israel end, so that it will no longer be a people before me eternally. Thus saith the Lord: When heaven above can be measured and the foundation of the earth can be fathomed, then shall I also reject the entire seed of Israel for all that they do, saith the Lord.

Jeremiah 31:35–37.

On the translation: Nothing to note.

GOD SPEAKS / יאמץ לבבך ומעדך יחלי

Luz., Div. Nr. 27. Harkavy I 57f.

Hope is the power that permits eternal life. God himself summons Israel to hope in this poem, which could not appear in the Bible, for it is filled with a certainty that only a thousand years of exile could make ripe in this way. Hope has now become the "greatest;" it has imbibed the powers of love into itself. The poem expresses this secret of Judaism in plain terms, that love here has become the hope of redemption – "You love most beautifully hoping for Him Who redeems you."

It is a hope not because of but in spite of everything. A hope whose end it is forbidden to reckon – for each reckoning has elapsed –; a hope which still hears out of the shame-prophecy of the Prophet

(Ezekiel 23)[52*] the proud "My sanctuary in her" contained in the name of the female form of Oholibah [Jerusalem] which symbolizes Israel's immorality; a hope which, with the Midrash on Jacob's answer (Genesis 33:14)[53*] to the rash brother, senses the historical irony of him who walks slowly and still reaches his goal in the end; a hope which knows well how fragile its bearer is and how yet just at the breaking point the immortal powers of renewal also dwell in him. It is a hope which has the courage to set the Heavenly King against all the earthly kings.

On the translation: Line 1: "May your heart be strong and hope for your day." – Line 4: "For Oholibah is Your Name and ..." – Line 6: "... and move away."

FESTIVAL OF LIGHTS / יחד באורך אל נאור

Luz., Div. Nr. 70. Harkavy II 9ff.

This song is dedicated to the Sabbath of the winter Festival of Lights. It takes its images from the prophetic passage of this day: of the priest, first soiled and then dressed in clean garments; of the call to grace; and of the two olive trees (Zechariah 2:14-4:7). From the breadth of Scripture it takes the symbolism of Light: of God and of man; of the primordial creation; and of the final redemption. From the depth of the people's consciousness it takes this world-encompassing symbolism of light fused with national liberation and purification that the Festival celebrates. For the lights, whose oil seemed to be almost gone, yet which then lasted in a miraculous in-spite-of-that, these lights, around which the tradition of the Festival revolves, might rightly mean to the people during these eight days the divine light of the Psalm (36:10),[54*] where it may look upon its own light of life and destiny.

On the translation: Stanza 3, lines 3f.: "and may you bless / the seed of the pious ones on the day when you curse, ..."

52*Ezekiel 23 concerns the rebuking and reproaching of Samaria's harlotrous dealings with the Assyrians, and Jerusalem's like dealings with Babylon.

53*Genesis 33:14: Let my lord, I pray thee, pass over before his servant: and I will lead on slowly, according to the pace of the cattle that goes before me and the children, until I come to my lord to Se'ir.

54*Psalm 36:10: For with thee is the fountain of life: in thy light we see light.

MORNING SERVICE / כל כוכבי בקר לך ישירו

Luz., Div. Nr. 45. Harkavy II 89. Brody-Albrecht 100. Brody-Wiener 154.

One of those little poems that are intended for the prayer-leader in communal worship as an introduction to the customary morning-prayer, something like Bach's Preludes for the organists before the chorale. The small praying community in the first dawn, surrounded by tranquility, but around this in a worldwide distance are two huge circles, the circle of the stars and the circle of the angels, and from all three the same song of praise, – Israel the lonely centre of the world, whose song [*Laut*] the heavens echo.

On the translation: Nothing to note.

LIGHT / יומם ולילה הלל לאדני

Luz., Div. Nr. 34. Harkavy II 87. Brody III 74f. Badisches Gebetbuch 372.

Israel can be the centre of the universe because the line of world time goes through its centre. This centre, however, in the poem in question is shown also as a point. In the remarkable verse where the poet replies to God's crushing question to Job (38:24): "In which way does One Light divide itself into the world?", instead of the crushed "I do not know," he gives that meekly yet boldly trusting answer which dissolves the mystery of creation in the command of revelation: This mysterious way of the original Light – it can be none other than the one which You have determined for me as my way. And thus in these ten lines, through which all the light of heaven and earth streams, the line can be drawn from the luminosity of the divine countenance to the reflection of this luminosity in the human countenance; this line, which leads from the original light of creation and the created lights over flashing Sinai to the eyes of the one praying during the Festival of Revelation [Shavuot], to which the poem belongs, is – One Light.

On the translation: Nothing to note.

CONQUERED DARKNESS / יונת אלם צקי לחשך

Luz., Div. Nr. 66. Harkavy II 63f.

The relation of the creation of light and the renewal of the expiring light of the people, the people whose sanctuary stands grounded on

the world's foundation-stone, is an inexhaustible topic. Here it is un-
furled from the concept and rhyme-word of darkness [*Finsternis*]. For
into the passage of the morning prayer for which this poem is intended, as most of its kind are, there enters also Isaiah's great word
(45:7),[55*] of the God who creates the light and darkness. The poem
revolves around this And.

On the translation: Stanza 1, lines 1 – 5: "Dove of silence, pour out
your whispers, / you defeated one in the dwellings of Meshech, / and
raise your soul to God, / your banner, horse and rider! / Who lets the
light of your sun rise," – Stanza 3, line 5: "... and they confessed to
their Creator and knew:"

ON REED SEA DAY / יגילון באור מזרחך יום חילך

Luz., Div. Nr. 20. Harkavy II 82f. Brody III 42.

Light, the light of the sunrise and the joy of the creation of the morning stars (Job 38:7)[56*] surges also around the edges of this poem,
which belongs to the Passover day on which the passage is read out
about the drowning of the Egyptian pursuers in the Reed Sea and Israel's song of triumph. Its inner lines however are filled entirely with
today's prayers of the multitude to whom the miracle once happened.
They know themselves in its shadows and as its lasting property, yet in
whose transitory world they are the poor and the suffering ones. They
know the synagogue with its divine authority and divine word as the legal owner of the site of the former and the future sanctuary, the "Little
Temple," as it is called in connexion with the talmudic interpretation
of a passage in Ezekiel (11:16). Still more: they know themselves in oppression and obscurity as the promised Messiah, Isaiah's servant of
God, whose world-atoning suffering and world-redeeming magnificence the poet understood as Israel's destiny also in his philosophical
work, as have so many from times of old right up to Hermann Cohen.
And because the people preserve in this knowledge the connexion of
the millennia, they may wait for the last miracle, which they implore,
quite simply as a parable of the first, the original miracle, which this
day as every day brings home to it. For the last miracle will of course be

---

55* Isaiah 45:7: I form the light, and create darkness: I make peace, and create
    evil: I, the LORD do all these things.
56* Job 38:7: or who laid its cornerstone; when the morning stars sang togeth-
    er, and all the sons of GOD shouted for joy!

greater than the first, but not different. The God of world-renewal is Israel's God of old.

On the translation: Line 4 "heavy load" and line 10 "out of the night"
are additions.

MY KING / יפעת מלכי חרא ותגל

Brody-Albrecht 106f.

But because God will rejuvenate the world, He is Himself therefore
eternally young. Thus the people see Him with Scripture and interpretation "with black locks on the day of the battle." Thus – in lines of
four-syllables, and in every case a five-syllable line as the fanfare of the
stanza's conclusion – the poet sings, with the flourish of jubilation of
this hymn, of the appearance and the manifestation of the beauty of
his King.

For this is at the same time source and mouth of all Jewish faith in
the Messiah: that after all God Himself is the Redeemer, "He Himself
and no other". It may also carry the Davidic king on its waves between
the source and mouth of the river of hope, indeed in its final widening, the entire suffering and exalted people. All this could still be
mythology – and because aimed towards the future, it is therefore
uncontrollable, but no better than a mythology attached to the past –
without that, without the transmission, never forgotten, of all messianic expectations to the only sure "King, Helper, Redeemer, Shield."

He Himself is the One who now – first stanza – will raise the banner
of redemption, the One who – second stanza – carries out the Prophets' proclamation of punishment on Babylon and – third stanza –
sends out the glad messenger of the approaching salvation to the other
city, to Jerusalem. The same One who – concluding stanza – in the
original gift of light and lights gave to the creation sign and guarantee
of all future redemption, as it is called up in these "Songs of Light" of
the morning prayer. The "Arise, let there be light!" of the joyful messianic message (Isaiah 60:1)[57*] becomes the renewal of the "Let there
be light!" – of the word of the first creation.

Meanwhile, between the light-invoking divine words of the beginning and of the end of days, stands the human being. He is not forgotten, for all God's might; indeed it is the whole meaning of the belief in
the Messiah that he is not forgotten. For the Messiah, whose royal pro-

---

57* Isaiah 60:1: Arise, shine; for thy light is come, and the glory of the LORD
    is risen upon thee.

cession surrounded by the host of armies, the glad messenger tells us
to behold, is indeed wholly a man. So very much a man, although yet
Son, begotten today (Psalm 2:7)[58*] that his "Path of Light" caught
sight of by his Father Himself can only be a path to the light. The life
of David (2 Samuel 11 – 19), precisely in this his return from guilt,
blindness and outrage through the divine atonement of the most painful House-and-Throne-Battles, becomes the turning point for the re-
covery in the crossing of the Jordan at Gilgal (2 Samuel 19:41).[59*]
That day brings the awareness to the humiliated one who was just now
(19:22),[60*] for the first and only time in his history addressed as Messiah, the awareness that now finally in truth he is "King over Israel"
(19:23),[61*] and out of this consciousness of divine forgiveness brings
the strength to forgive his greatest enemy in whose curses the divine
curse had been personified for him – this life just in its quite human
reversal becomes the model for the messianic King. For he may now
ride on a donkey or come with the clouds of heaven, and he may await
his hour as an unrecognized beggar, or in the cave guarded by Elijah
himself, this One [Ein: i.e., man with his sins] and Two-fold one [Dop-
pelte: i.e., man with God] is knowledge, certainly above all prophecy
and interpretation: man in and out of his sins, and not otherwise, is
called to be a work-partner of God; and God Himself is the true and
only Redeemer.

On the translation: Stanza 1, line 1: The beauty of my king / may appear and become visible, line 3b: and may he banish the one who ban-
ishes, – Stanza 2, lines 1f.: See, he makes / the city (Is. 25:2) a heap of
stones. // Suddenly a messenger comes / to gather the gleaning! [zu
lesen die Lese] – Stanza 4, line 1: … of light, line 3: blotted out his
wickedness, / then he returned to his Lord.

58* Psalm 2:7: I will tell of the decree: the LORD has said to me, Thou art my
   Son; this day have I begotten thee.
59* 2 Samuel 19:41: Then the king went on to Gilgal, and Khimham went on
   with him: and all the people of Jehuda conducted the king, and also half
   the people of Yisra'el.
60* 2 Samuel 19:22: But Avishay the son of Zeruya answered and said, Shall not
   Shim'i be put to death for this, because he cursed the Lord's anointed?
61* 2 Samuel 19:23: And David said, What have I to do with yuou, you sons of
   Zeruya, that you should this day be a hindrance to me? shall there any man
   be put to death this day in YUisra'el, for do not I know that I am this day
   king over Yisra'el?

OUT OF DISTRESS / יעבור עלי רצונך

Luz., Div. Nr. 21. Harkavy I 57. Brody-Wiener 169.

When one seeks to reject the Jewish people's uniqueness through the frontdoor of reason, it forces a re-entry through the backdoor of faith in paroxysms of hatred of the Jews (which has never taken on greater forms than it has in the last hundred and twenty years, when one seeks to explain the Jew as totally ordinary). This uniqueness consists in the fact that this people see themselves just as they are seen from the outside. The whole world names the Jewish race [*Stamm*] rejected and chosen; nd the race itself, instead of opposing the words of the others, confirms them. Only that the thing assumes from without the form of an external correlation [*Zusammenhang*], that is, of an outer- and therefore of an historical-succession. Whereas from within an inner inseparability is experienced and the cups of the curses and of the blessings are related to one another in such a manner that they can only overflow into one another, if ever one is full to the brim.

On the translation: Line 10: "And I am yet the young plant of your right hand!" – Line 12: "… from your heavenly dwelling!"

TO THE REDEEMER / יונה נשאתה על כנפי נשרים

Luz., Div. Nr. 74. Harkavy I 64ff. Brody-Albrecht 112f.

This mournful song has been included in the countries of Polish ritual as a redemption hymn in the liturgy of the last Sabbath during the time of sadness between the Festivals of Freedom and Revelation [Passover and Shavuot]. This is owing to its refrain, taken, even though with a shift in meaning, word for word from the Book of Ruth (4:4),[62*] which is read on the Festival immediately following this Sabbath. Or, actually, not really with a shift in meaning; for the people's cry of despair for their only Redeemer is meant no less earnestly and immediately and really than Boaz' words to Ruth's next-of-kin who is dutybound to redemption payment. The earnestness and the importance

---

62* Ruth 4:4: And I thought to advise thee of it, saying, Buy it in the presence
   of the inhabitants, and in the presence of the elders of my people. If thou
   wilt redeem it, redeem it: but if thou wilt not redeem it, then tell me, that I
   may know: for there is none to redeem it besides thee; and I am after thee.
   And he said, I will redeem it.

of the concept of justice weighs on and binds also the Jewish concept
of redemption, which has absolutely nothing of sky-blue, or only the
sky-blue of a beautiful summer day, that arches over a green earth.

In form, the hymn belongs to those that are metrically free; yet the
original develops a certain metrical bond in that most of the verse-
halves contain only two words, that is, two strong-stressed syllables.
Through the rhyme arrangement a further bond comes up which at
the same time is carried through not as strictly as elsewhere. Word-
plays, remote allusions to the Bible then bracket the externally looser
shapes from within, so that a certain approach to the "*Piutim*" [hymns]
of the other (older and younger) branch of our poetry emerges, to the
Italian-Polish-German school which has come out of the great name
Kalir. In any case, poems of this kind are somewhat less foreign to the
Jews of today who are at home in the tradition than those strictly metrical ones which constitute the particular fame of the Spanish school.

The mournful underlying tone of this poem is also greatly determined by the fact that the Scriptural word, with which each stanza
ends and with which the refrain therefore rhymes, obtains this rhyme
either from the word for grave and underworld or from forms of the
word "*bitten*" [to ask (for)], which sounds similar to this word. Thus the
cry for redemption here really rises up out of the depths of the grave.

On the translation: Stanza 1, line 6: Yet she in secret – ...; line 7: instead of the enemy: of the son of Dishan and Dishon (Gen. 36:20). –
Stanza 2, line 2: for Mizza and Shammah (Gen. 36:17) ... it; lines 3f.:
"suitor" as well as "consecration" and "horns" are additions; lines 5f.:
My tent: a temple of idols for Ahalibama (Gen. 36:41)! And Ahaliba
(Is. 23:4) what can she still hope and how much! Stanza 5, line 4: ...
into my dwelling and my innermost sanctuary.

EXCURSUS: AN ARTISTIC PLAY ON WORDS
קוראים בלבב שלם /

Luz., Div. Nr 76. Harkavy I 67f. Brody III 63.

You should implore from ardent hearts
so that Jerusalem may be called blessed.

I cried for years and bore suffering
Between snake's poison and deceit.
I found no pasture, I never set up
A camp. Bestow Your compassion upon me.
Waft away my woe lightly like a dream.

Lord, make my step steady,
Build anew my stronghold,
Enemy's people, a celebration for me, You
Avenger, strain Your strainer,
And my jewel, may it be mine anew.

And on guard in the night and greyness
I watch out for my oppressor, trembling.
Put him straight who trusts in idols!
That which makes him full of himself,
Consecrate to a scorching flame.

Snatch Your people from death's gate,
Already they do not ask, silly fools,
When the day of salvation will come, whose glory
Will feed the hungering heart with bliss.
As if it does not spew its guilt.

As a banner may Your salvation lead us,
Your people – gather them forever and ever.
Oh, that He would come down again,
The One Who snatched the enemy in the dark,
Let Him plant anew the bough on Zion.

Flehen ihr aus Herzen heiß
Sollt, dass Salem selig heiß'.

Jahre schrie und Leiden trug
Zwischen Schlangengift und -trug.
Weide fand nicht, Lager schlug
Nie ich. Mir dein Mitleid leih's,
Weh mein Weh weg traumgleich leis.

Herr, den Schritt mir feste du,
Neu bau meine Feste du,
Feinds Volk, mir zum Feste, du
Rächer, deine Seihe seih's
Und mein Kleinod, mein neu sei's.

Und in Acht in Nacht und Grau
Hab ich meine Dränger, grau
Mich. Zurecht, wer Bildwerk trau',
Weis! womit er groß sich weiß,

Weiß ergluehnden Flammen weih's.

Dein Volk reiß aus Todes Tor.
Schon fragts nicht, ein blöder Tor,
Wann der Heilstag komm', des Glor
Hungernd Herz mit Wonne speis'.
Als ob seiner Schuld nicht spei's.

Als Panier dein Heil uns führ',
Dein Volk – samml' es für und für.
O daß neu hernieder führ',
Der den Feind in Dunkel reiß',
Neu auf Zion pflanz' das Reis.

That which breaks out in many of these poems – very powerfully especially in the previous hymn "To the Redeemer" – rules this piece absolutely: the joy in wordplay, more accurately, the similar sounds in
words with different meanings. It is surprising that such artistry has not
proven much more offensive; one cannot deny this poem a certain
charm, even beauty in several places. But just because it makes an appearance only in a concentrated fashion, which everywhere runs
through Jehuda Halevi's and, to a much lesser degree, other Spanish
poetry, so here the question may be raised: on which relation with the
language does this poet base what is for us such unpoetic conduct?

Spanish poetry is actually precisely what one calls classical. In its cradle lay – grammar. In contrast to Kalir's poetry, for its birth has awaited
the origin of a scientific grammar of the Hebrew language. It is situated under the law of correctness of language. It has nothing of Kalir's
stormily baroque rules with the possibilities of the language, of this
bold creativity, to which everything possible in language is allowed. It
allows itself what is real in language, only what is – authenticated in
Scripture. That creativity as this classicism are both something very different from what they would be in a living, spoken language. The
"Scripture" ["*Schrift*"], not the "spoken language" ["*Sprache*"], is the
norm here, which those audacities bypass and into which this reveren-
tial awe is captivated. They are therefore fixed, not as in the elastic
boundaries of an oral language that are there overstepped, here es-
teemed.

The fixedness of the boundaries produces all by itself a very baroque
Baroque and a very classicized Classical, when it is at all possible in a
living language where every audacity nevertheless has a suitable for-
bear and the determination for awe has a practically unlimited field of
opportunities. He who, like the Spaniards, is resolved on the respectful

persistence holding out on the inside of the borders will plough through the bounded sphere which he calls his own, until no speck of unfruitful ground is left. The means for that is the young science of grammar.

It is inseparable first of all from what we would call lexicography. It is even perceived in these early times as a lexicographic scientific aid. It even serves after all to fathom the word-sense of the Scriptures. And the astonishing phenomenon – astonishing surely only for a rationalistic conception of language that sees in the language a method and consequently symbols in the words (but all primitive science of language is thus rationalistic) – the astonishing phenomenon then, that like-sounding words can have the most highly awkward different meanings, and this at least to some degree is cleared up through grammar. Thus the vocabulary of the Scriptures grows wider and for the first time is expanded before the observing eye. The poets however now solemnize the acquisition of this fortune by freely dealing with it anew and by taking a word, which in the Scriptures occurs only once, and which one thus "hardly knows" in natural usage. The whole fortune of this treasure of language, which the twenty-four extant books of the Old Hebrew literature encompassed, has become for the first time through this Spanish poetry an entirely conscious possession for the people, and becomes such still today for anyone who entrusts himself to the leadership of this master which newly arranges the precious treasures in the museum of the Bible in an enduring way: now this, now that gem is drawn near into the right light and thus the whole is saved from a museum-like torpor. That is the national-historical meaning of the assuredly childish play as this poem practises it.

On the translation: I indicate in this poem only the real deviations from the meaning, as the necessity for a deviating formulation is understood in the numerous plays on words. Stanza 1, lines 4f.: Never the flock, which becomes fat in the corn and when he turns round their prison like a dream. Stanza 3, lines 4f.: … let them go in darkness and roast them on the coals of the image.

LOOKING UPWARDS / ימין עזך אל ויד עזרך

Luz., Div. Nr. 17. Harkavy II 5. Brody III 150.

People have often asked why the Jewish people have persisted through all despair; and many more or less clever, therefore more or less stupid answers have been given. This poem can teach the true reason which disallows any plural "reasons." It begins with the cry out of the abyss of despair, which is so deep that the one called, only cried to to start with – can be cried to, called into question, charged with allegations. And in this cry of doubt and of blasphemy, which exceeds all Biblical models, because they are approached by the poisonous juices of a doubting and blasphemous philosophy, – still almost in this cry itself the eye recognizes in the one cried to the one around whom the stars circle; and the mouth acknowledges, breathing freely the might of the one who commands the hosts of heaven; and the heart sinks down enchanted into the view of the divine glory – and has forgotten all despair.

On the translation: Nothing to note.

BRIDE OF ISRAEL'S SABBATH / יקר יום שבת תנדיל

Luz., Div. Nr. 79. Harkavy II 11f.

On earth the Sabbath walls in the "union of peace and life" in whose sanctified region the people take refuge from the world of the nations. The separation, which in the last minute of the day of rest is articulated as its essence [*Wesen*], is the same, which already the first morning of creation brought into the world – between light and darkness – and which then was first of all renewed and deepened by the revelation: between holy and profane, between Israel and the nations. The Sabbath song immerses itself into this division – with all the fire, with all the passion, but also with all the jealousy that is peculiar to every love, and especially to such a love so surrounded by scoff and scorn. Indeed, it looks in this song practically as if the union of peace and life were not the meaning of the Sabbath, but instead the division between Israel and the nations which results from that union. This way of thinking has been called ill-will [*Ressentiment*]; but it is not that. Ill-will would be the case if the rejection were the central issue and not merely a peripheral – really peripheral! – consequence. The inner bliss of the possession of truth, of the claim to the royal blessing of the day, which God, as is indicated with reference to the great consecration passage of the day read on the eve of the Sabbath, commanded above all other solemn calls to holiness (Leviticus 23:3).[63*] It originates from the creation itself, ultimately of the priestly duty of the whole people (Exodus 19:6).[64*] All this inner wealth is so great and fulfilling that all prickli-

---

[63*] Leviticus 23:3: Six days shall work be done: but the seventh day is the sabbath of solemn rest, a holy gathering; you shall do no work: it is the sabbath to the LORD in all your dwellings.
[64*] Exodus 19:6: and you shall be to me a kingdom of priests, and a holy nation. These are the words which thou shalt speak to the children of Yisra'el.

ness towards the outside can never be as prickly as that blissfulness can be blissful.

And of course – if the reading is correct which has dared to conjecture the translation for the concluding lines without taking into account the passage of Ezekiel which is their immediate basis (36:23)[65*] in connection with the call of the Psalmist to "all heathens" to praise the Lord (Psalm 117:1)[66*] and passages like Malachi 1:11,[67*] then also here the view opens to the outside. It is a view to which the other text of the departure of the Sabbath opens, which, in contrast to the one mentioned above, is meant to distinguish, not the Sabbath from the workday, but the sanctity of the Sabbath from that lesser sanctity of the holiday. There all the divisions are named that are usually named at the Sabbath's parting – between holy and profane, between light and darkness, between Israel and the nations, between the Sabbath and the workday – but then in the concluding sentence that seals it God is praised, who distinguishes between – holy and holy.

Significantly, the concluding lines are delivered in the following form: In Levi's camp may you be sanctified if the heathens defame you. In itself nothing can be said against this text; it is based on the passage referred to from Ezekiel and does not interrupt the poem. This soil based version of the translation is only a possibility. But that it definitely is. The two versions differ from one another only by one Hebrew character, and that is the most easily interchangeable one. The small divergence from the written word of Scripture that underlies these lines could have been felt by the poet just as a stimulation. As proof that such a thing does happen, let the relationship of Gabirol's poem No. 57 of the Bialik edition, twentieth couplet, to Judges 1:1[68*] be cited, where the play occurs even with the same word roots as here. And that the inner tendency for an inclusion of the heathens is present is consonant with the author of the book of the *Kuzari*; which

65* Ezekiel 36:23: And I will sanctify my great name, which was profaned among the nations, which you have profaned in the midst of them; and the nations shall know that I am the LORD, says the LORD GOD, when I shall be sanctified in you before their eyes.

66* Psalm 117:1: Oh praise the LORD, all you nations: praise him, all you peoples.

67* Malachi 1:11: For from the rising of the sun until it goes down, my name is great among the nations; and in every place incense is burnt and sacrifices are offered to my name, and a pure offering: for my name is great among the nations, says the LORD of hosts.

68* Judges 1:1: Now after the death of Yehoshua [Joshua] it came to pass, that the children of Yisra'el asked the LORD, saying, Who shall go up for us against the Kena'ani [Canaanites] first, to fight against them?

rigorously holds fast the pre-eminence of Israel also for the future, but even so in its entire content is a missionary-writing – of course a Jewish one. It therefore knows as little an inner as an outer *coge intrare* [bring together to enter], but which, without such a forcible ingathering opens the gate only to the one who knocks out of his own world history, which gives him the impetus and does not actually state the answer to his questioning, even if only with a "we are like this," but fundamentally only points to an answer with a "look here."

On the translation: Stanza 1, line 5: The mockery of Kedar (Gen. 25:13) and Dishon (Gen. 36:20, and elsewhere) – ... Stanza 2, lines 7f.: Fruit of his commandment is a tree of life; in his shadow we live among the heathens. – Stanza 3 [4], line 2: ... in her hand as a support! – Stanza 4, lines 7f.: see what is said in the Note.

HOME / צאן אבדות בדלות להו בדלות להו

Luz., Div. Nr. 77. Harkavy I 69. Brody-Albrecht 118f.

The hour of the parting of the Sabbath is the critical hour of Jewish existence. Into the Sabbath all that this life can know and anticipate of perfection has converged; and now there threatens the sudden fall from the heights reached during the twenty-five-hour ascent directly into the abyss of the workday. Thus precisely in the last hours with their "Third Meal," an excitement is gathered which comprises equally messianic yearning and exilic despair. And Elijah the Prophet, whose return as the harbinger of the Messiah was the last word of the Biblical prophecy (Malachi 3:23),[69*] he is present in these hours – as an absent one is present, around whom all the thoughts and words of a group of people revolve.

This atmosphere is condensed in the song, which does not refer to the departure of the Sabbath itself with any word and only once, at the beginning, mentions both Elijah and the Messiah. Already in the rhythm of the individual line, which flows every time from a broad, graphic first half into the short moaning of the second half. Even stronger in the development, which this rhythm experiences in the surrounding lines where that second half not merely rhythmically, but

---

[69*] Malachi 3:23: Behold, I will send you Eliyya, the prophet, before the great and terrible day of the LORD.

also in its linguistic content, becomes the monotonous pleading, pressing cry: let, oh let, oh let ... .

On the translation: Pre-stanza, lines 1 and 2: "... bring to rest. Lead them through Elijah and the Mes- / siah." – Stanza 1, line 2: "When the saviour reveals himself / to the penitent ones." – Stanza 2, line 4: "Perform a miracle! my staff / let it blossom." Line 5: "... and all my doing / let it prosper." – Stanza 3, line 1: "... from drought," but also an antithetical play on words with "Zion." Line 5: "Roaring sea, which already covers me, / let it rest."

THE MIRACLES OF ELIJAH
אוחוחינו התמהמהו איה אליה אליהו /

Luz., Div. Nr. 80. Harkavy II 13f.

This is a song of Elijah as it is recited at the hour of the departure of the Sabbath. A wholly popular simple series of the miracles of the great "Tishbite" (1 Kings 17:1)[70*] which only through the repeated sound of the rhyme is reminiscent of the re-pitched and lamenting question of the beginning, from the bold earthly entrance of the successor Elisha (2 Kings 2:14)[71*] in which that rhyme – in the original the name Elijah himself – has its home. Until at the end the despairing where of the beginning changes into a hoping when – questionable, but the former a questioning groping into the darkness, the latter a hastening to the distant yet certain Light.

For miracles consistently fail to appear when a Where seeks them. They want to be implored with a When.

On the translation: Stanza 2, line 4: In the original there is still the statement of place of the miracle: Mount Karmel. – Stanza 3, line 4: "whom you know" is an addition. – Stanza 7, line 4: The work of God, for it is powerful.

70* 1 Kings 17:1: And Eliyyahu [Elijah] the Tishbi, who was of the inhabitants of Gil'ad, said unto Ah'av, As the LORD GOD of Israel lives, before whom I stand, there shall not be dew or rain these years, but according to my word.

71* 2 Kings 2:14: and he took the mantle of Eliyyahu [Elijah] that had fallen from him, and struck the water, and said, Where is the LORD GOD of Eliyyahu? And when he had also struck the waters, they parted to one side and to the other: and Elisha went over.

THE JEW / יריבוני בך הלכי חשכים

Harkavy II 31. Brody II 268.

An echo of the prophetic polemic. The eternity of the people expresses itself also this way: that nothing which was once actual loses its
actuality. The eternal people make eternal even their adversaries.

On the translation: Nothing to note.

THE PROMISE / יונות השתו שכם

Luz., Div. Nr. 75. Harkavy I 9f.

A conversation between God and his banished doves, as Israel is called
in connection with passages like Song of Songs 2:14, 5:2, 5:12, 6:9,[72*]
and Psalms 56:1 and 68:14,[73*] Isaiah 60:8,[74*] Ezekiel 7:16,[75*] Hosea
7:11.[76*] Here, as elsewhere, it is more a naming [Heißen] than an actual allegorical being [Sein]. The metaphor practically slips through
the poet's fingers; at the beginning of the third stanza the people
strike up the call of longing of the Psalm (55:7),[77*] which just in the

_____

72* Song of Songs 2:14: O my dove, who art in the clefts of the rock, in the secret places of the cliff, let me see thy countenance, let me hear thy voice;
for sweet is thy voice, and thy countenance is comely. 5:2: I sleep, but my
heart wakes: hark, my beloved is knocking, saying Open to me, my sister,
my love, my dove, my undefiled: for my head is filled with dew, and my locks
with the drops of the night. 5:12: His eyes are as the eyes of doves by the
water courses, washed with milk, and fitly set. 6:9: My dove, my undefiled is
but one; she is the only one of her mother, she is the choice one of her that
bore her. The daughters saw her, and called her happy; and the queens and
the concubines praised her.

73* Psalm 56:1: Be gracious to me, O GOD, for men long to swallow me up: all
day long the foeman oppresses me. 68:14: When you lie among the sheep
folds you shall shine like the wings of a dove covered with silver.

74* Isaiah 60:8: Who are these that fly as a cloud, and as the doves to their win-
dows?

75* Ezekiel 7:16: And those fugitives that escape, shall be on the mountains like
doves of the valleys, all of them moaning, every one for his iniquity.

76* Hosea 7:11: Efrayim is also like a silly dove without heart: they call to
Mizrayim [Egypt], they go to Ashshur [Assyria].

77* Psalm 55:7: And I said, Oh that I had wings like a dove! for then I would fly
away, and be at rest.

mouth of doves would be entirely impossible; and from then on the metaphor is dropped.

This is not a shortfall of poetic power, which of course would show up in any adherence to the metaphor, but rather an unpoetic-supra-poetic [*undichterisch-überdichterisch*] intent to penetrate into the image-less truth of prose, through every metaphor, which language's penchant for imagery puts into the speaker's mouth again and again. The Biblical style is poetic only against its will. The most inadequate approach to the Psalms, for instance, is to take them as "poetry." This atmosphere lacks exactly what necessarily belongs to all art, even the "truest," the most confessional: the delight in the play, more accurately in the mask. Bad enough that the word itself, because it is just not merely the word of this moment, but always already carries the traces of past destinies in its face, always has something masklike! Thus this speaker, for whom what matters is the truthfulness of the word, will not bind himself to the one word, rather, scarcely said, will say it again in a different way, – and thus the poet of this circle will not bind himself to the single image.

There is an apparent exception. The images of the kingdom, of the childlike, bridal and marital love do not stand under this law of the image to be dropped. The reason is that indeed they are images, but, not copies, rather the originals. A copy here is rather the inner-worldly reality of these relationships which we know only in mixtures and muddiness and whose pure form becomes manifest only in the divine-human connection. Only before God does a wholly pure homage kneel, only in God does a wholly pure trust rest, only to God does a wholly pure longing lament, only to God does a wholly pure thanks give thanks.

The dove image is used here because the underlying tone of the whole poem – and the source of its round-rhymes – is the promise of "rest." Rest in the homeland which now in conformity with the Mosaic prophecy (Leviticus 26:34 and 43),[78*] lies fallow in order to bring back the Sabbath-year neglected by its inhabitants, and over whose soil, renewed at the end of time, will stride once again the "seven shepherds and eight kings" whose return the Prophet (Micah

---

78* Leviticus 26:34: Then shall the land enjoy her sabbaths, as long as it lies desolate, and you are in your enemies' land; then shall the land rest, and enjoy her sabbaths. 43 The land also shall be forsaken by them, and shall enjoy her sabbaths, while she lies desolate without them: and they shall make amends for their iniquity: because, even because they despised my judgements, and because their soul abhorred my statutes.

5:4)[79*] has prophesied and, following the Talmudic interpretation of
the prophecy, the consciousness of the people awaits. Rest, for which
those driven away have been made worthy, not through their relationship to one another, but, as it is said in profound recognition of Jewish
essence, through their relationship to God, through the indefatigable
protection of hope which in days to come the now hidden love of the
father for his children must newly awaken in stormy might. The third
exile has gathered into itself the suffering of the first two, the Egyptian
and the Babylonian, but also the promise collects into itself the might
of the Law and of the Prophets. The power of the last stanzas surpasses
the might even of the Biblical word, just as the suffering of the present
surpasses the sufferings of the past, because it is present. The Biblical
promises are altogether purely future, they have the threat for a back-
ground. Thus they are with one voice divine and comprise the always
two-voiced present only in the form of the condition – "if you … ,
then … ." But here we have the full two-voiced divine-human reality,
and the promise shines, not as a conditional either-or, but as a radiant
yes into the night of sorrow and repentance and return which are already present in the other voice. Thus has the moment drawn near.

On the translation: Stanza 1, line 6: Region of Tiberias and Janocha
(Hos. 16:6f.). – Stanza 3, line 6: he let arise the seven and eight (see
the Note). – Stanza 4, line 7: Upon the cherub of salvation I ride. –
Stanza 5, line 1: Is it too little for you …

LOVE OF THE ENEMY / מאז מעון האהבה היית

Luz., Div. Nr. 58. Harkavy I 61. Brody-Wiener 169.

We will do as little justice to the "Love your enemy" of the Sermon on
the Mount as to other great realities if we regard it as an ethical postu-
late, that is from the viewpoint of unreality. The Christian love of the
enemy is a reality, when it – can be nothing else. It assumes this position of being incapable of being anything else when the Church or the
individual follows the original command of Christendom: to be mis-
sionaries. The love of the enemy then becomes the strongest weapon
for conquering the world, the enemy is loved as the future brother.
   Jewish love of the enemy should then be something entirely different, if it is to be real. For here the reality is not the one with the grace-

_____

[79*] Micah 5:4: And this shall be peace; when Ashshur [Assyria] shall come into
   our land, and when he shall tread in our palaces, then shall we raise against
   him seven shepherds, and eight princes of men.

filled mercies of the the conquest, but with those mercies of a community being defeated. Thus here love of one's enemy will arise at the point that Jehuda Halevi unveils in this poem. For it is a matter of unveiling; the real is seldom the immediately expressed; the word, when it tries to become objective, easily falls into the unreal. Thus, here the objective truth is unveiled, precisely because it is uttered entirely subjectively. The Jew loves in his enemy the one who extends divine judgement. Because he takes this judgement upon himself it becomes his own – and there remains for the Jew, as opposed to all other human beings, nothing else besides, for he alone does not have the Jews at his disposal to carry the guilt. The love with which a human loves God becomes life's law for all love with which he can love humans, even to extremes – but is there an extreme for love? – of the love of the enemy. "From the beginning you were the firmament of love."

On the translation: Line 6: "for he pursues the slain one, whom you slew." – Line 8: "... spurned, honour!"

MIRACLE OF LOVE / ייטב בעיניך נעים שירי ומיטב מהללי

Luz., Div. Nr. 26. Harkavy I 57. Brody-Wiener 170.

With this poem, as by the way also with the previous one, in spite of the last line, it might seem doubtful whether they rightly stand in this section and do not rather belong to the previous one. The longing of suffering in this one is expressed in such an enormously personal way that, in spite of the powerful third couplet which expresses that underlying consciousness of the Jewish people, in all depravity still to be chosen, one will find it difficult to accept that Jehuda Halevi here lets the people speak. The whole error lies already in this formulation. The poet does not let them speak, he speaks. He speaks not behind the mask of the people, but out of the people of whom he is himself a member. Only as a member of the people does he know originally what he knows. But – and in this But now comes the excuse for that error and at the same time its entire erroneousness – what he has experienced originally as a member of the people he is now capable of experiencing also personally in the accountability of his own soul. In genuine experiences there lies a power to propagate and to transmit. Not in the sense as if the first experience would become a symbol for others; rather precisely because the first experience is not a symbol, it can leap over. A symbol would remain in its own circle. Where the Jewish people have become a symbol, as in the Christian world, they reach only the nations with their symbolizing power. For the Jew himself however it does not become symbol, and on that account everything is transferred that he has experienced in the people, into the singular life of his soul. It is exactly the same as with the love for God over-leaping into the love for men. He who has grasped these things at some time will become very careful in religio-historical constructions and will dare no longer on the basis of the literary finding – "Literature is the fragment of fragments" – to ascribe to Jeremiah a "personal piety," which Isaiah "in his wholly politically oriented religiosity" did not "yet" have. And he will no longer pose a prize question about "the I in the Psalms," even if he is the chair of theology of a Prussian university.

On the translation: Nothing to note.

ANGRY LOVE / ידידי השכחת חנותך בביו שדי

Luz., Div. Nr. 11. Harkavy I 55. Brody III 4. Brody-Wiener 169f.

The reality of the love between God and Israel, as the Prophets, the Song of Songs, and the *Midrash* have expressed it, is shown in this: that it has not found its end in being expressed, in the way a "poet's" love finds its end in the poem that expresses it. Instead, this love goes further through time in an inexhaustible reality. Thus in this poem for the morning services of the Festival of Freedom [Passover], accompanied already by the Song of Songs, we are swept into an outburst of the abandoned loved ones, cast out already for a thousand years into the wretchedness of exile, as those classical witnesses of this love simply do not know it, because at that time, at the beginning of the millennium there was not yet any reason for such a frightful outburst. In these words there is no note of a penitent mood, only the judicial indignation about the faithlessness of the beloved, to whom she has sacrificed everything. The history of two millennia, from Sinai through the Persians, Greeks, Romans up to the Islam of the present, crowds together on a witness bench in the reproaches of the three middle couplets. And then comes the outcry, which one scarcely dares to believe one has heard, where Israel as the one human being stands erect before the one God and binds God's omnipotence to the redemption which he owes to it, Israel. For there is no other who waits for him, there can be no other, the power of love tolerates no outside; what *is*, is in it (love); what is not in it, *is* not.

Jewish? No, for all love forgets in the love that there is still an otherside of love, an It beside Me and You. Jewish? Oh yes, for the power to express this truth is only given to the human since and because there is – the Jew.

On the translation: Line 4: "and Seïr and Mount Paran and Sinai and Sin, bear witness for me." – Line 8: "tormented under the Persian yoke, / hardened in Greek fire."

DREAM VISION / יאירון כוכבי נשפי

Luz., Div. Nr. 37. Harkavy II 6.

A dream vision of the Daughter of Zion; of the ever young, never old one, whose youth already was an autumn rich in fruit and whom therefore the renewal may always approach in the form of return. Return of the youthful autumn, return of the youthful finery, return of the youthful union, which happened with the beloved and to him and in her at the same time. But that vision a return to her and this one – even still in the dream – a return which is encumbent upon her herself.

On the translation: Nothing to note.

FAITHFULNESS / יודעי הפיצני ימי עני

Brody III 20f.

The Jewish primeval word, out of which the world gained its belief, actually means faithfulness; it is a word of reciprocity. This reciprocity has always remained over the Jewish concept of the relationship of God and man; it has assumed shapes most incomprehensible to a foreign eye; the old Eisenmenger[13] who distinguishes himself from his modern successors and copyists, in still taking honest pains concerning the things he wanted to "discover," groups under the heading "What abominable and vicious representations the Jews have of God the Father," a series of haggadic passages filling many pages, of which one is always more splendid than the other.

The poet probably has in mind one of these passages in the powerful conclusion of this dialogue which already almost covers over the lament itself with the pride of one who may regard himself as better than his oppressors. Of their end, moreover, he is certain from the angelic speech which Daniel heard (8:13f),[80*] and with the sweetness of the

---

80* Daniel 8:13f: Then I heard one holy one speaking, and another holy one said to that certain one who spoke, How long shall be the vision concerning the daily sacrifice, and the transgression of desolation, to give both the sanctuary and the host to be trodden under foot? 14 And he said to me, For two thousand and three hundred evenings and mornings; then shall the sanctuary be restored.

Song of Songs: namely the famous Talmudic question, what is written
in God's prayer boxes. For even God puts on prayer thongs, just as the
man does it as a sign of his love for God – Maimonides notes in the
"Book of Love" [Song of Songs] in his great Code the stipulations
about their composition and putting them on. In man's prayer boxes
there is written the confession of God's uniqueness with the added
command of love for God (Deut. 6:4ff)[81*] – but what stands in those
which God "puts on"? "And who is like your people Israel, a unique
tribe on earth?" (1 Chronicles 17:21).[82*] To the human's confession of
faith to the unique God there echoes back God's confession of faith to
the unique people – to the people for whom the fates of the Patriarchs, Isaac's readiness for sacrifice, Jacob's cunning and suffering concerning the fight of the firstborn, Abraham's friendship with God –
have become traits in their three-thousand-year countenance.

On the translation: Stanza 2, lines 4f.: Hagar's, Moab's and Ammon's
son, / despising the word of the "Holy One" and of the "Unknown
One" (Dan. 8:13f.) – Stanza 3, line 2: "Pluck there spikenards and lil-
ies." Lines 6f.: "And the loved ones / lead back into my dwelling
place." – Stanza 4, line 2: "For I have exchanged you with no other
people."

LOVE'S SOLACE / מה לאחותי כי חשבה

Sachs 38f. Harkavy II 29f. Brody-Wiener 160.

A conversation between God and Israel, the "Sister-Bride" of the Song
of Songs (4:9; 4:11; 4:12; 5:1 and 5:2)[83*] which steers, right from the
beginning, with all its round-rhymes towards the famous words of love.
It begins with consolation to which – second and third stanzas – incon-
solable despair answers, whereup on the consolation starts in again in
reinforced tones and speaks in a very divine way for the length of the

---

81* Deuteronomy 6:4ff: Hear, O Yisra'el: The LORD our GOD is one. 5 And
    thou shalt love the LORD thy GOD with all thy heart, and with all thy soul,
    and with all thy might. 6 And these words, which I command thee this day,
    shall be in thy heart.
82* 1 Chronicles 17:21: And who is like thy people Yisra'el, a singular nation
    on the earth, whom GOD went to redeem to be his own people, to make
    thee a name of greatness and awesomeness, by driving out nations from be-
    fore thy people, whom thou didst redeem out of Mizrayim [Egypt]?

fourth stanza, then – last stanza – in a very human way and thus leads
into the word which is the most human-most divine of all the words.

On the translation: Stanza 1, line 6: "… already it draws near." – Stanza
2, line 4: "… Fruit of my doing I eat." Line 5: "of widowhood" is an addition. – Stanza 3, line 3: "… how is she not freed?" – Stanza 4,
lines 2f.: "I bring honour back to my camp / I eradicate the stranger
from my son's inheritance."

FINDING AGAIN / מה אתנה בכפר עפר שארח

Luz., Div. Nr. 69. Harkavy I 72ff.

In this totally humanly sweet love conversation, in which the sweetheart is called by the pet name of worldly love poetry (The beginning
could be translated: "How can I … to my Friedel"), the future moment
of reunion is dreamfully anticipated. All that is today past and today
present and today still future is united there on the one level of the
past and is made present as such a past in the intimate "Do you still
know?" "Do you remember?" "A year ago at this time" of the love conversation: the love of Abraham, the Psalmic songs of Israel, Isaiah's
promise of Redemption after he suffered his twofold punishment (Isaiah 40:2),[84*] the Book of Divine Judgement, mockery and profanation
of the turbid present, the promise of a lasting remnant (Isaiah 10:20ff

---

[83*] The Song of Songs 4:9: Thou hast ravished my heart, my sister, my bride;
thou hast ravished my heart with one of thy eyes, with one link of thy neck-
lace. 11: Thy lips, O my bride, drop as the honeycomb: honey and milk are
under thy tongue; and the scent of thy garments is like the scent of Levanon.
12: A garden enclosed is my sister, my bride; a spring shut up, a fountain
sealed. 5:1: I am come into my garden, my sister, my bride; I have gathered
my myrrh with my spice; I have eaten my honeycomb with my honey; I have
drunk my wine with my milk. Eat, O dear ones, and drink; drink deep, O
loving companions. 2: I sleep, but my heart wakes: hark, my beloved is
knocking, saying, Open to me, my sister, my love, my dove, my undefiled:
for my head is filled with dew, and my locks with the drops of the night.
[84*] Isaiah 40:2: Speak comfortably to Yerushalayim, and cry to her, that the war
service is ended, that her iniquity is pardoned: for she has received of the
LORD's hand double for all her sins.

inter alia),[85*] the guarantee of help for him who remains quiet (Isaiah 30:15),[86*] the horror that God had uttered through the mouth of the Prophet (Isaiah 1:14)[87*] in the face of Israel's sacrificial festivals, the rejoicing of the groom of the Song of Songs (5:1) who comes into his garden, and the call of the bride who saw him escape like a fleeting hart (Song of Songs 8:14)[88*] – all that and still more becomes, in the exchange of the "lovers finding each other again," newly sweet present, which rises from the trembling of the first glad presentiment to the rejoicing of the final fulfilment.

On the translation: Stanza 1, lines 9f.: "So I intend for my children / love of Terah's son." – Stanza 2, line 5: "Doubled measure of punishment ..." – Stanza 3, lines 7 – 10: In Edom's people and Epher's / I cried ardently to You / from prison in groans of grief; / the ornament of the head of consecration fell. – Stanza 4, lines 1f.: "Silence! was it not for salvation that / I left you as a remnant." – Stanza 5, line 3: "there came to the garden of praise ..." lines 9f.: "Return! God's splendour is / inflamed above you."

AWAKE / יִשַׁן וְלֵבוּ עֵר

Brody III 67.

No longer a dialogue as the final poems of the preceding part, but only one is still speaking, the One. Thus no longer present tense, but rather future, no longer drama, but rather vision. The lament, which is always an expression of the present, is silenced; also comfort, promise, even hope, which all of course look into the future, but out of the

---

85* Isaiah 10:20ff: And it shall come to pass on that day that the remnant of Yisra'el, and such as are escaped of the house of Ya'aqov, shall no more again rely upon him that smote them; but shall rely upon the LORD, the Holy One of Yisra'el, in truth. 21 A remnant shall return, even the remnant of Ya'aqov, to the mighty GOD. 22 For though thy people Yisra'el be as the sand of the sea, yet a remnant of them shall return: total destruction is decreed but overflowing with righteousness.

86* Isaiah 30:15: For thus says the LORD GOD, the Holy One of Yisra'el; in ease and rest shall you be saved; in quietness and in confidence shall be your strength: and you did not wish it.

87* Isaiah 1:14: Your new moons and your appointed feasts my soul hates: they are a trouble to me; I am weary of enduring them.

88* The Song of Songs 8:14: Make haste, my beloved, and be thou like a gazelle or a young hart upon the mountains of spices.

present, are now silent; only the purely present future speaks, the call, the "Be ready" of the hour that has come, finally come. And it speaks out of the mouth of Him Who has brought about the hour, Who through all contradictions of His Being [Wesen] and in the successive waves of our destiny maintains the love for His own, – of the Lord of the future.

On the translation: Nothing to note.

THE HAPPY MESSAGE / יונת רחוקים נגני היטיבי

Luz., Div. Nr. 6. Harkavy I 74f.

This poem, in itself not very significant, belongs here all the same owing to its motive. For rightfully has his publisher Luzzatto assumed – Geiger's opposition[14] and that of others has not convinced me – that it arose under the immediate influence of the news about the appearance of a messianic pretender, as more of these are witnessed elsewhere for that century. It is not Jehuda Halevi's way to manipulate situations to his poems. And where a dream or a face is the cause, then he says so. Thus it will have been a real news item, believed for a short or a long time.

Thus even Jehuda Halevi would have paid the price for his belief. For the expectation of the Messiah, by which and for the sake of which Judaism lives, would be an empty theologumenon, a mere "idea," idle babble, – if it were not over and over again made real and unreal, illusion and disillusion in the form of "the false Messiah." The false Messiah is as old as the hope of the genuine one. He is the changing form of this enduring hope. Every Jewish generation is divided by him into those who have the strength of faith to be deceived, and those who have the strength of hope not to be deceived. Those having faith are better, those having hope are stronger. The former bleed as sacrifices on the altar of the eternity of the people, the latter serve as priests before this altar. Until the one time when it will be the reverse, and the faith of the faithful becomes the truth, and the hope of the hoping becomes the lie. Then – and no one knows whether this "then" will not happen even today – then the task of those who hope comes to an end, and the one who still belongs to the hopeful and not to the faithful when the morning of that day breaks, risks the danger of being rejected. This danger hangs over the apparently unimperilled lives of those who hope.

Hermann Cohen once said to me – he was already over seventy –: "I am still hoping to experience the beginning of the Messianic time." By

this he, who had been a believer in the false Messiah of the nineteenth
century, meant the conversion of the Christians to "pure monotheism"
of his Judaism, something which he thought he saw ripening in contemporary liberal Protestant theology. I was surprised by this vehe-
mence of the "soon, in our days" and dared not say that *these* signs were
not signs to me, but rather replied only that I believed I would not experience it. To which he responded: "But when do you think then?" I
did not have the heart to name *no* date and said: Only after hundreds
of years. But he understood: only after a hundred years, and cried:
"Oh, please say fifty!"

On the translation: Line 12: "... / the house of love – enlarge it."

THE CALCULATION OF SALVATION / יונת רחוקים נדדה יערה

Luz., Div. Nr. 43. Harkavy I 74f.

Thus is the appointed time of redemption calculated. Again and again.
And yet every calculation collapses, so that it is already said in the Talmud, all appointed times have passed, and there remains only the
power of return.[15] Jehuda Halevi's lifetime indeed falls wholly into
such an epoch where the calculated appointed time had passed: one
had hoped for redemption in the thousandth year of the exile, thus according to the historical chronology of the time, in the year 1068 of
the Christian era. Sixty-four years – the poet transcribes the number
according to the dove-imagery of the poem with the sum of the numerical value of the letters of the word "vanish" [*entschwebe*], which the
translation of course can only reproduce very remotely, – sixty-four
years have now already elapsed in suffering; the past years are counted,
the future no longer dares to arrive at any calculation. No longer
dares? Yet precisely out of the despair of all calculating the flame of the
power of faith shoots up anew, as once for the Prophet (Jeremiah
20:9)[89*] out of his desperate attempt "no longer to remember" the
Name, and carries heavenward with a final force the "He will come!" of
the Psalm (50:3),[90*] which in the seemingly so artificial rhythm of the
poem seems to have waited in vain from the beginning for His coming.

On the translation: Line 7, see the Note. – Line 15: May our God come ...

89* Jeremiah 20:9: Then I said, I will not make mention of him, nor speak any
more in his name. But his word was in my heart as a burning fire shut up in
my bones, and I was weary with containing myself.
90* Psalm 50:3: Our GOD comes, and does not keep silence: a fire devours before him, and it is very tempestuous round about him.

IN THE SANCTUARY / אלהי משכנותיך ידידות

Luz., Bet. 54. Luz., Div. Nr. 51. Harkavy I 8f. Brody II 160.

The Jewish people's longing for Zion has never been merely the longing for rest from the torment, but always also a wish for a higher life
out of a lesser. When, on the Sabbath and the Festivals when the re-
quests for earthly needs should be silenced, the daily prayer omits the
request, may God blast into the great trumpet for our deliverance –
the request for the reinstitution of the sacrificial service is not silenced
there also:

> May you be gracious, o you God our God,
>   To your people Israel and to their imploring
> And send anew the holy custom to the chamber of Your house.
> And firebrands and prayers of love, oh receive them in grace, God.
> And forever shine the brightness of your grace upon Israel's service.
>   And may our eyes see,
>   how you return home to Zion mercifully gentle.
> Praise now, praise to you, oh God,
>   who lets his radiance dwell anew on Zion.

His dream placed Jehuda the Levite in the middle of his brothers serving in the Temple. He reveled in the sight of the sacrifice. They represented to him the re-instated immediacy of God's nearness. In the same
century Maimonides depicted accurately in his Code [of Jewish Laws]
how the laws of sacrifice would be again instituted after the rebuilding of
the Temple. But in his philosophical work [*Guide to the Perplexed*], linking
it to Leviticus 17:7,[91*] he deals with the law of sacrifices as a mere peda-
gogical concession of Moses. Today this and the prayers for its re-institution have become an embarrassment, among the reformists generally
admitted as such, among the orthodox not admitted.

The reasons given for the rejection of sacrifices are so weak that they
are obviously not true. For the horror over the "murder of innocent
animals" has to be taken as only comical and insincere in the mouth of
a regular non-vegetarian. But whatever is said beyond this relates as
much to sacrifice as to every other visible and established cultic act,
which renders in concrete vividness the relationship between the natural need for taking nourishment and the one who is giving the nourishment. And that is indeed the purpose.

91* Leviticus 17:7: And they shall no more offer their sacrifices to the demons,
    after whom they have gone astray. This shall be a statute for ever to them
    throughout their generations.

But in spite of this there is also an intuitive difference even for the one who is fully clear about this. Also for him the prayer for the re-institution of sacrifice is also for him a difficult prayer. But it should be so. It is the difference between the prayer that is prescribed and the one that is born of the moment in that the latter bursts forth out of the immediate need, whereas the former is intended to teach the one who prays to feel a need which otherwise he would not feel. This is especially applicable to the prayers for the messianic time, in so far as they are not a mere matter of redemption from the pressure of the present. The human is so far inrooted into every life, even into the most difficult, that he has a reason, indeed always to wish for change to some extent, but to shrink away from a radical change. And such a radical change, *the* radical change, is the messianic time, which to be sure puts an end to the hell of world history, but also to its ambiguities and apparent dearth of responsibilities. Then everything will be visible, and the human shrinks away from this absolute visibility and from the unequivocal responsibility that is bound to it, just as – from God's nearness at death, for which he may likewise yearn, yet without being able to free himself from the love of life, even of a deficient and sinful life. For the change is too radical. He should learn however to pray for this radical change, even if this prayer is difficult for him, right up until the time when the change has come.

That God is also with the human in this present world of imperfection, of confusion and of ghostlikeness, or rather, that the human can be with Him, can find a way to Him is that which Jehuda Halevi experiences as he awakes out of his dream again into this world. It would be a lie if the yearning wanted to forget what it already possesses, but it would be death if that possession wanted to forget to yearn.

On the translation: Nothing to note.

SOLOMON'S TAPESTRIES

יריעות שלמה איך בתוך אהלי קדר /

Luz., Div. Nr. 41. Harkavy I 59. Brody-Wiener 158.

This poem, which in many places has found admittance into the liturgy of the summer days of mourning for the destruction of Jerusalem, the heart indirectly over the greatest possible distance of objectivity. It does not speak out of the destiny of those afflicted, but dramatizes this destiny into a dialogue between the "tapestries of Solomon" and a wanderer who knew them in their former splendour and now happens upon them again in the Bedouin tent of the Ishmaelite. Thus the lament for the tapestries, the sorrow and the hope, together with the knowledge of the closeness of Israel to God, in a bold turn compared to the stars (Isaiah 40:26),[92*] is put into the wanderer's mouth, and sorrow, lament, consciousness and hope come back out of this estrangement even more fervently into the breast of the one praying.

On the translation: Lines 17f.: "Their radiance as once at the beginning / may he let return again at the end."

TEARS AT NIGHT / ירושלים האנחי

Harkavy I 15. Brody III 187.

The lament for Zion, to which three weeks of the summer belong, is not, however, silent throughout the entire year. It blends into every other lament. Thus it makes its lament even through the night-lamentations of the time in the autumn before the great Days of Judgement and Atonement, and blends the tear for Zion with the confession of sins, and Zion's hope with the plea for forgiveness.

On the translation: Stanza 1, lines 7f.: "... , if I do not think of You." – Stanza 2, line 2: "... rooms." – Stanza 4, line 6: "and he gives salvation to her [Israel] out of Zion."

THE CITY ON HIGH / יפה נוף משוש תבל

Luz., Bet. 53. Luz., Div. Nr. 1. Harkavy I 7. Brody-Albrecht 35. Brody II 167f. Brody-Wiener 183.

In this poem that starts with the Psalmic vision of the city built on high (48:3),[93*] there are strains which repeatedly occur in the poems of longing and of the voyage up to the great Song of Zion, and yet here these strains could still be poetic turns, grown out of the living literature intended for cultic use during the summer weeks in which this

---

92* Isaiah 40:26: Lift up your eyes on high, and behold who has created these things, that brings out their host by number: he calls them all by names; because of the greatness of his might, and because he is strong in power, not one is missing.

93* Psalm 48:3: Beautiful for situation, the joy of the whole earth: mount Ziyyon, the sides of the north, the city of the great King. GOD is known in her palaces for a fortress.

poem has actually found admittance – if the last line did not contain an almost shamefully hidden hint, from which one can sense that the poet has, as did many thousands in later centuries, a personal serious desire to die in Jerusalem. For this is not, as one might think, a continuation of the previous couplet, but the hidden meaning of the concluding couplet, which, with the word for "clods of earth" ["*Scholle*"], alludes to the one of the two single places of its occurrence in Scripture, and yet avoids making the allusion apparent to the reader through the use of other words of that verse – Job says of the dead "the clods of the valley shall be sweet unto him" (Job 21:33).

On the translation: Line 12: "until it is entirely mixed."

BETWEEN EAST AND WEST / לבי במזרח ואני בסוף מערב

Luz., Bet. 53. Luz., Div. Nr. 7. Harkavy I 7f. Brody II 155. Brody-Wiener 179.

Jehuda Halevi's longing for Zion, the split of the person between East and West, which he himself intensified even further through the vow that he could fulfil only in Zion, is a turning point in the history of Jewish exile. For a millennium, after the heroic convulsions of the first centuries had ebbed in the study halls of Babylon, the longing for Zion remains a dead commodity – "religion." With the millennium after the destruction of the Temple, at the beginning of which Jehuda Halevi was born, there begins the streaming back of Jewish life into the ancient land. Only a century later did the emigration of the French scholastics begin with any historical importance; but Jehuda Halevi's lonely spiritual destiny is the first beacon of the new movement which then carries on to our present, only with the one yet invigorating breathing space of the century following Mendelssohn, in which the leading Western Jewry sought radically to deny the connexion.

On the translation: Nothing to note.

REPLY / דבריך במר עבר רקוחים

Luz., Bet. 54ff. Luz., Div. Nr. 86. Harkavy I 16ff. Brody II 164ff. Brody-Wiener 181f.

This famous man's resolve is well known, and he is admonished for it in the form of a poetic letter. We can ascertain the letter's contents only from his reply, which in every instant shows how immense his resolve would have appeared at that time.

The writer of this letter is unknown and yet appears to us as if he *is* known, as if we could point him out by name, not in one but in a hundred shapes. Even the assimilated Jew belongs to the eternal metaphorical expressions of Judaism. And his arguments have remained – should one say: shockingly? – the same: Jerusalem no longer concerns us today, because, just as when David conquered it, it is again inhabited by the "blind and lame" (2 Samuel 5:6,8),[94*] by foreign nations. And this unhistorical-historical argument unites itself then as now with the unphilosophical-philosophical (only the unpolitical-political is missing, but that would be inappropriate in the case of a single individual). And the philosophy that must be upheld in order to give relief to the national forgetfulness, then as now, is derived from the Greeks, who know only of beginningless and endless eternity, not of a one Eternal, who establishes beginning and end.

The answer sings with its quote from Psalm 122:8f[95*] immediately in the same way the undying double-ring of the love for Zion, God, and the people: for the Temple's sake and for the brother's sake Jerusalem remains for us what it was. In a special way the argumentation enters fully on the "historical" defence of the "no-longer" and refutes it with reference to the situation of the "not-yet" corresponding to us, namely the time of the Patriarchs, for whom the land, which was ever so little their property, yet was holy. Between-times, the answer refers to orgies, which piety celebrates for the dead and with which the piety purchases its liberty at the expense of the real future-bearing realization of the living, and prizes the land as the sole sure place of refuge and as the places of historical memories as well as of eschatological hopes. And it knows itself to be on the mainstreets, compared to which all the decisive turns and protests of the word of the other are only tortuous side-paths.

The words of one have been forgotten; the answer has endured.

On the translation: Nothing to note.

94* 2 Samuel 5:6,8: And the king and his men went to Yerushalayim to the Yevusi [Jebusites], the inhabitants of the land: who spoke to David, saying, Unless thou remove even the blind and the lame, thou shalt not come in here: thinking, David cannot come in here. 8 And David said on that day, Whoever smites the Yevusi and gets up to the aquaduct, and smites the lame and the blind, (they are hated of David's soul) – Therefore the saying, The blind and the lame shall not come into the house.

95* Psalm 122:8f: For my brethren and companions' sakes, I will now say, Peace be within thee. For the sake of the house of the LORD our GOD I will seek thy good.

THE PILGRIM / הציקתני תשוקתי לאל חי

Luz., Bet. 62f. Harkavy I 20f. Brody II 172ff. Brody-Wiener 183f.

The emigration has not been easy for Jehuda Halevi. The poem shows what he has given up. And as in moments of parting everything which one is leaving seems to collect together, and as one grasps fully only at the moment of loss what one has had, thus the poet circumscribes here in fourteen lines the circle of life, which he has lived and loved all the years: family, friends, a circle of schoolmates, of whom he has gilded a few names, the synagogue to which his poetry, the study hall to which his thought has been dedicated, the rhythm of the Jewish year with its Sabbath and Festivals, his fame as a poet which wove around him in the land. Only briefly does he speak of the difficulties of being a pilgrim to which he submits himself; already they are swallowed up by the image of yearning, surrounded by all the sweetnesses of his language for that which beckons him at the goal of his journey. One senses: it is really the "yearning for the living God" which allows him to give up a world that is living to him without complaint – almost without complaint. Almost without complaint – this poem preserves the faint tones of the complaint, which still ring in him.

On the translation: Line 1: ... to the living God. – Line 4: ... and my friends, my brothers. – Line 21 I understood just as little as anyone before me. Brody's interpretation, which as a translator one would have to render something like: "and I cease to bow and scrape and fawn," for me goes against the taste and the connection; the conjectures of the others are to my mind too bold.

ALL WEIGHS LIGHTLY / לך נפשי בטוחה או הרדה

Luz. Nr. 9. Harkavy I 31ff. Brody II 170.

Both the metre and the content of this poem are the same as the preceding one. But so different is the mood that one hardly notices this similarity. The poet's fantasy flies ahead of the dragging course of the journey and anticipates the future. Anticipated is the passionate, divinely heard Your of the pilgrimage; anticipated is the elaborately described terror of the sea voyage on the Christian vessel in Islamic waters; anticipated also is that which in the previous poem is the entirely present content: the sorrow concerning those whom he is leaving. Even this seems here as he *will* feel it, not as he feels it today. And that is why, instead of the many names and blessings of life, which the former poem radiates with the golden lustre of the hour of parting, only two, only the two nearest, only this innermost ring of his heart, only the wound which no time will allow to heal: his only child concerning whom he reveals here at this unreserved moment of sorrow what she was to him, and concerning her son, who is clearly still a very young grand-child who bears his name. And then the single word of the whole which is not in the future form: leicht wiegt das alles gegen deine Liebe [all weighs lightly compared to your love] – indicating the point of the present moment, of the present moment which longs for God, out of which all the anticipation took place. Out of which also the last takes place, that of the fulfilment, of the goal, when he will bring his heart there in the holy places as burnt offering – the sacrifice of the heart for the poet, who dreams of the restoration of the visible sacrifice, not meant as its substitute, but as good as in the prophetic-psalmic battle over the sacrifice, as completion and elevation – , and last of all of the final fulfilment, of the final goal: the grave in the holy earth, which shows to him the deed of his life. For as such did the poet mean this end of his life. He had experienced so rich a life, as he showed it beforehand as such in the paradoxical – the most real and the most moving of all philosophical book-conclusions, the conclusion of the *Kuzari*. It therefore stands along with Plato's *Phaedo*, in fact, *above* Plato's *Phaedo* – for no Plato stands here between the Socrates of the dialogue and him who dies in actuality.

On the translation: Line 4: ... in all inconstancy and fleetingness. Lines 5f.: "over dark flood" and "over cypress woods" are additions. Lines 19f.: in the original reversed. Line 23: ... , – he cleaves my liver – . Line 24: ... of all riddles. Lines 29f.: ... and regard my heart bound as a burnt-offering upon Your altar.

THE COMPULSION / יום נכספה נפשי לבית הועד

Luz., Bet. 57. Luz., Div., Nr. 8. Harkavy I 8, Brody II 167.

And yet, in spite of all the yearning of the pilgrim, still stronger is the anxiety for that which he must give up, for the life in which he was deeply rooted at home for more than fifty years, the horror of homelessness. Here something happens that gives him what he is still lacking: the compulsion. Now he goes gladly.

What it is that has happened he does not reveal. We do not know what event made leaving home attractive or even a necessity for him. It is already almost fantastic that he reveals even that much. For this is something about which people are mostly silent, although perhaps everyone experiences it at some time. For it wounds their pride at the deepest point.

Man seeks his honour in action. But there is in every such action a moment when man loses courage, precisely because he has staked all of it. If at this point a compulsion did not come, which did not help the action to be born, it would never see the light of the world. But this compulsion comes. The human has a right to it, which is recognized by God.

All praying is in the last resort a prayer for this compulsion, all thanking a thankfulness for it. But the bashfulness, which surrounds the prayer, has its basis here.

On the translation: Nothing to note.

PRAYING / אלהי אל תשבר משברי ים

Luz., Bet. 65. Luz., Div. Nr. 2. Harkavy I 23. Brody II 168.

How strangely this little prayer on the sea journey sees the high tide and wind and God's mercy only as vehicles of yearning! If it is stilled, – then the wave may rest, the sea dry up. "May the world not go under, may heaven not collapse, before I may be with my beloved!"

On the translation: Nothing to note.

THE FLOOD / הבא מבול ושם תבל הרבה

Luz., Bet. 65f. Luz., Div. Nr. 3. Harkavy I 23f. Brody II 169. Brody-Wiener 183.

This is probably the most beautiful among the poems of this sea voyage. It is equally free from the cheap bombastic as from the just as cheap moralizing, to both of which the topic could easily be lured, and remains in the circle of the most immediate facts. For the poet there belongs to this circle the Biblical memory, which must necessarily become present for him, through the loneliness of the high sea: the Flood. He expresses the most natural human feeling on the sea, the horror not yet robbed of its good conscience through any sentimentality about nature. And just out of this undiluted feeling he at once takes the simplest and most powerful word and image. And finds just in this purity of view the courage for the great ending that dares – and may dare to face the raging of the monstrous sea with the exultation of his own heart which makes the pilgrimage to the goal.

On the translation: Line 4: "did we go to the place of suffering?" – Line 6: "in waste land I would know pleasure."

EXCURSUS: STORM / יועץ ומקים במרום שחקים

Luz., Bet. 74ff. Brody II 176ff. Brody-Albrecht 97f. Brody-Wiener 184ff.

(J) Yes, He plans and performs
even surrounded by clouds
– yet as far as the sea
His judgement reaches.

Is the deed the fame of man?
When His counsel is far,
it remains false pomp,
effort without weight.

Out of the land's prison
to the sea gladly sets to work
the heroic strength,
which makes a path for itself.

But sin turns
the rudder, the journey goes
westward, and see
how it moves eastward.

Until he notices:
neither nimbleness nor learnedness
helps for a safe journey
and never gives the direction.

Reflecting then,
trembling, he recognizes
what still in the middle of the spell
his sighing says:

Where do I go here
before Your spirit
and where do I flee, alas,
Your countenance!

(H) The waters surge high
in the blowing of the whirlpools
and go across the seas
towering, rippling.

The sky is black night,
The raging of the water roars,
The abyss of hell awakens
with a deep roar of thunder.

The boiling water howls,
the noise of the sea booms,
ah, woe, who is there to reconcile
the raging horror.

But force swallows itself up:
the torrent bursts asunder!
it half sinks, half rises
up mountain high.

The little ship, how it chases
upwards, downwards! the eye
loses courage, enquires
of the crew after the construction.

My heart grows rigid like stone.
I await: will someone ransom it from the pain
as Moses once did
for his two siblings?

I would cry to the Lord
imploring aloud, how gladly,
but sins – do they not
block the way?

(U) And the waves circle 'round
and the hammering of the east splits
the cedars of the ship and hurls
the masses of foam around.

The spine of the ship struggles out,
and the keel of hte shiop trembles,
there is no more winged pair
waving around the ship's mast.

Then there is boiling without fire;
courage is scarce;
the rudder itself resists
the helmsman.

The ship's master tame and mute,
and ship's crew lame and bent,
and ship's man grudging and stupid
and the ship's look-out empty.

And little ship – it tosses and pounds
as if frenzy fumes about it,
the fist lets go, uncramped,
thankless, what is too hard for it.

And Leviathan, hero
in the sea's floor, orders
in the tent of the wedding feast
his entire army as guests.

And the ocean's prince holds
his hand fast to its pledge –
there is no support,
and no light of hope!

(D) The eyes look afar
to You, to the Lord,
I gladly offer to You
the multitude of prayers.

I tremble inside
and I stand here afraid,
and bring the sound of crying to You
as once did Jonah.

In a crown of reeds the sea –
I think of it constantly, desire
only one thing: how can I honour
it truly in the song?

That Jordan's river flowed
back, I pluck out of that
happiness like Eden for me,
apparent to Him,

Who sweetens bitter wetness,
so that the day still greets kindly,
which was angry and desolate,
before a day of strife.

The two eyes fly
up, seeking Him,
Whose paths lead through
the danger of wild water,

The glow of the earth –
out of His fury;
he breathes: see, the woolly thickness
is resting round about.

(A) He turned the fury
from his servant, so that he
breathes courage anew, he who now
does not rest in the night.

From on high downwards flowed
the word which full of peace sounded
in the rancour of hell –
then the battle became quiet.

And the storm's passionate drink
grew smooth like cream
so that fear sank away
and trust awakened.

Then the ear of the oppressed flock
hearkened above to the heavens,
and a chorus of mercy
it hears nearing softly.

So close the message of salvation to them,
the people in distress,
whom prison, despot and oppression
had made weary, paralysed.

Those who experience the storms and torment
like the ship, be radiant
yet again
in the splendour of the psalms of thanks:

Move away, faithfulness, out of the innermost
because the glory of the Lord
surrounds you anew!

Ja plant und vollbringt
auch wolkenumringt
er, – meerferne doch dringt
hin Sein Gericht.

Mannes Ruhm die Tat?
wenn ihr ferne Sein Rat
bleibts falscher Staat,
Bemühn ohn' Gewicht.

Aus Landes Haft
zum Meer froh aufrafft
sich die heldische Kraft,
die Bahn sich bricht.

Doch Sünde dreht
das Steuer; Fahrt geht
nach West hin, und seht,
wie Ost zu es sticht.

Bis er gewahrt:
nicht gelenk, nicht gelahrt
hilft zur sichern Fahrt,
und gibt nimmer die Richt'.

Einkehrend alsdann
erkennt bebend er an,
was noch mitten im Bann
sein Seufzen spricht:

Wo geh ich hin
vor Deinem Geist
und wo flieh ich, ach,
Dein Angesicht!

Hoch walln die Seen
in der Wirbel Wehn,
und meerüberhin gehn
sie getürmt, sie kraus.

Himmel schwarze Nacht,
Gewässers Toben kracht,
der Höllabgrund erwacht
mit tiefem Donnerbraus.

Der Flutkessel stöhnt,
des Meer Lärm erdröhnt,
ach weh, wer versöhnt
den ertosenden Graus.

Doch Kraft selber verschlingt
sich: der Schwall er zerspringt!
halb sinkt er, halb schwingt
er berghoch hinaus.

Das Schifflein wie es jagt
aufwärts, abwärts! es zagt
das Aug, und es fragt
der Mannschaft nach des Baus.

Mein Herz starrt wie Stein;
ich harr': lösts wer der Pein,
wie einst Mose sein
Zwiegeschwisterpaar, aus?

Ich schriee zum Herrn
wohl lautflehend, wie gern,
doch Sünden – versperrn
den Weg sie nicht?

Und rings Woge kreißt,
und Osts Haemmern zerreißt
des Schiffs Zedern und schleißt
Gischtmassen umher.

Schiffs Dorn entstrebt,
und Schiffs Kiel erbebt,
Schiffs Mast umschwebt
kein Flügelpaar mehr.

Da kocht es ohn' Feu'r;
der Mut macht sich teu'r:
sich selbst setzt das Steu'r
dem Steu'rmanne zur Wehr.

Schiffs Herr zahm und stumm,
und Schiffs Knecht lahm und krumm,
und Schiffes Mann gram und dumm,
und Schiffs Ausguck leer.

Und Schifflein – taumelt und stampft,
wie wenn Rausch es umdampft,
die Faust läßt entkrampft,
danklos, was ihr zu schwer.

Und Levjathan, Held
in Meers Flur, bestellt
in Hochzeitmahls Zelt
zu Gast sein gesamt Heer.

Und Fürst Ozeans Hand
hält gar fest ihr Pfand –
nicht gibts Unterstand,
und kein Hoffnungslicht!

Die Augen fern
schaun zu Dir auf, zum Herrn,
ja Dir opfre ich gern
der Bitten Schar.

Ich erzittre in mir
und bang steh ich hier,
und bring Schreiens Laut Dir
wie einst Jona dar.

In Schilfs Kranz das Meer –
ich denks stets, begehr
nur einzig: wie ehr
im Lied ichs wahr?

Daß Jordans Flut zurück
geströmt, draus pflück
ich mir edengleich Glück
Ihm offenbar,

Der Naß, bittres, süßt,
dass noch hold der Tag grüßt,
der zornig und wüst,
ein Tag Haders erst war.

Die zwei Augen fliehn
empor, suchend Ihn,
des Pfade durchziehn
Wildwassers Gefahr.

Der Erde Glut –
aus seiner Wut;
er haucht: sich da ruht
rings Flockenschicht.

Abwandte die Wut
vom Knecht er, dass Mut
er neu haucht, der ruht
nun nicht in Nacht.

Von Höhn niederwärts quoll
Wort, das friedereich scholl
in Höllengroll –
da schwieg stille die Schlacht.

Und Sturms Eifertrank
ward sahnegleich blank,
dass Furcht fern versank
und Zutrauen erwacht.

Da horcht bedrückter Schar Ohr
zu Höhn himmelempor,
und Gnadenchor
hörts nahen sacht. –

So nah' des Heils Bot-
schaft ihm, dem Volk in Not,
das müd Kerker, Despot
und Druck starr gemacht.

Die Sturm erfahren und Qual
gleich dem Schiffe, erstrahl
zum anderen Mal
in Dankespsalms Pracht:

Entschreit', Treue, aus stern-
los wolkdunkler Nahct Kern
weil die Glorie des Herrn
dich neu umflicht!

Since its discovery and publication by Luzzatto this poem has become
perhaps Jehuda Halevi's most celebrated poem after the Song to Zion.
It owes this fame doubtless partly to the surprise that Jehuda Halevi or

indeed "one at that time" "could already do such a thing." Heine's images of the North Sea and surely also the worldly tendencies in the modern Hebrew poetry have stood as godfathers to this poem in the enthusiasm of the nineteenth century and haunt also the numerous translations.

In fact it is a glittering show-piece, today one would probably say: recitation piece; poetically it stands far beneath a little poem like "The Flood," to name something topically related. But Jehuda Halevi's art, technique, may perhaps be studied in this piece precisely for this reason.

It is enormously objective. One could even doubt whether it really owes its origin to the poet's journey to Zion in view of the quarters of heaven [cardinal points], which the fourth quatrain of the first stanza names, if this abstraction of the experienced reality did not fit so well into the poem, which nowhere mentions the poet's purpose for the journey. It is a wholly general I that gets a hearing here, and in the beginning not even that.

The first stanza is of course purely gnomic; it anticipates in greatest generality the content of the whole, arranged with the most conscious art, as again within it the first quatrain which gives the theological foundation to the moral content of the stanza. The subject of the stanza is "the human." The human, who puts to sea full of self-confidence and through the sea-voyage is led to atonement and to recognition of the divine judgment, so that he learns to speak the words of the Psalmist in their truth (Psalm 139:7).[96*] Then the actual content of the poem begins.

The content is apportioned to the four stanzas in such a way that the second and third deal with the storm, the fourth and fifth with the rescue. And the description of the storm, with the exception of one place presently to be discussed, is entirely in the objectivity of the third person, without I, detached; while in the description of the rescue the fourth stanza lets the first person predominate, the I of the speaker; the fifth the personal third person, conveying address as it were, of the blessing. And these two parts are now interlocked by the same means through which the two just characterized halves of the second part are riveted to each other by a means which, if it were not a product of the highest artistic consciousness, could be only incompetence, and an easily avoidable one and, in addition, so that one must be sure to notice it, an incompetence distributed in strict symmetry over the poem: the first quatrain couplets of the third stanza, the first of the fourth

---

96* Psalm 139:7: Where shall I go from thy spirit? or where shall I flee from thy presence?

and the last of the fifth, that is to say, the mid-point of the first and the cornerstone of the second part are locked together by the same rhyme, sometimes even by the same rhyme-words, of which one, the divine name of mercy, "Lord," stands in all three and only in them – otherwise the name of God does not occur in the poem. The first of these three places, which are spread over the poem as the rhyme-bond of the two tierces, allows the I of the poem and God's names to fall in for the first time right into the raging of the elements that are set loose, really God-less and I-less, the latter however still in the third person and the former still timid and in its awareness of sin not yet soaring up to the call. The whole second half of the storm part must still pass and the independence of the elements must have intensified to the horrors of mythical personification – the two concluding quatrains of the third stanza – until man overcomes in the most extreme fear his fear of calling to God. That fourth stanza's introduction of the quatrain marks the moment of this call. And the stanza further develops this call, that is the first half of the second part, the sketch as it were for a poetic prayer to be uttered in dangerous waters: since Jonah's fate is the sole case of a Biblical parallel, thus other cases in which the might of God has proven itself over the wet elements, must be drawn upon for help, the miracle at the Reed Sea (Exodus 14) and at Jordan (Joshua 3), the sweetening of the bitter waters (Exodus 15:22-25)[97*] and the gushing forth of the waters of strife (Exodus 17:1-7).[98*] Finally the prayer cul-

---

97* Exodus 15:22-25: So Moshe brought Yisra'el from the Sea of Suf [Red Sea], and they went out to the wilderness of Shur; and they marched three days in the wilderness, and found no water. 23 And when they came to Mara, they could not drink of the waters of Mara, for they were bitter: therefore the name of it was called Mara. 24 And the people murmured against Moshe, saying, What shall we drink? 25 And he cried to the LORD; and the LORD showed him a tree, which when he had cast into the waters, the waters were made sweet: there he made for them a statute and an ordinance, and there he tested them.

98* Exodus 17:1-7: And all the congregation of the children of Yisra'el journeyed from the wilderness of Sin, by their stages, according to the commandment of the LORD, and pitched in Refidim: and there was no water for the people to drink. 2 Wherefore the people did strive with Moshe, and said, Give us water that we may drink. And Moshe said to them, Why do you strive with me? why do you tempt the LORD? 3 And the people thirsted there for water; and the people murmured against Moses, and said, Why is it that thou hast brought us up out of Mizrayim [Egypt], to kill us and our children and our cattle with thirst? 4 And Moshe cried to the LORD, saying, What shall I do to this people? they are almost ready to stone me. 5 And the

minates, according to Isaiah's words (Isaiah 43:16),[99]* of the God who makes a pathway in strong waters, in the simple recognition of the divine omnipotence over wind and weather. And here, from the concluding quatrain of the fourth to the introductory quatrain of the fifth stanza, occurs that other above-mentioned full rhyme equation and almost full rhyme-word equation, through which the beginning of the fulfilment becomes the rhyme to the end of the prayer. And as now the fulfilment has been consummated and the waters have been transmuted again, like the trial-drink of jealousy (Numbers 5) – which according to the Talmud did not kill the body of the unjustly suspected man, but made it fruitful – there the poem sees, in what has happened, the allegory of the "assaulted, tormented" maiden Israel (Isaiah 54:11);[100]* and it names and rhymes now for the third time the name of God, now again no longer in the form of address, but not as the first time out of timidity, but out of certainty, and with the naming of the divine name calls down blessing upon those now addressed, the people.

On the translation: Stanza 2, line 24: the text names Aaron and Miriam (Num. 12). – lines 26 – 28: "but I fear my sins, / that my imploring / might become an encumbrance." – Stanza 3, line 16: "the scout blind." – Stanza 5, line 15: in the text only one angel of mercy.

SPOKEN TO THE HEART / אמר בלב ימים

Luz., Bet. 73. Harkavy I 31. Brody II 174.

The essential content of the great hymn imparted in the foregoing Excursus here in six epigrammatic lines. And yet not an epigram, rather in the sublimity of their rhythm with the now roaring, now rejoicing

---

LORD said unto Moshe, Pass before the people, and take with thee of the elders of Yisra'el; and thy rod, with which thou smotest the river, take in thy hand, and go. 6 Behold, I will stand before thee there upon the rock in Horev; and thou shalt smite the rock, and there shall come water out of it, that the people may drink. And Moshe did so in the sight of the elders of Yisra'el. 7 And he called the name of the place Massa and Meriva, because of the strife of the children of Yisra'el, and because they tempted the LORD, saying, Is the LORD among us, or not?

99* Isaiah 43:16: Thus says the LORD, who makes a way in the sea, and a path in the mighty waters.

100* Isaiah 54:11: O thou afflicted, tossed with tempest, and not comforted, behold, I will lay thy stones with fair colours, and lay thy foundations with sapphires.

force of the concluding lines of two syllables a genuine lyrical poem,
more than that ambitious hymn.

On the translation: Line 4: and His Name stands firm eternally.

CALM AFTER THE STORM / התרדף נערות אחר חמשים
Fragment (line 65 to end)

Harkavy I 30f. Brody II 163. Brody-Wiener 181.

These lines form the conclusion of a long poem in which the poet admonishes himself to forego finally the pleasures of his world at home
and to decide upon the pilgrimage. The anticipated description of the
anticipated discomforts of this journey, especially of a sea-storm, then
fills the major part of the poem. The description in its technical mastery and "facility" ["*Gekonntheit*"] is strongly reminiscent of the poem
which was contained in the Excursus "Storm," in which anyway at least
the suspicion that it was produced already before the journey, could
not be suppressed. But then the concluding lines come, which,
whether written later under the actual impression or having originated
in ingenious anticipation, in any case belong to the greatest works that
Jehuda Halevi has composed. It is an entirely objective composition,
image upon image, view upon view, – yet every view sweeps its full
curve. In all the profusion there arises no crowding of vision, rather
out of all images only one image, that of the sea resting at night.

On the translation: Line 8: "… like flames and like fire."

TO THE WEST WIND / זה רוחך צד מערב

Luz., Bet. 66f. Harkavy I 24f. Brody II 171f.

Thus there is also among the poems of Jehuda Halevi one "To Zephyr."
And not among the love songs, rather among the songs of the pilgrimage, – which of course are songs of a love as well. And in sweetness this
is second to none of the famous poetry about the west wind of world
literature; it praises the damp wings because they carry the ship to the
place of love's yoke. The rhyme-word "wind" itself already has in Hebrew the melting sweetness, as its German brother-word has the gentle
softness. And out of this underlying atmosphere of breezes and fragrance, without disturbing them, the poet can yet say everything, as his
high office, shared with children and fools, demands. He can, immediately after the humorous shrug of his shoulders in the penultimate

couplet, which smiles at the binding of the creature to a "creature," cross over into the last couplet's sublimity which looks up to the One Who – with the word of the Prophet – "created the winds" (Amos 4:13).[101*]

On the translation: Line 14: ... , which is brought to a boil. Line 16: now is surrounded and now dispatched!

IN THE HARBOUR / הרף שאון ים

Luz., Bet. 77f. Harkavy I 37f. Brody I 10f.

But a continuing east wind drives the ship from its course and forces it to land in Egyptian harbours. From the open sea, whose roaring had filled the poet's ear for a week now, it steers into the harbour of Alexandria. And then what we had least expected happens: with the thought of his host, whom he will seek there, the sweet habit of existence, of the old life that he will find again in Egypt's happy and cultured Jewish community, gain power over the weak human- and poet-heart of the pilgrim who had believed that he had already cast behind him all earthly bonds. Already in this first moment with such a power that he remembers in the mere imagination of a familiar roof only with an outcry – of course of exultation, but yet staggering in its piercing suddenness – that his roof will be where there are roofs no longer. Thus this cry at the moment of landing calls the life-yearning soul of the one who lands, who yet thinks of travelling "tomorrow," back to the self-imposed order of the high goal. And then for all that the "tomorrow" becomes – months.

On the translation: Lines 1f.: ... until the master's face draws near to the kiss of the disciples.

EGYPTIAN SOIL / ראה ערים והתבונן פרזות

Luz., Bet. 109. Harkavy II 3. Brody II 180.

When he thus passes through the land, everywhere a guest of the Jewish great, everywhere celebrated, everywhere lovingly pressed to stay,

---

101* Amos 4:13: For lo, he that forms the mountains, and creates the wind, and declares to man what is his thought, that makes the morning darkness, and treads upon the high places of the earth, The LORD, The GOD of hosts, is his name.

he can justify the delay to himself: that here too is historical soil and that the honour which he bestows on Egypt is meant for the scene of Jewish primal history [*Urgeschichte*]. So much is this poem tuned to the key of self-justification, that people have even suspected that they are hearing here not the voice of the poet himself, but rather the admonition of one of the Egyptian friends who asks him to abandon his strange obstinacy with regard to the pilgrimage and to remain in their midst. Such a distribution of voices to different persons is surely hardly necessary; the following poem, definitely by Jehuda Halevi as assumed by the conclusion, shows how he himself had been gripped by the magic of the historical soil; now the voices speak in him himself, which would like to warn him, if he had not wanted to be "all too righteous" and if not, what is enough for others also must be enough for him.

On the translation: Nothing to note.

THE RIVER / אלהי פלאך דור דור דור ירחש

Luz., Bet. 91. Luz., Div. Nr. 47. Harkavy I 45f. Brody II 183f.

Historical memories adhere to rivers in a different way from the way they do to firm land. For the elapsed centuries have altered the land in many ways, although, no, because it is firm; but the river, which flows through the land, just because it never for a moment was the same, still today is the same as thousands of years ago. Thus he speaks even more immediate testimony of that which happened to and with him than does the land around.[16]

On the translation: Nothing to note.

THITHER ... / נטה בי אלי צען

Luz., Bet. 91f. Luz., Div. Nr. 4. Harkavy I 46. Brody II 183.

But just the river also awakens the old lament of longing. For its much ramified high tide could carry the vessel which could lead the poet from the northeastern "Tunisian" branch of the Nile Delta – and Tunisia is, according to the Septuagint, the Biblical Zoan – on one of the narrow cross connexions to the seas of the Suez Narrows and from there into the Red Sea. Thus he loses himself totally in the yearning and forgets for once his inner conflict. Or could those concluding lines be genuine, with which the poem is included in many places in the rite of the summer weeks of mourning for the Fall of Jerusalem and which former publishers rejected because of their metrical divergences from the rest, while precisely these divergences speak rather for genuineness, at least for familiarity of their author, with the fine points of Arabic metre.

> That is why my heart is so very
> > sick and disquieted.
> Tomorrow becomes night through
> > my sinful flesh and blood.
> My bosom wholly pines away
> > and languishes for the mountain of myrhh,
> Life so yearns towards home
> > in the protection of the body.

> Drum krankt gar sehr dies mein
> > Herz und bekümmert sich,
> Morgen wird Nacht ja durch
> > mein sündig Fleisch und Blut.
> Mein Busen vergehet ganz
> > und schmachtet zum Myrrhenberg,
> Leben begehrt so nach
> > Hausung in Leibes Hut.

Then the divided consciousness of the delay, arising through his own fault, would fall like a hammerblow even into this poem in the spondee $[- - - -]$ shift of the iambic rhythm of yearning $[/ - - , - //]$.

On the translation: Line 2: "the waters" is an addition.

FOREBODING / אם רצון נפשכם

Luz., Bet. 110. Harkavy I 161. Brody I 211.

And then out of all the confusion of the feeling once again the simple word of the truth of the heart breaks through – indeed it cannot be otherwise. The poem is part of a poetic epistle, just as several are preserved from the Egyptian months; by accident that part of the letter prefacing the poem is lost, the one following makes no reference to it. But it is already clear. The poet entreats the Egyptian friends by their friendship to let him go. This time no balancing of the advantage of the Holy Land over the also-advantages [Auchvorzügen] of Egypt, no argumentation, no poetic niceties. Only very quiet words, but the heart is speaking. And the longing for the grave in the holy earth, which wells up again and again, joins now with the anxious presentiment, that if he hesitated any longer the destiny, his destiny could overtake him earlier. And plea, restlessness, and presentiment join in the quiet prayer at the end. He who prays like this has – at least at this moment – found himself again.

But how could it possibly have been that he lost himself? Whoever would ask like that does not know how narrow is the space that is left to the human and his freedom with regard to that which is last and decisive. If ever an entire life has ripened the fruit of a single action, then this. And yet the compulsion must have come in order that the action actually was begun to be done. And as if there were a danger that the action could still even then presume too much and could forget the formerly promised gratitude for every step that allowed it to achieve advancement, its strength is paralysed once more immediately before the final realization; the waters of earthly life threaten to engulf anew the swimmer and he must again, in distress and out of necessity, learn to pray – the prayer of distress, the totally sudden prayer – a prayer that is surprising even to the one who is praying, as it breaks forth here for him from the request to the friends, from the restlessness of the feet, from the trembling of the heart, not quite in the form of a prayer, only the thought of a prayer, a desire for praying.

God gives the human the freedom for the highest decision, for that exactly, only for that. But in giving it, he nevertheless retains the powers of realization in his treasure and freely gives out of it precisely to the one who has decided only upon an ever renewed call. For he does not want to make himself superfluous through the gift of freedom, but rather the reverse is required. He supports the human with a today, and thus makes himself the Lord of the tomorrow. That is why the human must tremble about his today, as long as a tomorrow can still come; and if the divinely sent compulsion stood at the beginning of the realization, so at the end, nearly at the goal, the compulsion stands as propeller of the fear [Angst], the divinely inspired fear, that following this today there might be no tomorrow. And then finally in this fear the deed will nevertheless be born, which the today raises into the eternal tomorrow.

On the translation: Line 2: … , that I may go to my Lord.

ODE TO ZION / ציון הלא תשאלי לשלום אסיריך

Luz., Div. Nı. 16. Harkavy I 10ff. Brody II 155ff. Brody-Wiener 179f. Besides in the usual collections of songs of lamentations for the Ninth of Av.

This Song of Lament is recited every year on the Ninth of Av, the day of the burning of the First and Second Temple, in all synagogues of the world. It is only one among a lot of brothers and sisters, of which in addition a whole series are directly imitative of it, up to the metre, up to the rhyme and up to the opening words. For Jehuda Halevi created the genre. He was the first to take over that metre of Arabic poetry which in its effect through the shift of a thirteen- or fourteen-syllable line acquires a remarkable likeness to the elegiac metre of the ancients, a similarity which yet, apart from the fact that there the longer line takes precedence, disappears again through the tremendous dragging heaviness of the last line's exit of three stresses. He gave to this verse-metre through the chosen rhyme, although he had also used it otherwise, for instance in love-poems – it is the feminine pronoun of the second person indicative of possession – , thus perhaps unconsciously, a suggestion of the "Ach" with which Jeremiah's songs of lament read aloud on that day begin, a suggestion which, as one surely has correctly noticed, has contributed to making this rhyme the classical rhyme of that day's Songs of Lament. But all that is foreground. The effect of the poem rests on something else: on the reality of the address, only seldom achieved and always striven after in all poetry, so, in short, in the truth of the first word: "Zion!"

Zion is the one addressed. She is not in any way "personified" – that would require that something still rings through of her being [*Sein*] before the address. But that is not the case. Zion is only there in the address, she is only the addressed one. Not she, but everything else, excepting the poet alone as the addressing one, drops back into the third person and gains life only insofar as it is taken up in the "you" which returns more than sixteen times in the rhyme and in the line. Not only do the people lose any other existence than that of the "Yours" ["*Deinen*"], but the one otherwise addressed, the simply addressed one, God Himself, is only He whose Spirit poured onto "Your great ones" ["*Deine Grossen*"], is only "Your Creator," "Your Light," the one who "revealed Himself to your Prophets and Seers," who – last intensification – "Himself desires you as a dwelling place." This enduringly burning flame of the presence in undiminished glow, through thirty-four couplets, two times – the first time barely noticeable apart from the brief interruptions – the poet would not have possessed the power to ignite it, and not *as* poet: it is the thousands of years, those in the past as in the future, of the people, out of which the power of this immediacy streams towards him. This power is great enough that those sources themselves can sink away from him and now, in the backflow continuing ever since, the power of this immediacy yearly streams in again to the sources out of which it has come.

That twice mentioned interruption of the flame of the "You" links the flow of the poem, running otherwise in the uninterruptedness of the lament. Longing is the word of the first third up to the fifteenth couplet, longing which penetrates through question, wish, praise, and dreaming anticipation of the fulfilment, until it – sixteenth line – breaks out into a jubilation of the delight that forgets the longing itself. Just in this jubilation it awakes from the dreamed fulfilment to the consciousness of the suffering and of the I – seventeenth to twenty-first couplets. This awakening is sudden enough, to break through for a moment, even grammatically, the magic circle of the I and You, of which the charmed dream in the sixteenth couplet was incapable: in the twenty-second couplet the rent-out I no longer speaks with Zion but instead apostrophes for the duration of two couplets its very suffering – "Cup of suffering oh let … ." But just into this apostrophe Jerusalem's destiny presses in, and in the twenty-fourth couplet in renewed address, which now continues till the end, Zion is again addressed: "Zion you circle of splendour …" And now it is no longer dreaming longing, but neither any longer awakened despair, but bright, manly consciousness, clear inspired vision, knowledge of Israel's suffering and of Israel's greatness, and knowledge that both are destined to crown Zion with an eternal crown. And thus the last couplets may forget the lament and rejoice beforehand the future jubilation: Blessed is he who awaits and experiences it and perceives.

One usually treats the story as legend that Jehuda Halevi, at the goal of his pilgrimage and in sight of the Holy City, was killed by an Arab with his song on his lips. It is without a doubt a legend. But there is still less doubt that the story cannot have been much different. He who composed this poem, it must have accompanied him into his hour of death. There is no room left for anything else.

On the translation: Line 10: "And where the pure ones at other time … You …" Line 20: "… God revealed Himself." Line 24: "with lament" is an addition. – Page 149, line 3: "woodland," "vineyards," "south" for Jaar, Karmel, Gilead. Lines 21f: "… when I think of Ohola and Oholibah." Line 24: "like a wall" is an addition. Page 150, lines 9f.: "Shinear and Patros … , when your Thummim and Urim …"

PART TWO

Responding to Rosenzweig's Halevi Book

CHAPTER ONE

Placing the Halevi Book, Rosenzweig, and the Star

The History of the Halevi Poetry Translations

Rosenzweig's supplementary essay to *The Star of Redemption* contains the signpost that piqued my curiosity and prompted the enquiry which has resulted in this book. The essay, "Das neue Denken" ("The New Thinking"), was addressed to the first, very daunted readers of *Star* (1921). Four years after its publication, Rosenzweig perceived with dismay that few had read the book, and that those who had done so could not grasp what he believed to be a simple, though new, philosophic method.[1] While a fair amount of attention has subsequently been given to both the *Star* and "Das neue Denken," especially since the late 1950s, in the United States, Israel, France, and once again in Germany, no scholar has passed through that significant gateway, leading both into and beyond the *Star*, which states: "The Notes to my *Jehuda Halevi* contain instructive examples of the practical application of the new thinking."[2]

Rosenzweig's designation, "Notes," is a modest one. More accurately, the Notes are profound philosophically reflective essays which display the praxis of the *Star*'s system. By opening this gate, which Rosenzweig himself has unlocked, we can move freely on and between the territories of the *Star* and of the Notes, asking and discovering how the Notes exemplify speech-thinking.

The Notes represent an important portion of Rosenzweig's later work. They may indeed be his greatest contribution to modern Jewish thought in terms of content as well as philosophical genre. The content of almost every note, or reflective essay, is worthy of substantial scholarly response. By definition of the speech-thinking method, moreover, the content of a responsive commentary will also participate in the method. That is, even the attempt through this book to understand how the speech-thinking method of doing philosophy is done is at once already to operate in part within the method. Thus a tension emerges in an attempt to define a system which, in its praxis, wants to be open to the never systemizable: the freedom of addressing speech, and the ever-surprising new events which are created by and arise from living. The effect hoped for here is simply to widen the slight, almost hidden opening of the gateway in that single sentence that claims the Notes to the Halevi poetry offer an example of the philosophical method as explicated in the *Star.* To fulfil this hope, then, the primary aim becomes an attempt to explore how Rosenzweig applies that which he designates as one demonstration of a practical aspect of the theory of speech-thinking.

Rosenzweig began the Halevi project at the end of 1922, the year following the publication of the *Star,* and only months after he had been diagnosed as having amyotrophic lateral sclerosis with progressive paralysis of the bulba.[3] In 1920, however, Rosenzweig, the increasingly observant Jew, had already whetted his appetite for translating from Hebrew, and by the time he fell ill the taste for this activity had grown so sweet to him that no malady could detract from its enjoyment. By 25 October 1925 Rosenzweig could write to Martin Buber that for the past five years his "literary development" had taken place in translating.[4] This development involved not only the act itself of translating but the exploration and experience of different period styles.

From prayer cycles Rosenzweig turned to medieval hymns and poems which, though secondary, had been incorporated into the Jewish liturgy. The first translation from Hebrew was the grace after meals which observant Jews recite daily. Rosenzweig's purpose and aim was to familiarize, in their native tongue, the assimilated and non-observant Jews in Germany with their ever more forgotten and abandoned Jewishness. By 1921 he had completed the entire Friday evening liturgy, for both home and synagogue. This work proved popular. In an undated letter of 1925 Rosenzweig wrote a German translation of the Kol Nidre, the prayer sung on the eve of Yom Kippur.

Primarily, however, apart from the collaborative Bible translation work with Buber, Rosenzweig's translation energies were spent on the poems of Jehuda Halevi. He achieved the remarkable feat of rendering the poems with rhyme, acrostics, and Arabic metre intact. I have not yet, incidentally, found any English translation of a collection of Jehuda Halevi's hymns and poems which approximates, even as a pale shadow, the German language feat accomplished by Rosenzweig.[5]

THE HALEVI-ROSENZWEIG KINSHIP

Both Jehuda Halevi and Rosenzweig perceive themselves as speaking within a wider conversation in which either the Bible is the focal point or God's word participates. In this sense and context, both are providing biblical commentary and consciously sharing in and trajecting the speech of revelation through time. The Notes can be read as a separate work, as its own speech, or even as individual essays, albeit all as response dependent upon the poems (and the Bible) and as address dependent upon the reader. Nahum Glatzer's book offers excellent samplings of about ten Notes, for instance, presenting them without the poems, and arranging them with other of Rosenzweig's writings on similar themes.[6]

In his address to his own readers Rosenzweig at the same time unfolds and acts out his own philosophy. One of Rosenzweig's reasons for translating the poems was to prove that the German language could (as can any) be stretched to incorporate Arabic metre, as the Medieval Spanish Jews had proved before him for the Hebrew language. There is a further twofold reason: to demonstrate the importance, possibility, and imperative of translating between languages and across generations, and to show that true conversation takes place only after true translating of another's speech into one's own. Rosenzweig's primary purpose with the Halevi book is to encourage his own readers to learn to speak Halevi's speech as their own. Both the translations and the Notes support this purpose. The translations draw Halevi into the German language. The Notes expand upon certain details of the form and content of the poems and respond to philosophical and theological issues. My own conversation and enquiry concern not (directly) Jehuda Halevi, but rather Rosenzweig.

In his Afterword to the translation, Rosenzweig indicates the larger conversation revolving around the poems and the Notes, in which all humans can partake in every age with their own fresh and particular speech:

In these poems one can encounter the always renewed words of humility and devotion, of despair of and trust in redemption, of world-aversion and longing for God, of repentance of sins and of faith in mercy – one can do it, but one does not thereby remove the fact from the world that the heart of the poet and the hearts of those for whom he has composed are full of these feelings and wish to see expression for them. The lie has many possibilities, the truth only a few, at base always only one. That it does not become tiresome to say anew this always One again and again testifies to its enduring power. In the mouth of the lover the word of love never becomes old, the word from the mouth that shams love already withers when it is spoken for the first time.[7]

In order further to understand the attraction Jehuda Halevi held for Rosenzweig and why his interest was sustained in translating and responding to the poems until the end of his life, some information regarding the poet's own life and thought will prove illuminating. Born c.1080 in Toledo, Spain, Jehuda Halevi studied the Talmud, philosophy, Arabic literature, and medicine at the academy of Isaac Al-Fasi in Lucena, near Cordova. Upon his return to Toledo he practised as a physician and began to write the poetry that gives him his chief fame. His increasing sensitivity to religious feelings and beliefs led him to the major decision of his life: to undertake the pilgrimage to Jerusalem, where he wished to die.

Jehuda Halevi is in some regards a precursor of the existentialist religious philosophers. His philosophy, like Rosenzweig's, stems from and develops along with a personal standpoint. This existential thrust, namely philosophy out of life history, can, according to Rosenzweig, achieve an empirical philosophy. When this experience is grounded in the concept of revelation and based on the logical positing of three separate elements of reality, personal experience may play a part in philosophizing. This sort of personal experience means one's own life course only in so far as it experiences revelation (and along with it a knowledge of creation and revelation). It is experience which is open to every person, not, for instance, the sort of private and/or privatized religious experience open only to a few. Rosenzweig's "new thinking" is distinct especially in this method whereby he balances the subjectivity of the person with the objectivity of the concept of revelation. Because the concrete "thusness" of existence can be comprehended only through experience, however, experience must be the starting point for thought. The empiricism of this philosophy differs from the usual meaning of the term. Rosenzweig means empiricism in the sense of grasping and contacting existence precisely in its concreteness. Unlike the special sciences which describe the being of phenomena completely devoid of quality and value, the experience sought here relates to the being and to the significance and value of things.

Not only do both Rosenzweig and Jehuda Halevi make personal experience the starting point for philosophy, both also display a kinship in their respective life experiences and thought. Parallel to Jehuda Halevi's turning away from courtly life is Rosenzweig's abandonment of university intellectualism. Both men broke from the prevalent philosophies of their day, and both embraced a radical return to Judaism in its classical and traditional forms at a time when their contemporary Jews were living increasingly assimilated lives. Neither belongs to a philosophic school, but each wrote one major philosophic work, *The Kuzari* and *The Star of Redemption*, respectively, from the standpoint, not of philosophic proofs of God, but of experience and life with God. Both verified the beliefs presented in their books by living them.

Jehuda Halevi lived during the period of the reconquest of Spain by Christians from the north. He belonged by birth and tradition to the upper stratum of court Jewry. In the second half of his life, having witnessed the destruction of successive Jewish communities caught between the Christian and Islamic armies, he made a radical break with court attitudes toward life. Ceasing to write poems of homage to Jewish grandees, he began a new way of writing and thinking that reflected upon Israel's destiny. His break concerned his rejection of the whole foundation upon which Spanish Jewry rested: culture of the senses and mind; love-making and philosophy; economic dependence on the princely courts and political security that relied upon the princes' favour. Profoundly aware that the political and the religious are inextricably related for the Jew, Halevi saw that along with the return to Zion must be a return to God: the return to traditional Judaism with all its transcendent claims as a means of renewing power in the faith.

Halevi's anti-rationalist stance parallels Rosenzweig's charge against idealism: it cannot attain to ultimate truths. The anti-rationalist tone of the *Kuzari* makes it unique among all the products of Jewish mediaeval thinking. Halevi believed that philosophy entails over-dependence on human reason, and as such is an enemy in Judaism's midst. Propositions in philosophy, he claims, can always be argued both ways; even at best they never pierce deeper than the surface of the argument. He reasserts the original historical character of the Jewish faith. To him, metaphysics cannot yield truth: ultimately the real source of religious truth is revelation. Through philosophy, that which attempts, in the will to know, to reach God through autonomous human efforts, the human mind becomes, or seeks to become, as eternal as the truths it assimilates. Chief among the objects it comprehends is God. To Halevi, communion with God is a gift of God, not a product of human effort. Revelatory or historical religion is basically different from the intellectual religion of the philosophers, and God is a radically different being in both. Philosophy is primarily the knowing of God, involving the serenity of the theoretic attitude; and religion is living with God, a dynamic of longing to be with him, in and through love.

As does Rosenzweig, Halevi finds serious fault with the methods and conclusion of traditional philosophy. Both writers, however, uphold the foundations of philosophy in its enquiry into origins when philosophy is abetted by theology. Halevi combatted above all the Aristotelian axiom of the eternity of matter and the Neoplatonic theory of the emanation of the world from spheres. To Rosenzweig also this theory and axiom are unacceptable, and indeed impossible to one who believes in creation and redemption, namely a real beginning and a real ending of the world.

Because the religious life involves the dynamic of yearning, Halevi saw prayer and worship as the apex of the pious person's life. Through prayer one's everyday life acquires a permeating power by which to live. A chief element of piety is joy in God. The pious one's full bliss is communion with God, whereby that person anticipates, in this world, the bliss of the world to come and feels assured of eternal life.

Halevi's greatness and fame lie mainly in his religious poetry. His liturgical poems are especially distinguished by almost unrivalled beauty, deep feeling and mastery of the Hebrew language. Liturgy for Rosenzweig, too, is the apex of speech, for it entails not only communion with God but harmonious communal speech. By Rosenzweig's lifetime many of Jehuda Halevi's poems had been incorporated into the Jewish prayer book, and as such constitute speech commonly spoken by the Jewish community. Jehuda Halevi himself is viewed as a central and classical figure in Judaism. One of Rosenzweig's aims was to draw his contemporaries, whom he defined as living on the periphery of Judaism, into its core. A present-day response to a classical text, Rosenzweig believed, would help to achieve this aim: not so much that the ancient text might speak, but more that those living today might speak old words either in new forms or with fresh voices and thus aspire to the correspondence between innermost essences and external practices and forms. On the capacity of poetry and prayer to remain vigorous both despite and due to repetition, Rosenzweig wrote in his 1923 article, "Apologetic Thinking":

Prayer and poetry are unremittingly at home in being clothed in words over and over again; it is well that a written interpretation reflects them in a thousand facets; well does a mystic immerse himself deeply into them to the point of mythological hypostasis: he becomes word, meaning, form, but not dogmatic formula, not – with the one great exception from all other such works, that of Jehuda Halevi's *Kuzari* – philosophy. He is inspired with and transported by presence [*Dasein*], he is roused by all immediate expression of presence – but whenever he consciously attempts to expound concerning sheer presence, he is unable.[8]

THE ROSENZWEIG-BUBER KINSHIP

Rosenzweig dedicated his Jehuda Halevi book to Martin Buber, whose advice he sought during the course of the work, and whose encouragement in large part saw the book through. While Martin Buber is better known than Franz Rosenzweig, and while their correspondence displays a mutual impact and love, it would nevertheless be a misapprehension to surmise that Buber exercized the greater influence in terms of language, speech, and translation. Their renowned translation of the Bible was sparked by Rosenzweig's work on Jehuda Halevi. Maurice Friedman has remarked:

The stepping stone to the translation itself was the translation of the mediaeval philosopher Jehuda Halevi's poems, which occupied Rosenzweig in 1923. Rosenzweig had frequently turned to Buber for advice, and he dedicated the book to him. Along with the particular examples they soon reached the point where they discussed with each other the problematic of translation in general and the task of the translator. Without being aware of it they found themselves impelled to ask: Is the Bible translatable? Has it already been really translated? What remains still to be done? How is it translated in this age?[9]

Rosenzweig exercised a forceful influence on Buber's *I and Thou*. Before committing his book to writing, Buber, upon Rosenzweig's invitation, gave an oral presentation of it in a course from 15 January to 12 March 1922 at the Freies Jüdisches Lehrhaus. In preparing his lectures in December 1921, Buber read *The Star of Redemption*, which had been published in that same year. Then, in their correspondence from September 1922 which dealt with the galley sheets of *I and Thou*, Rosenzweig seriously questions the systematic construction of the book. Rivka Horwitz has examined this correspondence and analyzes the differences between the lectures and the book. She writes: "Most abundant is the material concerning the influence of Rosenzweig in general, and of his dialogical thinking in particular, both in the last stages of the composition of *I and Thou* and in Buber's subsequent writings ... Rosenzweig's influence can no longer be doubted; only its extent may be differently evaluated."[10]

In comparing the lectures and *I and Thou*, Horwitz pinpoints two major issues that bespeak Rosenzweig's influence: "The first, and by far the more consequential, issue concerns Buber's concept of dialogue, which is central to *I and Thou* but which is almost completely absent from the manuscript of "Religion als Gegenwart." The second concerns the gradual elimination of the terms "realization" and "orientation." "Realization" especially, which is tied to the mystical notion of unification propounded by Buber in 1913, is freely employed in the Lectures, but was abandoned as an important philosophical term after 1923.[11]

Horwitz also points out that the central importance of language occurred to Buber only after that stage in his development represented by the lectures,[12] and that Rosenzweig sensed Buber's lack of clarity regarding the importance of language. After a discussion with Buber concerning dialogue and the *Star*, Rosenzweig wrote to his wife on 4

January 1922 that Buber did not quite see it right, and "speech I will teach him in Frankfurt."[13] Buber came to include speech or language as a cardinal action of the human being "precisely in the months during which Buber maintained a close, personal relation with Rosenzweig."[14]

The point here is not so much to argue who influenced whom but to emphasize that Rosenzweig believed he had already clearly worked out a speech theory by the time of writing the *Star*; it is this speech theory, unchanged by any subsequent influence, which he applies in the Halevi book. While Rosenzweig's debt for ideas on language do not lie with Buber, the debt for the writing of the book, particularly the Notes, does indeed lie with Buber. When Rosenzweig wrote to Buber to ask permission to dedicate the Halevi book to him, he told him, "This little book does owe its origins to you – to your praise and your insistence – and even its form, because but for your urging I would never have pulled myself together to do the prose additions."[15]

Rosenzweig believed that both his Halevi work and his friendship with Buber were gifts. In a tender letter to Buber he later explained that this was why the book rightly should be dedicated to him: "The book now dwells at the center of my life – which speaks not only for the book but against my present life. But, contrary to everything else I have been doing now, it is not something like an obligation, viz., something to be tackled as well as may be, nothing still to be finished, such as, e.g., the Cohen piece [Rosenzweig's introduction to Hermann Cohen's *Jüdische Schriften* (Jewish Writings) (Berlin 1924)], but purely a gift of this and only of this time. This is why it really has to be dedicated to you, since you are yourself such a gift to me."[16]

THE ROSENSTOCK-ROSENZWEIG KINSHIP

By far the greatest influence on Rosenzweig for ideas on language, and one to whom he explicitly states his indebtedness with regard to his speech-thinking philosophy, is Eugen Rosenstock-Huessy. A full ten years prior to Rosenzweig's initial interchanges with Buber, Rosenstock-Huessy had taught the method to Rosenzweig. And with regard to the *Star*, Rosenzweig writes in "Das neue Denken": "But for this decisive influence in the accomplishment of the book I am indebted not to them [Feuerbach and Hermann Cohen] but to Eugen Rosenstock, whose now published "Angewandte Seelenkunde" ["Practical Knowledge of the Soul"], had lain before me in a rough draft for a year and a half when I began to write."[17]

The profundities, problems, and complexities involved in the relationship between these two men who shaped each other's lives and thinking still have not yet been sufficiently brought to light. Robert Gibbs' focus on this neglected area is therefore encouraging; he offers a lengthy and sensitive treatment of Rosenstock's influence on Rosenzweig with regard to language theory in his *Correlations in Rosenzweig and Levinas*.[18] My own discussion of the relationship between these two men will continue in the chapter on translating.

THE SPEECH-LANGUAGE KINSHIP

Gibbs also correctly notes that Rosenzweig's theory of speech is not so rigorously developed as those of more recent language theorists, and yet that Rosenzweig's theory does differ from all others.[19] Here I wish only to state that Rosenzweig does not explicitly distinguish or differentiate any shades of meaning between the words "speech" and "language." The German word "Sprache" means both. Anglophone literature translates "Sprachdenken" with the term "speech-thinking," the francophone with "la pensée du langage." Within the context of Rosenzweig's writing, however, subtle differences between speech and language can be determined. True speech, according to Rosenzweig, is spoken or written language that addresses a specific other person and expects and awaits, however many years the wait may be, a response. Speech is seen as a divinely given faculty that is common to and among all people. At the same time, employment of this faculty by a person, community, or nation gives rise to expression that is particular to individual speakers or individual groups. Because speech is a shared human faculty, however, particularities of speech are, according to Rosenzweig, divinely decreed and commanded to be bridged by translation, both within the same language and between different languages. The true purpose of individual and communal speech and speaking is to achieve understanding and peace among all peoples. The achievement of this purpose will effect the understanding of each language by all other languages through translation. Rosenzweig calls this ultimate achievement the one language, a notion which will be more fully explored in the two following chapters.

THE TASK OF PLACING ROSENZWEIG AND HIS STAR

To attempt to make definitive statements on the place of Franz Rosenzweig in any context is an arduous task. His greatness was sensed from the start; some claim that he is the greatest Jewish thinker of this century; many professional philosophers admit that his thought and his style of expressing it nearly defy understanding. Reactions to Rosenzweig have been scattered, both in time and place, but more often

than not he is highly regarded. Recognizing his greatness and his potential as an important voice in post-modern discourse, both Jewish
and otherwise, an increasing number of thinkers have recently been
intensifying their perseverence in their efforts both to understand and
to place him. This process of placing him thus joins with and depends
upon a simultaneous process of coming to grips with the complexities
of his philosophical system, *The Star of Redemption*, of studying more extensively and deeply his other writings.

By attending to a work which Rosenzweig himself valued at least as
much as he did the *Star*, I aim to participate in this process of understanding and placing him. His Halevi book, requiring its own place,
serves as an example of the practical application of the philosophy
set out in the *Star*. As such, it deserves some sustained attention. The
timeliness of this attention, I suggest, is due in part to two welcome
monographs which contribute with magnificent strides to a better
comprehension of Rosenzweig's opaque magnum opus: Stéphane
Mosès' *System and Revelation: The Philosophy of Franz Rosenzweig* (English
translation by Catherine Tihanyi, 1992; original French, 1982), and
Robert Gibbs' *Correlations in Rosenzweig and Levinas* (1992). These
scholars, while their readings are at variance in some important ways,
have achieved the monumental feat of rewording, that is re-present-
ing, along with clear analyses, the dense knots of thought of the *Star*.
The value of these two contributions cannot be overrated: the effects,
including the anticipated comparisons of the two readings, can only
serve to force further clarification and attention to the details of the
precipitous routes through which Rosenzweig tried to lead his readers.
With these works now standing supportively behind us, or alongside
us, a firmer place for Rosenzweig's *Star* is prepared. Consequently, an
entry into and exploration of the *Star*'s praxis, the Halevi book, becomes appropriate.

I wish to return to Mosès and Gibbs, but before arriving back at
these more solid bases, I want first to offer an outline of the sporadic
and sometimes slippery places Rosenzweig has held till now, and where
conducive, to indicate a link with the Halevi work. Rosenzweig's tenu-
ous hold has been due almost as much to historical circumstances as to
the difficulties in understanding his innovative thought. After the Second World War, Rosenzweig's thought, particularly his ahistorical
notion of Judaism, was discounted by many as entirely dated (or out-
dated), inadequate, and even a naïve mockery of questions facing the
fact of the Holocaust. Levinas, whose own thought always faces the
Holocaust, writes in the introduction to Mosès' book: "Today, fifty
years after Rosenzweig's death, his voice, silent for so long, is reaching
us again. In many respects, and perhaps mostly because of the 'quiet-

ism' that characterizes it, it is a voice from before 1933, before Nazism, before the Holocaust. And yet this much is certain: at the high level where we find it, this work is still today asking the true questions of our time."[20]

By way of reaching our own times, I shall try as briefly as possible (1) to record the slight notice taken of Rosenzweig during his lifetime and to note the now familiar reasons for this, (2) to view Rosenzweig in the context of the Patmos Circle, (3) to trace Karl Löwith's insights into parallels between Heidegger and Rosenzweig, (4) to register recently revived interest in Germany, (5) to review the Israeli response, (6) to discuss the current Francophone response, and (7) to note the rapidly occurring, firmer hold and further dissemination of Rosenzweig's thought which is taking place in North America today. The intention here is to speak primarily of the reception of Rosenzweig's thought, but in thus speaking, some of the thought itself of the new thinking method will of course be displayed. Our subsequent return to Mosès, and to Gibbs, will afford a more focused view in terms both of projecting a place for Rosenzweig through a consideration of the *Star*'s innovative thought and of moving toward the Halevi book. I set these historical aspects in a separate chapter for two reasons. Those new to Rosenzweig's thought may appreciate such a group portrait of Rosenzweig. This multifaceted portrait, moreover, is inextricably, but only indirectly related to the task at hand. I prefer therefore to keep what might have been endnote information more visible, more temptingly placed in the forefront, welcoming further work on each facet displayed here.

Early Obscurity

During his lifetime, Rosenzweig made almost no impact on philosophical or theological thought. Apart from his influence on Martin Buber, and vice versa, no famed figure of the time seems to have been shaped or shaken by Rosenzweig's radical stance, namely his conception of German idealism as the culmination of a philosophical tradition, coupled with his conception of a new philosophy built upon the foundations of that perfected tradition. Two reasons, bearing upon circumstances rather than upon his thought, account for Rosenzweig's nearly invisible movements on the intellectual world during his lifetime. One was of his own engineering, the other out of his hands. The first reason is that Rosenzweig withdrew completely from university life. Hence he himself forestalled any reception in that arena. With regard to the university, he chose not to effect change from within. Such a tactic, true, within the contemporary German academic world, would likely have failed. The *Star* is not a book for common consumption. It requires the time and trained intellect that only, or almost only, those in a university setting or position can devote to it. Even so, Rosenzweig was surprised and disappointed over the dearth of readers – of astute and responsive readers – of the *Star.* He had expected more of a commotion.

The second reason colours the first in a different hue. Upon his turning away from the university, Rosenzweig did indeed direct himself to a new audience, the Jewish community, and here he did employ the strategy of working from within. In the Freies Jüdische Lehrhaus he tried to teach of and in the speech-thinking method, which itself includes working from within, and here he propounded the central ideas of the *Star:* the three elements of reality, their respective essences, their relationships in time. Foreshadowed, but unforeseen, darkly unimaginable circumstances intervened. Not only did Rosenzweig's illness cut short his teaching and administrative career, but the Holocaust prevented virtually all the Lehrhaus students from reflecting upon and furthering his thought. Rosenzweig did in this case choose an audience which he correctly believed he could inspire and influence. The Lehrhaus was generally a successful enterprise. But even there it is doubtful whether his students were fully grasping his thought. According to Nahum Glatzer, "He was simply unable to realize the intellectual limitations of even intelligent, university-trained men and women ... Thus, his direct and immediate influence extended to a small group of men and women; only indirectly, through intermediaries, through his explanatory essay ["The New Thinking"], and finally, through the example of his life, did his word reach wider circles."[21] Circumstances nevertheless largely muted this initial audience's response and therefore Rosenzweig's own speech.

Two men with whom Rosenzweig had close relationships were more inspirational for him than he was for them, although his effect upon them was by no means slight. Hermann Cohen represented for Rosenzweig the philosopher *and* human being; Eugen Rosenstock-Huessy the intellectual *and* man of faith. He considered both as whole men, that is to say, men who did not dualize or divorce knowledge and faith, and as such he respected them profoundly.

Rosenzweig met Hermann Cohen (1842–1918) in 1913. It was through Cohen, the neo-Kantian philosopher and leader of the Marburg School, that Rosenzweig first began to find the satisfaction in Judaism that Rosenstock-Huessy had found in Christianity. When Cohen and Rosenzweig met, the former's thought had moved away from its stress on the significance of the elements of flux and becoming and was distinguishing clearly between God as being and the world as becoming. Being and becoming Cohen saw as correlatives, and as such mutually dependent, God needing human beings as much as they need God. Instead of reason being uppermost, the I-thou language of correlation had come to the fore.[22] Rosenzweig believed that Cohen had "advanced with a powerful surge far beyond the philosophical movement of the nineteenth century, into the philosophical country of the future."[23] In Cohen's view, the human being is not merely *beside* another human being, as for Kierkegaard with the *Nebenmensch*, but actually a *fellow* human being, the *Mitmensch*. This idea of correlative partnership permeates Rosenzweig's writing. But as the later work of Hermann Cohen is relatively unknown beyond the circle of intellectuals concerned with modern Jewish thinkers, a wider audience for Rosenzweig was not yet to branch from this venue.

Eugen Rosenstock-Huessy, as already stated, stands in a special position. He and Rosenzweig regarded each other as alter egos, not simply as communicating Jew and Christian. As Harold Stahmer aptly phrases it: "They were dedicated to the *word* – to a common speech which each viewed as *the* fundamental vehicle for discovering meaning and truth at that moment ... The authority of each tradition was represented in and through the named individuals as an ontological reality – as a part of his actual being, rather than as an intellectual system of thought and doctrine which stands over against and judges human deeds."[24]

Not only did Rosenstock-Huessy introduce Rosenzweig to the speech-thinking method and practise it with him, often painfully, in their actual lives,[25] but the essay of "decisive influence," "Angewandte Seelenkunde" (literally, "Applied Knowledge of the Soul"), had actually been written specially for Rosenzweig.[26] It was largely upon this essay that Rosenzweig, in response, based and built his part two of the *Star*, that part devoted to the concept of revelation.

"Applied Knowledge of the Soul" holds that the body and mind do not present a dichotomy in the human being, but are two facets of the same thing. The soul, Rosenstock-Huessy maintains, uses the one and the other at appropriate times in order to express itself. Moreover, the soul's utterances occur because and only after it has been spoken to. Superficial philosophers of language, according to Rosenstock-Huessy, confuse the ability to speak with the necessity to speak. "When a person is confronted by the need to speak, however, he no longer sees speech as a tool by which he can make himself understood. Rather, he is seized by speech because things demand to be understood by him; because a man wants to be fully comprehensible, or because God wishes to become audible to him."[27]

In the *Star* Rosenzweig picks up, reacts to, complements and expands key features from "Practical Psychology." He affirms the relationship between God and human beings. He understands the soul as a gift from God. He regards the soul, once called by God, as having a mission, a burning desire, that compels it to share itself with other souls, lest it subside into another form of isolation. This other form constitutes the attempt at sustaining for too long a private love duet with God, unsung in the world of human beings, restricted to God. Such a form of isolation results, according to Rosenzweig, in a shrivelled soul which claims to "know" and to "love" God. Actually such a partially awakened soul remains unfulfilled as long as it does not seek expression in interhuman speech. Rosenstock-Huessy sees the soul as having stages of development and transformation that are grammatical and durational: the use of soul-language resolves the dichotomy between mind (I) and body (it) in the "you" of the soul. Finally, the "we" of souls is not a plural of one plus one plus one, but is communal expression that fuses a piece of the world into eternity.

Rosenstock-Huessy accepted the position of Professor of Social Philosophy at Dartmouth College in 1935, held it until 1957, and died at his home in Norwich, Vermont in 1973. Despite the publishing of his voluminous writings, he has to date had no enormous effect in respect to implanting his own or Rosenzweig's thought in North American intellectual soil. Rosenstock-Huessy, then, as Cohen before him, cannot be said to have paved any smooth roads into Rosenzweig's thought.

The Patmos Circle

In a wider, looser context Rosenzweig can lay claim to a place among his contemporaries through his connection with the Patmos Circle.

The Patmos Circle was a group particularly active during the immediate, shattered post-World War I period. Serious social, philosophical, and theological thinkers were deeply concerned with the collapse of what had seemed the supremacy of reason and with finding once again, but along new lines, and remolding fresh meaning and orientation for life. Rosenzweig was not a member of the Circle, but in company with such diverse thinkers as Hans and Rudolf Ehrenberg, Karl Barth, and Nicholas Berdyaev, was a contributor to the Circle's periodical, *The Creature*. Noteworthy among the original members of the Patmos Circle are Leo Weismantel, Werner Picht, Hans Ehrenberg, and Karl Barth.

The bond that united both members of the group and contributors to the periodical was their evaluation of the effects of the idealism, historicism, and positivism of the nineteenth century upon their own time. They judged their age as suffering primarily from a distortion of speech. Stahmer neatly sums up their common position: "The problem as the Patmos group viewed it was characterized by an absence of real personal encounter, together with a lack of a common language able to bridge the cultural and academic compartmentalization which prevailed not only in academic circles but at every level of European and, especially, German culture."[28]

Rosenstock-Huessy, a later member, states the aims of *The Creature's* editors, who included the Catholic Joseph Wittig, Martin Buber, and the psychiatrist Victor von Weizsäcker:

"The Creature" represented the sum of the struggles of Kierkegaard, Feuerbach, Dostoevsky, Nietzsche and William James. They had all discovered, that no one has really anything to say, if they all say the same thing. The creature does not speak as God does. A husband does not speak as his wife, nor does a Christian as a Jew, nor a child as a professor. For that very reason and solely for that reason are they able to speak to, and must they speak to, one another ... What the editors of "The Creature" discovered, were the spiritually nourishing processes experienced by genuinely speaking and existentially thinking persons.[29]

While the members of the Patmos Circle and the contributors to *The Creature* were rooted in a common purpose and were mutually supportive and responsive to each other, the authors branched out in compatible but diversely individual directions. Most well known among the works of the period is Buber's *I and Thou*, but independently of Buber and Rosenzweig, others developed their own philosophies of the dialogical I-thou: Karl Jaspers, Gabriel Marcel, and Max Scheler. Unlike Buber, both Rosenstock-Huessy and Rosenzweig appreciate and insist on the value of I-it speech as well, that is, formal and impersonal speech that ensues when the human being is speaking about the world.

For all the fruits associated with the Patmos Circle it was nonetheless not a school. While certain thinkers in the group are well known today, it is not the name Patmos Circle that brings them renown. Stahmer writes: "It should be remembered ... that the Patmos Circle, that small group of 'co-speakers and listeners,' was in fact, a small personal community within a larger impersonal culture. The Patmos Group was an island set apart which gave its inhabitants time and nourishment for speaking to the social needs which its members faced."[30]

Karl Löwith's Attention to Rosenzweig

Europe's attention to Rosenzweig outside Germany, and other than in France, remains much the same now as during Rosenzweig's lifetime.

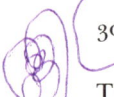

The philosopher of some stature and one-time student and teacher under Heidegger, Karl Löwith, has, however, indicated ways in which Rosenzweig might be included in studies of Heidegger's thought.[31]

Löwith, formerly of Marburg, notes that European universities knew Rosenzweig by name from his published dissertation, "Hegel und der Staat" (1920), but that as late as 1928 *The Star of Redemption* was still entirely unknown.[32] Only four years after his 1939 departure from Europe did Löwith himself begin to read the 700 pages comprising Rosenzweig's correspondence which had been recommended to him by a friend. "The impression Rosenzweig's personality made was so strong that thereupon I procured also his principal work in philosophy, *The Star of Redemption* and his collected *Shorter Writings* and perused these more than 1000 pages at one stretch."[33] What had particularly struck him was the similarity between Rosenzweig's and Heidegger's starting points. "If Heidegger ever had a 'contemporary' who would deserve of such a denotation in a more than external sense, it was this German Jew whose own thoughts were not even remotely known to Heidegger or his pupils."[34] Heidegger was known to Rosenzweig, who interpreted him by claiming that he "*de facto* though not consciously – represented the 'new thinking' of the old Cohen."[35] Hermann Cohen, a teacher of Rosenzweig's, undermined Idealism in his *Religion of Reason* through its main concept of correlation between the human being and God, and between individual human beings, and, in Rosenzweig's estimation, anticipated the "new thinking." Like Rosenzweig's *Star*, Cohen's *Religion of Reason*, however, "remained wholly unknown."[36]

The common starting point of Heidegger and Rosenzweig is the individual in the finitude of existence preceding all established civilization. Both philosophize in opposition to their scholarly milieu *in philosophos* and simultaneously *in theologos* – to echo Rosenzweig's terms – because they regard themselves as both at the same time. Their meaning of "is" differs from the traditional concept of essence. To them, the consideration of what the world is – water to Thales; spirit to Hegel – offers only a conceivable generality, but fails to determine the reality of experience and the particular event that "I only know because I happen to be involved in it and because my historical existence is constituted by it."[37] Essence knows nothing of time; reality is grasped only in time. The taking seriously of time and of the grammatical tenses, Löwith points out, is characterized in Heidegger's terms such as *alltäglich, jeweils, zunächst, schon immer, im voraus* and *um-zu*.

Rosenzweig and Heidegger branch apart from their common starting point in three major areas. The first divergence occurs at the point of the other person. Others, to Heidegger, are simply each peculiar ones who are mere beings "together" with me. To Rosenzweig the other is partner, the You belonging to an I, by which relation the I acquires an altered meaning.

The second point of divergence occurs where Heidegger's concept of existence as "being-in-the-world" is distinguished from Rosenzweig's concept of relationship of human and God and world. To Heidegger, the existence of the human being and of the world is an "undivided phenomenon." Löwith indicates the unnaturalness of Heidegger's conception by noting that Heidegger "is compelled to compound the 'undivided phenomenon' by means of three hyphens (being-in-the-world). Yet one who is so intimately acquainted with language and has his thinking proceed from it, ought to have become aware that it cannot be a mere accident if language lacks a common word for the existence of man and that of the world."[38]

The purpose of the whole of part one of the *Star* is to demonstrate simply the impossibility of tracing the three elements back to each other. They are connected by "and" and are not forced into unity nor are the world, the human being, and the temporal God of the world without a beginning in creation.

Third, Heidegger's "freedom towards death" stands against Rosenzweig's eternal life. Heidegger, in conceiving of existence as really independent and as having no authority above itself except death, nevertheless stops short of the Stoic view which holds suicide to be a sort of ultimate wisdom. According to Löwith, this was due to Heidegger's unconscious adherence to the Christian view that suicide is a sin. At the same time, Heidegger's concept of resolute existence shows his anti-Christian and irreligious thrust.

Rosenzweig, on the other hand, sees suicide simply as unnatural because it is contrary to the nature of life. Death as dying, however, belongs to life. Unlike Heidegger's resolve to take oneself upon oneself and that only freedom makes us true, Rosenzweig speaks of recognizing one's creatureliness and being open to revelation and the promise of eternity.

According to Löwith, the concept and understanding of time is left open to and beckons further philosophical enquiry. He recognizes: "A serious attempt has been made in the nineteenth century, it is true, to restore eternity to life – be it that of the cosmos or that of the biblical God, but it was doomed to failure. Kierkegaard's "eternal instant" and his discourse on God's "immutability" as well as Nietzsche's *paradoxon* of the "eternal recurrence" sprung from the insight that we need eternity to be able to withstand the time. But convincing in all this is not the eternity they were aiming at, but the criticism of time with which they started."[39]

Current Interest in Germany

From 7 to 11 December 1986, an international congress was held in Kassel, Germany, to commemorate the hundredth anniversary of Rosenzweig's birth. Close to seventy papers were contributed from all parts of Europe, Israel, and the United States.[40]

In his foreword to the published papers, Wolfdietrich Schmied-Kowarzik discusses the unchanged status of Rosenzweig in Germany since his lifetime. He states that Rosenzweig's generally unknown position arises not only from consequences of his illness but also from the mode of delivery of much of his thought: largely in the form of personal correspondence.[41] Further, Schmied-Kowarzik notes that not only did the Holocaust preclude Lehrhaus students from building upon Rosenzweig's thought and method, but that, immediately upon Rosenzweig's death in 1929, Jewish contributions to knowledge began to be radically uprooted from German soil. Only now, he says, decades after World War II, have the first appropriations and assessments of Rosenzweig's thought begun to be reseeded in that thinker's native soil. The symposium held in Kassel, then, had this purpose in mind: to endorse, support and consolidate this new beginning in order to foster the rediscovery of the philosopher Rosenzweig in Germany.[42]

From the contributions from America and Israel, Schmied-Kowarzik deduced that although Germany had all but forgotten Rosenzweig, there had been an unbroken regard for him elsewhere. Israel and the United States seemed particularly interested in him for his knowledge and teaching of Jewish belief, while Christian churches turned to him for guidance in dialogue.

The papers presented at the symposium can be roughly divided as follows: volume 1 focuses more on the life and historical impact of Rosenzweig, and is entitled *Die Herausforderung jüdischen Lernens*; the second volume addresses the more strictly philosophical-systematic content, and is titled *Das neue Denken und seine Dimensionen*. The contributors include people who represent longtime, solid scholars of modern Jewish thought, among them: Bernhard Casper, Emil Fackenheim, Paul Mendes-Flohr, Nahum Glatzer, Martin Goldner (the last secretary of the Lehrhaus), William Hallo, Rivka Horwitz, Reinhold Mayer, Stéphane Mosès, Natan Rotenstreich, Norbert Samuelson, and Harold Stahmer. While Emmanuel Levinas, a Holocaust survivor, refuses to touch German soil, he did nevertheless send to the congress words of greeting and encouragement.[43]

The impact of this meeting can of course not yet be measured. The fact that it took place is perhaps the most important feature to be noted so far.

The Responses of Rosenzweig's Israeli Critics

Michael Oppenheim's comprehensive survey of Rosenzweig's reception in Israel[44] shows that, particularly since 1970, interest in Rosenzweig has been steadily increasing and that this interest covers a wide range of areas in Rosenzweig's thought.

In 1960 some of Rosenzweig's shorter writings began to be translated into Hebrew. The *Star* was translated in 1970. Until about 1970 Rosenzweig's anti-totalizing system was rejected in Israel. Ernst Simon provided the first significant statement on Rosenzweig when, in 1956, he explained that the lack of interest was due less to the lack of translations than to the dominant Israeli intellectual climate. On one side secular rationalism went hand in hand with assigning the highest value to the state. On the other side many religious groups, in the face of traditional Judaism, viewed theology and philosophy with suspicion.

Since 1970 the attention to Rosenzweig has ranged from sharp disagreement to welcoming appraisals. The extremes are represented by Jacob Fleischman and Ehud Luz. Basing his conclusions on Rosenzweig's earlier writings, Fleischman criticizes Rosenzweig's apparent anti-Zionist stance as being the outcome of his Christian and German Idealist influences. Luz, on the other hand, detects in Rosenzweig a gradual, complex move towards Zionism, especially evident from the time of the Lehrhaus and of his Halevi book.

Most Israeli critics stand between these two extremes, but severe censure is stamped upon Rosenzweig's statements that the true Jewish homeland is the diaspora and that the Jewish people are a- or meta-historical. Eliezer Schweid points shrewdly to a particular inconsistency: Rosenzweig rejects as limited the neo-orthodox definition of the Jew as the one who performs *mitzvot*; yet he himself narrowly defined Judaism as communal liturgy and the individual's inner life.

From another angle, some who hold reservations about the state's possible achievement have turned to Rosenzweig for guidance. These include Samuel Hugo Bergman and Baruch Kurzweil, who reflected seriously on Rosenzweig's caution that the eternal purpose of Jewish existence would be thwarted by a return to history.

Most favourably judged are Rosenzweig's views and works on Jewish education which concern the return of the Jew to Judaism. Oppenheim cites Ernst Simon's contention that these writings point "to the next revolution, after Zionism, in the lives of the Jewish people: their 'spiritual auto-emancipation.' "[45] The two presuppositions underlying Rosenzweig's education system are invariably upheld: the Jews are one, eternal people; and individual Jewishness is relevant to each individual's every perception and activity.

Another area of positive response is to Rosenzweig's understanding of Jewish law and Rosenzweig's own relevance to Jewish life. In regard to the law, Rosenzweig is valued more highly than is Martin Buber, because Buber dismissed the personal significance of the law. Rosenzweig's undogmatic approach to the law involves the individual's path toward self-understanding and development, and many thinkers, notably Yehoshua Amir, have been profoundly impressed by it.

Most doubted among his Israeli critics is Rosenzweig's belief that a full return to tradition could be accomplished in the diaspora by means of such schools as the Lehrhaus.

Concerning the response to the *Star*, Theodore Dreyfus affirms Rosenzweig's influence on philosophers and historians of philosophy in Israel. Dreyfus wrote that "those who struggled with the relationship between general philosophy and Jewish philosophy in Israel between the 1930s and the 1970s walked in the wake of this great German-Jewish thinker."[46] Moshe Schwarcz came to believe, with Rosenzweig, that revelation is the bridge between philosophy and theology and points beyond dogmatic philosophic idealism and historical relativism. Thus, for both Rosenzweig and Schwarcz, revelation combines individual religious experience and objective event in the divine plan.[47]

The Israeli commentators often acknowledge Rosenzweig's philosophy of speech-thinking as his legacy for today. Eliezer Schweid and Samuel Bergman offer the best accounts of this aspect of Rosenzweig's thought. Schweid emphasized and expanded the following ideas: "The information that we can glean from language transcends what any one individual can experience. Within the language of any community there is the record of the people's past experiences as well as the limits or possibilities of what it can experience in the future."[48]

Samuel Bergman focuses on the link between revelation and speech, agreeing that the true dialogue among human beings is the one that continues the dialogue that God first started with humankind.

Nathan Rotenstreich takes Rosenzweig much to task over one such area of "universal horizons," over what he calls Rosenzweig's highly ambiguous concept, "common sense," which, Rosenzweig claims, provides his system with the necessary elements – God, human being, world. Rotenstreich says Rosenzweig never elucidates the way in which "common sense" arrives at this conclusion, and thus Rosenzweig is philosophically unsound with regard to the existence of God.

Jacob Fleischman also questions the philosophical authority of Rosenzweig, relegating his philosophical work to an "anti-rationalistic" theological stance that relies upon the author's personal religiousness. Moreover, Rosenzweig's "Judaism," he argues, is not true to Jewish history, but instead his reaction to German thinkers such as Goethe, Hegel, and Schelling.

Paul Mendes-Flohr holds that Rosenzweig's significance rests in his capacity to speak to modern Jews who both are sensitive to theological and religious questions and take a critical stand before the Jewish tradition. He has published two fine volumes which I want to mention here as an extension of Oppenheim's study before completing the survey of the Israeli response. Paul Mendes-Flohr is arguably the most outstanding, as well as most prolific bearer of Rosenzweig's thought. He sets much of his work in the wider context of other Jewish thinkers, most notably Martin Buber. He is the editor of *The Philosophy of Franz Rosenzweig*,[49] which offers a selection of essays arising from the symposium organized on the occasion of the fiftieth anniversary of Rosenzweig's death for the Fourth Jerusalem Philosophical Encounter and sponsored by the Shmuel Hugo Bergman Centre for Philosophical Studies at the Hebrew University of Jerusalem in the spring of 1980. As Mendes-Flohr notes in the Introduction, the aim is to elucidate the continuity of Rosenzweig's philosophical contribution with that of German Idealism. According to Mendes-Flohr, in the *Star* Rosenzweig sets his "theocentric affirmation of Judaism" as a particular (other) which has a bearing on the highest questions of human existence (the universal). Rosenzweig sees and intends this mutual exchange between the theological and the philosophical as a "system of philosophy," not one of Judaism or of religion. The Halevi book, as practical application of the *Star*, should likewise be characterized as philosophy. *The Philosophy of Franz Rosenzweig* includes essays covering a wide range of details in Rosenzweig's thought: concepts of language, of experience, of responsibility, of history, of Jewish mysticism, of meta-. In terms of the major principle of separation of elements (man, God, world) in Rosenzweig's system, whose bridging is the overall theme of the Halevi book, the essay by Nathan Rotenstreich on meta- provides an important entrée. He clearly and accurately describes Rosenzweig's use of meta- to mean outside, or before, the truths of relating and not as a static, non-relational above. This notion of meta- opens to possibilities of completion (or perfection) the physical, the logical, the ethical aspects of God, world, and human respectively. That is, whereas in traditional philosophy meta- designates an attribute, quality, or essence of inaccessability, in the new thinking under the framework of revelation the meta- is precisely that which is, through time, accessible.

Paul Mendes-Flohr's *Divided Passions*[50] attempts (successfully), in thematically and hermeneutically related essays, sociologically and culturally to understand the phenomenon of the Jewish intellectual, the tension between Jewishness and universality. About this rich and rewarding volume I wish here to state only that the majority of the essays discuss aspects of Rosenzweig's thought. Moreover, two sections of the volume are devoted to the postmodern notions of "other" (here the Jewish intellectual) and "openness." Of these two sections, "On the Bivalent Way" and "At the Crossroads," Mendes-Flohr writes:

One will note how such giants of modern Jewish thought as Martin Buber and Franz Rosenzweig perforce place Judaism (namely, its conception of God, ritual piety as structured by divine law, and the covenant elevates Israel as "a people apart" from the nations of the world) and Jewish solidarity (as expressed through Zionism) in the dock to be defended before a forum of modern, "universal" opinion. But not all modern Jewish thought need be apologetic, as indeed Buber and Rosenzweig themselves manifestly indicate in other expressions of their life and thought … The quest for parity – for a bivalent way – has been replaced by an open-ended – unselfconscious, unapologetic – plurality of possible alliances between one's Jewishness and the universal horizons of one's intellect and concern.[51]

Michael Oppenheim concludes his own review by indicating two features of Rosenzweig's thought that will prove important to the current social, political, and intellectual Israeli context. He writes:

First, some of Rosenzweig's insights might find sympathy with those who are looking for a corrective to the surging religious-nationalist ideology. This may be the time to remember Rosenzweig's desire to distinguish between the eternity of Judaism and the Jewish people, and the transitory pursuits of all nations that enter the historical arena. Second, Rosenzweig's presentation of a dynamic and pluralist Jewish spiritual life, which demanded that the mitzvoth be seen as catalysts and not as obstacles to new developments within Judaism, will continue to be valued by many Israeli thinkers.[52]

It should also be mentioned, though it is too early for assessment, that from 12 to 17 July 1992, the Tenth Annual Conference of the International Center for University Teaching of Jewish Civilization, held at Hebrew University, Jerusalem, had as its theme for the Continuing Workshop in Jewish Philosophy, "Paradigms in Teaching Jewish Philosophy. The Medieval Era: Judah-Halevi. The Modern Era: Franz Rosenzweig."[53] Participants who focused particularly on Rosenzweig included Richard Cohen, Paul Mendes-Flohr, Robert Gibbs, Gershon Greenberg, Rivka Horwitz, Irene Kajon, Ephraim Meir, Eliezer Schweid, and me. From the participants' unanimous agreement that meeting together was very profitable and enlightening, it can be hoped that further fruits arising from the study and teaching of

Rosenzweig's thought are slowly ripening in Israel, Europe, and North America.

The Current Francophone Response: Levinas, Mosès

The francophone world reacted almost at once to its reception of the French translation of *The Star of Redemption* [*Stern der Erlösung*] in 1982.

Emmanuel Levinas, nearing the end of his substantial philosophical career, strongly endorses Rosenzweig as a man and as a Jew, as philosopher and religious thinker. Rosenzweig's influence upon Levinas runs so deep, and so extensively do his writings speak with Rosenzweig, that Levinas could observe in relation to his *Totality and Infinity*: "We were impressed by the opposition to the idea of totality in Franz Rosenzweig's *Stern der Erloesung*, a work too often present to be cited."[54] Levinas both participates in and precedes the francophone literature that has emerged since the 1982 French translation. His *Totality and Infinity* was published in French in 1961 and in English in 1969. In 1963 he published a biographical article on Rosenzweig.[55] In 1982 Levinas reiterated his position regarding Rosenzweig, namely that instead of making a scientific inventory of Rosenzweig's individual works or seeking to outline his development as a thinker, Levinas takes all of Rosenzweig's ideas "*en bloc*" and, in fusing them into his own thought, develops them further.[56] Levinas displays a marked bond with Rosenzweig in the following areas: an anti-totalizing worldview, as regards the political and social implications as well as philosophical and theological matters; the view of the self in the face of the other as neighbour; the notion that love is as strong as death; incorporation of a positive evaluation of Christianity within a Jewish worldview; and most important, what Levinas names "l'essentiel du projet – conscient et lucide – de Rosenzweig, [le rapprochement de] la philosophie de l'expérience et de l'attitude théologique."[57] Levinas' interest in and support of Rosenzweig will doubtless bring about even wider attention, prompting further understanding of both Rosenzweig's and Levinas' thought.

Wendell S. Dietrich of Brown University reviewed the original French version of the current major Francophone contribution to Rosenzweig studies.[58] Stéphane Mosès' *Système et révélation: La philosophie de Franz Rosenzweig*,[59] is both influenced and prefaced by Levinas' social theorist interpretation of Rosenzweig. As intimated, I suggest that the recent English translation of this book, along with Robert Gibbs' *Correlations in Rosenzweig and Levinas*, will shortly spark a plethora of reactions, especially in North America. In his review, Dietrich proposes to indicate how the francophone literature sets standards for work in departments of Judaic studies. Dietrich calls this literature francophone and not French because it is not exclusively the product of France. Mosès, for example, now resides in Israel. Nor is this literature exclusive to the Jewish community and its interests and concerns. The authors publish in a variety of general academic journals, including *Archives de philosophie* and *Recherches de sciences religieuses*.

In the preface to Mosès' work, and elsewhere (*Totalité et infini*), Levinas calls attention to Rosenzweig in certain specific regards. First, unprecedented in previous Jewish thought is Rosenzweig's assigning to Christianity, alongside Judaism, the role of being one of the two great historical realities. To Rosenzweig, these two are always in complementary interaction but also unceasingly theologically opposed.

Second, Levinas emphasizes Rosenzweig's claims against all previous major systems, from Thales to Hegel, which reduced reality to one element, for the irreducible reality of each mode of being: world, human being, God.

Third, according to Levinas, Rosenzweig's doctoral dissertation, an interpretation and critique of Hegel's theory of the state, also shows Rosenzweig to be more than an existentialist thinker in Kierkegaard's way: he is also a social theorist. To Levinas, "Rosenzweig saw the deadly import of Hegel's claims for the totalizing reality of history and its inevitably developing social and cultural dynamisms ... As a witness against these totalizing dynamisms of Western culture, Rosenzweig interposed the social reality of the Jewish people 'beyond history' in eternity, already 'with God.' "[60]

This third point in Levinas' interpretation is the one that informs Mosès' book, and in Dietrich's opinion it is this social theoretical dimension of Rosenzweig's theory of Judaism that will have the most important impact on the expansion of understanding Rosenzweig among his anglophone audiences. Moreover, to Dietrich the connection between Levinas' and Rosenzweig's thought shows Rosenzweig to be more in continuity with the interpretations of Judaism during the late 1800s as ethical monotheism than is generally allowed. Levinas' own ethical monotheism is decisively oriented by recognizing the "visage" of the other as the other confronts me. That other declares, "Thou shalt not kill," and challenges me to acknowledge the neighbour's claims as radically superior to the obligation to the self.

Dietrich examines two specific contributions made by Mosès. One is the theme of system and revelation, and the other is what he terms "the modern political presence of Israel."[61] In contrast to the theological stand of his Protestant neo-orthodox contemporaries, Rosenzweig avoids reducing theological thought to the theme of revelation. He aims to reestablish the theme of creation, and to interpret redemption as fulfilling the command to love the neighbour and as human transforming of the created world. To Mosès, the *Star* evidences Rosenzweig's "struggle to overcome the temptation to construct a Hegelian system of revelation, in which revelation is thoroughly assimilated without remainder to a rational totality."[62] Further, Rosenzweig's theory of knowledge, to be verified finally only at the end of time by God, is "broken up out of the future." At the same time, the explicit social realities of Christianity and Judaism represent the site where God's revelatory truth is encountered. Recognition of the irresoluble disagreement between Judaism and Christianity guards against "premature systematic closure."[63]

Judaism for Rosenzweig is religious community and ethnic collectivity, and the simple existence of the Jewish people provides the ethical witness against all totalitarianism. Is Rosenzweig's stand then open to the possibility that the ethnic reality might be expressed in the presence of the modern state of Israel? Is Rosenzweig simply anti-Zionist?

By no means a full-blown Zionist, Rosenzweig does uphold the Zionist critique of the diaspora, that is: "Zionism's challenges can prompt the Jewish people to forsake their complacent settling down in the West; the Zionist challenge reinforces awareness of the distinctive ethnic dimension of the people."[64]

Mosès wants to go deeper. Within Rosenzweig's system, a Jewish state would not attribute absolute validity to its own existence and actions because it would not perceive itself as embracing messianic nationalism. Indeed, it would see itself as a redemptive projection and "partial realization of a properly ordered future set of social and political arrangements."[65] This political refusal at the heart of the Jewish vocation "functions to relativize the import of any such realization."[66]

Dietrich brings to bear a final point in his assessment and locating of the francophone literature. Since the 1930s French intellectuals have been involved in reappropriating Hegel with a special regard to neo-Marxist and existentialist versions, and as well carefully reappraising the late nineteenth century German philosophical world from Nietzsche to the neo-Kantians. All this comports well with the kinds of interests Rosenzweig studies arouse, and according to Dietrich will prove Rosenzweig has a future in the academic world far more solid than his past has been.

Rosenzweig in North America

Unlike the francophone world, North America has, by comparison, been slow to respond to the English translation of the *Star*, presented in 1971 by William H. Hallo.[67]

Nahum N. Glatzer, Rosenzweig's friend, was the first to introduce Rosenzweig to North America, through his still very helpful *Franz Rosenzweig: His Life and Thought* (1953). With a selection of diary entries, letters, and biographical information followed by a judicious choice of translated excerpts from a wide range of Rosenzweig's various writings, Glatzer offers a fair introduction to new students and pointers for more seasoned scholars. The book was reprinted in 1961 and 1975, with updated bibliographies.

In 1964 Rivka Horwitz published "Franz Rosenzweig on Language," one of the earliest pieces to appear in the u.s.

Rather than enter a detailed or extended discussion of each appearance of scholarly attention to Rosenzweig on this continent, I prefer to indicate a feature of Rosenzweig's reception here. It is that of sporadic scholarship. That reception is sporadic in terms both of response to the scholarship itself and of the reasons for attending Rosenzweig in the first instance. This feature of sporadic scholarship was already predicted by a discerning reading of the *Star* by one of the first reviewers. Hans Ehrenberg wrote, in the 29 December 1921 edition of the *Frankfurter Zeitung*:

The book offers in places great difficulties. Nevertheless it makes the reader – into a listener, and it is easier to listen further than to read further. It is much too much full of music not to stir up soon also in us the echo of a melody which then resounds further until the melody of the book comes to an end. So it offers us the fullness of life, contained in the container of thought. Content and form are of a piece. Therefore there streams out of it a fragrance like from tree which stands in full bloom. And yet this fragrance does not obscure. It is certainly not to be called a fruit, visible schools it will make with difficulty. Yet it will have an effect as a living person himself has an effect, atmospheric and penetrating, and will creep into the heart like all that has itself originated from the heart and was nourished with the blood of love.

The long and sporadic listening to the *Star* over the past two decades in North America is just now really catching hold in a stronger swell of responsive voices which join with those who have already spoken.[68]

Paul Mendes-Flohr, significantly, was a student of Glatzer's at Brandeis, and since then has listened deeply and beckons others to do likewise.

Soon after the appearance of the English version of the *Star*, as turned out also to be the case with Buber, several thinkers were attracted by Rosenzweig's argument that Judaism and Christianity are the two dials which most accurately reflect reality and divine truth. An example of such attention is Maurice G. Bowler's "Rosenzweig on Judaism and Christianity – The Two Covenant Theory" published in *Judaism* in 1973.[69]

Michael Oppenheim represents a scholar who, like Löwith, came to admire Rosenzweig through another European philosopher. In this case Oppenheim discovered parallels in Kierkegaard's and Rosenzweig's thought, and wrote his dissertation on this theme. He has since written numerous articles and one book in connection with Rosenzweig.[70] He intended to examine the North American response upon conclusion of his study of the Israeli response, but after beginning his research decided it might be more valuable to speak of Rosenzweig's relevance than to study those who still did not see it. Out of this came his latest book, *Mutual Upholding: Fashioning Jewish Philosophy Through Letters*. I am deferring a brief discussion of this volume until chapter 4.

There have been isolated articles written by some of the finest scholars of modern Jewish thought, including Arthur Cohen and Steven Katz. Michael Fishbane has written an important and exquisitely clear chapter in his book *Garments of Torah*, "Speech and Scripture: The Grammatical Thinking and Theology of Franz Rosenzweig."

Norbert Samuelson concentrates on and has offered interesting insights into the difficulties and fruitfulness of the mathematical aspects of the *Star*'s philosophy.

Aware that I am omitting mention of other scholars whose writings appear in U.S. publications, I think that an immediate turn to Robert Gibbs is nevertheless fitting at this point. While the *Star* may justifiably not be designated as a fruit, *Correlations in Rosenzweig and Levinas*, in the fullness of its response, may so be called. It may not be capable of forming a school; much more important, it may be conducive to the bearing of further fruits.

Robert Gibbs, with his *Correlations in Rosenzweig and Levinas*, provides a sensitive, careful analysis and reading of the *Star of Redemption*, by which he renders the move toward the system's practical application in the Halevi book a natural step. He renders this valuable service, interestingly enough, unintentionally and inadvertently. Of course I am not claiming that no one but Gibbs has understood the *Star*. But by rendering the system more readable and understandable from a fresh angle, he has created that vista necessary to be able to see what is being applied in the Notes. Rosenzweig himself, though he so obviously saw a firm and complementary link between the *Star* and his Halevi work, never saw more need to show the way across from the one work to the other than by that short, direly insufficient statement quoted above: "The notes to my *Jehuda Halevi* contain instructive examples of the practical application of the new thinking."

Gibbs' brilliant book is valuable throughout, though as noted, its reception and eventual impact cannot be predicted. My restriction here to two of his points of course does not do justice to his work, but it is these points specifically which I see as opening the way to this present book.

Gibbs argues convincingly that Rosenzweig was not replacing reason with experience as the key epistemological organon. Rather, in order to revive and buttress the healthy growth of ailing philosophy, Rosenzweig draws into philosophy the concept of revelation from theology. Speech and experience arise out of this concept, and only so does speech or experience become an organon for knowing. Moreover, Rosenzweig was not replacing reason at all. He affirms it and uses it as the objective foundation of his philosophical system. In the explanatory essay to the *Star*, "Das neue Denken," Rosenzweig writes of part one where he, through mathematic logic, enquires into the essences of God, human, and world: "And the difficulty, for example the concept of the Nothing [Nichts], 'the Nought' [*der Nichtse*], which here appears to be only a methodological helping concept, reveals its inner meaning only in the short concluding passage of the volume and its final meaning not until the concluding book of the whole. What is written here is still nothing other than simultaneously leading the old philosophy *ad absurdum* and its salvation."[71] Thus Rosenzweig was attempting to salvage, not to submerge, reason and to reorient philosophy from a base of reason. Gibbs states: "The move from logic, to speech as performance, to a philosophical sociology is the central design of the work, and as such is not a random progression. Rather it displays Rosenzweig's keen and profound vision – that the task of Jewish thought (and, I would add, of contemporary philosophy) requires the connection of these different spheres of reflection."[72]

Rosenzweig, having relied on reason as the proper foundation of philosophy, now builds upon it. He moves into the sphere of relationships between the elements, asking now, "What happens?" rather than, "What is?" Reason cannot build the bridges between the elements, but speech, under the open framework of revelation, can and does. Thus, "Rosenzweig augmented philosophy not with religious experience, which is the common view of his work, but with theological concepts."[73] That Rosenzweig was not selling out reason to experience is important. He was, as Gibbs points out, worried that the viewpoint philosophers, Schopenhauer, Kierkegaard, Nietzsche, would lead to oversubjectivity and collapse the required rigour of objectivity in philosophy.

How does this relate particularly to the Halevi book? First, Rosenzweig's designation of the book as the practical application of his philosophy is a strong argument in favour of Gibbs' claim concerning experience. Never does Rosenzweig indicate that his own personal, ex-perienced life as believing, observant Jew is an application of his phi-losophy. No one would deny that Rosenzweig indeed did live by his philosophy, but clearly this is not what he meant by "application." By "application" he means, rather, doing philosophy by the method of the new thinking. The philosophical quest is still one which seeks to dis-cover ultimate truths for all, not merely to disclose individually experi-enced truths. At the same time, because Rosenzweig, through reason, maintains that reality comprises three irreducible elements – human, God, world – each of which is equally transcendent to each other, he also maintains the following. In order to arrive at the ultimate truths of these elements, their connections and relationships require explora-tion. This he suggests can be achieved only through the concept of rev-elation, which includes the concepts of creation and redemption as well. The Notes to the Halevi poetry attempt to philosophize in this mode. The stress here emphatically is not on the personal experience of Halevi or Rosenzweig, although the event(s) of revelation necessar-ily touch the person personally and protects him or her from being swallowed into a totalizing "all is" philosophy.

This brings us to the second point Gibbs makes which is pertinent to the Halevi book. We retain, he observes, "modern" in our name for contemporary philosophy.[74] Modern philosophy's project, to Gibbs (to Rosenzweig, the project of the whole tradition, from Parmenides to Hegel), is characterized by an attempt to know all by means of logic and reason. The failure of this project is familiar; the crisis spawned by its failure is still with us in the form(lessness?) of post-modernity. Rea-son, being, human, God, world – all may have been damaged in the fall, but they are all, after all, still here. The fact that reason cannot know all (partly by trying to draw history into its allness, and the freely acting human being) does not preclude the possibility that other modes of knowing may open to more knowledge than reason alone does. The retention of "modern" in post-modern, according to Gibbs, denotes that we still want to know all. "Modern philosophy does not simply disappear in the 'postmodern discourse'. Instead, the *modern* in 'postmodern' continues to play a vital role as the aspiration toward to-tal knowledge against which the complaint (*post-*) is lodged."[75]

"Other," therefore, has become of paramount importance in the postmodern discourse. By insisting on the separation of the elements, Rosenzweig's thought, too, is invariably focusing on otherness. Others to the all which reason could not encircle and, in its attempt to take up all space, thus displaced: time (Chronos, that elusive and neglected god of the Greeks); the living I who dies a particular death – my death, your death; free deeds or acts of will which cannot be determined beforehand; word which, in the fullness of word and response, always requires another; the theological concept of revelation – these "others" are Rosenzweig's philosophical concerns. "Other" to Rosenzweig involves and permits transcendence and immanence by turns; periods or events of nondisclosure become times of distance (and not knowing) between the elements. Immanence, likewise, is not a state of being, but an event in time. The route to knowing, the path to learning truths, for Rosenzweig is always nourished by that other element, time.

The Halevi book thus seeks to explore, to arrive at, and to express truths, through speech, through always (at least) two voices, through revelation. Rosenzweig's method of doing philosophy does not merely take into account the "other," that is, God and world and other human beings in the world; more remarkably, it listens to the other in the actual philosophizing.

THE FORM OF THE HALEVI BOOK

To Rosenzweig, form discloses content, and the two may not be disconnected. Form-in-itself is empty, and content-in-itself is lame.[76] The form in which Rosenzweig presents his Halevi book is crucial to giving the content wings and to disclosing the method of the new thinking. The most recent edition of the Halevi book has abandoned the original form,[77] which had always been in this order: translations of the poems, divided into four sections – God, Soul, People, and Zion – each with an equal number of poems; an afterword to the translation; and finally Rosenzweig's notes. In a letter to Martin Buber dated 8 January 1921, he explained his reasons for this ordering of the book, and stressed his desire to have the Poems placed fully separate from his Notes:

That even a book which was constructed exactly in reverse will be read in this way, that I experienced after all in the *Star*. – Now I therefore by no means would want the insolent Afterword as conclusion of the book, rather really the conclusion of the last Note. The Afterword works only when it, just as now, is fastened at the front and at the back. The connection of Poems and Notes, however, will be made impressive by a very much stronger means. That is the Index at the front, which strikes the reader's eye enormously by its symmetry, contains two numbers for every poem, a straight one and a cursive one, the first leads to the Poem itself, the second to the Note.[78]

Later, on 1 April 1924, Rosenzweig reiterated to Buber how important he considered his work on translation *as* translation. Reference to the paralytic disease, in part, underlies the comment: "I have always said it: for my translations I'll go to heaven, on earth I can expect no reward."[79]

The first edition of *Jehuda Halevi: Sechzig Hymnen und Gedichte* appeared in 1924, published by Oskar Wöhrle, Konstanz. Rosenzweig was delighted and enchanted with the publisher's achievement in the visual presentation of his book. In his translations of the poetry, he clearly held that this sacred poetry, in the artform of speech, requires conformity to its beauty in the conveying to others. In this first edition, an additional poem, as a digression, in order to explain something further about Halevi and his poetry, is set into the Notes section of the book. The translated poem is followed by one of the lengthier notes, of two-and-a-half pages. Rosenzweig muffles this poem from the voice which is speaking in the poetry section because he does not regard it as genuine speech to which a response is possible. The note to this digression, "Exkurs: Sturm" ("Exkursus: Storm"),[80] begins:

Since its discovery and publication by Luzzatto [Luzzatto, *Divan des Jehuda Ha-Levi*, Lyck, 1864] this poem has become perhaps Jehuda Halevi's most celebrated poem after the Song to Zion. It owes this fame doubtless partly to the surprise that Jehuda Halevi or indeed "one at that time" "could already do such a thing." Heine's images of the North Sea and surely also the worldly tendencies in the modern Hebrew poetry have stood as godfathers to this poem in the enthusiasm of the nineteenth century and haunt also the numerous translations.

In fact it is a glittering show-piece, today one would probably say: recitation piece; poetically it stands far beneath a little poem like "The Flood" [the poem Rosenzweig has just finished commenting on], to name something topically related. But Jehuda Halevi's art, technique, may perhaps be studied in this piece precisely on account of this.[81]

By the beginning of 1925, the year he wrote to Buber that his literary development had been due to translating, Rosenzweig had completed translating thirty-four additional Halevi poems, two of which would be suppressed as digressions. One of these, Rosenzweig argues, is erroneously attributed to Halevi; the other is a highly contrived artistic play on words. In 1927 Lambert Schneider in Berlin published the second edition with the title *Zweiundneunzig Hymnen und Gedichte,* with three "Excursus" poems, their attendant notes embedded in the Notes section of the book. Rosenzweig had planned a third edition of 100 poems, plus the suppressed three.[82]

In 1983 Rosenzweig's son, Rafael, published a third edition, cited above, altering the second edition with four major changes:

1 With the intention of easing the reader into the material and the style of translation, he placed the Nachwort (Afterword) as a Vorwort (Foreword).

2 With the same intention, he placed each translated poem directly before the corresponding note, enmeshing two sections, so that now we have poem, note, poem, note, and so on, rather than an entire section of poems only followed by an entire section of Notes only.

3 Due to this altered set-up, it is impossible to show that the three Excursus poems are suppressed in the Notes section, for there no longer is one. Thus Rafael Rosenzweig's title, *Fünfundneunzig Hymnen und Gedichte des Jehuda Halevi*, becomes misleading. Only ninety-four are properly Halevi's, according to Rosenzweig, and only ninety-two represent Halevi's genuine speech.

4 Rafael Rosenzweig precedes each German translation with the original Hebrew text, in accordance with his father's often expressed wish that any reader who knows both languages should be able to look over his shoulders as he is working.[83] The accompaniment of the Hebrew is of course commendable, as this complies with the author's wishes.

I contend that Rosenzweig's ordering of the sections of his book, Poems, Afterword, Notes, was a conscious and deliberate demonstration in itself of the speech-thinking method. The most superficial sketch of the time-conscious process is as follows. Jehuda Halevi sings his songs. He is the first human speaker. Rosenzweig hears (translates) them into his own language. The Afterword is Rosenzweig's reflection on what takes place in the hearing phase. And it is more than that. I suggest that the deliberating care Rosenzweig took to plan the form of his Halevi is made irrefutable by the following excerpt from a letter Rosenzweig wrote to Buber on 17 June 1924:

[Christian Florens] Rang is then the third to notice that the Afterword does not belong. The first two are I and You. But now the funny thing, and what I knew beforehand: only the Afterword prevents the reader from discarding the book to begin with. Now almost everyone has a bad conscience that he does not like the poems. And precisely because of the insolence they read it. The Afterword is the absurd delight – not merely of the asses, but also of the in-spite-of-all ones. There is no change from Viktor of Imago's [by Spitteler] great perception: If there is a signboard on the left "Entrance to Paradise" and on the right a poster "Lecture on Paradise," they will all run to the right.[84]

The translations, then, are blocked off at their conclusion by a wide central panel from Rosenzweig's own speech in his own response to

Jehuda, as second, other speaker, in the form of his Notes. The Notes likewise are blocked into their own space. The two speakers, Halevi and Rosenzweig, together, within the framework of revelation, as will be shown, demonstrate what is called "full word" in the speech-thinking philosophy. Further analysis of these stages in speech will be undertaken in the following chapters, especially 2, 3, and 4.

In this book, references to the original German of the Afterword and the Notes will be as follows: (190/72). The first page number refers to the 1927 edition, the second to the 1983.[85] The excerpts from the Notes which are offered, found chiefly in chapters 4 and 5, are my translations, cited from part one.

CHAPTER TWO

Rosenzweig's Philosophy of Translation

ROSENZWEIG'S THREE-SENTENCE SUMMARY

Like Rosenzweig's philosophic system as a whole, his philosophy of translation is difficult to summarize. Yet Rosenzweig himself summarized it in a letter he wrote on 1 October 1917 to his baptized cousin, Rudolf Ehrenberg. In this letter Rosenzweig compresses into a few words principles of translation that he, in relation to his own experience, had been developing since 1913: "Translating is after all the actual goal of the mind [*Geistes*]; only when something is translated has it become really *audible*, no longer to be disposed of. Not until the Septuagint did revelation become entirely at home in the world, and as long as Homer did not yet speak in Latin [*lateinisch*] he was not yet a fact. In a corresponding way, also translating from person to person."[1]

All the components of Rosenzweig's philosophy of translation are concentrated here. The aim of this chapter is to unpack and analyze these ideas and to support them with other of Rosenzweig's writings. These principles grew directly from Rosenzweig's contact with the Jewish-born, Christianity-embracing professor of law and history, Eugen Rosenstock-Huessy. From this contact Rosenzweig took his momentous decisions to turn from monologic to dialogic thinking, to develop a systematic philosophy that expressed this view of life, and to live this philosophy as an observant Jewish man. Because of the role Rosenstock-Huessy played in the formative years of Rosenzweig's speech-thinking orientation, some of the analysis will focus on this formidable professor's incontrovertible impact upon his student and subsequent friend.

Before embarking on the more detailed analysis and expansion, sentence by sentence, an overview of the general thrust and sense of Rosenzweig's principles will first be supplied. At this first stage, the highly important aspect concerning his notion the "one language" will also be introduced.

The first sentence states that the goal of the mind is translating. "Mind" here carries with it as well the connotation of spirit [*Geist*], something more than an intellectuality based on reason alone. The effect of not achieving this goal of translating is the silencing of the original speech. This silencing is avoided only when someone other than the speaker hears the speech. Once heard, once audible, the speech is "no longer to be disposed of." When a person translates another's speech, the mind's activity of that other becomes *audible.* The purpose behind the goal of the mind rests on two minds for speech to attain a fully audible stage, but the responsibility is the translator's. Translating is equal to speaking as the means by which the mind's goal is reached. Neither the goal nor the purpose can be achieved in isolation. The original speech of one mind, sometimes unwittingly, depends on the translating mind of another person. It is the translator, not the original speaker, who brings the original speech into audibility. One's own speech is not ultimately one's own; it belongs to those who translate it, and then to still others who hear the translation. Even one's own speech is not originally one's own. It derives from others' speech.

The second sentence states that written texts become facts in the world because and only when they are translated from the original language into a foreign language. Committing speech to writing, as did Homer in poetic form, for example, does not preserve that speech in the sense of its assured perpetuation. Writing is a form of solitary expression that remains solitary until or unless heard by another's ear and spoken by that other's mouth. Even when one writes, for example, a letter, an essay, a book, a poem specifically intended to or for another or others, the writing depends on that other or those others in order to become a fact. Rosenzweig's famous letter to Meinecke[2] is an example of unheard speech which, in Meinecke's hands at least, did not become a fact. I shall be quoting and discussing this letter at length within a few pages. Writing down one's speech is a means by which thought formulated at that moment can be frozen until it reaches an ear to melt it into the river of life. A letter is not complete, truly audible, until answered. A book not read, a letter torn up unopened, a thought spoken to bewildered ears and uncomprehending eyes is frustrated into nonfact, alienation from the world. That which is a fact or at home in the world is that which is open, in which innumerable others may partake.[3]

Rosenzweig offers two examples, Homer and the Septuagint, and refers to their respective initial translations from the original into a foreign language. These examples are significant. Both texts grew up indigenous to a nation of people. The writers of these texts examined and narrated their people's history amid their own people. These writers were not intending objectivity in a modern historian's sense. In their observations the writers themselves are consciously members of their nation. The national history of which they tell, moreover, includes the people's relationship with and understanding of the divine.

Written texts like Homer's and the Septuagint can be seen, before translation, as a type of solitary expression by and for one body of people. After translation into a foreign language, not only a form and content of expression, but a whole people, and their own understanding of divine revelation, are translated into a new language and people. Only then does this people's "revelation" come to be "in the world," at home, a fact.

Expansion of language, and widening of the mind, therefore, takes place on the part of the translating nation, not on the part of the nation in which the original arose. The translated-into language, as well as the original, changes. The original changes in that it experiences a new stage of its life in the translation. The translated-into language experiences its own growth. Rosenzweig's first sentence states that translating [*Übersetzen*], not translation [*Übersetzung*] nor to be translated, is the mind's goal. Rosenzweig's examples indicate that translation spans not only from nation to nation, but from civilization to civilization and from religion to religion. Intergenerational speech is possible only through translation. Greece did not preserve Homer: Rome did. Moreover, because Homer and the Septuagint have come to be still alive today in numerous other languages, the proposition is implied here that one translation generates others, but that without that first translation any utterance will die.

The third "sentence" defines translation as an act that also operates within the same language, and not solely as an act that takes place between languages. The ideas of permanence and of factuality of person relate to everyday speech between humans. The human comes to be at home outside himself and a preserved fact only when translated by another. Hence one person's audibility and facticity depend first upon speech and second upon another's ear and mouth. Audibility holds the meanings of both being hearable and voiceable at once. Audibility, then, is an objective fact that comes to be once the time-requiring stages of speaking, hearing, translating, and responding have each taken their place. In other words, reality comes to be through the course of time, and truth depends upon its discovery in time. That is why Rosenzweig was wont to quote from Goethe:

> Why is truth so woefully
> Removed? To depths of secret banned?
> None understands in time! If we
> But understood betimes, how bland
> The truth would be, how fair to see!
> How near and ready to our hand![4]

Unlike Goethe, however, the last of the great pagans, Rosenzweig welcomed time and had faith in the not-yet. In his reassessment of faith in autonomous reason, Rosenzweig reoriented his thinking according to the principle that cognition is nourished by time and cannot remain independent of it. The world has a real beginning, middle, and end in creation, revelation, and redemption. Knowledge operates under this time-oriented framework.

This third sentence implies something else that is connected with views of time: the notion of there being ultimately only one language. The next chapter will address exclusively that integral aspect of Rosenzweig's philosophy of translation, which here is only implied. In the *Nachwort* to the Halevi book, Rosenzweig is explicit: "There is only one language."

By coupling the idea that the mind's true goal is translating with the idea that translating takes place also for those who speak the *same* (linguistic) language, Rosenzweig is hinting here at that notion he develops elsewhere: while there are many utterances, only one language really exists. That is, first, Rosenzweig is drawing a direct parallel between language and person. His ratio is: one language: another language:: one person: another person. Second, if audibility occurs only when speech is received in translation by another, then the issue here is understanding one another in the profoundest sense. The understanding takes place in time, and must have a future thrust: one speaks, *then* another translates. Third, under the framework of creation, revelation, and redemption, the ultimate vista is therefore a conclusion of time and of speech: the silence of understanding and peace. Translating is connected inextricably with a view and an aim to play a role in bringing about that final peace. Translating leads not toward a single linguistic language but toward multiple languages, each of which will have itself become the one language. Although the next chapter will try carefully to attend to several of Rosenzweig's writings in order to develop a clearer statement of the notion of the one language, here a few more remarks may at least lay a foundation for that discussion.

The true disparity of speech and understanding does not arise between languages themselves, in themselves. Apparent disparity, on the most surface level, is only technical. What makes the variously spoken languages of the world truly disparate is that each of the various languages is at various stages of speaking, or bringing to expression, its full potential. The fact that what different languages (or persons) say can be, and is, translated into another individual's or nation's or culture's different language or into another individual's speech of the same language, illuminates that fuller statement being implied here. As will be fully discussed later, Rosenzweig holds that *each* language holds in germ the capacity to speak the revelatory word of God. Thus the emphasis is on the essential oneness of all languages, not on their disparateness. In order to translate another's speech with a view toward this oneness, the aim, then, is not that everyone speak, say, English, but that each language bring to bloom its *own* capacity to speak the One Word of Truth. Any one language's (or person's or people's) utterance of divine truth in the world's necessarily manifold expression of it is neither a disparity with, nor an essential superiority over, other languages (or persons or peoples), but instead only temporary apartness until each language fully develops its seed.

Speech before translation cannot be related to anything beyond the speaker; it starts as speech separate from everyone but not as a disparate entity. Disparities, multiplicities, and fragmentedness do not occur in any one language. Disparity arises from unattended and untranslated solo utterances that seek or demand hearing, and yet are denied translation by the target language. These fly away as bits of a solitary mind; if they do not disappear, they land on misbegotten places and cause abominable transgressions. The goal of the mind, again, is to translate, not to be translated. The goal is one of absolute nonaggression, of welcoming inclusion. The slave's outcry against aggression upon the dignity and inherent freedom of the human being is an example of utterances often denied translation. Yet the Afghans once refused to translate the Soviet demands: an example of aggressive will forcefully aiming to be translated. What should be translated, eventually will be. What should not be, will eventually die. Whether worthy or not of translation, nothing is translated without the readiness and receptivity on the part of those who are to be the translators. Be that as it may, language itself stands firm. That all language can come to comply with its needs and desires to import new speech into itself whenever it is receptive and ready to do so, proves this. In speech-thinking, language is seen as a whole, or to-become-whole.

The direction for language growth then is more one of apparently, or presently, different languages moving together than one of veering apart. This converging is not a matter of merging languages. That too plays a part, but far from the major one. This part of merging is an apparent role, an effect more than an intention. Nor is the converging a matter of languages confounding or dissolving themselves into a total: instead, when a language incorporates into its own speech something spoken previously, or already, by a foreign language, the translating nation or person is giving birth to more of its potential. The seed was not implanted by but was already in the language which is doing the translating. But the translating language is giving birth to something really new in the world. That newness bonds for all time the two languages involved, but this is not the important thing. The important thing is that the birth-giving language has changed.

The following chapter will further explore this idea that each language has the potential, through its own seed, to become the one language, while at the same time remaining within the multiciplicity of languages. And should this potentiality be realized by every language, speech would no longer be necessary. All would have been both communicated and agreed upon. Discussion of the idea that a continued multiplicity of languages does not disturb or contradict the notion of there being at the same time a one language remains the next chapter's task.

Passages from Rosenzweig's other writings clarify and substantiate the principles and beliefs blueprinted in the three sentences. Rosenzweig himself upheld, tested, claims to have verified, and certainly further learned from his philosophy throughout his lifetime: during his major translation feats – the Jehuda Halevi poetry and the Bible translation with Buber and in his administrative and teaching duties at the Lehrhaus, as well as through his friendships. Since all that Rosenzweig wrote after 1913 was written not only consciously to other specific people but also as a conscious response to what was said before him, it is to be understood that underlying any examination of the principles is the fact that correspondence is a never-absent feature of speech-thinking.

The first sentence: Translating is after all the actual goal of the mind; only when something is translated has it become really audible, *no longer to be disposed of.*

If the mind's purpose and aim is to translate, then to think only in solitude would be contrary and a hindrance to that goal.

Translation in part involves communicating and being communicated to in written or oral speech. Speech, whether isolated in the mind, spoken speech that involves sound, or written speech that involves the eye, remains incomplete without another's mind that will respond: it remains abstract, disconnected from reality. Through communication, speech can be said to become concrete. Along these lines, Alexandre Derczansky offers a good starting point from which to consider the term speech-thinking: "Pour Rosenzweig, le discours n'est pas une matière abstraite, mais un souci communicatif dont les raisons lui sont internes et non pas extérieures ... Il insiste également sur le rapport de la parole et du langage et donne à la pensée le statut de la parole. C'est là d'ailleurs la raison pour laquelle il forge ce mot: Sprachdenken."[5] Speech-thinking, however, is more than communication, more than concrete. Communication can be one-directional: transference or informative communication, as in news broadcasts, brochures, pamphlets, lectures. Speech-thinking between any two human beings, whether or not of the same generation, whether or not they meet face to face, involves change on the part of the one addressed, *because* of being addressed. But between two live, face-to-face interlocutors the roles of the one who is speaking and the one who is addressed not only alternate, but appear to intermingle. The one who speaks is also listening for his cues as to how and what to speak to his or her listener. The speech of the one who is speaking at the moment is drawn out by the one who is listening at the moment. Speech-thinking, in its intergenerational sense, between, say, Homer and a senator in Washington, might, through the *Iliad*, alter the senator's views on human nature and war, leaving him questioning whether war is glorious or tragically futile. If the senator speaks and thinks differently thereafter, he will to some degree, have become a speech-thinker. He has experienced transformative communication. A sentence in E.V. Rieu's introduction to the *Iliad* nicely distinguishes between informative and transformative communication: "I would rather have the *Iliad* than a whole shelf of Bronze-Age war-reports, however accurate."[6] While Derczansky is right to distinguish between abstract and concrete, he does not penetrate into the spiritual aspect that, according to Rosenzweig, can accompany the concrete. Moreover, by stopping at the notion of the concrete, there is the risk of objectifying speech and language into mere tools. In an impassioned, biting passage, which for all that is not devoid of humour, Rosenzweig writes:

"Inadequacy of language," "limitation of thought," "our sensory experience," finally as a highlight the "God" formed by man in his image – this is how a theological problem is dealt with today! Even if we grant the soundness of these "theoretical-knowledge" imperfections (I frankly do not understand with which language, which thought, which experience we can compare our language, our thought, our experience in order to be permitted to confer upon them the grade of unsatisfactory), even if we grant that: in which other science is it permitted to place "theoretical-knowledge" lamentations instead of honest striving after the understanding of the facts themselves?[7]

The mind's intended mark lies beyond itself. The mark is relationship with God, other people. The mind misses its mark if it forgets God, other people, or even itself. Authentic thought drives toward expression. It does not reside enclosed and uncommunicative alone in any single mind. The mind's solitary speech will be "disposed of," die, unless heard, translated, and spoken into the language by another mind. Only the mind of another person or people can verify and vivify, renew and further engage one mind's speech and thereby bring it into truly vocal language in which yet others may partake. If the goal of the mind is mistaken as the desire to render one's own speech permanent, that view is merely an egotistical extension of the isolated mind. Such "permanence" that has no lifelines to other speaking minds is indeed only stagnation. Communication through translating, that is, through effort on the part of the hearer, who, having heard another is transformed and now speaks anew, is a communication that creates a permanence in the world. By "permanence" I wish to convey the precise meaning of "staying through," remaining, enduring, during worldtime. Such permanence resides in the world only because and when it is no longer locked in a mind, whether that mind is the mind of a person or a nation or a community. This sort of communication reaches from outward, centres itself in a person or in a nation or community, and speaks again outward into the world. This speaking outwardly is an orientation for someone and to someone other than self.

The simplest and most accurate meaning of "to translate" is to understand what another is saying and to be able to express this in one's own modes of speech. Understanding is always the first step – and the last. In a letter to Rosenstock-Huessy dated 24 July 1918 Rosenzweig reveals, in the live and specific context of friendship, how for him translation is not a matter of reiterating in synonymous words what the speaker says. Yet to speak within a language requires a base of synonymy that functions as common ground. Synonymy means that the frame of reference is already firmly established: ready availability of synonyms means that what is being said has already been translated and is already a fact upon which both parties rely. Differences will arise from this ground, but not necessarily disparities:

> You have been able to speak the language of your faith nearly unconstrained, in the certainty that I would be able to translate it for myself. And the simple solution to the puzzle lies there. Our faith (and therefore our works as well) is different. If faith were something absolutely separate, we would really not be able to say a word to one another. Translation wouldn't exist either. But faith is nothing beyond hope. And hope we have in common, both since our faith is different and because it is. The common property of hope enables me to trans-

late your faith into my language. And therefore we can really speak of those things "of which it is worthwhile for men alone to speak". You are utterly forgetful – or you would still have recalled another line of poetry in which all this was said shortly and well: "My enemy in space, my friend in time."[8]

A distinction is made in this letter between faith and hope. What makes translation possible between Jew and Christian is not faith. This difference in faith will remain until the end of time. But faith is not "absolutely separate." Faith is not the ultimate in inter-human and God-human relationships. The common property of hope that ultimately faith will not matter, although it does matter now "in space," is that which transcends different faiths and that which thus makes translation both possible and imperative. With the synonymous base of hope, the two people can speak. Form always requires space: Judaism and Christianity each take their place in space, and translation is not intended to render sameness in space. Hope requires not space, but time. Thus, the actual common base that permits translation is time. Faith that operates without hope promotes faith only: that is, form and not ultimately the one God. Faith without hope promotes differences that lead to disparity. Such hopeless faith forgets time. It forgets to believe that time has a beginning and will have an end. To hope and to pray for that end is the ultimate of faith: that there will be a Last Day, and that there will be peace.

Translated, words become "audible." It is with good reason that, in some circles, much has been made of Rosenzweig's and Rosenstock's relationship.[9] Because their correspondence provides a lively example of speech-thinking and at the same time the content addresses the method itself, it is rightly taken seriously by scholars. This correspondence, moreover, offers a glimpse of how true it is that Rosenzweig's philosophy sprang from life, from experience, and led back "into Life."[10]

This sort of communication to Rosenstock-Huessy, or to anyone, would have been barred from the Rosenzweig who had followed Hegel, Rosenzweig the assimilated Jew who had fancied Judaism a quaint relic in modernity and belief in God not possible to any intelligent twentieth century person. Let us take a brief backward glance at the transitional and transformative period of Rosenzweig's life in which Rosenstock-Huessy played the major role. This will be helpful because it shows not merely the influence that Rosenstock-Huessy had upon Rosenzweig, but more importantly some of the stages that take place self-consciously in a speech-thinking encounter.

The foregoing letter excerpt is a piece of a conversation between a certain Jew and a certain Christian. Rosenzweig and Rosenstock-

Huessy did not speak to each other like this at the start of their relationship. During 1912 and 1913 the two men engaged in almost daily
discussions concerning the inadequacy of "university" philosophy with
regard to human spiritual life. Rosenstock-Huessy had personally
solved the problem in his own life led as a Christian, which Rosenzweig
had come to respect. Rosenzweig, on the other hand, was speaking
from the standpoint of the intellectual with a dilemma. After a heated
conversation in July 1913, Rosenzweig decided to take up his own Jewish path toward Christianity, through the Jewish calendar for one year,
which would, he believed, prepare him for baptism. Rosenzweig describes that evening in July 1913, in that famous passage in which he
highlights the unreality and hypocrisy of dualizing oneself between a
person of faith and one of reason.

In that night's conversation Rosenstock pushed me step by step out of the last
relativist position that I still occupied, and forced me to take an absolute standpoint. I was inferior to him from the outset since I had to recognize for my part
the justice of his attack. If I could then have buttressed my dualism between
revelation and the world with a metaphysical dualism between God and Devil
[he meant to say if he could have split himself into two halves, a religious and a
worldly one] I should have been unassailable. But I was prevented from doing
so by the first sentence of the Bible. This piece of common ground forced me
to face him. This has remained even afterwards, in the weeks that followed, the
fixed point of departure. Any form of philosophical relativism is now impossible to me.[11]

Three months later, in October 1913, Rosenzweig observed Yom
Kippur as a Jew on the way to baptism. That day's experience led him
to decide to remain a Jew, or more precisely, to become a believing, observant Jew. Fearing after his decision that he was not yet strong
enough in his power to speak as a Jew in the face of Rosenstock's
power to speak as a Christian, Rosenzweig interrupted relations with
Rosenstock-Huessy. But by December 1916 Rosenzweig could write:
"The real adventure and achievement of the last few months was for
me my correspondence with Rosenstock. You know (or should be able
to know) that I expected, dreaded, and postponed the inevitable second discussion with him since November 1913. It was to be the test of
my new life ... Now the task is completed."[12]
    This new life was the life of the speech-thinker, the philosopher who
was also man of faith, not outside his philosophizing but in its very
core. This new life involved rejecting the arena where solitary thought
was the professed norm – the German university. This is expressed in
Rosenzweig's letter of August 1920 to his former history professor

(1908–10), Friedrich Meinecke, who had offered Rosenzweig a professorship at the University of Freiburg. By this time the *Star of Redemption* had been completed, the Lehrhaus had been operating under Rosenzweig's leadership since 1 August 1920, the Patmos Circle was meeting and publishing, and Rosenzweig had lived through seven Jewish calendar years.[13] What Rosenzweig wrote to Meinecke manifests a sense of the apologetic,[14] perhaps in the foreknowledge that still Meinecke would not be able to translate who Rosenzweig had become into his own life.[15] The letter's language indeed remained foreign to Rosenzweig's former professor. It has often been quoted; it seems again and again worth reading. It displays Rosenzweig's trust in the powers of speech, but perhaps as well a degree of naïveté?

In 1913 something happened to me for which *collapse* is the only fitting name. I suddenly found myself on a heap of wreckage, or rather I realized that the road I was then pursuing was flanked by unrealities. Yet this was the very road defined for me by my talent, and my talent only … I felt a horror of myself … Amidst the shreds of my talents I began to search for myself, amidst the manifold for the One. It was then … that I descended into the vaults of my being, to a place whither talents could not follow me; that I approached the ancient chest whose existence I have never wholly forgotten, for I was in the habit of going down at certain times of the year to examine what lay uppermost in the chest: those moments had all along been the supreme moments of my life … (This time, however, my hands dug deeper, bringing up armfuls of treasures.) These, indeed, were my own treasures, my most personal possessions, things inherited, not borrowed! By owning them and ruling over them I had gained something entirely new, namely the right to live – and even to have talents; for now it was *I* who had the talents, not they who had me … I had turned from a historian (perfectly "eligible" for a university lectureship) into an (utterly "ineligible") philosopher. The one thing I wish to make clear is that scholarship no longer holds the centre of my attention, and that my life has fallen under the rule of a "dark drive" which I'm aware that I merely *name* by calling it "my Judaism." The scholarly aspect of this whole process – the conversion of the historian into a philosopher – is only a corollary, though it has furnished me with a welcome corroboration of my own conviction that the "ghost I saw" was not the devil; it seems to me that I am today more firmly rooted in the earth than I was seven years ago. The man who wrote *The Star of Redemption* to be published shortly by Kaufmann in Frankfort – is of a very different caliber from the author of Hegel and the State [Rosenzweig's dissertation]. Yet when all is said and done, the new book is only – a book. I don't attach any undue importance to it. The small – at times exceedingly small – thing called [by Goethe] "demand of the day" which is made upon me in my position [as head of the Jüdisches Lehrhaus] at Frankfurt, I mean the nerve-wracking, picayune, and at the same time very necessary struggles with people and conditions, have now become the real core of my existence – and I love this form of existence despite the inevitable annoyance that goes with it. Cognition no longer appears to me as an end in itself. It has turned into service, a service to human beings (not, I assure you, tendencies). Any kind of tendentious work is not only distasteful but downright impossible to me. Cognition is autonomous; it refuses to have any *answers* foisted on it from the outside. Yet it suffers without protest having certain *questions* prescribed to it from the outside (and it is here that my heresy regarding the question seems to me worth asking). Scientific curiosity and omnivorous aesthetic appetite mean equally little to me today, though I was once under the spell of both, particularly the latter. Now I only inquire when I find myself *inquired of.* Inquired of, that is, by *men* rather than by scholars. There is a man in each scholar, a man who inquires and stands in need of answers. I am anxious to answer the scholar *qua* man but not the representative of a certain discipline, that insatiable, ever inquisitive phantom which like a vampire drains him whom it possesses of his humanity. I hate that phantom as I do all phantoms. Its questions are meaningless to me. On the other hand, the questions asked by human beings have become increasingly important to me. This is precisely what I meant by "cognition and knowledge as a service": readiness to confront such questions, to answer them as best I can out of my limited knowledge and my even slighter ability. You will now be able to understand what keeps me away from the university and forces me to follow the path I have chosen: not an extreme degree of consciousness [Meinecke thought that Rosenzweig was suffering from Post-War disillusionment, and had entered a "spiritualized" form of Judaism] (lucidity of this kind I can only summon when I am called upon to vindicate myself, as I am now) but precisely that "dark drive" to which you appeal in your letter ... Now a great weight has been lifted from my heart, for when we parted in Berlin I was extremely distressed over my failure of communication.[16]

Rosenzweig had arrived at the conviction that Hegel represents the "last philosopher" of a 2500-year tradition. He had achieved the zenith of the solitary mind's excursions. From Iona to Jena, philosophical dialogues, according to him, had been "fixed": the outcome was known at the beginning because they were the "dialogues" of a single mind, self speaking with self.[17] Rosenzweig's own life of speech-thinking, steadily developing from 1913, convinced him that solitary thought does not take into account full reality. Nor is it capable of arriving at human truths that reflect the divine Truth. The relating of one's thought within one's life is a test of the verity of the mind's concepts.

To Meinecke, Rosenzweig reports that "cognition and knowledge," while autonomous – and by implication, because autonomous – are not ends in themselves. Cognition and knowledge that come to be contained in the fortress of the human mind are to stand in readiness of service to those outside who have their questions to ask, as well as in openness to the possibility of shaking the fortress of the mind's foundations by answering those questions.

Those who are outside the mind's fortress and are asking the questions, as humans, not as scholars, are the ones who lead us to the achievement of the mind's true goal. Autonomous knowledge that delivers up its "findings" as an unalterable package upon those outside and upon whom, moreover, the "right" questions are imposed hinders human growth of knowledge of reality and truth. Reality and truths come to be known only in experience with others, and those others define our questions: "Now I only inquire when I find myself inquired of," Rosenzweig writes in that letter.[18] Thus cognition and knowledge become a service.

An especially sensitive and insightful Rosenzweig scholar, Michael Oppenheim, observes that Rosenzweig's own experiences in and through conversation enabled him to learn of and to promote the power of dialogue: "In later years Rosenzweig could speak of the immense possibilities of a meeting between people, when both stand facing one another with trust and openness, because he had experienced all of this with Rosenstock."[19] Oppenheim also highlights the speech-thinker's profound trust in coming to learn truths derived from the life experience of ourselves and of others: "The importance of recognizing the bridge between life and thought was once underscored by Rosenzweig in a statement he made about the great nineteenth century figure, Søren Kierkegaard. Rosenzweig wrote that "behind each paradox of Kierkegaard one sees biographical *absurda*, and for this reason one must credit." Here Rosenzweig, in a brief allusion to Tertullian's maxim, gives expression to one of his most characteristic ideas: the verification of concepts takes place in the *life* of the thinker."[20]

In order to be translated the mind that is inquired into must disclose itself and be able to reveal itself. Second – and simultaneously – that mind, expressing itself in written form, must display a vulnerability which a specific other can tap: the inquirer, who finds himself at a specific moment in need of hearing the original. And third, the mind inquired into must be amenable to being received – not necessarily or even usually simultaneously – by that other. Rosenzweig is speaking from the point of view of the translator. This is to be stressed. The mind's true goal is translating, he writes. It is not to seek to be translated. The human reaches outward to hear what is outside the self, does not (merely) thrust her- or himself out to be heard. Thus for the mind to achieve its true purpose it would have to take the part of the listener. In this role as listener, the listening mind takes an even more active part than the speaker. Once interested in or atune to any originating speech, God's or another human being's, the listener, in order to become translator, must seek or be open to self-revealing on another's part. He must attract the other's speech toward his own, and into it, however dissonant or foreign-sounding his own speech may at first appear in his translating efforts. He must especially attempt, then, to incorporate that other's speech into his own language. The incorporation eventually dissolves the apparent dissonance. The original is not subsumed into the new language. It has rather expanded it, given it a fresh, healthy, new moment of growth.

When considering especially the written word and translating, we might amend that partial truth of *verba volant, scripta manent* [spoken words fly away, written words endure]. Permanence depends more upon whether a word reaches reception or not, and less upon whether it is spoken or written. But the written word, because captured in a visible physicality, does offer a type of permanence that is denied to the spoken word. The written word can be read by those outside the "intimacy" of two speakers, such as letter writers; or of the "one-way intimacy" that arises between one speaker, such as the bookwriter, and many readers. The permanence inherent in the written word is framed within boldness and daring on the part of the speaker: translated or not, there is a thereness to the written word, and this thereness is conducive to replay for the hearer, through rereading. Rosenzweig's spoken words *had* flown away from Meinecke's understanding, but Rosenzweig's writing down what he had tried to communicate beforehand indicates Rosenzweig's courage in trying to communicate in such a way *ut scripta manant* [so that written words might endure].

It is the *reception* of a word, whether spoken or written, that perpetuates it, or its full spokenness with a view to permanence. Rosenzweig expressed this in a letter to Margrit Rosenstock-Huessy, Eugen's wife, during the early stages of writing *The Star,* on 2 November 1918:

I have the greatest reserve towards burning letters. I've never done it when it wasn't absolutely necessary. Words blow away or rather they transform themselves into answers. [*Wort* becomes *Ant-wort.*] But a written word, writing in general, means that the person wasn't satisfied with moments of looking at one another and the present, but rather was creating permanence, bridges across the distances in space and time. Anything which has withstood this test, the test of small permanency, doesn't have to be scared of the large permanency – the most fleetingly written word has withstood it ... One may forget a spoken word, but one has to preserve written ones, at least as long as one is "preserved oneself", that is, as long as one lives. The human life is the large permanency of which the written word has brought its proof of capability by overcoming the small permanency. The letters that I have received from someone are to me like a piece of his life that has been given into my custody; I would feel as though I were dealing deathblows, were I to burn them; so I find it hard even with indifferent letters; I have even usually saved invitations, if they were in writing. The fleeting character, which even written words have, is accepted and dissolved in the answer, just as with spoken words. A letter which has been answered is not "too intimate" anymore. I approach a letter with hesitation and shyness only as long as it is unanswered; but regardless of what the answer is like, it admits the letter, eradicates its fleeting character, and what remains is a permanent one.[21]

It cannot be overstressed that this true goal of the mind involves dependence on another, and this dependence holds both for the one who is to be translated and for the one engaged in translating. A fully audible word is always reducible to two people, never to one. Between those two, the task is greater for the listener, the one translating. The speaker, the original, after all, is disclosing what he or she already knows at that time. He may struggle to express himself clearly; he may be speaking *to* someone specific; he may change his mind at another time and know something different or something more; he at least however knows what he *wants* to say. But he cannot force the translating activity to take place by another.

A new emphasis upon words themselves emerges. Only a word which is picked up by another or others than the one or ones who already know a given speech, and which is incorporated into another's language, only that word partakes in full reality and leads to truth. In connection with the stages of the word from utterance to translation, Rosenzweig wrote in his introduction to part two of the *Star*, the section most evident and explicit concerning new turn in the speech-thinking method: "What was finished as thought reverts as word into a new beginning. For the word is mere inception until it finds reception in an ear, and response in a mouth."[22] In book 2, part two, Rosenzweig concludes this idea:

"We will henceforth proceed from real word to real word, not from describing one species of word to another as we did in describing creation. This accords with the wholly real employment of language, the centre-piece as it were of this entire book, at which we have here arrived ... we recognize the actual word ... as word and response."[23]

In word and response a two-step operation takes place in the responding alone. Rosenzweig tried to discover and to define an essential principle of translation in addition to the need for accuracy in any translated piece; he wrote on 10 March 1921 to Gershom Scholem concerning this.[24] Technically the art of translation can achieve error-free success. Yet the translated piece may still be inaccurate from the point of view of the original. The following excerpt from this letter raises the notion that the translator engages in a special two-way listening: to the speaker whom he wishes to translate, and to the language into which he wishes to translate. This operation goes on in all translating from one mind to another, which is to say in all fully voiced speech, but the steps are particularly clearly noticed in translating from one language into another:

Only one who is profoundly convinced of the impossibility of translation can really undertake it. Not by any means of the impossibility in translation in general (that isn't the case at all; rather all life beyond one's own soul is conditioned by the possibility of this miracle, as you so rightly call it), but the impossibility of the particular translation he is about to embark on. This special impossibility is different in every case. In this case its name is: Luther. And not Luther alone – he is only the point of intersection where the newest and the oldest meet – but more precisely: Notker, Luther, Hölderlin. The German language, in the names of these three men, has become a Christian language. Anyone who translates into the German language must to some extent translate into Christian language... It will be most Christian of all for Christian texts, less so but still strongly Christian for the "Old Testament," much less with biblical passages that have been incorporated into the text of a basic prayer, even less for Bible quotations in hymnal prayers and, in fact, in hymns in general. Any arbitrary or deliberate evasion at all is impossible here.[25]

Besides understanding the speaker, then, one must also be able to perceive the limitations of one's own modes of expression. One's own modes of expression can – indeed must – be stretched to accommodate the speaker in order for translation to be at all possible. If the stretching is not necessary, then what is being translated is nothing new in the translated-into language. German speakers had already been successful in stretching their language in this regard with respect to the Christian message.[26] Luther's Bible translation had brought Christian language indelibly into the German language. Anyone speaking something new into his or her own language, translating thoughts into truly audible words, must exercise this stretching of language. Three great German speakers, Notker, Luther, and Hölderlin spoke new spirit into German; they changed German for as long as it will be spoken. All heard new voices from outside their own minds, translated these voices, and spoke them into their own language. Hölderlin, with his exquisite poetry, not only composed a new German in terms of content and style, at the same time he also introduced into German the spirit of Greek poetry by using Greek metre. Hölderlin's achievement was based on the meaning of translation in Rosenzweig's sense: he translated something other than, and in addition to, words. Rosenzweig, in his *Nachwort* to the German translations of the poems of Jehuda Halevi, states that he has proved that Hebrew poetry can be translated into German in strict keeping with rhyme and metre; any future "translations" in the free style are simply, he says, laziness.[27] The spirits of foreign languages that have been translated into the German language are now never to be "disposed of." They have a permanent voice that lives in an expanded German.[28]

The second sentence: Not until the Septuagint did revelation become entirely at home in the world, and as long as Homer did not yet speak in Latin he was not yet a fact.

This "sentence" refers to bridging languages by translation. To Rosenzweig all speech is translation.[29] He does not take the philosophical identity word "is" lightly.[30] He really does mean identification here. Thus all translation is also speech. Yet not all languages can be bridged at once, and no one can all at once speak all the languages of the world – and yet he can. Two enormously important aspects become more brightly visible now: the aspect of time, and the already mentioned aspect of the one language. As I have repeatedly said the discussion of the one language is being deferred until the next chapter. Crucial here, however, is that notion, alluded to above, that each language contains in germ the potential to speak the one language. It takes time for a seed to germinate and to grow.

In any discussion of time, considerations of grammar and tenses are helpful, if not needed. Since time is such an indispensable aspect in speech-thinking, Rosenzweig also calls his philosophy grammatical thinking. His preferred label is "absolute empiricism,"[31] which purports Rosenzweig's view of the concreteness of speech as an epistemological organon.

In the case of two individuals who are speaking face to face or even letter to letter the present tense may only appear to be predominantly at play. But the time element which entails all three primary tenses between two contemporary humans who speak to each other is just as important and just as necessary as it is when speech is spoken across ages. Rosenstock-Huessy's motto "*Respondeo* etsi *mutabor* [I respond *although* I shall be changed], expresses the effects upon translators during and after their relationship with the one translated. A reorientation occurs. It is in this sense that taking time and taking another person seriously mean the same thing to a speech-thinker. This means that the tenses are not interchangeable. The present is based on a foundational past.

The past is always projecting into a future. The beginning, middle, and end of a life are related to the beginning, middle and end of the world: creation, revelation, and redemption. We *live* in the middle, in revelation. On being asked what revelation meant to him, Rosenstock-Huessy replied to Rosenzweig: orientation.[32] Rosenzweig adopted this meaning. The response and participation of the translator, as a listener into the past, and as a speaker in the present and into the future, always orient his present. In turn, the translator reorients the present of those who hear him creating new presents based on past and future.

Translating takes place in the present. The tenses are clear cut but on a continuum: an event that is past is a fact, not to be changed; an event that is present is that which is being experienced now; and an event that is to become or to happen is future. No event is without reference to time. No event, including the event of truth, can be designated simultaneously past, present, and future. Truth is not timeless.

Translating mediates events and understanding among human beings through time. The mediation of translation is the same thing that occurs in direct conversation within the same language. Timelessness is especially shunned by the speech-thinking method. Rosenzweig sees timelessness as the aberrational aspect to which thought aspires, what it purports to "have" and strives to "be" in its automonous realms that go nowhere and thus become phantoms. For reality, for concrete reality, for the concrete reality of speech, time is required and welcomed. Thought, in that it relates to no tenses, is indeed timeless.

Timelessness, to Rosenzweig, must not be construed as eternity which has no access to temporality. Timelessness has a relationship with eternity only at the end of time. Eternity, during the span of revelation, is not the absence of time. The major difference between time and eternity is that eternity is not created, and time is. Time was created precisely in order to relate to eternity.[33]

Eternity is that aspect of present reality that transpires in translating. How in the instance of translating does eternity transpire? Eternity of what? Eternity of language? Eternity of the original speaker? None of these. A present that links two people in translatable peace and understanding is a present that is also eternal. God is the sole element of reality whose essence is eternal: an eternal past in creation, an eternal present in revelation, and an eternal future in redemption. Eternity of the creator of language who transpires through his corollary creature time is that which is experienced in human speech through time. Through these creations, language and time, the creative spirit flows, for God the creator himself uses language. God lifted (lifts) himself out of his eternality, his essential realm, and acts in his creation time.

The human, living in his "natural" time-span of life, experiences eternity wherein God meets time.

That fundamental problem Rosenzweig came to have with Idealism involved the correlation between language and death. Language could not offer Idealism what it demands: calculability, finality, accountability. Language, "this voice, which resounds in man without apparent reason but the more realistically for that,"[34] cried out to the deaf ears of Idealism that death, being universal, is nevertheless not nothing: it is real, new, and individual in each case. A death – a life – will not be subsumed and reduced to an all. With its inherent relationship to time, language is also related to eternity. It is "a growth amidst all growing life [and] ... nourishes itself on language. Yet it is distinguished from this life precisely because it does not move freely and capriciously over the surface, but rather sinks roots into the dark foundations beneath life. Idealistic logic, however, thinks it must remain entirely in these dark subterranean foundations. Without knowing it, [Logic] thus rather drags the life of the above, into which it does not dare to grow, down into the nether world. [Logic] transforms the living into a realm of shadows.[35]

Only through the creative spirit can and do past, present, and future find for themselves a certain mutuality. Eternity *and* time, that is, the oneness of eternality and the plurality of the tenses, interconnect and are bridged by the creative spirit. Here there is no "versus." It is truly a matter of "and." Rosenzweig, among the several labels he reluctantly contrived for his new philosophy, also named it the "and" philosophy.

From the first sentence of Rosenzweig's summary we learn that to him a permanence occurs whenever speech becomes audible. The intention of translating is not to render language permanent, but to fulfil it. At this stage we can better see that the permanence arising from translating is not a permanence of language itself or of anyone's particular speech. The permanence is rather one of a mutuality of understanding, but a mutuality only in an imbalanced sense, only from the point of view of the translating language. The peace arrived at between two or more speakers, however momentary, endures as a peace which reaches an eternal plane and is eternally incontrovertible. The truth of peace remains as God's Truth. When experienced and expressed in time, in the present, truth is thus also permanent in the sense that it endures beyond time, after the end of the world. Alexander Altmann summarizes this meaning of permanence, and underlines that neither truth nor eternity can be monologically or solitarily understood. Moreover, rather than perceiving present moments as touching upon eternity, the speech-thinker would contend that it is more accurate to say that truths touch upon and relate permanently to eternity, but that truths can be reached only in the present, in present meetings. Altmann writes that according to speech-thinking: "Truth is revealed through speech as expressing the intercommunication of one mind with another. It is not the formal truths of logic in their timeless, abstract, systematic character that are really vital and relevant, but rather the truths that are brought out in the relationships of human beings with God and with one another – truths that spring from the presentness of time and yet reach out into the eternal."[36]

Translating for Rosenzweig entails, therefore, certainly quantifiable accuracy, but much more important than that, the resultant transformations that comprise an irreversible growth in spirit of the language translated into. The growth in spirit is the growth in the expressibility of truth in a specific language. Rosenzweig would say with Rosenstock-Huessy that "speech is that energy which makes us partake in the six or seven thousand years of civilized life on earth."[37]

In an essay titled "Scripture and Luther's Translation," Rosenzweig further elucidates the principle of permanence, as it relates to the translation of great literary works:

In a certain sense, every great work in one language can be translated into another language only once. The history of translation shows typical phenomena. First there are a number of interlinear translations, with the modest aim of serving trots, and free "creative" renderings that seek to make accessible to the reader the meaning – or what the translator considers the meaning – of the text. Then, one day, a miracle happens and the spirits of the two languages mate. This does not strike like a bolt out of the blue. The time for such a *hieros gamos*, for such a Holy Wedding, is not ripe until a receptive people reaches out toward the wing-beat of an alien masterpiece with its own yearning and its own utterance and when its receptiveness is no longer based on curiosity, interest, desire for education, or even aesthetic pleasure, but has become an integral part of the people's historical development ... A good translator will translate the foreign book into something indigenous.[38]

Thus, one language truly meets and mates with another, dependent upon the reaching out of the language ready to translate, to expand, to grow. That all languages do not at once, do not now, meet each other – technically they can – is due not to a faultiness in speech's means of communicating thought. It is due rather to the requirement of time, to waiting for the right time when the common ground necessary for translation to take place, that base of synonymy, emerges: in the case of literary works, the creative spirit embodied in one language is yearned for by another. "To need time means: to be able to anticipate nothing, to have to wait for everything, to be dependent on the other for what is ours. All this is entirely unthinkable to the thinking thinker, while it co-responds to the 'speaking thinker.' "39

Thus the creative spirit is not a diffusive, nebulous breath that vaporously enwreathes the world skimming worldly surfaces wherever it will. Rather it is *in* the world, *of* the world; created and creative. Language, like the world, is to be completed, to be realized. The creative spirit that bridges generations that the translator lures into his present, that yet reaches out to the eternal and to the permanent, is in the world because it is part of the world's created composition:

The world is – a new feature! – composed of imponderables and ponderables, heaven and earth. Not, for example, as even the politician perhaps all too gladly would concede: heaven *has* created earth. No, it does not stand behind and leave to hell the entire foreground, rather heaven *and* earth, both created, from the "foreground". Power wants to gain everything by force. And precisely this – thought upon doves' feet – rules the world. The spirit ... The peace of the seventh day, which yet itself is a work, itself only completes the creation: Power knows only of the world of six days. It would like to deny the Sabbath. But it belongs to the world – to the created world. The day when there is no weighing, the day of imponderables, of the positive rest – itself a part of creation. The peace which "belongs *to it*", as does the battle.40

Thus the creative spirit is not a force: it does not impose itself upon listeners. The listeners will listen when they ... will listen.

Introducing the word "spirit". Of spirit*ual* is not the point ... The spirit creates works. Wherein is it differentiated from artwork? Even the work of art *itself* as a spiritual work – wherein does it differentiate itself from the same thing as work of art? As spiritual work it is *expansive*, not bound to the aesthetic effect. The spirit *in*spirits everything. (Art beauti*fies* nothing but itself.) A fully spiritual world would be "beautiful" ... Against the notion of the "spiritual": it involves a separation, just what the spirit may not claim. And what it yet cannot do without. It needs the non-spiritual – and yet may not leave it non-spiritual. At the end everything must be spiritual. (The spirit produces its audience.) ... The soul, not the spirit is that which may lead out beyond the creation. The spirit belongs *to* the creation.41

"The creative achievement of translating can lie nowhere else than where the creative achievement of speaking itself lies."42 To translate is to speak again. It is to renew speech, the truth that is unfolded in speaking. The responsibility of the translator is not merely to be true to the speech being translated: he or she is at the same time being faithful to and has faith in future speakers. Otherwise he would not translate formally. Furthermore, in translating formally, the translator expects response by future readers and speakers in their turn:

In speaking and listening, the "other" need not have my ears or my mouth – this would render unnecessary not only translation but also speaking and listening. And in speaking and listening between nations, what is needed is neither a translation that is so far from being a translation as to be the original – this would eliminate the listening nation – nor one that is in effect a new original – this would eliminate the speaking nation. These could be desired only by a mad egoism intent on satisfying its own personal or national life and yearning to be in a desert surrounded oasis. Such an attitude is utterly out of harmony in a world created to be not a wilderness but a place to contain every kind of people.[43]

The second sentence has revealed many aspects of Rosenzweig's philosophy of translation. Translating is not a self-contained act that functions as a transference of interior thought to another interior and setting it down as fixed. The translator is a responder: his or her own speech depends upon another's speech. The translator becomes part of a larger conversation. The task is to translate one person's speech to others and *for* other persons' speech. Full reality of speech – anyone's speech, including God's – is not yet completed while language lives and grows. Thus it is impossible for any language to make final, definitive statements about reality in the present incompleteness of any single language. Every language's boundaries are still in the process of expanding from within, through its own speakers who have something new to say; and from without, through drawing in foreign speech which has not yet been expressed in the "mother" tongue, through translation. As long as there are still subsequent responders and rejoinders, no one human mind, no philosophic system or theological dogma can contain or control what "is." According to the speech-thinker, each human being, however, can partake in all speech that has ever been conversed:

The Scriptures constitute the first conversation of mankind, a conversation in which gaps of half and whole millennia occur between speech and response. Paul tried to find the answer to the question of the third chapter of Genesis [The Hiding of Adam from God after eating of the Tree of Knowledge] by questioning the words of the twentieth chapter of Exodus [The Giving of the Law]. Augustine and Luther repeated his answer, but each added his own answer to it. The former replied with his theory of the *Civitas Dei*, the latter with his *Epistle to the Councilmen*, in which he requested the establishment of Christian schools. In every instance a new phase in this conversation is introduced by translation, translation into the language of tragedy, translation into the language of the *Corpus Juris,* and into that of the *Phenomenology of the Spirit.* No one knows when this conversation will come to an end, but then, no one knows when it began. And so it cannot be determined by the peevishness, arrogance, or complacent cleverness of any man, but only by the will, the knowledge, and the wisdom of Him who wrought the beginning.[44]

The third "sentence": In a corresponding way, also translating from person to person.

At least two scholars have, understandably and to a degree justifiably, criticized Rosenzweig for not satisfactorily explaining human-to-human contact in speech.

Nahum Glatzer, in "The Concept of Language in Rosenzweig's Thought," states that from the supplementary essay to the *Star,* "Das neue Denken,"

One gains the impression that the *Star,* which uses the method of speech-thinking, is indeed concerned with the word exchanged between human beings ... But when we go back to the *Star,* we are confronted with the fact that word, speech and language take place in the sphere between God and man ... The most telling examples for speech-thinking Rosenzweig could offer came from the realm of man's relationship with the divine ...
We may ask whether the change – from the religious meaning of language to the role of speech in inter-human relations – is due to a conscious development: Is it not more than an attempt to make explicit in "The New Thinking" what lay dormant between the lines of the *Star?* This question I am unable to answer.[45]

Rivka Horwitz, in her article "Franz Rosenzweig on Language," writes that according to Rosenzweig, "Every person is in the present moment, here and now, in the center of *his* time. In a meeting man's life is concentrated; his past as well as his future are with him. Rosenzweig thinks that man as a center orders the external world in accordance with his experience [*Star* 127-8]. Unfortunately, he did not develop this principal theme; he merely left it as an idea."[46]

These criticisms point to the difficulties involved in any exposition of the vitality of speech-thinking. I shall not argue that Rosenzweig did indeed entirely surmount these difficulties in the *Star.* Yet, if only by a route beyond the gateway of the *Star,* it seems to me that Rosenzweig did find appropriate and successful ways in his attempt to "make explicit" "the role of speech in inter-human relations," and to "develop this principal theme" of the human in the present and centre of his own time. While the critiques of Glatzer and Horwitz hold to a degree, I suggest that few attempts to make explicit the *Star*'s boundedness as philosophical system would have been untenable. For example, to generally describe interpersonal relationships that were not his own, and therefore events that he could not really know by experience, would defeat the very presence that Rosenzweig asserts. Nor would it have worked to describe those relationships that were his own and that he therefore did know by experience. With the tenet, as Horwitz stated, that a meeting is in the present moment, how does one write a description in "merely a philosophical system,"[47] as Rosenzweig designated the *Star* to be, of something so present as live speech between an I and a You, without falling into the lie of the objective description for an event that is not a thing in the first place and defies objectification? If I would argue that Rosenzweig succeeded in making explicit the role of speech, I would do it from his reading of the Song of Songs as the "focal book of revelation."[48] Buber, perhaps bravely, but in some places rather unfortunately has risked this attempt. His works have popularly been discussed in maudlin terms tending toward a general, universal, sentimental, pervasive "love" rather than toward the specific love from particular person to particular person to which the philosophy of experience attests. Beyond the gate of the *Star* Rosenzweig "described" inter-human speech in the only way it could and should be done: by simply doing it, in the writing of the *Star* on army postcards, in teaching at the Lehrhaus, and in the testimony of his correspondence. I have already noted that he yearned to speak physically, but that his illness forbade it.

Interestingly, the criticism is not levelled at Rosenzweig's really equally vague "descriptions" of divine-human speech. Just as Rosenzweig never described in objective terms any specific relationship between humans, including any of his own, he likewise never described in objective terms, that is outside the present moment, any human-divine encounter. While this lack of criticism in itself indicates that such speech experiences are readily understood or accepted, it also indicates that those ready accepters view human-divine discourse as radically different from speech between human and human. To the speech-thinker, human-divine conversation is the root of human-human speech, and is that which nourishes and authenticates all speech. Neither Glatzer nor Horwitz mentions the important and inseparable connection the *Star* elucidates between human-divine and human-human speech.

In meetings between two, whether between God and a human or being, or between two people, so much happens from gesture, glance, nuance, vocabulary confined to the particular two – with their intertwined past that involves only those two and with the double present that converges in the meeting – that it would be perhaps impossible and at least unseemly to attempt to offer descriptions to third parties. Like Anselm, Rosenzweig could only "philosophize about" events of meetings between persons from immediate experience. He preferred speak *to* rather than *about* God, and in conversation with human beings, to permit God as a third speaker. Thus, Rosenzweig's reading of the Song of Songs as "more than simile" seems to me to offer an answer to Glatzer's and Horwitz's questions. Here, the human being, loved by God, aware of the love, and loving in return, finds she must break the love-circle in order to enlarge it. She must encounter her neighbour, and she must do so in such a way that she encounters him *with* God. It is from Rosenzweig's analysis of the Song of Songs that we learn he maintains that God is a partner in authentic inter-human speech.

A second partial answer to the two above criticisms lies in Rosenzweig's translation of the Jehuda Halevi poetry with the accompanying Notes. In the Notes, Rosenzweig *lives* with Jehuda Halevi as one lives with a person in the event of conversation. Rosenzweig listens *to* him in the translations, and speaks *with* him in agreement in the Notes. Halevi's poems are all either direct speech to God or theological and philosophical reflections. In the Notes Rosenzweig speaks not so much about Halevi as he does *to* the readers of the Notes. Rosenzweig includes Jehuda Halevi in his address to the reader, as if in a three-person conversation. To Rosenzweig it *is* a conversation involving three.[49] While the reader is the primary addressee, Jehuda Halevi appears to play the part of the one who in a live conversation would be participating by listening to the primary speaker and listener, and is yet included in the conversation by the speaker's frequent side-glances at him, the unspoken: "As you say," "I see you feel," "As you have experienced." Rosenzweig is asking, "Am I understanding you right?" to Jehuda Halevi, coupled with: "What do you say, Reader?" The reader is hearing Rosenzweig's words, but is constantly aware of their dependence on the one who "spoke" to Rosenzweig first in this conversation. Rosenzweig seems averse to categorizing, with one definition, inter-human speech and, with another definition, divine-human speech. The key to authentic speech, to Rosenzweig, is God's being there when human beings are in conversation.

Within one layer, Jehuda Halevi remains a real person who displays an integrity of experience and speech. His speech in the form of fixed, written words is not a text disassociated from a person. The text is more than the vehicle of his person; speech and person perform in mutuality: they are vehicles to each other. This mutuality keeps Jehuda

Halevi's presence intact. A history of the life of Jehuda Halevi, on the other hand, would not bring Jehuda's own presence to the reader.

In another layer, Rosenzweig remains a real and separate person from Jehuda Halevi. "Not for a moment," Rosenzweig emphatically printed in his Afterword to the Notes, "do [these translations] want to make the reader forget that he is reading poems not by me but by Jehuda Halevi, and that Jehuda Halevi is neither a German poet nor a contemporary."[50] Translating another's words into one's own speech does not subsume the speech of that other's presence. Indeed, Rosenzweig opens his Afterword with the statement that his selection of poems wishes to give to the reader an idea of Halevi as a great Jewish poet who composed in Hebrew. "So it was not my aim to make the reader believe that Jehuda Halevi composed in German, nor that he composed Christian church songs, nor that he is a poet of today, even if only a *Familienblatt* poet of today – all this as far as I can see the aims of my predecessors in translation, especially the most recent ones."[51] Rather, the act of true translating expands, alters and orients the present of the one translating. The Notes, fixed in writing, ensure the presence of Rosenzweig in Germany of the 1920s; the poetry ensures Jehuda Halevi's presence in mediaeval Spain. The Notes constitute an example of applied speech-thinking because (1) they concretely demonstrate the step of translation prior to response, (2) the response derives from this step, and (3) thus two presents meet. A fuller consideration of these three important points appears in chapter 4.

When Rosenzweig guided the first readers of the *Star* who misunderstood or did not understand at all what the *Star* was saying[52] by pointing them to his Notes to the Jehuda Halevi poetry as an example of practical application of speech-thinking, it seems that few followed this guide-post. Rosenzweig remarked that he could understand how the *Star*'s audience was disappointed, but not the readers of the translated poetry with Notes, presented as they were "in a tempting hors-d'oeuvre format."[53] In "The New Thinking," he again tries to lead his readers, not only into and through his book, but beyond the last pages of the *Star*, which conclude with that well-known imperative "Into Life!" He encourages his first readers in this way:

Here the book ends. For what is still coming is already beyond the book, a "Gate" out into the no-longer-book. No-longer-book is the enraptured-terrified recognition that in this beholding of the "world-image in God's countenance," in this grasping of all being in the immediacy of a moment [*Augenblick*] and blink of the eye [*Augen-blick*] the borderline of humanity is entered. No-longer-book is also the becoming aware that this step of the book onto the borderline can only be atoned through – ending the book. An ending which is at the same time a beginning and a middle: to enter into the middle of everyday of life. The problem of the philosopher goes through the whole book, especially through the three introductions. Only here does it find its definitive solution. Philosophizing should continue further, indeed further. Everyone should philosophize some time. Everyone should some time look around from his own stand- and life-point. But this look is not an end in itself. The book is not goal which has been reached, not even a temporary one. One must be responsible for it instead of it carrying itself or being carried by others of its kind. This responsibility happens in everyday [Alltag] life. Only in order to recognize and to live the day as every-day [All-tag], the day of the life of the All [All] had to be traversed.[54]

Notwithstanding Rosenzweig's charge to move on, Nahum Glatzer legitimately writes: "But when we go back to the text of the *Star* ..."[55] Rosenzweig himself recognizes and distinguishes between the limitations and possibilities of speech within philosophical books and the living of a philosophy outside books:

The first pages of philosophical books are held in specially high esteem by the reader. He believes they are the basis for all that follows. Consequently he also thinks in order to refute the whole it's enough to have refuted these pages. Hence the enormous interest in Kant's teaching of space and time in the form [*Gestalt*], in which he developed it at the beginning of the Critique. Hence the comical attempt to "refute" Hegel from the first three strokes of his logic, and Spinoza from his definitions. And hence the helplessness of the general reader in the face of philosophical books. He thinks they must be "especially logical," and understands by this the dependence of every following sentence on every foregoing; so that therefore when the famous one stone is pulled out of a famous work "the whole collapses." In truth that is nowhere less the case than in philosophical books. Here a sentence does not follow from the one preceding, but much rather from the one following. He who has not understood a sentence or a paragraph is little helped if he, in the conscientious belief that he must not leave anything behind that is not understood, reads it again and again or even starts over again from the beginning. Philosophical books deny themselves of such a methodical strategy of the *ancien régime*, which intends to allow no fortress left behind unconquered; they want to be conquered napoleonically, in a bold attack on the enemy's central force, after whose conquest the small border-fortresses will fall on their own. He who therefore does not understand something, most surely may expect illumination, if he boldly goes on reading. The reason for this rule, which is difficult to understand for the beginner, and, as the cases cited above show, also for many a non-beginner, lies in the fact that thinking and writing are not one. In thinking one stroke really strikes a thousand connections. In writing these thousand must be nicely and cleanly arranged on the string of thousands of lines. As Schopenhauer said, his book wants to impart only a single thought which, however, he could not ever impart more briefly than in the entire book. When a philosophical book then is worth reading at all, then certainly it is only when one either does not understand or at least falsely understands the beginning. For otherwise the thought which it imparts is scarcely worth re-thinking [*Nachdenden*], since one plainly already knows it, if one knows righ at the beginning "what this is leading to." All this is valid only for books; only they can be written and read without regard for passing time. Speaking and hearing stand under other laws. Of course, only real speaking and hearing, not that sort which reviles itself as a "lecture" and during which the hearer must forget that he has a mouth, and becomes at best a writing hand.[56]

Where *can* evidence of the laws under which speaking and hearing stand be found expressed in order further to reply to the criticisms of Horwitz and Glatzer? The *Star is* concerned with but cannot demonstrate "word exchanged between human beings" any more than it can demonstrate word exchanged between human beings and God. Yet an understanding of what the speech-thinker means by human-to-human speech, based directly as it is upon word between God and human, will result from a careful reading of the *Star*'s consideration of human-divine encounters.

Until now reference to God as speaker has been minimal. But *that* God speaks bestows upon word the ability to breathe comfortably in both spiritual and worldly realms. Speech entails the concrete and the spiritual. Since in the method of Rosenzweig, speech is the commonly shared bridge of communication also between God and human, then trust in the possibilities of speech and language in inter-human speech is absolute. Moreover, within Rosenzweig's discussion of human-divine meetings, the principal theme Horwitz refers to – the human as the experiential centre of his or her time who thereby orders the external world – is indeed developed: "And language is easily trusted, for it is within us and about us; as it reaches us from 'without,' it is no different from language as it echoes the 'without' from our 'within.' The word as heard and as spoken is one and the same. The ways of God are different from the ways of man, but the word of God and the word of man are the same. What man hears in his heart as his own human speech is the very word which comes out of God's mouth."[57]

Since God speaks to all, and with absolute trust in language, each human must both speak to others in a way that translates the words of God that he or she hears and listen to others in a translating frame of mind.

God's primary speech addressed to the human, that is, God's self-revelation, gives the human purpose in and for life: through the mutually contingent imperatives common to both Judaism and Christianity – Love me, love your neighbour – the human is commanded to act for God and for other humans.

God's statements about himself never tell *what* he is, but always decree *that* he is, and *who* he is in relation to the human: *your* God. Nor does God state the human *is* such-and-such, and the world *is* so-and-so. The creator of the world and of the human speaks in no logically static formulae. Rather, when the creator reveals, he relates to the world and to the human with the dynamics evoked by commands: "The imperative belongs to revelation as the indicative to creation ... As the object of experience ... the noun ceases to be thing. It no longer exhibits the basic character of the thing, that of a thing among others. Now it is subject and hence something individual. On principle it occurs in the singular. It is something individual, or rather someone individual. Just this was anticipated, in its turn, in the creation of man, the first individual, the 'image of God.' "[58]

The point of creation is createdness, not contingency or derivation: thus each element – God, world, and human – stands on its own. For understanding reality, then, what each *is* becomes the less important question in the move from creation to revelation than what each *does to* the other and what each *is for* the other. The imperative is a necessary grammatical category to link God and human. God's primary commands, love me and love neighbour, at once create a relationship among the three elements.

Creation is the beginning of the world, and the world on general includes the world of humans as well as of other particulars. From the world's point of view, revelation is the midpoint; but from the individually named human's point of view, revelation is both the midpoint, because based on the past, and the beginning, because at revelation the human becomes human: he or she is addressed.

With the summons of the proper name, the word of revelation entered the real dialogue. With the proper name, the rigid wall of objectness has been breached. That which has a name of its own can no longer be a thing, no longer everyman's affair. It is incapable of utter absorption into the category for there can be no category for it to belong to; it is its own category. Nor does it still have its place in the world, its moment in occurrence. Rather it carries its here and now with it. Wherever it is, there is a midpoint and wherever it opens its mouth, there is a beginning. In the intricate world of things there was no midpoint or beginning at all; the I, however, together with its proper name, introduces these concepts of midpoint and beginning into the world. In keeping with its creation as man and at the same time as "Adam," the I is midpoint and beginning within itself. For it demands a midpoint in the world for the midpoint, a beginning for the beginning of its own experience. The I longs for orientation, for a world which does not just lie there in any old arrangement, nor flow past in any old sequence, but a world which supports the inner order inherent in the I's experience on the solid base of an external order ... Thus both the midpoint and the beginning in the world must be provided to experience by this grounding, the midpoint in space, the beginning in time. These two, at least, have to be named, even if the rest of the world still lies in the darkness of anonymity ... the spatial taking-place of revelation and its temporal having-transpired live on today in separate media, the former in God's congregation, the latter in God's word: at one time, however, both must have been founded at a single blow. The ground of revelation is midpoint and beginning in one; it is the revelation of the divine name ... For name is in truth word and fire, and not sound and fury as unbelief would have it again and again in obstinate vacuity. It is incumbent to name the name and to acknowledge: I believe it.[59]

The name is of utmost importance. The name is particular. God calls upon humans one by one, calling each by name; and each human calls upon God in his or her individuality, from name to name. With name, the direction of movement from particular to universal is especially apparent and real. Neither the human nor God can be objectified when the name is in the vocative, and properly, the name is always only in the vocative. As God calls each by name, so the human is, one by one, to call each human in his path – his neighbour – by name. The specific other insisted upon by speech-thinking is derived from and based on this calling by God. Regions of anonymity in the world are dark regions to the speech-thinker, regions not yet lightened in love. Whatever accords with a proclamation of God's name is true speech and worthy – needful – of translating. What gives a person the key to recognizing the proclamation of God's name in others' speech?

According to Rosenzweig, we can all know what is to be listened to and translated by attending to our hearts. The capacity to translate and the judgment of the worthiness of speech – our own or others' – does indeed come from recognition of words that have already been spoken into the human heart by God. In the course of listening, when something faintly recognizable beats in our hearts, something as yet unuttered by our mouths strikes a chord of recognition of the divine word that has already been spoken into the heart, then that which is recognized is speech that becomes our enthusiastic goal to translate.

How, then, does hearing an utterance from a source outside the heart but speaking into it spark recognition? Recognition denotes to know again, to meet again. Rosenzweig speaks of "hearing in the heart", and experience replaces logic as primary source for knowing reality. One experiences hearing. One does not deduce or adduce hearing. It happens. Hearing one's name called initiates an experience for that particularly called person. Rosenzweig's contentions in the *Star* that one hears God's word in the heart and that revelation is both midpoint and beginning are phrased succinctly to a friend in 1921: "The Bible is precisely *in this way different* from all other books. All other books one can get to know only in reading them. What stands in the Bible one can learn to know in two ways: 1) in that one hears what it says, 2) in that one hearkens to the beat of the human heart. (Induction is both.) *The Bible and the heart say the same thing.* That is why (and *only* why) the Bible is 'Revelation.' "[60]

An excerpt from Rosenzweig's "Scripture and Luther's Translation" is pertinent here also. Two ideas are presented: (1) that the human's life illumines the Scriptures, and not vice versa, and (2) that every human life belongs to everything in the Scriptures, but that not everything in the Scriptures belongs to each life. These two ideas emphasize the notion of translating from particular human to particular human, whether or not living in the same generation.

Modern man is neither a believer nor an unbeliever. He believes and he doubts. And so he is nothing, but he is alive. Belief and unbelief "happen" to him and all that he is required to do is not run away from what is happening but make use of it once it has happened ...

Whoever lives in this way can approach the Bible only with a readiness to believe or not to believe, but not with a circumscribed belief that he finds confirmed in it ... As a searchlight detaches from darkness now one section of the landscape and now another, and then leaves these again dimmed, so for such a man the days of his own life illumine the Scriptures, and in their quality of humanness permit him to recognize what is more than human, today at one point, and tomorrow at another, nor can one day ever vouch for the next to yield a like experience ...

Luther reasoned that he must – on occasion – grant Hebrew a place in German, that he must expand his own language to accommodate Hebrew "instruction" and "solace of our conscious." Should not this same kind of reasoning beget new reverence for the word in us who do not know *what* words may, some day, yield instruction and solace, who believe that the hidden sources of instruction and solace may flow from every word in this book?

And must not such reverence renew our reading, our understanding, and hence our translating?[61]

Since all of God's word is *intended* for every human, and yet since each hears it in measures and paces according to his own life's experiences, and further, since life's experiences are different, God's word can be and is spoken in different words by different humans. The differences in human speech do not necessarily therefore entail ultimate difference. Of the words Rosenzweig used for the *Star*, writes in "Das neue Denken":

But the "Jewish book"? [sic] as is indicated already by the title page? I would like to be able to speak as softly as the poet when he concludes his powerfully far-reaching fugue on the theme of the cosmic beauty with the unforgettable preface: It appeared to me in form of youth, of woman – to be able to say truthfully what I now have to say. I received the new thinking in these old words, thus I have returned it and passed it on, in them. There would have come to the lips of a Christian, I know, instead of mine, words of the New Testament, to a pagan, I think, surely not words of his holy books – for their ascent leads away from the original language of humankind, – not to it – , but perhaps entirely his own words. But for me these ones. And yet this is a Jewish book: not one that deals with "Jewish matters," for the books of the Protestant Old Testament scholars would be Jewish books; but one to which there come the old Jewish words for what it has to say, and precisely for the new things it has to say. Jewish matters are, as matters generally are, at all times past; but Jewish words, even if old, take part in the eternal youth of the word, and when the world is opened to them, then they renew the world.[62]

Since God speaks to the human heart, whoever listens to the beats of his or her own heart will recognize divine speech (or otherwise) in others' lives.

Just as with translating between languages, where in each language all other languages already exist in potential, so with translating from person to person. Another's speech, when arising out of the human-divine encounter, may be seem initially different from one's own, and hitherto unuttered in one's own language. Such speech of the other *can* nevertheless be translated: it is potentially present in every human heart's capacity for hearing all of God's word. It *must* be translated into the heart because God commands: Love as I have loved. The faint recognition happens because hearing God's word spoken by another human is to re-hear what God has already spoken. It is faint because it has not yet been actualized by having become truly vocal.

To translate from human to human, then, is to enact the commandment of love of neighbour.

Now this fulfillment of God's commandment in the world is not, after all, an isolated action but a whole sequence of action. Love of neighbour always erupts anew. It is a matter of always starting over from the beginning ... It must be an act of love wholly lost in the (present) moment ... If it were to emerge as infinite affirmation, then it would be not an act of love but a purposive act. Then it would no longer emerge, fresh as the moment, from the volitional orientation of character. Rather its relationship to its origin in this orientation would be one of subservience, conclusive and concluded once and for all.[63]

To love outward to the whole world is to act in one solitary thought. "Love" here is merely a static attitude, an ineffective emotion – nothing unique, special, real, or eruptive happens.

In the "Urzelle" of the *Star*, written to his baptized cousin Rudolf Ehrenberg[64] in letter form, Rosenzweig's insights regarding love of neighbour tumble forth with a compelling swiftness of conviction:

The world whose sublime spirit teaches the human being to know the brothers in the forest and shrub, and bush and water and allows him nevertheless to feel bound herein and herewith directly that nothing perfect was given to the human being. Instead of these easily and cheaply found brothers everywhere, to whom he stands in "relationship," the human has in the "connection" in the first instance only *himself* as his own likeness; the word of neighbourly love, a well-tempered matter-of-course, here becomes a voice of trumpets, for it is not said to the human in whose breast's purity surges an aspiration for voluntary *submission*, but to the deaf I, buried in its own I-ness, to this I, about which nothing can be presupposed except this, that it loves *itself*. But that is why, *after* this word has opened up the deaf ear, the human now recognizes in the neighbour now really the one who is like him, recognizes him not merely as B2, B3 and so on, as co-habiter of the same world ... For he recognizes him only as It, only as his brother in the forest and grove in rock and water; rather I recognize that he *is not He She It, but rather an I*, an I like me, not a co-inhabiter of the same directionless and centreless space, not a travel acquaintance on the trip through time without beginning and end, but my brother, the consors [consort] of my destiny, for whom "things are" exactly as for me, who also sees only one track before him as I do; my brother not in the world, in woods and grove, in bush and water, but in the Lord.[65]

This recognition of which Rosenzweig speaks is the recognition that the eternal God has spoken as well to that other. That that other is also creature in creation, like him created by the creator, exactly *like* him, but not him. A bridge is required in order to awaken the recognition of the likeness, the recognition of the centred space in time. Time, but not the centres, will end. The end is the goal toward which all travel; the link between each distinct human being is the speech of God into the heart of each person. Before God's speech into the heart, the human cannot hear in love any other human being and thus cannot engage in authentic speech. Love of neighbour happens only after

God has spoken to the individual, and happens because of this address, but the love of neighbour is nevertheless encumbent upon the
individual human to fulfil. God does not create love between humans.
He creates the possibility and commands its fulfilment. Just as God in
present, centred revelation speaks to each human, one by one, and
one to one, so love of neighbour is also "as I have loved you," to be
brought about one by one, and one to one. In the *Star* this love of the
specific neighbour is again stressed:

Precisely here in the commandment to love one's neighbour, his self is definitely confirmed in its place. The world is not thrown in his face as an endless
melée, nor is he told, while a finger points to the whole melée: you. That is you
– therefore stop distinguishing yourself from it, penetrate it, dissolve in it, lose
yourself in it. No, it is quite different. Out of the endless chaos of the world,
one nighest thing his neighbour, is placed before his soul, and concerning this
one and well-nigh only concerning this one he is told: he is like you. "Like
you," and thus not "you." You remain You and you are to remain just that. But
he is not to remain a He for you, and thus a mere It for your You. Rather he is
like You, like your You, a You like You, an I – a soul.[66]

To Rosenzweig the self is an incomplete part of the human: it is what
the human manifests before revelation. The self is incapable of love: it
is capable only of soliloquy, of monologue, as the hero in pagan Greek
tragedy. The Greeks, according to Rosenzweig, expressed the truth of
the three elements of reality. But their definition of reality was limited
and lacking because the elements were conceived in isolation and not
in relation to one another. Without the correct designation of relation,
the human – love – is incomplete. God's speech awakens the deaf and
autonomously speaking self to become the hearing soul that is now capable of dialogue. "The blossoming tree of love always reaches towards
animating love only with the buds that have already opened."[67] An
opened bud is a soul, and a soul is one who is conscious of God and
has experienced God. Only one who has experienced God can know
her- or himself, and therefore others also, as souls. None of the three
elements are or can ever be totally alone: they will always confront
each other. And confrontation is always facing, always present.

Thus Rosenzweig cannot explain, lay out flat, explicate, unfold
present revelation. Nor can the Bible. Language, Rosenzweig asserts, is
more than analogy, and more than true analogue. The presentness of
our experience in present revelation is really as it is written in the Song
of Songs. It is speech speaking.

"The analogue of love permeates as analogue all of revelation,"[68] not as a pointer or indicator, rather as direct lover to the be-

loved. The I and Thou of human discourse is the I and Thou between God and human. In language the distinction between immanence and transcendence disappears. The Song of Songs is an "authentic," that is "worldly" love lyric, and for this reason, genuinely "spiritual."[69]

Abraham J. Heschel, who views time as Rosenzweig does, in distinguishing between time and space, notes: "Exclaimed Rabbi Akiba: 'All of time is not worthy as the day on which the Song of Songs was given to Israel, for all the songs are holy, but the Song of Songs is the holiest of holies." In a realm of spirit, there is no difference between a second and a century, between and hour and an age."[70] A moment can become eternity, depending on what it contains.

Love simply cannot be "purely human." It must speak, for there is simply no self-expression other than the speech of life. And by speaking, love already becomes superhuman, for the sensuality of the word is brimful with its divine super-sense. Like speech itself, love is sensual – supersensual. To put it another way, simile is its very nature and not merely its decorative accessory. "All that is transitory" may be "but simile." But love is not "but simile"; it is simile in its entirety and its essence; it is only apparently transitory: in truth, it is eternal. The appearance is as essential as the truth here, for love could not be eternal as love if it did not appear to be transitory. But in the mirror of this appearance, truth is directly mirrored.[71]

What Heschel means by claiming there is no difference in spiritual time between a second and a century is what Rosenzweig is claiming by eternity in the event of love.

In Rosenzweig's grammatical analysis of the Song of Songs, he examines the fact that this is the sole book in the Bible that opens with a comparative, "better than wine." This comparative at once asserts a point of view that negates all other points of view. This "better," that is, present revelation, picks up precisely where creation left off: "very good." The I who expresses this viewpoint, who had death as the "ultimate and consummate of creation,"[72] now asserts the transition from creation to revelation: "Love is strong as death." This sentence is the only assertion of fact in the whole of the Song of Songs; it is the only possible reflection about love. Everything else has to be spoken, "for love is – speech, wholly active, wholly personal, wholly living, wholly – speaking."[73] The rest of the Song of Songs, beyond this assertive, objective sentence that "the living soul, loved by God, triumphs over all that is mortal,"[74] is subjective present speech. "A downpour of imperatives descends on this evergreen pasture of the present and vitalizes it."[75]

But in the immediate revelation of love, something is lacking. While all shame dissolves ("I am very dark, but comely") in the outpouring of

love, in the peace of being loved, and in the "mine" uttered by the beloved, still, the love between the two lacks something and is not fulfilled. "Would that you were my brother," the beloved sobs. Calling by
name is not enough. It demands reality.

The name ought to be the truth. It should be heard in the bright light of "the
street," not whispered into the beloved ear in the dusk of intimate duo-soli-
tude, but in the eyes of the multitude ... Love after all remains between two
people; it knows only of I and Thou, not of the street. Thus this longing cannot be fulfilled in love, for love is directly present in experience and manifests
itself only in experience ... If this longing is to be fulfilled, then the beloved
soul must cross the magic circle of belovedness, forget the lover, and itself
open its mouth, not for answer but for her own word ... And only in her heart
of hearts may she hold fast to that dictum of the ancients which, on this her
path from the miracle of divine love out into the earthly world, gives force and
dignity to that which it experienced in that magic circle: "As he loves you, so
shall you love."[76]

The name is of central importance to Rosenzweig's philosophy of
speech-thinking. He was delighted with Margarete Susman's review
which first appeared in *Der Jude: Eine Monatsschrift* and later, in English
translation, in *The Jew: Essays from Martin Buber's Journal,* Der Jude,
1916–1928, selected, edited, and introduced by Arthur A. Cohen.
What delighted Rosenzweig particularly was Susman's heading her review with a quotation from the *Star:* "A name is not sound and smoke,
it is word and fire. The name must be named and professed: I believe
in it."[77] In connection with Susman's and Otto Gründler's[78] favourable
reviews of the *Star,* Rosenzweig writes to his cousin Gertrud Oppenheim: "The trumpet of fame is not usually tuned as fast as that, at least
not as far as good things are concerned. And the other consequence
"so it's just not a good thing" I am vain enough not to draw. I wonder
what you said to the fact that Susman really fishes out the core-sen-
tence and made it into a motto, and more than that, in the form I
think in which I had originally written it at that time in the spring of
1917 to you, I still see myself sitting and writing. Just as I also still know
the day when I wrote the sentence in the ✡ and knew at the same
time: this is the most central word of the whole book."[79]

With the proper name, first and last name, the danger of universaliz-
ing or totalizing "the" human being is lessened. As God speaks to each
human being individually, so to is each human being to love: one specific neighbour after another. Thus while each human being is loved
by God, the only possible expression of the reality of this love is the
outward love toward the nearest neighbour. This love of neighbour is

not merely a matter of volition: "It is quite true that its origin lies solely in volition, but man can express himself in the act of love only after he has become a soul awakened by God. It is only in being loved by God that the soul can make of its act of love more than a mere act, can make of it, that is, the fulfilment of a – commandment to love."[80]

If to speak authentically is to express love toward the neighbour, and if there is ultimately only one language, it follows that there must be a root-sentence of that One Language which can recognizably resound in every authentically uttered speech. That root-sentence must be a verbal manifestation of an unalterable fact of the One Truth: clearly, the root-sentence must be "God is good." But "God is good" is a sentence in the indicative mood and is thus a judgment statement, a solitary factual assertion. In order that it might be expressed in accord by two people, or by a community, the root-sentence of the one factual truth must have a future-oriented trajection, and say: "for God is good."

This anticipates and begins to infringe upon the material of the next chapter, so maybe the most profitable thing to do is once more to read the three sentences, offer a brief summary of the analysis, and go on to that next chapter. "Translating is after all the actual goal of the mind; only when something is translated has it become really *audible*, no longer to be disposed of. Not until the Septuagint did revelation become entirely at home in the world, and as long as Homer did not yet speak in Latin he was not yet a fact. In a corresponding way, also translating from person to person."

The goal of the mind, translating, leads to the achievement of the ultimate, revealed purpose of creation: redemption, that is to say, peace and harmony among all, God, human, and world. Thus to translate is not merely to communicate successfully but also to transform one another toward that peace of wholeness. The attainment of such a goal requires dialogical thinking as distinguished from solitary thinking. One might even call speech-thinking "trilogical" because God becomes a partner in conversations between two people. A person who translates hears and verifies the original speaker's words. Put differently, one's own words are verified only when truly received by another. Translating averts solitary self-delusion that can occur in thought as an activity that wants to be autonomous.

Cognition and knowledge that are arrived at through translating are not ends in themselves. Rather, they are means to service in the world, to specific people, and to God. The mind, when translating, mediates understanding among human beings through time, whether that timespan is within one lifetime or crosses two or more generations. More than cognition, an accord is reached through translating. This accord is like redemption in that it acquires a permanence, but the translation's permanence remains in time. The peace of redemption is at the end of time, and ends terrestrial temporality. Redemption began with time, at creation. The period of revelation means the period of translating. Translating brings about the permanences in world-time. These permanences are perceived as partaking of the creative spirit [*Geist*], and they contribute to the irreversible growth of each language spirit towards its destiny of sharing in the one language of humankind.

Speech between God and the human being is not radically different from speech between human and human. The word is at home in both spiritual and worldly realms, and trust in language is therefore absolute. God's word can be spoken differently by different people because one's speech is dependent upon one's experience: these differences among speakers require translation into the fullness of the one language.

"There is Only One Language"

PHILOSOPHICAL CONCEPTUALIZING OF A UNIVERSAL LANGUAGE

"There is only one language," Rosenzweig states in the Afterword (153/3). "Nothing shows so clearly that the world is unredeemed as the diversity of languages," he writes in the *Star*.[1] How can it be decided what Rosenzweig means by an essential oneness of language? Nowhere in his writings does he systematically unfold what appear ultimately to be categorical statements or decrees concerning oneness among languages. "Proofs" at present are, of course, impossible, but verification in history and in life are indeed possible, according to Rosenzweig, and even more: history and life provide the locus where it is imperative to test the verifiability of truths. Bold attempts need to be made at unravelling Rosenzweig's notions of the oneness of language. Without fully incorporating or understanding this aspect of speech-thinking, any description of the method would be both incomplete and significantly wrong.

Two divergent paths cut roughly through the density of Rosenzweig's briefly stated, twofold claim that there is only one language and that such a notion is inseparably connected with the concept of redemption. A recent scholarly and entertaining book on translation theories of the Western tradition, *The Translator's Turn*, by Douglas Robinson,[2] offers one pathway of entry. The other path trickles in a thin stream from some philosophical rivers which influenced Rosenzweig. The most notably influential figure in this stream for Rosenzweig is Feuerbach. These paths, though originating divergently, do open to a common clearing where further illumination may be possible. From there a detailed picture might then be painted. The fine, glimmering brushstrokes which Rosenzweig himself paints regarding language are overshadowed by his own broader, recurring strokes, that perhaps at first do not seem to be related to the glimmering ones. This glimmer needs to sparkle in its own right, as well as be seen as integral to the whole picture. That is to say, once the glimmer is released, it catches the light in the clearing, and displays those details crucial for the understanding of Rosenzweig's larger canvas.

The following two sections will not be direct explications. Nor are they defenses of Rosenzweig's method, though I do defend it later. Nor are they even intended to stand as subsequent supports for Rosenzweig's view; I shall argue from other angles than these. The next two sections are placed here really simply to clear the way to understanding of the notion of the one language, and to indicate how notions of universal languages are at least as old as the Babel story.

TRANSLATION THEORISTS WHO IMPLY A UNIVERSAL LANGUAGE

In the world's well of words and languages various sources can come to commingle in such a way that the resulting interflow enriches, perpetuates, and enlivens *each* of the sources. In this metaphor, the commingling is based on the likeness between the analogues: wateriness and language content. We will return to this metaphor, but a different metaphor will serve better to begin with: land and language content. The focused discussion after this section and the next one will show that the basis of the one language entails a tension between potential, future likeness and presently actualized likeness among languages. Here the metaphor of land, with arability and space and depth available on land, serves better than waterways. For the speech-thinking method, the belief that any language has its own resources for being stretched and for accommodating alien utterances is the key to translating, for only with this belief can anyone reveal and display each language's kernel potentialities. The visible, tonal, audible differences evident in content and form between any target language's present expression and its capacity for expression in the face of the source language are *the* important things to be detected by the listener, by the translator. The listener, the translator, who wishes to speak as the one to whom he listens speaks, foresees, forehears, in his or her own language territory, the possibilities for the cultivatation of verbal expression. He picks up from what is already realized in the source language that which is about to be unearthed from the target language's soil. This is like watering one's own seeds which are known to be deep down in the soil. Detecting, for example, a beautiful chestnut tree in full conical bloom on another's land, and confident that one's own soil can nourish a sim-

ilar botanical creature, a person can, in an utterly nonrapacious manner, glance homeward, and slowly, gently, carefully till his own soil until
he succeeds in growing a similar tree. Its sameness may be surrounded
by chill, rocky, dry mountains, however, and not by the cool lakes of
the warm, humid territory where the tree was first seen. The newly
grown tree may be clothed with an altered bark and leaf formation in
the new climate, and its blossoms may not appear to be the same to
certain eyes that view the two trees in the two lands. But the translator
knows that he has not sullied, touched, helped, hindered, the original
land of the tree. He knows only that he has altered his own landscape,
and is grateful for the new aspect. Just so, Thomas Mann's *Der Zauber-
berg*, in the language of the original, does not look like or sound like
Thomas Mann's *The Magic Mountain* translated by H.T. Lowe-Porter.
The arability of one's own land fits, in part, with Rosenzweig's notion
of the one language.

No other translation theorist quite makes the claims that Rosenzweig makes. According to Robinson in *The Translator's Turn*, and as is
commonly held, mainstream and dominant ideology of translation in
the West stems from the great ideologues: Plato, Paul, and Augustine.
Robinson contends that the three resultant principles of translation
theory have consistently been dualism, instrumentalism, and perfec-
tionism.[3]

With regard to language, indeed with regard to his entire philosophy, Rosenzweig emphasizes a non-dualistic view: his is an "and-philos-
ophy," not fully like, but neither unlike the notion of *coincidentia
oppositorum*. He insists on a noninstrumentalist definition of language: language is not a tool; each language has its own spirit. He insists, too, on a world created which is not-yet-perfect but which will-
have-been-perfect at the end of time. "Creature," after all, in German
[*Kreatur*] as in English, is derived from the future perfect root of the
Latin verb "creare."

Several important translation theorists do point to the notion of
there being essentially only one language with regard to transformative perfecting of the world.[4] None, however, trace the notion to the
lengths that Rosenzweig does. Robinson, from the point of view of an
experienced translator, writes:

Purpose ... at the broadest level of generalization, is what I call throughout
this book therapeutic or transformative, personal and political change; agency
is translation and/or translation theory as equipment for living. We would live
better and make the world a better place to live: purpose. And I see no reason
not to put every act, every translation and every translation theory, every class
taught, every book written or read, to work toward the attainment of those

goals: agency. It is sentimental to talk this way, I know; academics are supposed to be disinterested, which in practice (since we can never conform to the ro-bot-ideal of perfect value-free neutrality) means either uninterested or cynical. I am neither. I believe in this, and I will do it no matter what you think. If I do it well enough, I might get you to believe in it too.[5]

Many theorists, Robinson notes in relation to the notion of one lan-guage at the base of the multiplicity of languages, make a claim for a backward glance to a "golden age" of perfect language. With this claim, the golden age mentality urges that we must retrieve the once pure form. Judaism and Christianity, too, at times engage in a theolog-ically dressed yearning backward toward a "Garden of Eden" sense of purity. More common in Jewish and Christian theological categories is a teleologically oriented praying for the future, an expectation of a promised new paradise. This yearning backward toward to a perfec-tion, whether deemed possible or impossible to retrieve, only partially shares in this golden age view prevalent among the ancient Greeks and Romans, who viewed the world as endless, sometimes in cycles or ages.

Rosenzweig's view of the one language has much more to do with transformation toward an end than with the retrieval or re-formation of something past. However, we have also seen that to Rosenzweig, the one language endures, is carried forward through the generations. We have seen that according to Rosenzweig, the Bible can be read in two ways: by listening to the beats of one's heart or by hearing/reading the Bible. The biblical language, the Bible, is already the one language. Its translation, from heard heartbeats, or from understanding the bibli-cal word, is required in the world's languages. The one language is not restricted to the Bible, for the heart has its own full part in it.

Christian and Jewish thought, as is well known, in late Hellenism and again in the Middle Ages repeatedly analyzed, and often lamented the loss of a once-perfect past. This way of thinking arose each time from an impassioned study of the largely passion-repressing Greek philosophical thought.

Bible translating, as Robinson points out, has been the exemplum for all Western translation theory. Thus it is ironic, according to Robin-son, that the translation theorists who point to a universal language have overlaid and overridden that future-oriented biblical view by the backward glance of the golden age interpretation. Robinson does not note that teleological discussion with reference to the world to come appears explicitly *only* in the Christianly canonized Bible and not in the Hebrew Bible. In Jewish thought the first talk, and understanding, of the world to come begins with the Sages.

These universal language theorists who are geared toward retrieval pick up the golden age attitude from the story of the Tower of Babel as well as from the Greeks. With this past world in mind, they look backward to a day of communication through speech which will not be barred by multiple languages incomprehensible one to the other. This view is that such harmony is possible again. Thus the notion of a common language among all humankind is presumed also to be connected with harmonious relations. What these theorists ignore is that the *content* of the heavenward-tower builders' speech was loathesome to God. When all spoke one language, what the Greeks call hybris took place collectively among all the peoples of the earth. There is nothing to suggest that "hybris" was *caused* by the universal language, but no amount or type of logic could conclude, based on the Babel story, that a linguistically same universal language helps to bring about a peace that is blessed by God. The common aim of the Babel Tower builders desecrated divine speech by making it serve only human ambition. In this sense, that is to say, in the sense of the human desire to be independent of God by attempting to fit his infinite power and knowledge into the finite human capacity for power and knowledge, the Babel story parallels the Garden story.

Rosenzweig makes no mention of the Tower of Babel in his discussion of the one language.

The Translator's Turn not only embodies an exceedingly interesting history of translation theory, but Robinson wrote it explicitly in a dialogic mode, with the Third Partner, God. It reads much as would a book in the speech-thinking method, especially as Robinson infuses it, overtly but not annoyingly evangelically – that is, honestly – with his own religious beliefs. Like Rosenzweig in "Das neue Denken," Robinson, who is Lutheran, openly talks about the religious influence and his tradition's vocabulary in his mode of expression.

Robinson proposes his own translation theory: that speaking human beings actually *feel* language, in a concrete "gut" sense, in their bodies. Language, he contends, is something we carry with us, something which grows and transforms individuals, communities, and nations. He speaks of wanting "to explore some of the ways translators can *act* ... and more importantly, to create themselves as (more) fully alive human beings."[6] He connects his somatic theory of language and translation with a consideration of Bakhtin's theory for translation studies. Robinson suggests that an implication

Might be that in the translator's body, somatically charged words of two or more languages are always multiply entangled. The boundaries between languages that Buber imagined as impregnable barriers to successful translation are likewise anxious fictions maintained socially and politically – not real walls. After fourteen years of living in Finland, eighteen years of speaking Finnish, my Finnish is so much a part of my somatic/linguistic understanding of myself and my world that it often invades my English speech, in the form of literal translations of words and phrases, actual Finnish words, and language switches ... between English and Finnish. Somatically, inside my body, English and Finnish are not really separated from each other; there is no boundary, no territorial border between them, no sign saying "No trespassing." They conflow freely. In different moods, or different speech contexts, I have varying access to English and Finnish words; sometimes I feel that I cannot say a thing in English and have to use Finnish; other times I feel that my Finnish would be useless for what I have to say ... George Steiner describes a similar merging of languages in his own "mind" (I would say body) ... but unlike Steiner, who was raised trilingual, I first heard Finnish when I was sixteen. Sheer dialogical exposure to Finnish, not some mystical process of bilingual language acquisition, did this to me, swirled Finnish and English around inside my body in an undividuated mass.[7]

Robinson writes of the translator in the face of the wall-lessness between languages, and continuing to use his water image, calls the translator one who "opens up the floodgates, which were only momentarily closed (by an act of univocalizing will) anyway."[8] This idea of there being no necessary boundaries between languages suggests what Rosenzweig says: languages are intended to meet without encroaching upon each other in any aggressive fashion. An interesting passage implicitly considers possibilities of translation between academic disciplines in a different way from the now popular and promoted and praised "interdisciplinary approaches." The Robinson passage is interesting in connection with Rosenzweig, who wrote to his mother that it was a pity he had hadn't read Max Weber's *Judentum* when he had intended to, during the War and at the time of writing the *Star*. Weber, Rosenzweig wrote, was saying the same thing historically that he himself was saying philosophically, even though Weber wouldn't see it that way.[9] Robinson, for his part, observes, in a metaphoric turn to water droplets of clouds:

The Finnish brain scientist Matti Bergstroem suggests another way of imagining this process: in his model, words (syntactic structures, etc.) are generated by the cerebral cortex but are carried out into the world by what he calls "clouds of possibility," chaotic masses of interpretive multiplicity generated by the brainstem. Without these clouds of possibility, language would be univocal, homophonous, monoglot – pre-Babelian, in fact, unscattered, in the stable logical unity fantasized by cortically idealizing linguists. The clouds, which

Bakhtin would identify as the stuff of heteroglossia, allow not only for multiplicity of interpretation and linguistic variation in time and space but also for the richness of emotional association and connotation that characterizes our response to (use of) language. Without the clouds of possibility, language would be like the electronic transfer of data: neutral, logical, mechanical.[10]

Robinson glosses over Rosenzweig, mentioning him in passing, and even then as subjugated to Buber. Because Robinson's book is so utterly thorough, this suggests that Rosenzweig's theories (and practice) of translation really are little known by some who might enjoy a closer acquaintanceship. We all know that to know something or someone only a little often is to know even, or especially, that little bit in a wrong way. Rosenzweig is misrepresented through some misunderstandings of his and Buber's theory when Robinson states: "I would much rather read a really strange, alien translation of the Bible like the Buber-Rosenzweig ... Granted, you would not go into New Guinea and translate like that; this is a mode of translation almost exclusively for the jaded and sated intelligentsia, no matter what translators like Buber and Rosenzweig say."[11]

In this passage, Robinson suggests that Rosenzweig (and Buber) are obviating the path to a wider understanding among humans of God's word. Instead, they are only serving to specialize and to particularize language. Their intent, he states, consciously contrary to their own claim, is to be heard and understood by a few élite. At the same time, Robinson also, by finding fault with Buber and Rosenzweig precisely for this charge of particularity or exclusivity, argues implicitly – in a very different way from Buber and Rosenzweig – for a universally understood language through which no one language or person is excluded. Robinson is suggesting an a priori route to understanding the Bible by means of translation. Was or is no one left out in any great original piece of writing? If everyone learned the linguistic languages of the Bible, would everyone be included in the understanding? Several points with regard to Rosenzweig's theory need clarification right here.

Robinson has not taken seriously enough the intention of the Buber-Rosenzweig translation. For one of their intentions is to bring the written word to oral expression. Thus the Buber-Rosenzweig translation of the biblical texts, in the unfamiliarity of their German language version, can be a jarring, unpleasant novelty to any German reader who has until now been accustomed to the Luther translation. I would argue that the Buber-Rosenzweig translation is actually easier to read and to understand than the Luther version.[12] Ease is not the prime issue, but rather accuracy in tone and contour as well as in technicalities. Luther's may be the best *Christian* translation of the Bible into German; the Buber-Rosenzweig work may be the best Jewish-oriented German translation. I suggest that familiarity more than readership is at issue here for Robinson, and includes an underestimation of human understanding and an overestimation of the so-called élite.

The initial stimulus for the Buber-Rosenzweig translation at any rate was that the two translators had agreed on the following: German-Jewish readers of the Bible who knew no Hebrew and were therefore restricted to the Luther Bible were at the same time restricted to a Christian(ized) version of Hebrew Scriptures. Luther, too, unnoted by Robinson, originally wrote not only for one specific group but against another specific group. Buber and Rosenzweig were not writing their translation against Christianity or against anyone. They believed that they were filling a deficiency in the German language. The work was done for a specific group; Baber and Rosenzweig did not know that most of that group would be murdered. That Buber completed the task not only after Rosenzweig's death but *after* the Holocaust is an important factor, which I shall not, however, consider here. Although in synagogues the readings at the time were always done in Hebrew, there were some Jews in the many assimilated communities who could read Hebrew phonetically without understanding the meaning of the words. Rosenzweig and Buber did not want services or prayers to be said in any language but in the biblical, medieval, and other "Hebrews." They were seeking to serve as vehicles for the understanding of services and prayers among fellow German-Jews. And that is all.

To conclude these remarks sparked by a reading of Robinson, two points: (1) Clearly the notion of a universal language is a common one among those who think about language and more especially when they are thinking about translation; (2) Rosenzweig's position on language and translation, certainly for those beyond the small world of immediate Rosenzweig scholars, has barely been touched by any theorist in these recent decades of a proliferation of work on language theories. If, however, Rosenzweig's stance can be conceptually, intellectually imaginable, the question then becomes: is that stance realistic, realizable, practical? The following section will try to answer this two-sided question using the imagery of both water and land.

PHILOSOPHICAL FLUX AND FLUCTUATION

What then is the meaning of this notion that all languages are virtually one? Do not the tinkling of those mystical bells that Rosenzweig hears as a distortive din seem to ring? Is this a turn into some phantastic philosophical flight? Does Hegel's reasoned, universal All now chime with appealing and solid tones of finality, drowning out that future, distantly perceived, symphonic harmony of all speakers in unison? Before straying too far from Rosenzweig's own claims, let us glance at some of those streams of thought which flowed, and still flow, in firm lands leery of the Hegelian trend. Sound philosophical territory from which to build will be on those grounds which denote where and how Rosenzweig stands in regard to the categories of the particular and the universal.

Rosenzweig's approach to the particular and the universal is opposite to that of the Kantian school. To the Kantians, experience provides the particular content which the general form of knowledge articulates into a unity of experience. To Rosenzweig, the particular is the residence of all dynamism and activity. The universal functions as absorber of the particular. Thus the universal's sole function is to draw the particular toward itself wherein the particular will rest.[13]

Since Rosenzweig's philosophy moves from the particular to the universal in specific stages of growth, the universal language cannot yet be, for particular births and deaths are still taking place and not all individual speech has been spoken. In the growing stages an individual's language as a particular speaks into and is absorbed into the ultimate one and universal language.

The notion of these stages of growth is in opposition to Aristotle – he attributes to matter the striving for form and general lawfulness, whereas Rosenzweig's view of the world as a living growth understands the world as becoming: "Everything that becomes, bursts into existence and seeks therein its place ... All of this applies equally to man insofar as he is part of the world, but at a certain time in his life, man's essence is aroused within him, which places him beyond the world. Until then, he is part of the world, and afterwards he is part of it by virtue of his natural existence, which includes both his body and his soul. Human forms of association ... are creatures within the world, and are essentially of the same type as all other creatures within the world."[14]

The essence awakened in a human which places him beyond the world was discussed in the previous chapter: God's love and the ensuing response to divine love in love of neighbour. Human associations, which include associations arising in love of neighbour, are creatures, just as are the individual humans within any association.

Language too, as Julius Guttmann notes, is creature, and, in speaking, language is as individual as the one speaking. The identity of person and speech has already been addressed. Since associations consist of persons, individual languages along with the humans come to be unified in associations. An association, be it in the form of a state or of only two people, in order to communicate, shares in a common language. Since speech, although identified with person, is spoken in a direction moving outward from the person (per-sona), it at the same time remains separate. Speech is a separate creature from the person. A person's speech may be claimed to be his very own; but once spoken it certainly ceases to be that person's only. It belongs to the one(s) spoken to as well. A characteristic of speech is that once spoken, while it still may be identified with the speaker, it no longer belongs to the speaker. He or she may lay claim to the words, may stand behind them, or later reject them with new speech. But no one may own words once he has placed them, quite literally, outside himself. Only in the actual present process of speaking/writing can a person's speech appear to be precisely at that moment his own – or more accurately, an identification with himself. Speech, once listened and responded to, becomes a shared property, a newly formed creature. And indeed, even before speaking, one draws upon speech that is outside of oneself: one is taking a shareholding in which one comes to have a say in the to-date oneness of language. This is what Rosenzweig means when he writes that speech is common to all, and is all around us, and can be easily trusted.[15]

Speech functions as the particular input, and language itself, any language, functions as forming the eventual full oneness. Language, because still growing, as is evidenced by new speech that changes personal or national lives, verifies Rosenzweig's scheme of reality: the All, the universal is not yet. The world's essence, which according to Rosenzweig's enquiry is Logos, offers up that knowledge which augmentatively resides in the world for the purposes of ongoing disclosure and tapping.

Before speaking, one needs to draw from the public well of language. A person responds to the portion drunk in varying manners and degrees, whether refreshed, unquenched, embittered, angered, inspired to add, to alter, to agree, to dispute. Accordingly, the speaker then forms his own utterance in response to the public accumulation of particular speech that has been spoken before. Each particularity of speech brings about alterations and fresh drops into the common well. Whenever new particular speech is uttered and heard, the one who hears will thereupon speak in response to this ever-nourished spring.[16]

Strong agreement between speakers will prompt the one who has drunk to speak anew and forcibly in a language of agreement. Language of agreement is not repetitive. The one who speaks in agreement speaks in either other words, or in newly expressed ones that will also mean the same thing, and with the same burning passion of the very first utterance. The word "Amen," for example, denotes full affirmation and agreement. Amen is not a passive word that merely permits or wants continuity in a situation so that what is already believed or stated remains unchanged and untouched. It rather spurs varied responsive action. In language, strong affirmation tends to *seek* ways in which to ensure continuity of another person's speech. And this means to speak again and again that person's speech, be it divine or human, in different words in different times and situations, precisely in order to say the same things. Even – or especially – among voices which strongly agree and strive together toward fresh expression of a saying said before, there can be heard an actual growth toward the one language of humankind. This can occur in liturgical speech.

What of strong disagreement? As Guttmann points out, for Rosenzweig the three elements of reality, God, world, and human, each has two causes in it configuration: a static, passive one (a Yea), and a dynamic, spontaneous one (a Nay). The Yea corresponds to the universal, and the Nay to the particular. For the human element of reality, the self is the universal. Because each self is defiant in its "I am here, I and none other," because each self universally declares this same claim for itself, this very peculiarity constitutes the universal aspect of the human. In the human's universal attribute, then, there inherently exists a constant statement, in silence or aloud, which asserts a boundary that delineates difference among individual selves. Strong agreement – the Amen – builds a permanent residence in the growing universality of the *world*. In strong disagreement, the notion of the accumulative contours, ripples of speech in language become distinct. For example, "from Iona to Jena," mainstream philosophers affirmed reason and a concept of totality with regard to reality. A nay-sayer to the mainstream first needs to understand that mainstream, that is say yes to it, in order to say no. He is saying no *to* something; and in subsequent creative, reactive speech the nay-sayer adds something to what is already there in language. He forces that which is there either to take on new meaning or to move now in a different direction. Among those of others, Rosenzweig's own No to German Idealism is meant to be heard as a no of admiration at the Hegelian feat of culminating mainstream philosophy: he is saying that there is no point to taking Hegel and Hegelianism any further. To say more along Hegelian lines would be mere repetition and stagnating staticity, not a vibrant affirmation. Affirmation of something wants to move further, beyond that which has been affirmed – until nothing at all is left to affirm. This is what Rosenzweig means when he claims that as long as many languages exist redemption is not-yet.

The aim of Rosenzweig's nay-saying to Idealism is not at all to bring about the abolition of philosophy. Rather, Idealism, redirecting into a new orientation – that is, now stretched along the creation-revelation-redemption trestle – can reaffirm philosophy's goal and purpose: to discover and uncover, to depict still inclusively all spheres of reality in a cohesive whole. Rosenzweig's speech *into* philosophy can therefore be labelled as an addition to the cumulative character of philosophical language, especially by virtue of his No. Most important, among benevolent communities a strong disagreement always takes place with a view to ultimate agreement, as opposed to coercion for any sort of submission or subjugation of one to the other. Rosenzweig saw that such an alteration of the face and function of philosophy was possible through the speech-thinking method. He addressed himself to contemporary philosophers who were dissatisfied with Idealism as well as to future philosophers; simultaneously, he gratifully glances backward to the philosophical feats achieved from Aristotle to Hegel.

From the point of view of the *world*, the human being is a particular, only one particular within a multiplicity of bursting phenomena. In the configuration of the world, the finite side is attracted by the infinite side: the philosopher by the whole, the thing by the concept. The community lies on the Yea side of the world's configuration, and the becoming world configures from man to community. The activity of content leads to the passivity of form in the world. The human alone is a particular only.

In the new thinking, the unity of existence, with which philosophy began, is no longer the beginning point of thought. It is its end. Unity is not the presupposition. Yet it is presupposed for a final future. The potent aspect of the human is kindled when the human being meets a particular individual in his or her particular expression of speech. This potency comes to real power when a human being translates disparateness into association, by a Yea or Nay. Once empowered, that Yea or Nay at that moment comes to reside in the passive, perfecting, universal of the world's configuration. Since the dynamic energy enters and resides at rest in the world, the world is necessarily growing. The world's configuration, unlike God's and the human's, is still to come to be.

The end toward which the world is striving depends upon its attaining fullness of the language spirit of oneness. While God has in the first instance of the world – in creation – predetermined its last instance, the human being's task is – concurrently with and congruous to God's eternal promise and plan – in volition and by his own acts, to create this final end of unity and fullness.

The multiplicity of languages in the world, in Rosenzweig's philosophical/theological/life view, thus necessarily moves toward a unity.

THE RIVER WIDENS: FEUERBACH

In addition to providing explication, this chapter intends to conform as much as possible with the method of the new thinking. With this sketching of human, God, and world, the opposing logics of the old and the new thinking have also been briefly stated. As is the case in the realm of logic, both the old and the new thinking can be argued for or against. Rather than argue one way or the other, I prefer to turn to another of Rosenzweig's conversants, also a cross-current to mainstream philosophy: Feuerbach. Feuerbach, that fiery brook, appealed immensely to Rosenzweig. In "Das neue Denken" he designates Feuerbach as the discoverer of speech-thinking *in philosophy.* Sensitive poets and healthy-minded people with common sense always thought this way, Rosenzweig asserts. Feuerbach's great service to philosophy was to give speech thinking its *rites d'entrée.* Excerpting several of Feuerbach's insights, formulated as principles for future philosophy, will show how Rosenzweig built upon the former's speech and responded with the full-fledged philosophic system of the *Star.*

Rosenzweig, the one-time Hegelian, saw in philosophy a dominant thread that was woven into and embroidered upon in every school from Greece to Germany: an attempt to derive the many from the one. Hegel tied all the loose ends into a firm systematic knot that ironically turned out also to be philosophy's self-choking noose. Feuerbach considered Hegel's system as knowing "only *subordination* and *succession*; co-ordination and co-existence are unknown to it."[17] Relational co-existence, the core of speech thinking, requires both space and time. While Idealism had reduced both space and time to a static all, Feuerbach insists upon "the tolerance of space," because space allows everything co-existence, each thing occupying its rightful place in space, uninfringed upon by other things. The natural relation of things in space is co-existence and not subordination. Feuerbach writes of time: "To be sure, the last stage of development is always the totality that includes in itself the other stages, but since it itself is a definite temporal existence and hence bears the character of particularity, it cannot incorporate into itself other existences without sucking out the very marrow of their independent life and without robbing them of the meaning which they can only have in complete freedom."[18] Further: "Whatever enters into time and space must also subordinate itself to the laws of time and space ... Whatever becomes real, becomes so only as something determined. The incarnation of the species with all its plenitude into one individuality would be an absolute miracle, a violent suspension of all the laws and principles of reality; it would indeed be the end of the world."[19]

While Hegel starts with abstract notions of being, Feuerbach's starting point is real being, the human him- or herself. "Feuerbach believed that the degradation of man was a direct consequence of subordinating man, of deriving the purpose of his life, from a 'higher' order of transcendent reality – the divine being of theology and the Absolute of the Hegelian philosophy."[20]

Rosenzweig's views on solitary thought were presented in chapter 2. Feuerbach's precursive distrust of solitary thought in its claiming to be able to arrive at real truths is underlined in several of his principles, three of which are notable: an imperative; a description of the real character of thought as interactive with and verified only by others' thoughts; and an insight that the essence of the human as moral and thinking being functions only in community. Rosenzweig carried out the imperative; he expanded the descriptive into the relational activities and impacts between human and human, human and world, and human and God; and he clarified the essence of man to be, not an identity of reason and being, but Ethos. First, Feuerbach's imperative: "Think as one who exists, as one who is in the world and is part of the world, not as one in the vacuum of abstraction, not as a solitary monad, not as an absolute monarch, not as an unconcerned, extra-worldly God; only then can you be sure that being and thought are united in all your thinking."[21]

Second, on the inter-dependence of everyone's thinking upon others' thinking, Feuerbach writes: "You think only because your thoughts themselves can be thought, and they are true only if they pass the test of objectivity; that is, when someone else, to whom they are given as objects, acknowledges them as such. You see because you are yourself a feelable being. Only to an open mind does the world stand open, and the openings of the mind are only the senses."[22]

Third, Feuerbach anticipates what was to become one of Rosenzweig's most special contributions, the powers of relationships in life over the vaporously dubious powers of that spectre, *Das All.* The role of the human in the world is not a duality between the one and the many, but a mutuality of particularity and relationality. Relationality takes into account, indeed depends upon the reality of the laws of space. "The single man in isolation possesses in himself the essence of man neither as a moral, nor as a thinking being. The essence of man is contained only in the community, in the unity of man with man – a unity, however, which rests on the reality of the distinction between I and You."[23]

Rosenzweig's personally lived verification of the value of speech-thinking flowed through the documented storms and the calms of his interchanges, primarily with Rosenstock-Huessy, and certainly with other people who touched his life. But Feuerbach grounded the corrective philosophical bedrock in the ever-flowing river of philosophy, dammed Idealism, and set Rosenzweig free to build his philosophical houseboat.

ROSENZWEIG'S VIEW OF THE LIGHT OF GOD IN LANGUAGE

One language experiences another language in such a way that the foreign language alters the native one. The relational potency of experience and translation is operative here. This power journeys along the tortuous and tributaried river that empties into the universal language of humankind. The actualization of the universal language, that is accord among all humans, will mark the end of the creature language. Language, with the world, becomes wholly enspirited, perfected. The river-ocean image is helpful: rivers remain distinct one from the other, are replenished and nourished and grow or diminish in their own right. Yet, at the same time, rivers are fed by and feed into other rivers, each of which is itself distinct. All rivers flow into a larger, permanent body. A body of water which loses for some reason the nourishment of its sources, its springs, very slowly, imperceptibly at first, dries up. Its death begins at the moment it is no longer met with its sources. The large (universal) is dependent on the small (particular). For living large bodies of water, in this image an ocean, both ocean and river continue to live and grow separately. Some rivers will interflow before entering the ocean, others will not. The nonvariant, the eternal, the permanent, is the ocean; the variants are the rivers. Languages, like rivers, can die; but each leaves behind its permanency in another language, as Old High and Middle High German have done in Modern German. Latin and Greek live more than linguistically in English. No river on its own can be The River; no language on its own can be The Language. The universal, the eternal, the permanence, all reside outside the particulars, but is related to each. Neither all of the individual, particular rivers, nor each particular language necessarily need interconnect or interact in order to reach or, more accurately, on the way to that Whole. Adding the parts together cannot render the whole. The particulars relate, one to the other, quite simply – *when* they are relating. The character of relating very much relies upon being bound to time and timing.

While human activity and creativity are involved in reaching of the one language, the content of the accord is not a humanly decided one. It is not arrived at by means of reason alone; nor does a study of the designs or desires of the human will alone determine the content of the one language. It is an accord decided upon eternally by God. The accord does not pertain to a demonstration of only humanly orchestrated goodness of intra-human professions of love. Such love is selfishly possible between selves that are not yet souls. Rather, the harmony, the wholeness, the peace among humans, pertains ultimately to what Rosenzweig designates as the soul beloved of God: "'God said, Let there be light,' – and what is the light of God? It is the soul of man."[24]

To return to the analogy, if the ocean is the universal language, and the rivers the languages, the languages are moving to something that is already there. The rivers do not determine what the ocean is: they flow into it. And the rivers do not determine that they flow into the ocean. The laws of the world determine not only that they shall flow into the ocean. The laws forbid them to flow merely among themselves. The similarity of wateriness in these analogues of river and ocean evokes that of relationship.

This sort of river-ocean analogy fails with regard to light; and, since few human beings have had the experience of being deep under water and of seeing how light refracts through water of varying clarities and depths, maybe the better path to take is one which turns now directly to a consideration of light itself, which is less tangible, but is capable of contact by its own activity.

The Light of God is refracted through individually, divinely beloved souls. This light, from the human point of view, and from that of the world as well, is intended to become one light. From the point of view of God as eternal God, the lights are indeed already one light, the eternal future light. From the point of view of God who acts in time, his light is seen by him, too, as refracted in individual souls. In time, God can even limit his own eternality: he can bring about events for and with the human, events which reside in the realm of the particular: he can, according to Rosenzweig, see, smell, draw near, draw far away, while at the same time always only giving one message at a time. An amusing account to Buber of what happened after one of Rosenzweig's lectures at the Freies Jüdisches Lehrhaus goes as follows: "By the way, someone asked me after the lecture if I really believed that God, for example, could smell. 'Yes, of course – when I stink." Dia ton anthropon! [for the sake of the human!]."[25]

The oneness of the Light of God is simultaneously for the human's and God's good. God created the "good" world with future perfection in the world's germcell of Logos. Thus, from God's *then* monologic point of view, revelation and redemption are already also enfolded. The "very good" human, through divine revelatory love, experiences that which is "better" than only createdness and creatureliness. This "better" is precisely what requires translation: God's action and God's love are demonstrated in speech, lived and verified in human life both in the same generation and from generation to generation. Only speech uttered from a divinely enlightened soul can be authentic speech, and speech that speaks truths. Inter-human speech that is perceived as happening *only* between human beings and without the third "silent partner" or with no listening to and translating God's speech – such speech, such language, takes no real part in the germcell-oneness of that creature, language. Inter-human speech, when perceived as autonomous, ignores entirely one of the elements of reality: God. It also ignores the world *as* perfecting its created Logos, *as* multiplicities of life-forms other than the human being. Inter-human speech can purport to be objective: observing "facts," not imparting them as they wish to disclose themselves. Speech without God attends only the human being. As noted, speech confined between God and a human being denies the world: such speech affirms fellow-selves, but denies fellow-souls.

GOD SPEAKS AND REVEALS IN THE SAME ACT

God speaks to the human, and the human speaks both to God and to the world of humans and other creatures. Where, or how, is God's speech to be heard? Again, according to Rosenzweig, God speaks in two places: the Bible and the heart. We have seen how, to a Rabbi in Göttingen, Rosenzweig explained that these channels and vehicles of God's self-revelation say the same thing. God *also* speaks to the heart that which he speaks in the Bible. This speaking to the heart is the *only* reason that the Bible is "revelation."[26] This is the chronological order of the birth of authentic speech: from God to human, from human to God, from human to human. Language began first with God, and in the following chapters there will be some discussion of who, God or human, takes the first step in human-divine conversations, and what sorts of demands and expectations occur in the actual conversations. For now, we can say that for God language began at creation and begins in his revelation already at creation. Those who speak without acknowledging God as an element of reality are partaking of the creature, language, in a way that is not fully relational. Word is both human and divine.

The human being, then, does not create his or her own speech, though he may be one who creatively pours into or draws from the available well of language. Speech was created for the human in an elastic, extensive way so that it might be possible to be creative in speech. A person may utter and formulate and express what he himself has not before expressed. Such expression will appear creatively new if no one else in his generation is saying what he is saying. If he is speaking fittingly, insightfully, for his own generation those things which others have said in former generations in ways fitting or insightful for their own, he is creatively reaffirming, through translation, the life of a particular river which now flows in his own course of life, and the course of life of his times.

To listen so carefully as to recognize sameness and difference between utterance entails listening both to God in our hearts and to other creature speakers. The recognition of either sameness of speech or difference of speech is detected primarily by listening to the tones and the contours of God's voice's speech, and not primarily by determining linguistic similarities and dissimilarities. The mind's *and* the heart's effort and goal are to translate old – the oldest – truths into ever new language until the oneness of tone and contour reaches across the whole world.

An utterance will appear to be that of a genius if what a person says elucidates a current historical or social or some other important event or condition. It is likewise the case when someone presents or creates a revolutionary turning point in history. Change and elucidation are *always* manifested through speech. A painting, after all, may be worth a thousand words, but these words, at some time, in the audience's or viewers' speech-world, must be spoken words if the artwork is to live. A visual work of art or a nonvocal or vocal musical work of art provide, for example, a new way to say what has once been spoken, or a way to say something that has not yet, in a particular time and relating to a particular event, been spoken *to* or *for* a particular person or group. The audience, perhaps unknown to the artist, perhaps centuries after the artist's lifetime, regardless decides on this "to" and "for" – in words or speech or in a "school" of derivative artists. The freezing of time in an artwork, from the audience's or viewer's standpoint in historical and personal time, is gradually or suddenly melted by the ear or eye into the time-requiring story the art tells, the statement it makes, the judgment it concludes.

Only the separateness in space and time of the three elements of reality permits this creative aspect of speech to grow. Only through separateness are relational events possible. Each event *is* new under the sun from the human point of view. History does not reveal patterns, but rather a time- and light-line from a real beginning, through a real middle, to a real end of time and light in the world. The liturgical year reveals, as does the weekly round from Shabbat to Shabbat, a repetitive cycle, but only repeatedly to remind the human being of this real beginning and middle and end.

God and the world and man! The And was the first word of experience; thus it must also return in the ultimacy of truth. Still in the truth itself, in the ultimate truth, which can be only One, an And must be planted; this truth, differently than the truth of the philosophers, which is permitted to know only itself, must be truth for someone. If it should be nevertheless the one truth, so it can be truth only for the One. And thereby it becomes necessary that our truth is manifold, and that "the" truth changes into "our" truth. Truth in this way ceases to be what truth "is," and becomes that which as true – wants to be verified. The concept of the verification of the truth becomes the basic concept of this new theory of knowledge which replaces the old theories of non-contradiction and of objects, and intends in the place of the concept of static objectivity of those theories, a dynamic one.[27]

Truth is preserved by the burning, passionate concreteness of the reality of the fiery word whose flames speak out of the full fire of the Name.[28] It is not that truth validates reality, nor that validates reasoning being. Truth for the world is not law but content, and truth therefore underlies reality and shines through it.[29] Thus truth for the world "is" not, but rather it comes to be: truth, as it is imparted from the manifold to the One Truth comes to be preserved in the world. It is the activity of temporal revelation *en route* to the eternality of redemption. The permanence of truth is created in the world through rendering words lasting, that is, by speaking them to someone who has an ear and a mouth that respond to these words. And the ultimately spoken truth is to be speech of accord, not strife and not divisiveness: "No enmity between humans can be allowed to be more than relative, lest a world totally at war perish."[30]

God, *not* in his past creative act, when he is secluded and alone and purely creative, but in his present self-revealing act, which God perpetuates by ever anew so acting, reveals (or conceals) nothing but himself to (from) the human. He speaks "something" to someone – his presence, his distance, his message. God's speech, after the past fact of creation, is never, *never* again self-monologue. His speech is ever after speaking to the human. It is always asking for response and, in turn, responding to human response. God's speech is never less than dialogue. His own monologue ended with his creative words: "Let there be ..."

Dialogue invariably requires two grammatical cases. It uses the dative, and always simultaneously the accusative. God speaks his self to the human. Whenever God speaks he is revealing himself. This identity of speech and person in God is reflected in the human image.

HUMAN SPEECH: THE CONTENT OF THE ONE LANGUAGE

In order that human speech might reflect in its manifold, refracted rays the One Truth and Light of God, it must transform – that is, translate – those divine words into humanly uttered words that each can hear in his and her heart or can read in the Bible: that is, not that which we as independent selves speak from our hearts *of* flesh, but that which God speaks to our dependent hearts *as* flesh, and that which humans before us have already translated for the events and realities of their times.[31]

If, *in* love for God, love of neighbour is the decorous response to returning God's love, what precisely is it that is primarily to be translated and spoken to the neighbour and among humans? Most simply it is that God has revealed himself and his name. To us. For us. "God is not a concept but the right name; and the whole Bible is nothing but the search for God's right name. On the other hand, man is not found except in his conversation with his brothers."[32] On the impossibility of conceptualizing God, Rosenzweig maintains that only that which is absent can be made into a thing, a concept: "Whatever has a name can be talked about, can be talked to, depending on whether it is absent or present. God is never absent and that is why there is no concept of God (of the false gods definitely, but of the true, none). God is the only one whose name is at the same time his concept; whose concept is at the same time his name."[33]

If God's name cannot fully – or separately from all else but logic – be conceptualized as *N*ame, it nevertheless can be partially understood through *n*ame*s*. In this sense human speech is *not* inadequate when it talks about God. In inter-human speech God must be talked to, addressed as the ever-present third party – or more precisely, as first partner. In the *Star* Rosenzweig designates the enactment of liturgy as the time when God formally and consciously is that third party. Speech in liturgy is in accord, in praising and in thanking God. God is addressed in community. The only possible underlying statement of accord about God is in the form of a future-oriented conclusion which is already now drawn about the world. The statement of accord which gives the reason for the accord, and which is to be spoken by all at the really realized redemption, is this: for God is good.[34] The congregation speaks to God in unison and in absolute agreement in uttering this presently drawn and believed future-oriented conclusion. The Amen stands firmly at the end of communal prayer.

In the case of God the identity of speech and person is readily understandable because we cannot see God but can only trust in his

Word. In this sense and context, J.G. Hamann's words are significant: "Speak that I may see thee!" wrote Hamann, whom Rosenzweig admired and wanted to carry forward, "This wish was fulfilled in the creation, which is a speaking to the creature through the creature." Only in this way can the human speak of God if he or she is to speak authentically and truly, to speak in the way that speech is spoken by the creator: the human does not speak of God, but once having heard God, he cannot help but let God's Light shine through his speech, outward to the world. God speaks to the creature, and to the world through the creature. To use a lesser light image, the lit candle shines with its own flame, as does God's Light. An unlit candle may be lit from this first one. This second one cannot relight the already lit candle, but it can, like the first, give its light to other candles without diminishing or even changing its own. The transformation takes place in each newly lit candle. The life of each candle stands on its own wax stem. The wax stem does not intermingle with any other. While the light holds true for all, and while what holds true for all is shared, each lit candle maintains and retains its own particularity. But each is *for* the other. Rosenzweig describes the understanding of God's name through names in his lecture notes on the science of man. He holds that we say only, "I am" and never "I am not." What, then, he asks, stands on the other side of the "I am" if not "not"? The legitimate opposite is the partner, "*to* whom is said 'the' you, but with the opposite [grammatical] sign of the 'are'." Only because the same things hold true for both the I and the you is speaking to another possible. Rosenzweig writes in these lecture notes: "I am I? No, I am Franz Rosenzweig. 'Your Franz Rosenzweig' ... Your you. The one to whom you say you."[35]

Identity of speech with the speaker can perhaps be best illustrated by an aberration in which the speaker is volitionally disassociated from his self-uttered speech. Truths are suppressed, lies prevail in such a disassociation. Rosenstock-Huessy offers these characteristically forcible words: "The modern mind declares anybody who keeps from writing for money to be a fanatic or "nuts" ... Words have lost their meaning. Names have lost their appeal. The publishers instead of consulting the Gallup poll should ask themselves if books did not depend for their very existence during the last four hundred years on some strange identity of the speaker and the words he spoke, and whether probably the time for books is over as this identity is lost."[36]

Rosenzweig meant this same thing when he advocated that it is not new books that are needed, but a new (Jewish) person.[37] Later A.J. Heschel was also to urge: "What we need more than anything else is not textbooks but text people." Whenever speech and person are not identified, then what is being said cannot be true speech, and the human not a true human being who is created to be and to live in God's image.

Speech is intended to open, to open *to* truths. It opens first always to, and among, two or more speakers. If speech remains between only two, however, it becomes inauthentic. It closes itself off from others, and thus muffles and precludes possibilities for the mind's goal of translating, which was lengthily discussed in chapter 2. Rosenzweig's pejorative remarks about the "mystic" are critical of speech restricted to God and one human being. He makes the claim that, while authentic speech for the human *begins* here, this is truly only inception. Conception and concretization of speech develop with the human neighbour. In a parallel way but importantly on a different track, with his perjorative remarks about the "nature mystic" Rosenzweig means that the communion between human and nature (the world) is not the end of knowledge, not the arrival at God's Truth. This is so because the Logos of the world is still *meta-*, still to become realized, and therefore simply cannot yet be wholly known. Thus the outcome is the same for any speech that results in this sort of attempted permanent closure between two of the elements of reality or between two representatives of the same element, namely the human being. The effect, as well as the result, is an aggressively contumaceous arrogance toward, and a temporary blockage of the growth of the one language.

Closures of any sort always divide something from something else and are in themselves neutral. But an immobile stillness here between two humans, within the natural movement of the world, and in the face of the commandments of God to love him *and* the neighbour, stiffens into an idolatry of idleness. The potentiality around closures occurs at the moment one chooses to move beyond the borders of erstwhile closures. Speech which opens to the one language does itself close around the growing of perfection of the world, *in* the world. The sparks of God's Light and Truth, once and whenever they touch the world, reside in the world, and a new "place" is marked off in time in the world. Each time a new love between two people takes place as an event, that love is reflected at once, both now and beyond time, in eternity. The world will pass away, the love does not.

Closures in temporality and "closures" in eternity are not ultimately the same: eternity seals, through temporality, that which becomes silence and light in the final future. There are no closures, no boundaries, in the that world, the world to come. The physical and spiritual worlds do not merge in temporality: there are the created heavens, there is the created earth. Both are created. This, too, will be looked at more closely in the following chapters. The two realms are bridged but not subsumed the one to the other. In the final future, even the heavens are perfected, and come to their end – and beginning.

Anyone who ignores one of the elements' essences – meta-physicality for God, meta-ethicality for the human, meta-logicaltiy for the world – and does not attempt ultimately to get beyond the meta- for each, that is to fulfil, as far as it is given to the human to do, the true purpose of each element: the "after" the meta-. A division that closes off and seals true speech, speech that relates the three elements according to their respective characters, marks a boundary line between reality and nonreality, that is between truth and nontruth. Thus boundaries are a positive aspect in the temporal world: boundaries between particular human beings, between the three elements, between temporality and eternality, between this world and that world.

The creature language enfolds into itself the truly possible spokenness of the the one language. The human opens his or her speech by hearing in and listening to this world. Human and divine speech take place in time. The closures of love and accord are enfolded in that world to Come, right now, at any temporal moment, and are recorded in the Book of Life.[38] During revelation, speech – divine and human – remains within the rippling contours of the perfecting enfoldments of this world.

GRAMMAR OF DIALOGUE

If there is only one language, it can be only that language which the one who created language decreed speech to be: accusative and dative, that is, speech whose contents are intended for someone who is addressed. The original "content and form" of the one language is God. If the Bible's meaning is God's name, then the Bible is God's name is humanly utterable and expressible speech. Words spoken in interhuman, worldly speech are intended to be for and to the human, as well as for and to God, because he reveals himself in language, ultimately one language only, however expressed and uttered in the multiplicities of possibilities for human languages.

The original content and form must be carried over in the form of speaking-speech from human to human. Rosenzweig maintains that form and content need to be seen as necessarily joined, impossible to disconnect without distorting the meaning. Content and form together serve understanding adequately in translation: "Wherever talk of faith is not struck dumb to prose of a mere 'content,' it has to – it cannot be otherwise – serve all manner of expression, to harmonize all tones, to want to have all supposedly firm, planned out 'contents' translatable for itself, only by grace of the fleeting moment of the expressive orality." And: "The living word, the flown, whose flight leaves behind deep in the ground, the empty form-in-itself and the lame content-in-itself."[39]

Our truths are contained and expressed in our individual languages. Our love of neighbour is the expression of our love for God. Given that God is the founder and foundation of love of neighbour, then at all times our expression is an expression *to* someone *for* someone. In Rosenzweig's letter to Meinecke (chapter 2), he writes of knowledge as service *to* another human being, and if to a scholar, to that scholar qua human being. We speak to someone for our love of God if we are expressing what God spoke and speaks to our hearts. We are speaking not his One Truth in our multiple and still growing languages, but rather our truths that have come to us individually and collectively (at Sinai, or at Golgotha, for example). Each recipient of God's Truth who looks around at the world of other speaking human beings hears, must hear, that this (his or her own and every other's) truth which each human being hears is necessarily manifold. Many folds are enfolded, and many are already unfolded. Indivisible *Truth* is yet divided among us all; *our* truths are sometimes kin, in the same fold, sometimes not. Our many languages in and by themselves are not untrue. But they will not and cannot be the Whole Truth of the All until the relationships of God, human being, and world are completed in the fullness of time, in the fullness of translating our many-folded speech into the smooth, calm waters of the one language.

At the same time, God obviously did not give a bit of his Truth only to this one person and a bit only to the other person. God himself does not split his indivisible Truth. He is after all, One: His speech-person identity cannot speak a multiplicity of truths. But: in an event in time, in an event of a human-divine meeting, God gives to this specific person or people a message – in a command, in comfort, in punishment, in reward, in guidance – that is appropriate and particular to that person or people at *their* particular moment in time and in understanding of the Whole.[40] God's Truth, then, becomes clear to human beings only according to the life experiences of the individual recipients. More accurately, he does not deny his Truth to anyone *for* that one's needs at each moment in life. It is we humans who are split, universally particular. Thus our particularity necessitates that we hear God's speech to us as specific event. God speaks particular speech to the particular human. What we hear is the particularity of the events of God's repeated love-speech forging its way into the universal – the All. The essential aspects of both God and human, that is meta-physicality and meta-ethicality, are there in time, in germ. The human being *can* be wholly ethical. God *shall* again fill in a miracle greater than that of creation, the whole "space" and "place" of the All. The human and God are already configured as elements. The realization of their respective essences, physicality and ethicality, will take place in time. Essentially, then, in germ, in time, the essences themselves cannot be changed. This immutability of essence is non-paradoxically connected with growth, and this non-paradox is called by Rosenzweig meta-physics and meta-ethics. Only the world, as meta-logical, is not-yet *as* essence. The move into the universal means the move into the world, the move of the world. From the world's point of view, then, the particularity of the human, his individual ethicality, *is* not-yet. In the world-becoming-universal, the human being must relate in ethically sound, increasingly re-sounding, communities.

Truth appears quantifiable and divisible only at the human level of capacity for Truth in time. None of us *is* God and we know God only because he speaks to us in love and only in so far as we listen or ask him to speak to us. The divisibility, therefore, between the many languages occurs only for the human side in the conversations between God and human and between human and human. The meeting of languages happens when there is a bridging of humanly perceived divine truth between diverse languages. God speaks to the hearts of humans. Humans, in order to translate God's One Language, need to listen to the hearts of other men and women. The one language requires translation from heart to heart, and translating from heart to heart, speech to heart from heart, and translating from human to human.

In our hearts we do hold some truths that are more important, stronger even than the truths held in our own particular lives: we humans have died for some truths, and some we now maintain we would die for. This is never the case for truths derived or learned from logic. The (lost?) lives of many in history verify this distinction between truths of logic and divine truths. Rosenzweig discusses the verification and realizability of truth in life in "Das neue Denken": "From those most unimportant truths, of the type two times two is four, on which people readily agree, without any other cost than a little brain grease ... the path leads over the truths which have cost man something, on towards those which he can verify not otherwise than with the sacrifice of life, and finally to those whose truth can verified only upon generations of risked lives ... Only with God himself does the verification reside, only before Him is the truth One. Earthly truth thus remains split – split into two, like the extra-divine factuality, like the primeval facts of world and man.[41]

The summary might be: When God speaks to the human being, the human can then speak divine words. No single human's translation of God's speech can be the translation of all of God's word. This is because God's language is the created vessel *and* vehicle, for the purpose of unfolding in time, of his eternal One Truth, which is also Love.

CONVERSATION IN THE HUMAN GENERATIONS

God speaks in every generation from the beginning at creation. From the monologic speech of the act of creating, God moves into speech between himself and his creature, the human being. Each person lives and speaks concretely in his or her generation alone, but can be audible, that is can be translated into, as many generations in interrupted or unbrokenly continued fashion, as he is heard anew. Only the Bible has been spoken and heard in some place in every generation, before its writing down in the human heart, and after its writing down by listening to it, to the heart, or to both. This historical fact of Bible translating through the generations is a verification of the drive toward the one language.

God creates time as that first condition of the universe that is necessary for the possibilities of the combinations of relationship between God, world, and man and the human being. God limits his own eternality for the duration of world-time. This he does so that he may himself speak in time, act in time, partake in human and worldly events, or even bring to pass actual events. When God interrupts the flow of worldly time by a divinely decided-upon event, though it may appear to fit nicely into ordinary time, such an event is a miracle. There will be much more to say about this in the discussion of the notes to the poems (especially chapter 4). God speaks in time so that his former and present speech, as acts that take place in grammatical tenses, might be translated and spoken in the world, *among* human beings, again and again. The first thing God created was space; the first thing God blessed was time.

A person's speech can endure beyond the terrestrial life of a human being. It can be and remain speech that tells a "piece" of the truth of God's speech, and that the person has at one time told to someone to whom he or she has spoken or written. The ones who leave these legacies have themselves in their turn, wittingly or unwittingly, translated a divine utterance which came directly from divine speech spoken into his heart or from another human being's mouth. Truth remains in the world in order that the world might grow to its promised perfection. Truth comes to reside and remain permanent in the world because its truth of its Logos alone concurs with the permanent divine law of the world. The divine law means to pace off that first created creature, space, and to fill it, through the divinely blessed creature, time, with love for the neighbour, the one who is nearest to us at any moment.

Our neighbour can be one even from another generation, if at that moment that person is the nearest one. To Rosenzweig, Jehuda Halevi was no less than a neighbour.

Whenever speech is linked by translating through the generations, the creative spirit of the growing world is infused into a language that one can speak. Whenever this is done, the one who translates has stretched his presently spoken language, has stretched his mind [*Geist*], to open to the changes for which that mind has been born. In the Nachwort, Rosenzweig writes of the renewal of language through an alien spirit of original language.

The task of translating is entirely misunderstood if it is seen as the Germanizing of what is foreign ... Will this not be asking something impossible of language with this task to reflect the foreign tone in its foreignness: not to Germanize what is foreign, but rather to make foreign what is German?

Not the impossible but rather the requisite, and the requisite not merely in translating ... He who has something to say, will say it in a new way. He becomes the creator of language. After he has spoken, the language has a different face from before. The translator makes himself the mouthpiece of the foreign voice, which he makes audible over the gulf of space or time ...

[The language] will experience a renewal, just as if a new speaker had stood up within the language itself. But still more. For indeed the foreign poet calls into the new language not merely what he himself has to say, but rather he brings along with it the heritage of the general language-spirit of his language to the new language, so that here not merely a renewal of the language occurs through the foreign person, but rather through the foreign language-spirit itself.[42]

THE MULTIPLICITY OF LANGUAGES

Many languages out of the well of the multiplicity of languages have died in the sense that they are no longer spoken today. Middle High German, Old Norse, Sanskrit, Latin, Classical Greek, Biblical Hebrew, Aramaic, Q'ran Arabic, and more remain written and fixed as physically, visually manifest, possibly still oral, embodiments in various depths of eternal truth, all written down at specific moments in historical time. Although in the eternal realm, which is infinitely there, God's word is one, from the human point of view, and from the world's point of view, God's word can increase. God decrees and commands that it does in the world, through time.

In the previous chapter it was claimed that the direction of translation among world languages leads toward the one language of humankind. This oneness, we said, is the ultimate telos of the multiplicity of languages. But in their presently divided state of multiplicity, languages also divide. Choices are available to the human to translate or not to translate what is foreign into the home language. Besides, the choices for translating, in a nonparadoxical way, are also dependent upon such conditions as how much one, a nation, a community, wishes, needs, or is ready to translate another's speech. Translating depends on time and timing. In Rosenzweig's own historical moment, there was no talk of so-called pluralism, religious or otherwise, but it seems to me that before the notion arose in certain circles, Rosenzweig had already a clearer picture that we do today of the intentions and meaning of authentic dialogue and of pluralism, and this I claim *despite* his grave shortcomings with regard to Confucianism, Islam, and the East Indian religions. Rosenzweig found it easier to be gentle with Hellenic mythology than with any currently lived religious form other than Judaism and Christianity. This is presumably because he himself could relate both Judaism and Christianity to Hellenic influences, but not to other influences. While Rosenzweig's vision was wide and indubitably beautiful, and even viable, he himself was restricted, as all of us are, to his own world. His world was one of wealth, not only of soul and spirit and intellect, but also economically. His world was restricted to the Germany that had witnessed and experienced the horror of the First World War; he himself of course experienced it from the Balkan Front and from an army hospital bed. His world grew narrower in all the physical senses of the word, when his movements were restricted to bed living, to one room, to being prevented from speaking orally. His philosophical vision, however, I maintain, was not distorted, but perhaps sadly all the clearer for this. That he found a way to continue to be a speech-thinker, through letter writing, through Halevi, through Buber, that he continued to uphold what he wrote in the *Star* even from this nearly immobile position, is nothing less than, quite literally, remarkable – something to be noticed.

In Rosenzweig's view, the only sin that the human commits happens *prior* to revelation. The human is capable of becoming conscious of this sin *only* upon revelation. That sin is, simply: not having returned God's love. The awareness, the sudden knowledge of not having loved, shames the human self before God. This moment of shame opens the human being's potential also to create love-events. The shame at once falls away. The divinely addressed human being, now as awakened soul, is ready to speak to as well as to be spoken to from human soul to human soul, not merely from self to self. He is therefore also now ready to bridge multiplicities through translating.

God begins to love a human being, not, of course, at the precise moment when revelation is received, but he loves the human quite simply as he loves all his creation. From the beginning of time. To the end of time. Only for God is love both event and attribute. For the human being, and between human beings, love is *always* a new or a renewed event, and *never* a state. A careful reading of Rosenzweig needs to take this point into serious consideration, as did Gershon Greenberg in that very fine, barely attended paper at Harvard in 1973. He states that he disagrees with Rotenstreich, a Rosenzweig critic, who holds that love is an attribute. In a valuable, very important footnote to his paper, Greenberg writes (with page references to either Hallo's translation [111] or to the 1930 German edition of the *Star*, which appeared, as was Rosenzweig's wish, in three separate volumes [II/111]):

Love is not *identical* with God's essence – which forever remains concealed (381). Indeed, God's essence dissolves in his love (*Gottes Wesen ist ... zergangen in seiner ... Liebe*; III/168). But it is deeper than the truth. The "God is truth" means that God's essence is the *Urgrund* of truth, "that all truth is truth only by virtue of deriving from him." The divine essentiality that God is truth is that God reveals himself to man (*göttliche Sich – Offenbarung*) and loves him (III/165-66).

We differ from Rotenstreich's view that love is an attribute of God, and that while truth represents the objective view, which is in God's reality prior to revelation – the transcendental dimension – love represents the intra-revelational dimension, the subjective aspect (*Ha-Mahshava*, II, p. 242, and *Jewish Philosophy*, p. 211). Rosenzweig states that God is within his act of love, is one with it. "Love is not an atribute, but an event – and no attribute has any place in it. God's love does not mean that love befits him like an attribute as does, say, the power to create." The thrust of SE [Der Stern der Erlösung] is to show that God is not only a pre-relational transcendental object. God is both truth and love, but if Rosenzweig had to rest at one point, it would be around revelation. "The letters of love are forged around intellect" (III/156, 163, [164, 381-382, 93]).[43]

Only God is one, only God can be one love and one truth and simultaneously act in the particular events in time. The human being can only love his or her neighbour one at a time, in time, and not "all neighbours" all at once in a timeless so-named "loving state."

Present, personal revelation means that God has *now* revealed this love specifically to this human being at this specific moment in time. Thus the human being, who lives under the grand framework of time, that is creation, revelation, and redemption, *besides* through theological or traditional dogma, also speaks qua specific human being, and never loses his particularity of his own soul, of his own standpoint for understanding. Greenberg, too, discloses Rosenzweig's double admonition with regard to subjective, personal understanding, and I quote, two decades later, the same juxtaposed passages; the "But," placed with precision, is Greenberg's:

Extreme subjectivity means being deaf and blind (II/24, [106]).

But:

If philosophy wants to be true, it must be *erphilosophiert* from the real standpoint of the one philosophizing. There is no other possibility for being objective, than to proceed (*ausgeht*) honestly from one's subjectivity. The duty of objectivity requires only that one *besieht* the entire horizon, not that one sees from a different standpoint than that in which one began, or even from "no standpoint at all." One's own eyes, to be sure, are only one's eyes. But it would be stupidly bourgeois, to believe that one had to pluck out one's own eyes, in order to see clearly. (*B und T, 1. Band* 597) [44]

This self-disclosure by God and this soul-receiving cannot be taken away. Yet it can be taken amiss by the revealed-to human. Love and speech, we have seen, Rosenzweig deemed incomplete when they do not take into account all the three elements of God, world, and human. I return to this for a moment in order to lead us to the section on the profound trust in language in the speech-thinking method of doing philosophy. The "mystic," as Rosenzweig describes him or her, is one such incomplete human lover; he rebels. He does not open himself to the world, that is, to other humans, as God does:

Loved only by God, man is closed off to all the world and closes himself off. What is uncanny for every natural feeling about all mysticism, as well as objectively disastrous is this: that it becomes such a cloak of invisibility for the mystic. His soul opens for God, but because it opens only for God, it is invisible to all the world and shut off from it. The mystic rotates the magic ring on his finger in arrogant confidence, and at once he is alone with "his" God, and incommunicado to the world. This becomes possible for him only by virtue of the fact that he wants wholly and solely to be God's favourite and nothing else. He must treat [the world] as if it were not – created ... This thoroughly immoral relationship to the world is thus utterly essential for the pure mystic if he wants, for the rest, to assert and preserve his pure mysticism. The world must close itself off against the arrogant seclusion of man. And instead of coming to life as discoursing figure, man, whom we already saw opening up, is swallowed back into seclusion. [45]

The previous chapter stressed the openness of the translator to others' speech. The "mystic," who would "possess" the truth is interested in self-absorption, self-abandonment, or self-empowerment through his or her communion with God. Since he can have no power over God, he turns God's love for him into power over other humans. By closing himself off from the world, he abuses the real and intended power that was divinely imbued in him. His speech becomes impositional, it wants to force its way upon the thought of others. At the same time, it wants to bar the often rightful and needful path of others' speech, which he is meant to beckon into his "own" speech. His own say is all that counts. He cannot hear his fellow man and is thus incapable of achieving the true goal of the mind. He wants to hear only God. His direct line to God he sees as unique. In abandoning the world he mistranslates God's light into the darkness of his interior. He blinds himself by refusing to watch for the lights that shine forth from others.

Light always shines outward: God's Light shines outward into the soul of the human. Human light, which is kindled from the divine revelation needs, too, its specific places, surfaces, faces, on which and into which to shine. To the human, light is only apparent when it touches. Light does not speak: light is silent. The "mystic" sees himself as already there, already redeemed, in no need of speech. He fancies himself as already shining in the silent light of redemption. But that one light can only full *be* at the end, when the world is no longer. The "mystic," then, is lying; directing language onto a miscreant path – into non-communication, into non-growth. In his inactivity he actively divides language and humans. When language is fully created into the one language, only then may speech end between humans and between God and humans. With regard to the contrast between the "todays" of presently speaking revelation and the consummation of speech in the silence of redemption, Rosenzweig writes:

Light does not discourse, it shines. It does not by any means seclude itself in itself, for it shines outward, not inward. But in shining outward, it does not give itself up, as does speech. Light does not sell itself, it does not give itself away, like speech, when it expresses itself. Rather it is visible by remaining wholly in itself. It does not really shine outward, it only shines forth. It shines, not like a fountain, but like a face, like an eye which is eloquent without the lips having to move. Unlike the muteness of the protocosmos, which had no words yet, here is a silence which no longer has any need of the word. It is the silence of consummate understanding. One glance says everything here. Nothing shows so clearly that the world is unredeemed as the diversity of languages. Between men who speak a common language, a glance would suffice for reaching an understanding; just because they speak a common language, they are elevated above speech. Between different languages, however, only the stammering word mediates, and gesture ceases to be immediately intelligible as it had been in the mute glance of the eye. It is reduced to a halting sign language, that miserable surrogate for communication.[46]

Thus language is a conveyer, carrying something from the innermost of the human being to the outside and into his innermost. We speak because we are *not* in accord, we speak *until* we are. Once we attain the true goal of the mind [*Geist*], translating from other languages than our own, and reaching understanding among all men and women, language too will rest in the universal all.

In the Afterword to the translations, Rosenzweig discusses the idea that the one language means an accord among all languages reached by means of translating between them:

That such a renewal of one language through a foreign one is at all possible certainly presupposes that just as the language itself has given birth to each of its speakers, so too all human speaking [*Sprechen*], all foreign languages, which ever were spoken and ever will be spoken, are contained in it in germ-cell at least. And that is the case. There is only one language. There is no language trait of one language that does not evidence itself, at least in germ, in every other language, be it in dialects, nurseries, peculiarities of trades. Upon this actual oneness of languages and upon the dependent commandment, namely that of universal human mutual understanding [*Verständigung*], is based the possibility as well as the task of translating, its Can, May and Shall. One can translate because in every language is contained the possibility of every other language; one may translate if the translator can realize this possibility through cultivation of such linguistic fallow land; and one should translate so that the day of that harmony [*Eintracht*] of language, which can grow only in each individual language, not in the space "between" them, may come.[47]

Diversity of languages then is to remain until the time of redemption. The promise and pre-view of redemption and the knowledge of creation's character of having a beginning and an ending ensure that creature language shall endure throughout all the ages of man. Language is validated at creation, and the goal – the commanded goal – of reaching full accord among humans compels us to endeavour to translate new utterances into our speech, by listening for and to God, and for and to true speech among people.

Language, as paganly spoken, already revolves around the three elements, God, human, and world. The one language, however, is that language which does and shall relate experientially the three elements in time: in creation, revelation, and redemption.

TRUST IN LANGUAGE: PHYSICAL AND SPIRITUAL
MUTUALITY OF SPEECH

Within language Rosenzweig claims the occurrence of a mutual reflection of spiritual and physical (soul) worlds. Creature language is shared in the mutual use of it by God and the human being. It is both divine and terrestrial at the same time. It is not spiritual merely when speaking of "spirituality," not physical merely when discussing a leaf's greenness. Language can be both.

Language as creature belongs to the physical and temporal world. Language – transmitted by mouth and pen, received by ear and eye, as visible and audible – is thus materially concrete in that it is sensible. It was created when God spoke during his creative act, before speech began to be realized in the world. As a creation of God and as a gift to the human, it is a separate entity and not an attribute of either. It can be therefore logically reified, as contemporary deconstructionists well know. In things that seem to be "merely" things the wise never place their trust. Yet speech-thinkers share an incontrovertible, unshakeable trust in word and speech and language.

Are the senses not also of the spirit? Feuerbach's Principle 41 leads to the sensible and sensitive conclusion that we as humans are compelled to put faith in language:

We feel not only stones and wood, not only flesh and bones, but also feelings when we press the hands or lips of a feeling being; we perceive through our ears not only the murmur of water and the rustle of leaves, but also the soulful voice of love and wisdom; ee not only mirror-like surfaces and specters of colour, but we also gaze into the gaze of man. Hence, not only that which is external, but also that which is internal, not only flesh, but also the spirit ... is an object of the senses ... Empiricism is therefore perfectly justified in regarding ideas as originating from the senses; but what it forgets is that the most essential sensuous object for man is *man himself*; that only in man's glimpse of man does the spark of consciousness and intellect spring. And this goes to show that idealism is right in so far as it sees the origin of ideas from man understood as an isolated being, as mere soul existing for himself; in one word, it is wrong when it derives the ideas from an ego that is not given in the context of its togetherness with a perceptibly given You. Ideas spring only from conversation and communication. Not alone but only within a dual relationship does one have concepts and reason in general.

It takes two human beings to give birth to a man, to physical as well as spiritual man; the togetherness of man with man is the first principle and the criterion of truth and universality. Even the certitude of those things that exist outside me is given to me through the certitude of the existence of other men besides myself. That which is seen by me alone is open to question, but that which is seen also by another person is certain.[48]

A person who intercepts an idea from conversation and communication and does not regard it, as all ideas are, as an inception, but thinks about it henceforth as if it were the monopolized property of self, and does not give back in speech that intercepted idea with his own additions which have developed in solitary thought, destroys himself – and sometimes others in his sphere – as a person. Any school of philosophy that adheres to such a reification of language with the inherent proprietary notions that are fitting for things will, if it becomes the predominant philosophy in the world, despite or because of "rights of ownership" tyrannically seep its way into the foundations of all schools that run and shape the world. A great, grievous evil is the result: for such a philosophical base around the globe, taken to its logical and practical conclusions, dictates unilaterally (for it cannot speak): there will be no communication among humans. With thought and being identified concurrently with the reification of language, the human too becomes a thing.

Speech was created in the solitude of God and was not the true communicative speech of the world but a decreeing sort of speech that decreed how the world was to be, and thus includes revelation. There was a time when God was and the world and man were not, and only at creation did the triadic relationship become possible. In part one of the *Star*, Rosenzweig describes God as placing an arch-Yea behind every word, thus validating language for all who speak, which is to say for everyone. The passage is important:

For speech is truly mankind's morning gift from the Creator, and yet at the same time it is the common property of all the children of men, in which each has his particular share and, finally, it is the seal of humanity in man. It is entire from the beginning: man became man when he first spoke. And yet to this day there is no language of mankind; that will only come to be at the end. Real language, however, is common to all between beginning and end, and yet is a distinct one for each; it unites and divides at the same time. Thus real speech includes everything, beginning, middle, and end. It is the presently visible fulfillment of the beginning, for in its countless forms it is today the visible criterion of man, whom, so we may say, language makes human. And it includes the end, for even as the individual language of today, or as the language of the individual, it is completely dominated by the ideal of coming to a perfect understanding which we visualize as the language of mankind.[49]

We have spoken of identity of speech and person. There is also an identity of speech and the capacity to realize worldviews. Individual language states a worldview, and a stated worldview can come to be. It strives to be realized beyond speech and in the world. In his lecture notes, "The Science of the World,"[50] Rosenzweig states that the world, being passive, offering itself to us for knowing, must be knowable. But yet, he notes, it seems impossible for us to say just what it is. What we doubt about the world is its reality. In that case, Rosenzweig asks, is each person the creator of his or her own world? The artist of the world of art, the politician of the world of power? Concerning the co-incidence of conceiving and realizing worlds, in conjunction with the assertion that the secret of the spirit [*Geist*] is that it is created spirit, Rosenzweig writes with much emphasis:

Must not one of these world creators really have created a world, a real world? And the world, which perhaps is not real, will become real in the creative act of humankind? For which room is even left precisely through the still-not-realness of the world. For that which I "conceive" through my conceiving becomes a real *concept, that* at least, *this* reality, this *created* reality, would then be not to be doubted. And thus the doubt of the reality of the world leads wholly of its own accord to the belief in the creative power of the spirit [Geist] ... Each worldview indeed wants to *realize its* world, which of its kind *becomes* real; and which does not after all remain stuck merely in the worldview.[51]

Thus language, in its relation to how the world comes to be, comprises concreteness and spirit [*Geist*]. What ultimately unites distinct worldviews? At the base of every worldview is something independent of views, Rosenzweig claims, and "if the viewing itself may colour the surfaces of things, the 'base of things' must nevertheless really be really just as it is."[52] The worldview of God the creator, revealer, and redeemer is *the* worldview, as spoken at creation and in revelation, in the promise. But built into this foundational worldview is dependence upon time: the worldview which is to realize its world is that world which will become real.

God's speech in his solitude created both a world and a worldview. It is the worldview at the base of all worldviews. God revealed his worldview to the world of humans, and decrees it for the world in which humans live. God's worldview is truly a worldview: for the world, for world-time, and beyond. The promise is devoid of descriptions of the world to come beyond time. That it will come is the primary statement for that world. The concentration is on this world. This day and not that day. Nor does God speak of pre-world, before time. What counts for the human is the today. Yet the today, revelation, counts as nothing without knowledge that creation happened and that redemption will come to pass for the human: that there is a beginning and there will be an end. Endless we are not: were we endless, then language would likewise be endless with continual accumulation or recycles or isolated private pockets for the frivolous use of each of us. Tenses would make no sense. A beginning and an end denote connection and relation among tenses, movement, progression, change, and growth from a starting point to the fullness of death.

GOD THE TRANSLATOR

Once God has spoken to a particular human heart, and its soul awakes, she awakens to the capability of speaking the language that is ultimately universal for other humans, for God's ears, and in the world's en-souling reception. Speech that does not affirm "He is good" has no archetypal, divine Yea supporting it. Each word individually, unlike the complete sentence, of course does have the archetypal Yea standing behind it, or else speech could not possibly grow through the growth of the human soul. Only those affirming God would be capable of speech, and we know that this is not the case. Because the purpose and goal of speech is to affirm God through love of neighbour, of each nearest neighbour one at a time, then love must be event and not attribute even for God. Otherwise his commands, which are related to events, would be meaningless. None of his commands are universal, as is his law.

In order to communicate with God one needs to know: what language does God understand? What language will God accept? To which words will he respond? Which words will fall away from his ears? Certainly he will hear and affirm into the final seal and permanence of eternal silence and light those words which make whole, make peace among humans.

Words that fall away from God's ears are utterances that abuse the ultimate wholeness of language. Within this knowledge remains human choice. Choosing the abusive aspects of language is possible to the point of obliterating the primary sense, or experience, of choice. Constantly renewed and remembered knowledge of God minimizes the possibility of choosing speech that abuses language's ultimate oneness. Instead, the renewing and the remembering encourage the human to translate the creator's speech into widening revelatory circles and links through world time. Liturgy renews and remembers God's great communications to the human, and instructs us how to respond to God's communications.

Liturgy most of all is a large prayer for redemption, praises God and his creation, and affords speaking with communal accord. But because liturgical speech preglimpses eternity, there is no dialogue here. Individual speech is precluded from liturgy; in liturgy all congregants agree. Prayer takes its place here in time, but is spoken and heard in unison. The congregants say We, and forget their individual names. No spontaneous conversation takes place here.

Outside church or synagogue humans speak more often with "I" or an addressed "You" than with a "we," even in associations. Strictly speaking, each person speaks consciously as himself, always remembering his name: I, my first name and my last name, say my words on behalf of myself or even on behalf of somebody else, but I speak them. Even the I, with name, who speaks on behalf of somebody else, remembers his or her own name. He has been called by name to represent his nation, for example, and thus the choice to respond as a "we," is really "my" delegation, in which the I is still nevertheless prominent. Speech addressed to God outside liturgical speech is in the form of the specific human whose own name calls upon God's name. In speech to others, the universal language speaker will be speaking to those others in *both* his own name *and* in God's name.

God's capability of translating, that is, his listening to and his responding to human speech addressed to him, sustains the base of the one language. No religion, a purely human creation according to Rosenzweig, has a more privileged access to God than any other. In explaining the new thinking in terms of divine revelation, Rosenzweig writes:

Revelation as "ever renewed" is the content of the second volume [of the *Star*] just as "always true" is the content of the first. It deals with the visible and audible, thus manifest reality; its forerunner deals with its dark-mute secret presupposition ... because and insofar paganism in its historical forms forgot or denied this revelation to Adam, who was as little a pagan as a Jew or Christian, this historical paganism, which was rigidified into a form for itself, of course is not at all perpetual; precisely in its independence and having become form it has no part in reality. The temples of the gods have rightly collapsed, their statues are rightly in the museum, their service, as far as it was set in order and ruled, may have been a single enormous error – but the fast and fervent prayer with struggled up to them out of a tormented breast, and the tears which the Carthaginian father, who sacrificed his son to Molech, poured, cannot have remained unheard, nor unseen. Or is God supposed to have waited for Sinai or even for Golgotha? No, as little from Sinai or from Golgotha do the roads lead upon which He is reached with certainty, that He can just as little have refused to meet even him who sought Him on the mountain-trails surrounding Olympus. There is no temple built which would be so near to Him that a person would be permitted to be confident of this nearness, and none which would be so far from Him that His arm could not easily reach even to there, no direction out of which He could not come, none out of which He would have to come, no block of wood in which He does not one time take up a dwelling, and no Psalm of David which always reaches His ear.[53]

Different religions, insists Rosenzweig, are merely forms of living that more and less accurately conform to reality. What God hears is his One language's various translations. What is dissonant with his word he shuns from translation into eternity. The base of the one language is the fact of God's creating language. The pinnacle of language is its completion when it will, being complete, be no longer necessary. It will fall away, maybe sigh, transformed into silent light.

Just as the weekdays lead up to the perfection of the holy time of the Sabbath, so the world days of speech lead up to the perfection of the One Language of accord at redemption. Whatever is to be impermanent – business dealings, money matters – is not permitted to be spoken of on the Sabbath. Before Yom Kippur each Jew is required to make peace with his brother. The Christian is not entitled to partake of communion when at strife with the members of his community. God hears words that entreat peace, wholeness, oneness among humankind that is in alliance with God's word.

Real listening is love, and whatever is worthy of being translated, and is translated, constitutes speaking the one language. Likewise, to reject what is not worth translating, is also ultimately to speak the one language.

CONCLUSION

The one language is the language that will be spoken within existing, diverse languages. English, French, and German, for instance, will not be replaced by one specific, different language, and least of all by any sort of Esperanto. Nor will languages merge together as one. Yet each language has in itself the potential to grow into that one language. Speech is both divine and human; and words spoken are destined to reach agreement and perfect understanding between God and human, and between human and human.

This perfect agreement will render speech unnecessary. Thus the ultimate purpose of speech is not to communicate but to draw to a conclusion, based on all that has gone before in creation and revelation, so that there will be the peace of silence. The conclusion that will both precede that silence and open to the day of redemption is: "For God is good."

Until that time, Rosenzweig defines each language as growing toward a fullness of spirit [Geist] through translating. Therefore, while each language in itself possesses the potential for becoming the one language, different languages are dependent upon each other. Through translation, the translating language experiences and meets another language. Translating nurtures and increases the creative spirit [*Geist*] in language which traverses both between contemporary lives and across generations. This creative spirit grows irreversibly and shines through all languages, for the creative spirit is God's presence and self-revelation. Each time two people express love in word and response a permanence occurs in temporality and is reflected into eternity. Each time a language learns how to express in a new way that God is good, that language is closer to becoming the one language.

Languages, however, cannot be in complete harmony with one another until each language states absolutely that God is good. The statement that God is good is expressed in love of neighbour, each neighbour successively. Concurrent with the final, universal arrival of the one language, then, universal love will take place among human souls. But this universality must be reached from the direction of the particular to the universal and by means of the particular relating to the particular, through time.

The Notes as Application
of The New Thinking

This chapter explores three areas. The largest comprises a spanning across the basic features of speech-thinking as applied in the Notes. The attention Alan Udoff gives to one of the notes fills several pages and offers a hint of the extent to which a single note can merit consideration.[1] The chapter concludes in an area still barely excavated with regard to possible layouts and further findings: the scope of speech-thinking as philosophical genre.

BASIC FEATURES OF SPEECH-THINKING IN THE NOTES

Most of the ways in which the Notes embody and exemplify the speech-thinking method are easily identifiable. Five readily apparent features can be attended to by only a brief exposition before emphasizing three less obvious ones. The obvious features comprise: (1) speech in multiple levels, (2) the aspect of religious experience, (3) the presence of the individual person, (4) direct address, and (5) distinctions between eternality and temporality. Less apparent in their full significance are the following three features: biblical language, the root-sentence, and suddenness or eruption.

By features I mean those topical or surface characterizations of the poems and of Rosenzweig's way of doing philosophy. One can recognize features by seeing them, as it were, as facts or facets, by observing them without engagement with them. In the concluding chapter themes will be audited. By themes I mean those topics which are developed or discussed in the Notes, upon which further reflection is invited. There, with the themes, an engagement which conjoins philosophizing with living is meant to be transparent. If vision is the image for understanding of features, then for the themes probing microscoping equipment or the inner eye or the soul serves better for finding meanings. One feature and one theme will overlap: that of eternality and temporality.

Speech in Multiple Levels

The Notes involve speech that occurs in multiple levels.[2] Jehuda Halevi directly addresses God in nearly every poem. Because his direct addresses to God are shaped in poetic form, Halevi intends to engage co-singers who can also address God by means of his poems. That is to say, Halevi wants listeners to his words in addition to God *and* speakers of his words other than himself. He thus already, through form, signifies a desire for an co-resonating inclusion of others' – inter-humanly other – speech. Through co-recitative poetry, people can speak in self-consciously, simultaneously voiced speech to God which addresses him with the expectation, or request, that he hear and in some way respond to the speakers. In this simultaneity of multiple human speakers, each one who speaks, prays, sings, or even reads Halevi's hymns can speak *also* through his own voice and stand affirmatively behind the words as if they were his own. The "we" which is involved here represents the speech-thinking's tenet of the "we" as an "I" and an "I" and an "I" and on and on, that is to say as community and not as a collectivity or totality of "I"s that are subjugated by the "we." Each "I" is equi-vocal, equally audible in this sort of speaking in unison. Moreover, from this simultaneity of individual voices arising out of a multiplicity of "I"s there is expressed a "we" that can, nonetheless, be reduced to no fewer speakers than two, but certainly to as few as two. A solitary singer of a poem by Jehuda Halevi can be in conversation with God, and here the humanly uttered "we" is, as it were, a "soft we" of poet and fresh speaker. The new speaker utters a "we" that is only faintly aware that someone else composed the words he is now saying. Many of the poems are repeated and/or heard in congregational or liturgical situations. Halevi did not compose his poetry in these liturgical situations, but in many poems he explicitly points and refers to the Jewish calendar of holy times and occasions.

The speech of the Halevi book as a whole, as Rosenzweig presents it, comprises an inception of a conversation between the book's (Rosenzweig's and Halevi's) words and each reader of the book.

The Notes themselves can be read as constituting secondary speech, spoken, that is, after Rosenzweig's co-recitation with Halevi in the translations. The possibility for co-recitation between Halevi and Rosenzweig rests, of course, on Rosenzweig's translating effort. For the German who knows neither Hebrew nor a language into which

Halevi has already been translated, the possibility for co-recitation with Halevi was created by Rosenzweig. These possibilities for co-recitation are visually displayed in the Poem section of the book. The secondary speech of the Halevi book, the Notes, is both reflective of Jehuda Halevi's words and responsive. Thus Rosenzweig stretches the German language to accommodate a medieval mind's speech and to make it audible in German. He also carries forward the original speech and extends it, certainly not in the translations but in the reflections and responses. Rosenzweig does not intend, beyond the translating stage, to speak as a medievalist, but as a German Jew of the 1920s.

The translating is keen listening, both to the originating speaker and to the untapped resources in one's own language potential. This means that Rosenzweig, here at the reception stage of speech, is preparing for his own speaking. This accomplished translating phase gives to Rosenzweig's reader both the immediateness of Halevi's speech and the mediation of the German language. Rosenzweig wanted to achieve the mind's goal of translating, to make the poems audible in a new language. All this echos what we saw Rosenzweig say in the *Star*: that authentic word is word and response.

Jehuda Halevi addresses the world as well as God. He addresses it as creature – created components are praised. He also speaks outward, into the world as creature which is also filled with his fellow human beings. The world is all else that is neither himself nor his community of fellow Jews nor God. Specific human beings he loves – his daughter, his grandson, his friends in Egypt – these he speaks of as fellow-souls. His love for specific fellows is poignantly described in his pain at leaving his family and friends in Spain, and later in departing from his hospitable friends in Egypt, who have been trying to persuade him to stay on a little longer. This address to fellow human beings thus lives permanently, but in a fixed, concretely tangible and audible artform in his written poetry. Halevi composed for contemporaries; we possess the compositions eight centuries later.

While Halevi speaks outward to others (the address moment), and while others may speak with him in singing his hymns (the we moment), there is recorded in the poetry the poet's own speech as human being, to God, world, and with other human beings. In that the poetry was also composed for posterity, the address to fellow human beings is not fixed for those who are still alive or have not yet been born; for these, of any faith or of none, the poetry remains open to answers. That Jehuda Halevi repeatedly does receive answers and still speaks inter-humanly today is evidenced through his place in the Jewish Prayer Book, which in its turn remains open for others' participation.

But conversation to the speech-thinker is not a matter of ongoing speech and response only. The display of the growth of the one language – that is, the widening base of, and active hope for, agreement and harmony among people – has its place *in* but also *between* audible speech and vocal response: the translating *phase*, or, better: *moment*. When the original Hebrew poetry of Halevi is brought into the German language to the extent even of rhyme, metre, and acrostic, there is a distinguishing mark of the widening base and a hope fulfilled. This phase indicates understanding in the sense of alteration on the part of the listener, and here the alteration is evidenced by the German language itself. Thus the one who is responding, in the process of coming to understand someone else's speech, alters both his own speech and his innermost per-sona (through sound) before responding. And he is altered *because* another spoke to him, not because he was thinking out an issue or idea in solitary self-conversation.

In addition to the poetic form, which itself shows the need for an audience to hear and to respeak its intended spokenness, two notes attend this poetic intention by a special focus: the ones to "Gelobt!" ("Praised be He!" [171–2/24–5]) and "All meine Glieder" ("All my Limbs," [176–7/34–5]). Rosenzweig points out that each of these poems uses familiar phrases for its core, just as phrases of the Lord's Prayer would be for the Christian. By virtue of this familiarity the reader is already brought beforehand as it were into the conversation. This focus on revoiced familiar phrases, moreover, is an example of speech being picked up and taking on new life in fresh expression over centuries. Rosenzweig is critical of other translators of the poem "Gelobt!": "This emptying into the familiar sound of the prayer which in Jewish ritual plays a role with which "The Lord's Prayer" ["Our Father"] in Christian rituals can be compared – this emptying determines the effect of the poem: now in splendrous latitude, now in a sublime cascade, now in a ferocity brisk as a river, now in mysteriouus rustling. (No coincidence, then, that both the earliest and the most recent translators, simply omit the refrain, apparently because it is repeated five times and therefore would be "fatiguing")" (171/24).

The refrain's content, which I shall give here, is translated from Rosenzweig's German. The rendering is, therefore, by no means meant to be a translation of Halevi, for it is against the principles of translation *not* to translate from the original.[3] When, from here on, I provide a few lines of renderings from Rosenzweig's translations, I do so, as here, only so that the reader can have at hand, for the sake of staying on the same page, a paled copy of what Halevi is saying in a given poem. In each case, the poem should rightly be read at some time separately, on its own, preferably if possible, in the Hebrew. The refrain, then, which is expressed five times, is: "That He be praised, / Oh that He be garlanded, / Oh that He be extolled, / and consecrated."

For "All meine Glieder," Rosenzweig begins his note as follows:

There is a hymn contained in the Sabbath and Festival morning services where the transition is made from their preluding parts as it were to the main prayers. The one who says the prayers lets course broadly into this hymn all that he has only touched like a survey in the hasty "mumbling" of the wealth of the Psalms. The hymn is very old – the French medieval Jews in all seriousness ascribe it to the Apostle Peter – , the language of the Psalms resounds in it, but here heightened to the monumental. And the poets have allowed their ivy to twine around this edifice so that it is completely covered with it. Just as in the Catholic liturgy there are certain points of the mass-text upon which are built up the great phrases of the musical masses, so traditionally in Jewish liturgy there are firmly located points. In this prayer one such a place occurs over which the accompanying insertions have accumulated since the revival of our poetry after the Talmud-inspired centuries. It is the place where it leads, after a powerful messianically convoked crescendo, "every mouth," "every tongue," "every knee," "every heart," into the word of the Psalm, "as it is written" (Psalm 35:10), and in it for a moment into the individual praying person: "All my limbs must say: Lord, who is like unto You?" (176–7/34)

Rosenzweig, for his part, addresses both Jehuda Halevi and his contemporaries. While for the moment he closes, with each note, his own conversation with Jehuda Halevi and the particular poem, he opens another conversation with any reader of his book. This second conversation embraces both his own speech and that which Jehuda Halevi speaks, yet without confounding the two. By placing his Afterword to the translations as a wall between the Poems and the Notes, Rosenzweig emphatically separates his own voice from the voice of Jehuda Halevi. The Afterword itself begins with words to this separating effect, asserting that the translations want to be nothing but translations.

Jehuda Halevi was a great Jewish poet in the Hebrew language. This small selection seeks to give an idea of this to the German reader. So it was not my aim to make the reader believe that Jehuda Halevi composed in German, nor that he composed Christian church songs, nor that he is a poet of today, even if only a *Familienblatt* poet of today – all this as far as I can see the aims of my predecessors in translation, especially the most recent ones. Instead, these translations want to be nothing but translations. Not for a moment do they want to make the reader forget that he is reading poems not by me, but by Jehuda Halevi, and that Jehuda Halevi is neither a German poet nor a contemporary. In a word: this translation is not a free rendering, and if nevertheless here and there it is so, then only for need of rhyme. Basically my intention was to translate literally, and in approximately five-sixths of these lines of verse I may have succeeded. For the sixth sixth, where, even I, if only to the most careful extent, had to resort to "free renderings," here I formally beg the pardon of the reader. (153/1)

At the conclusion of each note, Rosenzweig is careful to indicate precisely which words he has added or altered for the sake of rhyme.

In any case, the one who is speaking, and to whom, and the dynamics of the speech can all be clearly detected. What is less transparent is how, as human being, one speaks at different times. For both "Gelobt" and "All meine Glieder," Rosenzweig delineates some alternating levels within the same human being. Each of the speech-streams which flow five times into the "That He be praised" refrain is occasioned by a different human mode: "The streams of the five stanzas which empty into the common ocean of the "Daβ gelobt ..." all come from a different direction. The first stanza starts from the position of the creature, of the creature to which the creature's demand for the Creator's help is rhymed immediately by his receiving this help. Heaven opens up to the one so conscious of the help, and blinded, he falls down" (171–2/24).

When, as Rosenzweig puts it, "the second stanza [of "Gelobt"] dares to open its eyes again," the human creature looks around and observes nature. Swinging up then through the spheres to the first mover, who does not move himself, the human again falls down, overcome by the vision of the heavenly throne. This tension between the high heavens and the earth beneath shakes the poet, and he moves to another direction. He knows that even now he has seen "only a glimpse," but that his knowledge is not a mere "only" but that "only" in the form intended for the human being, as the treasure of his being [*des Wesens Hort*]. Again he falls. The next direction is looking to the world of human beings around him: he sees that humans are to feel a "free and joyous acceptance of this dependence," to recognize providence and to expect judgment. Now he is tranquil. The final direction from which the poet's speech to God takes place is from the innermost regions of his breast. He cannot repose in his calm of acceptance: he knows he is not wise, that he is nothing. Still, he looks up again to God's greatness: "And shuddering from this feeling of the mystery over him, he stammers the words of the prayer [*Daβ gelobt*] which, now whispered in solitude, carry further, as when in the beginning they had been accompanied by the chorus of the Creation and of the created spirits" (17ø/ø5).

The occasion of indistinguishability between different speakers' speech occurs only where there is utter agreement. The growth of the one language, a speaking as a "we" of particular, nonsubmersible "I"s is thus evident here, as well as in "All meine Glieder": "Jehuda Halevi's hymn deepens into this moment where the We, the "Breath of all things living" – the opening words of the prayer – sinks into the I. "My limbs," "my songs," "my spirit," "my plumage," "my driving force," "my heart," – always again "my": it is man, the individual man before God. He is not looking inwards, he is extending himself outwards; he only says My in order to place that which is his again and again at God's feet. He says I, but only to forget Himself. Again and again his words begin with My and end again and again with: to You" (177/34–5).

The familiarity of phrases, too, shows the growth of the one language in that such phrases in praise of God's goodness are already agreed upon and are repeated over many generations. Psalmic praying speaks in unison by virtue of the voices of one century joining with those of another. Familiar phrases are not timeless but are made sempiternal by being newly spoken in time, in a swelling chorus.

Religious Experience

Religious experience, in consonance with theological concepts of revelation, is plainly at the base of Jehuda Halevi's words and actions. Such experience is intimately known to Rosenzweig, as his sympathetic, confirming response to the poet shows. Rosenzweig repeatedly and emphatically reminds the reader of the place and propriety of religious experience, as he does in discussions of his definition of the "mystic" in the *Star* and elsewhere, as noted above. Meetings with God are not the end point of faith, but rather the beginning point: for life in the world, and for life beyond the world.

The Personal Aspect of Speech-Thinking

Not only for the reasons of valuing individual religious experience is speech-thinking deemed as a philosophy devoted to personal dimensions. The speech-thinking method of philosophy is associated with the personal dimension also because speech itself is tied to particular persons and to God as per-sona, *and* because both human and divine speech are joined to action and events in life.

Nothing could be less atuned to the method than "value-free" scholarship and the aims of absolute objectivity. But the method is personal only in the sense that, when used, a specific "I" is not merely speaking but addressing a specific "you" whose response is awaited. Thus the

uniqueness of each person is protected in this philosophy. Speech protects the uniqueness of the three elements, including the individual
human being, because behind the "I" is the name, one's own name,
and facing the "I" there is the "you" with his or her own name. A free-
standing otherness is welcomed – required and needed for speech-
thinking. When the very act of philosophizing is dependent on otherness, then boundaries are imperative between each pair of "others" to
some one (or thing).

In the new thinking, there is no transgression of boundaries by any
itself-bounded other element. The relating between boundaries here
does not take place via the defenseless chinks in these boundaries
which the reductionist old thinking could find so easily. Traditional
Western philosophy finds all borders defenseless, invadable. Reduction
of one to the other, the making the "same" of what is really other is its
goal: to arrive always at one, one universal, and to work from that one
standpoint. The political implications, and results of this way of thinking have proved it to be a horror to most of the world's peoples.

In the new thinking, openness and boundedness as features at the
same time means openness *only* through the concepts of creation, revelation, and redemption. To these categories the personal experience of
the individual *is* subject. Immanence and transcendence to each "other"
are characterized as alternating events. The event of revelation each
time, at Sinai, Golgotha, or in a personal meeting, is itself a relationship
between the easily violable boundaries of God and man. But divine revelation commands that there be relationships across the boundaries of
the three elements. If relationships can never involve fewer than two,
boundaries must remain. If two cannot reduce further, these two must
co-relate in order to know anything important of the other.

The poetry discloses not so much Jehuda Halevi's private thoughts
on any matter in his life as it discloses his awakened soul's conversations with God or fellow human beings at every step. Jehuda Halevi's
particular participation in the conversation renders the poetry personal, this specific I speaking and listening to this specific You in the
context of events. The note to "All meine Glieder" ("All my Limbs")
has demonstrated this concept of the I: "These are my very own limbs
which are praising You only" (176–7/34–5). This is important for
Rosenzweig's view of personal revelation. The specific I can respond to
and address God, in his or her heart and life, because God addresses
each human specifically. According to the speech-thinker, an I that
sees himself as speaking in solitude, as "to all the world" or as a "free-
standing" thinker, objectifies the self to a static entity.

The historical revelations of Sinai and Golgotha and personal revelation (Song of Songs) safeguard each other. Personal revelation is not

permitted to become fanatic, and historical revelation is not permitted to become an irrelevant past fact.

Direct Address

From the notion of immanence and transcendence as event, direct address and the name are of paramount interest to the speech-thinker. Wherever speech can be a speaking-to or a speaking about another, speaking-to must take precedence. Not one poem speaks about God; the closest to this third-person level or moment of speech occurs in a lament over God's distance. Yet even this lament remains in the form of address, which brings to the fore the importance of the name. Rosenzweig's notes on the nearness or distance of God elucidate the characteristics and significance of the name, notably in "Exkurs: Offenbarungstag" ("Excursus: Day of Revelation,"175–6/31–2). The name of God, Rosenzweig asserts, is at once God's name and concept. No one "has" a name. Each is given his or her name, each is called. It does not matter whether God draws near or remains far away nearly as much as it does that he has a name, that he can be called to and upon – even in anger. God's nearness or farness assigns to the human utterance degrees of expressibility. When near, God is inexpressible. When drawing far away, he is expressible. When utterly far away, he is provable. But since God is never absent, even when far away, according to Rosenzweig, he is always addressable. The trouble with proofs, Rosenzweig claims, like that proof fashionable at the time (the 1920s), namely God's being wholly other, is that proofs do not let God do exactly as he pleases when he pleases: each proof is a limiting of God to an entity or to an abstract idea.[4] In the speech-thinking method one learns truth through continued conversations with God, and with other humans, where the temporal and eternal, which also have their own borders, are bridged.

Eternity and Time

Jehuda Halevi alludes to the connection between eternity and time in every poem and is exceptionally explicit in "Gerichtstag," "Der Lohn," and "Welt" ("The Day of Judgment" 179/43–4; "Reward" 204–7/108–11; "World" 211–12/124–5).

"Gerichtstag" is a poem comprising five stanzas, the beginning letter of which forms the acrostic JHUDA. This is significant for the poem's meaning in that, while it may be sung by the "I" of another's name, it makes subtly clear that a specific soul composed this prayer. In the note, Rosenzweig writes of the multiplicity of singular souls as each

faces the Day of Judgment each year through the Jewish calendar, and
of eternality and temporality:

Judaism has kept alive the thought of the judgment of the world, which always
awakens in man when the seasons renew themselves and fall asleep when the
seasons decline and "yet all remains as before," in that it has drawn the
thought, irrespective of the end of the seasons, into the year. The New Year's
Day in the Autumn has become the "Day of Judgment" which places the individual once each year before the full dreadfulness of world judgment. Of a
world judgment of course only in the microcosmos of the soul, of all souls. For
the soul, for the souls, today the fate is sealed. To this internal knowledge, of
which the external realization must be lacking – for the end of the world, of
course, can happen only once, and not every year – the reading creates now at
least a substitute of this worldly reality in placing on the Today of this Day the
great Day of the World, its beginning and its messianic completion ... And besides there is reflected for him into that day – which makes the hearing of the
final trumpets a duty in the circle of Jewish duties and tells Israel to anticipate
the universal acknowledgment of God's dominion – there is reflected also the
destiny of the Patriarchs, exactly at the point where man feels his dependence
most intimately and yet at the same time quite concretely, at the point where
the unbeliever is as believing as the believer and the believer cannot be more
believing than the other. The reading places onto this day the reprieve of the
three barren mothers, Sarah, Rachel, Hannah; one of these three fates, that of
Hannah (1 Samuel 1), has therefore become the passage for this day of the
Last Judgment that is interwoven by the most ardent and most private prayers.
(179/43-4)[5]

In "Der Lohn" the subject under reflection is this world and that
world. Rosenzweig writes in response to this poem that to Halevi it is
self-evident that there is

full equivalence of the "sensual" and the "spiritual" reward, of nectar and of
wisdom. Here the poet seems to see as little a difference as does the Bible, for
which what one calls today other-worldly and what one calls today worldly also
hopelessly merges. Our concepts of That Side and This Side are Platonic; they
are much too static; they make out of this and that world two essences existing
side by side, whose chief difference to all practical purposes is that we believe
in this world and not in that one. In the sense of that unfruitful differentiation,
the other world, promised by God and hoped for by man, is other-worldly as
well as worldly: other-worldly, totally other-worldly compared to this world of
today; worldly, totally other-worldly for us who await it ...
But on this ground that final freedom has been able to grow up which, in the
exuberance of God's love, already felt in the world of now, scorns the bliss of

the future one, something *toto coelo* – really by a whole heaven – other than the arrogant Stoic scorn of the Kantians for reward, for here the loving one believes and knows that "an hour of bliss of the world to come is more than the whole of life in this world" [Pirke Avot, 4:22] and yet prefers the one hour of active nearness to God in this world to the whole life of the future world, from the utmost overflow of love, for which no future can any longer displace the entirely fulfilling present.

The little poem of six lines in the Soul section, "Welt," admonishes against over-worldliness. And Rosenzweig comments:

With few words the little poem says the same as many another does with many. The word in which it captivates the object of its denial and which I have translated with "world," actually means: time. The reason why the poet does not say, as does for example his great inspiration, Ghazali, "world," is a very noteworthy one. In the language of the Bible the word which is later used for "world" means "eternity." In later language of course "this" world and "that" world are differentiated, but "world" pure and simple can assume no pessimistic meaning; the word is too much filled with the meaning "eternity"; thus the word "time" must do, which contains no value judgment in the language of the Bible, neither positive nor negative. (211/124)

The note to "Gelobt," the poem that leads us into the Halevi book, states when Halevi is looking around at the world, that spatially the world is not sufficiently capacious to hold eternity, that is, all of God's greatness.[6] Temporally, however, eternity is experienced and comprehended, but only in events, in one experience and in another, in time whenever eternity breaks in. The whole of eternity can be neither seen nor known in one sweeping look; nor can it be expressed, even philosophically, in any one system; but when experienced in time, eternity can be recognized by the human being who experiences it.

The always-thereness (*Dasein*) of God, his ever-addressability, is nonetheless vividly depicted through the night-vision of the poem "Nachts" ("During the Night" 173/28–9). This poem, of only ten lines, also displays the acrostic JHUDA. The vision of God deflects Jehuda Halevi's world-weariness, that is weariness of temporality alone. In the experience of that world in the night-vision, God is wholly present: eternity is wholly present. Inasmuch as the experience is also event, as event it moves into the past. The human heart now, however, can move forward in time, strengthened with the enduring presence of the experience. Any experience of eternity must necessarily remain, eternally.

The one "definition," the one model of the Incomparable One ("Keiner sonst!" ["None Other!"] 178/39), is simply God's flowering of love. This one model is a model which requires time even from the point of view of God in his relationship with human beings, but at the same time each flowering is a manifestation of eternity. Each flowering in the course of time represents, or, more accurately, presents, an instance of eternity. Thus love is equated with eternity. But a present coupled with eternity never recedes wholly into the past. Even though God acts also in the world in the aspects of past, present, and future, he never acts outside his eternal essence. All this correlates with the notion of the one language. "The great German scholar Lagarde,[7] whose bitterness was possibly still greater than his scholarship – and that says something – once said that for the Jews monotheism meant: of God there is only one model. What the truth of this is, that is, seen from the inside, if one does not already know it, is seen in this poem, which belongs to those that revolve around David's morning prayer" (178/39).[8]

This sense of God's acts being at once temporal and eternal is described in Rosenzweig's analysis of Balaam's visit to the courtiers of Balak.[9] Upon God's command, Balaam refused to go with Balak's first emissary. With the arrival of the second emissary, however, Balaam, still desirous of cursing Israel, again asks God; this second time God orders him to go. Rosenzweig asks, then, why it is that "God's wrath was inflamed that he thus went?" when God had just now, on second thought as it were, ordered him to go. Rosenzweig concludes: Balaam did not take God's once-spoken word as spoken for all time. Rosenzweig claims that the maxim "once doesn't count" does not apply to God. God's "once" is for all time. God's speech in arresting the moment stands for eternal significance. Balaam wanted to try again, "to start out again," to see if "this time" God's word 'newly starting' would suit his own desire to go." Rosenzweig writes, "If we are not satisfied with God's unequivocal first word, but, attempt what God, starting out again, speaks to us, then God without fail this time speaks the demon's words in our own breast."[10] This is an example of God's unchangeability, dependability, and fidelity through the changing tenses of past, present, and future. God's word is carried forward in the heart in the secure knowledge that what God speaks once means that he has spoken that particular speech for all time. God's word is for these reasons wholly trusted. He is not going to change his mind when he is commanding something.

In human-divine *conversations*, turns can occur: this is the point of conversation, a word which has the same root as conversion. Turns even in conversation, however, do not mean that that which is turned *from* does not remain a fact. The human parallel to this notion of any act's having durability and having no possibility of being annulled by a counteraction is found in the Note to "Menschenschwäche" ("Human

Frailty" 202–3/103–4). This note will be quoted again and discussed in the context of human free will in chapter 5. Here, this portion of the note points to an idea of the parellel: "The criminal judge may try to define how much intention and how much diminished responsibility is involved in an act. But wherever the act is not subsequently analysed, but operates in its present totality, this apparently meaningful difference becomes meaningless. Thus first of all for the violated world order, which demands restitution through a healing counteraction – a counteraction which always must retain something symbolic because indeed there are only immediate acts and no 'counteracts'" (202–3/103–4).

Later, in the People section, Rosenzweig's briefest note of all, to "Der Jude" ("The Jew" 231/178), has a similar idea of permanence in history: "An echo of the prophetic polemic. The eternity of the people expresses itself also this way: that nothing which was once actual loses its actuality. The eternal people make eternal even their adversaries."

The world is incapable of holding eternity in dimensions of space, and yet because the model of the One God is "the flowering forth of love," eternity is known by, appears to happen in, and *does* grow in, the dimensions of time. This is so both from the human point of view and from God the revealor who, for self-revelation, can and does give himself temporality.

The temporal and eternal worlds meet not only at death but also in life: in the "being-eternal-in-the-moment." The "being-eternal-in-the-moment" affords equal value to the sensual and the spiritual worlds, and human expression of divinely commanded love is to be both sensual and suprasensual. In the aspect of eternity, Rosenzweig agrees with the tradition that holds that this world and that world are the same, and destined to come together again in eternity. The soul is always leading up to the unmediated address. Belief in eternity as the ultimate reality is dependent on the belief in the beginning and end of time. This is shown in the note to the poem in the Zion section, "Antwort" ("Answer" 244–5/219–20), which explicitly stands in contradistinction to Greek-derived philosophy of beginningless and endless eternity. We do not have the letter to which Jehuda Halevi is replying, but someone has written to dissuade him from his resolve to get to Jerusalem. The reply "in every instance shows how immense his resolve would have appeared at that time" (244/219). The argument to which Halevi is replying is one which has remained, and thus the author "appears to us as if he *is known*, as if we could point him out by name, not in one but in a hundred shapes. Even the assimilated Jew belongs to the eternal metaphorical expressions of Judaism" (244/219) The argument is, "should one say: shockingly?" as it was then.

"Jerusalem no longer concerns us today, because, just as when David conquered it, it is again inhabited by the 'blind and lame' (2 Samuel 5:6, 8),[11] by foreign nations. And this unhistorical-historical argument unites itself then as now with the unphilosophical-philosophical (only the unpolitical-political is missing, but that would be inappropriate in the case of a single individual). And the philosophy that must be upheld in order to give relief to the national forgetfulness, then as now, is derived from the Greeks, who know only of beginningless and endless eternity, not of a one Eternal, who establishes beginning and end" (244/219). The note concludes with sentences powerfully reflecting Rosenzweig's view of verification by history: Jehuda Halevi knows that his argument in reply is "on the mainstreets, compared to which all the decisive turns and protests of the word of the other are only tortuous side-paths. The words of the one have been forgotten; the answer has endured."[12]

Besides these basic features of speech-thinking, there are three that are less evident because, as application of the *Star*'s system, they pervade the whole of the Notes, but are not displayed as specifically explicated principles. These have to do with, first, the language of the Bible, which of course will indeed be at once recognizable by those who are familiar with the biblical discourse; second, the root-sentence, which, too, may be recognizable by those who have immersed themselves in the *Star*; and, third, the eruptive characteristic of the speech-thinking method of enquiry into truths, as opposed to truth enquiries that want to arrive there by predictable gradations of logical steps.

Biblical Language

As does Rosenzweig for the *Star*, so Jehuda Halevi in the poems relies upon and draws from the Bible for his underlying, initiating speech-text. Both Rosenzweig and Halevi are always responding to biblical texts. Neither sees the Bible as a prooftext but as a dialogical partner for life. The Bible for them reads or is heard as a text which informs and enlightens life lived in the present. This informing, as discussed, comes from the direction of the experience of the present, and not from the past's being imposed on the present. A person or nation or community understands present experience through a correlative biblical poem, story, commandment, prophecy, word of wisdom.[13]

But Jehuda Halevi depends on the Bible to the extent that he adheres to its written, fixed language. At the same time without, remarkably, veering at all from the biblical grammatical forms, he explores their full possibilities for oral speech. In his note to one of the three suppressed digressing poems, "Exkurs: Ein Sprachkunststück" ("Excursus: An Artistic Play on Words," 225–7/165–7), Rosenzweig writes that medieval Spanish poetry "allows itself what is real in language, only what is – authenticated in Scripture ... The 'Scripture' ['*Schrift*'], not the 'spoken language' ['*Sprache*'], is the norm here ... He who, like the Spaniards, is resolved on the respectful persistence holding out on the inside of the borders will plough through the bounded sphere which he calls his own, until no speck of unfruitful ground is left ... Thus the vocabulary of the Scriptures grows wider and for the first time is expanded before the observing eye."

Jehuda Halevi pioneers and fertilizes the medieval Hebrew germ of the one language in expressing that the Bible says the same thing in different ways. That he is speaking in tune with the biblical word has been verified by liturgical use. In the same Note to this digressive poem, Rosenzweig asserts that one does well to emulate the "leadership of this master which newly arranges the precious treasures in the museum of the Bible in an enduring way, now this, now that gem is drawn near into the right light and thus the whole is saved from a museum-like torpor" (227/167).

I cannot substantiate my conjecture here, but I suspect that Rosenzweig, who was profoundly influenced by his close work with Jehuda Halevi, had the following idea in mind: I think that, subsequent to the first publication of the *Star*, he decided to show more explicitly to his (assimilated) reader that he was aiming to present the biblical word as freshly spoken. I derive this from what Nahum Glatzer discloses in his Introduction to the *Star*, namely that Rosenzweig "himself abandoned his original position of considering the *Star* strictly as a *textus* when, shortly before his death, he asked me to prepare an extensive list of references to his Judaic sources to be included in the second edition of the work."[14] The *Star*, to be sure, invigorates the biblical speech by the fresh application Rosenzweig brings to it.

According to Rosenzweig, the distinctive quality of the Bible that marks its difference from all other books lies in its dialogical element. Rosenzweig posits that the dialogical element characterizes the entire Bible, but is demonstrated especially as the principle of the form of Bible storytelling, which Rosenzweig claims was discovered by Buber. This principle,

Which stretches the narration onto a trestle of question and answer, dictum and contradiction, sentence and addition, is evidenced in the Bible not only for the epic but also for the other great genres of style of the Bible, that is for the psalmic lyric, the prophetic rhetoric, indeed even for the legal casuistic. Of course its significance here is less. Chastising and promise, praise, prayer and thanks, law and proverb are much less in danger than the narrative of becom-

ing, as works of art, objects of "pure enjoyment" and thereby of losing their so-
lemnity, their connection with reality. The writtenness places itself upon them
only like a light gown; at the moment when the Psalms are prayed, the laws observed, the Prophets believed, they at once lose their monologic muteness,
they get a voice and call the eternal partner to a dialogue: the listening human
beings, the yielding God.[15]

It is the dialogue that renders the Bible present; hence it is the human
person in the existential moment who must bring the Bible's speech
into a present engagement and not the other way around. Speaking always takes place only in the present. The Bible story does *not* want to
transfer the listener out of his or her present: it wants the past to be
poured forth into his or her present.

Several passages in the Afterword also testify to the importance of
the scriptural word. There is a connection between exilic times and
Scripture. Rosenzweig's assessment of this connection characteristically reveals a way of interpreting both exile and the role of Scripture
which reverses a common view. Exile would no longer be exile if those
experiencing it felt at home wherever they reside in the world. In this
sense, the ones who experience exile must actually put their surrounding world into exile, make their own exile a kind of home, and be
proud of it. Scripture offers to the one who is in exile a home-in-exile,
not by imposing its word onto the present, but by being present to the
experience of exile. The experience renders the Bible meaningful, not
the reverse.

All Jewish poetry in exile scorns to ignore this being-in-exile. It would have ignored its exile if it ever, like other poetry, took in the world directly. For the
world which surrounds it is exile, and is supposed to remain so to it. And the
moment that it would surrender this attitude, when it would open itself to the
inflow of this world, this world would be as a home for it, and it would cease to
be exile. This exiling of the surrounding world is achieved through the constant presence of the scriptural word. With the scriptural word another present
thrusts itself in front of the surrounding present and downgrades the latter to
an appearance, or more precisely, as parable. Thus it is not that the scriptural
word is drawn out as parables for illustrations of present life, but exactly reversed, that events serve as illucidation of the scriptural word and become the
parable for this scriptural word. Thus the relationship is exactly the opposite to
what we imagine with the expression *Musivstil.*[16]

Quotations from the Bible are frequent and potently placed
throughout the Halevi poetry. In translating the poems, Rosenzweig
considers the question of translating the biblical quotations. First, a

quotation in Halevi "is by no means an adorning pendant, rather it is the label for the envelope of his speech."[17] Second, what were readily recognizable verses to Halevi's contemporary audience are not to Rosenzweig's. To Rosenzweig, the problem cannot be fully solved. While his solution is confined to his own time and place in a specific community, and would not be suitable for all times and places, it nevertheless, I think, pertains or is pertinent still today.[18] Rosenzweig decided that the question of translating the quotations is not helped by imparting in the commentaries the medieval reader's knowledge of the Bible:

For the Hebrew reader the bond with the scriptural word is no additional matter, but rather is a succession accompanying the reading of immediate connections of currents which precisely in their continuous sequence effect the fluorescing of what is being read ... The succession of the individual connections of currents can not be as fast as in Hebrew, simply because the scope for quoting the German Bible is less than for the Hebrew. But still, here there is also a certain scope for quoting – thanks to the Lutheran Bible, thanks to a few of the church-songs drawn from biblical passages and thanks as well to the fact that some biblical content is still known to people today. And because biblical quotation is less common in German, it is by comparison all the more powerful that even in sparser frequency it manifests a certain fluorescing. Thus the translator has the task of working out every Bible quotation of the text, which he wants to bring to awareness really as such, and possibly to substitute a quotation that is foreign to a contemporary with one more familiar to him. ... Incidentally, it helps today's reader that precisely the Books of the Bible still best known to the educated person today, like the Psalms, Isaiah, the Song of Songs, are the same ones that most often come to the lips of the Hebrew poet.[19]

Rosenzweig faced another challenge in translating the poetry. Halevi was so thoroughly acquainted with the Bible that he knew precisely which words to bring forward in their proper place and frequency. A word in the Bible used rarely, or only once, appears equally sparingly – and thus strikingly so – in the poems. Rosenzweig thinks he can meet this challenge, and transmits it to his own readers:

Jehuda Halevi particularly has the reputation of an effortless charm and special polish. People obviously think since they are pretty much without exception dependent on a dictionary, that Jehuda Halevi would have been as well. But he was more capable in Hebrew, not merely more than I, but even – let this be said in all modesty seemly to the author – than my critics. He was an intimate servant in the whole vast house of the Holy Language. And he had a feeling for whether a word belongs to the daily tableware of the language, or whether it was kept inm a locked cupboard only for special occasions. That for him the two keys turn equally easily in his hand testifies to his faithful diligence as a steward, which did not let even the less often used lock to rust, says nothing, however, about the difference of the chinaware, for which both keys open the latch.

... Even at the risk that readers whose knowledge of development of the German language has advanced only to the point of the Song of Songs, or for whome the discovery of the *Westöstliche Divan* and Hölderlin's hymns, to say nothing of more recent writings, still lies ahead, might find [my] German incomprehensible.

The Root-Sentence

The root-sentence of the one language which can branch outward into the world resides as both the centre and core of each langugae. For Rosenzweig the Bible is revelation, and the focal book is the Song of Songs. Because it is revelation, the Bible, like all books, will no longer be needed. The entire Bible, from narrative to prophets to wisdom, is intended to be primarily dialogical between the human being and God, and this dialogue is to occur again and again in interhuman forms, in love, in teaching, in knowledge.[21] Revelation is all audible, all word. Since for Rosenzweig God speaks to the human heart, revelation is new to and renewed in every human being who is born into this world and who attends to his or her own heart. When each of us speaks out responsively to what we hear, revelation has orally become special and specific to him in his own present. Most important, each person can therefore respond, not only to historical revelation meant for and spoken to all, but to revelation spoken to that person in particular.

Only *because* God speaks in this way to each particular human being does he speak revelation to all. Revelation is both universal law and particular command.[22] God loves and commands each human and thereby brings about direct speech, word, and response. "The obedience to the commandment [to love] cannot remain mute. It too must become audible, it too become word. For in the world of revelation everything becomes word, and what cannot become word is either prior or posterior to this world."[23]

Revelation does not merely result, for instance, as Kierkegaard would say, in God's awakening the human to full unselfish love. Nor does Rosenzweig claim, as Buber would, that revelation can occur as an effect of inter-human love: namely, that the human awakens to loving God as a result of speaking inter-humanly and of being-there for another. Rather, Rosenzweig's view is that because God speaks into each human's present time, each human's present comes to be understood to be as important as others' present times. This is in part what Rosenzweig means by saying that taking time seriously and taking a person seriously are the same thing. He also means that each of us, in personal revelation, is receiving differently *because* our particular times in life are *always* different, whether a century apart or on the same day.[24]

God reveals in his commandment to love. I believe that he says, "Your neighbour is like you, namely present to me like you. I speak to your neighbour, and your neighbour also converses with me. Be aware of me when you speak to one another: you each of you have a relationship with me." The self is neither suppressed nor forgotten: rather, a sense of humility arises in the human because he now has a perspective and respective view of the other, rather than an objective view of either his own self or of another self. Moreover, just as God awakens the self to become soul in revelation, so one human loving another enfolds soul into the world spirit's growth. "Where the dual has once applied, where someone or something has become neighbour to a soul, there a piece of the world has become something which it was not previously: soul."[25]

God commands that what is revealed both universally and particularly is to become audible in the world. The root-sentence for revelation, and of the One Language, is "He is good," he is "the roof over the house of language. It is the sentence true in itself ... All other linguistic formations must be capable of connection with this sentence ... The root-word of revelation opens a dialogue."[26] This root sentence asserts *that* He is good. Singing in unison, communally, the root-sentence for redemption is expressed in the phrase: "*For* he is good." All that Jehuda Halevi's poems and Rosenzweig's response express is translatable by others' voices until the end of time, because all that they say is an expression of the root-sentence of revelation.

The whole of the poetry comprises meetings between God and Jehuda Halevi. While these meetings are specific to Jehuda Halevi, they nevertheless constitute the themes of human-divine discourse that always repeat themselves, especially in the liturgical calendar year, which is intended to repeat specific meetings year after year. Jehuda Halevi composed with an intent beyond perfection of an artform.

The purpose, however, is in this case a performance by the cantor and the singing along of the congregation at set points of the liturgical year. The flow of the words known to all and of old has to be, uninterrupted by them, dammed up into the lakes, that bring into view unaccustomed shorelines. In the recurrence they are the variable, but because in their variation they are necessarily forced into a certain similarity. That is not conspicuous as long as they stand in their natural relationship to application; the different poems indeed were then divided by a full, really a full year full of events of the life of the synagogue. Repetitions were not experienced as such, or, as far as they are experienced, it is entirely in order. For this recurrence in the year is after all the essence of the festival. As in the final analysis repetition is altogether the great and only form which man has for expressing what is entirely true for him.[27]

The words which follow this discussion of repetitive speech are important with regard to why renewed words, as Jehuda Halevi composed them, can freshly, penetratingly, again and again, with vital passion, speak "of humility and devotion, of despair of and trust in redemption, of world aversion and longing for God, of repentance of sins and faith in mercy." In re-encountering these poems "one does not thereby remove the fact from the world that the heart of the poet and the hearts of those for whom he has composed are full of these feelings and wish to see only a few, at base always only one. That it does not become tired of saying anew this always One again and again testifies to its enduring power. In the mouth of the lover the word of love never becomes old, the word which from the mouth that shams love already withers when it is spoken for the first time."[28] These themes are always fresh, always present and alive on the lips of the one who expresses them: together these themes form the truth of the divine-human relationship. The truth of the divine-human relationship is always renewable through conversation.

The Eruptive Feature

The third feature which is inherent as a principle in the method, but is not readily apparent in the Notes as a whole piece of writing is the deliberateness with which speech-thinking perceives suddenness of turns in life. This feature is akin in important ways to (but not wholly like) Hamann's, Nietzsche's, Walter Benjamin's and others' insight that philosophizing needs to be done in aphoristic citation, form, and style, as a speaking to and a reflection of reality. Moreover, this feature in the new thinking perhaps best shows its move from the traditional drive toward system and reduction. Speech-thinking shuns the hypostatizations of logic and the conclusions of logic that want to be timeless. On the other hand, the method shuns equally notions of steady gradation or process. This is one reason why even the *Star*, written as "philosophical system," is difficult to read. There stands a gate at the end, not a conclusion saying: "There, and that is how things are." Rosenzweig philosophizes in the Halevi book out of the unpredictably episodic story of the (most of the time) steadfastly faithful and sometimes falteringly faithful Jehuda Halevi.

Jehuda Halevi opens his story with breathless, joyous, awe-filled lines as he praises God for his greatness and, as God's creature, asks for help. When God answers his call, Jehuda Halevi falls down, overcome first by the fact of the answer and then by the power of the heights. He sees that there is not enough room in the world for the eternity that redemption will bring. But he raises his eyes in a happy awareness of dependence and he trembles at the mystery of divine action upon him.

But so ardent does Jehuda Halevi's yearning for heaven become that he wishes for eternal sleep in order to see God, and to be with him unendingly. God gives Jehuda Halevi the gift of a dream, a night-vision of the divine glory.[29] Now, strengthened in his heart, he bows down to the source, the giver of the vision. In recognition of and in thanks to God, Halevi leads the poem "All meine Glieder" ("All my Limbs" 176–7/33–5), "after a powerful messianically convoked crescendo, from the familiar 'every mouth,' 'every tongue,' 'every knee,' 'every heart,' into the word of the Psalm, 'as it is written' (Psalm 35:10), and in it for a moment into the individual praying person: 'All my limbs must say: "Lord, who is like unto You?" ' " (176–7/34). The concluding paragraph of the note shows the turn of speech, almost the bursting out of speech, from the individual point of view, that is, from the individual's feelings and thoughts toward the other to whom and for whom these words are, literally, expressed. It also shows how the "I" is audible in the communal "we": "Jehuda Halevi's hymn deepens into this moment where the We, the "Breath of all things living" ... sinks into the I. "My limbs," "my songs," "my spirit," "my polumage," "my driving force," "my heart" – always again "my": it is man, the individual man before God. He is not looking inwards, he is extending himself outwards; he only says My in order to place that which is his again and again at God's feet. He says I, but only to forget himself. Again and again his words begin with My and end again and again with: to You" (177/35).

In the midst of his praise, Halevi ponders, with some urgency, What is the human being beside the incomparable? For this "leaf that withers ... knowledge of the Creator has its zenith in not asking questions" (note to "Der Unvergleichliche" ["The Incomparable One"] 177/37). Who is this leaf that withers other than the one who "finds divine support for his life in the commitment to human duty" and "for whom the bliss of freedom awakens only out of the mystery which he remains to himself" and "who can realize his own particular will only through subordinating to His" (177/37). He must know only how to perceive God's uniqueness as His unceasing outflowing of love. "For the uniqueness of God is the exclusiveness of love. Of God there is only One Model" ("Keiner Sonst!" ["None Other!"] 178/39).

How does a human being not only bear but return such love? The enormous difficulty in loving the infinite God from the heart of a finite form is complicated by this: "The refuge for the most ardently desired thing is under the eternal arms, but the eternal countenance no one sees and remains alive … The solution of this predicament and conflict lies, however, as the solution of all predicaments and conflicts, with the lover, with his strength for the For All That, who endures the For-All-That, and who For-All-That permits Himself to be endured. Here then it is the human's prerogative and his strength to demand that God – love him in return" (Note to "Die Liebenden" ["The Lovers"] 178–9/40–1).

There is also a liturgical time for this demand that God give his love in return for human love. The middle hours of Yom Kippur, the holy day which ends in the closest permissible nearness between God and a Jew, involve a distance between God and the individual person when the human confesses his or her sins before his Lord. But the human audaciously *demands* forgiveness, because God has *promised* his love, to be there always.[30]

In his response in his life to the command to love God Jehuda Halevi retains both the suprasensual and the sensual: "May my life and blood be a glory for you, as long as I still have breath in my throat." He opens "Dein Gott" ("Your God" [35–7/56–7]) with exclamatory imperatives:

Still slumbering? Hasn't your rest been sufficient?
Renounce the fool's derisions!
Look upon heaven's steps of the spheres,
Move towards the arch-eternal rock's service!
Thus moves the fleet of stars.
But enough, not more rest?
Up! call to your God!

Later, he has:

rise up at midnight,
to tread upon the footprints of the great ones,
who, the splendour of the Psalms on their tongues,
with reflection, reflective constantly,
spent their day fasting,
their night with praying,

God a shaft in their heart,
they are planets around the throne –
Climb up your way, up, with might,
to Him, to your God.

All this compelling, commanding tone gives the impression of the human effect on God, and on the human effectiveness for drawing positive changes in life. The theme of the inadequacy of the human being again occurs in the penultimate of the six stanzas, this time in comparison with the beast, and again offers a key to human powers in the possibilities of approaching God:

Man's particular good distinguished from
the beast: such a small nothing.
Only: his gazing radiated around the shelter
– the heart's vision! not the eye's illusion –
…
But thus, flesh and blood,
you approach your God.

And finally, in the sixth stanza, comes this command:

You, endure His final judgment
and live! Leave the blustering
Which is intent on 'When?' and 'Where?',
'What is below?' and 'What is above?' –
No, rather you be wholly and simply
with Him, with your God.

It is God who takes care that your foot does not stumble, that your arm does not grow weak.

The imperative mood runs through the poems of this section: Seek peace, pursue God. ("Sein Friede" ["His Peace"] 38/59). Don't you know he is the "Lord of Peace" and "The one who makes peace?" He is the God of all, Lord over all other gods. The refrain for "Das All" ("The Universe" 39–42/60–4) rings:

God only He
in the divine halls!
He the Lord
of Lords all![31]

And he is the same God, whether far or near, because he has a name and can be called upon. Don't you see, Halevi urges, this world is created to be like *that* world, to reflect it in its praising of God and in its outflowing flowering of love?

Jehuda Halevi addresses God, and demands of Him, "Tell Your servant, here I am," in reference to the well-known utterances of Adam, Abraham, Moses, and others who say, at once or eventually, "Here I am" הינני in their respective words, attitudes, and times. This demand is not so much a reversal of God's demand that the human being say Hineni הינני but a demand for reciprocity. This idea, this demand, opens the Soul section. When God answers, "Here I am," the exiled soul suddenly blooms. When God says, "You are my slaves alone," the soul yearns for the near God, the God of the heart, where he has set up a dwelling. The note to "Knechte" ("Slaves" 211/123) is brief to match the four-line poem and refers to Leviticus 25:42 and 55, where the Torah has, "They are my slaves," meaning those slaves who are freed in the fiftieth year. Rosenzweig holds that from this source "a good part, the best part, of all subsequent world history has flowed," and that the poet here has "filled also the cup of this epigram, which begins quite epigrammatically as a tightly argued summary of all the disseminated moral wisdom which ever was to be known, and ends quite lyrically, with the Book of Lamentations' cry of longing (3:24) for the God of the heart."

The Sabbath, for all the soul's adventures during the workdays, brings, every seventh day, the day of the soul, when she feels peace, is at peace, at home. In her origins and in her ultimacy, the soul is a stranger in this world. She yearns to return to her pristine state at birth, to her place of birth.

Jehuda Halevi repeats in one poem in the Soul section the biblical assertion that the Jewish people will live until the end of the world. Therefore hope can always be alive. Hope is always youthful and rejuvenating. Of God's Light (as considered in chapter 3 above) we discern the refractions, which shine out of individual souls. Each soul has her path that is particular to her alone. That path, for each soul, is meant to reflect, to blaze its own path, and warmly, passionately, to glow in each person's soul and to show in the soul's life's activities. Jehuda Halevi sees his own path, knowing that every rightly, individually followed path longs for and leads towards the final light of all: redemption.

Besides the Sabbath's peace, the pain of suffering on any right path can, both Halevi and Rosenzweig know, be alleviated – forgotten – because, and when, any human being, here the Jew, cries out to the responsive God with demanding accusations. But the Sabbath holds its own divine commands imposed on the human being. That day is set apart for the time when one is commanded to forget suffering, to re-

member to be joyful. The Jew who attains this peaceful bliss finds it difficult to re-enter day-to-day life from this separated holy time of the
Sabbath. The close of the day is intense with praying for Elijah the harbinger of redemption. And then, knowing that the final rest is promised, the weekdays are entered into once again with a refreshed soul.

Jehuda Halevi perceives the miracle of his life as the experiencing of
God's love. And the love and faithfulness are mutual: God, too, prays,
saying, "And who is like my people Israel?" And in a conversation between suffering Israel and God, Israel is consoled: "Love is strong as
death."

In the poem at the head of the Zion section, "Auf" ("Awake" 121/
201) Jehuda Halevi experiences another vision. It is unlike the one at
the beginning of the collection. Here he hears God say: "Up, awake, be
ready," and he dreams of an earthly future. He sees himself serving in
the Temple for the sacrifice. He awakes and finds, in all wakefulness,
that God is still with him. For this he thanks God and utters a prayer
for the reinstitution of sacrifice in a dramatized dialogue between a
traveller and the curtains of Solomon. This traveller remembers the
distant past, and reminisces to the deeply listening Jehuda about those
early days. In the remembering, his desire for these days to return, in
the at-any-moment future, at the moment of redemption, becomes fervent. (From here until the conclusion of this chapter, the story will be
told without nearly as many specific, interruptive, references to the
specific poems and the notes. Much from both the poems and the
notes will for different reasons be cited in the final chapter.

Jehuda Halevi, now about to become a traveller himself, feels split,
torn between East (Zion) and West (Spain). Someone tries to dissuade
him from going on his pilgrimage,[32] arguing from the then "modern,"
newly studied and understood Greek philosophical standpoints, but Jehuda Halevi refutes him by insisting that the divine promise endures
and that the land is holy, as it was for the patriarchs. No Jewish contemporaries were embarking on a journey such as Jehuda Halevi pro-
posed.

Resolved as he is, he is nevertheless pained at parting – from the
children he will kiss no more, his friends, the garden he had planted
and watered – but he believes that God is with him, that this is his right
path, and he asks himself why, then, he should be anxious and fearful.
He avows that because he has been given life, he will bring praise to
God's name, and thanks for ever and ever. His imagination sends him
forward onto the sea waters, aware of their horrors; and he projects his
pain, thinking of the ones whom he will most miss: his daughter and
his young grandson, also called Jehuda. Indeed, he might not have
gone through with his plan, but God suddenly gives him a sense of

compulsion. He now departs with gladness, praying en route that the
end will *not* actually arrive before he reaches his destination.

A storm arises. God anwers the poet's request that it might be stilled.
And Jehuda Halevi describes the great stillness of the sea at night. He
glorifies the waves and the west wind for carrying the ship forward –
and the creator of the waves and the wind.

But an east wind drives the ship to harbour in Egypt. Jehuda Halevi
dwells for awhile on that land that is laden with the meaning of Jewish
history. He assures himself that his sojourn is for this reason worship-
ful. His friends beg him to stay even longer, but the Nile River reopens
Jehuda Halevi's yearning – and his compulsion is renewed.

In closing, Jehuda Halevi composes a long poem to Zion: yearning
for Jerusalem, and then, with sure knowledge of the final crowning day
of redemption, he accompanies his yearning with rejoicing.

The eruptions of passion, of feeling, of resolution are all based on
meetings and conversation. They resist being framed into systematic
thought. Crescendos, not of logic but of events, build up in time so
that the poetry makes sense only as a story. J.G. Hamann, whom Rosenzweig admired and who also believed language to be sacred, wrote
against the idea that rational religion consists of universal intelligible
truths, saying: "I know of no eternal truths save those which are unceasingly temporal,"[33] and, "System is in itself a hindrance to truth."[34]

I have traced the story the poetry presents in order to show how the
philosophy of speech-thinking views life as an eventful, episodic path,
and how a philosophical method can be tied directly to events and actions in life and, indeed, springs from life. In the note to "Seele im
Exil" ("Soul in Exile," 197–8/94–5), Rosenzweig highlights and affirms the reality of the soul's broad and deep capacity for suddenness
of change in her life, which is "incomprehensible through logic, but
absolutely authentic."

On one level Rosenzweig intends the poetry to be read as story. On
another level, still in keeping with the story form, he means his responses to be read as so many smaller conversations within the whole,
event by event. In his Afterword he asks:

How could I prevent the reader of this collection of translations from behaving
as a reader, in other words, how could I bring him to consume the poems not
like cherries but like peaches, that is not to begin the next one when he still
has hardly finished the previous one, but instead each neatly one by one and
and with deliberation and with the idea: Perhaps there will not be one like this
so soon.

The Notes are supposed to serve this purpose. Of course, not this alone. They
should accomplish besides the usual purpose of notes, to impart, while keep-

ing to civilized manners, that is, more in passing and as if he already knew it all, the things useful for the understanding of the poem, which he surely does not know. But the main purpose is the other: to induce the reader to take each poem as a thing for itself, just as the poet has composed it as a thing for itself and just as the singer and the hearer, in that place for which it is meant, sang and heard it, sings and hears it, will sing and hear it. Thus, to change the reader from a reader and consumer into a guest and friend of the poem.[35]

The invitation to be a guest and friend indicates another level of speech: the reactions and participation of those invited. Each of the levels – the story as a whole, the story in its parts, and the reader's response – is episodic in nature, and is not a mere component within a gradual, predictable process.

SCHOLARLY ATTENTION TO THE NOTE ON MIRACLES

The scant number of guests and friends, as well as the neglect of scholarly attention to the Notes to the Halevi poetry, leaves these reflective essays as still new territory to explore in Rosenzweig's thought. Rosenzweig's statement that the Notes offer an example of the practical application of speech-thinking can result in much more reading, study, and comment than I am carrying out here. The latest compendium of Rosenzweig scholarship, published in 1988,[36] scarcely glances in the Notes' direction. But with Alan Udoff, we have a treatment of Heidegger's and Rosenzweig's re-origination of texts.[37] Udoff attends to the note to "Heilig" ("Holy" 193–4/82–3).[38] He discusses genre and develops instructive, interesting, and inventively sensitive definitions which cover an important, indeed core, feature of the speech-thinking genre. He refers only to this note, as for his purposes, he need refer to none other. He therefore provides a model of how even only one note is filled with material for substantial further reflection and commentary.

Udoff develops an illuminative term, "originative thinking." By this he means the way in which thought is both a return to origin and a laying bare of its presence. Through such a term he creatively captures the aspect in speech-thinking which distinguishes it from mere communication, or general conversation, by stressing the *event* of two who meet within the space of a text: "Meeting within ... the space of originative thinking."[39] Udoff turns to the note which addresses belief in miracles, particularly, it would seem, because of the sentence: "Thus the miracle becomes the germ-cell of holiness which is alive so long as it retains connection with this its origin, so long as it continues to be miraculous." This means to Udoff that the presentness of the miracle is laid bare, as opposed to the "natural" explanation given after the fact, the sort of explanation even the Bible provides for the parting of the Red Sea. This presence, Udoff contends, brings it about that "a virtual world of borders defining seemingly endless domains of dwelling and discourse face us."[40] Udoff designates this genre not the genre of margins, but the genre *as* margin.[41]

This analysis corresponds to the supporting source from Rosenzweig, which Udoff presents with regard to the borders of the Torah. First, we do not know Torah's borders. Nor do we know how far the tent-pegs of Torah can be moved outward. Nor even do we know which of our deeds is sure to move them outward. Second, we can be sure that the tent-pegs are moved outward through – at least in part – our own human means and efforts. But third, we must be careful when our deeds draw borders around us and take from our deed its most noble sphere: that we need only to be sons and daughters in order to be builders.[42]

What Udoff, of course, does not highlight, because it is not explicitly within the bounds of this particular note, is Rosenzweig's idea of expanding borders, something discussed above in connection with the one language and the divine commandment of love of neighbour: that the expansion is commanded to continue, and each time an expansion is sealed between two, it must be opened anew with new specific neighbours. Udoff does not get at the idea of singular actions that take place one at a time and events whereby the whole world becomes in-spirited. In designating the genre as margin, Udoff is adhering to a notion of alienation in speech. Yet rather than destroy the contention Rosenzweig so carefully constructed regarding permanence, Udoff actually strengthens the argument for in-spiritment. The permanences that result from love-meetings, such as a divinely wrought miracle provided for God's people would be, does indeed become a fenced-off area which can never again be disturbed: it will live forever. These are what I have termed closure meetings in the chapter 3. The state of alienation is a state not yet alive. Hence, in terms of the one language, the margins will remain, but at harmonious (peaceful) border crossings.

Udoff quotes Bakhtin: "The event of the life of the text, that is, its true essence, always develops *on the boundary between two consciousnesses, two subjects.*"[43] Rosenzweig would wholeheartedly agree with this, especially in conjunction with Udoff's remark that the path along which dialogical thinking leads is limited by a certain topic, a certain text – in this instance, creation.[44]

Rosenzweig's prime concern, and I think Udoff's, is not merely the "life of the text"; at most, life that grows within a text, or texts that are produced out of life and in life. "Play" is a frequent term in Udoff's essay, and he relies to a degree on Derrida. With speech-thinking's absolute trust in language, however, the method is ill-suited to deconstructionist categories and views. While deconstructionists do show an appreciation of the openness of texts, they are more concerned with the reactions and conversations that ensue among readers of a written work than with an actual conversation between writer and reader.

Rosenzweig's emphasis is indeed both upon the text and the speaking speaker. But from here on, and only because the this enquiry and Udoff's are asking different questions, we will have to part company. To Rosenzweig, Jehuda Halevi does not produce "text" but rather speaks. In speech-thinking, the text itself, as text disassociated from speech, as object in itself, does not apply. Text *and* audience are required, as *two* speaking subjects. No text, until heard, until translated, is a fact. Factuality of text occurs only when it is heard and responded to. Or as discussed in chapter 2, text for a speech-thinker comprises word and response. The context for speech-thinking is as broad and as long as the time between creation and redemption. In this breadth and length, "each has his particular share" in that "common property of all the children of men."[45]

Jehuda Halevi's and Rosenzweig's dependence on the Bible as multiply factualized text is not like dependence upon other kinds of texts. As far as speech-thinking is concerned, the Bible is not and never was a text like any other. Because the Bible is read or heard as dialogue, and because this dialogue is meaningful only if transported into the present, any classification of it as text collapses. As present, it is changeable, expandable, and still open and living. A text, as text in dialogue, has only a past tense in that the text, its speech, is a fact – a thing done. Because the Bible is revelation, it is also a fact being accomplished at every now and will be done away with only at the final future. The Bible is the supreme book because of its *always* dialogical element. That is not to claim, as Rosenzweig notes in "Das neue Denken," that other books may not also fall into this non-text category. Good texts with authentic speech always do. But this: No other book has been translated into as many languages as has the Bible. This is, to Rosenzweig, the historical proof of the growth of the one language.

The notion of being "limited by a certain text" does not hold for speech-thinking. The "certain text" represents the gift of speech itself: the possibility of individual utterances. This gift does not limit, but is intended to bring about, the opposite of limiting with regard to the

good: again, the gift of speech is a gift common to all, and in the translations and in the Notes, the one increasingly incapable of physical
speaking could still speak. If a primary goal of speech-thinking is to
lead to the One Language, this will take place in speaking and not in
texts. "Language ... constantly renews itself in living speech."[46]

A possible "fixed" text for speech-thinking might be in liturgical
prayer: speech in unison that glimpses and senses eternity by speaking
in key with the one language. Liturgy, unlike the Bible, however, is not
so fixed in immutable writing, but is fixed in a community. The community has the right to change its liturgical texts, and carefully does so
from time to time. Liturgy points strongly to the spokenness and cen-
tredness of speech. "To be able to pray: that is the greatest gift presented to the soul in revelation."[47] Every prayer is a variation of the
root-sentences of revelation (God is good) and of redemption (for
God is good). The prime thrust of Rosenzweig's remarks on miracle is
this: for Rosenzweig, it is not the miracle itself that is brought to the
present, but rather the *possibility* of praying for miracles, that is, the
possibility of speaking with God. Prayer renders the past miracle alive,
and even to live again, even in the present – both for the prayed-for
miracle in the past and for the possibility of praying for miracles now.
"The sole condition for its coming to pass is that one can pray for it,"
Rosenzweig writes in this note on miracles (194/83).

Thus, if any "text" is to be determined, that text is not creation, not
miracle, but rather a form of speaking itself. The transformative powers of speech are at their height in prayer, both for the human being
and, according to Rosenzweig, for God. To pray for miracles is to believe also that human beings have an effect on God. When God answers a prayer, any prayer, while the moment still remains with the flow
of temporality, that moment is raised "from the stream of moments"
(194/83). Udoff's analysis focuses on none of the transformative or
eternal aspects of speech of which Rosenzweig writes in the note.

Speech and languages do have borders, but they can be crossed.
Indeed, they must be crossed. This is the chief aim of translating, of
understanding another's speech or language: to cross wholly into what
is read (heard), cull from it any good which does not yet express itself
in one's own speech or language, and help it to grow in one's own language, *as* one's own language. Rosenzweig himself asserted that he
understood a poem only after translating it. Of the crossing of the border into "Im Heiligtum" ("In the Sanctuary" 240–2/206–8), he wrote
to Martin Buber: "I especially love this poem; for a whole week I
sniffed around it before I plunged into it."[48] How entirely borders can
be crossed is expressed in what Rosenzweig wrote about his Jehuda
Halevi book: "The book now lives in the centre of my life."[49] And Trud-

chen Oppenheim, with real insight, had written to Rosenzweig, with reference to the note to "Antwort": "You let Jehuda Halevi speak and you speak about him, but *you* speak; and you have glided over onto his track with your own more than you had done even in the *Star*."[50] Thus, the work that represents an example of Rosenzweig's philosophical method lives in the centre of his life. Rosenzweig agrees so wholeheartedly with Jehuda Halevi at times that he speaks with Halevi. There Something like an overlay of two consciousnesses even perhaps occurs, rather than an idea of boundary between consciousnesses.

If, then, the "text" lives on the edges of speech, the true essence in the speech itself is found in its content and form. Borders, however, are neither broken down nor made fuzzy by speaking participants. Each has his or her say: but the life is in the speaking, the rendering oral what is said or written. There is a direction between the borders of speech that arises from the receptivity and the addressability of speakers. Udoff sensitively states that "performative reading" brings messages into "a space of actualized encounter," and "the text *as other* becomes dialogically present," making "possible in life what is impossible in theory: genuine communication."[51] This, too, can conform to speech-thinking as genre, but we do have to be cautious with analogies to performances. A case in point is the enacted liturgical text, the performance which, unlike others, is meant to be real, meant to have only participators, "actors," and no spectators other than God. In his article on storytelling techniques, Rosenzweig conveys speech-thinking as something different from a performance sort of communication, which wants to make the hearer forgetful of his or her present and carry him into a different world of the past. In speech-thinking, an event of circumstance in a person's or a people's life draws out the meaningfulness of another person's or people's words. One of the reasons for Rosenzweig's criticism of the sermon is that it imposes something upon a present that was not there naturally. It is not performance but dialogue that captures the person in the present:

It is part of that book-destiny of the Bible that its portions that arise out of dialogue again and again call up the human partner of the dialogue. Again and again the Psalms evoke the praying ones, the Laws observers, the Prophecies believers. The biblical narrative cannot count on such a regeneration of its listeners, because it always was and remains a narrative of something long past. It must content itself with the listeners whom the Law, Prophecy and the Psalm again and again lead to it [the narrative] from their newly awakened active ones, hoping ones, loving ones. It cannot make these listeners into an audience that seizes the word from its lips. Thus it had to remain for them in an epic past and a graphic distance. But then it entraps the listeners distanced from it through time in the net of the hidden dialogue that is extended through it. It makes the distant listeners into participating speakers of a conversation, which under the cover of its epic past stretches itself in full, anecdotal present and which in word and reply, dictum and contradiction, statement and addition, gives to the ones aroused to deed, hope and love the one thing that they still lack. And it gives it to them so modestly that it does not dogmatically paralyse deed, hope, love; no, it airily inspires: Knowledge, Learning, Revelation.[52]

I suggest we need to take care when we include the element of theatricality in the speech-thinking genre, or use terms borrowed from Calvin O. Schrag, such as "personae" for speakers who wear "changeable masks" and designating liturgical forms as "theatricalizations."[53] Jehuda Halevi's poems can be per-formed by per-sonae. So if theatricalization or performance means a beautification through form and content, then, yes. And if "personae" means changing masks due to changing events and different people with whom we wish to speak authentically, and for this we require a variation of speech, then, yes.

The expression "the text *as other*" strikes an interesting note, not unlike counterpoint: while genuine communication certainly does not take place with a thing, a text, when emphatically designated as other, forces upon the idea of text the otherness which pertains between people. Rosenzweig does not read or respond to Jehuda Halevi as if he were a text, but as a person who is already in the course of a dialogue. It is significant that Rosenzweig suppressed "Exkurs: Ein Sprachkunststück" ("Excursus: An Artistic Play on Words" 225–7/165–7) *as* an excursus, because it is not personal speech but a "glittering show-piece," to which Rosenzweig responds only to point out some of the great linguistic achievements in medieval Hebrew poetry. One who does not believe, with Rosenzweig, "in the inseparability of spirit and language" would consider "the text as other person."[54] The poet himself, just as Gertrud Oppenheim notes regarding Rosenzweig himself, remains always a particular voice, even when composing for a people, as spokesperson. At no time does the poet permit the reader to forget the human urgency and vibrancy in the words spoken by a specific and real person. "I began to take care," Rosenzweig remarks in the Afterword, "that the translated poems liked to should as far as possible supply, in terms of content and form, a collective picture of the poet."[55] This is why Rosenzweig refrains from describing Jehuda Halevi the person in the Afterword: "A better, because direct, opportunity for this will be given in the Notes to the individual poems."[56]

SPEECH-THINKING AS PHILOSOPHICAL GENRE

Can there possibly be, within the genre as margin, an ongoing genre for philosophy that would engender the speech-thinking method? Publications of thinkers' correspondence would seem to serve as suitable forerunners. But as conscious speech-thinkers, future correspondents would need to focus upon specific topics, showing especially their mutual transformation through responding to each other, to each other's texts-as-others. Rosenstock-Huessey's *Judaism Despite Christianity* offers a glimpse of this sort of thing. So does the correspondence between Buber and Rosenzweig during the time when they were translating the Bible.

Another possibility is something along the lines Rosenzweig achieved through his Notes. Poetry of course is specially conducive to dialogical writing because each poem provides a whole speech in itself. Notes to Hölderlin, William Blake, Matthias Claudius, or any other great poet, for example, could also be remarkably compelling.

The speech-thinking genre is only at its very beginnings and still requires pioneers. Michael Oppenheim's book, *Mutual Upholding: Fashioning Jewish Philosophy through Letters*,[57] comprises letters to and responses from friends with whom he has discussed at length, and over the course of several years, subjects such as revelation, what it means to be a person, God as person, and the use of anthropomorphic metaphors for language pertaining to God. Together, these letters and replies provide us with a conscious, active speech-thinking book. Oppenheim has attempted, I would say remarkably successfully, to convey through letters that such a philosophical genre is valuable, practicable, and powerful. At any event, Oppenheim's book represents the first conscious practical application, since the Notes, of the philosophy-in-life which Rosenzweig theorized in the *Star*'s system.

Oppenheim – with some profound insights expressed with that courageous frankness and forcefulness which is permitted between friends – draws into his conversations two other real questions of special pertinence today, the questions of religious pluralism and of women's voices. Two letters are addressed to Christian scholars, one is to an orthodox rabbi, one to a reconstructionist rabbi, and two to a scholar and feminist who is married to the just-mentioned orthodox rabbi. Their shorter replies are all, like the longer letters written by Oppenheim, equally frank and critical. Some replies, however, display an awkwardness and a contrived manner in writing, perhaps due to the public forum suggested by the author for letters between friends, perhaps due to some inattention to the letters that are so well written to them.

It would seem in any case that the philosopher who wishes to uphold Rosenzweig's method would do well to look into the Notes and attempt his or her next philosophical endeavour in a form that suits a speech-thinking genre. To turn speech-thinking into an abstract discussion only of the method is counter-productive both to the *Star* and to the Notes. Such a discussion would be valuable only if considered as the translating phase.

Rosenzweig maintains that the so-called forum of dialogue among academicians still remains in the category of thought-thinking. This is primarily because the interchange is not live speech: not so much because it is in written form, but more because it is hurled into general space, to the general scholar. Yet, as was certainly the case for Rosenzweig in his reading of Jehuda Halevi, it may equally be the case that the individual scholar on occasion in reading finds himself to be "you" who is being unwittingly addressed by the "I" of the author. Certainly this was the case for Rosenzweig vis-à-vis Jehuda Halevi. In the main, however, although intellectual dialogue addresses an issue, it does not address person as person. Reactions to such dialogue are therefore again directed to the general forum, so that what might be construed as scholarly conversation is really what Rosenzweig calls a phantom, as discussed in chapter 2. Thus an abstraction grows around issues instead of a concrete relationship which might have a real effect upon the participants and out of which concrete effects upon events and issues in life might more readily ensue. In traditional scholarly debate, there most often emerges a pasting together of no truly interconnected conversations. Hence comparisons are a prevalent sort of scholarly endeavour. One demonstrates how this scholar refutes that, and heaps new fillers into the hole of refutation.

It could be noted again that Rosenzweig's refutation of Hegel was not of Hegel's system as such. The refutation was aimed rather against any continued perpetration of Hegelianism when Hegel had already conclusively marked the successful end of the Greek philosophical enterprise. Rosenzweig does not wish to raze past philosophy to ignominious extinction, but to affirm what has been accomplished. That accomplishment has reached completion. To prevent its certain decay, Rosenzweig carefully sods over philosophy's now forceless and impotent soil. He fertilizes it with theology's concept of revelation so that it might have new life and continued growth.

Furthermore, in a discussion of mere issues nothing much more than a game of wits is at stake. When associating words absolutely with the self, another real self is needed to whom to speak these words. This other self's response addresses both issue and person, and both are thereby further enlivened. As the conversation continues, and while each person's speech can be distinguished one from the other's, the happening of mutual transformation cannot be dissociated. The enterprise becomes dual, but not a dualization. The happening cannot be seen in terms of a comparison but in those of a story of interaction. Until Hegel, when logic was the prime tool and aim of philosophy, the interaction of philosophers as persons was not an issue. With Rosenzweig and his insistence upon three separate elements of reality, along with his insistence that truth is reached only by the spanning of the three elements, philosophy becomes relational, experiential, dialogical and never isolated or monological. Philosophy, done with the new thinking method, now comes to promote this bridging in its own philosophizing efforts.

CHAPTER FIVE

The Sub-themes of Revelation In the Notes

SEVEN SUB-THEMES

The Notes to the poems display various aspects or sub-themes within the conceptual framework of revelation.

The first sub-theme to which attention might be drawn arises from the concept of creation, which the new thinking perceives as the factual foundation of present reality. The immutable past of creation stands firmly at and as the base of revelation. Creation, deep in the past, remains unchanging. Yet even so it is also charged with fertility, abidingly, vibrantly connected with revelation and redemption. Creation, as hidden past, is the locus of the limits of the "old" thinking's enquiry. In the event of creation, according to the new thinking's enquiry into origins, the separateness of the elements is established. The new thinking, unlike the old, welcomes the separateness and spurns attempts at fusions into totalities. At the moment of creation, for the duration of world-time, the three elements of God, human, and world are determined as mutually transcendent to one another. Only thus are the possibilities for relating among the elements eventuated. This concept of mutual transcendence and independent stature, then, constitutes the first sub-theme: the factualities of the three elements of reality are irreducible to one another. This concept spawns the second sub-theme: the soul's consciousness that *only* separateness allows for relationship, but that the separateness itself does not necessitate relationship.

This second sub-theme, revolving around notions of relationship, pertains to the awakening of the soul. God awakens her to the consciousness of separateness, of individuality and uniqueness. The uniqueness of the individual human being resides in the particular soul, not in the self. The human self is universal, common and identical to all. Each human soul is *like* all other souls, but none is ever the same as another's.

Once awakened by God to the fact of the individuality of the soul, the human being subsequently knows, and knows again and again, that his or her soul can, and is commanded to, relate to the elements other than herself, that is, God, world, and each other human being he or she meets. This knowledge and this commandment together comprise revelation, and revelation's path from creation to redemption. The Notes to the poems do not, as does Rosenzweig's analysis of the Song of Songs in the *Star*,[1] describe the moment and the path of the soul's awakening by God and her approach in love to her neighbours in the world. Here, with his reflections on the poems, Rosenzweig speaks of the soul as already awake, aware of her particular path which can be no one else's. Even so, even when awake, she is not always steadfast in her approach to and reception of the world or of God. But the soul, whether trembling, terrified, suffering, or blissful, experiences soaring upsurges in which she repeatedly and joyfully recognizes that she lives and that she will live, and that her love and her being loved are stronger than death.

The second sub-theme, the life of the soul, opens to the third: the bridging, through speech and experience, between God and the human being, and between human beings themselves. In this third sub-theme the possibilities and the contours of such speech and experience are often colourfully, dramatically portrayed in the Notes. In the new thinking, when the concept of revelation enhances logic and brings about a new epistemological mode, human experience is seen as both contained in revelation and yet also maintaining its own autonomous ground. That is, divine revelation depends upon the human's experiencing it, and necessarily involves human experience. However, while experience holds its own ground, genuine experiences with other human beings, the world, and God are genuine *because* they are indwelt by the revelatory word. This sub-theme, then (as do the others), relates to experience only in so far as experience relates to revelation.

Although revelation reveals much, much still remains hidden. The fourth sub-theme tends to questions of knowing and not-knowing, and the limits of both; the fifth is that of the limits of human free will. Although the final two sub-themes persistently pervade the Notes, they have already been considered during the course of this book, and will here be discussed even more briefly than the first five. The sixth sub-theme is eternity and time, the seventh, the notion of the one language. We are confronted throughout by the non-systematic, non-totalizing method of Rosenzweig's philosophical method and the results of his method.

Excerpts from the Notes will serve as guides on the exploration through the sub-themes. In the *Star,* for purposes of explanation, the first and second sub-themes do follow in order – that is, from the factualities which are separate elements to the awareness of relational possibilities. The sub-themes gathered from the Notes do not intend to show a specific chronology either in themselves or in the order of their appearance. The experiences involved in the sub-themes are experiences which every soul does or will experience, at different times according to the various moments of the soul's life and to different degrees. Halevi's experiences follow the order of his own life events from that point where the poem-story begins: departure from Spain, raptures in Egypt, fear of not completing his pilgrimage, nearing Zion. He makes sense of every experience through the manifold treasures of revelation.

Another reader of the Notes may be drawn to sub-themes other than the ones I consider here or may maintain that others such as the liturgical, to which I allude here only in passing, are more important. A consideration of the liturgical aspect and use of the poems and Rosenzweig's relevant observations would be worth another book, as might several clusters of notes.

For the ease of the reader, the page references for the German originals follow the quoted texts in the same way as previously: 1927 edition/1983 edition.

The Separateness of the Elements

In his response to "Heilig" ("Holy") toward the conclusion of the God section, Rosenzweig distinguishes forms of separateness beyond those which are set out in creation. The factualities of human, God, and world in the new thinking are transformed into vital activities of shifting configurations. The miracle of the past creation is, of course, not merely that there was once upon a time a creator, but that *this* creator of the past created this one creation with which he himself continues to relate. Besides creating the two elements, human and world, that are set apart from himself, God also, in the course of time, makes holy, or sets apart, other occurrences that happen in time. Especially set apart are miracles, the existence of the Jewish people, and the path of Christianity. All these separations of holy times and events and existences are set in world time, and all are connected with eternity in time. A miracle is that which is set apart in time *as* eternal. To be set apart, or made holy, *in time* means that something other than time is inset *into* chronological time. Time remains but at the same time is displaced. Here, in the miracle, there is room for both time and eternity.

That we can pray for a miracle to come to pass is itself a miracle. Praying is a bridge between time and eternity. Decorum, in the Greek sense of the word, in praying for a miracle is exercised with the question, When? not Where? And decorous interpretation of miracles is not a *post factum* explanation through logic, which can always be done, but an acknowledgment that the miracle *is* a miracle because it occurred exactly when it did. Under this miracle of the one creation, the greatest miracle to be prayed for in time is the fulfilment of God's creation: the event of redemption, and the end of time.

In this long note to "Heilig" ("Holy"), Rosenzweig guides his reader beyond reflecting upon the deep, abiding past of the creation and its ensuing multiplicity of separations, through miracle, between time and eternity. Rosenzweig wonders, with Jehuda Halevi, at the creator God who ultimately dissolves all separation and division:

God's work is at one time the quiet, almost inaudible work of the first beginning; and there everything remains, for the time being, standing as it stands ... Strict believers in Kant could well come to the idea that it actually would alter nothing if one were to surrender to the "religious position": God as the creator of starry heavens and conscience. But this "position" is not to be purchased so cheaply. God is not merely the one who was. He is not merely base, supporter, of the world and of the human. For, surely, this is an empty faith, a mere "surrender," if it lacks the experience of the living present, indeed if it does not directly spring from it. Without the God who takes action, powerfully working in the day of our present life, the quiet and inaudible, which preserves the world and our hearts that he created, becomes a fairy tale, no, worse: a dogma ... Only the revelation of things set apart teaches us to revere the Creator even in "natural things." Only the tremors of holiness sanctify the everyday of the profane ...

The Creator, who created only One Creation, laughs at the divisions that the human being tries to establish, and lets them again and again be flooded over by the onslaught of primordial chaos. But the divisions which God Himself establishes stretch out over the whole creation and make manifest in their becoming the Oneness and the All-ness of the silent secret of the one creation. (193–4/82-3)

Here Rosenzweig has taken exception to "dogma," by which he means lifeless dogma, for elsewhere he writes with a different slant. However tidy a dogmate package can be presented, it will have value only if it can intimate God as relational to our lives in time. The dogmatic formula contains its value precisely in its tidiness, as well as its wrapping, for in the unwrapping it can come to renewed life.

The poem "Gewaltiger" ("Mighty One") is densely packed with the awe of the mystery of God and with the creature's timidity at approaching him, the one whom we yet can never touch or see. Rosenzweig writes here positively, though conditionally, of dogma: "This enormous concentration, with respect to content, is achieved by the means which man generally has for transmitting his knowledge about God for himself and others across the ages: the dogmatic formula. Precisely because it is frozen, it awakens an infinity of co-vibrating tone, if only the formula is brought rightly to those hearing it." This little poem bursts with exclamations: "The Incomparable!" "The Creator!" "The Invisible!" "The Manifest to the Heart!" And, with a Talmudic reference, "The All-Embracing 'Space'!" (173/26).

"Gelobt!" ("Praised be He!"), the long poem which precedes "Gewaltiger," ("Mighty One"), carefully describes the sort of awakenness which is experienced in the tension between separateness and relationship, between the height of bliss in receiving help from God when help is asked for and the depths of being humbly awe-stricken in knowing that one has approached God. This poem, to Rosenzweig, portrays the condensation of the dogmatic formula. "Gelobt!" ("Praised be He!") "brings rightly to those hearing it" the dogmatic formula in "Gewaltiger" ("Mighty One"). The order of the placement of the poems and the responses of the corresponding notes is interesting: Rosenzweig has the poem depicting the lifelfulness of experience *before* the poem comprising the dogmatic formula. In these notes he describes a situation in which one encounters the formula before the understanding of it through experience. There is a parallel here in understanding the Bible.

For all this experience of nearness to God, for all this knowledge, for all his having an Ezekiel-like vision, "Man reaches more deeply into his breast. He is not wise, he is – Nothing. And yet out of this last and innermost experience of his Nothingness he looks up again to the greatness of his Lord. Trembling, only now does he express the last thought which his thinking has reached: he perceives, is conscious only of the divine action; upon God Himself he – he says it with the same words with which God denies power to the Tempter over Job's life – may 'not lay a hand'" (172/25).

The separateness of the elements also means of course that each element is different in its essence. Rosenzweig suggests that the poem "Der Unvergleichliche" ("The Incomparable One") "can induce man to reflective comparison: 'What is he beside the Incomparable, he, the very comparable?'" (177/37). But later, in the Soul section, the note to "Leben" ("Life") has: "The one acknowledges the One – Hermann Cohen referred to this poem in his great defence when he proclaimed to his students his mature perception of the necessary 'transgression' from 'ethics' to 'religion,' the perception that before the unique God even man becomes unique, one, alone" (214/133).

If God is absolutely incomparable, then what does this uniqueness mean? Monotheism? As noted in a different context in the previous chapter, Rosenzweig writes in response to "Keiner Sonst!" ("None Other!"): "The great German scholar Lagarde, whose bitterness was possibly still greater than his scholarship – and that says something – once said that for the Jews monotheism meant: of God there is only one model" (178/39). Rosenzweig's reading is that this poem discloses the truth of the idea of one model. The "no one but you," the "no one else," and the "no second" of the poem express the "true root word of faith in the One" (178/39). This root word derives from the question the handmaids pose in the Song of Songs, What is your Friend among other friends, oh you most beautiful among women? The poem "surges up in the answer out of the wavy crests of the song of praise, of the destiny of being called (Jer. 20:9), of the suffering of martyrdom, and of the present time in history, over all of which, at the conclusion, it rises monumentally. For the uniqueness of God is the exclusiveness of love. Of God there is only One Model" (178/39).

With love as the relationship between God and human being, the difficulties, rather than easing, seem to compound. All love, says Rosenzweig in response to "Die Liebenden" ("The Lovers"), is difficult, and love for God is the most difficult. All love, he says, contains an element of unhappiness: the desire to love and the having to love are infinite, but the capacity for loving is finite. To love God can be the experience of the unhappiest of love, for such love "comes close to the human being, the closest – and draws itself away from him again into the most distant distance ... The refuge for the most ardently desired thing is under the eternal arms, but the eternal countenance no one sees and lives." How then can the beloved of God return God's love? Rosenzweig concludes that the solution "lies ... as the solution of all predicaments and conflicts, with the lover, with his strength for the For-All-That, who endures the For-All-That, and who For-All-That permits himself to be endured. Here then it is the human's prerogative and his strength to demand that God – loves him in return" (178– 9/40–1).

Encroachment on the territory of the sub-themes of the bridging between the elements and of knowing and not-knowing is being risked here, but I think the foregoing note as well as the following two that I want to mention can be claimed peacefully as also the rightful territory of the separation of the elements. The issue in the notes to "Der Fern- und-Nahe" ("The Far-and-Near One") and "Der Name" ("The Name") is to delineate the notion of the drawing near to and drawing far away of both God and human.

For "Der Fern-und-Nahe" ("The Near-and-Far One") Rosenzweig deliberately uses hyphens. The hyphens link the space and motion aspects of God in respect to his creation. The hyphens neither dualize, nor set in opposition or even in tension, two aspects of God. We, in our humanly lived lives may feel the tension in our experiences of God; but this hyphenated name for God, The Far-and-Near One, gives us access to the fact that, far or near, God is God. The hyphens illustrate what Rosenzweig writes in the note: that which is comprehended last by human thinking and first by Jewish thinking is that the faraway and the near God are the same God. In the same way, too, there is no division between the unknown God and the revealed, between the creator God and the redeemer. But for God, too, his creation of time permits him to behave differently in different times. In the note, "Der Fern-und Nahe," Rosenzweig says: "We theologians cannot help but make prescriptions for God's conduct out of our knowledge. We know that God can be known only in His presence, and at once we make out of this a law for Him: that He does not permit Himself to be known in His absence. In truth, however, we could easily leave it to Him as to when and how and what of Himself He wants to be known. And we have to say only what we know in utter calm or in utter unrest – but whether in calm or in unrest is not up to us; that is as accurately as we can – and this accuracy *is* up to us" (189/70).

Thus, while the new thinking may emphatically claim that the elements can be reduced to no fewer than three, and that one can, from "old" philosophy, even determine the respective essences of each of these three elements, the new thinking makes fewer and fainter claims for the predictability of movement and of relationships. The following excerpt discusses all this. The one to whom God draws near from whom he goes and far away, the human being, has a say in the matter of God's proximity, and that human say in the matter, moreover, is neither humanly nor divinely predictable.

Even in the most dreadful nearness the human can look away and then does not know in the least what has happened to him. And in the farthest distance the glance of God and of the human can burn into one another, so that the coldest abstractions become warm in the mouth of Maimonides or Hermann Cohen – more than all our distressed prattle. Near, far, it doesn't matter! What does matter is that here as there, what is spoken is spoken before His countenance – with the You of the refrain of our poem, the You that never turns away for a moment. (190/71)

This notion of proximity in connection with addressing God touches upon the human's right and strength to demand God's love as expressed in the note to "Die Liebenden" ("The Lovers"). This notion is also linked to the response to "Der Name" ("The Name") where the point is made that one who has a name and is present can be called, and God is never absent. "The paradox that God is near and far at the same time is smashed to pieces by the fact that he has a name. Whatever has a name can be spoken of and spoken to, depending on whether it is absent or present. God is never absent and that is why there is no concept of God (of the false gods definitely, but of the true none). God is the only one whose name is at the same time his concept, whose concept is at the same time his name. One names God only God, and each name has only this meaning" (190/72).

To Rosenzweig, as to most people, and as is well known, the name for God is decided from Exodus 3:14, where God tells Moses what he should say to the people when they would ask who had sent him. Not "being" but "being-there" is the concept which must shine through the name for God. In "Der Name" ("The Name"), Halevi uses the concrete word "dwell" for the being of God that is far away from the world. Normally, Rosenzweig notes, this word "dwell" designates God's glory dwelling on earth, among his people, and in his house. Here Rosenzweig shows that this "most abstract word imaginable" is used for the "dwelling in the crushed heart." He writes:

The Boreh Olam, the Creator of the world, does not mean here, as one would have thought, something distant as indicated by the content of the words. But rather: in popular speech words are filled with emotion, and with the God of the heart, the heart does not forget for a moment He is the one who "is." So here the spark does not merely jump back and forth between the two poles of far and near; but rather the poles themselves are each laden with two polar charges, only ordered differently. The Creator above the world sets up a "dwelling," and the abstract God of Philosophy has "being" in the crushed heart. (191/73)

The Awakened Soul

The awakened soul is that which has been awakened by a moment alone with God in personal divine revelation. That moment remains as and with the soul's past, and the person with the awakened soul knows he or she loves God, and will explode or shrivel up if he cannot be given a way to obey the command to love God. The corollary love commandment, that of human love, to love the neighbour, gives to the human being an outlet for his outpouring of love for God. Rosenzweig explained this in the *Star* and taught it at the Lehrhaus.[2] The soul who wishes to stay in her aloneness with God is one who resists obedience to the second love commandment. Thereby she stunts her growth, cannot ultimately obey the contingent first commandment, and eventually she returns to her unrevealed-to state – but now not as merely an unawakened soul and a proudly defiant self, but as a sick soul. "Having found God is not the end, but rather itself a beginning. Seeking and finding are here differentiated not as present tense and perfect tense, but rather both are future tense, only the former a temporal future and the latter an eternal future. Both speak the word of yearning" (in the note to "Umkehr" ["Return"], in some places read on the morning of Yom Kippur, 204/107). This yearning speaks from life, and it is experienced for a prescribed day each year, on Yom Kippur, the day when souls are divinely judged. Here, at the moment of this poetic utterance, the "cloak of good works has fallen off. Man, naked and uncovered, can cover himself with no other righteousness than with that of God Himself" (203/107). Only when speaking from the midst of life, only in that soulful yearning on Yom Kippur, only because the soul is permitted so to yearn on Yom Kippur, may she seek a day of solitude with God.

Jehuda Halevi's soul forgets neither the revelation at Sinai nor his own experiences of revelation, but Halevi's soul can falter, and she can be diminished in her strength. The soul who remembers her past knows, in her suffering, weak moments, to whom to pray, and what to pray for: to be refreshed under a renewed revelatory moment.

For human beings there are two kinds of certainty of divine help. The one is the certainty of the one to whom help has already been given [i.e., Sinai] … There is however a depth of despair in which that certainty fails, because even the memory of the former help itself chokes in it. When in this way that which is nearest is for man removed into the distance of unbelievability, then there remains only the help which comes to him from the furthest distance; then, and only then, is it time for the final appeal, for the appeal to the Creator, not in the cultic prayer, where also other laws serve for this, but rather in the fervent prayer of the heart. For in this depth of despair nothing more than the creature remains of man, and thus it is indeed the Creator alone with whom he can learn anew to believe in the Revealer and to hope for the Redeemer. (From the note to "Der Helfer" ["The Helper"], 195–6/85)

At other times the soul tilts the delicate balance in all that is revealed, and fragments revelation, stressing one aspect especially, responding only to that aspect. While human souls do and must respond to revelation in "pieces," that is, according to personal, social, historical, economical, political events and geographical and other sorts of life-setting situations and sudden accelerations of Fortuna's Wheel, still, imbalances in the world's road toward redemption can be humanly orchestrated. We have seen this, for example, in Rosenzweig's

view of the "mystic" and his view that the modern anthropological inquiry overweights the self at the reductive expense of God and world.
At times, too, the soul can become almost over-aware of, or overly concerned with, the eternal future and can reduce creation and revelation
to redemption.

"Seele im Exil" ("Soul in Exile") is about the soul when she is yearning for redemption. This turn of the soul of the poet is not one of loss
of belief, but one of belief to the point of pained yearning for the actualization of the divine promise. She senses a loneliness, a sense of being unfulfilled. This experience of the soul seems to be decorous in a
devoted soul like Halevi's. Such an experience of "pushing," displacing
time, makes sense in one who was at that time en route on his pilgrim-
mage, midway on his journey to secure his grave on the soil of the Holy
Land. The poem portrays a speaking soul, who expressses her feeling
of loneliness in the world: "like the Patriarchs (Gen. 23:4) the soul is
only a stranger and sojourner on earth, but the homeland is promised
to it" (in the note to "Kehr um, Kehr um!" ["Return, Return!"], 216–
17/137).

At first there was a lamenting, pale, tormented backward glance, from couplet
to couplet, to the bliss in God's mansion before birth, lost by the descent to
earth: then after the nadir is reached, or rather immediately at this nadir,
comes the reversal which, from the despairing consciousness of withering,
achieves in a wonderful soaring (incomprehensible through logic, but absolutely authentic) the certainty of the new blossoming – a certainty not despite
this withering but out of it. And from then on the tone changes, and the transitions of the couplets become proudly assured triumphal cries of a conqueror
over life. (198/94–5)

With characteristic wit and humour, Rosenzweig defends this "absolutely authentic" turn of the soul which is, however, "incomprehensible
through logic." The turn is too sudden for logic. It wants steps, not
leaps. "This lack of transition in this two-part poem – shocking to the
'modern man's' need for gradualness – this change of mood is violently unfounded because at its profound depth powerfully founded, is
the same as that which could be familiar to this modern man after all
from countless Psalms, as long as his own experience knows nothing of
it; if he did not prefer rather to cut these Psalms into two halves, and
by attributing each to different authors, he then protects himself from
the disconcerting experience of what can happen in a human soul"
(198/95).

The note to "Der Aufstieg" ("The Ascent") affirms as authentic the
sudden turns which can happen in, or to, or by a soul: "Here soul is

not first the restless wanderer, but right away the ascending one, indeed the ascended, the conqueress – God's daughter, who worships among God's sons" (217/138).

One paragraph of the note to "Diese Seele Hier" ("This Soul Here") offers a simply expressed view, but one of the most crucial in the new thinking: "The soul is not a thing. On this truth all psychology runs aground, from Aristotle and Thomas [Aquinas] to Häckel and Wundt. The appearance that it must nevertheless be a thing, "matter," "something," is raised up by the fact that, like things it is "here." But things can be "here" just as easily as they can also be "there." The soul can always only "be here." A soul "there," a soul in the third person – there is no such thing. The soul is always present – my soul, your soul, our soul, hence always: this soul here" (207/114).

This view of the soul as "always present" and therefore "not a thing" is reminiscent of Rosenzweig's words about God's presence and about resisting attempts to make him an abstract concept. But the soul, according to Rosenzweig, does have a place, an in-between two poles. Only one of these poles characterizes God's "place." In the note to "Wahn und Wahrheit" ("Illusion and Truth"), which immediately follows the one which claims that the soul is not a thing, Rosenzweig names these poles as illusion and truth, world and service, and masks and countenance. These poles, he claims, "lie in the same line of vision for the soul which moves between them. By getting entangled in illusion, she perseveres also in service and stands before the divine countenance. The soul's 'spiritually destined order,' 'bodily form,' and 'secret vision' are not one, but they coincide in this poetic life, whose oneness is precisely a oneness of the before and after. Even in 'olden Jewish' life this oneness is only too often split apart" (208/117).

To the soul is given a beloved, which comes to her in the form and time of a day. The Sabbath remembers the moment of creation, and therefore even the oneness of all before time was created; the Sabbath as well foreglimpses the oneness of the all after the fulfilment of time. Thus on the Sabbath, the oneness of the before and after, experienced in the soul, coalesces in a whole, a peace, שלום. On this day the soul does not move between two poles, but rests. The soul prepares herself like an all-loving lover, and greets her beloved Sabbath as her destined mate. Every week, the weekdays lead to this zenith of the experience of oneness of the before and after. The special beauty of love on this day is that consciousness is permitted of the eternality of love, though it takes place in time.

The beautifully tender poem, "An den Sabbat" ("To the Sabbath"), sings an ode to all the days of the week, appreciating each as it is connected to and leads to the Sabbath, the day of full, restful reunion with the beloved. Each stanza concludes with "Awake happily, O Day, awake happily, you, my Seventh One!" ("Glück auf, o Tag, Glück auf, mein Siebter Du!"). "Then," writes Rosenzweig, "the sixth stanza empties into the wonderful comparison with the prescription for the 'seven days of the banquet,' the seven-day wedding celebration during whose length the whole 'seven blessings' of the marriage ceremony may always be newly repeated in the blessing at the table when new guests, 'new faces' in the language of the law, join at the table: thus the Sabbath is welcomed as a 'new face,' like a bride, but not as guest, rather himself as the always new groom, the beloved of the soul" (213/129). All week the soul is not far away from her beloved, as the concluding line of each stanza especially expresses – you, my Seventh One! – and in this sense she does live in an in-between here, holding in her line of vision again and again the beloved seventh day. "And thus the poet drinks to the Sabbath the cup of love in this song, which nowhere departs from the immediacy of the address, of I and You" (213/129).

Rosenzweig remarks that, although mystical thinking arrived late at this idea of the Sabbath as the "day of the soul," this idea was included in the purpose and meaning of the Sabbath from its very origins. And in these origins there is a sense of oneness during the Sabbath day that differs from that oneness of bridegroom union, of the before and after. In its origins the Sabbath portrayed, besides a oneness of before and after, also a oneness of now: a oneness of "religious" and "social" aspects. The "fundamental chord" of the poem "Frei" ("Free") not only intones that "blissful sigh of relief and that perfecting of the soul's coming to itself," but it also strikes this other "fundamental chord of the Sabbath," of the union of the "religious" and the "social."

Should one like to play off the "social" meaning of the command of the Sabbath, as the formulation of the fifth Book of Torah [Deuteronomy] emphasizes it, against the "religious" meaning of the second Book [Exodus], our poem demonstrates the folly of such a risky undertaking with its joining of the first and third couplets through that blissful word [*Ruhtag*, day of rest] which, taken from the rest of the Most High, yet is applicable to the sigh of relief of the servant (Ex. 23:12). Each separation of the "social" from the "religious," or the reverse, makes the social an eternally open question, the religious an ever ready answer. The separation deprives that question of the healing power of recurrent possibilities of answers, and deprives this answer of the verification of recurrent possibilities of being questionable. The freedom of the servant is devoid of content if it is not freedom of the master; the freedom of the master is unreal if it does not transform into freedom of the servant. For each is master and each is servant. (213–14/130)

When the "religious" aspect is isolated, it appears to deliver up ever-ready, standing, static answers, as an authoritative master might do. When the "social" aspect is isolated and seeks healing power from the "religious," only one answer can be expected. When the social and religious are inter-dependent, the master-servant relationship dissolves. What appears in its place is the freedom of repeated interchange. In speech, in genuine conversation, both speakers are free. When healing powers are asked about, answers recur, that is to say, newly stated answers which fit the new situation and verify former answers. The religious (the master) is real freedom only when the social (the servant) is also permitted freedom – to speak again and again, to receive answers again and again. In speech both the religious and the social are master and servant. The religious serves to answer the social, and the social serves to fulfil the religious. This idea in this tightly packed note parallels Rosenzweig's notion that genuine subjective experience arises out of the the objective character of revelation, out of its factual past-ness. That is, people may experience revelation in different ways and measures, but it is open to all, and it conditions all experience. Without the informing fact, form, and content of revelation, social activity remains too open, without borders, a contentless freedom. When the religious borders close in on themselves, rendering the religious free from having to answer again and again in different ways to questions out of the struggles of social life, then the "religious" is denied vibrancy in life, offers only mechanically muttered answers, and is meaninglessly ineffective in changing concrete temporality.

The considerations of this day of the soul, which dissolves borders between the "social" and the "religious," brings us to the sub-theme of speech and experience under the concept of revelation, where, to Rosenzweig, speech is both human and divine.

The Bridges of Speech and Experience

"Nachts" ("During the Night") describes a vision Jehuda Halevi experiences in sleep, "as if his heart 'had been allowed to stand by at Sinai.' The experience of today confirms and repeats the historical Revelation" (174/28). The experiential repetition of revelation consists in God revealing always and again only himself in revelation, always and again only to the human being, not only as a people, but also to each particular soul. God reveals himself (accusative) to the human being (dative). "This accusative and dative in its union is the peculiar content of revelation" (174/29). The experiential confirmation of revelation must follow immediately "from this bond established here between God and human," and "whatever cannot verify its unmediatedness to this bond, does not belong to it" (174/29). Thus, as Rosenzweig asserts in the note to the next poem, "Ereignis" ("Event"): "Revelation is experience and event. Genuine experience only, because and when it also has been event, genuine event only, because and when it can become experience again and again" (174/30). This relationship between experience and event thwarts every attempt either to confine God to the present tense of experience or to deny him entry into the world of event. "But God does not permit his roads to be impeded. Event is not farther from Him than experience, nature is not more inaccessible than the soul. Nor, as the fearful ones dread, will He be pulled down into coarse objectivity; he has already taken care of that ... [As] the Midrash knows how to report: that the nations heard each a different thing and answered each a different thing. The answer is what matters – here also" (174/30).

In *both* the "social" *and* "religious" meanings of revelation, the human "answer" to revelation is given: that is to say, in the terrestrial world where social and religious events take place. The awakened soul, carrying in herself the strength she is given from revelation, that is the strength through God's love to fulfil the commandment to love her neighbour, can and must now move, as it were, away from God to the world of human beings.

Rosenzweig seems nowhere fully or precisely or explicitly to describe or prescribe speech which takes place between human beings, other than to say that the speech must embody, enact, and convey that love which God gives to each soul, ultimately to the extent to which God loves. This was discussed at length in chapter 2 in connection with the critiques of Rivka Horwitz and Nahum N. Glatzer. Here we can take the discussion further.

The love of neighbour is a commandment which is not so much fulfilled as always being fulfilled in ever-renewed actions of loving each neighbour, each nearest person, one by one throughout the soul's earthly life. Thus love, or loving, is not an attribute, love is not even an attitude, in general or in particular. Love is a concrete *event* that – because it is event – requires renewal in new events if it is to live. If the world's fulfilment is to be all-love, this fulfilment is not therefore a *state*, but a culmination – a telos – of a multiplicity of particular love actions and events.

While each soul bears the responsibility to take a share in fulfilling the love commandment, the commandment will not ultimately be fulfilled until all neighbours fulfil it, and can say "we." The sort of speech that involves love toward the neighbour can therefore only be characterized as "loving as God loves," through particular meetings. Thus each encounter between neighbours becomes a unique event.

In the context of being near to or far away from God, Rosenzweig suggests that God, as the far-and-near one, helps Jehuda Halevi to understand the problem of the purpose of the world, "about which the philosophy of religion of that time toiled (190/72)." The purpose, Rosenzweig asserts, is that the commandment to love the neighbour be fulfilled. The fulfilment of this purpose of the world – love of God and the neighbour – must literally and actually take place *in* the world. One's own being therefore must be seen as being-there *both* for itself *as well as* for others, that is to say, for other human beings, for God, and even for the world in the sense of contributing to its growth to perfection. The soul awakens and sleeps. The self, on the other hand, is always conscious of itself: the proud, defiant self always risks overriding the soul. The "mystic," in believing he is close to God is actually all "self" and not a *soul* in the world. When it experiences its own being, however, the self is indeed close to God. When it moves toward other human beings it is far from God, but only at this distance can it obey the commandment to love the neighbour: "Everything created has a double function: first, it is simply wholly there, has being, self-being, is a purpose in itself. But then ilt is also there for the sake of something else, in the final resort for the sake of everything else. In its selfness it experiences the near God, in its bondedness to the other the far God. For the far God is the God of the world, which always is the whole, and a whole made up of totally different parts. The near God is the God of the heart, of the heart which is never so much Self and only Self as when it suffers (190–1/72–3).

Thus direct speech with God, *after* revelation, becomes necessary and or appropriate only under specific conditions at specific times. Liturgical speech comprises this "I" and this "I" and this "I", each of whom forgets the self and who can come together say to "we" as souls. Liturgical speech thus lies in a category other than, or as an intermediary between, human-divine speech and human-to-human speech. The "we" as "we souls" forms a prelude to the one language of mankind in that liturgical speech speaks with a "we." The "we souls" is of course not restricted to synagogue and church settings. It can be "in the street" between two or more at *any* time. But liturgical content, liturgical tone, what is prayed for, all clearly bely that liturgy is self-consciously preredemptive speech: it prays *for* redemption. Liturgical speech, moreover, specifies and teaches, is open to and answers to, "times" and "events" of life's paths. Times are set for praise, asking for forgiveness, asking for help, mourning for the temple, seeking comfort and healing from the one who can give help, praying for redemption, peace. In addition to prescriptive prayers, the liturgy contains those for unexpected turns in life's path, such as mourning for loved ones.

Outside the liturgical speech of the "we," there arise moments of the need for the spontaneous prayer of the "I", the "I" alone, when it fears this sense of aloneness. The yearning for God can be the most intense in suffering. Jewish liturgy expresses a response to *every possible human suffering of the soul.* Jehuda Halevi has appropriated *added* "we" *to* liturgy in several ways. And his poems speak as a "we" especially because he can speak as an "I" *of his people.*

But even in the severest of suffering, even in the direst need to speak, the would-be spontaneity of speaking to God can just as suddenly become a muteness of hesitation, a sudden fear: How do "I," a puny "I", approach "him"? The need to utter a fervent prayer in all spontaneity can dissolve into desperately deliberating the propriety of initiating speech with God. Experience testifies, therefore, that the question of who begins divine-human conversations is not at all theoretical. "Rather," as Rosenzweig writes in the note to "Heimkehr" ("Homecoming"), "it is a real question of the real heart of the human... The real question emerges because the human always senses his own lack of power whenever he stands before God, and thus necessarily must await and request the first step from God. And yet at the same time he hears that which he cannot help but hear: that God demands the first step from him, from the human" (180/49).

In three other poems, "Treue," "Liebestrost," and "Wiederfinden" ("Faithfulness," "Love's Solace," "Finding Again"), which conclude the People section, real human-divine conversations take place. Alternating stanzas are given to the mouth of the human and the mouth of God.

But "Heimkehr" ("Homecoming") provides a good example of this fearful hesitation to approach God. The poem is connected with the noon hours of the Day of Atonement, and it portrays the unwillingness of both God and the human to initiate the conversation, except on the demanded condition of each that the other guarantee a response. This mutual hesitation that precedes real conversation is based on the Midrash to Lamentations 5:21 and Malachi 3:7. Once the condition is agreed to, it does not matter who begins. A response *is* promised, no matter who speaks first. And only then, with the trust in the mutual promise, does the conversation open in the poem.

In all conversations, however, Rosenzweig observes that the one who is right gets the last word. At the actual end of the world, of course, God will have that last word. Rosenzweig asks, then: Why does this poem, which comprises four double stanzas (J-J; H-H; U-U; D-D) of alternating divine and human speech, have only the one stanza of human speech (A) in its conclusion? The poem is attached to the midday hours of Yom Kippur. And midway through that day God's word cannot yet be conclusive. "And if the human being is to be the one to speak that which is God's thing, then the last word – or the day, of life, of history – can be only the word that stands behind all God's speech – in the way in which the human can take this divine 'I' into his mouth, namely as a profession of the 'He' " (182/51). The day ends with precisely such a human profession, which solves the question of the last word, for both the poem and the day:

At this moment he is as near to God, as close to his throne as human beings can be. In the rapture of this nearness the "You" is silent to him, not merely the You of his cry of despair, but also the You of his yearning and of his love. Like the angel under the throne he turns around and professes, testifies to – Him. But he is permitted to anticipate this highest, final moment because a few minutes later when the sound of the ram's horn (Lev. 25:9) announces the close of the holy day, he will again recite the evening prayer of his everyday life that has broken through once again: Forgive us, our Father, for we have sinned. (182/51)

But the praying for forgiveness during Yom Kippur itself is boldly demanded. At most other times, the praying is uttered feebly and fearfully. The poem "Hör" ("Hear") shows and exemplifies this fearfulness. "Heimkehr," however, is not a peaceful interchange; it is all demand. Rosenzweig defends the right of the human boldly to demand that he be forgiven: "People have been terrified about this, have found blasphemous this demand of man for forgiveness – quite literally – for God's sake. They have even gone so far as erasing the words from the prayers. And certainly this is as ridiculous as the clever psychology children use with their parents: it serves my father right if I freeze my hands – why doesn't he buy me any gloves! But after all – isn't this parent-psychology right?" (183/53).

In the note to "Hier bin ich" ("Here I am"), the question – and answer – as to who initiates divine-human conversations takes on an ironic twist with an amusing but astute point at its end. This is achieved through an instance of an innocent confusion as to who actually *has* spoken first. Rosenzweig tells the story of a feeble-minded man named Mendele, who lived in a southern Black Forest village. One day when he was busy at chopping wood in the square beside the synagogue, some local boys decided to have a bit of fun. They would call Mendele's name and then hide to watch his reaction. At the third call, Mendele throws down his axe and runs into the synagogue, up to the raised middle section where the Torah is read, and calls out in Hebrew: "Here I am." Rosenzweig connects this touching story with the poem, as follows:

Man can call "Here I am," because the echo returns out of God's mouth. The poem longs, laments, atones and prays for this divine "Here I am" in twenty-three beats of its rhyme until the twenty-fourth, where the answer to the longing, lamenting, atoning and praying rhymes with it.

And the answer is not merely longed, lamented, atoned and prayed for: No, the divine answer must be so humanly spoken that in this poem a moment can arrive where the answer is demanded almost with a threat: "but when I suffer ..." The human heart has the inalienable right to deny again and again the great truth of Revelation, that suffering is a gift from God, whenever it becomes a theological schematization, as it does again and again, and to reinstate against this the primaeval position of nature. For this position suffering is suffering and nothing else. God answers only the word that rises out of the depth of all human powers, of the created as well as of the awakened. (196/91)

To Rosenzweig, boldness is often justified on the part of the human speaker in the face of God. Indeed, Rosenzweig claims that bold – actually blasphemous – human speech to God is the reason for the Jewish people's persistence through all despair. The poem "Aufblick" ("Looking Upwards"), according to Rosenzweig, teaches that this boldness is the one and only reason for Jewish survival. "It begins with the cry out of the abyss of despair, which is so deep that the one called, only cried to to start with – can be cried to, called into question, charged with allegations" (227/168). Almost still in his cry, the doubting, despairing one recognizes the great God to whom the heavenly hosts bow, "and the heart sinks down enchanted into the view of the divine glory – and has forgotten all despair" (227/168).

Still the exile persists, and this is unsettling to the Jewish soul. Rather than perceive the exile as a cause or reason for despair, the Jew can instead *demand* the *faithfulness* of God to his promise of the ultimate bliss of the wholeness of redemption. The Prophets, the Song of Songs, and the Midrash all tellingly demonstrate that the love between Israel and God is not satisfied with conclusive declarations, as can be found in "love poetry." Love between Israel and God lives *in time,* and the expressions of this love vary with changing events through history. In contrast to any timeless, declarative statement of love, Rosenzweig, in his response to "Zürnende Liebe" ("Angry Love"), writes about the love between Israel and God, which endures through the exile which at this point has persisted for a thousand years.

In this poem for the morning services of the Festival of Freedom [Passover], accompanied already by the Song of Songs, we are swept into an outburst of the abandoned loved ones, cast out already for a thousand years into the wretchedness of exile, as those classical witnesses of this love simply do not know it, because at that time, at the beginning of the millennium there was not yet any ground for such a frightful outburst. In disputatious indignation about the faithlessness of the beloved, to whom whe has sacrificed everything. The history of two millennia, from Sinai through the Persians, Greeks, Romans, up to the Islam of the present, crowds together on a witness bench in the reproaches of the three middle couplets. And then comes the outcry, with one scarcely dares to believe one has heard, where Israel as the one human being stands erect before the one God and binds God's omnipotence to the redemption which he owes to it. For there is no other who waits for Him, there may be no other, the power of love tolerates no Outside; what *is*, is in it [love]; what is not in it, *is* not.

Jewish? No, for all love forgets in the love that there is still an Other-Side of love, an It beside Me and You. Jewish? Oh yes, for the power to express this truth is only given to man since and because there is – the Jew. (235/187–8).

While he writes "because there is – the Jew," Rosenzweig saw neither the *Star* nor his Halevi book as a specifically Jewish book other than in the sense that the words are spoken by a Jewish man who speaks in a Jewish way. With regard to the *Star*, Rosenzweig says: "I received the new thinking in these old words, thus I have returned it and passed it on, in them. There would have come to the lips of a Christian, I know, instead of mine, words of the New Testament, to a pagan, I think, surely not words of his holy books – for their ascent leads away from the original language of humankind, not towards it like the earthly path of revelation – but perhaps entirely in his own words. But for me these ones."[3]

In the very brief note to the poem "Der Wahre" ("The True One") (183/54), which addresses truth, Rosenzweig states that for both Jewish feeling and the Hebrew language, "Truth" and "the One Who is True" mean the same thing. "Thus this poem as a matter of course also finds its beginning in the first words of that prayer: in the command to love God (Dt. 6:5), which here now becomes the love of truth and yet retains all the sensual and suprasensual ardour of love for God. And he who has understood this 'and yet' will know what 'Jewish rationalism' is about, and that this rationalism may be very rational, and yet can never be as rational as it – is Jewish" (183/54). Rosenzweig concludes this note with a reference to Hermann Cohen, whom he viewed as a whole man – philosopher *and* believer, and of whom he claims: anyone who has known Cohen will understand this relationship between Jewishness and rationalism.

The last poem in the People section is "Wiederfinden" ("Finding Again") (116–17/196–8). Rosenzweig describes this poem as a "totally humanly sweet love conversation, in which the sweetheart is called by the pet-name of worldly love-poetry," and where "the future moment of reunion is dreamfully anticipated" (237/198). The poem *"Auf"* ("Awake") opens the Zion section, and Rosenzweig writes of it as if the conversation is continuing from the previous poem directly from the previous section. He observes that "only one is still speaking, the One. Thus no longer present tense, but rather future, no longer drama, but rather vision. The lament, which is always an expression of the present, is silenced; also comfort, promise, even hope, which all of course look into the future, but out of the present, are now silent; only the purely present future speaks, the call, the 'Be ready' of the hour that has come, finally come" (238/201).

The Limits of Knowing and of Not-Knowing

The note to the poem "Dein Gott" ("Your God") expresses the notion that if we were permitted to know of God *only* that he *is* God, then the answer to the question, What is God? would most adequately be answered simply by the tautology "God is God." If we can all conclusively say this concerning the question of our knowledge of God, then any kind of prayer calling to him would be in vain, looking up to the stars would be only an escape from the world, and those who claim to recognize God in the love duet of the Song of Songs would be deluded. No conversation can take place with pure being other "than those answers forbidden in the Talmud about When and Where, the Below and Above of Creation, and precisely not that intercourse of the whole and simple life (Dt. 18:9–15) which is opposed, by the Scriptures, to all such magic compulsion for knowledge" (184/57).

More than cognition of the existence of God, we are permitted to know this: that God is "your God." Thus, "just as we have to heed the limits of our knowledge, so too, and not less, the limits of our not-knowing. Beyond all our knowledge God lives. But before our not-knowing begins, your God presents Himself to you, to your call, to your ascent, to your readiness, to your glance, to your life" (184/57). This knowledge is granted only from revelation, that is, from an initiating experience of an event which brings to the knower a knowledge not from within his own self, or from his own reasoning powers, but from beyond the bounds of human flesh, mind, and soul. This knowledge can be confirmed only by subsequent verifying experiences of revelation. Stéphane Mosès describes Rosenzweig's views on revelation and human knowledge, stating: "In Revelation God entrusts himself into human finiteness and, consequently, confines himself in it. Revelation brings to light the aspect of God that human experience is capable of containing; the remainder withdraws and can only remain concealed. In this sense Revelation does not negate the finiteness of human knowledge; on the contrary, it founds it. If absolute Truth escapes man, it is not in spite of Revelation but because of it."[4] Just when philosophy reaches its limits of knowledge of (divine) being and is reeling at the edge of not-knowing, a capacity for knowing is again opened up. A *new* limit to our not-knowing is set, this time not by human reason, but by God. *Your* God becomes approachable, and as knowable as He wishes to be, through relationship with you.

Knowledge derived from relationship cannot be expressed in the verbal mood of the indicative. References to God as third person do not convey knowledge of "your" God. The Song of Songs expresses the kind of knowledge learned from relationship and expresses it *in* relationship. In certain of the speech of the Halevi poetry, too, especially in the poems which address God and hear God's address, events occurs now, and in each "now" when these texts are read again. The near God is experienced, is speaking, is listening. Only the far God can be spoken about, and only when far away can he be appropriately spoken about as "He," for instance the He of "Gelobt!" ("Praised be He!") (13–17/22–4). Concerning the possibilities of proving God, Rosenzweig maintains the tension of transcendence and immanence, that is to say the tension arising from the mobility involved in the freedom of both human and God to draw afar and to come near. "And when He is totally distant," Rosenzweig insists, "that is when he has totally distanced himself, we can even – deliver me up to the worldly arm of the law, you inquisitors of the new theology! – prove him" (in the note to "Der Fern-und-Nahe" ["The Far-and-Near One"] 189/70–1).

Rosenzweig's principle of there being no fewer than three irreducible elements of reality is intended to be a concrete statement of factualities, and not an abstract one of concepts or ideas. The three elements are no longer concepts, but factualities. When the separateness, or otherness, of God is characterized as merely an abstraction, Rosenzweig passionately counters this. Still addressing the "inquisitors of the new theology," he writes:

The possibility of the proof of God is the simple result of the fact that God, as you will never tire of repeating, is Wholly Other. Nay, not even a result. Rather this "wholly-other" is itself the modern proof of God, namely the residue of the other proofs thinned out to the outermost distance of abstraction. But the proofs reach, before this last point of distance, the point where they, each from its own distance, represent the accurate expression of what is here visible. Thus it is not at all a sign of being hopelessly lost with respect to knowing that God is the wholly perfect being or the first cause, or indeed even that He is the ideal of ethics. Rather, wherever it is expressed as honest knowledge, it is only a sign that at the moment of acquiring this knowledge, God really was very far away from the one who was acquiring it. But what does this mean: "honest knowledge"? Nothing other than what it always means. To say nothing about what does not concern us and what we ourselves do not concern. (189/71)

Just as abstract notions of otherness are impermissible in the principle of the three elements of reality, so too the same principle forbids any fusion or reduction between the elements. Nevertheless, as discussed before, one of the themes of the poem "Das All" ("The Universe") is that the universe, though separate from, does belong to, God, and Rosenzweig here distinguishes between those pantheists who reduce God to the world, to whom he is opposed as reductionists of God to world, and those who see God in nature, of whom he here, at least, approves. A hundred and fifty years have not yet passed, he writes, since the formulation of the "fundamental dogma of modern education and consequently also of modern religiosity, that one may not seek God in nature" (185/65), and therefore the modern reader of "Das All" ("The Universe") is alienated from the worldview of the poem.

At the source of this prejudice sits Kant with his refutation of the "physico-teleological proof of God," through which the previously obvious step from the Creation to the Creator all at once appeared forbidden even to the grounding of modern natural science. Truly only apparent; no one knew it better than Kant himself, Kant, who concludes the story of how he observed during one insect-scarce summer that the swallows were even pushing their young out of the nest with an outcry: For my understanding stood still, for there was nothing to do about it except to fall down and to worship. He had wanted to criticize the "proof" and not the "worshipping." (185–6/65)

In the same note, Rosenzweig explicitly, however, echoing the pantheist passages in the Star, acknowledges the danger in praising God out of nature. The poem itself hints at this danger, which is not so much one of reduction as of dismissing one of the elements, and of subsuming the individual human being – our own "I" – to the world. The world as element comprises all human beings other than ourselves. Thus human beings, in the plural, means "the world." Included is every component in the world, "man in general," human as element, human as self. The human as a component among all the multiplicities of the world is wholly worldly. The individual human being as distinct element – the I with its unique soul – is an element irreducible to the "good" world. The element, human being, is hindered in fully, finally, praising God's world when any one "I" suffers.

Thus Rosenzweig writes: "In the third stanza's last four lines there is an attempt, unbroken from nature, to overlook – not the human, that would be permitted, but – our very selves, and to drown out the seriousness of the individual destiny with an all too cheaply purchased Hallelujah, that is not with the particular body. Against this danger the Jobs and the Ivan Karamazovs remain, who believe in God, but do not accept his world, the eternally necessary antidote [Gegengift]" (187/65). Rosenzweig notes quietly that Jehuda is not in need of the antidote; he will not hastily sing Hallelujah, for he is a Jew.

The positive side of praising God out of nature took place during pre-Copernican times, when the human being "did not lose the courage really to look around himself now and to see also what he 'knew' " (186/66). The human saw the ordered spheres, the sun, the moon, the planets, at their various distances from the earth. "For one still had the good conscience that Below really was Below, and Above, Above ... 'Where one stands is always below." And because one knew it, so in that which was always under, and in that which was always above, and in that which was always between below and above, one could again not merely know the elements of all things, but rather see them" (186–7/ 66). Since Copernicus, the trust in seeing the world has been broken. And we no longer worship the now invisible heavens, because we no longer experience the work of God in them. The experience of seeing, of feeling ourselves to be below, of being in awe of what is above, has been usurped by reason's scientific truth that we have seen incorrectly. Reason, to Rosenzweig, has distorted the "truer" truths of pre-Copernican visual experience.

Wherever, then, knowledge by seeing ceased, there one always replaced the final cause with a system of between-powers, exactly as now at the limit of our calculated knowledge. The angel of mediaeval Aristotelianism and the basic understanding of modern physics approach this the most closely in that here, as there, the whole world believes in it; and concerning it, the uninitiated envisage for the most part nothing, the knowledgeable for the most part nonsense. For the spiritual righteousness which it brings upon itself has seldom been a case of expressing the really experienced thing purely, and not mythologically growing forth with those former knowledges that shoot up directly in the experience for the one experiencing. Real and great experiences of the work of God have been set down in the Talmudic study of the angels, but they have been all too lightly choked by the ramblings of fantastic reason lacking in experience, as the real and great knowledges of science have been choked through the ramblings of a fantasy that is a stranger to experience and a possessor of reason. (187/66)

This faraway world above us, which we could "see" in pre-Copernican times as the divinely created heaven, was no less a mystery then than it is now in terms of knowledge about death. But Rosenzweig claims that what is true "here" is true "there." Revelatory truth that the soul lives is no different there than here.

Of the things that happen in life we know something. Of death we know less and more, namely nothing and everything. Everything that it is for us the living, nothing of what it will be for us when dead. Knowledge of death from this-side is our most precious possession and through every increment is augmented in genuine knowledge; he who does not respect the secret of that Nothing of our hither-side knowledge of death from the other side, but attacks it, with the fools who exist under changing names in every age, loses as a punishment even that genuine knowledge of the universe [*Allwissenheit*] that he has. Indeed there is a relation between that which from here can be much better known to us than anything, only because it is totally unknown from there. It is the same thing that we see from here entirely and from there not at all. What is true here, is also true there. But this certainty, which does not allow the foot to stumble when it nears the border that separates the all-known from the all-unknown, does not illuminate the darkness wherein the unknown lies. (207/ 111)

While knowledge of death from this side may be our most precious possession, our *proudest* possession, Rosenzweig writes in his note to "Der Gott der Geister" ("The God of the Spirits"), is God's spirit. While the possession may not be taken away, our pride in it may be modified. God's spirit is manifested in the expressing of God's speech through humanly spoken speech. Pride arises in man when he forgets that his speech has this connection with divine speech and instead believes that he speaks autonomously. This pride adjusts itself when it understands that knowing what to say comes from God. The pride in this possession of God's spirit through speech was shaken, by a divine gentleness, for Moses at Exodus 4:16 and 22. "There remains for him, undoubted, the wisdom, the sparkle of the word, but he owes to wisdom and word the place at the heavenly throne, whence they spring. And certainly: the Tables of the Commandments stand in the heart of man – but God's finger has written them. And the soul has a nearby path to heavenly delight, but God's spirit must show that path to the soul. Always only a small But, upon which after all the 'self-glory' of the human spirit, his 'autonomies' are dependent" (192/80).

This dependence of human knowledge on God is reflected in another way by which God manifests his one path to the multiplicities of human lives. The first and final knowledge is God's, a knowledge of oneness of truth. How can this one truth be conveyed through world time? Rosenzweig finds an answer in this way: The notion that the line of world time goes through the centre of Israel permits Israel to be the centre of the universe. As the poem "Licht" ("Light") demonstrates, the centre can also be represented as a point – any point in that time line. This point is exemplified in the poem by its reference to Job. Here the poet replies to God's crushing question: In which way does One Light divide itself into the world? Rather than stammering a crushed, "I don't know," Job replies with an answer which is meek and yet boldly trusting at the same time. His answer "dissolves the mystery of creation in the command of revelation: This mysterious way of the original Light – it can be none other than the one which You have determined for me as my way" (220/151). Thus the line (Light) is carried forward at this point of recognition: recognizing both that God initiates the line in creation and that in revelation God commands that his light be refracted in world time. In this little poem of ten lines, then, "through which all the light of heaven and earth streams, the line can be drawn from the luminosity of the divine countenance to the reflection of this luminosity in the human countenance; this line, which leads from the original light of creation and the created lights over flashing Sinai to the eyes of the one praying during the Festival of Revelation [Shavuot], to which the poem belongs, is – One Light" (220/151). This echoes the passage which concludes the *Star's* introduction to part 2: "The human word is a symbol; with every moment it is newly created in the mouth of the speaker, but only because it is from the beginning and because it already bears in its womb every speaker who will one day effect the miracle of renewing it. But the divine word is more than symbol: it is revelation only because it is at the same time the word creation. "God said, Let there be light" – and what is the light of God? It is the soul of man."5

This one light, of course, has no end, but it does have a fulfilment, just as does the line of world time. The line begins as orientation in the miracle of creation, when the lights were created. "And because the people preserve in this knowledge the connexion of the millennia, they may wait for the last miracle, which they implore, quite simply as a parable of the first, the original miracle, which this day [the day during Passover when Israel's song of triumph is read out] as every day brings home to it. For the last miracle will of course be greater than the first, but not different. The God of world-renewal is Israel's God of old" (in the note to "Am Schilfmeertag" ["On Reed Sea Day"], 221/155).

In another note Rosenzweig writes of the correspondence between heaven and earth as one of a double-dominion, that is to say in which heaven and earth face and reflect each other. The poem, "Geweiht"

("Consecrated") (46–8/74–6], is placed in the morning services where Isaiah is portrayed at the moment when he hears the thrice holy of the heavenly host.

> For all the the "Below" corresponds to an "Above": thus should Israel echo the threefold-consecration of the angels on earth, Israel whose city faces the heavenly city of God – or as it is also written in memory of the preliminary form of the city during the wandering inthe desert: the earthly camp faces the heavenly. The hymn is entirely embued with the view of this divine double-dominion in heaven and on earth. This is miraculous, where the dominion unites the angelic powers of mercy and truth, which usually neutralize like fire and water, and where it confronts again at the destination the messengers it has sent out – for this divine double-dominion governs at the destination just as it does in the place of instruction. And it is no less miraculous where it steels the human powers of the people, to unlimited patience for suffering and untiring witnessing, the people whom the poet summons to come up to the angels. (191–2/ 76–7)

The notion that human powers are steeled for limitless patience to suffer and to witness brings us now to the sub-theme of human free will.

Human Free Will

In Rosenzweig's Lehrhaus lecture series on the "Science of the Man," he states that the pressing question which pertains to man is whether he is free, whether he has free will. (For God the question is whether he exists, for the world it is whether it comprises reality or illusion.) Humankind, to Rosenzweig, *is* free. The first choice involving free will occurs at a moment when he tries really to be alone, and yet finds he cannot be. The being-alone breaks out into "a question, a cry of pain, a shout of joy, in which he perceived that precisely *then* he was not alone. Afterwards he is certain of having *chosen*."[6] Rosenzweig means having chosen God. This attempted isolation teaches the human being something else about himself, it is a "having to," a "must" in terms of being with God. One *can* still deny God, but if one chooses God at that moment of attempted isolation, then *after* the choice has been made, one *must* henceforth walk *with* God. This "must" with a future-oriented thrust is contained in the choice. If he or she chooses God, he must be with God. The paradox in the juxtaposition of simultaneously choosing and having to constitutes the locus of Rosenzweig's understanding of human free will within time.

As the sections on the awakening soul in the *Star* also show, in the lecture notes the moment of isolation with God is portrayed as empow-

ering the human to enact the love commandment in the world: that
the real "I," the "I *And* God," knows God "from behind and looks the
others in the eye."[7] Thus present acts of free will are anchored in the
past moment of choice. They can depend on the silent, unuttered,
"we" of "I And God" for help in achieving these deeds.

Only three notes directly pertain to this particular issue: those to the
poems "Menschenschwäche," "Der Zwang," and "Vorgefühl" ("Human
Frailty," "Compulsion," and "Foreboding") (103–4/202–3; 227/247;
248–9/256–7). One note shows how the full burden of free will and
responsibility for his deed is placed on the human being. The next describes how compulsion to execute a rightly chosen deed comes from
God, even though, as the third shows, for the highest decision, God
gives freedom to the human being – freedom for the highest decision.

The note to "Menschenschwäche" ("Human Frailty") discusses the
wordplay in the poem on the root "schaffen" (to create), which can
have an active and a passive possibility for meaning, and "in its equivocal in-between position between creature and creator designates really
most accurately of all the place of our own weakness. This lies precisely
in the fact that we are strong, and yet that this strength breaks down
only when it is called for. In this desperate experience that our own being [*Wesen*] ceases again and again to be our own, time, the faithless
one, which we must nevertheless again and again trust, even through
its faithlessness, teaches us that our work belongs to us as little as does
our day" (202/103). Human weakness and strength are so close that
only for theoretical, abstract, legal purposes, can intentionality be extracted as something in itself and can questions of intentionality therefore be posed. The actual deed always comrprises a totality in the
present tense of its occurrence which renders subsequent analysis, by
means of abstracting intention, meaningless.

Thus first of all for the violated world order, which demands restitution
through a healing counter-action – a counter-action which always must retain
something symbolic because indeed there are only immediate acts and no
"counter-acts." Secondly, however, also before the divine grace which according to the great word of the Talmud, turns acts of intention into acts of madness. And finally, most astonishing, even for the doer's own consciousness,
which, when and because it is not permitted to face the deed, its own deed,
with attempts at scientific analysis, but must face the deed, which for it is still
present tense, a pressing, not disposed of, present tense, as an indivisible
whole and which consequently cannot know where the consciousness has
stopped and the confusion has begun. It must disdain for itself as an unworthy
evasion the appeal to its own creatureliness, which his advocate puts forth for it
loudly before God's throne – as does the poet of this poem. (203/103–4)

In "Der Zwang" ("The Compulsion") Halevi's yearning for journeying to the Holy Land is overpowered and blighted by his worry about
leaving his home of over fifty years and by the horror of having no
home. Then suddenly there comes to him just what is required – the
compulsion to carry out his intended deed – and he departs gladly.
Rosenzweig remarks that honour is sought in one's actions. "But there
is in every such action a moment when man loses courage, precisely
because he has staked all of it" (247/227). If just at this moment the
compulsion did not arise, the deed would not be done. But that compulsion, to which the human being has a right, and which right God
recognizes, does come. "All praying is in the last resort a prayer for this
compulsion, all thanking a thankfulness for it. But the bashfulness,
which surrounds the prayer, has its basis here" (247/227).

The note to the poem "Vorgefühl" ("Foreboding") again picks up
the the idea of help coming from God to carry out a deed, and again
that help comes just at the crucial moment. Halevi has been lingering
in Egypt, enjoying the company of his friends, who pressingly urge him
to stay a little longer, and yet he implores them to let him go on. He
has not yet achieved his goal; he is merely on the way. The confusion
he experiences is a blending of the yearning for a grave in the Holy
Land with the presentiment that he will die before he arrives. "And
then out of all the confusion of the feeling once again the simple word
of the truth of the heart breaks through – indeed it cannot be otherwise" (256/248). At the end of the poem he is praying quietly, and
Rosenzweig observes that the one who prays like this is one who has
found himself again, at least for that moment. Rosenzweig here presents interesting comments on what he perceives as the confusion
which can take place after the time of a freely willed decision, and after
as well the moment of the divine spur of compulsion which has lent to
the doer fledgling wings. A new fear – the fear of a fall mid-flight –
seizes the one whose deed has not yet flown to the mark. Rosenzweig
writes:

But how could it possibly have been that he lost himself? Whoever would ask
like that, does not know how narrow is the space that is left to man and his
freedom with regard to that which is last and decisive. If ever an entire life has
ripened the fruit of a single action, then this. And yet the compulsion must
have come in order that the action actually was begun to be done. And as if
there were a danger that the action could still even then presume too much
and could forget the formerly promised gratitude for every step that allowed it
to achieve advancement, its strength is paralysed once more immediately before the final realization; the waters of earthly life threaten to engulf anew the
swimmer and he must again, in distress and out of necessity, learn to pray – the

prayer of distress, the totally sudden prayer – a prayer that is surprising even to the one who is praying. (257/248–9)

Rosenzweig explains that, whereas God gives to the human the freedom for the highest decision, he also keeps the powers for its realization, and only gives them out freely to the one who has made the decision, only when that one repeatedly calls to him. "For he does not want to make himself superfluous through the gift of freedom, but rather the reverse is most needful ... and as the divinely sent compulsion stood at the beginning of the realization, so at the end, nearly at the goal, there stands as propelling force the fear [Angst], the divinely produced fear, that following this today there could be no tomorrow. And then in this fear finally the deed is indeed born, which raises the today into the eternal tomorrow" (257/249).

Eternity and Time

As the just-cited note to "Vorgefühl" ("Foreboding") reveals, Rosenzweig holds that eternity and time can break into each other. In the note to "Der Lohn" ("The Reward"), he writes explicitly: "Eternity can of course break into every moment, but what it then seizes is only just this moment. Life on the whole is contained in few moments in such a way that it can graasp them in these moments. At the moment of birth as a life ahead; in one or two moments during life as a decisive one; and in death as a perfected one. Thus, only in death as a real, "present" whole. This worldly reality has life only here, and to want here to withdraw it from the clasp of eternity would mean that life never would be allowed to be an experienced whole" (206–7/110–11).

If eternity can break into time, then temporality and eternality are separate spheres which, because separate, can be bridged *from either side*. In connection with sacred time enacted in the cycle of the liturgical year, Stéphane Mosès states that it "is this sacred time that Rosenzweig calls *eternity*. For Rosenzweig eternity is not a time indefinitely stretched out forward but rather a total immobilization of the present instant, a state of perfect equilibrium absolutely outside the flow of time."[8]

Time has been created out of eternity, it is a creature. Time's borders with eternity are like the borders between the human being and God, and a relationship is possible which concludes in fulfilment at the moment of redemption. Rosenzweig explains the end and goal of this time-world in its relationship to that eternal-world not through a scriptural passage but through Scripture itself as a whole. In the note to

"Welt" ("World"), he designates Scripture as a power of separation in the world, and offers the following analogy regarding this power:

Scripture has gone into the world as a power of separation. Just on that account it itself was not allowed to contain the final and most fundamental split which was meant to arise out of it. The cutting edge of a knife may not itself be cut into two. Thus Scripture itself does not have the schism of this and that world, which everywhere, even in Judaism, opens up under its breath, (and which because both worlds are known as equally real, is entirely different from the Greek "real" and "apparent" world). And just for this reason it is the guarantee that this opposite which it has called forth in the first place, is not final and that this and that world are destined to come together cone again in eternity, out of which they have separated from one another. (211–12/124)

In the poem "Antwort" ("Reply"), Halevi is replying to someone who has attempted to dissuade him from going to the Holy Land. Rosenzweig observes how comfortable it is to forget the Holy Land's abiding connection in time with eternity the moment classical Greek notions of time and eternity are resorted to:

Even the assimilated Jew belongs to the eternal metaphorical expressions of Judaism. And his arguments have remained – should one say: shockingly? – the same: Jerusalem no longer concerns us today, because, just as when David conquered it, it is again inhabited by the "blind and lame" (2 Samuel 5:6,8), by foreign nations. And this unhistorical-historical argument unites itself then as now with the unphilosophical-philosophical (only the unpolitical-political is missing, but that would be inappropriate in the case of a single individual). And the philosophy that must be upheld in order to give relief to the national forgetfulness, then as now, is derived from the Greeks, who know only of beginningless and endless eternity, not of a one Eternal, who establishes beginning and end. (244/219)

Universal Language

The chapter on there being only one language has already covered the aspects of this sub-theme: the peace of redemption, which is promised by God but which human beings are also commanded to actively participate in bringing about. We have seen that love of neighbour is to be embodied in speech which testifies to the goodness, the love of God. Three times a day, Rosenzweig notes, the main prayer concludes by reciting the plea for peace to the "Lord of Peace." The concluding prayer, as well as the Kiddush, ends with, "The One who makes peace in his heights, let Him also make peace upon us and all his people."

"This conclusion of the prayers," Rosenzweig writes in the Note to
"Sein Friede" ("His Peace"), "is also the final conclusion of human wisdom. But in order that it may become the conclusion of wisdom, it
must be the beginning of action. Of an action which is, of course, doing" (184/59).

Doing, in connection with the universal language (as described in
the chapter on translation), means in part translating afresh, speaking
anew, the biblical word of revelation. Through live speech the biblical
word lives and is meaningful. The liveliness depends upon current life-
events which light up the meanings in the Bible, and not the other way
around. The Bible, in its fixed speech, remains empty of meaning to
both individual and community unless and until one's own life events
are brought to it. One's own enlivening of the biblical speech can en-
liven it also for others. This is Jehuda Halevi's great gift to us in his poetry. Rosenzweig uses "Exkurs: Ein Sprachkunststück" ("Excursus: An
Artistic Play on Words") (225/165) to offer tribute to his dear poet. In
many poems Halevi shows his talent for and joy in wordplay. In this
poem wordplay is the reigning feature, and Rosenzweig remarks that it
is surprising that this concentrated artistry is not more offensive. Thus,
Rosenzweig opens a discussion on the beginnings of the science of
grammar in answer to his own question: "Upon which relation with the
language does this poet base what is for us such unpoetic conduct?" In
his answer, Rosenzweig describes how Jehuda Halevi actively contrib-
utes to the speaking of the universal language. The young science of
grammar, Rosenzweig claims,

Is inseparable first of all from what we would call lexicography. Indeed, it is
even perceived in these early times as a lexicographic scientific aid. Indeed it
serves to fathom the word-sense of the Scriptures. And the astonishing phenomenon – astonishing surely only for a rationalistic conception of language
that sees in the language a method and consequently symbols in the words
(but all primitive science of language is thus rationalistic) – the astonishing
phenomenon then, that like-sounding words can have the most highly awkward different meanings, and this at least to some degree is cleared up
through grammar. Thus the vocabulary of the Scriptures grows wider and for
the first time is expanded before the observing eye. The poets however now
solemnize the acquisition of this fortune by freely dealing with it anew and by
taking a word, which in the Scriptures occurs only once, and which one thus
"hardly knows" in natural usage. The whole fortune of this treasure of language, which the twenty-four extant boods of the Old Hebrew literature encompassed, has become for the first time through this Spanish poetry an
entirely conscious possession for the people, and becomes such still today for
anyone who entrusts himself to the leadership of this master which newly ar-

ranges the precious treasures in the museum of the Bible in an enduring way: now this, now that gem is drawn near into the right light and thus the whole is saved from a museum-like torpor. This is the national-historical meaning of the assuredly childish play as this poem practises it. (226–7/166–7)

Halevi's famous poem "An Zion" ("Ode to Zion"), which concludes the Zion section, is a song of lament which is recited on Tisha b'Av, the Ninth of Av, the day of the destruction of the first and second temples. The ode concludes in a forgetting of the lament, in a rejoicing beforehand of the future jubilation. Of this conclusion, written by one who has become filled with the knowledge that both Israel's suffering and greatness "are destined to crown Zion with an eternal crown," Rosenzweig comments: "Blessed is he who awaits and experiences it and perceives" (259/254). And the one who speaks in such words carries them for all time and into the silence of eternity:

One usually treats the story as legend that Jehuda Halevi at the goal of his pilgrimage and in sight of the Holy City, was killed by an Arab with his song on his lips. It is such without a doubt. But there is still less doubt that the story cannot have been much different. He who composed this poem, it must have accompanied him into his hour of death. There is no room left for anything else. (259/254–5)

Appendices

The Problem of the English Aids
to the Understanding of Rosenzweig's
Translations into German

In three distinct parts I will attempt to lay out the problem, which must remain insoluble, with regard to translating the poetry section of Rosenzweig's Halevi book. Understanding the problem can at most produce a soothing effect on an otherwise utterly upsetting situation.

The first part of this discussion simply provides a list of translation principles which were being debated in the early years of this century. The second describes the problem of translating precisely the Halevi book, which is in part itself a translation. The third presents further problems as assessed by Rafael Rosenzweig, Franz's son, but concludes on a pleasing note with two translations of Halevi poetry.

In 1922 J.P. Postgate, a translator of classical Greek and Latin authors and a scholar seasoned with fifty years' experience, published *Translation and Translations: Theory and Practice*. This book breathes the flavour of the times. Its concerns complement Rosenzweig's. Arising out of a similar pre-post-modern approach, Western theories of translation revolve around, and are nearly exclusively restricted to, the works of classical Greece and Rome, and hence of works primarily in verse. For this first part, obvious parallels can be drawn between Rosenzweig's and Postgate's respective comments on the views of the then famed translator from Berlin of Greek classics, Ulrich von Wilamowitz-Moellendorff (1848–1931). In the Afterword, Rosenzweig wittily disagrees with the translation theories of Wilamowitz, and Postgate finds cause to call him a misrepresenter, one whose translations are sham originals. For a full first-hand account of Wilamowitz's views, the preface to his edition of Euripides Hippolytos, "Was ist Übersetzen?" ["What is Translating?"], is reproduced in that excellent collection gathered by Hans Störig, *Das Problem des Übersetzens*. The only point here is to show, superficially, the principles being used and vigorously argued by various translators and to pinpoint the principle which most closely resembles the one I used for offering aid to English readers of the poetry section of Rosenzweig's Halevi book.

The second, very brief part of this appendix, based precariously on the pinpointed principle, will be an attempt to define the frustrating details of the particular translating problem here. It is a dilemma; all translators agree that one does not translate from a translation. In the case at hand, however, as will be disclosed, it is not possible to translate from the original.

In the third part, I give examples of problems unstated by Rosenzweig but brought to my attention through correspondence with his son, Rafael. This is notwithstanding Rosenzweig's care in showing changes he made in the transition from the original to the translation in his "On the translation" notations at the conclusion of each Note. I conclude with two translations from the original Hebrew, one by Nina Salaman, the other by Olga Marx. Somewhere in this book, Jehuda Halevi ought truly to sing in English.

TRANSLATION PRINCIPLES DISCUSSED IN THE 1920S

Postgate depicts and discusses eight principles and theories in an enthusiastically engaged manner. My aim here is barely more than to list; Postgate's animated style will be blunted here. Attention to Wilamowitz will be drawn where pertinent throughout the list of translating principles. All page references in parentheses are to Postgate's volume.

The first principle is faithfulness, and, although defined in widely sweeping variations, is a principle upon which all translators agree.

The second, hotly debated, principle is that translation is for the pleasure of the reader. Postgate disparagingly notes that to Wilamowitz "accurate translation" is an "unmixed evil" (24). Wilamowitz's dictum is that "Every translation is a travesty" (5); he thus applauds making the translation more elegant than the original. Postgate protests views like Wilamowitz's, and is appalled that the trend of the principle of translating with the reader's pleasure in mind, while not always professed, is "more often creeping into its practice" (5).

The third principle is a closely connected one: the translator here aims to produce a translation which pretends to be the original. Postgate again points a finger at Wilamowitz, who aims to achieve precisely this. Wilamowitz, as a contemporary example of a translator who seeks to create a "new original," holds that neither words nor sentences should be translated. Rather, he says, feelings and thoughts ought to be taken up and reproduced. In the reproduction of feelings and thoughts, the content, Wilamowitz thinks, is thus unchanged, and only the cover differs between original and translation. That is to say, he claims that the soul remains, but the body is changed, and that true translation is metempsychosis (7).

It follows, then, in the next link of connected principles, that as "original" the translation, that is, the translator, is the proprietor of the true original *and* of the translation. Concerning this fourth principle, note how Rosenzweig, in exacerbated dissent, insists in the Afterword to his own translations that the reader remain always aware that he is reading poems not by Rosenzweig, not by a contemporary, but by Jehuda Halevi from the Middle Ages.

The fifth principle contends that the faithful translator will convey the spirit and, where possible, the letter of the original. Postgate criticizes this principle by stating that the transfuser is too prone to lose both letter and spirit. The notion of translation of the spirit seems to concur with Rosenzweig's notion of translating the contours; at the same time, of course, Rosenzweig also wants the detailed relief of every letter. So, too, does Postgate, according to whom to lose one is at the same time to lose the other. As an example of the sacrifice of both letter and spirit, Postgate cites a passage in Wilamowitz's translation of Euripides, at Hippolytos 555–64. Postgate's evaluation is: "The serenity and sobriety of the Greek have disappeared to make room for a riot and turbulence of language more in keeping, were the scene the Teutoburger Wald and the occasion a Walpurgisnacht" (14).

Adding vigour to an original, dressing it up in modern styles of expression, and similar alterations represent the sixth principle. Postgate laments that following such a principle "may transform an original into something which itself is an accession to literature" (16) because it ministers and conforms to current tastes and shuns what might be read as anachronisms. Rosenzweig poses the humorous question in the Afterword about whether the Apollo Belvedere would really be enhanced if he were wearing a cutaway collar.

The seventh principle involves the sentimental theory which aims at literal translation. This most closely describes what I have done with the poems in their German translations, all the while maintaining, however, that what I have done does not fall under the category of translating, but only under that of an aid to understanding. Postgate defines this principle as "a translation which is the nearest intelligible rendering of the words of the foreign original, whether it would have been employed in the circumstances by a native writer or not" (17–18). The consistently literal translation is a "crib" and "has a value of its own; but it is as an aid to the understanding of an original, *not as a substitute therefor* [my emphasis]. A growing fashion in translation ... interpaginates translation and original. That this juxtaposition should affect the character of the translation, which thus plays a subordinate role, is very natural. That it ought to do so is by no means so clear." In the case of an "aid to the understanding of" a *translation* of an original, the subordination of this aid is by all means, of course, clearly deliberate and desirable.

The eighth principle represents one that Postgate himself was attempting to formulate and focus. It concerns the question of who is being considered in translating, the author of the original, or the prospective reader of the translation. Postgate states that it is "unfortunate that usage has not provided distinctive names for translation which primarily regards the Author and translation which primarily regards the Reader" (18). With the last principle discussed by Postgate, a question is raised that is cursorily answered later by Walter Benjamin in the first paragraph of his "Task of the Translator," also found in Störig's collection. I have come to agree with Benjamin that the consideration of the receiver does not prove fruitful in the appreciation of art or of an art form; and that the translator looks only at the original and does not consider the reader. This agreement adds to the problem of translating the Halevi book, and deserves frank exposition.

THE PROBLEM DESCRIBED

I have stated the problem above as a dilemma, that whereas one cannot translate from a translation, I cannot in this case do otherwise. Before stating precisely why the original cannot be used in this case, let me state, through Walter Benjamin, why one cannot translate from translations.

The higher the level of a work, the more does it remain translatable even if its meaning is touched upon only fleetingly. This, of course, applies to originals only. Translations, on the other hand, prove to be untranslatable not because of any inherent difficulty, but because of the looseness with which meaning attaches to them. Confirmation of this as well as of every other important aspect is supplied by Hölderlin's translations, particularly those of the two tragedies by Sophocles. In them the harmony of the languages is so profound that sense is touched by language only the way an aeolian harp is touched by the wind ... Where a text is identical with truth or dogma ... this text is unconditionally translatable. (*Illuminations*, 81; Störig, 194–5)

Had Rosenzweig's Halevi book been *only* a book of translations accompanied, say, by a preface, an introduction, a life of Jehuda Halevi, or the Afterword alone, translating from the original would of course have been the only choice open. His Notes, however, alter the picture and close the choice. So closely are the Notes tied to his own translations and to his technique of translation, so frequently are references made to precisely how Rosenzweig rendered this rhyme and that metre, this tone and that contour and to how he accommodated these in his translations, and so frequently does he refer to his own translated lines, that the Hebrew alone, or any English translations from the Hebrew *would no longer make any sense in connection with the Notes themselves.*

The Notes constitute an example of a practical application of Rosenzweig's philosophy, certainly in connection with the poems; but the poems, even in translation, are emphatically Halevi's voice, and the Notes, Rosenzweig's. The exemplification of the philosophy is in part to stress the fact of separate, individual voices and the right to the separateness. Translating, then, from Rosenzweig's translations, would blur Halevi's voice and would loosen the meaning attached to his voice on an English horizon distanced from the Hebrew through the German.

Further, my task was to translate *Rosenzweig's* book, and to follow this translation with a commentary. Rosenzweig's task was to translate *Halevi's* poems, and to follow *this* translation, that is to say this *listening* to Halevi with his own philosophical response.

The area of impossibility in my task of translation really is an area of impossibility: it is an area which is empty, in which there is nothing to translate. If I am not permitted to translate from a *translation* of an artwork, and yet, through weighting the attention on the Notes to the poems, I am not permitted to translate from the *original* of the artwork, then I have nothing to translate.

Here, then, I come to break another sound rule in translation principles and theories: I must consider my reader; I must consider the fact that one who knows German well would prefer to read the original Rosenzweig's Halevi book, and the only ones who would be tempted to read my translation would be those who have no German or too little for access to the original. I would much prefer to leave the German translations standing on their own, but, if translations are not possible, then I still must give *some* meaning, at the high price of sacrificing the beauty of both the Hebrew original and the German translation, to readers without German.

To conclude the definition of the problem: it would have been ridiculous to translate from the Hebrew; it would have been ridiculous to translate from a translation; yet it would have been ridiculous not to have given an aid, subordinated on left-hand pages, to English readers for the understanding of Rosenzweig's German translations, *whether or not these English readers know any Hebrew.* There was, and there is, no solution.

EXAMPLES OF FURTHER PROBLEMS,
AND TWO TRANSLATIONS

The 1983 Nijhoff edition of Rosenzweig's Halevi book, introduced and edited by Rosenzweig's son, provides two interesting footnotes in which Rafael Rosenzweig has detected errors. One is to "Zürnende Liebe" ["Angry Love"], the other to "Der Pilger" ["The Pilgrim"], on pages 187 and 223 respectively in the Nijhoff edition. The notes are as follows:

For "Angry Love," line 2 in Rosenzweig's translation reads: "und konntst mich verkaufen je/ du meinen Vertilgern just" ["and how could you ever sell me to my exterminators"]. The Hebrew is וְלָמָּה מְכַרְתָּנִי צְמִיתָת לְמַעְבָּדִי. Rafael Rosenzweig writes: "In the Hebrew text the last word of this line is 'למעביד', which would have to be translated in this connection with 'my enslavers'. 'My exterminators' used by FR [sic] would correspond to the Hebrew 'למאבידי' a reading which does not appear in any of the sources indicated in the second edition [i.e., the 1927 edition]."

For "The Pilgrim," the reference is to line 21: "und ich hör auf, zu gehn wo Weg und Steg ist" ["and I cease to go where there is road and path"]. Rafael Rosenzweig writes: "The literal translation reads: And I no longer walked on my souls and nose. In classical Hebrew nose and face are often synonymous. The wording, which is incomprehensible in the Hebrew connection, complies directly with the connection of the poem, if it is translated (or perhaps translated back) into the classical Arabic. 'Dshaba ala waj'hihi' (He walked on his face) means: he walked aimlessly, without paying attention to the road."

Other minor details include, for example, the following: for the poem "Heim"["Home"], Rafael Rosenzweig pointed out to me that, for Stanza 2, line 5, the Hebrew reads: וְאֶת מַמְּהוּ תַּפְרָח. In English this is: "And his staff he lets blossom." Rosenzweig translated the line with "be gracious, and let the scales of fate turn," but offers, in his On the translation notation, this alternative: "and all my doing / let prosper."

The first word in line 4 of Stanza 2 of "Treue" ["Faithfulness"], translated by Rosenzweig as "sons", is problematic. The Hebrew is הַגְרִי , which neither Rafael nor I understands, but which quite certainly does not mean "sons."

These examples show the further complexities in the area described as impossible. Possible, however, both quite outside and quite inside the bounds of Rosenzweig's book, are fine translations from the Hebrew of Jehuda Halevi's artistic and devotional beauty. Rosenzweig's feat of taking the acrostics, rhyme, and metre into German has not been achieved in English, but beautiful English versions have been written, and are certainly true to the spirit.

One of Nahum N. Glatzer's great gifts, as is evidenced in *Franz Rosenzweig: His Life and Thought*, his collection of Kafka's writings, *I am a Memory Come Alive*, and *Language of Faith* is his gift of character sketching. With a stress and a focus and a highlight on now just this detail and now just that feature, Glatzer succeeds, with suggestive lines, in sketching with both breadth and depth. In his *Language of Faith*, not only does he give the reader a profound sense of the themes and moods of devotional Hebrew poetry, but as well, by including only two poems by Jehuda Halevi, he gives a sense of the talent of this sweetest of medieval Hebrew poets.

The poem which Rosenzweig entitles "Der Wahre" ["The True One"] is presented in Glatzer's collection in an English translation by Olga Marx, entitled there "With All My Strength" (68–9). As well, eight lines of the poem Rosenzweig entitles "Der Fern-und-Nahe" ["The Far and Near One"] appears in Nina Salaman's translation, with the title "Lord, Where Shall I Find Thee?" (70–1).

For ease oof comparison and linkage among the three languages involved in the translations, four versions in succession appear here for each of the two examples. The original Hebrew is first. Then the English translations are followed by Rosenzweig's German translations. The English aids for access to the German appear last, and although they will be seen to be distant from the original, still, something of the truths Halevi sings echoes faintly through, indestructible.

בְּכָל לִבִּי אֱמֶת וּבְכָל מְאֹדִי
אֲהַבְתִּיךָ וּבְגָלוּיִי וְסוֹדִי
שְׁמָךְ נֶגְדִּי וְאֵיךְ אֵלֵךְ לְבַדִּי
וְהוּא דוֹדִי וְאֵיךְ אֵשֵׁב יְחִידִי
וְהוּא נֵרִי וְאֵיךְ יִדְעַךְ מְאוֹרִי
וְאֵיךְ אֶצְעַן וְהוּא מִשְׁעָן בְּיָדִי
חֲקָלוּנִי מְתִים לֹא יָדְעוּ כִּי
קְלוֹנִי עַל כְּבוֹד שְׁמָךְ כְּבוֹדִי
מְקוֹר חַיַּי אֲבָרֶכְךָ בְּחַיַּי
וְזִמְרָתִי אֲזַמֶּרְךָ בְּעוֹדִי

With all my strength and spirit, I adore
You, Truth, aloud and in my secret core.
I hoard your name. And who can rob this spoil?
He is my love. What other could I crave?
He is my light. How could my lamp need oil?
How can I falter, leaned on such a stave?
They mock – and do not know that mockery,
Because I praise your name, is praise to me.

Source of my life, your praise shall sound as long
As I can breathe my fervor into song.

Mit ganzer Kraft, Du Wahrheit, ganzer Seele
   hab ich Dich lieb, im Licht, in Busens Hehle.
Dein Name mein! – wo gäbs, der den mir stehle?
   Mein Liebster Er! – wen gäbs, der da mir fehle?
Mein Licht Er – meinem Docht gebrächs an Öle?
   Gäbs Wank? wo solchem Stab ich mich empfehle!
Ihr Hohn schmält – Toren! wird doch Hohngeschmäle
   ob Deiner Krone mir zum Kronjuwele!
Mein Lebensborn! sei Dir Ein Preis mein Leben
   und Sang, solang noch Hauch in meiner Hehle.

With all my strength, You, Truth, with all my soul
   do I love you, in the light, in the secret of my bosom.
Your Name is mine! – where could there be anyone, if someone stole
     it from me?
   My Beloved, He! – who could there be who would be missing
     there?
My Light, He! – could my wick be devoid of oil?
   Could there be stumbling? where I rely on such a staff?
Their mockery derides – fools! yet derisive mockery
   of your crown becomes for me the crown jewel!
My fountain of life! may my life be a praise for You
   and my song, as long as there is breath in me.

יָהּ אָנָה אֶמְצָאֶךָ
מְקוֹמְךָ נַעֲלָה וְנֶעְלָם
וְאָנָה לֹא אֶמְצָאֶךָ
כְּבוֹדְךָ מָלֵא עוֹלָם

דְּרַשְׁתִּי קִרְבָתֶךָ
בְּכָל לִבִּי קְרָאתִיךָ
וּבְצֵאתִי לִקְרָאתֶךָ
לִקְרָאתִי מְצָאתִיךָ

Lord, where I shall I find thee?
High and hidden is thy place;
And where shall I not find thee?
The world is full of thy glory.

I have sought thy nearness,
With all my heart I called thee,
And going out to meet thee
I found thee coming toward me.

Ja Gott wo wirst funden Du,
        des Raum hülln Ätherweiten.
Und wo nicht wärest funden Du,
        des Saum füllt Erdenbreiten.
...
Deiner Nähe wegen
        ging aus mein Herz, aufglomms zu Dir.
So kams Dir entgegen –
        sieh! entgegen kommst du mir.

God, where are You found,
        Whose space the breadths of aether veil.
And where would You not be found,
        Whose border fills the breadths of the earth.
...
For the sake of your nearness
        my heart went out, glimmered up to You.
Thus it came towards You –
        see! You come towards me.

Reversed Fronts
(A Translation of Rosenzweig's "Vertauschte Fronten", from Zweistromland [Nijhoff, 1984], 235–7)

Ten years after Hermann Cohen's death[1*] the first edition of his post-humously published work on the philosophy of religion was out of print. That first edition had stood under an unlucky star. Its text was more similar in parts to the indiscriminate copy of any manuscript of an old work than to a modern printed work and particularly to a work of Cohen, even in the first two-thirds, whose printing Cohen himself had still supervised: Cohen, true to his word, which was handed down by Robert Fritzsche:[2*] "The philological aspect must always be in order," consistently applied special attention to the production of the text of his works. In this second edition Bruno Strauss[3*] has made up for that "philological aspect" which had been neglected in the first edition, and with the most beautiful critical caution and most pious empathy established the most authentic wording in these circum-stances out of a collection of samples of possible textual corruptions – even long marginal notes of others, e.g., of the great Frankfurt Rabbi

---

* To accompany the section in chapter 4: "Scholarly Attention to the Note on Miracles." See chapter 4, n. 1.

1* Hermann Cohen (1842–1918), Professor of philosophy at Marburg 1873–1912. Neo-Kantian. In his later years a lecturer at the school of the Science of Judaism [Wissenschaft des Judentums].

2* Robert Arnold Fritzsche, born 1868, D.Phil., Librarian in Gießen, friends with Hermann Cohen.

3* Bruno Strauss (1889–1969), grew up in Marburg, studied classical antiqui-ty and German philology. Beginning 1918, high school teacher in Berlin. Emigrated in 1939 to the U.S.A. where he taught at a college in Louisiana.

Nobel,[4*] who gave help to his friend and teacher, had got into the text, quite as was the case with works from the time before the invention of printing!

The book even went under a false title during the nine years of its first run! It was called: "The Religion of Reason from the Sources of Judaism;" it is really called "Religion of Reason from the Sources of Judaism" without the aggressive and intolerant definite – and here really all too definite – article. Of course, what is intended is not the opposite, the indefinite article, which here really would be too indefinite. Rather Cohen means, equally far from an arrogant exclusion and comfortable everything-is-allowed, the part in the one and general religion of reason, to which the sources of Judaism which arise in its inheritance lead him. To him, these, to others, others. But to him, these. And of course: the sources are original sources, humanity drank from them. Only this historical consciousness mixes into the pious modesty of the permission to take part, a little of humble-joyful pride.

Thus is the Jewish side of the work, the task of a "Jewish ethic and philosophy of religion," which it had taken upon itself to solve within the scope of a collected work and to which it gave one of the few – one may already say today – classical solutions for Judaism, yet not the most important one at any rate at the present moment and for its philosophical situation not the most important. Today at least the classical character of the work is overshadowed by its actual meaning.

This actual meaning lies, as it could become visible only after Cohen's death, thus also beyond Cohen's own intention and insight. He had altogether a strange thinker's fate. The works of the time of his apprenticeship, which he drew up in Kant's workplace, especially the first, the work of the twenty-eight-year-old, then revolutionized the philosophical science of the time and were generally accepted, at least in their negative result, the antipsychologism of the Kantian interpretation, and till today, that is after almost sixty years, remained of unchanged validity. It was not as good for the works of the master-time: his own system was barely noticed outside the narrower school and even there stood in the shadow of the earlier writings which interpreted Kant; thus the great comprehensive system, for which the time ostensibly asked, entered, not into the time, rather alongside it, the

---

4*Nehemia Anton Nobel (1871–1922), classical and Talmudic scholar. Dissertation: "Schopenhauers Theorie des Schönen" ["Schopenhauer's Theory of the Beautiful"]. Zionist, co-founder of the religious Zionist movement, "Mizrachi" in 1902. Rabbi in Frankfurt. Professorship for Jewish theology at the University of Frankfurt.

off-centre work by a spirit who was very much moved by the time, yet foreign to it. And finally the old man, the seventy-year-old, draws up, within the plan of his system and confined and bound by it, the installation and extension which had originally not been planned and had actually been excluded; and with this completion he now steps not into his own time, but beyond it into ours.

For, that which only five years ago, when I expressed it in the introduction to Cohen's Jewish Writings, could be published as a personal opinion about the philosophical tendency of the present, has in the meantime become commonly familiar. In Davos, a short time ago, that conversation between Cohen's most distinguished pupil Cassirer[5*] and the current custodian of Cohen's Marburg chair, Heidegger, took place before a European forum, about which Hermann Herrigel[6*] reports in detail in the Hochschulblatt of the Frankfurter Zeitung of 22 April 1929, as a representative discussion between old and new thinking. And here Heidegger, the pupil of Husserl, the Aristotelian scholastic, whose occupation of Cohen's chair can only be felt as an irony of the history of thought by every "old Marburger," represented, in opposition to Cassirer, a philosophical position, precisely the position of our, the new thinking, which lies wholly in the line which derives from that "last Cohen."

For what else is it, when Heidegger, in opposition to Cassirer, gives the task to philosophy to reveal to the human being, to the "specifically finite being," his own "worthlessness in spite of all freedom" and to recall him "from the lazy aspect of a person who merely makes use of the works of the spirit, into the hardship of his fate," – what is this final formulation of the philosophical task other than that impassioned representation of the "Individuums quand même" against the "Learned-Bourgeois-Thought," that one must "honour the thinker in the soul and accordingly look upon the intellectual transport towards the eternity of culture as the main force and the particular worth of the poor

---

5*Ernst Cassirer (1874–1945), philosopher, interested in language. Emigrated to the u.s.a. in 1933.

6*Dr Hermann Herrigel (1888–?), theologian. Contributor to the Festschrift for Martin Buber of 1928: *Aus unbekannten Schriften* [From Unknown Writings]. Wrote an essay with the same title as Rosenzweig's, "Das neue Denken" ["The New Thinking"], in 1928. Herrigel's writings have had no significant effect.

human individual"7* (Cohen's letter to Stadler after Gottfried Keller's death), the vital personal source of that realization of the "later Cohen" which developed into a philosophy not until a quarter of a century later? If Heidegger said in Davos what he calls "existence," it could not be expressed by a concept of Cassirer: that just referred to introduction showed just with the help of the basic concept of the philosophy of Cohen's old age, namely the "correlation," how from it, as the later Cohen uses it, the start leads to the – to express it in Heidegger's language – "leap into existence." Not in vain is the chapter found in the old-age work, which is inspired and leaves all "Marburg" far behind, and which replaces the "engendering" reason of Idealism by the divinely created, reason as creature.

The survivors of the "school" – not Cassirer! – would like to make a schoolmaster out of the dead master. The living, progressing history of the spirit removes him from such a schoolboyish undertaking; it does not pay any attention to such claims and reverses the fronts when the dead Cid now sets out anew. The school dies with its schoolmaster; the master lives.

7*Rosenzweig is quoting here from a letter by Hermann Cohen. The letter is written to Ernst Stadler (1883–1914), of Strassburg, the German philologist and Expressionist poet, and translator of poems by Charles Péguy. The occasion of the letter is the death of Gottfried Keller (1819–1890), who is considered to be the greatest of the German-Swiss poets.

Notes to Part One

1 The German edition I am using is Franz Rosenzweig, *Jehuda Halevi,*
   Zweiundneunzig Hymnen und Gedichte, Deutsch, mit einem Nachwort und mit
   Anmerkungen, Der Sechzig Hymnen und Gedichte Zweite Ausgabe, Berlin:
   Verlag Lambert Schneider, 1927. See in Part II, Chapter 1, in the section
   on The Form of the Halevi Book for discussion of the third edition, published in 1983 by Kluwer.
   The English "renderings" of the poems, presented here on the left-hand
   pages, are not to be viewed as translations. They are not translations, but
   only a guide into the content of Rosenzweig's versions of the Halevi poems.
   One does not translate from translations of a literary or poetic work of art;
   one translates only from originals. My capabilities as a translator do not extend to poetry. In any case, I cannot bring Halevi's poems into English, neither from the Hebrew nor from the German, in any way that is remotely
   close to the level of Rosenzweig's achievement in German. The only fully
   satisfactory translation of the Halevi poems into English would be one that
   reflects Rosenzweig's feat in German: acrostics, metre, rhyme, tone, contours, all these intact in the new language. I have yet to see any of Halevi's
   poems truly and fully translated into English; how welcome this would be.
   See Appendix A for a fuller discussion of the problems of translating a
   book which itself is in part a translation.
   Glatzer, in his *Life and Thought,* provides translations from 14 of the
   Notes, two or three *in toto,* most excerpted. I chose, however, to keep this
   chapter consistently my own translation. It may be noticed both in the
   translations provided in Glatzer's book and in my own that the language in
   many places reads in a flowery, hymnic and even lofty style. This is appropriate not only to Rosenzweig's original German but also, I would argue, to
   the subjects addressed.

In the Notes to the Poems, moreover, Rosenzweig makes frequent references to biblical passages. For the ease of the reader, I have quoted these passages, as well as some references to lines from the poems, as footnotes, from the Jerusalem Bible translation. Please note, however, that the biblical passages are cited only, and not quoted, in the 1927 original. To differentiate these footnotes clearly from the endnotes, they are numbered as follows: 1*, 2*, 3* and so on.

AFTERWORD

1 A periodical of rather low literary standard.
2 Iwan Müller, editor of *Handbuch der klassischen Altertums-Wissenschaft.* Franz Schulze, German scholar active in the 1920s. Emil B. Cohn, translator of Jehuda Halevi; in 1921 he published a volume of translation which turned out to be the incentive for Rosenzweig's own translation enterprise. So inadequate was Cohn's work in Rosenzweig's estimation he could not help but try his own hand at the task. See Glatzer, *Life and Thought,* 122: Cohn's translations "annoyed me so much that verse came out of it." The left-hand pages of the poetry part in this volume are not intended to annoy, but only to guide the English speaker; still, perhaps they will similarly motivate someone to accomplish that which I cannot.
3 Ulrich von Wilamowitz-Moellendorf (1848–1931). Philologist. See his "Was ist Übersetzen?" ["What is Translating?"] in Hans Störig, ed., *Das Problem des Übersetzens.*
4 Also a periodical of a low literary standard.
5 Rosenzweig's Footnote: Fairness requires us not to conceal that the most important authority in the field of the history of classical antiquity, Eduard Meyer, has uncovered an alternate explanation why melancholy lies upon the faces of the Pharoahs from the centuries of the Middle Kingdom: heavy cares concerning government. So it can be read in his history of antiquity.
6 Biblical text of the Old and New Testaments, published by D.E. Kautzsch. The New Testament is in the translation of Carl Weizsäcker (1822–1899), Protestant theologian.
7 Heller, Die echten hebräischen Melodien [Genuine Hebrew Melodies], Frankfurt a.M., 3. Aufl. 1908.
8 The translation of the poem, page 217 ["Antwort"; "Reply"], makes an attempt at imitation by keeping the pre-rhyme vowels of the original. But it is unavoidable that the German reader here senses not so much the similarity of the last syllable, but rather the rhymes of the pre-rhyme syllables, which are scattered through the poem and which are incidental from the Hebraic feeling for rhyme

9 Rosenzweig's footnote: Sephardic (Spanish) and Ashkenaz (German) are the two most important pronunciations of Hebrew. The essential difference consists in the manner of reading some vocals [vowels] (e.g. Aulom – world; Ashkenaz, and Olam, Sephardic) and in the accent of the last syllables in Sephardic as opposed to the accent, in many cases, on the penultimate in Ashkenaz.

10 Stefan George (1868–1933). German poet, and translator of Baudelaire, Shakespeare, Dante, and contemporary poets.

11 Rosenzweig's footnote: An example of an exact rendering of the original rhythm is given in the poem "Exkurs: Sturm" ["Excursus: Storm"] pages 248ff. Only four syllables per line, constructed in German as double iambic, are rhythmically essential. The others are to fill out the line.

12 Eighth-ninth century Frankish secretary and biographer of Charlemagne.

13 A figure of speech or term that appears only once in the sources – in this case the Bible.

14 Fast Day in commemoration of the Destruction of the First and Second Temples.

NOTES TO THE POEMS

1 I repeat here what I mentioned in note 1 to the Poetry section. Nahum N. Glatzer, in his *Life and Thought*, includes translations from 14 of the 92 Notes, two or three *in toto*, most excerpted. After some thought, I chose to keep this chapter consistently my own translation. It will be noticed in both Glatzer's translations and my own that the language in many places reads in a flowery, hymnic and, to some ears, even a pompous style. This is appropriate not only to Rosenzweig's original German but also, I would argue, to the subjects addressed.

Rosenzweig makes frequent references to biblical passages. For the ease of the reader, I have quoted these passages in footnotes, from the Jerusalem Bible translation. To differentiate them clearly from the endnotes, they are numbered as follows: 1*, 2*, 3* and so on. In the original there are several footnotes by Rosenzweig; these footnotes are being placed here as endnotes 2, 5, 6, 9 and 15.

2 Rosenzweig's footnote: I am giving as many places as possible of discovery, not merely those of the standard editions, because I do not want to make it more difficult for the reader through scientific snobbery, to which I would have no right in this area anyhow, to use the edition which is perhaps within his range of reach or borrowing – in the sense of the Afterword's motto. – I will indicate the abbreviations: Luz., Bet. = Luzzatto,

Virgo filia Jehudae. Prag 1840. Luz., Div. = Luzzatto, Divan des Jehuda ha-Levi. Lyck 1864. Sachs = Religiöse Poesie der Juden in Spanien. 2. Aufl. Berlin 1901. Harkavy = J.J. Sammlung seiner Gedichte. 2 Bde. Warschau 1893 and 1895. Brody-Albrecht = Die neuhebräische Dichterschule der spanisch-arabischen Epoche. Leipzig 1905. Brody = Diwan J.H.'s. 3 Bde. Berlin 1901, 1909, 1910f. Brody-Wiener = Anthologia Hebraica. Leipzig 1922.

3 The remarks on the translations [Zur Übersetzung] which conclude each note display the exactness with which Rosenzweig at all times wishes to translate: any occasion on which he finds he must stray from the original in dictionary-literal word-translation for reasons of rhyme adherence or for reasons of capturing the language-spirit of the foreign tongue at the expense of a literally translated word, Rosenzweig indicates the place. He sometimes adds a word, for rhyme, for clarity, that would not be evidenced from a strict, schoolroom translation. Often, also, he offers an alternate rendering that could have served for his translated lines; but these alternatives are Rosenzweig's second choices. This first "Zur Übersetzung" section is accompanied by a footnote which reads: "See the conclusion of the Afterword. I have not mentioned here the paraphrases which convey themselves within the illustrative circle of the idea rendered, as for example the part for the whole (e.g. for "rivers:" "the river's waves") or affirmation through negated negation (e.g. "not ceasing" for "continuing"). To be sure, even these small freedoms are not desirable, but are nevertheless always comparatively harmless over against the dances of the paraphraser and free-renderer."

4 The collector of the Divan was Rabbi Jeshua.

5 Rosenzweig's footnote: Mishnah Chagiga (Festivals) 2. Each person who looks at four things, it would be for him as if he had not come into the world: what is above and what is below, what is ahead and what behind.

6 Rosenzweig's footnote: Mishnah, Avoda Sara (Idol Worship) 4, One asked the ancients in Rome: If HE did not permit idol worship – why did he not allow it to fall away? They answered: If they worshipped a thing that the world did not need, he would make it fall away; but they worship the sun, the moon, the planets and the stars – should His world be lost on account of their stupidity? Then one answered the ancient ones: if it is so for that one, He should let the idols be lost which the world does not need, and that which the world needs should remain. They answered: Then if we strengthened specifically the hands of those who worship what the world needs and then they would say: Recognize however that they are divine, for they were not made dispensible.

7 Rosenzweig is referring to the Hebrew grammatical form called *smichut*, in this case occurring in the word-form "soul *of*," "soul *belonging to*," after which is expected the designation of the owner, here, finally: "all Living

Things." While "all Living Things" is properly the genitive, it is only "soul" which shows inflection.

8 Baron Wilhelm von Humboldt (1767–1835), German philologist and diplomat; philosopher of language and translation who investigated notions of pure language.

9 Rosenzweig's footnote: Babylonian Talmud, Yoma, page 36b. There Moses spoke to the Holy, Praised be He: Lord of the World – at the hour when Israel sins before You, and practices return, turn their outrages into madnesses.

10 From Pirke Avot [Ethics of Our Fathers].

11 Ernst Häckel (1834–1919), Zoologist, Darwinist.

12 Wilhelm Wundt (1832–1920), Philosopher and psychologist.

13 Johann Eisenmenger (1654–1704), Orientalist, author of antisemitic writings.

14 Abraham Geiger (1810–1874), leader of Jewish religious liberalism in Germany, co-founder of the Wissenschaft des Judentums [Science of Judaism].

15 Rosenzweig's footnote: Babylonian Talmud: Tractate Sanhedrin, 97b: The Rabbi said: All ends of time have been fulfilled, and the matter depends alone upon return and good works.

16 In the 1924 edition of the Notes the poem is translated "Auf dem Nil" ("On the Nile"), and the Note, as does the title, differs. The earlier Note reads: "The ship's course leads past Egypt, and here again one of the splendid homelike worlds surrounds the pilgrim. But the splendour of the miracle that is fixed to the name of this soil outshines this world and admonishes him to break away whither the Patriarchs had set out. It is already the atmosphere of the scriptural writing, but not yet the air of the land."

Notes to Part Two

1 Rosenzweig had similar frustrations in other contexts. Nahum N. Glatzer writes concerning the otherwise successful Freies Jüdisches Lehrhaus (Free House of Jewish Studies), of which Rosenzweig was the head: "Rosenzweig's own lecture course, attended by about one hundred persons, was a failure. He was motivated by a passionate urge to teach, to interpret, to clarify. But he was simply unable to realize the intellectual limitations of even intelligent, university-trained men and women. He did not talk their language and they did not understand his. His listeners sensed his greatness; yet he did not want to be admired, but understood." (Glatzer, "The Frankfort Lehrhaus," 109).

2 "Das neue Denken," in *Der Mensch und sein Werk, Gesammelte Schriften*, 3, *Zweistromland: Kleinere Schriften zu Glauben und Denken*, 152. Henceforth referred to as "Das neue Denken." Other essays from the volume will refer to *Zweistromland*. Unless otherwise specified, all translations from the German texts are mine.

3 Rosenzweig's correspondence during the course of his illness does not often reflect his reaction to slow loss of speech. He did repeatedly, however, confide in his friend Gertrud (Trudchen) Oppenheim (1885–1976), with the following kinds of observations: "I am not taking my illness lightly. It is not being confined (but this please *between us!*) it would be painful to me if others notice it before it cannot be concealed, and perhaps it will mercifully pass over" (14 March 1922). "I myself am taking only the speech impediment hard ... You well know that right after I published the writing through the ✡ [Rosenzweig used the Star of David whenever he referred to the *Star*, and he wished all future editions of the book to display the symbol on the front cover], the speaking had become important; it was to me *the* still possible form of productivity. That such a restraint can be properly

overcome I do not believe" (27 March 1922). To another intimate friend, his cousin Hans Ehrenberg (1893-1958), he wrote in May 1922: "After the ✿ there remained for me only the oral and the practical." Quotes from letters appear in *FR: Gesammelte Schriften*, 1, *Briefe und Tagebücher*, 2. Band, 757, 761, 787, respectively.

This is all to point out that the Notes do indeed exemplify *one* possible example of the application of the speech-thinking method. Many others, such as continued teaching at the Freies Jüdisches Lehrhaus, became closed to Rosenzweig. See Glatzer, *Franz Rosenzweig: His Life and Thought*, for an account of how Rosenzweig, when nearly totally paralysed, continued to "speak" through the written word with the help of his wife, Edith.

4 *FR: Gesammelte Schriften*, 1, *Briefe und Tagebücher*, 2. Band, 1063. Henceforth referred to as *B und T, 1. Band* and *B und T, 2. Band*.

5 As noted, I have translated all the poems from Rosenzweig's German, for my own understanding and now for the reader's ease, into a literal, rather coarse English. A poetic sort of prose is the most I could manage at times; at other times only the sense. Rosenzweig's principle of there being only "one language" (see chapter 3) leads me firmly to believe that one more talented and knowledgeable than I will, or at least can, stretch the English language's resources to bring more fully into English the poetry of Jehuda Halevi. The versions in part 1 serve only as the crutches of content renderings for those who need them, and are to be entirely ignored by those who do not.

6 Glatzer, *FR: Life and Thought*.

7 In the 1927 edition, 167.

8 Rosenzweig, "Apologetisches Denken," in *FR: Gesammelte Schriften*, 3:678.

9 Friedman, *Martin Buber's Life and Work, vol. 2:53*.

10 Horwitz, *Buber's Way to I and Thou*, 24–5.

11 Ibid., 214.

12 Ibid., 182.

13 Ibid., 222.

14 Ibid.

15 From a letter dated 22 February 1923, translated in Glatzer and Mendes-Flohr, *The Letters of Martin Buber*, 301.

16 Ibid., n. 2.

17 "Das neue Denken," 152. "Angewandte Seelenkunde," written in 1916 for Rosenzweig, was first published in 1924 by Roether-Verlag, Darmstadt. An English translation is available: "Practical Knowledge of the Soul" (Norwich, VT: Argo, 1988). "Seelenkunde" is normally translated as "psychology," but the more usual word for psychology in German is "Psychologie." Rosenstock wanted the Greek meaning of "psyche" to be transparent, and so too presumably did the translators of the piece.

18 Gibbs, *Correlations*. See especially 62–7. Gibbs' book was published after I had completed the final manuscript for this one. Any parallels in interpretation were arrived at independently. My own reception of the Gibbs book, as will become evident, is positive; it is much too early, however, to make any statement on the value of his work or on its reception, impact, and influence. I suspect all will be both controversial and great, but several years more, of course, are required to prove me right or wrong.

19 I have recently been struck by similarities between Walter Benjamin's notion of the "pure language" and Rosenzweig's notion of the "one language." A careful reading of Benjamin's "The Task of the Translator" (his introduction to his translations of the poetry of Beaudelaire) alongside Rosenzweig's "Nachwort" to his Halevi translations prove mutually illuminating. As Stéphane Mosès briefly points out in his article, "Walter Benjamin and Franz Rosenzweig," there are certainly differences in their views, but I suspect they are not so great as Mosès contends (197–200).

20 Mosès, *System and Revelation*, 27.

21 Glatzer, "The Frankfort Lehrhaus," 109–10.

22 Stahmer, *"Speak That I May See Thee!"*, 157.

23 Ibid., 157.

24 Ibid., 161.

25 *Judaism Despite Christianity* is now a well-known volume which partially discloses the speech-thinking activity between the two men.

26 See the Introductory Note to Rosenstock-Huessy, "Practical Knowledge of the Soul."

27 Rosenstock-Huessy, "Practical Knowledge of the Soul," 19.

28 Stahmer, *"Speak That I May See Thee!"*, 121.

29 Cited in ibid., 122.

30 Ibid., 262–3.

31 Karl Löwith, "M. Heidegger and F. Rosenzweig or Temporality and Eternity," in 53–77.

32 Ibid. 53.

33 Ibid.

34 Ibid.

35 Ibid., 54–5.

36 Ibid., 54.

37 Ibid., 57.

38 Ibid., 63.

39 Ibid., 76–7.

40 These papers have been compiled in the two-volume publication, *Der Philosoph Franz Rosenzweig (1886–1929)*, Internationaler Kongress Kassel, 1986.

41 Ibid., vol. 1:36.

42 Ibid., 37.

43 Ibid., 17. Part of Levinas' message reads: "J'évoque avec espoir une pensée qui, pour la première fois dans l'histoire religieuse – pour la première fois dans l'histoire d'Israel – revendique pour le judaïsme et pour le christianisme la plénitude de leurs vérités à prolonger dans un dialogue – qui est probablement la forme initiale du Verbe. Dialogue sans compromis et sans dialectique – sans 'Aufhebung' – mais où, dans la fin d'une guerre bimillénaire, les souvenirs atroces et inoubliables du XXième siècle cesseront peut-être de séparer les hommes des hommes."

44 Michael Oppenheim, "The Relevance of Rosenzweig in the Eyes of his Israeli Critics," 193-206.

45 Ibid., 197.

46 Ibid., 200.

47 Ibid., 201.

48 Ibid., 201.

49 Mendes-Flohr, *The Philosophy of Franz Rosenzweig.*

50 Mendes-Flohr, *Divided Passions.*

51 Ibid., 16.

52 Ibid., 203-4.

53 While her work was not mentioned at the workshop, I have since learned of a doctoral dissertation in Hebrew by Dorit Orgad of the Department of Philosophy of Bar-Ilan University, submitted in November 1986, entitled "Franz Rosenzweig in Relation to Rabbi Jehuda Halevi." The Interlibrary Loan Department of Concordia University, Montreal, kindly gathered information on this writing, and as far as I can determine from a detailed and most interesting table of contents, the thrust is more weighted toward Halevi than Rosenzweig, with a focus on the study of liturgy and language of prayer.

54 Dietrich, "Franz Rosenzweig: Recent Works in French," 99.

55 Emmanuel Levinas, " 'Entre deux mondes'. Biographie spirituelle de Franz Rosenzweig," 137-49.

56 Levinas, "F. Rosenzweig: Une pensée juive moderne," in Levinas, *Les Cahiers de "La nuit surveillée",* 65.

57 Ibid., 68.

58 Dietrich, "Franz Rosenzweig: Recent Works in French," 97-103. Dietrich also presented a slightly varied version of this review at the Internationaler Kongress Kassel 1986: "Is Rosenzweig an Ethical Monotheist? A Debate with the New Francophone Literature," in *Der Philosoph Franz Rosenzweig (1886-1929),* 891-900.

59 Mosès, *System and Revelation.*

60 Dietrich, "Franz Rosenzweig: Recent Works in French," 99.

61 Ibid., 100.

62 Ibid., 100.

63 Ibid., 101.

64 Ibid.

65 Ibid.

66 Ibid.

67 William H. Hallo is the son of Rudolf Hallo (1896–1933), who taught at the Freies Jüdisches Lehrhaus.

68 Four of the most recent North American articles on Rosenzweig are: Maurice Friedman's "Dialogue, Speech, Nature, and Creation: Franz Rosenzweig's Critique of Buber's *I and Thou*"; Yudit Greenberg's "A Jewish Postmodern Critique of Rosenzweig's Speech-thinking and the Concept of Revelation"; and my "Rosenzweig Speaking of Meetings and Monotheism in Biblical Anthropomorphisms" and "Rosenzweig and the Name for God." Gershon Greenberg was one of the first non-German Jewish scholars in North American to show interest in Rosenzweig, even before the appearance of William Hallo's English translation of the *Star.* In 1969 Greenberg wrote a paper which he eventually presented at the Association for Jewish Studies Conference at Harvard in 1973. This truly avant-garde paper, which fell on unresponsive ears at the time, was published in German in two parts, as "Franz Rosenzweigs zwiespältige Gottessicht: Von der Zeit und Ewigkeit."

69 There has been some focus, much of it in conversation, and very little in writing, on Rosenzweig's unfavourable statements regarding Eastern religions and Islam. For an interesting analysis of the roots of Rosenzweig's views, see Shlomo Pines, "Der Islam im 'Stern der Erlösung': Eine Untersuchung zu Tendenzen und Quellen Franz Rosenzweigs." Pines' essay opens with this paragraph:"I shall try to demonstrate in this essay that a substantial part, perhaps indeed the majority of Rosenzweig's statements in the *Star of Redemption* concerning Islam were written in relation to and in discussion with the sections in Hegel's writings which also deal with the theme 'Islam.' Likewise it seems to me that Rosenzweig at times (without making explicit reference to this) uses the *Vorträge über den Islam* [*Lectures on Islam*] by Goldziher, which had appeared in 1920, shortly before the *Star of Redemption*, in order to get as it were a factual support for his standpoint. Occasionally this happens, wittingly or unwittingly, in a more tendentious manner from a simplification of history and of religious reality."

Gibbs, too, in his *Correlations*, faces this often ignored problem.

70 Michael Oppenheim's articles include: "Death and Man's Fear of Death in Franz Rosenzweig's *The Star of Redemption*"; "Taking Time Seriously: An Inquiry into the Methods of communication of Søren Keirkegaard and Franz Rosenzweig"; "Sons Against Their Fathers"; and "Franz Rosenzweig and Emmanuel Levinas: A Midrash or Thought-Experiment." Oppenheim's book, which will be cited in the following pages in context, is *What Does Revelation Mean to the Modern Jew?*

71 "Das neue Denken," 142–3.

72 Gibbs, *Correlations*, 14.

73 Ibid., 19.

74 In his chapter 2, "The Logic of Limitation," 34–56, Gibbs discusses in depth notions of knowing, not knowing, knowing that we do not know; here I am offering only a hint of his clear but complex text.

75 Ibid., 34.

76 "Das Formgeheimnis der biblischen Erzählungen" ["The Secret of the Form of the Bible Stories"] in *Zweistromland*, 819.

77 *FR: Gesammelte Schriften* IV 1. Band, *Sprachdenken Jehuda Halevi: Fünfundneunzig Humnen und Gedichte, Deutsch und Hebräisch, mit einem Vorwort und mit Anmerkungen.*

78 *B und T*, 2. Band, 938.

79 Ibid., 952.

80 In the 1924 edition, 167–70.

81 Ibid., 168–9.

82 In 1933 Schocken published a seventy-two-page, much abridged edition of Rosenzweig's Halevi book. (The 1927 edition is 262 pages.) Whereas the title is *Zionslieder*, the collection omits some poems of the Zion section and includes several poems from the Volk (People) section. For more details regarding this edition, please consult Appendix A.

83 See Rafael Rosenzweig's introduction to the third edition, xxiii.

84 *B und T*, 2. Band, 973.

85 Rafael Rosenzweig and I have corresponded since 1991. He knows my stand in choosing to use the 1927 edition, and defends his own. I continue to be indebted to him for taking the time and energy carefully to read several of my draft translations of his father's writings. His criticisms and exactitude are deeply appreciated, as of course is his rare word of praise.

CHAPTER TWO

1 *B und T, I. Band*, 460-1. The original reads: "Das Übersetzen ist überhaupt das eigentliche Ziel des Geistes; erst wenn etwas übersetzt ist, ist es wirklich *laut* geworden, nicht mehr aus der Welt zu schaffen. Erst in der Septuaginta ist die Offenbarung ganz heimisch in der Welt geworden, und solange Homer noch nicht lateinisch sprach, war er noch keine Tatsache. Entsprechend auch das Übersetzen von Mensch zu Mensch." I am calling these three sentences, despite the fact that the third is only a fragment and makes sense only in connection with the preceding two sentences.

2 See Glatzer, *Life and Thought*, 93–8, for the text of the letter and Glatzer's comments.

3 On the fleeting character of letters until answered, see Harold Stahmer, "The Letters of Franz Rosenzweig to Margrit Rosenstock-Huessy: 'Franz,' 'Gritli,' 'Eugen' and 'The Star of Redemption,' " 1:110–11.

4 From "Das neue Denken," translated in Glatzer, 196. The original is:

Warum ist Wahrheit fern und weit,
Birgt sich hinab in teifste Gründe?

Niemand versteht zur rechten Zeit!
Wenn man zur rechten Zeit verstünde:
So wäre Wahrheit nah und breit,
Und wäre lieblich und gelinde.

An alternate translation, which is less elegant, but emphasizes the aspect of time, might read:

Why is truth far and distant,
hiding itself in deepest depth?

No one understands at the right time!
If one did understand at the right time,
Then truth would be near and wide,
And would be sweet and gentle.

5 Derczanski, "Une pensée de la grammaire ou l'assomption du temps" in *Les cahiers de "La nuit surveillée"*, 116. The English is: "For Rosenzweig, the discourse is not an abstract topic, but a communicative concern whose rationalities are for him internal and not exterior ... he insists equally on the connection of the spoken word [*parole*] and of language and gives thought the status of the spoken word. This, moreover, is the reason for his inventing this word: Sprachdenken [speech-thinking]."

6 Rieu, in his introduction to Homer's *The Iliad*, xiv.

7 "Zur Encyclopaedia Judaica: Zum zweiten Band, mit einer Anmerkung über Anthropomorphism," in *Zweistromland*, 736.

8 In Stahmer, "Franz Rosenzweig's Letters to Margrit Rosenstock-Huessy, 1917–1922," 400.

9 Notably Rosenstock-Huessy, *Judaism Despite Christianity*; Stahmer, *"Speak That I May See Thee!"*, 106–82; "Franz Rosenzweig's Letters to Margrit Rosenstock-Huessy 1917–1922"; and "The Letters of Franz Rosenzweig to Margrit Rosenstock-Huessy: 'Franz,' 'Gritli,' 'Eugen' and 'The Star of Redemption' "; and Kamper, "Das Nachtgespraech vom 7. Juli 1913. Eugen Rosenstock-Huessy und Franz Rosenzweig" in *Der Philosoph Franz Rosenzweig (1886–1929): Internationaler Kongress Kassel 1986*, 97–104. Gibbs's *Correla-*

tions in Rosenzweig and Levinas gives a rather thorough, and very interesting account in terms of Rosenstock-Huessy's affect on Rosenzweig.

10 The concluding words of *The Star.*

11 In Oppenheim, *What Does Revelation Mean to the Modern Jew?*, 15; and in *Judaism Despite Christianity*, 32–3.

12 In Stahmer, *"Speak That I May See Thee!"*, 160.

13 Members of the Patmos group and editors of and contributors to the group's publication *The Creature* included Rosenstock-Huessy, Rosenzweig, Leo Weismantel, Werner Picht, Hans Ehrenberg, Karl Barth, Joseph Wittig, Martin Buber, Victor von Weizsäcker, and Nicholas Berdayev. Ibid., 122–3.

14 While Gershom Scholem finds much of value in Rosenzweig's *Star*, even here he detects an apologetic tendency. In a discussion of modern Jewish thinkers from Mendelssohn, explicitly including Rosenzweig, he writes, with characteristic forthrightness, that their "religious thought is apologetically oriented toward the respective categories of the dominant philosophies, from the Arabic Kalam and Aristotle to Kant, Hegel, Dewey, and even Heidegger. The outstanding characteristic of these theologies, regardless of their basic differences, is their strictly selective attitude toward tradition. They disregard anything traditional they find undigestible and by its nature unsuitable for apologetic purposes." "Reflections on Jewish Theology," 264-5.

15 For good discussions of the restrictions on unbaptized Jews at German universities in the first decades of this century, see Neusner, *The Academic Study of Judaism: Essays and Reflections*; and Meyers, *The Origins of the Modern Jew.*

16 In Glatzer, *Life and Thought*, 95–8.

17 See *Star*, 12.

18 Quoted in Glatzer, *Life and Thought*, 97.

19 In Oppenheim, *What Does Revelation Mean to the Modern Jew?*, 18.

20 Ibid., 14.

21 In Stahmer, "Franz Rosenzweig's Letters to Margrit Rosenstock-Huessy, 1917–1922," 386–7. Also, see Stahmer, "The Letters of Franz Rosenzweig to Margrit Rosenstock-Huessy: 'Franz,' 'Gritli,' 'Eugen' and 'The Star of Redemption.' " In this essay, Stahmer emphasizes that the writing of letters was an integral part in the composing of the *Star.* "Please note that Rosenzweig's practice of exchanging letters, and then circulating certain ones among his 'Kreis,' his 'group,' his small circle of close friends, was essential to the shaping of the *Star* at every stage of its development. The 'inner group' *during this period* consisted primarily of Eugen and Margrit Rosenstock and Rudolf and Hans Ehrenberg. The 'outer circle' of the group, if one may be permitted to characterize it in this fashion, consisted of Gertrud Oppenheim, Adele Rosenzweig, and Viktor von Weizsäcker. These groupings reflect the role these personalities played during this particular period in Rosenzweig's life based on the published as well as the new unpublished material" (129).

22 *Star*, 110.

23 Ibid., 174. Rosenzweig designates the notion "word and response" being "actual word" as the "center-piece" of the *Star*. On page 188 of the Hallo translation, there appears what Rosenzweig later, to Margarete Susman, termed the "kernel" of his philosophy. She heads her review of the *Star* with a quote from it: "A name is not sound and smoke, it is word and fire. The name must be named and professed: I believe in it." Rosenzweig whole-heartedly approved of every sentence of Susman's review. It appeared origi-nally in *Der Jude: Eine Monatsschrift*, in the Umschau section, 259–64, and has been translated by Joachim Neugroschel in Cohen's fine volume, *The Jew: Essays from Martin Buber's Journal, Der Jude, 1916–1928*, 276–85. In Feb-ruary 1922 Rosenzweig wrotes to Susman, stating how deeply she had un-derstood the book, and how much he appreciated her picking out the "kernel." He said he remembered writing the sentence in November 1918, knowing then that it expressed the heart of his book. See *B und T: 2. Band*, 752.

This heart-sentence of the *Star* is a reference to Goethe's *Faust*, part 1, where Faust relegates name to sound and smoke. Rosenzweig vigorously re-futes Faust's view. The setting is Margarete's garden, and Margarete asks Faust if he believes in God. The conclusion of Faust's reply is: "Gefühl ist alles; / Name ist Schall und Rauch, / Umnebelnd Himmelsglut." Albert G. Latham, a contemporary of Rosenzweig, translates the passage:

Margaret: Then thou believest not?

Faust: Thou winsome angel-face, mishear me not!
Who can name Him?
Who thus proclaim Him:
I believe Him?
Who that hath feeling
His bosom steeling,
Can say: *I believe Him not?*
The All-embracing,
The All-sustaining,
Clasps and sustains He not
Thee, me, Himself?
Springs not the vault of Heaven above us?
Lieth not Earth firm-stablished 'neath our feet?
And with a cheerful twinking
Climb not eternal stars the sky?
Eye into eye gaze I not upon thee?
Surgeth not all
To head and heart within thee?

And floats in endless mystery
Invisible visible around thee?
Great though it be, fill thou therefrom thine heart,
And when in the feeling wholly blest thou art,
Call it then what thou wilt!
Call it Bliss! Heart! Love! God!
I have no name for it!
Feeling is all in all!
Name is but sound and reek,
A mist round the glow of Heaven!

From Goethe's *Faust*, parts 1 and 2. Trans. Albert G. Latham. New York: E.P. Dutton, 1908.

24 The reference is to Rosenzweig's translation from Hebrew into German: "Grace after Meals," written for those guests in his home who knew no Hebrew.

25 In Glatzer, *Life and Thought*, 100–2.

26 Rosenzweig here states explicitly that whatever once is translated into a language resides there permanently. He does not, as far as I know, discuss the notion of evil speech. Nor, therefore, does he discuss what to do about it. He did not have to face Nazi language, for example, or Neo-Nazi speech. This was indeed addressed, within Germany, with attempts at a future oriented redress, by writers such as Heinrich Böll and Günther Grass.

27 The concluding paragraph of the Afterword, it may be recalled here, reads: "If I may express a wish, then it is the double one that the water-gauge established here on this small selection will soon overflow, but that not one of my successors in this region may have again the audacity of laziness to fall behind the measure of sufficiency reached here. The excuse that it 'doesn't work' now no longer is at anyone's disposal."

28 Rosenzweig, we have seen, states explicitly that whatever once is translated into a language resides in it permanently. He does not, as far as I know, enter into discussions of evil speech. It may be said here only that Buber *did* complete their jointly begun project to translate biblical Hebrew into the German language. Perhaps he believed, even after the Holocaust, in that principle of the one language and all the imperatives involved in that principle.

29 Ibid., 255.

30 See Rosenzweig's discussion of essence, the word "is," and so on, in connection with the "old" and the "new" thinking, in "Das neue Denken."

31 In "Das neue Denken" of 1925 Rosenzweig writes. "I would soonest have to agree to the label absolute empiricism; at least it would cover the special attitude of the new thinking in all three precincts, of the prehistoric world of concept, of the world of reality, of the supra-world of the Truth; that atti-

tude which likewise does not claim to know anything of the heavenly other than what it has experienced – but this really, even if philosophy already may denounce it as a knowledge 'on the other side' of all 'possible' experience; nor anything of the earthly which it has not experienced – but this not in the least, even if philosophy may already puff it up as a knowledge 'before' all possible experience," *Zweistromland*, 161.

32 See the 1916 correspondence between Rosenzweig and Rosenstock-Huessy in Rosenstock-Huessy, *Judaism Despite Christianity*, 77–170, especially 164–70.

33 See Mosès, *System and Revelation*, 269–71.

34 *Star*, 145.

35 Ibid., 145–6.

36 *Judaism Despite Christianity*, 26.

37 Rosenstock-Huessy, *Magna Carta Latina*, 176.

38 In Glatzer, *Life and Thought*, 256–7.

39 "Das neue Denken," 151.

40 "Die Wissenschaft von der Welt" in *Zweistromland*, 660–1.

41 Ibid., 661.

42 Nachwort, 154/3.

43 In Glatzer, *Life and Thought*, excerpt from Rosenzweig's "Scripture and Luther's Translation," 255.

44 Ibid., from "Scripture and Luther's Translation," 260–1.

45 Glatzer, "The Concept of Language in the Thought of Franz Rosenzweig," 183–4.

46 Rivka Horwitz, "Franz Rosenzweig on Language," 396–7.

47 "Das neue Denken," 140.

48 See *Star*, 198–205.

49 The conversational layers, of course, are much wider. One would be justified in arguing that the layers of voices begin (and end) with biblical voices and further discussions with rabbinic references, receptions, and allusions. A consideration of all these voices would involve a separate study. Appropriate and interesting in this regard would be a focus on reception theory. I am not addressing these wider layers here, nor is it within this book's purview to discuss reception theory.

50 Nachwort, 153/1.

51 Nachwort, 153/1.

52 Glatzer, in *Life and Thought*, includes a letter Rosenzweig wrote to his cousin Hans Ehrenberg on 11 March 1925: "Again and again I am amazed at how little its readers know it. Everybody thinks it is an admonition to kosher eating" (146).

53 Ibid., from a letter to Richard Koch dated 2 September 1928, 165.

54 "Das neue Denken," 160.

55 Glatzer, "The Concept of Language in the Thought of Franz Rosenweig," 183.

56 "Das neue Denken," 141–2.

57 *Star,* 151.

58 Ibid., 186.

59 Ibid., 186–8.

60 *B und T, 2. Band,* from a letter to Benno Jacob, 27 May 1921, 708–9.

61 In Glatzer, *Life and Thought,* from "Scripture and Luther's Translation," 257–8.

62 "Das neue Denken," 154–5.

63 *Star,* 215.

64 Rudolf Ehrenberg (1884–1969), a professor of medicine at Heidelberg, was also heavily engaged in theological thinking.

   I would like to mention here a few things about a cousin of Rosenzweig's father, Hans Ehrenberg (1893–1958). He held a doctorate in philosophy from Heidelberg (1909), and served as a Privatdozent until 1911 when he was baptized; he was ordained in 1925. Rosenzweig refers to him as a fellow "new philosopher" in "Das neue Denken" (1925), pointing the reader to Ehrenberg's by then published *Fichte.* This work and his *Die Parteien der Philosophie* (Leipzig, 1911) have not yet appeared in English.

   The earliest review of the *Star* was written by Ehrenberg, published in the *Frankfurter Zeitung* on 29 December 1921. Rosenzweig was pleased with it. He wrote to his cousin at the end of December 1921: "Your essay in the *Frankfurter Zeitung* is wonderful" (*B und T, 2. Bande,* 735). He took exception only to Ehrenberg's reading of the *Star* as setting philosophy and life in opposition. Rosenzweig contended that he was opposing not philosophy and life, but rather "the looking around" until one develops a philosophy and life. Indeed, Rosenzweig thought that philosophy and life *do* go hand in hand (Ibid., 735–6).

65 " 'Urzelle' " des Stern der Erlösung: Brief an Rudolf Ehrenberg vom 18.11.17,"in *Zweistromland,* 131–2.

66 *Star,* 239–40.

67 Ibid., 241.

68 Ibid., 199.

69 Ibid., 199.

70 Heschel, *The Earth is the Lord's & The Sabbath,* 98.

71 *Star,* 200.

72 Ibid., 202.

73 Ibid.

74 Ibid.

75 Ibid.

76 Ibid., 203–4.

77 See Ibid., 188.

78 Otto Gründler, "Eine jüdisch-theistische Offenbarungsphilosophie."

79 *B und T, 2. Band,* 757–8.

80 *Star,* 214.

CHAPTER THREE

1 *Star,* 295.

2 Other highly recommended comprehensive works of Western language theory are Wesley Morris, *Friday's Footprint;* and L.G. Kelly, *The True Interpreter: A History of Translation Theory and Practice in the West.*

In his brief essay, "Language," in *Contemporary Jewish Religious Thought: Original essays on critical concepts, movements, and beliefs,* ed. Arthur A. Cohen and Paul Mendes-Flohr, Josef Stern gives succinct and helpful attention is given to essentialist theories in Jewish thought.

Perhaps most important, and in direct connection with translation theories of language, is Hans Joachim Störig's collection of primary sources (in German) in *Das Problem des Übersetzens,* which includes Rosenzweig's "Die Schrift und Luther." The collection includes essays by those Rosenzweig did or would greatly admire: Buber's "Zu einer neuen Verdeutschung der Schrift"; Walter Benjamin's "Die Aufgabe des Übersetzers"; Nietzsche's "Zum Problem des Übersetzens"; and Wilhelm von Humboldt's "Einleitung zu 'Agamamemnon' " as well as essays by those with whom Rosenzweig disagreed: Goethe's "Drei Stücke vom Übersetzen"; and Wilamowitz-Moellendorff's "Was ist Übersetzen?"

The Störig book does not include any writings by Johann Georg Hamann, whom Rosenzweig liked enormously. Hamann was good friends with Kant and Herder. Of Herder's and Hamann's critique of Kant, Rosenzweig writes, in "Die Schrift und das Wort: Zur neuen Bibelübersetzung" of 1925: "For poetry is indeed the mother tongue of the human race – we must not neglect the Hamann-Herder wisdom" (*Zweistromland,* 782). It is Hamann's cohortative: "Speak that I may see thee!"

3 Robinson, *The Translator's Turn,* 38.

4 For a clear, brief, readable historical synopsis of Jewish essentialist views of language, see the "Language" entry by Josef Stern in Cohen and Mendes-Flohr, *Contemporary Jewish Religious Thought: Original essays on critical concepts, movements, and beliefs,* 543–51.

5 Ibid., 132–3.

6 Ibid., 131.

7 Ibid., 106.

8 Ibid., 107.

9 *B und T,* 2. Band, 717.

10 Ibid.

11 Ibid., 227.

12 I may be able to use myself as a test case here. My first experience with *any* German translation of the Bible was a reading of the Luther translation alongside the Buber-Rosenzweig one. I *also* had the Hebrew in front of me. It is not that Luther is inaccurate, but that Buber and Rosenzweig do, for

me at least, bring out the Bible's speech rhythms, and thus prompt better understanding as I read aloud.

13 Julius Guttmann, *Philosophies of Judaism*, 429.

14 Ibid., 430. `

15 *Star*, 154.

16 Remarkably, during the Holocaust the poets spoke poems and poetic prose we know, hear, and read still today.

17 Feuerbach, *The Fiery Brook: Selected Writings of Ludwig Feuerbach*. In the introduction by Zawar Hanfi, 13.

18 Ibid., 15.

19 Ibid., 14.

20 Ibid., 27.

21 Ibid., 36–7.

22 Ibid., 37.

23 Ibid., 244.

24 *Star*, 111.

25 *B und T*, 2. *Band*, 963–4, dated 21 May 1924, referring to Rosenzweig's course at the Lehrhaus, the Science of God, at the Freies Jüdisches Lehrhaus, given for the first time from 25 October to 22 December 1921. See also Rosenzweig's article on biblical anthropomorphisms, *Zweistromland*, 735–41, and his essay on the secret of the form of biblical storytelling, ibid., 817–29.

26 *B und T*, 2. *Band*, 708–9.

27 "Das neue Denken," 158–9.

28 See *Star*, 188.

29 Ibid., 14–15.

30 Eugen Rosenstock-Huessy, *I am an Impure Thinker*, 33.
The world did *not* end in the Nazi death camps. The souls did not perish in the realm of Nazidom. Names of souls, known and now maybe some unknown to presently living souls, live in memory in Yad Vashem, in hearts, in scholarly writings, in poems, in freshly spoken fiery words. Some victims did not even curse the world or God in that accursed time. Some have since decided that there can be no God. How do we understand that some did *not* make the decision that God can either not exist or not care? Would Rosenzweig himself still ask, *not* "Why were you utterly absent?" but "Why were you so far away, and why did you choose not to hear us, and if you heard us, not to help?"

31 That great influence on Rosenzweig, Rosenstock-Huessy, wrote, referring to William James, "Speech and thought came to him not as the individual gifts of an upstart but they entered him as they enter or should enter, all of us, as rays from the radiant crown of a gigantic family conversation" (Ibid., 27).

32 Ibid., 29.

33 "Der Name" ("The Name"), 190/72.

34 *Star*, 231.

35 "Die Wissenschaft vom Menschen," in *Zweistromland*, 645.

36 Eugen Rosenstock-Huessy, "Our Urban Goggles (1948)" in *Rosenstock-Huessy Papers*, vol. 1:6.

37 "The state of the world today may force us to postpone many desirable things, not for a better day but for a better century. It could hardly be asserted that the great urgency of the present moment is to organize the science of Judaism (*Wissenschaft des Judentums*] or to prompt both Jews and non-Jews to the endless writing of books on Jewish subjects. Books are not now the prime need of the day. But what we need more than ever, or at least as much as ever, are human beings – Jewish human beings, to use a catchword that should be cleansed of the partisan associations still clinging to it." From Franz Rosenzweig, *On Jewish Learning*, 55.

38 See Rosenzweig's lecture notes on the "Die Wissenschaft vom Menschen," in *Zweistromland*, 652.

39 "Das Formgeheimnis der biblischen Erzaehlungen," in *Zweistromland*, 818.

40 Ibid., 825–9.

41 "Das neue Denken," 159.

42 Nachwort, 154–5/3.

43 Gershon Greenberg, "Franz Rosenzweig's Dual Perception of God: from Time and in Eternity." Paper presented at the Association for Jewish Studies Conference, Harvard, 1973, 20. See chapter 1, n. 68.

44 This translation is Greenberg's.

45 *Star*, 207–8.

46 Ibid., 295–6.

47 Nachwort, 155/3–4.

48 Ludwig Feuerbach, *The Fiery Brook*, 231–2.

49 *Star*, 110.

50 "Die Wissenschaft von der Welt," in *Zweistromland*, 655–64.

51 "Die Wissenschaft von der Welt," in *Zweistromland*, 656.

52 Ibid., 655.

53 "Das neue Denken," 153–4.

CHAPTER FOUR

1 The discussion here could certainly be extended much further than I lead it. For example, my brief debate with Alan Udoff also revolves in part around Rosenzweig's review "Vertauschten Fronten" ["Reversed Fronts"]. In this short review Rosenzweig focuses on Hermann Cohen, Ernst Cassirer, and Martin Heidegger, treating issues thematically related to those raised in this book. A translation of "Vertauschten Fronten" is presented in Appendix B.

2 See chapter 2, n. 47.

3 See Preface and Appendix A.

4 For a fuller discussion of the notion that God and God's name mean the same thing, and on the dangers of naming God "The Eternal One," see Rosenzweeig's " 'Der Ewige': Mendelssohn und der Gottesname," in *Zweistromland*, 801–15.

5 Feminist writer Luce Irigaray has vehemently attacked Rosenzweig's grand successor, Emmanuel Levinas, for a myriad of things, like saying that truly to love a person means not even to notice the colour of his eyes. Irigaray also dislikes the "he" talk. She finds Levinas abstract, excluding of and therefore harmful to women. This quote from the note to "Gerichtstag" reminds me that, for my part, I continually find Rosenzweig to be a refined thinker whose "man's" and "he's," including the "Er," "Ihn," "Ihm" for God, although archaic, ring wholesomely in my soul. At the same time, it is touching (and perhaps worth the argument) to note that Everett Fox, in his *Genesis and Exodus: A New English Rendition with Commentary and Notes*, states in his prefatory "On the Name of God and its Translation" (xxxv–vi) that the Buber-Rosenzweig translation of the Bible introduced an "overly male emphasis through its constant use of HE, an emphasis which is not quite so pronounced in Hebrew." Fox chooses YHWH.

6 Here, as elsewhere, Rosenzweig makes non-explicit reference to views developed in Jewish mysticism. Nowhere does Rosenzweig, in any sustained fashion in writing, talk about Tzimtzum, or other ideas from Jewish mysticism. Moshe Idel and Scholem have referred to this feature of Rosenzweig's writing, the former with a positive critique, the latter with a negative one. See, for example, Gershom Scholem, "Franz Rosenzweig and His Book *The Star of Redemption*" (based on his 1930 review); and Moshe Idel, "Franz Rosenzweig and the Kabbalah," both in *The Philosophy of Franz Rosenzweig*, ed. Paul Mendes-Flohr, 20–41 and 162–71, respectively.

7 Paul Anton de Lagarde (1827–1891), Orientalist, author of antisemitic writings.

8 Rosenzweig here refers to five pertinent biblical texts:

O LORD, there is none like thee, nor is there any GOD besides thee, according to all that we have heard with our ears (1 Chronicles 17:20).

I am the LORD, and there is none else, there is no GOD beside me; And there is no GOD else beside me, a just GOD and a deliverer; there is none beside me (Isaiah 45:5 and 21). I am the LORD thy GOD from the land of Mizrayim, and thou knowest no God but me, for there is no saviour besides me (Hosea 13:4).

For who is GOD save the LORD? or who is a rock, save our GOD? (Psalm 18:32).

Then I said, I will not make mention of him, nor speak any more in his name. But his word was in mine heart like a burning fire shut up in my bones, and I am weary with containing myself, and I cannot (Jeremiah 20:9).

9 "Das Formgeheimnis der biblischen Erzählungen," in *Zweistromland*, 817–29.

10 Ibid., 825–6.

11 2 Samuel 5:6, 8: "And the king and his men went to Yerushalayim to the Yevusi [Jebusites], the inhabitants of the land: who spoke to David, saying, Unless thou remove even the blind and the lame, thou shalt not come in here: thinking, David cannot come in here. 8. And David said on that day, Whoever smites the Yevusi, and gets up to the aqueduct, and smites the lame and the blind (that are hated of David's soul) – therefore the saying, The blind and the lame shall not come into the house."

12 A complete translation of this note is also in Glatzer, *Life and Thought*, 359–60.

13 A recent example of this is an "orthodox" Jewish view that Sadam Hussein, in Desert Storm, was defeated on Purim. Whether or not the interpretation is correct is not the point here.

14 *Star*, in Introduction by Glatzer, ix.

15 "Das Formgeheimnis der biblischen Erzählungen," in *Zweitstromland*, 828.

16 Nachwort, 161/10.

17 Nachwort, 162/11.

18 I am not certain how to express this, but problems with Rosenzweig occur again and again because he is a pre-Holocaust thinker. Rosenzweig's community did have the Holocaust fall upon them. Rosenzweig, because he died young in 1929, was not of the Holocaust community in bodily fact, but in a way he was. If Nahum Glatzer found it so very important to introduce Rosenzweig's thought to America by the early fifties, then *this* conveyor of Rosenzweig's thought and person cannot be ignored for reasons beyond both men's scholarship. Neither Glatzer nor Rosenzweig was a "Holocaust thinker," but Glatzer is never charged with that with which Rosenzweig is charged: You can't know. Also, there is something about the speech at Yad Vashem which I can not yet figure out – the experience is only months' fresh – that pertains to speech-thinking, something to do with Rosenzweig's compelling reading of the Song of Songs, and love being stronger than death.

19 Nachwort, 162/11.

20 Nachwort, 163/12–13.

21 See "Das Formgeheimnis der biblischen Erzählungen," in *Zweistromland*, 817–29.

22 "Die Wissenschaft von Gott," in *Zweistromland*, 628.

23 *Star*, 178.

24 Levinas, that great bearer of Rosenzweig, speaks of the "multiplicity of people, each one of them indispensable" as "necessary to produce all the di-

mensions of meaning; the multiplicity of meanings is due to the multiplicity of people" (195). Levinas developed this idea in "Revelation in the Jewish Tradition" in *The Levinas Reader*, 190–210.

25 Ibid., 235.

26 Ibid., 231.

27 Nachwort, 167/16.

28 Nachwort, 167/17.

29 The poem describing this dream is "Ereignis" ["Event"], 21/30.

30 Several poems prompt Rosenzweig to reflect on demands between God and human being, notably "Heimkehr" ("Homecoming" 28–32 and 180–2/45–51). These are discussed under the theme of human-divine conversations in chapter 5.

31 Rosenzweig's translation from the Hebrew is: Gott nur Er / im Göttersaal! / Er der Herr / der Herren all!

32 This is the poem "Antwort" ("Reply"), referred to above, this chapter.

33 Stahmer, *"Speak That I May See Thee!"*, 86.

34 Ibid., 89.

35 Nachwort, 167–8/17.

36 *Der Philosoph Franz Rosenzweig (1886–1929)*. 2 vols. Internationaler Kongress, Kassel 1986.

37 Alan Udoff, "Rosenzweig's Heidegger Reception and the re-Origination of Jewish Thinking" in *Der Philosoph Franz Rosenzweig*, vol. 2, 923–50. See note 1 to this chapter.

38 This is the penultimate poem of the twenty-three collected for the God section. The corresponding note is nearly a full two pages, and is translated also in Glatzer, 289–91.

39 Alan Udoff, "Rosenweig's Heidegger Reception," 924.

40 Ibid., 928.

41 Lawrence Kaplan of McGill University's Department of Jewish Studies has recently informed me that Rosenzweig based his note on the passage by Nachmanides on miracles, though the two thinkers' readings of miracle differ.

42 See *Zweistromland*, 709.

43 Udoff, "Rosenzweig's Heidegger Reception," Bakhtin's emphasis, 948.

44 Ibid., 925.

45 *Star*, 110.

46 Ibid., 32.

47 Ibid., 184.

48 *B und T*, 2. *Band*, 900.

49 *B und T*, 2. *Band*, in a letter to Martin Buber, 12 May 1923, 933.

50 *B und T*, 2. *Band*, Rosenzweig is quoting Trüdchen Oppenheim in a letter to Martin Buber, 29 May 1924, 965.

51 Alan Udoff, "Rosenzweig's Heidegger Reception," 939.

52 "Das Formgeheimnis der biblischen Erzählungen," in *Zweistromland*, 829.

53 Alan Udoff, "Rosenzweig's Heidegger Reception," 935, 937–8, 947.
54 *B und T, 2. Band,* 1191, 965.
55 Nachwort, 166/15.
56 Nachwort, 168/18.
57 Oppenheim, *Mutual Upholding: Fashioning Jewish Philosophy through Letters.*

CHAPTER FIVE

1 *Star,* 198–204.
2 See especially the lecture notes on the science of God, human, and world, *Zweistromland,* 619–69.
3 "Das neue Denken," 155.
4 Mosès, *System and Revelation,* 264.
5 *Star,* 111.
6 "Die Wissenschaft vom Menschen," in *Zweistromland,* 649.
7 Ibid., 652.
8 Mosès, *System and Revelation,* 170.

Bibliography

Benjamin, Walter. "The Task of the Translator." In *Illuminations*, ed. and intro. Hannah Arendt, Trans. Harry Zohn, 69–82. New York: Schocken, 1968.

Bowler, Maurice G. "Rosenzweig on Judaism and Christianity – The Two Covenant Theory." *Judaism* 22, no. 4 (1973):477–81.

Buber, Martin. *The Letters of Martin Buber*, edited by Nahum N. Glatzer and Paul Mendes-Flohr. New York: Schocken, 1991.

Casper, Bernhard. "Franz Rosenzweig's Criticism of Buber's *I and Thou*." In *Martin Buber: A Centenerary Volume, Ben Gurion University of the Negev.* New York: KTAV Publishing, 1984. 139–43.

Derczanski, Alexandre. "Une pensée de la grammaire ou l'assomption du temps." *Les Cahiers de "La nuit surveillée"* 1, (1982): 115–18.

Dietrich, Wendell S. "Franz Rosenzweig: Recent Works in French." *Religious Studies Review* 13, no. 2 (1987): 97–103.

Feuerbach, Ludwig. *The Fiery Brook: Selected Writings of Ludwig Feuerbach*. Trans. Zawar Hanfi. Garden City, NY: Anchor, 1972.

Fishbane, Michael. "Speech and Scripture: The Grammatical Thinking and Theology of Franz Rosenzweig." In *The Garments of Torah: Essays in Biblical Hermeneutics*, 99–111. Bloomington & Indianapolis: Indiana University Press, 1989.

Fox, Everett. *Genesis and Exodus: A New English Rendition with Commentary and Notes.* New York: Schocken, 1990.

Friedman, Maurice. "Dialogue, Speech, Nature, and Creation: Franz Rosenzweig's Critique of Buber's *I and Thou*." *Modern Judaism* 13, no. 2, (1993): 109–18.

– *Martin Buber's Life and Work*, 2 vols. Detroit: Wayne State University Press, 1988.

Galli, Barbara E. "Rosenzweig Speaking of Meetings and Monotheism in Biblical Anthropomorphisms." *The Journal of Jewish Thought and Philosophy* 2, no. 2, (1993): 219–43.

– "Rosenzweig and the Name for God." *Modern Judaism* 14, no. 1 (1994): 63–86.

Gibbs, Robert. *Correlations in Rosenzweig and Levinas.* Princeton, NJ: Princeton University Press, 1992.

Glatzer, Nahum N. "The Concept of Language in the Thought of Franz Rosenzweig." In *The Philosophy of Franz Rosenzweig,* ed. Paul Mendes-Flohr, 172–84. Hanover and London: University Press of New England, 1988.

– "The Frankfort Lehrhaus." In *Leo Baeck Institute Yearbook* 1:105–22. London: East and West Library, 1956.

– *Franz Rosenzweig: His Life and Thought.* New York: Schocken, 1953.

– ed. *Language of Faith: A Selection from the Most Expressive Jewish Prayers.* New York: Schocken, 1975.

Goldy, Robert G. and H. Frederick Holch, trans. "Atheistic Theology: From the Old to the New Way of Thinking" by Franz Rosenzweig. *The Canadian Journal of Theology,* 14, no. 2, (1968): 79–88.

Greenberg, Gershon. "Franz Rosenzweig's zwiespältige Gottessicht: von der Zeit und Ewigkeit." *Judaica* 34, no. 1 (1978): 27–34; no. 2 (1978): 76–89.

Greenberg, Yudit Kornberg. "A Jewish Postmodern Critique of Rosenzweig's Speech-thinking and the Concept of Revelation." *The Journal of Jewish Thought and Philosophy* 2, no. 1, (1992): 63–76.

Gründler, Otto. "Eine jüdische-theistische Offenbarungsphilosophie." *Hochland* 19, no. 5, (1922): 261–3. (Available at the Leo Baeck Institute, New York City)

Guttmann, Julius J. *Philosophies of Judaism: The History of Jewish Philosophy from Biblical Times to Franz Rosenzweig.* Garden City, NY: Anchor, Doubleday, 1966.

Halevi, Jehuda. *Book of Kuzari,* trans. Hartwig Hirschfeld. New York: Pardes Publishing House, 1946.

– *Ein Diwan: Übertragen und mit einem Lebensbild versehen.* Trans. Emil Bernhard. Berlin: Erich Reiss Verlag, n.d.

– *Le "Diwan".* Traduit et présenté par Yaacov Arroche et Joseph G. Valensi. Postface de S.D. Luzzatto (1864). Montpelier: Editions de l'éclat, 1988.

– *The Kuzari.* With an introduction by H. Slonimksy. New York: Schocken, 1964.

Heschel, Abraham J. *The Earth is the Lord's & The Sabbath.* Cleveland and New York: Meridian, 1963.

Hölderlin, Friedrich. *Gedichte.* Stuttgart: Philipp Reclam, 1971.

Homer. *The Iliad.* Trans. E.V. Rieu. Harmondsworth, Middlesex: Penguin, 1950.

Horwitz, Rivka. *Buber's Way to I and Thou: An Historical Analysis and the First Publication of Martin Buber's Lectures: "Religion als Gegenwart".* Heidelberg: Verlag Lambert Schneider, 1978.

– "Franz Rosenzweig – On Jewish Education." *The Journal of Jewish Thought and Philosophy* 2, no. 2, (1993): 201–18.

– "Franz Rosenzweig on Language." *Judaism* 13, no. 4 (1964): 393–406.

– "Franz Rosenzweig's Unpublished Writings" in *The Journal of Jewish Studies* 20, nos. 1–4 (1969): 57–80.

Idel, Moshe. "Franz Rosenzweig and the Kabbalah." In *The Philosophy of Franz Rosenzweig*, ed. Paul Mendes-Flohr, 162–71. Hanover and London: University Press of New England, 1988.

Kafka, Franz. *I am a Memory Come Alive, Autobiographical Writings*, ed. by Nahum N. Glatzer. New York: Schocken, 1974.

Kelly, L.G. *The True Interpreter: A History of Translation Theory and Practice in the West*. Oxford: Blackwell, 1979.

Levinas, Emmanuel. " 'Entre deux mondes': Biographie spirituelle de Franz Rosenzweig." In *Difficile liberté: Essais sur le judaïsme*. Paris: Albin Michel, 1963. 235–60.

– "F. Rosenzweig, une pensée juive moderne." *Les cahiers de la nuit surveillée judaïsme*. Paris: Albin-Michel, 2nd ed., 1976.

– "F. Rosenzweig, une pensée juive moderne." *Les cahiers de "La nuit surveillée"* 1 (1982): 65–78.

Löwith, Karl. "M. Heidegger and F. Rosenzweig or Temporality and Eternity." *Philsophy and Phenomenological Research* 3, no. 1 (1942). Reprinted, New York: Kraus Reprint, 1963. 53–77.

Mendes-Flohr, Paul. *Divided Passions*. Detroit: Wayne State University Press, 1991.

– ed. *The Philosophy of Franz Rosenzweig*. Hanover and London: University Press of New England, 1988.

– and Jehuda Reinharz. "From Relativism to Religious Faith: The Testimony of Franz Rosenzweig's Unpublished Diaries." *The Leo Baeck Institute Yearbook*, 161–74. London: Secker & Warburg, 1977.

Meyers, Michael A. *The Origins of the Modern Jew*. Detroit: Wayne State University Press, 1967.

Morris, Wesley. *Friday's Footprint: Structuralism and the Articulated Text*. Columbus: Ohio State University Press, 1979.

Mosès, Stéphane. *System and Revelation: The Philosophy of Franz Rosenzweig*, Foreword by Emmanuel Levinas. Translated by Catherine Tihanyi. Detroit: Wayne State University Press, 1992.

– "Walter Benjamin and Franz Rosenzweig." *Philosophical Forum* 15, nos. 1–2, (1983–84): 188–205.

Neusner, Jacob. *The Academic Study of Judaism: Essays and Reflections*. New York: KTAV Publishing, 1975.

Oppenheim, Michael D. *Mutual Upholding: Fashioning Jewish Philosophy through Letters*. New York: Peter Land, 1992.

– "The Relevance of Rosenzweig in the Eyes of His Israeli Critics." *Modern Judaism* 7, no. 2 (1987): 193–206.

– "Taking Time Seriously: An Inquiry into the Methods of Communication of Søren Kierkegaard and Franz Rosenzweig." *Studies in Religion* 7, no. 1 (1978): 53–60.

– *What does Revelation Mean to the Modern Jew?* Symposium Series. Lewiston, NY: Edwin Mellen Press, 1985.

Orgad, Dorit. "Franz Rosenzweig in Relation to Rabbi Jehuda Halevi." Ph.D. diss., Department of Philosophy, Bar-Ilan University, 1986.

Pines, Shlomo. "Der Islam im 'Stern der Erlösung': Eine Untersuchung zu Tendenzen und Quellen Franz Rosenzweigs." *Jahrbuch der Universität Bar-Ilan* 22/23, (1978–88): 303–14.

Postgate, J.P. *Translation and Translations: Theory and Practice.* London: G. Bell and Sons, 1922.

Robinson, Douglas. *The Translator's Turn.* Baltimore and London: Johns Hopkins University Press, 1991.

Rosenstock-Huessy, Eugen. *I am an Impure Thinker.* Norwich, VT: Argo, 1970.

– ed. *Judaism Despite Christianity: The "Letters on Christianity and Judaism" between Eugen Rosenstock-Huessy and Franz Rosenzweig.* Tuscaloosa: University of Alabama Press, 1969.

– *Magna Carta Latina.* Pittsburgh: Pickwick, 1975.

– *The Origin of Speech.* Norwich, VT: Argo, 1981.

– "Practical Knowledge of the Soul." Norwich, VT: Argo, 1988.

– *Rosenstock-Huessy Papers*, vol. 1. Norwich, VT: Argo Books, 1981.

Rosenzweig, Franz. *Jehuda Halevi: Zionslieder, mit der Verdeutschung und Anmerkungen von Franz Rosenzweig.* Berlin: Schocken, 1933.

– *Jehuda Halevi: Zweiundneunzig Hymnen und Gedichte, Deutsch, mit einem Nachwort und mit Anmerkungen* (Der Sechzig Hymnen und Gedichte Zweite Ausgabe). Berlin: Verlag Lambert Schneider, 1927.

– *On Jewish Learning.* Trans. and intro. Nahum N. Glatzer. New York: Noonday Press, 1965.

– *Der Mensch und sein Werk, Gesammelte Schriften,* I *Briefe und Tagebücher,* 2. Bände, ed. Rachel Rosenzweig and Edith Rosenzweig-Scheinemann, 1979. II *Der Stern der Erlösung,* 1976. III *Zweistromland: Kleinere Schriften zu Glauben und Denken,* ed. Reinhold Mayer and Annemarie Mayer, 1984. IV *Sprachdenken* 1. Band: *Jehuda Halevi: Fünfundneunzig Hymnen und Gedichte,* ed. Rafael N. Rosenzweig, 1983. 2. Band: *Arbeitspapiere zur Verdeutschung der Schrift,* ed. Rachel Bat-Adam, 1984. The Hague: Martinus Nijhoff.

– "Das neue Denken." In *Der Mensch und sein Werk Gesammelte Schriften,* III *Zweistromland: Kleinere Schriften zu Glauben und Denken,* ed. Reinhold Mayer and Annemarie Mayer. The Hague: Martinus Nijhoff, 1982. 139–61.

– *Sechzig Hymnen und Gedichte des Jehuda Halevi, Deutsch, mit einem Nachwort und mit Anmerkungen.* Konstanz: Oskar Wöhrle / Verlag, 1924.

– *The Star of Redemption.* Trans. William W. Hallo. Notre Dame, IN: University of Notre Dame Press, 1985.

– *Understanding the Sick and the Healthy: A View of the World, Man, and God [Das Büchlein vom gesunden und kranken Menschenverstand].* Trans. Nahum N. Glatzer. New York: Noonday Press, 1953.

Salaman, Nina, trans. *Selected Poems of Jehudah Halevi, chiefly from the critical text edited by Heinrich Brody, Ph.D.* 4th impression. Philadelphia: The Jewish Publication Society of America, 1946.

Scholem, Gershom. "Franz Rosenzweig and His Book *The Star of Redemption*" (based on his 1930 review). In *Philosophy of Franz Rosenzweig*, ed. Paul Mendes-Flohr, 20–41. Hanover and London: University Press of New England, 1988.

Seeskin, Kenneth. *Dialogue and Discovery: A Study in Socratic Method.* Albany: State University of New York Press, 1987.

– *Jewish Philosophy in a Secular Age.* Albany: State University of New York Press, 1990.

Stahmer, Harold M. "Franz Rosenzweig's Letters to Margrit Rosenstock-Huessy (1917–1922)." In *Leo Baeck Institute Yearbook 1989 XXXIV,* 385–409. London: Secker & Warburg, 1989.

– "The Letters of Franz Rosenzweig to Margrit Rosenstock-Huessy: 'Franz,' 'Gritli,' 'Eugen' and 'The Star of Redemption.'" in *Der Philosoph Franz Rosenzweig (1886–1929),* Internationaler Kongress, Kassel 1986, 109–37. Munich: Verlag Karl Alber Freiburg, 1988.

– "*Speak That I May See Thee!*" *The Religious Significance of Language.* New York: Macmillan, 1968.

Störig, Hans, ed. *Das Problem des Übersetzens.* Stuttgart: Henry Goverts Verlag, 1963.

Susman, Margarete. Review of the *Star.* German original in *Der Jude: Eine Monatsschrift,* 259–64. Sechster Jahrgang, 1921–22. Berlin: Jüdischer Verlag. (Available at Montreal's Jewish Public Library.) English translation, by Joachim Neugroschel, in *The Jew: Essays from Martin Buber's Journal, Der Jude, 1916–1928,* ed. and intro. Arthur A. Cohen, 276–85. Tuscaloosa: University of Alabama Press, 1980.

Tewes, Joseph. *Zum Existenzbegriff Franz Rosenzweigs.* Meisenheim am Glan: Verlag Anton Hain, 1970.

Theunissen, Michael. Trans. Christopher Macann. *The Other: Studies in the Social Ontology of Husserl, Heidegger, Sartre, and Buber.* Cambridge and London: MIT Press, 1984. Originally published as *Der Andere: Studien zur Sozialontologie der Gegenwart.* Berlin: Walter de Gruyter, 1977.

Udoff, Alan. "Rosenzweig's Heidegger Reception and the re-Origination of Jewish Thinking" in *Der Philosoph Franz Rosenzweig (1886–1929),* Internationaler Kongress, Kassel 1986, 923–50. Munich: Verlag Karl Alber Freiburg, 1988.

Wolfdietrich Schmied-Kowarzik, ed. *Der Philosoph Franz Rosenzweig (1886–1929),* Internationaler Kongress, Kassel, 1986. Band I *Die Herausforderung jüdischen Hernens.* Band II *Das neue Denken und seine Dimensionen.* Munich: Verlang Karl Alber Freiburg, 1988.

Index

Address: Rosenzweig's, to Halevi, and to his own readers, 403
Amen: in communal prayer, 379; word of affirmation, 369-70
Amir, Yehoshua: on Rosenzweig and Jewish law, 308
"Apologetic Thinking": and vitality of repeated speech, 294

Bergman, Samuel Hugo: on Jews as outside history, 307; on Rosenzweig's speech-thinking contribution, 308
Buber, Martin: role of, in the Halevi book, 294-5, 296; Rosenzweig's influence on, 294-5

Cohen, Hermann: on being and becoming, 300-1; influence of, on Rosenzweig, 300-1; philosopher and believer, 452; and *Religion of Reason*, 304

Dietrich, Wendell: and francophone contribution to Rosenzweig studies, 311-12; on Mosès' contributions to Rosen-

zweig studies, 312; on the social-theoretical dimension of Rosenzweig's theory of Judaism, 407-8
Dreyfus, Theodore: on Rosenzweig's influence in Israel, 308

Eastern religions: Rosenzweig's shortcomings in the face of, 387
Ehrenberg, Hans: early review of *Star*, 314
Elements of reality: essences of, 384; irreducibility of, 434; in isolation in God's conception, 355; meta-essences of, 382; relating of, 434; separateness of, 377; taking into account of, for speech and love, 389
Eternity: of God in his use of time and language, 339-40; and time, 462; as transpiring in translating, 339
Exile: of Jewish people, 451-2
Experience: personal, in Jehuda Halevi's and Rosenzweig's philosophies, 292; of nearness to God,

438; as organon for knowing, 316; and revelation, 435

Feuerbach, Ludwig: as discoverer of speech-thinking, 372-4
Fleischman, Jacob: on Rosenzweig's "anti-Zionism," 307; on Rosenzweig's lack of philosophical authority, 308-9
Free will: in acts and "counteracts," 411; choice in, 459; compulsion in, 462; fear in, 462; and God's, 419; God's power in, 462; intentionality in, 460; limits of, 435
Freies Jüdisches Lehrhaus: arena for speech-thinking method, 300; and the Holocaust, 306; Israeli view of, 308; and lectures on Science of God, 375; and lectures on Science of Man, 459

German language: expanded by translations, 337-8
Germany: reception of, to Rosenzweig, 306
Ghazali: 409
God: the Creator, 436-8; far

and near, 439-41, 448, 450; identity of name and concept, 407; identity of person and speech, 379-80; uniqueness of, 438
Grammar: accusative and dative cases, 378, 382, 446; biblical forms of, 412-13; dative case, 377, 380, 383; of dialogue, 382; eternal future, 442-3; exclamations, 438; first person plural, 448-9; imperative mood, 350, 356; indicative mood, 356, 358, 454; and persons, 407; science of, 494-5, 661; tenses, 385, 410, 442; vocative case, 351

Halevi book: form of, 318-21; history of editions of, 318-21; re-ordering of, by Rafael Rosenzweig, 319-20; the three excursus poems and Notes, 319
Heidegger and Rosenzweig: connections between, 304-5; divergences between, 304-5

Islam: Rosenzweig's shortcomings in the face of, 387

Jehuda Halevi: biographical sketches, 292-4, 423-4; compared to Rosenzweig, 293-4; philosophy of, 292; and prayer in life, 294
Judaism and Christianity: hope as common ground in, 330; space and time in, 330

Kierkegaard, Søren: parallels with Rosenzweig, 315; Rosenzweig's appreciation of, 334

Knowing: limits of, 435; speech and experience as organons for, 316
Knowledge: of being, 453-4; of death, 457; of God, through relationship, 454; of life, 457; limit of, by God, 454; from revelation, 453
Kurzweil, Baruch: on Jews as outside history, 307

Language: absolute trust in, 349-50; biblical, as dialogical, 412-13, 414, 427; biblical, in the poems, 414-15; borders, 428; in correlation with death, 340; creative spirit working in, 342; expanding own resources of, 291, 343; expansion of, 337, 361, 401; expansion of, in speaker, 402; as instrument, 393; meetings of, 341; perfection of, 374; philosophical, 371; as physical and spiritual, 392; Rosenzweig's non-instrumentalist view of, 328-9; in *Song of Songs*, 355-6; stretching through translating, 386; through time, 391; universal and particular in relationship, 375
Language growth: direction of, 326; of expressibility of truth, 341; from particluar speech, 368; through translating, 324, 341; verification of the not-yet All, 369
Languages: dead, 386; multiplicity of, 371
Levinas, Emmanuel: indebtedness to Rosenzweig, 311; on Rosenzweig and Christianity and Judaism, 311-12; and Rosenzweig's

anti-totalizing philosophy, 311, 312; on Rosenzweig as social theorist, 312
Light: divine and human, 390; of God in individual souls, 422; in redemption, 422; shining like a face, 390
Listening: for likeness and unlikeness to God's speech, 377; in philosophy, 314
Liturgy: as apex of speech, 294
Love: as always fresh, 418; as analogue, 355-6; and anonymity, 351; commandments of, 350, 353-4, 357, 358, 416-17, 420, 426, 441-2, 447-8, 459-60; demanding God's, 440-1; as difficult, 439; divine flowering of, 409-10; equated to eternity, 410; equated to speech, 356; eternity in the event of, 356; as event, 388, 395, 447; and finitude of the human, 420; of God for human, 439; of God, in philosophy, 293-4; God's, since beginning of time, 387-8; God's promise of, 420; God's speech of, moving toward the universal, 383-4; as God's uniqueness, 419-20; growth of, in time, 411, 451; human return of, to God, 387-8; in indicative mood, 358; between Israel and God, 451-2; as listening, 397; the need to speak, 358; of neighbour, 353-5, 357-8, 388; of neighbour, as expression of love for God, 383; of neighbour, in *Star*, 355; permanence in, 426-7; as Rosenzweig's philosophical source,

314; self's incapacity for, 355; as sensual and su-prasensual, 411; of specific persons, 401; in speech, 291; and three elements of reality, 389; and waiting for the other, 389
Luz, Ehud: on Rosenzweig's "pro-Zionism" move, 307

Meinecke, Friedrich: as deaf to Rosenzweig, 335; Rosenzweig's letter to, 323, 331-3
Meta-: Rosenzweig's use of prefix, 309
Miracle: presentness of, 424
Mystic, the: nature, 455-6; pantheistic, 455; Rosenzweig's critique of, 381, 389-90, 405, 448

Name: behind speech, 396; calling by, 351-2, 396; as central to speech-thinking, 357-8; and direct address, 407; divine, 378; for God, 351, 423, 440-1; identity with concept in God's name, 407; individuality of, 351; and meaning of Bible as divine name, 382; presence of, 379; revelation of divine, 379; and truth and reality, 357; understanding of divine, through human names, 380; as unique, 406; as word and fire, 482, 497, n.23, 357
"Neue Denken, Das": See "The New Thinking"
"New Thinking, The": encouragement beyond Star, 347-8; on essences of the elements, 316; on import of Halevi book, 289; logical versus di-vine truths, 384; and reading philosophy books, 348-9; reference to Halevi book, 347

One language: and action in, 463-4; and Bible, 363, 427; blocking growth of, 381, 390, 395; and God's decree, 374-5; God's support of, 396; growth to-ward, 326, 369, 381, 402, 405; and human heart, 363; and language spirit, 371; multi-ple languages in, 325; and particular and uni-versal, 374; and redemp-tion, 360, 370; root-sentence in, 358, 416; in same and different lan-guages, 297; seed for, in each language, 327, 338, 391; statement of, 325
Other: dependence on, 341-2; God's speech to, 354
Otherness, welcoming of, 406

Patmos Circle: members of, contributors to, 302; pe-riodical of (The Creature [Die Kreatur]), 302-3; as reaction to World War I, 302
Peace: as truth and mutual understanding, 340
Philosophy: the "and," 362, 378; and concept of reve-lation, 432-3; existential-ist: experience and revelation in, 292; exis-tentialist, and French re-appropriation of Hegel, 313; existentialist, Je-huda Halevi as precur-sor of, 292; and Greek meaning of eternity, 412; Greek standpoints in Middle Ages, 423; Kan-tian, 368; and particular and universal, 368, 372-4; and particularity of human being, 371, 383; proofs of God, 454-5; re-ductionism in, 340, 406, 418, 455; reductionist, political implications of, 406; Rosenzweig's reac-tion to German Idealism, 370; speech-thinking, personal experience in, 405; speech-thinking, protection of unique-ness of person in, 406; timelessness in, 418; to-talizing, 317; Western tradition of totalizing, 370. See also Speech-Thinking
Postmodernism: the "other" in, 317-18; Rosenzweig as a re-source for, 317-18
Prayer: cycles, translated by Rosenzweig, 290; as transformative speech, 428

Reason: as distorter of truths, 456; foundation of, in new thinking, 316-17
Redemption: root-sen-tence of, 417
Religions: as forms to re-flect perceived reality, 396-7
Revelation: as experience and event, 447; concept of, as philosophical cate-gory, 317; historical and personal, 406-7; human experience of, 435; Je-huda Halevi's view of, 293; receiving, through time, 417; renewed mo-ments of, 442; as univer-sal and particular, 417
Rosenstock-Huessy, Eugen: influence of, on Rosen-zweig, 296-7, 301-2, 322;

as intellectual man of faith, 300; and the need to speak, 301; Rosenzweig's relationship with, 329-33; and words as way to truth, 301

Rosenstock-Huessy, Margrit, 335

Rosenzweig, Franz: his illness, 290

Rotenstreich, Nathan: on Rosenzweig's term "common sense," 308; on Rosenzweig's use of meta-, 309

Sabbath: given to the soul, 444-5

Schwarcz, Moshe: on Rosenzweig and revelation, 308

Schweid, Eliezer: on Rosenzweig's definition of Judaism, 307; on Rosenzweig's speech-thinking, 308

Scripture: illumined by life, 352; relationship to individual lives, 352; and relationship to world, 462-3

Self: awakening to soul in revelation, 417; becoming soul, 355; incapacity to love, incomplete part of human, 355

Silence: of accord, 327

Simon, Ernst: and Israeli rejection of Rosenzweig, 307; on Rosenzweig and Jewish education, 307

Solitary thought: autonomy of knowledge in, 334; and Feuerbach, 373; and Hegel, 333; versus knowledge as service, 334; mind missing mark in, 329

Song of Songs, as focal book of revelation, 416; and knowledge expressed in relationship, 454; language in, 355-6; love in, 346, 356, 453; Rosenzweig's analysis of, 356-7, 435; and uniqueness of God, 439

Soul: alone with God, as sick, 441-2; always present, 444; authentic speech of, 376; authentic turns in, 424, 443-4; awakening of, 434-5, 459-60; in isolation and in speaking, 302; as light of God, 375, 458; loneliness and yearning in a, 443; path to heaven, one for each, 457-8; place of, 444; recognizing other souls, 355; suffering of, 449;

Speech: and address, 401, 445; alienation in, 426; in Bible and human heart, 385; borders of, 428; as bridge, 435; communal, 400, 405, 417; co-recitative, 400-1; dependent on an other, 324; disagreement in, 370-1; divine, 453; divine, as dialogical, 378; divine, into human heart, 351-2, 354, 376, 383, 416; divine, as revelatory, 376; divine, in variations, 352-3; divinely derived, 457; and eternality of God's word, 410; for God, identity of person with, 379-80; human and divine, during revelation, 382; as human common property, 394; human versus divine, 376; human-divine, 344-7, 349, 355-6, 376, 400, 417, 449, 450-1, 452-3; human-to-human, 344-7, 349, 353, 356, 376; identity of person with, 378-80; and language, 297; levels in, 346-7, 400-5; liturgical, 370, 395, 400, 413, 417-18, 428, 436, 448-9; needing two speakers, 336, 381; as organon for knowing, 316; particularity of, 369; as prayer, 428, 442, 449, 453, 461-2; repetition in, 370, 418; sentence of accord, 379; as separate from speaker, 369; and silence, 325; solitary, 323-4, 406; written text, 426-30; through generations, 385; trust in, between God and human, 449; to world, 401; and worldviews, 394-5

Speech-thinking: as genre of margin, 424, 426; the need of two speakers for, 328-31; as philosophical genre, 431. See also Philosophy

Star: attention to 297-8; conclusion of, 347; early review of, by Hans Ehrenberg, 314; on God's presence as third party in liturgy, 379; inattention to, 299-300; as Jewish book, 452; on love of neighbour, 355; as opening to the Halevi book, 315; and relationship between elements of reality, 393; and the "Urzelle" ("Germcell"), 354

Storytelling: biblical, 413

Suffering: patience for, 459; and rejection of world, 455-6

Suicide: Heidegger's view of, 305

Temporality: and eternality, 408

Time: beginning and end of, 293, 377-8, 412, 434; bridging between, 462; bridging heaven and earth in, 381-2; in contrast to essence, 304; and creation, 350; as creature, 385, 462-3; ending in silence 325; enquiries into, 305; and eternity, 356, 407-8, 462; experience of eternity breaking into, 409; freezing of, in artwork, 377; God acting in, 385, 410; and grammatical tenses, 338-9; holy, 397; hope in, 330; and human soul in, 388; language through, 343-4; love in, reflected in eternity now, 381; as meaning "world," 409; need of, 341-2; as not infinite, 395; as nourisher for knowing, 318, 324-5; and permanence in, 335-6, 411; permanence in, for literary works, 341; permanence of speech in, 329; permanence of truth in, 340; and permanence of word in, 335; and person, 338-9, 416-17; relating in, 374; required for stages of speech, 324-5; and revelation, 351; and space,

356, 372-3; speech through, 291, 294, 297, 324; translating through, 291; verification of knowledge at end of, 313
Timelessness: as thought's aim, 339
Translating: of divine word, 351; as equivalent to speaking, 342-3; expansion of language through, 347; as fulfilling love commandments, 353-4; as goal of mind, 323, 401; and the intactness of the other, 347; languages changing through, 324; listening as prime principle in, 334-5; readiness for, 326; requirements for translator in, 334; Rosenzweig's personal history of, 290
Translation: Bakhtin's theory, 364-5; Buber-Rosenzweig Bible, 366-7; as commandment, 297; of divine deed and love, 475-6; essential principle of, 336-7; from heart to heart, 384; identity of

speech with, 338; impossibility of, 337; mainstream principles in theories of, 362; and a nation's need for, 387; philosophy of, summarized, 322; refusal of, 326; as renewing truths, 377; Rosenzweig's care in, 404; somatic theory of, 364-6; and transformation of the translator, 338-9
Truth: as becoming, 378; individual receipt of, 383; as unitive, 378
Truth(s): apprehension of, in present moment, 341
Truths: logical versus divine, 384

Universal language: theories of a, 363; Tower of Babel, 364

World: growth of, 371

Yom Kippur: 450; Rosenzweig's translation of Kol Nidre, 290

Zionism: Rosenzweig's position on, 307, 313